JUVENAL
THE SATIRES

JUVENAL
THE SATIRES

Edited with Introduction,
Commentary and Bibliography by

John Ferguson

Bristol Classical Press

First published in 1979 by Macmillan Education Ltd

This edition published in 1999 by
Bristol Classical Press
an imprint of
Gerald Duckworth & Co. Ltd
61 Frith Street
London W1D 3JL
e-mail: inquiries@duckworth-publishers.co.uk
Website: www.ducknet.co.uk

Reprinted 2001

A catalogue record for this book is available
from the British Library

ISBN 1-85399-581-9

Printed in Great Britain by
Antony Rowe Ltd, Eastbourne

Contents

Acknowledgements

The Latin text printed here is based on the Oxford Classical Text by
W.V. Clausen (1959), by arrangement with the Oxford University Press.
The principal divergences from the Clausen edition are listed on pages xxvi
and xxvii.

The author and publishers also wish to thank the following who have kindly
given permission for the use of copyright material: —
Oxford University Press for a table from Fowler's *Modern English Usage* (2nd
edition revised by Sir Ernest Gowers) © Oxford University Press 1965;
Oxford University Press for the use of Oxford Classical Texts edition from
Persius and Juvenal: Satires edited by W.V. Clausen (1959) © Oxford
University Press 1959;
Professors T. Reekman and H. Verdin for extracts from the article "Juvenal's
Views on Social Change" in the journal *Ancient Society* published by
Katholieke Universiteit, Leuven, Belgium.

Preface

A new annotated Juvenal seems needed: the last commentaries in English
were those of J.D. Duff, admirable and sensible (as even the waspish Housman
admitted), but dating from 1898, and somewhat expurgated, and, in America,
of H.L. Wilson (1903). The 'red Macmillan' edition by E.G. Hardy was 1883
(^{2}1891); Pearson and Strong's Clarendon Press edition 1887 (^{2}1892).
J.E.B. Mayor's magnificent commentary on Roman social life, though not on
Juvenal's poetry, actually goes back to 1869 (^{2}1872 ^{3}1878 ^{4}1889). All these
were selective.

There are four obvious reasons for a fresh commentary.

First, a great deal of attention has been paid to the text by Housman,
Knoche, Clausen and others, and to the interpretation of the text by
innumerable commentators in scholarly journals.

Second, our age is franker and more like Juvenal's. We do not need the
expurgated edition, whether for male or female readers, especially as we
know that we shall not grasp the full force and nature of Juvenal's satire if
we bowdlerise. Indeed, in a famous article Mason actually suggested that the
ninth poem, ugly and unpleasing as is its theme, is the key to our understanding
of Juvenal.

Third, critical judgement has changed. We pay more attention now to
structure, to the nature of satirical effect, to verbal details. The best work here
has been done in America by Anderson and others, again in the pages of the
journals. It is important that it be made available for the ordinary reader.

Fourth, the readership has changed, and the whole approach to classical
studies. Much less can be taken for granted: more guidance is needed through
the Latin, clear explanation of allusions. On the other hand it is inappropriate
to weigh down the commentary with complex grammatical and syntactical
exposition which may get in the way of the poetry, or with parallel passages;
except when these may be used in support of the textual reading, or to
illustrate the way Juvenal has built on earlier writers or later writers have
developed from Juvenal. I have not solved the problems of an edition to be
used alike in schools and universities: references may be overweighted for
some readers, too slight for others. I hope that Juvenal will hold both groups.

I must acknowledge a continual debt to Duff in making my own commentary.
It is impossible to avoid citing parallel passages which he too chose, and I have
not tried to do so, and I have always learned from his notes even when I have

disagreed with his interpretation. I must also express my indebtedness to Gilbert Highet's *Juvenal the Satirist*. It is hard to see why this has attracted so much disapprobation: it is far in advance of any other comprehensive treatment in English, being learned and humane. I have, as noted above, profited a great deal from the work of W.S. Anderson. I must express thanks to Professor G.B.A. Fletcher, who generously laid at my disposal his immense scholarship and saved me more than once from serious error; he has supplied many references. I am the more grateful because he does not approve of some of my views. Gratitude also to Dr Michael Coffey for constructive and helpful comments. Mrs Veronica Anstey kindly tried out some of the commentary in draft upon her sixth-formers, and I am grateful to her and to them for their comments. Mrs Kitty Chisolm has been most helpful in checking the work generally. Mr John Hunt has drawn the maps. None of these is responsible for errors of fact or judgement which remain.

I have borrowed a few phrases from some work I did for the Open University A291 *The Early Roman Empire and the Rise of Christianity* Units 6-7 *Petronius and Juvenal*. When one has said something as clearly and incisively as possible, it is mere affectation to search round for alternative phrases.

I was able to do some of the work on the hospitable campus of the University of Florida; the rest has been snatched from deanship. The bulk of the typing has been done by my friend Lesley Roff, whose high standards and warm interest have always been an encouragement. Karen Smith has been of great help in the final stages.

J. F.

Introduction

SATIRE

In 1669 Hans Jakob von Grimmelshausen published *Simplicissimus Teutsch*.
The frontispiece is a representation of Satire, with a satyr's head, woman's
body, wings, fishtail, different legs — one of a goat and one of a waterfowl —
wearing a shiny sword, holding an illustrated book with an obscene gesture,
and with masks on the ground before it. Some of the elements in this are
clear enough. Satire is both man and brute, humane and brutal. Satire wears
many faces. Satire is compounded of incongruities, and is not to be judged
by the ordinary criteria of literary criticism. Satire is equally at home on land,
sea or in the air. Satire has some of the creative and other qualities (including,
in male eyes, the unpredictability) of the female. Satire is devilish. Satire is
naked. Satire is obscene. Satire is winged like poetry. Satire pierces like a
sword. Satire's subjects (depicted in the book) are as various as life, and they
include crowns and castles, fools' caps, wars and ordinary living.

Early in this century, in his *Modern English Usage*, H.W. Fowler compiled
a useful table:

	Motive or Aim	Province	Method or Means	Audience
humour	Discovery	Human nature	Observation	The sympathetic
wit	Throwing light	Words and ideas	Surprise	The intelligent
satire	Amendment	Morals & manners	Accentuation	The self-satisfied
sarcasm	Inflicting pain	Faults and foibles	Inversion	Victim & bystander
invective	Discredit	Misconduct	Direct statement	The public
irony	Exclusiveness	Statement of facts	Mystification	An inner circle
cynicism	Self-justification	Morals	Exposure of nakedness	The respectable
the sardonic	Self-relief	Adversity	Pessimism	Self

Two useful books on the subject of satire were published in the early
1960s. In *The Art of Satire*, David Worcester calls satire 'the Proteus of
literature'. He analyses its constituents into three. The first is invective.

> The Satire should be like the porcupine
> That shoots sharp quilles out in each angry line.
>   Joseph Hall *Virgidemiarum*

'The comic butt of satire', wrote W.H. Auden in *The Dyer's Hand and Other Essays*, 'is a person who, though in possession of moral faculties, transgresses the moral law beyond the normal call of temptation.' Invective implies anger, or the appearance of it: it also implies rhetorical form. Further, satiric invective is not mere abuse: it shows 'detachment, indirection, and complexity in the author's attitude'. Again, satire uses the comic. 'Satire begins where laughter enters.' Under this head, Juvenal is the great satiric exemplar. The second constituent is burlesque.

> Bastings heavy, dry, obtuse,
> Only dulness can produce;
> While a little gentle jerking
> Sets the spirits all a-working.
>   Swift 'To a Lady'

'Burlesque-satire is historically the form developed for the informal observation of human nature and for the seemingly artless revelation of the writer's personality.' Its supreme exponent is Rabelais. The third constituent is irony, which may be allied with comedy or tragedy: its masters include Lucian, Chaucer and Swift.

Gilbert Highet, in *The Anatomy of Satire*, suggests that there are three main types of satire: monologue, parody and narrative. Monologue is linked to diatribe and the philosophical sermon, and is the primary pattern of ancient satire: Juvenal is its last grand master in Latin. Parody uses incongruity to take down a work of literature, or a form or an idea. Aristophanes used it: so did Petronius: so on occasions did Juvenal, and there are many examples from more recent times. Narrative-satire Highet calls 'the distorting mirror'. *Gulliver's Travels* and *Candide* are perhaps the two great narrative satires. But there are monologues, parodies and narratives which are not satirical. Highet offers a number of tests of satirical intent: open declaration of purpose; the offering of a satiric pedigree; the choice of a traditionally satiric subject (no safe guide this!); allusion to earlier satirists; the treatment of the theme in a concrete, personal and topical way; the use of forceful vocabulary and varied texture; the use of typical satiric devices, such as concentration on incongruous detail; the arousal of the satiric emotion, a blend of amusement and contempt.

There have been two other postwar treatments of satire which call for attention. One will be found in Northrop Frye's *Anatomy of Criticism*. He identifies two elements in satire. One is wit or humour founded on fantasy or a sense of the grotesque or absurd; the other is an object of attack. Pure denunciation is one frontier of satire; humour without denunciation is the other; satire involves both. Frye also notes that in satire observation is primary, but as the observed phenomena pass from the sinister to the grotesque they become more illusory and insubstantial. The balance needed for great satire is thus a fine one.

The other treatment was by Maynard Mack in an essay in *Yale Review* in

1951. Mack makes an interesting contrast between tragedy and satire. Satire, he suggests, depends on ethos; it depends on norms and a value-system. Tragedy is concerned with the inadequacy of all norms. Mack stresses the rhetorical element in satire, the element deriving from *laus et uituperatio*, the element too of fictionality. The main object of Mack's study is Pope, but his analysis can certainly be fruitfully applied to Juvenal.

SATURA

The Latin word *satura*, satire, has four possible derivations, according to ancient grammarians.

(a) *Satyrus*, a satyr. So, for example, Donatus in his *Life of Terence*. The satyrs were gross spirits of the woodland with animal-tails. In Greece at dramatic festivals three tragic dramas were followed by a satyr-play, containing knockabout humour, a strong sexual element, and parody. It is quite certain that this is not the derivation, but the similarity of the words may have affected the development of Roman satire, in the combination of a strongly dramatic element and (sometimes) sexual subjects: it has been argued that it was assimilation to the satyrs which changed the spelling from *satura* to *satira* and gave us our word.

(b) *Lanx satura*, a 'full dish', an offering at a harvest home, a bowl full of various vegetables and fruits. *Satur* means 'full' (compare our 'saturated'). Here the reference would be to the variety of themes. On the whole this seems the likeliest explanation.

(c) *Satura*, a sausage (though the ingredients sound more like the basis for a cake: raisins, polenta, pine nuts, honeyed wine, and sometimes pomegranate seeds). Here again the reference would be to the variety of the ingredients.

On the whole this seems a slightly less likely origin than the *lanx satura*, though there is an interesting parallel in *farsa*, a miscellaneous pudding, from which we derive our 'farce'.

(d) *Lex satura*, a law covering miscellaneous subjects. This is however a false derivation.

It is safe to say that the satire is named from its varied content but that there is some assimilation to the satyr-play.

Behind the Romans lie the Greeks, and behind Latin literature lies Greek literature. Greek literature is in some respects very artificial, and was rigidly categorised not merely by theorists but by practitioners. There is no category which corresponds either to our modern satire or to the Latin *satura*. When the Roman critic Quintilian wrote 'Satire is completely ours' he was on the face of it justified. Even after the Romans had developed the *genre*, the Greeks never took it up.

None the less there are categories of Greek literature which contributed to the formation of the *satura*:

(a) Parody and Burlesque. The best surviving example of this is a parody of Homeric epic entitled *The Battle of the Frogs and the Mice*.

(b) Invective (which the Greeks called Iambics from the metre usually used).

(c) The Animal Fable, which might be in prose or verse; the best-known examples were attributed to an Asiatic slave named Aesop. The Roman

Horace uses an animal fable charmingly in his well-known satire *The Town Mouse and the Country Mouse.*

(d) Comedy. Comic drama in fifth-century Athens enjoyed considerable freedom of topical allusion, and was an instrument for ethical and political comment on current issues and personalities.

(e) Mime. The mimes are sketches, with a solid basis in down-to-earth real-life situations: a woman is uncertain whether to take a lover, a naughty schoolboy is faced with a whacking; the interest of the situation is exploited without moral conclusions. The mimes undoubtedly contained a good deal of slapstick and of crude sexual humour.

(f) Diatribe. A diatribe is really an ethical sermon preached by a philosopher.

One individual approximates more closely in his works to the Latin *satura*. This was Menippus of Gadara. Unfortunately we know little about him except at second hand. He lived in the third century BC; he came from Gadara in Palestine (familiar enough from the Gadarene swine); he was once a slave, won his freedom, and became a citizen of Thebes. He was, it seems, a Cynic philosopher, and we may properly see his writings as a variant on the diatribe, and his purpose ethical preachment. His originality lay first in his literary vehicle, which was a medley of prose and verse, and second in his attitude, which the Greek writer Strabo called *spoudogeloios,* which is a coined word of the 'bitter-sweet' type, and means 'serious-laughing'. It has been interestingly argued (F. Dornseiff *Antike und Alter Orient* Leipzig [2]1959 I 234-5) that the mixture of prose and verse is a Semitic trait, being found in Jewish apocalyptic as in Daniel 2: 7 or the Qumran *War Scroll.* Such medleys were produced at Rome by Varro and Petronius. Northrop Frye has seen in it the ancestor of *Gulliver's Travels, Candide,* and the satires of Thomas Love Peacock and Aldous Huxley.

EARLIER ROMAN SATIRE

It will not be appropriate here to give more than a summary account of Roman satire before Juvenal. Wilamowitz once said 'There is no Roman satire; there are only Lucilius, Horace, Persius and Juvenal' (*Griechische Verkunst* 42 n 1). It is a perverse and provocative part-truth. There is Roman satire, but its several exponents make something very different of it. The story is best told under eight heads.

(a) Quintus Ennius (239-169 BC) was the first great Roman poet, and more than any other writer was responsible for the introduction into Latin of the Greek hexameter. He was born at Rudiae in southern Italy, and was trilingual, being fluent in Oscan, Latin and Greek. We know little of his life, but Scipio Africanus was his patron, and his literary career centred on Rome. His great achievement was the epic *Annales,* but he wrote plays as well, and four books of *saturae,* a new *genre* which he probably initiated. Thirty-one lines survive, but they are in a variety of metres. The *saturae* included an excellent animal fable, about the crested lark who did not move her young when the farmer asked his friends to reap the cornfield, nor when he asked his relatives to do so, only when he said he was going to do it himself. Another contained a

debate between Mors and Vita, but we do not know how it was handled.
Ennius also wrote a mock-heroic poem on gastronomy. For the rest we are
aware of some philosophical speculation, and of some improving moral
observations. Ennius was a monumental and original genius. Today we might
find the *saturae* heavy, but they were the work of an inventive pioneer.
(b) C. Lucilius (c. 180-102 BC) took up from Ennius, and it was his fiery
vigour which really established the *satura;* Horace in fact calls him the inventor
of the *genre* (*Serm.* 1,10,46-9). Lucilius's poetry was regarded as *carmen
maledicum;* he was concerned with denunciation of individuals and society,
and set a precedent which Juvenal was to follow. About 1400 lines survive
from his work, but many of them are cited for grammatical peculiarities, and
it is difficult to get a sense of continuity, or to see the work as a whole. The
style is crude, forceful and often conversational. The poems include parody
and literary criticism. But Lucilius's main aim was moral preachment; he is in
the tradition of the diatribe; and he attacked superstition, greed, bad temper,
grumbling, superficiality and other vices. Some of his writing is political; it is
characteristic that to celebrate the triumphant return of Scipio Aemilianus
from Spain he attacked his patron's detractors rather than praising his patron;
in general he is strong against political twisters. Lucilius stood for *libertas,* a
word which gives us our 'liberty', but which is wider in scope. For Lucilius it
meant uncensored expression of political and social criticism, but later genera-
tions thought that *libertas* in Lucilius went with a lack of central personal
commitment, and an indifference to literary values.
(c) M. Terentius Varro (116-27 BC) is important for introducing the Romans
to satire after the fashion of Menippus. A voluminous and learned writer, he
wrote no less than 150 volumes of *Menippean Satires.* The 600 fragments are
mainly in verse, but this reflects the interests of grammarians, not the
proportions of the original. We can see that dialogue was extensively used,
and we can trace some historical references, but we know more of titles than
content; they are often cryptic and sometimes in Greek. Such titles are 'How
long?' and 'It's waiting, isn't it?' (reminders of the imminence of death), 'Got
you' (on luck), 'The pot's found its lid' (on marriage), 'Tut! Tut!' (on
flattery), 'Man-chester' (on family life). We know a little more of one or two
of the satires. 'Sixty Years Old' is an anticipation of the Rip Van Winkle
theme. 'You don't know what the late evening's bringing' is a kind of manual
on the conduct of dinner parties.
(d) Q. Horatius Flaccus, Horace, (65-8 BC) is certainly the best loved of the
Roman satirists. His father was a freedman, seemingly of the Epicurean
persuasion, who gave his son a good education. The young man was in Athens
when Brutus passed through, and was caught up in the liberation movement,
fighting with the losers at Philippi. He lost his family property but was
pardoned, and given an administrative post, and turned to writing verse. About
35 BC he published a collection of *sermones,* conversation-pieces (but note our
'sermons'). He claims to be in the line of descent from Lucilius (*Serm.* 1,4,56)
and in the second book published four years later, uses the word *satura* (2,1,1).
But Horace is brief and disciplined, where Lucilius was loose and frenetic. His
themes are not so different from those of his predecessors; he writes of avarice

or lust or hypocrisy or ambition. Some of his themes were later taken up by
Juvenal: *sit finis quaerendi* (1,1), or the tedium of official duties in Rome (2,6),
or the horrible dinner-party (2,8). So were some of his devices, such as epic
parody (1,7). Horace uses reminiscences, anecdotes, animal fables, to make or
illustrate his points. He is philosophical; he retains many Epicurean values; his
preachment is less harsh than that of the Cynics. He is whimsical rather than
wounding; and he is never selfrighteous; he is aware of his own weaknesses.
His poems are urbane, anecdotal, sensible, genial, likeable. For all this, as Rudd
has shown, his critique is no less searching. Alexander Pope summed him up
neatly in *An Essay on Criticism:*

> *Horace* still charms with graceful Negligence,
> And without Method *talks* us into sense,
> Will like *a Friend* familiarly convey
> The *truest Notions* in the *easiest way.*

Later, after a period in which he concentrated on lyric poetry, he returned to
sermones, only now he called them epistles or letters. Porphyrio says that
these are identical with the satires in style and subject matter, except that the
satires are addressed to someone present, the epistles to someone absent.

(e) *Ludus de Morte Claudii* is an anonymous skit on the death of Claudius. It
is often attributed to Seneca, because Seneca also wrote a skit called *The
Pumpkinification of Claudius (Apocolocyntosis).* There is no reason for think-
ing the two works the same: no doubt there were other such skits. Like
Varro's satires, this is a medley of prose and verse, brilliant, trenchant,
economical, savage. It uses three traditional themes (though it is hard to be
sure how far they had entered satire), the ascent to heaven, the council of the
gods, and the descent to the underworld. There is parody, of historical
writing, of epic, of tragedy (Seneca's *Hercules Furens*), even of the style of
Augustus, as well as an ironical use of quotation. The portrayal of Claudius is
masterly and unfair; but we do not expect fairness from satirists. The result
is very funny. This is a minor masterpiece in its own field.

(f) T. Petronius Niger (d. AD 66) was *arbiter elegantiae* to Nero's court, who
left behind him some verses and a long, bawdy, racy novel in the form of a
Menippean satire, about the adventures of three dissolute young men, one of
whom is under the curse of impotence. Only fragments survive, though these
include extended episodes. We have perhaps a tenth of the whole. The story
is strung on the thread of epic parody, with a free use of literary allusion.
There is a profession of realism, but the realism when more closely inspected
is a combination of concentration and caricature. There is also a deal of
fantasy.

   Much of the satire has to do with sex: indeed the title is *Liber Satyricon,*
the book of satyr-themes. These are told with a lusty enjoyment which his
readers across the ages have shared. But Gilbert Highet (in *TAPA* 42 (1941)
176ff) has suggested that there is a serious moral purpose. Extravagant
indulgence in 'sticky honeyballs of phrases' is death to good taste in language;
extravagant indulgence in overeating leads to constipation; extravagant
indulgence in sex leads to the destruction of sex. All the sexual situations are

painful or ridiculous or both, and Encolpius's impotence is a warning against indiscriminate indulgence. The work thus becomes a kind of Epicurean sermon against *luxuria*. To this view we may add the analysis by William Arrowsmith (in *Arion* 5,3; 1966) to the effect that in *The Satyricon* death, food and wealth are interacting themes, so that Encolpius's impotence is a symbolic death brought on by *luxuria*, and the ultimate meaning of his restoration is the reassertion of life. This theme of *luxuria*, represented by sexual indulgence, is important in Juvenal.

Petronius brings many gifts to his theme: slapstick humour, wordplay, and parody; some excellent characterisation; the capacity to tell a good story within his longer narrative, often depending on an unexpected twist (as in 'The Widow of Ephesus' which Christopher Fry dramatised as *A Phoenix Too Frequent*); and biting satire, on religion, superstition, legacy-hunting, bad taste, love, the *nouveaux riches*.

(g) Aulus Persius Flaccus (AD 34-62) was a Stoic who wrote six satires in intolerably difficult Latin; he disclaims poetic inspiration but writes in verse. The poems are indebted to Lucilius, and particularly to Horace, but he has none of Horace's charm. He is sometimes biting, never amusing, always intense, always moralistic. The first satire treats literary values, the second (which gave Juvenal the theme for his tenth) right and wrong objects of prayer, the third the need for moral earnestness, the fourth self-knowledge, the fifth the relation between freedom and virtue, the sixth the proper use of riches. Persius has some gifts of imagery, but the main impression is one of ethical earnestness; he lacks Juvenal's brilliance.

(h) Between Horace and the Neronian age we can trace no writers of *saturae*; Phaedrus's animal fables are the nearest thing. But the Flavian age, unpromising as it was for free speech, produced three whom we can name. Manilius Vopiscus was an Epicurean who wrote *saturae* among other occasional verses (Stat. *S* 1,3,103). One Silius, of whom we know nothing for sure, was a satirist (schol. in Juv. 1,20). Turnus was a more important figure (Mart. 7,97; 11,20; schol. in Juv. 1,20; 1,71; Rut. Nam. 1,603; Sid. Ap. 9,266; Joh. Lyd. *Mag.* 1,41), though only a couple of lines survive and we get no real impression of the man and his work. Quintilian (10,1,94) implies that there were others.

LIFE OF JUVENAL

Our knowledge of Juvenal is derived from four sources.

(a) The ancient lives. These are derived from one, which is attributed by most scholars to the fourth century:

> Iunius Iuuenalis libertini locupletis incertum est filius an alumnus, ad mediam fere aetatem declamauit, animi magis causa quam quod se scholae aut foro praepararet. deinde paucorum versuum satura non absurde composita in Paridem pantomimum poetamque eius semenstribus militiolis tumentem genus scripturae industriose excoluit; et tamen diu ne modico quidem auditorio quicquam committere ausus est. mox magna frequentia

magnoque successu bis ac ter auditus est, ut ea quoque quae prima fecerat
inferciret nouis scriptis:

> quod non dant proceres, dabit histrio. tu Camerinos
> et Bareas, tu nobilium magna atria curas?
> praefectos Pelopea facit, Philomela tribunos.

erat tum in deliciis aulae histrio multique fautorum eius cottidie
prouehebantur. uenit ergo Iuuenalis in suspicionem, quasi tempora figurate
notasset, ac statim per honorem militiae quamquam octogenarius urbe
summotus est missusque ad praefecturam cohortis in extremam partem
tendentis Aegypti. id supplicii genus placuit, ut leui atque ioculari delicto
par esset. uerum intra breuissimum tempus angore et taedio periit.

It is exceedingly difficult to know what credence to put in this. There is no
date of birth or death: even the reference to Paris, like much of the rest, could
be derived from the satires. The initial statement, however, that Juvenal was
the son or adopted son of a freedman, must rest on an independent tradition,
and may be cautiously accepted. The tradition of his banishment, though
implausible as it stands, is widespread, and Juvenal certainly seems to show
expert knowledge of Egypt.

Other lives give additional information, a birth-date in AD 55, the name of
his mother and sister Septumuleia and brother-in-law Fuscinus. The difficulty
lies in seeing how these could have been independently preserved: most
scholars therefore think it more likely that they are fifteenth-century inven-
tions to add verisimilitude to a bald and unconvincing narrative.

(b) The inscription from Aquinum (*CIL* X 5382)

> [CERE] RI SACRVM
> [D IV] NIVS IVVENALIS
> [TRIB] COH [I] DELMATARVM
> II VIR QVINQ FLAMEN
> DIVI VESPASIANI
> VOVIT DEDICAV[ITQ] VE
> SVA   PEC

We have independent knowledge of Juvenal's association with Aquinum
(3,319). We also know that he mentions Ceres Helvina (3,320), and always
treats Ceres with respect (6,50; 9,24; 10,112; 14,219; 14,263; 15,141). We
can confidently state that this pertains either to him or to a close relative.
But which?

(c) The satires. The satires give us a few dates. The firmest is the latest:
Juvenal dates the cannibalism in Egypt explicitly to AD 127 (15,27). But
there are others. 1,49-50 refers to the trial of Marius Priscus: this took place
in AD 100. The comet of 6,407 is likely to be that of November 115. Caesar
in 7,1 is likely to be Hadrian. We can thus form a reasonable chronology for
the writing, or at least publication, of Juvenal's works:

> Book I   (1-5)   c. 110
> Book II   (6)   c. 116

Book III   (7-9)   c. 120
Book IV   (10-2)   c. 125
Book V   (13-6)   c. 130

As the last satire is unfinished we may reasonably assume that his death took place about 130. At 11,201-4 he seems to be elderly: so his birth will be somewhere around AD 60 or earlier.

We are less certain than we used to be about using the satires as evidence for Juvenal's way of life. A poet is liable to adopt a *persona*, or more than one. Still, with reservations, we may draw some deductions — birth in Aquinum (3,318-21), an education in grammar and rhetoric (1,15-6 and often), a deep and intense knowledge of Rome, and some acquaintance with Egypt (15,45) and perhaps with Britain, a comfortable competence allowing him to live in Rome with a second home in the country (6,57; 11,66), a dislike of foreigners especially from the east, an awesome loathing of Domitian and general disgust with the power élite at Rome, a possible but not certain homosexuality combined with a contempt for pathics and a strong misogyny.

(d) References in other authors. There are six of these in literary sources, three of them from Martial, who was evidently a close friend, as well as a literary associate from whom Juvenal likes to take a theme and work it up.

Martial, 7, 24, 1-6 (AD 92)

> Cum Iuuenale meo quae me committere temptas,
> quid non audebis, perfida lingua, loqui?
> te fingènte nefas Pyladen odisset Orestes,
> Thesea Pirithoi destituisset amor,
> tu Siculos fratres et maius nomen Atridas
> et Ledae poteras dissociare genus.

7, 91, 1-2

> De nostro, facunde, tibi, Iuuenalis, agello
> Saturnalicias mittimus ecce nuces.

12, 18, 1-9 (AD 101)

> Dum tu forsitan inquietus erras
> clamosa, Iuuenalis, in Subura
> aut collem dominae teris Dianae
> dum per limina te potentiorum
> sudatrix toga uentilat uagumque
> maior Caelius et minor fatigant,
> me multos repetita post decembres
> accepit mea rusticumque fecit
> auro Bilbilis et superba ferro.

Ammianus Marcellinus, 28,4,14

> Quidam detestantes ut venena doctrinas, Iuuenalem et Marium Maximum curatiore studio legunt, nulla uolumina praeter haec in profundo otio contrectantes, quam ob causam non iudicioli est nostri.

Rutilius Namatianus, 1,603-4

> Huius uulnificis satura ludente Camenis
> nec Turnus potior nec Iuuenalis erit.

Sidonius Apollinaris, *Carm.* 9,269-73

> non qui tempore Caesaris secundi
> aeterno incoluit Tomos reatu,
> nec qui consimili deinde casu
> ad uulgi tenuem strepentis auram
> irati fuit histrionis exsul.

In addition the scholia or ancient commentaries occasionally give us informa-
tion. These fall into two groups. The less important are attributed to one
Cornutus, a medieval scholar who assumed the name of Persius's executor.
The more important are the *Scholia Pithoeana* and are found in the Codex
Pithoeanus (see page xxv) and the tradition stemming from it. They are of
multiple authorship, but seem to include material from the hand of an other-
wise unknown Probus writing in the second half of the fourth century. He
was a man of genuine learning and good sense.

We may attempt a reconstruction. The author's name was Decimus Junius
Juvenalis. He was born in Aquinum, perhaps in the middle 50s. His father was
a *libertus* and comfortably off. The friendship with Martial and the promin-
ence of Junii in Spain suggest the possibility of Spanish blood. The young man
had a good education; it is possible but not certain that he studied with
Quintilian. If the inscription refers to him he saw military service with the
first Dalmatian cohort. This might well have been in Britain under Agricola,
say in 78-80; he has a surprising number of references to Britain. On his
return he became priest of the newly-deified Vespasian, and held local
government office.

We now come to the question of his exile. It is an odd tradition if without
foundation. The lives attribute this to the attack on Paris in 7,90-2. Paris
was an actor who had influence at court. In 83 he was executed for a love
affair with the empress. In the later part of Domitian's reign references to
Paris were punished with death. The contorted evidence involves the follow-
ing factors: the impossibility of the seventh satire being written in the early
80s or even 90s; the fact that 7,87-9 would have been even more objection-
able; Martial's complimentary reference in 92 when Juvenal cannot have
been in disgrace; the death penalty; Juvenal's hatred of Domitian; his know-
ledge of Egypt. There seem two possible explanations. One is that Juvenal
offended Paris in 82, perhaps by a lampoon, and that the actor had him
packed off to Upper Egypt, perhaps with some military office: after Paris's
disgrace and death he was able to return. This seems to me the most likely.
The other is that Juvenal was exiled by Domitian for some lampoon, but not
mentioning Paris, in 93 or 94, returning after Domitian's death. I should
mention the ingenious but misguided view of P. Gérard, that Juvenal's
offence was given right at the end of his life to T. Aelius Alcibiades, a Graeco-
Oriental of great influence at Hadrian's court towards the end of his reign

and honoured by the theatrical companies of Rome and Ephesus (*PIR* 1,134). There are two problems about this: one that it makes 7,88-92 a later insertion; the other that it seems unlikely that Juvenal would be satirically punished by being given a military command in Upper Egypt at the age of 80.

If the first view is right, Juvenal returned to practise as a lawyer or rhetorician, since Martial in 91-2 describes him as *facundus* (7,91,1). After Martial returned to Spain he depicts Juvenal leading the life of a hanger-on of the aristocracy with a daily round of tedious duties (12,18,1-6). For the rest, the life is the poems. None of the ancient lives gives a date of death. One says that he pined away because of Martial's departure, which is too early. In one tradition he survived Hadrian: this would have made him very old, and does not explain the unfinished state of the sixteenth satire. Probably he died about 130.

Of his character and personality we have little impression. Pliny shines from his letters; we catch glimpses of Martial behind the epigrams; Juvenal remains elusive.

JUVENAL AS SATIRIST

Juvenal brings to satire first of all moral fervour: *si natura negat, facit indignatio uersum* (1,79). There is little comedy: when we laugh, our laughter has a hollow ring. Nor is he a philosophical preacher; though he has accepted some of Epicurus's attitudes he is no expounder of a systematic ethic. His intensity is rather tragic than didactic: Scaliger indeed called his satires 'tragical'. He has an intensity which blazes with a baleful light through even the 700 lines of the sixth satire.

The object of his satire is Rome, life at Rome, and particularly the life of the upper classes. He has his vision of the true traditions of Rome, and attacks all that falls short. So his chauvinistic jingoism attacks Greek and Jewish incursions into Roman life, but only to show that the Romans themselves are far worse. It is this that makes it hard to believe that the fifteenth satire, on Egyptian cannibalism, was meant to stand in isolation: we expect him to be saying 'But things quite as bad go on in Rome', and it is hard not to think that this was the purport of the sixteenth as planned. So too with the concentration on the upper classes. The women of Juvenal's grim gallery in the sixth satire belong to the establishment; when he turns aside for a moment to the lower classes (6,582), it is only a rhetorical device to intensify his assault.

It matters little whether Juvenal is donning a *persona* for his attack. The effect which he brilliantly produces is one of moral fervour. The historical Juvenal may have been detached and dispassionate, though I doubt it: his satire certainly is not. Some critics have impugned his sincerity because of his resolution to attack the dead (1,170-1). Syme notes that he does not attack the new aristocracy from Spain or Narbonensis, or contemporary sophists like Favorinus, Polemo and Dio. In fact Juvenal makes it clear that he is attacking the living under the likeness of the dead. This was courageous enough. Who is penning anything like the sixteenth satire in our present

military dictatorships? The implication of Satire 1 is that in Trajan's Rome
there is all the filth and corruption of which Juvenal writes. It is present
abuses which dip his pen in acid. We find ourselves asking: What was a cabinet
meeting like under Trajan? What was patronage of letters like under Hadrian?
Does not Juvenal's reference to Seneca under Nero (8,212) make us think of
Hadrian's elimination of C. Avidius Nigrinus? Hadrian was a musician too!

Juvenal took his themes from life. The first and third satires have an I-am-
a-camera feel about them. This does not prevent our placing them in a
literary tradition, for literary tradition is part of life for a writer and shapes
his sensibilities. So the Horrible Dinner Party of the fifth satire stands in a
line of descent from Horace and Petronius. But Juvenal adds to the literary
traditions which inform the satire. Greek epigrams had consisted in short
poems, suitable for engraving, usually in the elegiac metre, not necessarily
dependent on point or wit or closely illustrating actual life. Martial, a personal
friend of Juvenal, gave the epigram its modern connotation. He insisted that
his epigrams speak of life; they smack of man (Mart. 8,3,20; 10,4,10). And
he gave to his epigrams satirical point; his epigrams are satires in miniature.
Juvenal took hints from Martial and worked them up. In fact his Horrible
Dinner Party owes as much to Martial (Mart. 3,60; 6,11; 10,49) as to Horace.
Martial's 'Give us more of Maecenas; then there'll be Vergils in plenty'
(8,56,5) was worked up into the seventh satire. The picture of life in Rome
in the first satire (1,127-8) owes something to Martial (4,8,1-4). Juvenal's
Umbricius (3,41) echoes Martial (3,38,13-4). Proper names, Glaphyrus and
Matho and Naevolus and Saufeia are found in both; rare words and neat
expressions are taken up. The subjects of their satire are the same: the
hurly-burly of the capital, the contrast with the peace of the country,
niggardly patrons and their neglect of the liberal professions, philosophical
debauchees, the man who commits arson on his own property because of
the presents he'll receive from sympathisers, and, of course, women.
Clarence Mendell put the relationship between them well when he
described Juvenal as the scourge of his day, Martial as its commentator.
Or, as Gilbert Highet expressed it, 'One of Juvenal's most interesting
achievements was to make serious and positive poetry out of Martial's little
intimations of immorality.'

Juvenal was a serious writer. The seeming looseness of his writing is
illusory: a total of sixteen satires over the best part of a quarter of a century
does not suggest that they were tossed off lightly. Juvenal in fact (like
Catullus) uses bad verse to good effect. Nor is his structure as careless as
Friedländer and others have made out. He is a master of controlled rhetoric
and knows the force of digression and disproportion.

His style is, as Highet puts it, 'boldly original'. One would not readily
mistake a passage of Juvenal. He has two supreme gifts. One lies in the use of
rhetorical language. Epigrams flash from his page: *probitas laudatur et alget*
(1,74); *nemo repente fuit turpissimus* (2,81); *omnia Romae/cum pretio*
(3,183-4); *quis custodiet ipsos/custodes?* (6,0 31-2); *et propter uitam uiuendi
perdere causas* (8,84); *panem et circenses* (10,81); *mens sana in corpore sano*
(10,350); *numquam aliud natura, aliud sapientia dicit* (14,321) — these are

only a few. He uses rare words, foreign words, conversational words, archaic words to make a point. He alludes to earlier authors, sometimes to fit his words into a context, sometimes to parody. He loves the deflating twist in the tail which the Greeks called *paraprosdokian*. Umbricius's *quid Romae faciam? mentiri nescio* (3,41) is one example. More elaborate is *uiuendum recte, cum propter plurima, tum est his/idcirco ut possis linguam contemnere serui* (9,118-9). Along with this goes hyperbole. Boileau said that Juvenal's main characteristic was driving mordant hyperbole to excess. An excellent example appears in the tenth satire where he suggests that the diseases of old age are as many as the patients killed off by Dr Themison in a single autumn — the partners eliminated by a businessman named Basilus, the orphans defrauded by Hirrus, the men worn out by Maura's love in a single day, the schoolboys corrupted by a homosexual teacher (10,221). Inez Gertrude Scott, in *The Grand Style in the Satires of Juvenal*, has made a valuable study of rhetorical effects in the grand manner, analysing (after the ancient critical theorists) his imagery (ἐνάργεια), rhetorical questions, apostrophe, asyndeton and anaphora, hyperbaton, accumulation, variation, climax, periphrasis, metaphor, transferred epithets and hyperbole. Juvenal particularly practises amplification. Hyperbole is one example of this; accumulation is another; comparison and contrast (5,56-9) and emphasis on minor detail may also be added.

One other verbal device I must mention is ambiguity. Since William Empson, we have become more aware of this in English poetry, but, except for a pioneering work by W. B. Stanford, little attempt has been made to apply it to the analysis of classical writings. Ambiguities may be of various kinds. Simile and metaphor are ambiguities; we are reading at two different levels. Epic allusion is another; Juvenal uses this for both serious and comic purposes. A good example of syntactical ambiguity comes when an adverb is placed in relation to more than one word: commentators tend to say that it 'goes with' one rather than another, but this is not really so: it is ambiguous. There are various forms of pun, some sharply pointed, some casual wordplay. So at 5,38 *inaequales* marks the irregular surface and the unfair difference of treatment; at 6,91 *molles* means that the chairs are comfortable and their occupants highly sexed; at 10,22 *uacuus* is empty-handed and free from care; at 15,160 *macula* is the leopard's spot with allusion to moral blemish. Such effects are naturally common with sexual innuendo: the Romans had plenty of allusive words to sex-organs and sexual acts. It is important to remember sometimes that we may have to choose between two meanings in translation where a Latin word carries in itself a scope which we express by more than one word. It is important too to recognise that with a writer as careful as Juvenal it is likely that ambiguous effects are deliberate; even if they were unconscious, this would still tell us something about the working of his poetic mind.

Juvenal's other great gift is his capacity to convey a visual scene vividly with great verbal economy. We see this in the street-corner observations in the first satire (1,22-80), a succession of superb 'flashes', or from the same satire the curtained litter (1,124), or the poet at the stake (1,155). In the next satire we have the perverts with eyelids trembling as they daub on mascara

(2,93-5). Among many pictures in the third there is the street-scene (3, 243-
8), the dead man's servants busy at their household duties (3,261-4), the
brawl (3,291-9). Or again the marvellous cameos in the sixth satire, Messalina
in the brothel (6,115-35), or the rich lady making up her face or toying with
the fringe of her dress while a slave is being cruelly beaten (6,481-5). Or from
the tenth, the picture of Sejanus's statues dragged down and vilified, one of
the greatest of all pieces of word-painting (10,58-64). Many of his *exempla*
are characteristic of rhetoric, but he makes them unmistakably his own.

So he fortifies his attack on *luxuria*, on excess, and cruelty, and sexual
indulgence, and greed, and indifference to others, and triviality. He is attack-
ing aristocrats, but no non-aristocrat can feel self-righteous when reading
Juvenal. For his weapons still strike home; his grand pessimism forces us to
look freshly at ourselves; which is why he is still read.

JUVENAL AND SOCIAL CHANGE

In 1971 Tony Reekmans broke quite fresh ground in his brilliant article
'Juvenal's Views on Social Change' *Ancient Society* 2 (1971) 117-61. What
follows summarises some of his main points.

Juvenal accepts seven social categories, each with its own pecking order.

Extraction	Nobility	Liberty	Fortune	Business	Age	Sex
Romans	*patricii*	*ingenui*	*diuites*	liberal arts	*senes*	*uiri*
European Greeks	senatorial order	*libertini*	equestrian *census*	*militia*	*iuuenes*	*mulieres*
Eastern Greeks	equestrian order·	*serui*	*pauperes*	*artes ludicrae*	*pueri, puellae*	*semiuiri*
Barbarians	*plebs*		*humiliores*	*artes sordidae magistri uoluptatum* gladiators	*infantes*	

The ranks are distinguished by their own customs and habits.

Much of Juvenal's satire is directed against nonconformity: this is made
clear in the first satire when a eunuch or a Mevia adopts the style of a *uir*. He
attacks particularly nonconformity by members of the higher ranks: the
Romans who adopt Greek dress (3,67-8), or practise Egyptian or Jewish
religions (6,526-30; 14,101-2); the descent by nobles into the plebeian queues
(1,99-101) or the arena (6,250-1), and so on. This leads them to deny their
specific obligations, and to oust the lower orders from their natural customs.
But Juvenal also attacks the social climbers, the lower classes who ape the
rich (1,124; 7,144; 11,1-5, etc.), the women who behave like men, the
immigrants who take on Roman customs especially of the nobility, the
indocti who affect books and statues (2,4-7). The social problems all this

gave rise to are: renunciation and usurpation of rights; neglect of duties and lack of responsibility; abuse of power and breach of trust.

Reekmans goes on to discuss structural changes arising from status-inconsistency, and has a valuable table summarising his observations (I have in the second column used + for increased, – for diminished; in the third + for positive, – for negative; in the last L for levelled, R for reversed, I for increased).

Social categories	Social distance	Integration	Hierarchy
Romans — foreigners	–	+	LR
nobility — *plebs*	–	+	LRI
rich — poor	+	–	LI
freeborn — slaves	–		LR
men — women	–		R
higher — lower trades			L
elder — younger			R
Social positions			
husband — wife	+	–	R
owner — slaves		–	R
domina — slaves	–		
patronus — client	+	–	I
wife — *adulter*	–	+	
clients — freedmen	–		
clients — slaves			LR
orbi-captatores		+	I
teachers — pupils			R
clients (*inter se*)	–	–	R

It will be noticed in the last column that Juvenal is liable to complain sometimes that the hierarchical structure has been exaggerated, sometimes that it has been negated, and that he may even bring both complaints (seemingly contradictory) within the same social category. He does not establish connections between the three socio-structural dimensions represented by the three columns, though they are plainly connected. He is less interested in the interaction between cultural and structural changes than in the influence of the changed cultural pattern upon social structure.

Juvenal in fact fails to integrate himself with a changing world.

JUVENAL AND ROMAN SOCIETY

In the eighteenth century Edward Gibbon wrote: 'If a man were called to fix the period in the history of the world during which the condition of the human race was most happy and prosperous, he would without hesitation name that which elapsed from the death of Domitian to the accession of Commodus.' Yet this is the very period at the outset of which Juvenal was writing. Gibbon was more reconciled to autocracy than we are today, but

Juvenal never challenges the principle of autocracy. Gibbon writes with ironical undertones, but that is because he can see the decline and fall to come, not because he disavows the happiness and prosperity of the preceding period. Are we then to take Juvenal's depressed view or Gibbon's exalted view of the period?

Certainly the younger Pliny gives us a very different picture from Juvenal's. He was, he admits, inclined to idealise his friends (*Ep.* 7,28); he was charitable in temperament and comfortable in position; he shows us, as Sir Samuel Dill pleasantly put it, 'a society in which people are charmingly refined, and perhaps a little too good.' But even when allowances have been made, Pliny's society is a calm society, not frenetic like the world Juvenal depicts, a world of leisure and letters, endowed with a sense of public responsibility and private concern for others, enjoying alike the peace of the countryside and the innocent pleasures of urban fellowship.

If we look more widely, we are looking to the 'immeasurable majesty of the peace provided by Rome'. Haverfield called the Roman Empire the greatest experiment the world has yet seen in Free Trade and Home Rule. Travel was secure and swift, as it had never been, and was not to be for many centuries to come. Paul's freedom of travel is but one example. Flavius Zeuxis, a workman from Hierapolis in Phrygia, boasts in his epitaph that he has sailed past Cape Matapan no less than seventy-two times. A merchant from Mysia claims wide-ranging experience, including fifteen voyages to Rome, two to Germany, four to the Danube, two to Alexandria and more besides. It is important too that Roman government and Roman culture were reinforced by those from outside Rome, so that we have Spaniards, the Senecas and Lucan and Quintilian and Martial and Trajan and Hadrian, followed by those from Africa, Fronto, Apuleius, Tertullian and the Severi. Greek culture flourished; the Second Sophistic produced men of ability; there was original work in science and medicine; Epicureanism came to a new prominence; there were writers of near-genius, such as Plutarch and Lucian. The picture is not Juvenal's; can we discount Juvenal?

The answer is, of course, 'Yes and No'. The achievements of the Roman Empire were immense: it is not negligible to have given a wider area of the globe a longer period of peace than at any time in the history of man (with the possible but not certain exception of some eras in China) either before or since. Or we may think of the rule of law giving to life a solid and reliable framework, a protection against arbitrary oppression; and in this connection, we may think of the progressive humanitarianism of the legislation concerned with slaves, Claudius decreeing that a sick slave abandoned by his master, if he recovered, should go free, Hadrian banning the sale of boys and girls for prostitution, and declaring the murder of a slave a capital crime. To draw one's impressions of the second-century Empire exclusively from Juvenal can only produce unhistorical results. Juvenal does not profess to offer a reliable picture. In the first place, he concentrates almost exclusively on Rome. Rome and Alexandria, perhaps alone in the ancient world, suffered from what we today call 'inner city' problems and all the tensions of urbanisation. Secondly, Pliny speaks for the haves, for the establishment, for those in power; Juvenal dons the *persona* of the powerless. Gracious and generous living on the part of the upper classes is not incompatible with social injustice, often voiced not by those who are suffering most, but by those who are near enough to the privileged to feel excluded.

It is therefore important in reading Juvenal to look also at the positive achievements of the Romans during the first and second centuries; it is also important in evaluating those achievements to remember that there was another picture, caricatured perhaps, but also recognisable.

MANUSCRIPTS AND TEXTS

It is generally agreed that the best manuscript is a ninth-century codex in the Library of the Medical School at Montpellier, called the Codex Pithoeanus (P) after its sixteenth-century owner Pierre Pithon; this also preserves the ancient scholia; it has been corrected by four hands. No complete MS derives from this, though there are some fragments of the same tradition. The other MSS are generally inferior, but helpful when P is unclear. After the great work of Housman, there has been recent critical work by Knoche and Clausen. Clausen's Oxford text provides a convenient and reliable text with critical apparatus.

E. O. Winstedt in 1889 discovered in the Bodleian an eleventh-century MS with thirty-six additional lines in the sixth satire (see after 6,345). Their authenticity is controversial: they are rejected by Axelson and Knoche, favoured by Clausen, Courtney, Griffith and Highet. The lines are difficult, but fully worthy of Juvenal: if they are authentic they raise major questions as to how much more may have been lost.

Other small discoveries of some interest include a papyrus leaf of about AD 500 containing 7,149-98, unfortunately not very helpful (*Ant.*), a sixth-century fragment of 14,250-6, 268-91, 303-19, whose textual family is not quite clear (*Ambr.*), evidence of ninth-century readings for 2,32-89 and 3,35-93 left by a sheet glued to the cover of a textbook in Orleans (*Aurel.*).

One major question relates to interpolation. Jachmann has been the major exponent of this theme. Modern Juvenal scholars are divided between those who follow Jachmann and hold (sometimes pontifically) to a doctrine of extensive interpolation, and those who are more cautious and conservative, and take the view that the fact that lines are not up to Juvenal's best standard is no indication that he did not write them. I have no solution to offer on this. It is certain that there are some interpolations: in this text I have generally given the MSS the benefit of any doubt.

The text here presented has no claim to originality. It is based on Clausen. I have however accepted a number of readings different from his, mainly from more recent discussions and proposals; these are documented in the notes. I list below the principal divergences from his text; these do not include insignificant alterations in punctuation, the removal of obeli or square brackets, and one or two other minor matters. The object here is to present students with a readable text. I have not engaged in lengthy textual discussion, but generally refer to where the discussion may be found.

1,70	For *rubetam*	*rubeta* (PRV)
1,156-7	Line omitted	(Housman)
2,45	For *faciunt nam plura*	*faciunt peiora* (Bucheler)
2,168	For +*indulsit*+	*indulget* (Clausen)
3,109	For *aut*	*huic uel* (Green from Jacoby)
3,187	Change of punctuation	(Duff)
4,78-80	Change of punctuation	(Green)
4,128	For *in*	*per* (Housman)
6,12	For *rupto robore*	*rupe et robore* (Schotte)
6,50	For *uittas*	*uictus* (Giangrande)
6,107	For *sicut*	*sulcus* (Nisbet)
6,135	For *minimumque*	*summumque* (Courtney)
6,158	For *dedit hunc*	*gestare* (Housman)
6,167	For *Venustinam*	*Vetustinam*
6,195	For *relictis*	*ferendis* (Housman)
6,345	Insert 0 1-34 here	(Griffith)
6,09	For +*eupholio*+	*Euhoplo* (after Leo)
6,011	For +*pulsatamque arma*+	*pulsatoremque* (Leo)
6,415	For +*excitata*+	*experrecta* (Duff)
6,455	For *nec*	*haec* (Postgate)
7,16	For *gallica*	*Gallia* (ΦΣ)
7,22	For *expectanda*	*speranda* (Housman)
7,42	For *portas*	*porcas* (Jessen)
7,177	For *scindes*	*scindens* (PSΦ)
7,242	For *cura; sed*	*cures, et* (cod. det.)
8,7	For *Coruinum posthac*	*pontifices posse ac* (Housman)
8,112	For *nam*	*iam* (Bücheler)
8,161-2	Add *et* (161).	
	For *et* (162)	*iam* (Helmbold)
8,201	For *aut*	*et* (Nisbet)
8,220	For *Orestes*	*Oresten* (Jones)
8,241	For +*in*+	*sibi* (Jahn)
9,76	For *signabat*	*migrabat* (Highet)
9,118	For +*tunc est*+	*tum est his* (Housman)
10,54	For *quae*	*si*
10,175-6	Change of punctuation	(Housman)
10,183	For *quod*	*quid* and change of punctuation (Weber)
10,195	For *iam mater*	*Garamantis* (Ferguson)
10,197	For +*ille*+ *alio,*	*ardalio* (Giangrande)
10,313	For *irati*	*ex ira* (Clausen)
11,23	For *sumit*	*sumptus* (Heinrich)
11,156	For *raucus*	*draucus* (cod. det.)
12,14	For *et grandi ceruix iret*	*iret et a grandi ceruix* (Giangrande)
12,78	For *igitur*	*similis* (Housman)
13,23	For *furem*	*furtum* (Nisbet)

13,44	For *siccato*	*saccato* (Schurtzfleisch)
13,108	For *uexare*	*uectare* (Nisbet)
13,179	For *minimus*	*nimius* (Martyn: codd. det.)
13,213	For *sed uina*	*Setina* (Herel, Withof)
13,226	For *iudicet*	*uindicet* (Nisbet: codd. det.)
13,249	For *surdum*	*Drusum* (Courtney)
14,5-7	Change of punctuation	(Nisbet)
14,71	For *patriae*	*ciuis* (Housman)
14,229	For *et qui . . . conduplicari*	*quippe et . . . conduplicare* (Amyx)
14,269	For *+ac uilis+*	*adquirens* (Schreiber)
15,20	For *Cyaneis*	*Cyaneas* (cod. R. Stephani)
15,86	For *donauit*	*donasti* (Griffith)
15,143	For *ideo*	*adeo* (Nisbet)
16,18	For *+est igitur+*	*exigitur* (Bücheler)

GRAMMAR AND SYNTAX

(1) Nouns and Adjectives. Juvenal likes to use nouns adjectivally (3,110 *filia uirgo;* 4,33 *municipes siluros;* 15,22 *remigibus porcis* etc.).

He likes to use adjectives substantively (3,127 *pauper;* 3,240 *diues;* 13,55 *uetulo;* 14,11 *auarus* etc.).

He delights in periphrasis, especially in the use of an abstract noun rather than an adjective (4,39 *spatium admirabile rhombi;* 4,81 *Crispi iucunda senectus;* 4,107 *Montani uenter;* 13,184 *mite Thaletis ingenium*).

He uses proper names in the singular or plural, from mythology or history, in a representative capacity (1,61 *Automedon* of a charioteer; 7,94 *Maecenas* of a patron; 8,38 *Creticus aut Camerinus* of a blue-blooded aristocrat; 16,26 *Pylades* of a friend).

He takes rhetorical pleasure in allusiveness (1,20 *magnus Auruncae alumnus* of Lucilius; 5,45 *zelotypo iuuenis praelatus Iarbas* of Aeneas; 7,25 *Veneris marito* of fire).

He uses Greek terminations, usually to add to his scorn of things Greek.

Colloquial words, including diminutive forms, are common: the stock-in-trade of satire.

(2) Cases. In their simplest form the nominative represents the subject of the sentence, the vocative is the person addressed, the accusative limits the action of a verb, the dative is the person or thing indirectly concerned in an action. The genitive and ablative are more complex. The genitive is used when one noun depends on another in a variety of ways; an important use is the partitive genitive, where the genitive is the larger area from which a smaller quantity is taken. The ablative covers primarily origin in all its forms, or instrument. It should be remembered that case usage does not depend on a preposition: prepositions were originally adverbs, intensifying or clarifying the meaning.

Juvenal does not have many eccentric uses: but note 8,16 *attritus . . . lumbum;* 12,128 *uiuat . . . Nestora totum;* see notes. Internal accusatives are

common 1,16-7 *ut altum/dormiret; 14,295 aestiuum tonat.*
(3) Verbs. Tenses are fairly straightforward, and the usage is natural. Juvenal prefers the present to the perfect subjunctive in prohibitions: it is the more natural construction (14,203 *neu credas:* the perfect is found at 5,139; 14,48). The future participle is easily used to express purpose (7,116 *dicturus;* 8,130 *raptura*), destiny (1,18 *periturae;* 4,10 *subitura*), characteristic or likelihood (4,50 *dubitaturi;* 10,144 *haesuri;* 11,95 *factura;* 16,28 *excusaturos*). Once or twice an odd usage of a past tense is best explained as an imitation of the Greek aorist ('timeless'), e.g. 1,149 *omne in praecipiti uitium stetit:* 2,83 *nemo repente fuit turpissimus.*
    The simplest difference between indicative and subjunctive is simply that the latter is more remote, the former more vivid. This readily explains the so-called 'mixed conditionals', e.g. 6,98 *si iubeat coniunx, durum est conscendere nauem; 7,50 nam si discedas, . . . tenet . . ..*
    Juvenal uses *quamquam* and *quamuis* with the remoter subjunctive (11,205; 13,3), as well as with participles and adverbial phrases: these are normal Silver Latin usages.
    The infinitive is a verb-noun: at 14,30 *dat . . . ferre,* an apparent infinitive of purpose, really means 'gives for carrying'.
(4) Sentences. Juvenal often omits conjunctions, and this gives his writing a feeling of staccato abruptness. The different courses of Satire 5 and ambitions of Satire 10 are introduced without link. Similarly he avoids interrogative particles.
    Verbs are often omitted. This is obvious enough with the verb 'to be' (1,1 *semper ego auditor tantum?;* 13,26 *rari quippe boni*). Other verbs have also to be supplied (5,56 *flos Asiae ante ipsum* sc. *stat;* 13,182 *nempe hoc indocti* sc. *dicunt*). A particularly vivid ellipsis comes in rhetorical questions with *quo* and *unde* (8,9 *effigies quo tot bellatorum?* cf. 8,142; 14,56; 14,135; 15,61).
(5) On matters of syntax I have referred to E. C. Woodcock, *A New Latin Syntax* (London 1959).

METRE

(1) The terms 'long' and 'short' refer to the length of time taken to pronounce a sound. They are usually denoted by − ∪, but the musical signs ♩ ♩ (or ♩ ♪) give a clearer picture.
(2) A *vowel* is long or short by its natural pronunciation. The vowel sound is long in the southern English pronunciation of *bath,* short in the northern, long in *see,* short in *sit.* In Latin a long vowel is the extension of sound of a short one: a, a͡-a; e, e͡-e; i, i͡-i; o, o͡-o; u, u͡-u. Care should be taken in pronunciation to show this accurately (e.g. u is never sounded as in English *but,* but is closer to a shortening of English *too*). All diphthongs are obviously long, e.g. a͡-e.
(3) A *syllable* is long *either* if the vowel sound it contains is long, *or* if it ends in a consonant. The Romans 'carried on' from one word to the next, and indeed one sentence to the next, and where possible began a syllable with a consonant. In Satire 5,19 *quaeris? habet Trebius propter quod rumpere somnum* the syllabic division is *quae-ri-sha-bet-Tre-bi-us-prop-ter-quod-rum-*

pe-re-som-num. quae with its diphthong is long; so are *bet, us, prop, ter, quod, rum, som,* even though the vowel sound is short. In English the first syllable of *sit back* would be long, of *sit in* short. When r was involved as the second of two consonants the Romans were ambiguous, and sometimes divided it *pa-tris,* sometimes *pat-ris.*

(4) If a word ended in a vowel, or in *-am, -em, -im, -om, -um,* and the next word began with a vowel (or an aspirate), the Romans *elided* the final syllable of the first word, i.e. (as some think) omitted it, or, more probably, slurred it somehow, e.g. Satire 5,9 *tantin* (e) *iniuria cenae.* There seems to have been occasional *prodelision,* especially with *est,* e.g. *eundum 'st.*

(5) Latin had a word-accent. The matter is complex, and ancient grammarians are misleading, but it seems likely that this was a stress on one syllable (*mátter, sýllable, adóre*). In two-syllable words this was invariably on the first: *tíbi, fórma.* In three-syllable or longer words the accent fell on the penultimate if this were long (*parátus, recúmbas*), but on the antepenultimate if the penultimate were short (*cúrrĕre, quáttŭor*). Words of five syllables seem to have had a secondary accent (*ŏfficiórum*). It will be noticed that the English stress-accent is not consistent in this way; *réfuse* (garbage), but *refúse* (deny).

(6) The earliest Latin poetry seems to have been based on stress-accent, but the matter is controversial and does not help our understanding of Juvenal. This metre was known as Saturnian.

(7) Most extant Latin poetry before the medieval period is based on Greek practice, and follows Greek quantitative metres, i.e. musical rhythms.

(8) Juvenal wrote in the *dactylic hexameter catalectic.* The *dactyl* is a foot or bar in 4-time /♩ ♪ ♪/ with the spondee /♩ ♩/ admitted as its rhythmic equivalent. It is totally erroneous to treat the dactyl as a three-time waltz rhythm. A *hexameter* is a line of six bars or feet, but it is *catalectic,* because it is a syllable short. The rhythmic pattern then is

$$ ♩ \underset{\smile\smile}{♪♪} / ♩\underset{\smile\smile}{♪♪} / ♩\underset{\smile\smile}{♪♪} / ♩ \underset{\smile\smile}{♪♪} / ♩\underset{\smile\smile}{♪♪} / ♩ ♩(♪) $$

There is usually a dactyl in the fifth foot; Catullus and a group round him espoused the fifth-foot spondee, and were nicknamed the *spondeiazontes,* but even with them it was a special effect. The last syllable may be long or short.

(9) This metre was the metre of the old Greek epic bards, and was used in the two Homeric epics, and later in Latin epic. It was also, from the time of Q. Ennius and Lucilius through Horace and Persius to Juvenal the principal metre for the *satura.*

(10) There is a natural tendency, which should not be overdone, to stress the first beat of each bar. This is called the *ictus,* and is not to be confused with *accent.* Vergil in particular found that it was possible to create an effective balance between ictus and accent by (a) insisting on a stong caesura (a break between words after the first syllable) in the third foot, or, if not, in the second or fourth; (b) ending the line with *either* a two-syllable word preceded by a word of at least three syllables, *or* a three-syllable word preceded by a word of at least two syllables. This created generally a coincidence of ictus

and accent at the start, a clash in the middle, and a coincidence at the end.
Satires 1,1

Sḗmpĕr ḗ/g(o) āudī/tōr/ /tắn/tūm?/ /nūm/quắmnĕ rĕ́/pṓnam

Once the ear is acclimatised to this, variants can be introduced for special
effects e.g. Vergil's effect when the ox falls: we expect the line to end ⌣ ʋ ʋ /
⌣ —/ but we have *pro/cŭmbit hŭ́/mī bŏ̄s* with two offbeat accents, ending in
the monosyllabic thud. The satiric line is looser than Vergil's, but the effects
are still controlled, and Vergil is an inescapable voice in the background by
now.

(11) Juvenal breaks the expected rhythm in the last two feet more frequently
than Vergil, and indeed satiric verse is looser in structure than is epic. None-
the-less after a careful examination I am persuaded that he does this deliber-
ately, precisely in order to create a harsh effect.

(12) A second device that he uses to an unusual extent is the bucolic diaeresis.
This is a strong punctuation break at the end of the fourth foot. It has the
effect of breaking the line sharply into sections of four feet and two. Juvenal's
use of it is usually to draw attention to an epigram in the first four feet: it
marks it off memorably. Occasionally it is the words which follow which he
picks out.

(13) Assonance is a device of all poets. The Romans did not normally employ
rhyme: it was regarded as jingling, and therefore rhyme (or near-rhyme) is
usually used for a satirical effect (there is a remarkable example in Catullus 49
where *Marce Tulli* 'rhymes' with *-mas Catullus*). Alliteration is commoner: in
Juvenal it is often scornful, and *p* (rejection) or *c* and *t* (a sharp cutting sound)
is frequent for this purpose. But a general assonance, not merely of initial
letters, is common, especially one which plays on *m* and *n*.

(14) It will be clear that to read the line rhythmically is sometimes the only
way you can make sense of it. This may be true grammatically, e.g. to know
whether a first-declension noun or adjective is nominative or ablative: Satire
1,22-3 *Meuia Tuscum/figat aprum et nuda teneat uenabula mamma:* does
nuda agree with *Meuia, uenabula* or *mamma?* It is still more true of subtler
poetic effects.

(15) You must learn to read the line aloud, or at least hear it in your mind,
and in particular hear the rhythm which leads to the caesura and the rhythm
which leads away from it. There is no other way. In any event remember that
all ancient literature, prose and poetry, was meant to be heard, not read with
the eye, and is more rhetorical than much modern writing.

Glossary of Technical Terms

accent The natural stress on one syllable of a word.

accumulation Rhetorical device, consisting of the heaping up of parallel examples.

alliteration Succession of words with the same initial letter.

anaphora Pointed repetition of a word or phrase in successive clauses.

anastrophe Inverted word-order, with preposition following its noun, e.g. 14,202 *Tiberim ultra.*

antonomasia Replacing of one name by another, e.g. 7,25 *Veneris marito;* 10,112 *generum Cereris.*

apostrophe A 'turning away' to address an absent person.

asyndeton Absence of connectives as in 1,85-6; 3,73-8.

bucolic diaeresis A marked division of sense coinciding with the end of the fourth foot of a dactylic hexameter.

caesura A 'cutting': a break between words in the middle of a foot: in the dactylic hexameter 'strong' after the first syllable of a foot, 'weak' if falling between two short syllables. The main caesura divides the line into two unequal rhythmic units.

chiasmus A 'cross-pattern', created when the second of parallel phrases reverses the order of the first, e.g.

I cannot＼／dig
to beg ／＼I am ashamed

dactyl A foot or bar in 4/4 time consisting of one long note followed by two short ones ♩ ♪ ♪.

diaeresis A division between words coinciding with the end of a foot.

dittography Double-writing: repetition by a scribe of a word, combination of letters or phrase.

elision The omission or slurring of the last syllable of one word before a vowel beginning the next; in Latin when the previous word ends in a vowel or *m*, e.g. 6,635 *fin(em) egressi.*

ellipsis Omission of a word grammatically essential, e.g. 1,88-9; 10,72-3 where there is no verb.

enallage Variation of mood or tense in coordinate clauses e.g. 1,155-7; 7,185.

epanalepsis Repetition of the same word at the end of one line and start of the next, e.g. 2,135-6; 5,112-3; 6,279-80.

geminatio Repetition of the same word without break, e.g. 2,135-6.

hapax legomenon A word which occurs nowhere else.

haplography 'Single-writing': omission by a scribe of a group of letters similar to one already copied.

hendiadys Analysis of a single idea in two coequal parts, e.g. 10,152 *Alpemque niuemque* 'the snow-covered Alps' or 'the Alpine snows'.

hiatus An absence of elision; in Juvenal always coinciding with a strong caesura.

hyperbaton Moving words from their expected position.

hyperbole 'Overshooting', rhetorical exaggeration. Good examples are *Liburna* (3,240), *montem* (3,258), *antro* (4,21).

metonymy Replacing of one word by another. Quintilian says that it is more readily available in poetry than oratory (Q 8,6,73).

paraprosdokian An unexpected twist to a phrase, e.g. 8,158 *peruigiles placet instaurare — popinas;* 10,77-8 *suffragia nulli/ — uendimus* (for *damus*).

patronymic Name derived from a father's or ancestor's name.

periphrasis Indirect instead of direct description, either to skirt round a difficult or obscene subject, or for decorative purposes (Q 8,6,60).

pleonasm Use of more than one phrase with similar meaning.

polysyndeton Use of numerous connectives.

repetitio Repetition of the same word with a break, e.g. 1,102.

rhetorical question A question in form, but one which does not expect an answer, e.g. 1,1.

ring-form Structural device by which a poem or passage is given unity by 'coming full circle', so that the end picks up the beginning.

spondee A foot or bar in 4/4 time with two notes of equal length ♩ ♩.

syncope Contraction, e.g. *uincla* for *uincula* (3,310).

synecdoche 'Inclusive acceptance': the use of part for whole, e.g. 'sail' for 'ship'.

synizesis The blending of two vowels into a single syllable, e.g. *dein*.

transferred epithet The application of an adjective to a noun to which it cannot strictly apply, e.g. 13,116 *pia tura*.

zeugma Linking of two words in a similar construction readily applicable to either, but not easily to both at once, like Housman's parodic 'I go into the house with heels and speed.'

Bibliography

ABBREVIATIONS OF PERIODICAL TITLES

AJP	American Journal of Philology
Ath	Athenaeum
AUMLA	Journal of the Australasian Universities Modern Languages Association
CB	Classical Bulletin
CJ	Classical Journal
CP	Classical Philology
CQ	Classical Quarterly
CR	Classical Review
CW	Classical World
GR	Greece and Rome
HSCP	Harvard Studies in Classical Philology
J Ph	Journal of Philology
JRS	Journal of Roman Studies
Mnem	Mnemosyne
RCC	Rivista di Cultura Classica e Medioevale, Rome
REL	Revue des Etudes Latines
RFIC	Rivista di filologia e di instruzione classica (Torino)
RhM	Rheinische Museum
TAPA	Transactions and Proceedings of the American Philological Association
UCP	University of California Publications in Classical Philology
UCS	University of California Studies in Classical Antiquity
UTQ	University of Toronto Quarterly
YCS	Yale Classical Studies

SATIRE

Dryden, J. 'Discourse concerning Satire' in Kinsley, J. *The Poems of John Dryden* Vol. II Oxford 1958 pp. 601-70

Frye, N. 'The Nature of Satire' *UTQ* 14 (1944) 75-89 = (altd.) *Anatomy of Criticism* Princeton 1957 pp. 223-39

Highet, G. *The Anatomy of Satire* Princeton 1962

Hodgart, M. *Satire* London 1969

Kernán, A. *The Plot of Satire* New Haven 1965
Mack, M. 'The Muse of Satire' *Yale Review* 41 (1951) (also in Paulson)
Paulson, R. (ed.) *Satire: Modern Essays in Criticism* Englewood Cliffs 1971
Pollard, A. *Satire* London 1972
Sutherland, J. R. *English Satire* Cambridge 1958
Worcester, D. *The Art of Satire* New York 1960

CLASSICAL SATIRE

Cèbe, J-P. *La caricature et la parodie dans le monde romain antique des origines à Juvénal* Paris 1966
Coffey, M. *Roman Satire* London 1976
Duff, J. W. *Roman Satire: Its Outlook on Social Life* Berkeley 1936
Haight, E. H. *The Roman Use of Anecdotes in Cicero, Livy and the Satirists* New York 1940
Hendrickson, G. L. 'The Dramatic Satura and the Old Comedy at Rome' *AJP* 15 (1894) 1-30
Hendrickson, G. L. 'Satura, the Genesis of a Literary Form' *CP* 7 (1912) 177-89
Hendrickson, G. L. 'Satura Tota Nostra Est' *CP* 22 (1927) 46-60
Hopkins, H. M. 'Dramatic Satura in relation to Book Satura and the Fabula Togata' *TAPA* 31 (1900) 1-51
Ingersoll, J. W. D. 'Roman Satire: Its Early Name!' *CP* 7 (1912) 59-65
Knapp, C. 'The Sceptical Assault on the Roman Tradition concerning the Dramatic Satura' *AJP* 33 (1912) 125ff.
Knoche, U. *Die römische Satire* Göttingen [3]1971
Knoche, U. *Roman Satire* ET Bloomington 1975
Krenkel, W. (ed.) *Römische Satire* Rostock 1966
McKay, A. G. and Shepherd, D. M. *Roman Satire* Basingstoke 1976
Nettleship, H. 'The Original Form of the Roman Satura' *Lectures and Essays* II Oxford 1895 pp. 24-43
Ramage, E. S., Sigsbee, D. L. and Fredericks, S. C. *Roman Satirists and their Satire* Park Ridge, NJ 1974
Rudd, N. *The Satires of Horace* Cambridge 1966
Sullivan, J. P. (ed.) *Critical Essays on Roman Literature: Satire* London 1963
Terzaghi, N. *Per la storia della satira* Messina 1944
Tiddy, R. J. E. 'Satura and Satire' in Gordon, G. S. *English Literature and the Classics* Oxford 1912 pp. 196-227
Ullman, B. L. 'Satura and Satire' *CP* 8 (1913) 173-94
Ullman, B. L. 'The Present State of the Satura Question' *Studies in Philology* 17 (1920) 379-402
Van Rooy, C. A. *Studies in Classical Satire and Related Literary Theory* Leiden 1966
Weinreich, O. *Römische Satiren* Zürich 1949
Weston, A. H. *Latin Satirical Writing subsequent to Juvenal* Lancaster US 1915
Wheeler, A. L. 'Satura as a Generic Term' *CP* 7 (1912) 457-77
Witke, E. C. *Latin Satire: The Structure of Persuasion* Leiden 1970

JUVENAL: EDITIONS

Clausen, W. V. *A. Persi Flacci et D. Iuni Iuvenalis saturae* Oxford 1959
Duff, J. D. *D. Iunii Iuvenalis saturae XIV* Cambridge 1898 (rev. 1970)
Friedlaender, C. *D. Junii Juvenalis Saturarum Libri V* Leipzig 1895
Housman, A. E. *D. Iunii Iuvenalis saturae* Cambridge [2]1931
Knoche, U. *D. Iunius Iuvenalis: 'Saturae'* Munich 1950
Labriolle, P. de and Villeneuve, F. *Juvénal: Satires* Paris 1931
Lewis, J. D. *D. J. Juvenalis Satirae* London [2]1882
McKay, A. G. and Shepherd, D. M. *Roman Satire* Basingstoke 1976 (contains 1, 3, 4, 5, 7, 9, 10)
Mayor, J. E. B. *Thirteen Satires of Juvenal* 2 vols London [2]1872-8
Vianello, N. *Giovenale: Satirae* Turin 1935
Weidner, A. *D. Iunii Iuuenalis saturae, erklärt* Leipzig [2]1889
Wilson, H. L. *D. Iunii Iuuenalis saturarum libri V* Boston 1903

JUVENAL: TEXT AND REFERENCE

Courtney, E. 'The Transmission of Juvenal's Text' *Bull. Inst. Class. Stud.* 14 (1967) 38-50
Dubrocard, M. *Juvénal – Satires: Index Verborum: Relevés statistiques* Hildesheim 1976
Giangrande, G. 'Juvenalia: Emendations and Interpretations' *Eranos* 63 (1965) 26-41
Griffith, J. G. 'Author Variants in Juvenal: A Reconsideration' in *Festschrift für Bruno Snell* Munich 1956 pp. 101-11
Jachmann, G. 'Studien zu Juvenal' *Nachr. von der Akad. der Wiss. in Göttingen, phil.-hist. kl.* (1943) 187-266
Kelling, L. and Suskin, A. *Index verborum Iuvenalis* Chapel Hill 1951
Knoche, U. *Handschriftliche Grundlagen des Juvenaltextes* (*Philologus* Suppl. 33,1) 1940
Luck, G. 'The Textual History of Juvenal and the Oxford Lines' *HSCP* 76 (1972) 217-31
Nisbet, R. G. M. Review of W. V. Clausen *JRS* 52 (1962) 233-8
Wessner, P. *Scholia ad Iuuenalem uetustiora* Leipzig 1931

JUVENAL: TRANSLATIONS

Dryden, J. in Kinsley J. *The Poems of John Dryden* vol. II Oxford 1958 (1, 3, 6, 10, 16)
Gifford, W. *The Satires of D. J. Juvenalis, translated into English verse* London 1802
Green, P. *Juvenal: The Sixteen Satires* Harmondsworth 1967
Humphries, R. *The Satires of Juvenal* Bloomington 1958

JUVENAL: GENERAL

Anderson, W. S. 'Juvenal and Quintilian' *YCS* 17 (1961) 3-93
Anderson, W. S. 'Anger in Juvenal and Seneca' *UCP* 19 (1964) 127-96

Beaujeu, J. 'La réligion de Juvénal' in *Mélanges offerts à Jérome Carcopino* Paris 1966 pp. 71-81

Bodoh, J. J. 'Artistic Control in the Satires of Juvenal' *Aevum* 44 (1970) 475-82

Brugnoli, G. 'Il *dialogus* e Giovenale' *Riv. Cult. Class. e. Med.* 10 (1968) 252-9

Burrigs, E. E. 'The Religious Element in the Satires of Juvenal' *CW* 20 (1926) 19-21

Coffey, M. 'Juvenal Report for the Years 1941-61' *Lustrum* 8 (1963) 161-215

de Decker, J. *Juvenalis Declamans* Ghent 1913

Ebener, D. 'Juvenal' *Das Altertum* 10 (1964) 52-60

Ercole, P. 'La cronologia delle satire di Giovenale' *RFIC* 7 (1929) 184-207; 340-58

Ercole, P. *Studi Giovenaliani* Lanciano 1935

Fletcher, G. B. A. 'Juvenaliana' *Latomus* 35 (1976) 108-16

Ganger, F. *Zeitschilderung und Topik bei Juvenal* Diss. Greifswald 1936-7

Gérard, J. 'Juvénal et les associations d'artistes grecs à Rome' *REL* 48 (1970) 309-31

Gérard, J. *Juvénal et la réalité contemporaine* Paris 1976

Griffith, J. G. 'Juvenal, Statius and the Flavian Establishment' *GR* 16 (1969) 134-50

Harrison, E. L. 'Neglected Hyperbole in Juvenal' *CR* 10 (1960) 99-101

Hartmann, A. *De Inventione Iuvenalis* Basel 1908

Highet, G. 'The Philosophy of Juvenal' *TAPA* 80 (1949) 254-70

Highet, G. *Juvenal the Satirist* Oxford 1954

Jachmann, G. 'Studien zu Juvenal' *Nachr. d. Akad. d. Wiss. Göttingen phil.-hist. kl.* (1943) 187-266

Jefferis, J. D. 'Juvenal and Religion' *CJ* 34 (1939) 229-33

Kenney, E. J. 'Juvenal: Satirist or Rhetorician?' *Latomus* 22 (1963) 704-20

Knoche, U. Review of G. Highet *Juvenal the Satirist Gnomon* 29 (1957) 54-65

Labriolle, P. de 'Juvénal, peintre d'histoire' *Rev. Cours et Conf.* 31 (1930) 673-87

La Fleur, R. A. *A prosopographical commentary on Juvenal Book I* Diss. Duke 1973

Marache, R. 'Rhétorique et humeur chez Juvénal' *Hommages à Jean Bayet* Brussels 1964 pp. 474-8

Marchesi, C. *Giovenale* Rome 1921

Marmorale, E. V. *Giovenale* Bari ²1950

Martha, C. *Les Moralistes sous l'Empire Romain* Paris 1865

Martyn, J. R. C. *Friedländer's Essays on Juvenal* Amsterdam 1969

Mason, H. A. 'Is Juvenal a Classic?' *Arion* 1 (1962) 1,8-44; 2,39-79

Reekmans, T. 'Juvenal's Views on Social Change' *Anc. Soc.* 2 (1971) 117-6

Schütze, R. *Juvenalis ethicus* Diss. Greifswald 1904-5

Scott, I. G. *The Grand Style in the Satires of Juvenal* (Smith College Classical Studies 8) Northampton, Mass. 1927

Serafini, A. *Studio sulla satira di Giovenale* Florence 1957

Strefinger, J. *Der Stil des Satirikers Juvenals* Regensburg 1882

Thiel, A. *Juvenalis graecissans* Diss. Breslau 1901

Townend, G. B. 'The Literary Substrata to Juvenal's Satires' *JRS* 63 (1973) 148-60

Ullman, B. L. 'Psychological foreshadowings in the Satires of Horace and Juvenal' *AJP* 71 (1950) 408-16

Ullman, B. L. 'Miscellaneous Comments on Juvenal' in L. Wallach *The Classical Tradition* Ithaca 1966 pp. 274-84

Vico, P. de *Pensiero morale e religioso di Giovenale* Naples 1961

Waters, K. H. 'Juvenal and the Reign of Trajan' *Antichthon* 4 (1970) 62-77

Widal, A. *Juvénal et ses satires* Paris 1870

Wiesen, D. S. 'Juvenal and the Intellectuals' *Hermes* 101 (1973) 464-83

JUVENAL: LIFE AND PERSONALITY

Boissier, G. 'Juvénal et son temps' *Rev. des Deux Mondes* 87 (1870) 141-74

Brugnoli, G. 'Vita Iuvenalis' *Studi Urbinati* 37 (1963) 5-14

Dürr J. *Das Leben Juvenals* Ulm 1888

Dürr, J. 'Juvenal und Hadrian' in *Festschrift zu Otto Hirschfeld 60* Berlin 1903 pp. 447-51

Green, P. 'Juvenal and his Age' in *The Shadow of the Parthenon* London 1972 pp. 216-67

Highet, G. 'The life of Juvenal' *TAPA* 68 (1937) 480-506

Hild, J. A. *Juvénal: Notes biographiques* Paris 1884

Merchant, F. I. 'The parentage of Juvenal' *AJP* 22 (1901) 51-62

Meszaros, E. 'Zum Leben des Juvenal' *Archiv Philolog. Egyetemes Philologiai Közlöny* (1937) 219-27

Nettleship, H. 'The Life and Poems of Juvenal' *JPh* 16 (1888) 41-6 and in *Lectures and Essays* Oxford 1895 pp. 117-44

Pepe, L. 'Questioni Adrianee. Giovenale e Adriano' *Giorn. ital. di Filol.* 14 (1961) 163-73

Razzini, C. S. *Il diritto romano nelle satire di Giovenale* Turin 1913

Strack, C. *De Juvenalis exilio* Frankfurt 1880

Syme, R. *Tacitus* 2 vols Oxford 1958 pp. 499-500

Wiesen, D. 'Juvenal's Moral Character: an Introduction' *Latomus* 22 (1963) 440-1

JUVENAL AS A SOCIAL CRITIC

Barbu, N. I. 'Les esclaves chez Martial et Juvénal' *Acta Antiqua Philippopolitana* (1963) 67-74

Colton, R. E. 'Juvenal and Martial on the Equestrian Order' *CJ* 61 (1966) 157-9

Duff, J. W. *Roman Satire: Its Outlook on Social Life* Berkeley 1936

Ebener, D. 'Juvenal, Mensch, Dichter, Gesellschaftskritiker' *Altertum* 10 (1964) 55-60

Flores, E. 'Origini e ceto di Giovenale e loro riflessi nella problematica sociale delle satire' *Ann. Fac. Lett. Napoli* 10 (1962-3) 3-32

Hellegouarc'h, J. 'Les idées politiques et l'appartenance sociale de Juvénal' in *Studi in Onore di Eduardo Volterra* 2 (1969) 233-45

Knoche, U. 'Juvenals Mass-Stäbe der Gesellschaftkritik' *Wiss. Zeitschr. U. Rostock Gesellsch. und sprachwiss Reihe* 15 (1966) 453-61

Krenkel, W. 'Römische Satire und römische Gesellschaft' *Wiss. Zeitschr. U. Rostock Gesellsch. und sprachwiss. Reihe* 15 (1966) 471-7

La Fleur, R. A. '*Amicus* and *Amicitia* in Juvenal' *CB* 51 (1975) 54-8

Lepore, E. 'Un sintomo di coscienza occidentale all' apogeo dell' Impero' *Riv. Stor. Ital.* 60 (1948) 193-203

Marache, R. 'La revendication sociale chez Martial et Juvénal' *Riv. cult. class. med.* 3 (1961) 30-67

Reekmans, T. 'Juvenal's Views on Social Change' *Ancient Society* 2 (1971) 117-61

Sherwin-White, A. N. *Racial Prejudice in Imperial Rome* Cambridge 1967

Varcl, L. 'Die soziale Grundlage der Literatur bei den Satirikern des 2 Jahrhund. u. Zr.' *Acta Antiqua Philippopolitana* (1963) 305-12

Wiesen, D. 'Juvenal's Moral Character: an Introduction' *Latomus* 22 (1963) 440-71

JUVENAL: DEBT TO EARLIER WRITERS

Colton, R. E. 'Juvenal and Propertius' *Traditio* 23 (1967) 442-61

Ercole, P. 'Stazio e Giovenale' *Riv. indo-greco-ital. di filol., lingua, antichita* 15 (1931) 43-50

Gehlen, J. *De Juvenale Vergilii imitatore* Diss. Erlangen 1881

Highet, G. 'Juvenal's Bookcase' *AJP* 72 (1951) 193-209

Joly, D. 'Juvénal et les "Géorgiques" ' *Hommages à Jean Bayet* Brussels 1964 pp. 290-308

Lelièvre, F. J. 'Parody in Juvenal and T. S. Eliot' *CP* 53 (1958) 22-6

Lelièvre, F. J. 'Vergil and Juvenal's Third Satire' *Euphrosyne* 5 (1972) 457-62

Rebert, H. F. 'The Literary Influence of Cicero on Juvenal' *TAPA* 57 (1926) 181-94

Schneider, K. *Juvenal und Seneca* Diss. Wurzburg 1930

Scivoletto, N. 'Presenza di Persio in Giovenale' *Giorn. It. Fil.* 16 (1963) 60-72

Scott, I. G. *The Grand Style in the Satires of Juvenal* (Smith College Classical Studies) Northampton, Mass. 1927

Syme, R. *Tacitus* 2 vols Oxford 1958 pp. 776-8

Thomas, E. 'Ovidian Echoes in Juvenal' in N. Herescu (ed.) *Ovidiana* Paris 1958 p. 505-25

Thomas, E. 'Some Aspects of Ovidian Influence on Juvenal' *Orpheus* 7 (1960) 35-44

Wagenigen, J. van 'Seneca et Juvenalis' *Mnem.* 45 (1917) 417-29

JUVENAL AND MARTIAL

Anderson, W. S. '*Lascivia* vs *ira:* Martial and Juvenal' *UCS* 3 (1970) 1-34

Barbu, N. I. 'Les esclaves chez Martial et Juvénal' *Acta Antiqua Philippopolitana* (1963) 67-74

Boissier, G. 'Relations de Juvénal et de Martial' *Rev. Cours et Conférences* 7 (1899) 2. 443-51

Colton, R. E. 'Juvenal and Martial on Literary and Professional Men' *CB* 39 (1963) 49-52.

—— 'Cabinet Meeting, Juvenal's Fourth Satire' *CB* 40 (1963) 1-4

—— 'Juvenal 14 and Martial 9,46 on the Building Craze' *CB* 41 (1964) 26-7

—— 'Dinner Invitation, Juvenal 11, 56-208' *CB* 41 (1965) 39, 41-5

—— 'Juvenal's Second Satire and Martial' *CJ* 61 (1965) 68-71

—— 'Juvenal and Martial on the Equestrian Order' *CJ* 62 (1966) 157-9

—— 'Echoes of Martial in Juvenal's Third Satire' *Traditio* 22 (1966) 403-19

—— 'Some Rare Words used by Martial and Juvenal' *CJ* 67 (1971) 55-7

—— 'Echoes of Martial in Juvenal's Twelfth Satire' *Latomus* 31 (1972) 164-73

—— 'Cruelty and Vanity. Juvenal 6,490; 6,502-6 and Martial' *CB* 50 (1973) 5-6

—— 'Juvenal and Martial on Women who Ape Greek Ways' *CB* 50 (1973) 42-4

—— 'Juvenal's Thirteenth Satire and Martial' *CB* 51 (1975)

Marache, R. 'Le revendication sociale chez Martial et Juvenal' *RCCM* 3 (1961) 30-67

Nettleship. H. 'The Life and Poems of Juvenal' *JPh* 16 (1888) 41-6 and in *Lectures and Essays* Oxford 1895 pp. 117-44

Salanitro, N. *Gli epigrammi di Marziale a Giovenale* Naples 1948

Wilson, H. 'The Literary Influence of Martial upon Juvenal' *AJP* 19 (1898) 193-209

JUVENAL'S INFLUENCE

Alden, R. M. *The Rise of Formal Verse Satire in England under Classical Influence* Philadelphia 1899

Collignon, A. 'Victor Hugo et Juvénal' *Rev. d'Hist. Litt. de la France* 16 (1909) 259ff.

Colton, R. E. 'Ausonius and Juvenal' *CJ* 69 (1973) 41-51

Gabotto, F. 'Appunti sulla fortuna di alcuni autori romani nel medio evo' *Biblioteca delle scuole italiane, Verona* 3 (1891) 40-54

Highet, G. *Juvenal the Satirist* Oxford 1954 pp. 179-232

Hild, J. A. 'Juvénal dans le moyen âge' *Bull. de la Faculté de Poitiers* 8 (1890) 177-89; 9 (1891) 39-54; 106-22, 235-52

Sanford, E. M. 'Renaissance commentaries on Juvenal' *TAPA* 79 (1948) 92-112

Maps

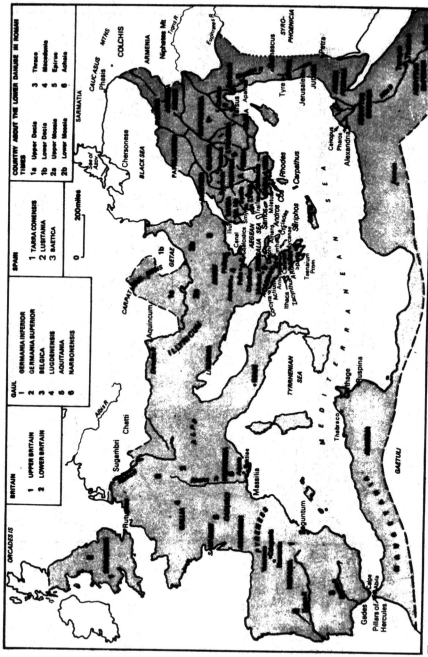

The Roman World

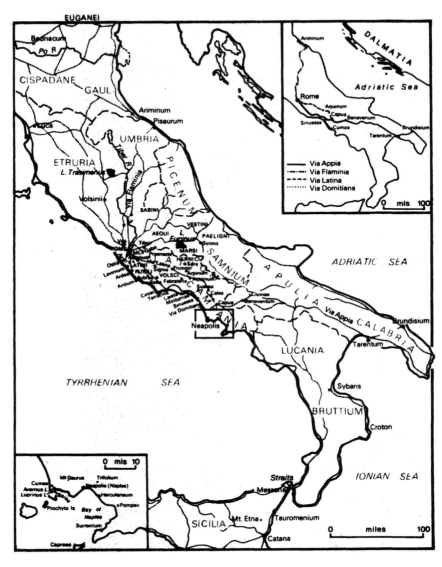

Italy

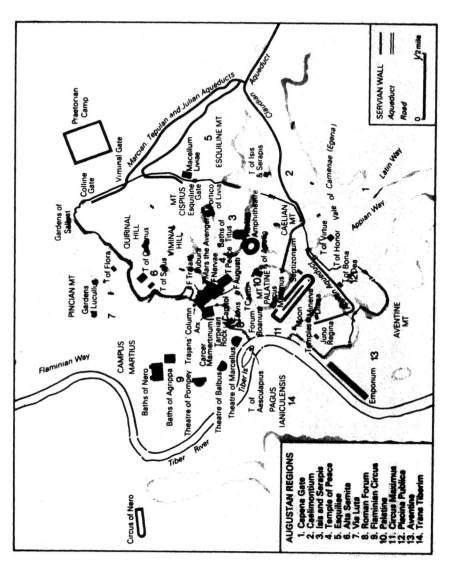

The City of Rome

The Satires

BOOK ONE

1

Semper ego auditor tantum? numquamne reponam
uexatus totiens rauci Theseide Cordi?
inpune ergo mihi recitauerit ille togatas,
hic elegos? inpune diem consumpserit ingens
Telephus aut summi plena iam margine libri   5
scriptus et in tergo necdum finitus Orestes?
nota magis nulli domus est sua quam mihi lucus
Martis et Aeoliis uicinum rupibus antrum
Vulcani; quid agant uenti, quas torqueat umbras
Aeacus, unde alius furtiuae deuehat aurum   10
pelliculae, quantas iaculetur Monychus ornos,
Frontonis platani conuolsaque marmora clamant
semper et adsiduo ruptae lectore columnae.
expectes eadem a summo minimoque poeta.
et nos ergo manum ferulae subduximus, et nos   15
consilium dedimus Sullae, priuatus ut altum
dormiret, stulta est clementia, cum tot ubique
uatibus occurras, periturae parcere chartae.
cur tamen hoc potius libeat decurrere campo,
per quem magnus equos Auruncae flexit alumnus,   20
si uacat ac placidi rationem admittitis, edam.
    cum tener uxorem ducat spado, Meuia Tuscum
figat aprum et nuda teneat uenabula mamma,
patricios omnis opibus cum prouocet unus
quo tondente grauis iuueni mihi barba sonabat,   25
cum pars Niliacae plebis, cum uerna Canopi
Crispinus Tyrias umero reuocante lacernas
uentilet aestiuum digitis sudantibus aurum
nec sufferre queat maioris pondera gemmae,
difficile est saturam non scribere, nam quis iniquae 30
tam patiens urbis, tam ferreus, ut teneat se,
causidici noua cum ueniat lectica Mathonis

plena ipso, post hunc magni delator amici
et cito rapturus de nobilitate comesa
quod superest, quem Massa timet, quem munere palpat   35
Carus et a trepido Thymele summissa Latino;
cum te summoueant qui testamenta merentur
noctibus, in caelum quos euehit optima summi
nunc uia processus, uetulae uesica beatae?
unciolam Proculeius habet, sed Gillo deuncem,   40
partes quisque suas ad mensuram inguinis heres.
accipiat sane mercedem sanguinis et sic
palleat ut nudis pressit qui calcibus anguem
aut Lugudunensem rhetor dicturus ad aram.
quid referam quanta siccum iecur ardeat ira,   45
cum populum gregibus comitum premit hic spoliator
pupilli prostantis et hic damnatus inani
iudicio? quid enim saluis infamia nummis?
exul ab octaua Marius bibit et fruitur dis
iratis, at tu uictrix, prouincia, ploras.   50
haec ego non credam Venusina digna lucerna?
haec ego non agitem? sed quid magis? Heracleas
aut Diomedeas aut mugitum labyrinthi
et mare percussum puero fabrumque uolantem,
cum leno accipiat moechi bona, si capiendi   55
ius nullum uxori, doctus spectare lacunar,
doctus et ad calicem uigilanti stertere naso;
cum fas esse putet curam sperare cohortis
qui bona donauit praesepibus et caret omni
maiorum censu, dum peruolat axe citato   60
Flaminiam puer Automedon? nam lora tenebat
ipse, lacernatae cum se iactaret amicae.
nonne libet medio ceras inplere capaces
quadriuio, cum iam sexta ceruice feratur
hinc atque inde patens ac nuda paene cathedra   65
et multum referens de Maecenate supino
signator falsi, qui se lautum atque beatum
exiguis tabulis et gemma fecerit uda?
occurrit matrona potens, quae molle Calenum
porrectura uiro miscet sitiente rubeta   70
instituitque rudes melior Lucusta propinquas
per famam et populum nigros efferre maritos.

aude aliquid breuibus Gyaris et carcere dignum,
si uis esse aliquid. probitas laudatur et alget;
criminibus debent hortos, praetoria, mensas,   75
argentum uetus et stantem extra pocula caprum.
quem patitur dormire nurus corruptor auarae,
quem sponsae turpes et praetextatus adulter?
si natura negat, facit indignatio uersum
qualemcumque potest, quales ego uel Cluuienus.   80
    ex quo Deucalion nimbis tollentibus aequor
nauigio montem ascendit sortesque poposcit
paulatimque anima caluerunt mollia saxa
et maribus nudas ostendit Pyrrha puellas,
quidquid agunt homines, uotum, timor, ira, uoluptas,   85
gaudia, discursus, nostri farrago libelli est.
et quando uberior uitiorum copia? quando
maior auaritiae patuit sinus? alea quando
hos animos? neque enim loculis comitantibus itur
ad casum tabulae, posita sed luditur arca.   90
proelia quanta illic dispensatore uidebis
armigero! simplexne furor sestertia centum
perdere et horrenti tunicam non reddere seruo?
quis totidem erexit uillas, quis fercula septem
secreto cenauit auus? nunc sportula primo   95
limine parua sedet turbae rapienda togatae.
ille tamen faciem prius inspicit et trepidat ne
suppositus uenias ac falso nomine poscas:
agnitus accipies. iubet a praecone uocari
ipsos Troiugenas, nam uexant limen et ipsi   100
nobiscum. 'da praetori, da deinde tribuno.'
sed libertinus prior est. 'prior' inquit 'ego adsum.
cur timeam dubitemue locum defendere, quamuis
natus ad Euphraten, molles quod in aure fenestrae
arguerint, licet ipse negem? sed quinque tabernae   105
quadringenta parant. quid confert purpura maior
optandum, si Laurenti custodit in agro
conductas Coruinus ouis, ego possideo plus
Pallante et Licinis?' expectent ergo tribuni,
uincant diuitiae, sacro ne cedat honori   110
nuper in hanc urbem pedibus qui uenerat albis,
quandoquidem inter nos sanctissima diuitiarum

maiestas, etsi funesta Pecunia templo
nondum habitat, nullas nummorum ereximus aras,
ut colitur Pax atque Fides, Victoria, Virtus   115
quaeque salutato crepitat Concordia nido.
sed cum summus honor finito conputet anno,
sportula quid referat, quantum rationibus addat,
quid facient comites quibus hinc toga, calceus hinc est
et panis fumusque domi? densissima centum   120
quadrantes lectica petit, sequiturque maritum
languida uel praegnas et circumducitur uxor.
hic petit absenti nota iam callidus arte
ostendens uacuam et clausam pro coniuge sellam.
'Galla mea est' inquit, 'citius dimitte. moraris?   125
profer, Galla, caput. noli uexare, quiescet.'
    ipse dies pulchro distinguitur ordine rerum:
sportula, deinde forum iurisque peritus Apollo
atque triumphales, inter quas ausus habere
nescio quis titulos Aegyptius atque Arabarches,   130
cuius ad effigiem non tantum meiiere fas est.
uestibulis abeunt ueteres lassique clientes
uotaque deponunt, quamquam longissima cenae
spes homini; caulis miseris atque ignis emendus.
optima siluarum interea pelagique uorabit   135
rex horum uacuisque toris tantum ipse iacebit.
nam de tot pulchris et latis orbibus et tam
antiquis una comedunt patrimonia mensa.
nullus iam parasitus erit. sed quis ferat istas
luxuriae sordes? quanta est gula quae sibi totos   140
ponit apros, animal propter conuiuia natum!
poena tamen praesens, cum tu deponis amictus
turgidus et crudum pauonem in balnea portas.
hinc subitae mortes atque intestata senectus.
it noua nec tristis per cunctas fabula cenas;   145
ducitur iratis plaudendum funus amicis.
    nil erit ulterius quod nostris moribus addat
posteritas, eadem facient cupientque minores,
omne in praecipiti uitium stetit. utere uelis,
totos pande sinus. dices hic forsitan 'unde   150
ingenium par materiae? unde illa priorum
scribendi quodcumque animo flagrante liberet

simplicitas? "cuius non audeo dicere nomen?
quid refert dictis ignoscat Mucius an non?"
pone Tigillinum, taeda lucebis in illa   155
qua stantes ardent qui fixo gutture fumant,
   <   >
et latum media sulcum deducit harena.'
qui dedit ergo tribus patruis aconita, uehatur
pensilibus plumis atque illinc despiciat nos?
'cum ueniet contra, digito compesce labellum: 160
accusator erit qui uerbum dixerit "hic est."
securus licet Aenean Rutulumque ferocem
committas, nulli grauis est percussus Achilles
aut multum quaesitus Hylas urnamque secutus:
ense uelut stricto quotiens Lucilius ardens   165
infremuit, rubet auditor cui frigida mens est
criminibus, tacita sudant praecordia culpa.
inde ira et lacrimae. tecum prius ergo uoluta
haec animo ante tubas: galeatum sero duelli
paenitet.' experiar quid concedatur in illos   170
quorum Flaminia tegitur cinis atque Latina.

2

Vltra Sauromatas fugere hinc libet et glacialem
Oceanum, quotiens aliquid de moribus audent
qui Curios simulant et Bacchanalia uiuunt.
indocti primum, quamquam plena omnia gypso
Chrysippi inuenias; nam perfectissimus horum,   5
si quis Aristotelen similem uel Pittacon emit
et iubet archetypos pluteum seruare Cleanthas.
frontis nulla fides; quis enim non uicus abundat
tristibus obscenis? castigas turpia, cum sis
inter Socraticos notissima fossa cinaedos?   10
hispida membra quidem et durae per bracchia saetae
promittunt atrocem animum, sed podice leui
caeduntur tumidae medico ridente mariscae.
rarus sermo illis et magna libido tacendi
atque supercilio breuior coma. uerius ergo   15
et magis ingenue Peribomius; hunc ego fatis
inputo, qui uultu morbum incessuque fatetur.

horum simplicitas miserabilis, his furor ipse
dat ueniam; sed peiiores, qui talia uerbis
Herculis inuadunt et de uirtute locuti   20
clunem agitant. 'ego te ceuentem, Sexte, uerebor?'
infamis Varillus ait, 'quo deterior te?'
loripedem rectus derideat, Aethiopem albus.
quis tulerit Gracchos de seditione querentes?
quis caelum terris non misceat et mare caelo   25
si fur displiceat Verri, homicida Miloni,
Clodius accuset moechos, Catilina Cethegum,
in tabulam Sullae si dicant discipuli tres?
qualis erat nuper tragico pollutus adulter
concubitu, qui tunc leges reuocabat amaras   30
omnibus atque ipsis Veneri Martique timendas,
cum tot abortiuis fecundam Iulia uuluam
solueret et patruo similes effunderet offas.
nonne igitur iure ac merito uitia ultima fictos
contemnunt Scauros et castigata remordent?   35
    non tulit ex illis toruum Laronia quendam
clamantem totiens 'ubi nunc, lex Iulia, dormis?'
atque ita subridens: 'felicia tempora, quae te
moribus opponunt. habeat iam Roma pudorem:
tertius e caelo cecidit Cato. sed tamen unde   40
haec emis, hirsuto spirant opobalsama collo
quae tibi? ne pudeat dominum monstrare tabernae.
quod si uexantur leges ac iura, citari
ante omnis debet Scantinia. respice primum
et scrutare uiros, faciunt peiora; sed illos   45
defendit numerus iunctaeque umbone phalanges.
magna inter molles concordia. non erit ullum
exemplum in nostro tam detestabile sexu.
Tedia non lambit Cluuiam nec Flora Catullam:
Hispo subit iuuenes et morbo pallet utroque.   50
numquid nos agimus causas, ciuilia iura
nouimus aut ullo strepitu fora uestra mouemus?
luctantur paucae, comedunt coloephia paucae.
uos lanam trahitis calathisque peracta refertis
uellera, uos tenui praegnantem stamine fusum   55
Penelope melius, leuius torquetis Arachne,
horrida quale facit residens in codice paelex.

notum est cur solo tabulas inpleuerit Hister
liberto, dederit uiuus cur multa puellae.
diues erit magno quae dormit tertia lecto.   60
tu nube atque tace: donant arcana cylindros.
de nobis post haec tristis sententia fertur?
dat ueniam coruis, uexat censura columbas.'
    fugerunt trepidi uera ac manifesta canentem
Stoicidae; quid enim falsi Laronia? sed quid   65
non facient alii, cum tu multicia sumas,
Cretice, et hanc uestem populo mirante perores
in Proculas et Pollittas? est moecha Fabulla;
damnetur, si uis, etiam Carfinia: talem
non sumet damnata togam. 'sed Iulius ardet,   70
aestuo.' nudus agas: minus est insania turpis.
en habitum quo te leges ac iura ferentem
uulneribus crudis populus modo uictor et illud
montanum positis audiret uulgus aratris.
quid non proclames, in corpore iudicis ista   75
si uideas? quaero an deceant multicia testem.
acer et indomitus libertatisque magister,
Cretice, perluces. dedit hanc contagio labem
et dabit in plures, sicut grex totus in agris
unius scabie cadit et porrigine porci   80
uuaque conspecta liuorem ducit ab uua.
    foedius hoc aliquid quandoque audebis amictu;
nemo repente fuit turpissimus. accipient te
paulatim qui longa domi redimicula sumunt
frontibus et toto posuere monilia collo   85
atque bonam tenerae placant abdomine porcae
et magno.cratere deam. sed more sinistro
exagitata procul non intrat femina limen:
solis ara deae maribus patet. 'ite, profanae,'
clamatur, 'nullo gemit hic tibicina cornu.'   90
talia secreta coluerunt orgia taeda
Cecropiam soliti Baptae lassare Cotyton.
ille supercilium madida fuligine tinctum
obliqua producit acu pingitque trementis
attollens oculos; uitreo bibit ille priapo   95
reticulumque comis auratum ingentibus implet
caerulea indutus scutulata aut galbina rasa

et per Iunonem domini iurante ministro;
ille tenet speculum, pathici gestamen Othonis,
Actoris Aurunci spolium, quo se ille uidebat   100
armatum, cum iam tolli uexilla iuberet.
res memoranda nouis annalibus atque recenti
historia, speculum ciuilis sarcina belli.
nimirum summi ducis est occidere Galbam
et curare cutem, summi constantia ciuis   105
Bebriaci campis solium adfectare Palati
et pressum in faciem digitis extendere panem,
quod nec in Assyrio pharetrata Sameramis orbe
maesta nec Actiaca fecit Cleopatra carina.
hic nullus uerbis pudor aut reuerentia mensae,   110
hic turpis Cybeles et fracta uoce loquendi
libertas et crine senex fanaticus albo
sacrorum antistes, rarum ac memorabile magni
gutturis exemplum conducendusque magister.
quid tamen expectant, Phrygio quos tempus erat iam   115
more superuacuam cultris abrumpere carnem?
    quadringenta dedit Gracchus sestertia dotem
cornicini, siue hic recto cantauerat aere;
signatae tabulae, dictum 'feliciter,' ingens
cena sedet, gremio iacuit noua nupta mariti.   120
o proceres, censore opus est an haruspice nobis?
scilicet horreres maioraque monstra putares,
si mulier uitulum uel si bos ederet agnum?
segmenta et longos habitus et flammea sumit
arcano qui sacra ferens nutantia loro   125
sudauit clipeis ancilibus. o pater urbis,
unde nefas tantum Latiis pastoribus? unde
haec tetigit, Gradiue, tuos urtica nepotes?
traditur ecce uiro clarus genere atque opibus uir,
nec galeam quassas nec terram cuspide pulsas   130
nec quereris patri. uade ergo et cede seueri
iugeribus campi, quem neglegis. 'officium cras
primo sole mihi peragendum in ualle Quirini.'
quae causa officii?' 'quid quaeris? nubit amicus
nec multos adhibet.' liceat modo uiuere, fient,   135
fient ista palam, cupient et in acta referri.
interea tormentum ingens nubentibus haeret

quod nequeant parere et partu retinere maritos.
sed melius, quod nil animis in corpora iuris
natura indulget: steriles moriuntur, et illis   140
turgida non prodest condita pyxide Lyde,
nec prodest agili palmas praebere luperco.
uicit et hoc monstrum tunicati fuscina Gracchi,
lustrauitque fuga mediam gladiator harenam
et Capitolinis generosior et Marcellis   145
et Catuli Paulique minoribus et Fabiis et
omnibus ad podium spectantibus, his licet ipsum
admoueas cuius tunc munere retia misit.
    esse aliquos manes et subterranea regna,
Cocytum et Stygio ranas in gurgite nigras,   150
atque una transire uadum tot milia cumba
nec pueri credunt, nisi qui nondum aere lauantur.
sed tu uera puta: Curius quid sentit et ambo
Scipiadae, quid Fabricius manesque Camilli,
quid Cremerae legio et Cannis consumpta iuuentus,   155
tot bellorum animae, quotiens hinc talis ad illos
umbra uenit? cuperent lustrari, si qua darentur
sulpura cum taedis et si foret umida laurus.
illic heu miseri traducimur. arma quidem ultra
litora Iuuernae promouimus et modo captas   160
Orcadas ac minima contentos nocte Britannos,
sed quae nunc populi fiunt uictoris in urbe
non faciunt illi quos uicimus. et tamen unus
Armenius Zalaces cunctis narratur ephebis
mollior ardenti sese indulsisse tribuno.   165
aspice quid faciant commercia: uenerat obses,
hic fiunt homines. nam si mora longior urbem
indulget pueris, non umquam derit amator.
mittentur bracae, cultelli, frena, flagellum:
sic praetextatos referunt Artaxata mores.   170

3

Quamuis digressu ueteris confusus amici
laudo tamen, uacuis quod sedem figere Cumis
destinet atque unum ciuem donare Sibyllae.
ianua Baiarum est et gratum litus amoeni

secessus. ego uel Prochytam praepono Suburae;   5
nam quid tam miserum, tam solum uidimus, ut non
deterius credas horrere incendia, lapsus
tectorum adsiduos ac mille pericula saeuae
urbis et Augusto recitantes mense poetas?
sed dum tota domus raeda componitur una,   10
substitit ad ueteres arcus madidamque Capenam.
hic, ubi nocturnae Numa constituebat amicae
(nunc sacri fontis nemus et delubra locantur
Iudaeis, quorum cophinus fenumque supellex;
omnis enim populo mercedem pendere iussa est   15
arbor et eiectis mendicat silua Camenis),
in uallem Egeriae descendimus et speluncas
dissimiles ueris. quanto praesentius esset
numen aquis, uiridi si margine cluderet undas
herba nec ingenuum uiolarent marmora tofum.   20
    hic tunc Vmbricius 'quando artibus' inquit 'honestis
nullus in urbe locus, nulla emolumenta laborum,
·res hodie minor est here quam fuit atque eadem cras
deteret exiguis aliquid, proponimus illuc
ire, fatigatas ubi Daedalus exuit alas,   25
dum noua canities, dum prima et recta senectus,
dum superest Lachesi quod torqueat et pedibus me
porto meis nullo dextram subeunte bacillo.
cedamus patria. uiuant Artorius istic
et Catulus, maneant qui nigrum in candida uertunt,   30
quis facile est aedem conducere, flumina, portus,
siccandam eluuiem, portandum ad busta cadauer,
et praebere caput domina uenale sub hasta.
quondam hi cornicines et municipalis harenae
perpetui comites notaeque per oppida buccae   35
munera nunc edunt et, uerso pollice uulgus
cum iubet, occidunt populariter; inde reuersi
conducunt foricas, et cur non omnia? cum sint
quales ex humili magna ad fastigia rerum
extollit quotiens uoluit Fortuna iocari.   40
quid Romae faciam? mentiri nescio; librum,
si malus est, nequeo laudare et poscere; motus
astrorum ignoro; funus promittere patris
nec uolo nec possum; ranarum uiscera numquam

inspexi; ferre ad nuptam quae mittit adulter,   45
quae mandat, norunt alii; me nemo ministro
fur erit, atque ideo nulli comes exeo tamquam
mancus et extinctae corpus non utile dextrae.
quis nunc diligitur nisi conscius et cui feruens
aestuat occultis animus semperque tacendis?   50
nil tibi se debere putat, nil conferet umquam,
participem qui te secreti fecit honesti.
carus erit Verri qui Verrem tempore quo uult
accusare potest. tanti tibi non sit opaci
omnis harena Tagi quodque in mare uoluitur aurum,   55
ut somno careas ponendaque praemia sumas
tristis et a magno semper timearis amico.
    quae nunc diuitibus gens acceptissima nostris
et quos praecipue fugiam, properabo fateri,
nec pudor obstabit. non possum ferre, Quirites,   60
Graecam urbem. quamuis quota portio faecis Achaei?
iam pridem Syrus in Tiberim defluxit Orontes
et linguam et mores et cum tibicine chordas
obliquas nec non gentilia tympana secum
uexit et ad circum iussas prostare puellas.   65
ite, quibus grata est picta lupa barbara mitra.
rusticus ille tuus sumit trechedipna, Quirine,
et ceromatico fert niceteria collo.
hic alta Sicyone, ast hic Amydone relicta,
hic Andro, ille Samo, hic Trallibus aut Alabandis,   70
Esquilias dictumque petunt a uimine collem,
uiscera magnarum domuum dominique futuri.
ingenium uelox, audacia perdita, sermo
promptus et Isaeo torrentior. ede quid illum
esse putes. quemuis hominem secum attulit ad nos: 75
grammaticus, rhetor, geometres, pictor, aliptes,
augur, schoenobates, medicus, magus, omnia nouit
Graeculus esuriens: in caelum iusseris ibit.
in summa non Maurus erat neque Sarmata nec Thrax
qui sumpsit pinnas, mediis sed natus Athenis.   80
horum ego non fugiam conchylia? me prior ille
signabit fultusque toro meliore recumbet,
aduectus Romam quo pruna et cottana uento?
usque adeo nihil est quod nostra infantia caelum

hausit Auentini baca nutrita Sabina?   85
quid quod adulandi gens prudentissima laudat
sermonem indocti, faciem deformis amici,
et longum inualidi collum ceruicibus aequat
Herculis Antaeum procul a tellure tenentis,
miratur uocem angustam, qua deterius nec   90
ille sonat quo mordetur gallina marito?
haec eadem licet et nobis laudare, sed illis
creditur. an melior cum Thaida sustinet aut cum
uxorem comoedus agit uel Dorida nullo
cultam palliolo? mulier nempe ipsa uidetur,   95
non persona, loqui: uacua et plana omnia dicas
infra uentriculum et tenui distantia rima.
nec tamen Antiochus nec erit mirabilis illic
aut Stratocles aut cum molli Demetrius Haemo:
natio comoeda est. rides, maiore cachinno   100
concutitur; flet, si lacrimas conspexit amici,
nec dolet; igniculum brumae si tempore poscas,
accipit endromidem; si dixeris "aestuo," sudat.
non sumus ergo pares: melior, qui semper et omni
nocte dieque potest aliena sumere uultum   105
a facie, iactare manus laudare paratus,
si bene ructauit, si rectum minxit amicus,
si trulla inuerso crepitum dedit aurea fundo.
praeterea sanctum nihil huic uel ab inguine tutum,
non matrona laris, non filia uirgo, nec ipse   110
sponsus leuis adhuc, non filius ante pudicus.
horum si nihil est, auiam resupinat amici.
[scire uolunt secreta domus atque inde timeri.]
et quoniam coepit Graecorum mentio, transi
gymnasia atque audi facinus maioris abollae.   115
Stoicus occidit Baream delator amicum
discipulumque senex ripa nutritus in illa
ad quam Gorgonei delapsa est pinna caballi.
non est Romano cuiquam locus hic, ubi regnat
Protogenes aliquis uel Diphilus aut Hermarchus,   120
qui gentis uitio numquam partitur amicum,
solus habet, nam cum facilem stillauit in aurem
exiguum de naturae patriaeque ueneno,
limine summoueor, perierunt tempora longi

seruitii; nusquam minor est iactura clientis.   125
   quod porro officium, ne nobis blandiar, aut quod
pauperis hic meritum, si curet nocte togatus
currere, cum praetor lictorem inpellat et ire
praecipitem iubeat dudum uigilantibus orbis,
ne prior Albinam et Modiam collega salutet?   130
diuitis hic seruo cludit latus ingenuorum
filius; alter enim quantum in legione tribuni
accipiunt donat Caluinae uel Catienae,
ut semel aut iterum super illam palpitet; at tu,
cum tibi uestiti facies scorti placet, haeres   135
et dubitas alta Chionen deducere sella.
da testem Romae tam sanctum quam fuit hospes
numinis Idaei, procedat uel Numa uel qui
seruauit trepidam flagranti ex aede Mineruam:
protinus ad censum, de moribus ultima fiet   140
quaestio. "quot pascit seruos? quot possidet agri
iugera? quam multa magnaque paropside cenat?"
quantum quisque sua nummorum seruat in arca,
tantum habet et fidei. iures licet et Samothracum
et nostrorum aras, contemnere fulmina pauper   145
creditur atque deos dis ignoscentibus ipsis.
quid quod materiam praebet causasque iocorum
omnibus hic idem, si foeda et scissa lacerna,
si toga sordidula est et rupta calceus alter
pelle patet, uel si consuto uolnere crassum   150
atque recens linum ostendit non una cicatrix?
nil habet infelix paupertas durius in se
quam quod ridiculos homines facit. "exeat" inquit,
"si pudor est, et de puluino surgat equestri,
cuius res legi non sufficit, et sedeant hic   155
lenonum pueri quocumque ex fornice nati,
hic plaudat nitidus praeconis filius inter
pinnirapi cultos iuuenes iuuenesque lanistae."
sic libitum uano, qui nos distinxit, Othoni.
quis gener hic placuit censu minor atque puellae   160
sarcinulis inpar? quis pauper scribitur heres?
quando in consilio est aedilibus? agmine facto
debuerant olim tenues migrasse Quirites.
haut facile emergunt quorum uirtutibus obstat

res angusta domi, sed Romae durior illis   165
conatus: magno hospitium miserabile, magno
seruorum uentres, et frugi cenula magno.
fictilibus cenare pudet, quod turpe negabis
translatus subito ad Marsos mensamque Sabellam
contentusque illic Veneto duroque cucullo.   170
pars magna Italiae est, si uerum admittimus, in qua
nemo togam sumit nisi mortuus, ipsa dierum
festorum herboso colitur si quando theatro
maiestas tandemque redit ad pulpita notum
exodium, cum personae pallentis hiatum   175
in gremio matris formidat rusticus infans,
aequales habitus illic similesque uidebis
orchestram et populum; clari uelamen honoris
sufficiunt tunicae summis aedilibus albae.
hic ultra uires habitus nitor, hic aliquid plus   180
quam satis est interdum aliena sumitur arca.
commune id uitium est: hic uiuimus ambitiosa
paupertate omnes. quid te moror? omnia Romae
cum pretio. quid das, ut Cossum aliquando salutes,
ut te respiciat clauso Veiiento labello?   185
ille metit barbam, crinem hic deponit amati;
plena domus libis uenalibus. "accipe et istud
fermentum tibi habe." praestare tributa clientes
cogimur et cultis augere peculia seruis.
   quis timet aut timuit gelida Praeneste ruinam   190
aut positis nemorosa inter iuga Volsiniis aut
simplicibus Gabiis aut proni Tiburis arce?
nos urbem colimus tenui tibicine fultam
magna parte sui; nam sic labentibus obstat
uilicus et, ueteris rimae cum texit hiatum,   195
securos pendente iubet dormire ruina.
uiuendum est illic, ubi nulla incendia, nulli
nocte metus. iam poscit aquam, iam friuola transfert
Vcalegon, tabulata tibi iam tertia fumant:
tu nescis; nam si gradibus trepidatur ab imis,   200
ultimus ardebit quem tegula sola tuetur
a pluuia, molles ubi reddunt oua columbae.
lectus erat Cordo Procula minor, urceoli sex
ornamentum abaci, nec non et paruulus infra

cantharus et recubans sub eodem marmore Chiron,   205
iamque uetus Graecos seruabat cista libellos
et diuina opici rodebant carmina mures.
nil habuit Cordus, quis enim negat? et tamen illud
perdidit infelix totum nihil. ultimus autem
aerumnae cumulus, quod nudum et frusta rogantem   210
nemo cibo, nemo hospitio tectoque iuuabit.
si magna Asturici cecidit domus, horrida mater,
pullati proceres, differt uadimonia praetor.
tum gemimus casus urbis, tunc odimus ignem.
ardet adhuc, et iam accurrit qui marmora donet,   215
conferat inpensas; hic nuda et candida signa,
hic aliquid praeclarum Euphranoris et Polycliti,
haec Asianorum uetera ornamenta deorum,
hic libros dabit et forulos mediamque Mineruam,
hic modium argenti. meliora ac plura reponit   220
Persicus orborum lautissimus et merito iam
suspectus tamquam ipse suas incenderit aedes.
si potes auelli circensibus, optima Sorae
aut Fabrateriae domus aut Frusinone paratur
quanti nunc tenebras unum conducis in annum.   225
hortulus hic puteusque breuis nec reste mouendus
in tenuis plantas facili diffunditur haustu.
uiue bidentis amans et culti uilicus horti
unde epulum possis centum dare Pythagoreis.
est aliquid, quocumque loco, quocumque recessu,   230
unius sese dominum fecisse lacertae.
    plurimus hic aeger moritur uigilando (sed ipsum
languorem peperit cibus inperfectus et haerens
ardenti stomacho); nam quae meritoria somnum
admittunt? magnis opibus dormitur in urbe.   235
inde caput morbi. raedarum transitus arto
uicorum in flexu et stantis conuicia mandrae
eripient somnum Druso uitulisque marinis.
si uocat officium, turba cedente uehetur
diues et ingenti curret super ora Liburna   240
atque obiter leget aut scribet uel dormiet intus;
namque facit somnum clausa lectica fenestra.
ante tamen ueniet: nobis properantibus obstat
unda prior, magno populus premit agmine lumbos

qui sequitur; ferit hic cubito, ferit assere duro 245
alter, at hic tignum capiti incutit, ille metretam.
pinguia crura luto, planta mox undique magna
calcor, et in digito clauus mihi militis haeret.
nonne uides quanto celebretur sportula fumo?
centum conuiuae, sequitur sua quemque culina. 250
Corbulo uix ferret tot uasa ingentia, tot res
inpositas capiti, quas recto uertice portat
seruulus infelix et cursu uentilat ignem.
scinduntur tunicae sartae modo, longa coruscat
serraco ueniente abies, atque altera pinum 255
plaustra uehunt; nutant alte populoque minantur.
nam si procubuit qui saxa Ligustica portat
axis et euersum fudit super agmina montem,
quid superest de corporibus? quis membra, quis ossa
inuenit? obtritum uolgi perit omne cadauer 260
more animae. domus interea secura patellas
iam lauat et bucca foculum excitat et sonat unctis
striglibus et pleno componit lintea guto.
haec inter pueros uarie properantur, at ille
iam sedet in ripa taetrumque nouicius horret 265
porthmea nec sperat caenosi gurgitis alnum
infelix nec habet quem porrigat ore trientem.
    respice nunc alia ac diuersa pericula noctis:
quod spatium tectis sublimibus unde cerebrum
testa ferit, quotiens rimosa et curta fenestris 270
uasa cadant, quanto percussum pondere signent
et laedant silicem. possis ignauus haberi
et subiti casus inprouidus, ad cenam si
intestatus eas: adeo tot fata, quot illa
nocte patent uigiles te praetereunte fenestrae. 275
ergo optes uotumque feras miserabile tecum,
ut sint contentae patulas defundere pelues.
ebrius ac petulans, qui nullum forte cecidit,
dat poenas, noctem patitur lugentis amicum
Pelidae, cubat in faciem, mox deinde supinus: 280
[ergo non aliter poterit dormire; quibusdam]
somnum rixa facit. sed quamuis inprobus annis
atque mero feruens cauet hunc quem coccina laena
uitari iubet et comitum longissimus ordo,

multum praeterea flammarum et aenea lampas.   285
me, quem luna solet deducere uel breue lumen
candelae, cuius dispenso et tempero filum,
contemnit. miserae cognosce prohoemia rixae,
si rixa est, ubi tu pulsas, ego uapulo tantum.
stat contra starique iubet. parere necesse est;   290
nam quid agas, cum te furiosus cogat et idem
fortior? "unde uenis" exclamat, "cuius aceto,
cuius conche tumes? quis tecum sectile porrum
sutor et elixi ueruecis labra comedit?
nil mihi respondes? aut dic aut accipe calcem.   295
ede ubi consistas: in qua te quaero proseucha?"
dicere si temptes aliquid tacitusue recedas,
tantumdem est: feriunt pariter, uadimonia deinde
irati faciunt. libertas pauperis haec est:
pulsatus rogat et pugnis concisus adorat   300
ut liceat paucis cum dentibus inde reuerti.
nec tamen haec tantum metuas; nam qui spoliet te
non derit clausis domibus postquam omnis ubique
fixa catenatae siluit compago tabernae.
interdum et ferro subitus grassator agit rem: 305
armato quotiens tutae custode tenentur
et Pomptina palus et Gallinaria pinus,
sic inde huc omnes tamquam ad uiuaria currunt.
qua fornace graues, qua non incude catenae?
maximus in uinclis ferri modus, ut timeas ne   310
uomer deficiat, ne marra et sarcula desint.
felices proauorum atauos, felicia dicas
saecula quae quondam sub regibus atque tribunis
uiderunt uno contentam carcere Romam.
    his alias poteram et pluris subnectere causas,   315
sed iumenta uocant et sol inclinat. eundum est;
nam mihi commota iamdudum mulio uirga
adnuit. ergo uale nostri memor, et quotiens te
Roma tuo refici properantem reddet Aquino,
me quoque ad Heluinam Cererem uestramque Dianam   320
conuerte a Cumis. saturarum ego, ni pudet illas,
auditor gelidos ueniam caligatus in agros.'

4

Ecce iterum Crispinus, et est mihi saepe uocandus
ad partes, monstrum nulla uirtute redemptum
a uitiis, aegrae solaque libidine fortes
deliciae, uiduas tantum aspernatus adulter.
quid refert igitur, quantis iumenta fatiget   5
porticibus, quanta nemorum uectetur in umbra,
iugera quot uicina foro, quas emerit aedes
[nemo malus felix, minime corruptor et idem]
incestus, cum quo nuper uittata iacebat
sanguine adhuc uiuo terram subitura sacerdos?   10
sed nunc de factis leuioribus. et tamen alter
si fecisset idem caderet sub iudice morum;
nam, quod turpe bonis Titio Seiioque, decebat
Crispinum. quid agas, cum dira et foedior omni
crimine persona est? mullum sex milibus emit,   15
aequantem sane paribus sestertia libris,
ut perhibent qui de magnis maiora locuntur.
consilium laudo artificis, si munere tanto
praecipuam in tabulis ceram senis abstulit orbi;
est ratio ulterior, magnae si misit amicae,   20
quae uehitur cluso latis specularibus antro.
nil tale expectes: emit sibi. multa uidemus
quae miser et frugi non fecit Apicius. hoc tu
succinctus patria quondam, Crispine, papyro?
hoc pretio squamae? potuit fortasse minoris   25
piscator quam piscis emi; prouincia tanti
uendit agros, sed maiores Apulia uendit.
qualis tunc epulas ipsum gluttisse putamus
induperatorem, cum tot sestertia, partem
exiguam et modicae sumptam de margine cenae,   30
purpureus magni ructarit scurra Palati,
iam princeps equitum, magna qui uoce solebat
uendere municipes fracta de merce siluros?
incipe, Calliope. licet et considere: non est
cantandum, res uera agitur. narrate, puellae   35
Pierides, prosit mihi uos dixisse puellas.
     cum iam semianimum laceraret Flauius orbem

ultimus et caluo seruiret Roma Neroni,
incidit Hadriaci spatium admirabile rhombi
ante domum Veneris, quam Dorica sustinet Ancon,   40
impleuitque sinus; neque enim minor haeserat illis
quos operit glacies Maeotica ruptaque tandem
solibus effundit torrentis ad ostia Ponti
desidia tardos et longo frigore pingues.
destinat hoc monstrum cumbae linique magister   45
pontifici summo. quis enim proponere talem
aut emere auderet, cum plena et litora multo
delatore forent? dispersi protinus algae
inquisitores agerent cum remige nudo,
non dubitaturi fugitiuum dicere piscem   50
depastumque diu uiuaria Caesaris, inde
elapsum ueterem ad dominum debere reuerti.
si quid Palfurio, si credimus Armillato,
quidquid conspicuum pulchrumque est aequore toto
res fisci est, ubicumque natat. donabitur ergo,   55
ne pereat. iam letifero cedente pruinis
autumno, iam quartanam sperantibus aegris,
stridebat deformis hiems praedamque recentem
seruabat; tamen hic properat, uelut urgueat auster.
utque lacus suberant, ubi quamquam diruta seruat   60
ignem Troianum et Vestam colit Alba minorem,
obstitit intranti miratrix turba parumper.
ut cessit, facili patuerunt cardine ualuae;
exclusi spectant admissa obsonia patres.
itur ad Atriden. tum Picens 'accipe' dixit   65
'priuatis maiora focis. genialis agatur
iste dies. propera stomachum laxare sagina
et tua seruatum consume in saecula rhombum.
ipse capi uoluit.' quid apertius? et tamen illi
surgebant cristae. nihil est quod credere de se   70
non possit cum laudatur dis aequa potestas.
sed derat pisci patinae mensura. uocantur
ergo in consilium proceres, quos oderat ille,
in quorum facie miserae magnaeque sedebat
pallor amicitiae. primus clamante Liburno   75
'currite, iam sedit' rapta properabat abolla
Pegasus, attonitae positus modo uilicus urbi.

anne aliud tum praefecti? quorum optimus atque
interpres legum sanctissimus — omnia quamquam
temporibus diris tractanda putabat inermi   80
iustitia. uenit et Crispi iucunda senectus,
cuius erant mores qualis facundia, mite
ingenium. maria ac terras populosque regenti
quis comes utilior, si clade et peste sub illa
saeuitiam damnare et honestum adferre liceret   85
consilium? sed quid uiolentius aure tyranni,
cum quo de pluuiis aut aestibus aut nimboso
uere locuturi fatum pendebat amici?
ille igitur numquam derexit bracchia contra
torrentem, nec ciuis erat qui libera posset   90
uerba animi proferre et uitam inpendere uero.
sic multas hiemes atque octogensima uidit
solstitia, his armis illa quoque tutus in aula.
proximus eiusdem properabat Acilius aeui
cum iuuene indigno quem mors tam saeua maneret   95
et domini gladiis tam festinata; sed olim
prodigio par est in nobilitate senectus,
unde fit ut malim fraterculus esse gigantis.
profuit ergo nihil misero quod comminus ursos
figebat Numidas Albana nudus harena   100
uenator. quis enim iam non intellegat artes
patricias? quis priscum illud miratur acumen,
Brute, tuum? facile est barbato inponere regi.
nec melior uultu quamuis ignobilis ibat
Rubrius, offensae ueteris reus atque tacendae,   105
et tamen inprobior saturam scribente cinaedo.
Montani quoque uenter adest abdomine tardus,
et matutino sudans Crispinus amomo
quantum uix redolent duo funera, saeuior illo
Pompeius tenui iugulos aperire susurro,   110
et qui uulturibus seruabat uiscera Dacis
Fuscus marmorea meditatus proelia uilla,
et cum mortifero prudens Veiiento Catullo,
qui numquam uisae flagrabat amore puellae,
grande et conspicuum nostro quoque tempore monstrum, 115
caecus adulator dirusque, a ponte, satelles,
dignus Aricinos qui mendicaret ad axes

blandaque deuexae iactaret basia raedae.
nemo magis rhombum stupuit; nam plurima dixit
in laeuum conuersus, at illi dextra iacebat   120
belua. sic pugnas Cilicis laudabat et ictus
et pegma et pueros inde ad uelaria raptos.
non cedit Veiiento, sed ut fanaticus oestro
percussus, Bellona, tuo diuinat et 'ingens
omen habes' inquit 'magni clarique triumphi.   125
regem aliquem capies, aut de temone Britanno
excidet Aruiragus. peregrina est belua: cernis
erectas per terga sudes?' hoc defuit unum
Fabricio, patriam ut rhombi memoraret et annos.
'quidnam igitur censes? conciditur?' 'absit ab illo   130
dedecus hoc' Montanus ait, 'testa alta paretur
quae tenui muro spatiosum colligat orbem.
debetur magnus patinae subitusque Prometheus.
argillam atque rotam citius properate, sed ex hoc
tempore iam, Caesar, figuli tua castra sequantur.'   135
uicit digna uiro sententia. nouerat ille
luxuriam inperii ueterem noctesque Neronis
iam medias aliamque famem, cum pulmo Falerno
arderet. nulli maior fuit usus edendi
tempestate mea: Circeis nata forent an   140
Lucrinum ad saxum Rutupinoue edita fundo
ostrea callebat primo deprendere morsu,
et semel aspecti litus dicebat echini.
surgitur et misso proceres exire iubentur
consilio, quos Albanam dux magnus in arcem   145
traxerat attonitos et festinare coactos,
tamquam de Chattis aliquid toruisque Sygambris
dicturus, tamquam ex diuersis partibus orbis
anxia praecipiti uenisset epistula pinna.
atque utinam his potius nugis tota illa dedisset   150
tempora saeuitiae, claras quibus abstulit urbi
inlustresque animas inpune et uindice nullo.
sed periit postquam cerdonibus esse timendus
coeperat: hoc nocuit Lamiarum caede madenti.

5

Si te propositi nondum pudet atque eadem est mens,

ut bona summa putes aliena uiuere quadra,
si potes illa pati quae nec Sarmentus iniquas
Caesaris ad mensas nec uilis Gabba tulisset,
quamuis iurato metuam tibi credere testi.   5
uentre nihil noui frugalius; hoc tamen ipsum
defecisse puta, quod inani sufficit aluo:
nulla crepido uacat? nusquam pons et tegetis pars
dimidia breuior? tantine iniuria cenae,
tam ieiuna fames, cum possit honestius illic   10
et tremere et sordes farris mordere canini?
    primo fige loco, quod tu discumbere iussus
mercedem solidam ueterum capis officiorum.
fructus amicitiae magnae cibus: inputat hunc rex,
et quamuis rarum tamen inputat. ergo duos post   15
si libuit menses neglectum adhibere clientem,
tertia ne uacuo cessaret culcita lecto,
'una simus' ait. uotorum summa. quid ultra
quaeris? habet Trebius propter quod rumpere somnum
debeat et ligulas dimittere, sollicitus ne   20
tota salutatrix iam turba peregerit orbem,
sideribus dubiis aut illo tempore quo se
frigida circumagunt pigri serraca Bootae.
    qualis cena tamen! uinum quod sucida nolit
lana pati: de conuiua Corybanta uidebis.   25
iurgia proludunt, sed mox et pocula torques
saucius et rubra deterges uulnera mappa,
inter uos quotiens libertorumque cohortem
pugna Saguntina feruet commissa lagona.
ipse capillato diffusum consule potat   30
calcatamque tenet bellis socialibus uuam.
cardiaco numquam cyathum missurus amico
cras bibet Albanis aliquid de montibus aut de
Setinis, cuius patriam titulumque senectus
deleuit multa ueteris fuligine testae,   35
quale coronati Thrasea Heluidiusque bibebant
Brutorum et Cassi natalibus. ipse capaces
Heliadum crustas et inaequales berullo
Virro tenet phialas: tibi non committitur aurum,
uel, si quando datur, custos adfixus ibidem,   40
qui numeret gemmas, ungues obseruet acutos.

da ueniam: praeclara illi laudatur iaspis.
nam Virro, ut multi, gemmas ad pocula transfert
a digitis, quas in uaginae fronte solebat
ponere zelotypo iuuenis praelatus Iarbae.   45
tu Beneuentani sutoris nomen habentem
siccabis calicem nasorum quattuor ac iam
quassatum et rupto poscentem sulpura uitro.
si stomachus domini feruet uinoque ciboque,
frigidior Geticis petitur decocta pruinis.   50
non eadem uobis poni modo uina querebar?
uos aliam potatis aquam. tibi pocula cursor
Gaetulus dabit aut nigri manus ossea Mauri
et cui per mediam nolis occurrere noctem,
cliuosae ueheris dum per monumenta Latinae.   55
flos Asiae ante ipsum, pretio maiore paratus
quam fuit et Tulli census pugnacis et Anci
et, ne te teneam, Romanorum omnia regum
friuola. quod cum ita sit, tu Gaetulum Ganymedem
respice, cum sities. nescit tot milibus emptus   60
pauperibus miscere puer, sed forma, sed aetas
digna supercilio. quando ad te peruenit ille?
quando rogatus adest calidae gelidaeque minister?
quippe indignatur ueteri parere clienti
quodque aliquid poscas et quod se stante recumbas.   65
[maxima quaeque domus seruis est plena superbis.]
ecce alius quanto porrexit murmure panem
uix fractum, solidae iam mucida frusta farinae,
quae genuinum agitent, non admittentia morsum.
sed tener et niueus mollique siligine fictus   70
seruatur domino. dextram cohibere memento;
salua sit artoptae reuerentia. finge tamen te
inprobulum, superest illic qui ponere cogat:
'uis tu consuetis, audax conuiua, canistris
impleri panisque tui nouisse colorem?'   75
'scilicet hoc fuerat, propter quod saepe relicta
coniuge per montem aduersum gelidasque cucurri
Esquilias, fremeret saeua cum grandine uernus
Iuppiter et multo stillaret paenula nimbo.'
    aspice quam longo distinguat pectore lancem   80
quae fertur domino squilla, et quibus undique saepta

asparagis qua despiciat conuiuia cauda,
dum uenit excelsi manibus sublata ministri.
sed tibi dimidio constrictus cammarus ouo
ponitur exigua feralis cena patella.   85
ipse Venafrano piscem perfundit, at hic qui
pallidus adfertur misero tibi caulis olebit
lanternam; illud enim uestris datur alueolis quod
canna Micipsarum prora subuexit acuta,
propter quod Romae cum Boccare nemo lauatur,   90
[quod tutos etiam facit a serpentibus atris.]
mullus erit domini, quem misit Corsica uel quem
Tauromenitanae rupes, quando omne peractum est
et iam defecit nostrum mare, dum gula saeuit,
retibus adsiduis penitus scrutante macello   95
proxima, nec patimur Tyrrhenum crescere piscem.
instruit ergo focum prouincia, sumitur illinc
quod captator emat Laenas, Aurelia uendat.
Virroni muraena datur, quae maxima uenit
gurgite de Siculo; nam dum se continet Auster,   100
dum sedet et siccat madidas in carcere pinnas,
contemnunt mediam temeraria lina Charybdim:
uos anguilla manet longae cognata colubrae
aut glacie aspersus maculis Tiberinus et ipse
uernula riparum, pinguis torrente cloaca   105
et solitus mediae cryptam penetrare Suburae.
    ipsi pauca uelim, facilem si praebeat aurem.
nemo petit, modicis quae mittebantur amicis
a Seneca, quae Piso bonus, quae Cotta solebat
largiri; namque et titulis et fascibus olim   110
maior habebatur donandi gloria. solum
poscimus ut cenes ciuiliter. hoc face et esto,
esto, ut nunc multi, diues tibi, pauper amicis.
    anseris ante ipsum magni iecur, anseribus par
altilis, et flaui dignus ferro Meleagri   115
spumat aper. post hunc tradentur tubera, si uer
tunc erit et facient optata tonitrua cenas
maiores. 'tibi habe frumentum' Alledius inquit,
'o Libye, disiunge boues, dum tubera mittas.'
structorem interea, ne qua indignatio desit,   120
saltantem spectes et chironomunta uolanti

cultello, donec peragat dictata magistri
omnia; nec minimo sane discrimine refert
quo gestu lepores et quo gallina secetur.
    duceris planta uelut ictus ab Hercule Cacus   125
et ponere foris, si quid temptaueris umquam
hiscere tamquam habeas tria nomina. quando propinat
Virro tibi sumitue tuis contacta labellis
pocula? quis uestrum temerarius usque adeo, quis
perditus, ut dicat regi 'bibe'? plurima sunt quae   130
non audent homines pertusa dicere laena.
quadringenta tibi si quis deus aut similis dis
et melior fatis donaret homuncio, quantus
ex nihilo, quantus fieres Virronis amicus!
'da Trebio, pone ad Trebium. uis, frater, ab ipsis   135
ilibus?' o nummi, uobis hunc praestat honorem,
uos estis frater. dominus tamen et domini rex
si uis tunc fieri, nullus tibi paruolus aula
luserit Aeneas nec filia dulcior illo.
iucundum et carum sterilis facit uxor amicum.   140
sed tua nunc Mycale pariat licet et pueros tres
in gremium patris fundat semel, ipse loquaci
gaudebit nido, uiridem thoraca iubebit
adferri minimasque nuces assemque rogatum,
ad mensam quotiens parasitus uenerit infans.   145
    uilibus ancipites fungi ponentur amicis,
boletus domino, sed quales Claudius edit
ante illum uxoris, post quem nihil amplius edit.
Virro sibi et reliquis Virronibus illa iubebit
poma dari, quorum solo pascaris odore,   150
qualia perpetuus Phaeacum autumnus habebat,
credere quae possis subrepta sororibus Afris:
tu scabie frueris mali, quod in aggere rodit
qui tegitur parma et galea metuensque flagelli
discit ab hirsuta iaculum torquere capella.   155
    forsitan inpensae Virronem parcere credas.
hoc agit, ut doleas; nam quae comoedia, mimus
quis melior plorante gula? ergo omnia fiunt,
si nescis, ut per lacrimas effundere bilem
cogaris pressoque diu stridere molari.   160
tu tibi liber homo et regis conuiua uideris:

captum te nidore suae putat ille culinae,
nec male coniectat; quis enim tam nudus, ut illum
bis ferat, Etruscum puero si contigit aurum
uel nodus tantum et signum de paupere loro?   165
spes bene cenandi uos decipit. 'ecce dabit iam
semesum leporem atque aliquid de clunibus apri,
ad nos iam ueniet minor altilis.' inde parato
intactoque omnes et stricto pane tacetis.
ille sapit, qui te sic utitur. omnia ferre   170
si potes, et debes. pulsandum uertice raso
praebebis quandoque caput nec dura timebis
flagra pati, his epulis et tali dignus amico.

BOOK TWO

6

Credo Pudicitiam Saturno rege moratam
in terris uisamque diu, cum frigida paruas
praeberet spelunca domos ignemque laremque,
et pecus et dominos communi clauderet umbra,
siluestrem montana torum cum sterneret uxor   5
frondibus et culmo uicinarumque ferarum
pellibus, haut similis tibi, Cynthia, nec tibi, cuius
turbauit nitidos extinctus passer ocellos,
sed potanda ferens infantibus ubera magnis
et saepe horridior glandem ructante marito.   10
quippe aliter tunc orbe nouo caeloque recenti
uiuebant homines, qui rupe et robore nati
compositiue luto nullos habuere parentes.
multa Pudicitiae ueteris uestigia forsan
aut aliqua exstiterint et sub Ioue, sed Ioue nondum   15
barbato, nondum Graecis iurare paratis
per caput alterius, cum furem nemo timeret
caulibus ac pomis, et aperto uiueret horto.
paulatim deinde ad superos Astraea recessit
hac comite, atque duae pariter fugere sorores.   20
    anticum et uetus est alienum, Postume, lectum
concutere atque sacri genium contemnere fulcri.
omne aliud crimen mox ferrea protulit aetas:

uiderunt primos argentea saecula moechos.
conuentum tamen et pactum et sponsalia nostra   25
tempestate paras iamque a tonsore magistro
pecteris et digito pignus fortasse dedisti?
certe sanus eras. uxorem, Postume, ducis?
dic qua Tisiphone, quibus exagitere colubris.
ferre potes dominam saluis tot restibus ullam,   30
cum pateant altae caligantesque fenestrae,
cum tibi uicinum se praebeat Aemilius pons?
aut si de multis nullus placet exitus, illud
nonne putas melius, quod tecum pusio dormit?
pusio, qui noctu non litigat, exigit a te   35
nulla iacens illic munuscula, nec queritur quod
et lateri parcas nec quantum iussit anheles.
    sed placet Vrsidio lex Iulia: tollere dulcem
cogitat heredem, cariturus turture magno
mullorumque iubis et captatore macello.   40
quid fieri non posse putes, si iungitur ulla
Vrsidio? si moechorum notissimus olim
stulta maritali iam porrigit ora capistro,
quem totiens texit perituri cista Latini?
quid quod et antiquis uxor de moribus illi   45
quaeritur? o medici, nimiam pertundite uenam.
delicias hominis! Tarpeium limen adora
pronus et auratam Iunoni caede iuuencam,
si tibi contigerit capitis matrona pudici.
paucae adeo Cereris uictus contingere dignae,   50
quarum non timeat pater oscula. necte coronam
postibus et densos per limina tende corymbos.
unus Hiberinae uir sufficit? ocius illud
extorquebis, ut haec oculo contenta sit uno.
magna tamen fama est cuiusdam rure paterno   55
uiuentis. uiuat Gabiis ut uixit in agro,
uiuat Fidenis, et agello cedo paterno.
quis tamen adfirmat nil actum in montibus aut in
speluncis? adeo senuerunt Iuppiter et Mars?
    porticibusne tibi monstratur femina uoto   60
digna tuo? cuneis an habent spectacula totis
quod securus ames quodque inde excerpere possis?
chironomon Ledam molli saltante Bathyllo

Tuccia uesicae non imperat, Apula longum,
sicut in amplexu, subito et miserabile gannit.   65
attendit Thymele: Thymele tunc rustica discit.
ast aliae, quotiens aulaea recondita cessant,
et uacuo clusoque sonant fora sola theatro,
atque a plebeis longe Megalesia, tristes
personam thyrsumque tenent et subligar Acci.   70
Vrbicus exodio risum mouet Atellanae
gestibus Autonoes, hunc diligit Aelia pauper.
soluitur his magno comoedi fibula, sunt quae
Chrysogonum cantare uetent, Hispulla tragoedo
gaudet: an expectas ut Quintilianus ametur?   75
accipis uxorem de qua citharoedus Echion
aut Glaphyrus fiat pater Ambrosiusque choraules.
longa per angustos figamus pulpita uicos,
ornentur postes et grandi ianua lauro,
ut testudineo tibi, Lentule, conopeo   80
nobilis Euryalum murmillonem exprimat infans.
nupta senatori comitata est Eppia ludum
ad Pharon et Nilum famosaque moenia Lagi,
prodigia et mores urbis damnante Canopo.
inmemor illa domus et coniugis atque sororis   85
nil patriae indulsit, plorantisque improba natos
utque magis stupeas ludos Paridemque reliquit.
sed quamquam in magnis opibus plumaque paterna
et segmentatis dormisset paruula cunis,
contempsit pelagus; famam contempserat olim,   90
cuius apud molles minima est iactura cathedras.
Tyrrhenos igitur fluctus lateque sonantem
pertulit Ionium constanti pectore, quamuis
mutandum totiens esset mare. iusta pericli
si ratio est et honesta, timent pauidoque gelantur   95
pectore nec tremulis possunt insistere plantis:
fortem animum praestant rebus quas turpiter audent.
si iubeat coniunx, durum est conscendere nauem,
tunc sentina grauis, tunc summus uertitur aer:
quae moechum sequitur, stomacho ualet. illa maritum   100
conuomit, haec inter nautas et prandet et errat
per puppem et duros gaudet tractare rudentis.
qua tamen exarsit forma, qua capta iuuenta

Eppia? quid uidit propter quod ludia dici
sustinuit? nam Sergiolus iam radere guttur   105
coeperat et secto requiem sperare lacerto;
praeterea multa in facie deformia, sulcus
attritus galea mediisque in naribus ingens
gibbus et acre malum semper stillantis ocelli.
sed gladiator erat. facit hoc illos Hyacinthos;   110
hoc pueris patriaeque, hoc praetulit illa sorori
atque uiro. ferrum est quod amant. hic Sergius idem
accepta rude coepisset Veiiento uideri.
    quid priuata domus, quid fecerit Eppia, curas?
respice riuales diuorum, Claudius audi   115
quae tulerit. dormire uirum cum senserat uxor,
sumere nocturnos meretrix Augusta cucullos   118
ausa Palatino et tegetem praeferre cubili   117
linquebat comite ancilla non amplius una.
sed nigrum flauo crinem abscondente galero   120
intrauit calidum ueteri centone lupanar
et cellam uacuam atque suam; tunc nuda papillis
prostitit auratis titulum mentita Lyciscae
ostenditque tuum, generose Britannice, uentrem.
excepit blanda intrantis atque aera poposcit.   125
continueque iacens cunctorum absorbuit ictus.
mox lenone suas iam dimittente puellas
tristis abit, et quod potuit tamen ultima cellam
clausit, adhuc ardens rigidae tentigine uoluae,
et lassata uiris necdum satiata recessit,   130
obscurisque genis turpis fumoque lucernae
foeda lupanaris tulit ad puluinar odorem.
hippomanes carmenque loquar coctumque uenenum
priuignoque datum? faciunt grauiora coactae
imperio sexus summumque libidine peccant.   135
    'optima sed quare Caesennia teste marito?'
bis quingena dedit. tanti uocat ille pudicam,
nec pharetris Veneris macer est aut lampade feruet:
inde faces ardent, ueniunt a dote sagittae.
libertas emitur. coram licet innuat atque   140
rescribat: uidua est, locuples quae nupsit auaro.
    'cur desiderio Bibulae Sertorius ardet?'
si uerum excutias, facies non uxor amatur.

tres rugae subeant et se cutis arida laxet,
fiant obscuri dentes oculique minores,   145
'collige sarcinulas' dicet libertus 'et exi.
iam grauis es nobis et saepe emungeris. exi
ocius et propera. sicco uenit altera naso.'
interea calet et regnat poscitque maritum
pastores et ouem Canusinam ulmosque Falernas—   150
quantulum in hoc!—pueros omnes, ergastula tota,
quodque domi non est, sed habet uicinus, ematur.
mense quidem brumae, cum iam mercator Iason
clausus et armatis obstat casa candida nautis,
grandia tolluntur crystallina, maxima rursus   155
murrina, deinde adamas notissimus et Beronices
in digito factus pretiosior. hunc dedit olim
barbarus incestae gestare Agrippa sorori,
obseruant ubi festa mero pede sabbata reges
et uetus indulget senibus clementia porcis.   160
      'nullane de tantis gregibus tibi digna uidetur?'
sit formonsa, decens, diues, fecunda, uetustos
porticibus disponat auos, intactior omni
crinibus effusis bellum dirimente Sabina,
rara auis in terris nigroque simillima cycno,   165
quis feret uxorem cui constant omnia? malo,
malo Vetustinam quam te, Cornelia, mater
Gracchorum, si cum magnis uirtutibus adfers
grande supercilium et numeras in dote triumphos.
tolle tuum, precor, Hannibalem uictumque Syphacem   170
in castris et cum tota Carthagine migra.
'parce, precor, Paean, et tu, dea, pone sagittas;
nil pueri faciunt, ipsam configite matrem'
Amphion clamat, sed Paean contrahit arcum.
extulit ergo greges natorum ipsumque parentem,   175
dum sibi nobilior Latonae gente uidetur
atque eadem scrofa Niobe fecundior alba.
quae tanti grauitas, quae forma, ut se tibi semper
inputet? huius enim rari summique uoluptas
nulla boni, quotiens animo corrupta superbo   180
plus aloes quam mellis habet. quis deditus autem
usque adeo est, ut non illam quam laudibus effert
horreat inque diem septenis oderit horis?

quaedam parua quidem, sed non toleranda maritis.
nam quid rancidius quam quod se non putat ulla   185
formosam nisi quae de Tusca Graecula facta est,
de Sulmonensi mera Cecropis? omnia Graece:
[cum sit turpe magis nostris nescire Latine.]
hoc sermone pauent, hoc iram, gaudia, curas,
hoc cuncta effundunt animi secreta. quid ultra?   190
concumbunt Graece. dones tamen ista puellis,
tune etiam, quam sextus et octogensimus annus
pulsat, adhuc Graece? non est hic sermo pudicus
in uetula. quotiens lasciuum interuenit illud
ζωὴ καὶ ψυχή, modo sub lodice ferendis   195
uteris in turba, quod enim non excitet inguen
uox blanda et nequam? digitos habet. ut tamen omnes
subsidant pinnae, dicas haec mollius Haemo
quamquam et Carpophoro, facies tua conputat annos.
    si tibi legitimis pactam iunctamque tabellis   200
non es amaturus, ducendi nulla uidetur
causa, nec est quare cenam et mustacea perdas
labente officio crudis donanda, nec illud
quod prima pro nocte datur, cum lance beata
Dacicus et scripto radiat Germanicus auro.   205
si tibi simplicitas uxoria, deditus uni
est animus, summitte caput ceruice parata
ferre iugum. nullam inuenies quae parcat amanti.
ardeat ipsa licet, tormentis gaudet amantis
et spoliis; igitur longe minus utilis illi   210
uxor, quisquis erit bonus optandusque maritus.
nil umquam inuita donabis coniuge, uendes
hac obstante nihil, nihil haec si nolet emetur.
haec dabit affectus: ille excludatur amicus
iam senior, cuius barbam tua ianua uidit.   215
testandi cum sit lenonibus atque lanistis
libertas et iuris idem contingat harenae,
non unus tibi riualis dictabitur heres.
'pone crucem seruo.' 'meruit quo crimine seruus
supplicium? quis testis adest? quis detulit? audi;   220
nulla umquam de morte hominis cunctatio longa est.'
'o demens, ita seruus homo est? nil fecerit, esto:
hoc uolo, sic iubeo, sit pro ratione uoluntas.'

imperat ergo uiro. sed mox haec regna relinquit
permutatque domos et flammea conterit; inde   225
auolat et spreti repetit uestigia lecti.
ornatas paulo ante fores, pendentia linquit
uela domus et adhuc uirides in limine ramos.
sic crescit numerus, sic fiunt octo mariti
quinque per autumnos, titulo res digna sepulcri.   230
    desperanda tibi salua concordia socru.
illa docet spoliis nudi gaudere mariti,
illa docet missis a corruptore tabellis
nil rude nec simplex rescribere, decipit illa
custodes aut aere domat. tum corpore sano   235
aduocat Archigenen onerosaque pallia iactat.
abditus interea latet et secretus adulter
inpatiensque morae silet et praeputia ducit.
scilicet expectas ut tradat mater honestos
atque alios mores quam quos habet? utile porro   240
filiolam turpi uetulae producere turpem.
    nulla fere causa est in qua non femina litem
mouerit. accusat Manilia, si rea non est.
conponunt ipsae per se formantque libellos,
principium atque locos Celso dictare paratae.   245
    endromidas Tyrias et femineum ceroma
quis nescit, uel quis non uidit uulnera pali,
quem cauat adsiduis rudibus scutoque lacessit
atque omnis implet numeros dignissima prorsus
Florali matrona tuba, nisi si quid in illo   250
pectore plus agitat ueraeque paratur harenae?
quem praestare potest mulier galeata pudorem,
quae fugit a sexu? uires amat. haec tamen ipsa
uir nollet fieri; nam quantula nostra uoluptas!
quale decus, rerum si coniugis auctio fiat,   255
balteus et manicae et cristae crurisque sinistri
dimidium tegimen! uel si diuersa mouebit
proelia, tu felix ocreas uendente puella.
hae sunt quae tenui sudant in cyclade, quarum
delicias et panniculus bombycinus urit.   260
aspice quo fremitu monstratos perferat ictus
et quanto galeae curuetur pondere, quanta
poplitibus sedeat quam denso fascia libro,

et ride positis scaphium cum sumitur armis.
dicite uos, neptes Lepidi caeciue Metelli   265
Gurgitis aut Fabii, quae ludia sumpserit umquam
hos habitus? quando ad palum gemat uxor Asyli?
    semper habet lites alternaque iurgia lectus
in quo nupta iacet; minimum dormitur in illo.
tum grauis illa uiro, tunc orba tigride peior,   270
cum simulat gemitus occulti conscia facti,
aut odit pueros aut ficta paelice plorat
uberibus semper lacrimis semperque paratis
in statione sua atque expectantibus illam,
quo iubeat manare modo. tu credis amorem,   275
tu tibi tunc, uruca, places fletumque labellis
exorbes, quae scripta et quot lecture tabellas
si tibi zelotypae retegantur scrinia moechae!
sed iacet in serui complexibus aut equitis. 'dic,
dic aliquem sodes hic, Quintiliane, colorem.'   280
'haeremus. dic ipsa.' 'olim conuenerat' inquit
'ut faceres tu quod uelles, nec non ego possem
indulgere mihi. clames licet et mare caelo
confundas, homo sum.' nihil est audacius illis
deprensis: iram atque animos a crimine sumunt.   285
    unde haec monstra tamen uel quo de fonte requiris?
praestabat castas humilis fortuna Latinas
quondam, nec uitiis contingi parua sinebant
tecta labor somnique breues et uellere Tusco
uexatae duraeque manus ac proximus urbi   290
Hannibal et stantes Collina turre mariti.
nunc patimur longae pacis mala, saeuior armis
luxuria incubuit uictumque ulciscitur orbem.
nullum crimen abest facinusque libidinis ex quo
paupertas Romana perit. hinc fluxit ad istos   295
et Sybaris colles, hinc et Rhodos et Miletos
atque coronatum et petulans madidumque Tarentum.
prima peregrinos obscena pecunia mores
intulit, et turpi fregerunt saecula luxu
diuitiae molles. quid enim uenus ebria curat?   300
    inguinis et capitis quae sint discrimina nescit
grandia quae mediis iam noctibus ostrea mordet,
cum perfusa mero spumant unguenta Falerno,

cum bibitur concha, cum iam uertigine tectum
ambulat et geminis exsurgit mensa lucernis.   305
i nunc et dubita qua sorbeat aera sanna
Maura, Pudicitiae ueterem cum praeterit aram,   308
Tullia quid dicat, notae collactea Maurae.   307
noctibus hic ponunt lecticas, micturiunt hic
effigiemque deae longis siphonibus implent   310
inque uices equitant ac Luna teste mouentur,
inde domos abeunt: tu calcas luce reuersa
coniugis urinam magnos uisurus amicos.
    nota bonae secreta deae, cum tibia lumbos
incitat et cornu pariter uinoque feruntur   315
attonitae crinemque rotant ululantque Priapi
maenades. o quantus tunc illis mentibus ardor
concubitus, quae uox saltante libidine, quantus
ille meri ueteris per crura madentia torrens!
lenonum ancillas posita Saufeia corona   320
prouocat et tollit pendentis praemia coxae,
ipsa Medullinae fluctum crisantis adorat:
palma inter dominas, uirtus natalibus aequa.
nil ibi per ludum simulabitur, omnia fient
ad uerum, quibus incendi iam frigidus aeuo   325
Laomedontiades et Nestoris hirnea possit.
tunc prurigo morae inpatiens, tum femina simplex,
ac pariter toto repetitus clamor ab antro
'iam fas est, admitte uiros.' dormitat adulter,
illa iubet sumpto iuuenem properare cucullo;   330
si nihil est, seruis incurritur; abstuleris spem
seruorum, uenit et conductus aquarius; hic si
quaeritur et desunt homines, mora nulla per ipsam
quo minus inposito clunem summittat asello.
atque utinam ritus ueteres et publica saltem   335
his intacta malis agerentur sacra; sed omnes
nouerunt Mauri atque Indi quae psaltria penem
maiorem quam sunt duo Caesaris Anticatones
illuc, testiculi sibi conscius unde fugit mus,
intulerit, ubi uelari pictura iubetur   340
quaecumque alterius sexus imitata figuras.
et quis tunc hominum contemptor numinis, aut quis
simpuuium ridere Numae nigrumque catinum

et Vaticano fragiles de monte patellas
ausus erat? sed nunc ad quas non Clodius aras?   345
    in quacumque domo uiuit luditque professus   01
obscenum, tremula promittit et omnia dextra,
inuenies omnis turpes similesque cinaedis.
his uiolare cibos sacraeque adsistere mensae
permittunt, et uasa iubent frangenda lauari   05
cum colocyntha bibit uel cum barbata chelidon.
purior ergo tuis laribus meliorque lanista,
in cuius numero longe migrare iubetur
psyllus ab Euhoplo quid quod nec retia turpi
iunguntur tunicae, nec cella ponit eadem   010
munimenta umeri pulsatoremque tridentem
qui nudus pugnare solet? pars ultima ludi
accipit has animas aliusque in carcere neruos.
sed tibi communem calicem facit uxor et illis
cum quibus Albanum Surrentinumque recuset   015
flaua ruinosi lupa degustare sepulchri.
horum consiliis nubunt subitaeque recedunt,
his languentem animum seruant et seria uitae,
his clunem atque latus discunt uibrare magistris,
quicquid praeterea scit qui docet. haud tamen illi   020
semper habenda fides: oculos fuligine pascit
distinctus croceis et reticulatus adulter.
suspectus tibi sit, quanto uox mollior et quo
saepius in teneris haerebit dextera lumbis.
hic erit in lecto fortissimus; exuit illic   025
personam docili Thais saltata Triphallo.
quem rides? aliis hunc mimum? sponsio fiat:
'purum te contendo uirum.' 'contendo.' 'fateris?
an uocat ancillas tortoris pergula?' noui
consilia et ueteres quaecumque monetis amici,   030
'pone seram, cohibe'. sed quis custodiet ipsos
custodes, qui nunc lasciuae furta puellae
hac mercede silent? crimen commune tacetur.
prospicit hoc prudens et ab illis incipit uxor.   034
[audio quid ueteres olim moneatis amici,   346
'pone seram, cohibe.' sed quis custodiet ipsos
custodes? cauta est et ab illis incipit uxor.]
iamque eadem summis pariter minimisque libido,

nec melior silicem pedibus quae conterit atrum 350
quam quae longorum uehitur ceruice Ṡyrorum.
    ut spectet ludos, conducit Ogulnia uestem,
conducit comites, sellam, ceruical, amicas,
nutricem et flauam cui det mandata puellam.
haec tamen argenti superest quodcumque paterni 355
leuibus athletis et uasa nouissima donat.
multis res angusta domi, sed nulla pudorem
paupertatis habet nec se metitur ad illum
quem dedit haec posuitque modum. tamen utile quid sit
prospiciunt aliquando uiri, frigusque famemque 360
formica tandem quidam expauere magistra:
prodiga non sentit pereuntem femina censum.
ac uelut exhausta recidiuus pullulet arca
nummus et e pleno tollatur semper aceruo,
non umquam reputant quanti sibi gaudia constent. 365
    sunt quas eunuchi inbelles ac mollia semper
oscula delectent et desperatio barbae
et quod abortiuo non est opus. illa uoluptas
summa tamen, quom iam calida matura iuuenta
inguina traduntur medicis, iam pectine nigro. 370
ergo expectatos ac iussos crescere primum
testiculos, postquam coeperunt esse bilibres,
tonsoris tantum damno rapit Heliodorus.
(mangonum pueros uera ac miserabilis urit 373A
debilitas, follisque pudet cicerisque relicti.) 373B
conspicuus longe cunctisque notabilis intrat
balnea nec dubie custodem uitis et horti 375
prouocat a domina factus spado. dormiat ille
cum domina, sed tu iam durum, Postume, iamque
tondendum eunucho Bromium committere noli.
    si gaudet cantu, nullius fibula durat
uocem uendentis praetoribus. organa semper 380
in manibus, densi radiant testudine tota
sardonyches, crispo numerantur pectine chordae
quo tener Hedymeles operas dedit: hunc tenet, hoc se
solatur gratoque indulget basia plectro.
quaedam de numero Lamiarum ac nominis Appi 385
et farre et uino Ianum Vestamque rogabat,
an Capitolinam deberet Pollio quercum

sperare et fidibus promittere. quid faceret plus
aegrotante uiro, medicis quid tristibus erga
filiolum? stetit ante aram nec turpe putauit   390
pro cithara uelare caput dictataque uerba
pertulit, ut mos est, et aperta palluit agna.
dic mihi nunc, quaeso, dic, antiquissime diuom,
respondes his, Iane pater? magna otia caeli;
non est, quod uideo, non est quod agatur apud uos.   395
haec de comoedis te consulit, illa tragoedum
commendare uolet: uaricosus fiet haruspex.
    sed cantet potius quam totam peruolet urbem
audax et coetus possit quae ferre uirorum
cumque paludatis ducibus praesente marito   400
ipsa loqui recta facie siccisque mamillis.
haec eadem nouit quid toto fiat in orbe,
quid Seres, quid Thraces agant, secreta nouercae
et pueri, quis amet, quis diripiatur adulter;
dicet quis uiduam praegnatem fecerit et quo   405
mense, quibus uerbis concumbat quaeque, modis quot.
instantem regi Armenio Parthoque cometen
prima uidet, famam rumoresque illa recentis
excipit ad portas, quosdam facit; isse Niphaten
in populos magnoque illic cuncta arua teneri   410
diluuio, nutare urbes, subsidere terras,
quocumque in triuio, cuicumque est obuia, narrat.
    nec tamen id uitium magis intolerabile quam quod
uicinos humiles rapere et concidere loris
experrecta solet. nam si latratibus alti   415
rumpuntur somni, 'fustes huc ocius' inquit
'adferte' atque illis dominum iubet ante feriri,
deinde canem. grauis occursu, taeterrima uultu
balnea nocte subit, conchas et castra moueri
nocte iubet, magno gaudet sudare tumultu,   420
cum lassata graui ceciderunt bracchia massa,
callidus et cristae digitos inpressit aliptes
ac summum dominae femur exclamare coegit.
conuiuae miseri interea somnoque fameque
urguentur. tandem illa uenit rubicundula, totum   425
oenophorum sitiens, plena quod tenditur urna
admotum pedibus, de quo sextarius alter

ducitur ante cibum rabidam facturus orexim,
dum redit et loto terram ferit intestino.
marmoribus riui properant, aurata Falernum   430
peluis olet; nam sic, tamquam alta in dolia longus
deciderit serpens, bibit et uomit. ergo maritus
nauseat atque oculis bilem substringit opertis.
    illa tamen grauior, quae cum discumbere coepit
laudat Vergilium, periturae ignoscit Elissae,   435
committit uates et comparat, inde Maronem
atque alia parte in trutina suspendit Homerum.
cedunt grammatici, uincuntur rhetores, omnis
turba tacet, nec causidicus nec praeco loquetur,
altera nec mulier. uerborum tanta cadit uis,   440
tot pariter pelues ac tintinnabula dicas
pulsari. iam nemo tubas, nemo aera fatiget:
una laboranti poterit succurrere Lunae.
inponit finem sapiens et rebus honestis;
nam quae docta nimis cupit et facunda uideri   445
crure tenus medio tunicas succingere debet,
caedere Siluano porcum, quadrante lauari.
non habeat matrona, tibi quae iuncta recumbit,
dicendi genus, aut curuum sermone rotato
torqueat enthymema, nec historias sciat omnes,   450
sed quaedam ex libris et non intellegat. odi
hanc ego quae repetit uoluitque Palaemonis artem
seruata semper lege et ratione loquendi
ignotosque mihi tenet antiquaria uersus.
haec curanda uiris. opicae castiget amicae   455
uerba: soloecismum liceat fecisse marito.
    nil non permittit mulier sibi, turpe putat nil,
cum uiridis gemmas collo circumdedit et cum
auribus extentis magnos commisit elenchos.
[intolerabilius nihil est quam femina diues.]   460
interea foeda aspectu ridendaque multo
pane tumet facies aut pinguia Poppaeana
spirat et hinc miseri uiscantur labra mariti.
ad moechum lota ueniunt cute. quando uideri
uult formonsa domi? moechis foliata parantur,   465
his emitur quidquid graciles huc mittitis Indi.
tandem aperit uultum et tectoria prima reponit,

incipit agnosci, atque illo lacte fouetur
propter quod secum comites educit asellas
exul Hyperboreum si dimittatur ad axem.   470
sed quae mutatis inducitur atque fouetur
tot medicaminibus coctaeque siliginis offas
accipit et madidae, facies dicetur an ulcus?
        est pretium curae penitus cognoscere toto
quid faciant agitentque die. si nocte maritus   475
auersus iacuit, periit libraria, ponunt
cosmetae tunicas, tarde uenisse Liburnus
dicitur et poenas alieni pendere somni
cogitur, hic frangit ferulas, rubet ille flagello,
hic scutica; sunt quae tortoribus annua praestent.   480
uerberat atque obiter faciem linit, audit amicas
aut latum pictae uestis considerat aurum
et caedit, longi relegit transuersa diurni
et caedit, donec lassis caedentibus 'exi'
intonet horrendum iam cognitione peracta.   485
praefectura domus Sicula non mitior aula.
nam si constituit solitoque decentius optat
ornari et properat iamque expectatur in hortis
aut apud Isiacae potius sacraria lenae,
disponit crinem laceratis ipsa capillis   490
nuda umeros Psecas infelix nudisque mamillis.
'altior hic quare cincinnus?' taurea punit
continuo flexi crimen facinusque capilli.
quid Psecas admisit? quaenam est hic culpa puellae,
si tibi displicuit nasus tuus? altera laeuum   495
extendit pectitque comas et uoluit in orbem.
est in consilio materna admotaque lanis
emerita quae cessat acu; sententia prima
huius erit, post hanc aetate atque arte minores
censebunt, tamquam famae discrimen agatur   500
aut animae: tanta est quaerendi cura decoris.
tot premit ordinibus, tot adhuc conpagibus altum
aedificat caput: Andromachen a fronte uidebis,
post minor est, credas aliam. cedo si breue parui
sortita est lateris spatium breuiorque uidetur   505
uirgine Pygmaea nullis adiuta coturnis
et leuis erecta consurgit ad oscula planta.

nulla uiri cura interea nec mentio fiet
damnorum. uiuit tamquam uicina mariti,
hoc solo propior, quod amicos coniugis odit   510
et seruos, grauis est rationibus. ecce furentis
Bellonae matrisque deum chorus intrat et ingens
semiuir, obsceno facies reuerenda minori,
mollia qui rapta secuit genitalia testa
iam pridem, cui rauca cohors, cui tympana cedunt   515
plebeia et Phrygia uestitur bucca tiara.
grande sonat metuique iubet Septembris et austri
aduentum, nisi se centum lustrauerit ouis
et xerampelinas ueteres donauerit ipsi,
ut quidquid subiti et magni discriminis instat   520
in tunicas eat et totum semel expiet annum.
hibernum fracta glacie descendet in amnem,
ter matutino Tiberi mergetur et ipsis
uerticibus timidum caput abluet, inde superbi
totum regis agrum nuda ac tremibunda cruentis   525
erepet genibus; si candida iusserit Io,
ibit ad Aegypti finem calidaque petitas
a Meroe portabit aquas, ut spargat in aede
Isidis, antiquo quae proxima surgit ouili.
credit enim ipsius dominae se uoce moneri.   530
en animam et mentem cum qua di nocte loquantur!
ergo hic praecipuum summumque meretur honorem
qui grege linigero circumdatus et grege caluo
plangentis populi currit derisor Anubis.
ille petit ueniam, quotiens non abstinet uxor   535
concubitu sacris obseruandisque diebus
magnaque debetur uiolato poena cadurco
et mouisse caput uisa est argentea serpens;
illius lacrimae meditataque murmura praestant
ut ueniam culpae non abnuat ansere magno   540
scilicet et tenui popano corruptus Osiris.
   cum dedit ille locum, cophino fenoque relicto
arcanam Iudaea tremens mendicat in aurem,
interpres legum Solymarum et magna sacerdos
arboris ac summi fida internuntia caeli.   545
implet et illa manum, sed parcius; aere minuto
qualiacumque uoles Iudaei somnia uendunt.

spondet amatorem tenerum uel diuitis orbi
testamentum ingens calidae pulmone columbae
tractato Armenius uel Commagenus haruspex;   550
pectora pullorum rimabitur, exta catelli
interdum et pueri; faciet quod deferat ipse.
Chaldaeis sed maior erit fiducia: quidquid
dixerit astrologus, credent a fonte relatum
Hammonis, quoniam Delphis oracula cessant   555
et genus humanum damnat caligo futuri.
praecipuus tamen est horum, qui saepius exul,
cuius amicitia conducendaque tabella
magnus ciuis obit et formidatus Othoni.
inde fides artis, sonuit si dextera ferro   560
laeuaque, si longe castrorum in carcere mansit.
nemo mathematicus genium indemnatus habebit,
sed qui paene perit, cui uix in Cyclada mitti
contigit et parua tandem caruisse Seripho.
consulit ictericae lento de funere matris,   565
(ante tamen de te) Tanaquil tua, quando sororem
efferat et patruos, an sit uicturus adulter
post ipsam; quid enim maius dare numina possunt?
    haec tamen ignorat quid sidus triste minetur
Saturni, quo laeta Venus se proferat astro,   570
quis mensis damnis, quae dentur tempora lucro:
illius occursus etiam uitare memento,
in cuius manibus ceu pinguia sucina tritas
cernis ephemeridas, quae nullum consulit et iam
consulitur, quae castra uiro patriamque petente   575
non ibit pariter numeris reuocata Thrasylli.
ad primum lapidem uectari cum placet, hora
sumitur ex libro; si prurit frictus ocelli
angulus, inspecta genesi collyria poscit;
aegra licet iaceat, capiendo nulla uidetur   580
aptior hora cibo nisi quam dederit Petosiris.
si mediocris erit, spatium lustrabit utrimque
metarum et sortes ducet frontemque manumque
praebebit uati crebrum poppysma roganti.
diuitibus responsa dabit Phryx augur et inde   585
conductus, dabit astrorum mundique peritus
atque aliquis senior qui publica fulgura condit.

plebeium in circo positum est et in aggere fatum.
quae nudis longum ostendit ceruicibus aurum
consulit ante falas delphinorumque columnas   590
an saga uendenti nubat caupone relicto.
    hae tamen et partus subeunt discrimen et omnis
nutricis tolerant fortuna urguente labores,
sed iacet aurato uix ulla puerpera lecto.
tantum artes huius, tantum medicamina possunt,   595
quae steriles facit atque homines in uentre necandos
conducit. gaude, infelix, atque ipse bibendum
porrige quidquid erit; nam si distendere uellet
et uexare uterum pueris salientibus, esses
Aethiopis fortasse pater, mox decolor heres   600
impleret tabulas numquam tibi mane uidendus.
transeo suppositos et gaudia uotaque saepe
ad spurcos decepta lacus, saepe inde petitos
pontifices, salios Scaurorum nomina falso
corpore laturos. stat Fortuna inproba noctu   605
adridens nudis infantibus: hos fouet omni
inuoluitque sinu, domibus tunc porrigit altis
secretumque sibi mimum parat; hos amat, his se
ingerit utque suos semper producit alumnos.
    hic magicos adfert cantus, hic Thessala uendit   610
philtra, quibus ualeat mentem uexare mariti
et solea pulsare natis. quod desipis, inde est,
inde animi caligo et magna obliuio rerum
quas modo gessisti. tamen hoc tolerabile, si non
[semper aquam portes rimosa ad dolia, semper   614A
istud onus subeas ipsis manantibus urnis,   614B
quo rabidus nostro Phalarim de rege dedisti.]   614C
et furere incipias ut auunculus ille Neronis,
cui totam tremuli frontem Caesonia pulli
infudit. quae non faciet quod principis uxor?
ardebant cuncta et fracta conpage ruebant
non aliter quam si fecisset Iuno maritum
insanum. minus ergo nocens erit Agrippinae   620
boletus, siquidem unius praecordia pressit
ille senis tremulumque caput descendere iussit
in caelum et longa manantia labra saliua:
haec poscit ferrum atque ignes, haec potio torquet,

haec lacerat mixtos equitum cum sanguine patres.   625
tanti partus equae, tanti una uenefica constat.
    oderunt natos de paelice; nemo repugnet,
nemo uetet, iam iam priuignum occidere fas est.
uos ego, pupilli, moneo, quibus amplior est res,
custodite animas et nulli credite mensae: 630
liuida materno feruent adipata ueneno.
mordeat ante aliquis quidquid porrexerit illa
quae peperit, timidus praegustet pocula papas.
fingimus haec altum satura sumente coturnum
scilicet, et finem egressi legemque priorum   635
grande Sophocleo carmen bacchamur hiatu
montibus ignotum Rutulis caeloque Latino.
nos utinam uani. sed clamat Pontia 'feci,
confiteor, puerisque meis aconita paraui,
quae deprensa patent; facinus tamen ipsa peregi.'   640
tune duos una, saeuissima uipera, cena?
tune duos? 'septem, si septem forte fuissent.'
    credamus tragicis quidquid de Colchide torua
dicitur et Procne; nil contra conor. et illae
grandia monstra suis audebant temporibus, sed   645
non propter nummos. minor admiratio summis
debetur monstris, quotiens facit ira nocentes
hunc sexum et rabie iecur incendente feruntur
praecipites, ut saxa iugis abrupta, quibus mons
subtrahitur cliuoque latus pendente recedit.   650
illam ego non tulerim quae conputat et scelus ingens
sana facit. spectant subeuntem fata mariti
Alcestim et, similis si permutatio detur,
morte uiri cupiant animam seruare catellae.
occurrent multae tibi Belides atque Eriphylae   655
mane, Clytaemestram nullus non uicus habebit.
hoc tantum refert, quod Tyndaris illa bipennem
insulsam et fatuam dextra laeuaque tenebat;
at nunc res agitur tenui pulmone rubetae,
sed tamen et ferro, si praegustarit Atrides   660
Pontica ter uicti cautus medicamina regis.

BOOK THREE

7

Et spes et ratio studiorum in Caesare tantum;
solus enim tristes hac tempestate Camenas
respexit, cum iam celebres notique poetae
balneolum Gabiis, Romae conducere furnos
temptarent, nec foedum alii nec turpe putarent   5
praecones fieri, cum desertis Aganippes
uallibus esuriens migraret in atria Clio.
nam si Pieria quadrans tibi nullus in umbra
ostendatur, ames nomen uictumque Machaerae
et uendas potius commissa quod auctio uendit   10
stantibus, oenophorum, tripedes, armaria, cistas,
Alcithoen Pacci, Thebas et Terea Fausti.
hoc satius quam si dicas sub iudice 'uidi'
quod non uidisti, faciant equites Asiani
quamquam et Cappadoces faciant equitesque Bithyni   15
altera quos nudo traducit Gallia talo.
nemo tamen studiis indignum ferre laborem
cogetur posthac, nectit quicumque canoris
eloquium uocale modis laurumque momordit.
hoc agite, o iuuenes. circumspicit et stimulat uos   20
materiamque sibi ducis indulgentia quaerit.
si qua aliunde putas rerum speranda tuarum
praesidia atque ideo croceae membrana tabellae
impletur, lignorum aliquid posce ocius et quae
componis dona Veneris, Telesine, marito,   25
aut clude et positos tinea pertunde libellos.
frange miser calamum uigilataque proelia dele,
qui facis in parua sublimia carmina cella,
ut dignus uenias hederis et imagine macra.
spes nulla ulterior; didicit iam diues auarus   30
tantum admirari, tantum laudare disertos,
ut pueri Iunonis auem. sed defluit aetas
et pelagi patiens et cassidis atque ligonis.
taedia tunc subeunt animos, tunc seque suamque
Terpsichoren odit facunda et nuda senectus.   35
    accipe nunc artes. ne quid tibi conferat iste,

quem colis et Musarum et Apollinis aede relicta,
ipse facit uersus atque uni cedit Homero
propter mille annos, et si dulcedine famae
succensus recites, maculonsas commodat aedes.   40
haec longe ferrata domus seruire iubetur
in qua sollicitas imitatur ianua porcas.
scit dare libertos extrema in parte sedentis
ordinis et magnas comitum disponere uoces;
nemo dabit regum quanti subsellia constant   45
et quae conducto pendent anabathra tigillo
quaeque reportandis posita est orchestra cathedris.
nos tamen hoc agimus tenuique in puluere sulcos
ducimus et litus sterili uersamus aratro.
nam si discedas, laqueo tenet ambitiosum   50
[consuetudo mali, tenet insanabile multos]
scribendi cacoethes et aegro in corde senescit.
sed uatem egregium, cui non sit publica uena,
qui nihil expositum soleat deducere, nec qui
communi feriat carmen triuiale moneta,   55
hunc, qualem nequeo monstrare et sentio tantum,
anxietate carens animus facit, omnis acerbi
inpatiens, cupidus siluarum aptusque bibendis
fontibus Aonidum. neque enim cantare sub antro
Pierio thyrsumque potest contingere maesta   60
paupertas atque aeris inops, quo nocte dieque
corpus eget: satur est cum dicit Horatius 'euhoe.'
quis locus ingenio, nisi cum se carmine solo
uexant et dominis Cirrhae Nysaeque feruntur
pectora uestra duas non admittentia curas?   65
magnae mentis opus nec de lodice paranda
attonitae currus et equos faciesque deorum
aspicere et qualis Rutulum confundat Erinys.
nam si Vergilio puer et tolerabile desset
hospitium, caderent omnes a crinibus hydri,   70
surda nihil gemeret graue bucina. poscimus ut sit
non minor antiquo Rubrenus Lappa coturno,
cuius et alueolos et laenam pignerat Atreus?
non habet infelix Numitor quod mittat amico,
Quintillae quod donet habet, nec defuit illi   75
unde emeret multa pascendum carne leonem

iam domitum; constat leuiori belua sumptu
nimirum et capiunt plus intestina poetae.
contentus fama iaceat Lucanus in hortis
marmoreis, at Serrano tenuique Saleiio   80
gloria quantalibet quid erit, si gloria tantum est?
curritur ad uocem iucundam et carmen amicae
Thebaidos, laetam cum fecit Statius urbem
promisitque diem: tanta dulcedine captos
adficit ille animos tantaque libidine uolgi   85
auditur. sed cum fregit subsellia uersu
esurit, intactam Paridi nisi uendit Agauen.
ille et militiae multis largitus honorem
semenstri uatum digitos circumligat auro.
quod non dant proceres, dabit histrio. tu Camerinos   90
et Baream, tu nobilium magna atria curas?
praefectos Pelopea facit, Philomela tribunos.
haut tamen inuideas uati quem pulpita pascunt.
quis tibi Maecenas, quis nunc erit aut Proculeius
aut Fabius, quis Cotta iterum, quis Lentulus alter?   95
tum par ingenio pretium, tunc utile multis
pallere et uinum toto nescire Decembri.
    uester porro labor fecundior, historiarum
scriptores? perit hic plus temporis atque olei plus.
nullo quippe modo millensima pagina surgit   100
omnibus et crescit multa damnosa papyro;
sic ingens rerum numerus iubet atque operum lex.
quae tamen inde seges? terrae quis fructus apertae?
quis dabit historico quantum daret acta legenti?
    'sed genus ignauum, quod lecto gaudet et umbra.'   105
dic igitur quid causidicis ciuilia praestent
officia et magno comites in fasce libelli.
ipsi magna sonant, sed tum cum creditor audit
praecipue, uel si tetigit latus acrior illo
qui uenit ad dubium grandi cum codice nomen.   110
tunc inmensa caui spirant mendacia folles
conspuiturque sinus; ueram deprendere messem
si libet, hinc centum patrimonia causidicorum,
parte alia solum russati pone Lacertae.
consedere duces, surgis tu pallidus Aiax   115
dicturus dubia pro libertate bubulco

iudice. rumpe miser tensum iecur, ut tibi lasso
figantur uirides, scalarum gloria, palmae.
quod uocis pretium? siccus petasunculus et uas
pelamydum aut ueteres, Maurorum epimenia, bulbi   120
aut uinum Tiberi deuectum, quinque lagonae.
si quater egisti, si contigit aureus unus,
inde cadunt partes ex foedere pragmaticorum.
'Aemilio dabitur quantum licet, et melius nos
egimus.' huius enim stat currus aeneus, alti   125
quadriiuges in uestibulis, atque ipse feroci
bellatore sedens curuatum hastile minatur
eminus et statua meditatur proelia lusca.
sic Pedo conturbat, Matho deficit, exitus hic est
Tongilii, magno cum rhinocerote lauari   130
qui solet et uexat lutulenta balnea turba
perque forum iuuenes longo premit assere Maedos
empturus pueros, argentum, murrina, uillas;
spondet enim Tyrio stlattaria purpura filo.
et tamen est illis hoc utile. purpura uendit   135
causidicum, uendunt amethystina; conuenit illi
et strepitu et facie maioris uiuere census,
sed finem inpensae non seruat prodiga Roma.
fidimus eloquio? Ciceroni nemo ducentos
nunc dederit nummos, nisi fulserit anulus ingens.   140
respicit haec primum qui litigat, an tibi serui
octo, decem comites, an post te sella, togati
ante pedes. ideo conducta Paulus agebat
sardonyche, atque ideo pluris quam Gallus agebat,
quam Basilus. rara in tenui facundia panno.   145
quando licet Basilo flentem producere matrem?
quis bene dicentem Basilum ferat? accipiat te
Gallia uel potius nutricula causidicorum
Africa, si placuit mercedem ponere linguae.
   declamare doces? o ferrea pectora Vetti,   150
cum perimit saeuos classis numerosa tyrannos.
nam quaecumque sedens modo legerat, haec eadem stans
perferet atque eadem cantabit versibus isdem.
occidit miseros crambe repetita magistros.
quis color et quod sit causae genus atque ubi summa   155
quaestio, quae ueniant diuersa parte sagittae,

nosse uolunt omnes, mercedem soluere nemo.
'mercedem appellas? quid enim scio?' 'culpa docentis
scilicet arguitur, quod laeuae parte mamillae
nil salit Arcadico iuueni, cuius mihi sexta   160
quaque die miserum dirus caput Hannibal inplet,
quidquid id est de quo deliberat, an petat urbem
a Cannis, an post nimbos et fulmina cautus
circumagat madidas a tempestate cohortes.
quantum uis stipulare et protinus accipe: quid do   165
ut totiens illum pater audiat?' haec alii sex
uel plures uno conclamant ore sophistae
et ueras agitant lites raptore relicto;
fusa uenena silent, malus ingratusque maritus
et quae iam ueteres sanant mortaria caecos.   170
ergo sibi dabit ipse rudem, si nostra mouebunt
consilia, et uitae diuersum iter ingredietur
ad pugnam qui rhetorica descendit ab umbra,
summula ne pereat qua uilis tessera uenit
frumenti; quippe haec merces lautissima. tempta   175
Chrysogonus quanti doceat uel Pollio quanti
lautorum pueros, artem scindens Theodori.
balnea sescentis et pluris porticus in qua
gestetur dominus quotiens pluit. anne serenum
expectet spargatque luto iumenta recenti?   180
hic potius, namque hic mundae nitet ungula mulae.
parte alia longis Numidarum fulta columnis
surgat et algentem rapiat cenatio solem.
quanticumque domus, ueniet qui fercula docte
conponit, ueniet qui pulmentaria condit.   185
hos inter sumptus sestertia Quintiliano,
ut multum, duo sufficient: res nulla minoris
constabit patri quam filius. 'unde igitur tot
Quintilianus habet saltus?' exempla nouorum
fatorum transi. felix et pulcher et acer,   190
felix et sapiens et nobilis et generosus
adpositam nigrae lunam subtexit alutae,
felix orator quoque maximus et iaculator
et, si perfrixit, cantat bene. distat enim quae
sidera te excipiant modo primos incipientem   195
edere uagitus et adhuc a matre rubentem.

si Fortuna uolet, fies de rhetore consul;
si uolet haec eadem, fiet de consule rhetor.
Ventidius quid enim? quid Tullius? anne aliud quam
sidus et occulti miranda potentia fati?   200
seruis regna dabunt, captiuis fata triumphum.
felix ille tamen coruo quoque rarior albo.
paenituit multos uanae sterilisque cathedrae,
sicut'Tharsimachi probat exitus atque Secundi
Carrinatis; et hunc inopem uidistis, Athenae,   205
nil praeter gelidas ausae conferre cicutas.
di maiorum umbris tenuem et sine pondere terram
spirantisque crocos et in urna perpetuum uer,
qui praeceptorem sancti uoluere parentis
esse loco. metuens uirgae iam grandis Achilles   210
cantabat patriis in montibus et cui non tunc
eliceret risum citharoedi cauda magistri;
sed Rufum atque alios caedit sua quemque iuuentus,
Rufum, quem totiens Ciceronem Allobroga dixit.
    quis gremio Celadi doctique Palaemonis adfert   215
quantum grammaticus meruit labor? et tamen ex hoc,
quodcumque est (minus est autem quam rhetoris aera),
discipuli custos praemordet acoenonoetus
et qui dispensat frangit sibi. cede, Palaemon,
et patere inde aliquid decrescere, non aliter quam   220
institor hibernae tegetis niueique cadurci,
dummodo non pereat mediae quod noctis ab hora
sedisti, qua nemo faber, qua nemo sederet
qui docet obliquo lanam deducere ferro,
dummodo non pereat totidem olfecisse lucernas   225
quot stabant pueri, cum totus decolor esset
Flaccus et haereret nigro fuligo Maroni.
rara tamen merces quae cognitione tribuni
non egeat. sed uos saeuas inponite leges,
ut praeceptori uerborum regula constet,   230
ut legat historias, auctores nouerit omnes
tamquam ungues digitosque suos, ut forte rogatus,
dum petit aut thermas aut Phoebi balnea, dicat
nutricem Anchisae, nomen patriamque nouercae
Anchemoli, dicat quot Acestes uixerit annis,   235
quot Siculi Phrygibus uini donauerit urnas.

exigite ut mores teneros ceu pollice ducat,
ut si quis cera uoltum facit; exigite ut sit
et pater ipsius coetus, ne turpia ludant,
ne faciant uicibus. non est leue tot puerorum   240
obseruare manus oculosque in fine trementis.
'haec' inquit 'cures, et cum se uerterit annus,
accipe, uictori populus quod postulat, aurum.'

8

Stemmata quid faciunt? quid prodest, Pontice, longo
sanguine censeri, pictos ostendere uultus
maiorum et stantis in curribus Aemilianos
et Curios iam dimidios umeroque minorem
Coruinum et Galbam auriculis nasoque carentem,   5
quis fructus generis tabula iactare capaci
pontifices posse ac multa contingere uirga
fumosos equitum cum dictatore magistros,
si coram Lepidis male uiuitur? effigies quo
tot bellatorum, si luditur alea pernox   10
ante Numantinos, si dormire incipis ortu
luciferi, quo signa duces et castra mouebant?
cur Allobrogicis et magna gaudeat ara
natus in Herculeo Fabius lare, si cupidus, si
uanus et Euganea quantumuis mollior agna,   15
si tenerum attritus Catinensi pumice lumbum
squalentis traducit auos emptorque ueneni
frangenda miseram funestat imagine gentem?
tota licet ueteres exornent undique cerae
atria, nobilitas sola est atque unica uirtus.   20
Paulus uel Cossus uel Drusus moribus esto,
hos ante effigies maiorum pone tuorum,
praecedant ipsas illi te consule uirgas.
prima mihi debes animi bona. sanctus haberi
iustitiaeque tenax factis dictisque mereris?   25
agnosco procerem; salue Gaetulice, seu tu
Silanus: quocumque alto de sanguine rarus
ciuis et egregius patriae contingis ouanti,
exclamare libet populus quod clamat Osiri
inuento. quis enim generosum dixerit hunc qui   30

indignus genere et praeclaro nomine tantum
insignis? nanum cuiusdam Atlanta uocamus,
Aethiopem Cycnum, prauam extortamque puellam
Europen; canibus pigris scabieque uetusta
leuibus et siccae lambentibus ora lucernae   35
nomen erit Pardus, Tigris, Leo, si quid adhuc est
quod fremat in terris uiolentius. ergo cauebis
et metues ne tu sic Creticus aut Camerinus.
    his ego quem monui? tecum mihi sermo, Rubelli
Blande. tumes alto Drusorum stemmate, tamquam   40
feceris ipse aliquid propter quod nobilis esses,
ut te conciperet quae sanguine fulget Iuli,
non quae uentoso conducta sub aggere texit.
'uos humiles' inquis 'uolgi pars ultima nostri,
quorum nemo queat patriam monstrare parentis,   45
ast ego Cecropides.' uiuas et originis huius
gaudia longa feras. tamen ima plebe Quiritem
facundum inuenies, solet hic defendere causas
nobilis indocti; ueniet de plebe togata
qui iuris nodos et legum aenigmata soluat;   50
hinc petit Euphraten iuuenis domitique Bataui
custodes aquilas armis industrius; at tu
nil nisi Cecropides truncoque simillimus Hermae.
nullo quippe alio uincis discrimine quam quod
illi marmoreum caput est, tua uiuit imago.   55
dic mihi, Teucrorum proles, animalia muta
quis generosa putet nisi fortia. nempe uolucrem
sic laudamus equum, facili cui plurima palma
feruet et exultat rauco uictoria circo;
nobilis hic, quocumque uenit de gramine, cuius   60
clara fuga ante alios et primus in aequore puluis.
sed uenale pecus Coryphaei posteritas et
Hirpini, si rara iugo uictoria sedit.
nil ibi maiorum respectus, gratia nulla
umbrarum; dominos pretiis mutare iubentur   65
exiguis, trito ducunt epiraedia collo
segnipedes dignique molam uersare nepotes.
ergo ut miremur te, non tua, priuum aliquid da
quod possim titulis incidere praeter honores
quos illis damus ac dedimus, quibus omnia debes.   70

haec satis ad iuuenem quem nobis fama superbum
tradit et inflatum plenumque Nerone propinquo;
rarus enim ferme sensus communis in illa
fortuna. sed te censeri laude tuorum,
Pontice, noluerim sic ut nihil ipse futurae   75
laudis agas. miserum est aliorum incumbere famae,
ne conlapsa ruant subductis tecta columnis.
stratus humi palmes uiduas desiderat ulmos.
esto bonus miles, tutor bonus, arbiter idem
integer; ambiguae si quando citabere testis   80
incertaeque rei, Phalaris licet imperet ut sis
falsus et admoto dictet periuria tauro,
summum crede nefas animam praeferre pudori
et propter uitam uiuendi perdere causas.
dignus morte perit, cenet licet ostrea centum   85
Gaurana et Cosmi toto mergatur aeno.
expectata diu tandem prouincia cum te
rectorem accipiet, pone irae frena modumque,
pone et auaritiae, miserere inopum sociorum:
ossa uides rerum uacuis exucta medullis.   90
respice quid moneant leges, quid curia mandet,
praemia quanta bonos maneant, quam fulmine iusto
et Capito et Tutor ruerint damnante senatu,
piratae Cilicum. sed quid damnatio confert?
praeconem, Chaerippe, tuis circumspice pannis,   95
cum Pansa eripiat quidquid tibi Natta reliquit,
iamque tace; furor est post omnia perdere naulum.
non idem gemitus olim neque uulnus erat par
damnorum sociis florentibus et modo uictis.
plena domus tunc omnis, et ingens stabat aceruos   100
nummorum, Spartana chlamys, conchylia Coa,
et cum Parrhasii tabulis signisque Myronis
Phidiacum uiuebat ebur, nec non Polycliti
multus ubique labor, rarae sine Mentore mensae.
inde Dolabellae atque hinc Antonius, inde   105
sacrilegus Verres referebant nauibus altis
occulta spolia et plures de pace triumphos.
nunc sociis iuga pauca boum, grex paruus equarum,
et pater armenti capto eripietur agello,
ipsi deinde Lares, si quod spectabile signum,   110

si quis in aedicula deus unicus; haec etenim sunt
pro summis, iam sunt haec maxima. despicias tu
forsitan inbellis Rhodios unctamque Corinthon
despicias merito: quid resinata iuuentus
cruraque totius facient tibi leuia gentis?   115
horrida uitanda est Hispania, Gallicus axis
Illyricumque latus; parce et messoribus illis
qui saturant urbem circo scenaeque uacantem;
quanta autem inde feres tam dirae praemia culpae,
cum tenuis nuper Marius discinxerit Afros?   120
curandum in primis ne magna iniuria fiat
fortibus et miseris. tollas licet omne quod usquam est
auri atque argenti, scutum gladiumque relinques
[et iaculum et galeam; spoliatis arma supersunt.]
quod modo proposui, non est sententia, uerum est;   125
credite me uobis folium recitare Sibyllae.
si tibi sancta cohors comitum, si nemo tribunal
uendit acersecomes, si nullum in coniuge crimen
nec per conuentus et cuncta per oppida curuis
unguibus ire parat nummos raptura Celaeno,   130
tum licet a Pico numeres genus, altaque si te
nomina delectant omnem Titanida pugnam
inter maiores ipsumque Promethea ponas:
[de quocumque uoles proauom tibi sumito libro.]
quod si praecipitem rapit ambitio atque libido,   135
si frangis uirgas sociorum in sanguine, si te
delectant hebetes lasso lictore secures,
incipit ipsorum contra te stare parentum
nobilitas claramque facem praeferre pudendis.
omne animi uitium tanto conspectius in se   140
crimen habet, quanto maior qui peccat habetur.
quo mihi te, solitum falsas signare tabellas,
in templis quae fecit auus statuamque parentis
ante triumphalem? quo, si nocturnus adulter
tempora Santonico uelas adoperta cucullo?   145
    praeter maiorum cineres atque ossa uolucri
carpento rapitur pinguis Lateranus, et ipse,
ipse rotam adstringit sufflamine mulio consul,
nocte quidem, sed Luna uidet, sed sidera testes
intendunt oculos. finitum tempus honoris   150

cum fuerit, clara Lateranus luce flagellum
sumet et occursum numquam trepidabit amici
iam senis ac uirga prior adnuet, atque maniplos
soluet et infundet iumentis hordea lassis.
interea, dum lanatas robumque iuuencum   155
more Numae caedit, Iouis ante altaria iurat
solam Eponam et facies olida ad praesepia pictas.
sed cum peruigiles placet instaurare popinas,
obuius adsiduo Syrophoenix udus amomo
currit, Idymaeae Syrophoenix incola portae,   160
hospitis adfectu, et dominum regemque salutat
iam cum uenali Cyane succincta lagona.
defensor culpae dicet mihi 'fecimus et nos
haec iuuenes.' esto, desisti nempe nec ultra
fouisti errorem. breue sit quod turpiter audes,   165
quaedam cum prima resecentur crimina barba.
indulge ueniam pueris: Lateranus ad illos
thermarum calices inscriptaque lintea uadit
maturus bello Armeniae Syriaeque tuendis
amnibus et Rheno atque Histro. praestare Neronem   170
securum ualet haec aetas. mitte Ostia, Caesar,
mitte, sed in magna legatum quaere popina:
inuenies aliquo cum percussore iacentem,
permixtum nautis et furibus ac fugitiuis,
inter carnifices et fabros sandapilarum   175
et resupinati cessantia tympana galli.
aequa ibi libertas, communia pocula, lectus
non alius cuiquam, nec mensa remotior ulli.
quid facias talem sortitus, Pontice, seruum?
nempe in Lucanos aut Tusca ergastula mittas.   180
at uos, Troiugenae, uobis ignoscitis et quae
turpia cerdoni Volesos Brutumque decebunt.
    quid si numquam adeo foedis adeoque pudendis
utimur exemplis, ut non peiora supersint?
consumptis opibus uocem, Damasippe, locasti   185
sipario, clamosum ageres ut Phasma Catulli.
Laureolum uelox etiam bene Lentulus egit,
iudice me dignus uera cruce. nec tamen ipsi
ignoscas populo; populi frons durior huius,
qui sedet et spectat triscurria patriciorum,   190

planipedes audit Fabios, ridere potest qui
Mamercorum alapas. quanti sua funera uendant
quid refert? uendunt nullo cogente Nerone,
nec dubitant celsi praetoris uendere ludis.
finge tamen gladios inde atque hinc pulpita poni,   195
quid satius? mortem sic quisquam exhorruit, ut sit
zelotypus Thymeles, stupidi collega Corinthi?
res haut mira tamen citharoedo principe mimus
nobilis. haec ultra quid erit nisi ludus? et illic
dedecus urbis habes, nec murmillonis in armis   200
nec clipeo Gracchum pugnantem et falce supina;
damnat enim talis habitus [sed damnat et odit,
nec galea faciem abscondit] : mouet ecce tridentem.
postquam uibrata pendentia retia dextra
nequiquam effudit, nudum ad spectacula uoltum   205
erigit et tota fugit agnoscendus harena.
credamus tunicae, de faucibus aurea cum se
porrigat et longo iactetur spira galero.
ergo ignominiam grauiorem pertulit omni
uolnere cum Graccho iussus pugnare secutor.   210
    libera si dentur populo suffragia, quis tam
perditus ut dubitet Senecam praeferre Neroni?
cuius supplicio non debuit una parari
simia nec serpens unus nec culleus unus.
par Agamemnonidae crimen, sed causa facit rem   215
dissimilem. quippe ille deis auctoribus ultor
patris erat caesi media inter pocula, sed nec
Electrae iugulo se polluit aut Spartani
sanguine coniugii, nullis aconita propinquis
miscuit, in scena numquam cantauit Oresten,   220
Troica non scripsit. quid enim Verginius armis
debuit ulcisci magis aut cum Vindice Galba,
quod Nero tam saeua crudaque tyrannide fecit?
haec opera atque hae sunt generosi principis artes,
gaudentis foedo peregrina ad pulpita cantu   225
prostitui Graiaeque apium meruisse coronae.
maiorum effigies habeant insignia uocis,
ante pedes Domiti longum tu pone Thyestae
syrma uel Antigones seu personam Melanippes,
et de marmoreo citharam suspende colosso.   230

quid, Catilina, tuis natalibus atque Cethegi
inueniet quisquam sublimius? arma tamen uos
nocturna et flammas domibus templisque paratis,
ut bracatorum pueri Senonumque minores,
ausi quod liceat tunica punire molesta.   235
sed uigilat consul uexillaque uestra coercet.
hic nouus Arpinas, ignobilis et modo Romae
municipalis eques, galeatum ponit ubique
praesidium attonitis et in omni monte laborat.
tantum igitur muros intra toga contulit illi   240
nominis ac tituli, quantum sibi Leucade, quantum
Thessaliae campis Octauius abstulit udo
caedibus adsiduis gladio; sed Roma parentem,
Roma patrem patriae Ciceronem libera dixit.
Arpinas alius Volscorum in monte solebat   245
poscere mercedes alieno lassus aratro;
nodosam post haec frangebat uertice uitem,
si lentus pigra muniret castra dolabra.
hic tamen et Cimbros et summa pericula rerum
excipit et solus trepidantem protegit urbem,   250
atque ideo, postquam ad Cimbros stragemque uolabant
qui numquam attigerant maiora cadauera corui,
nobilis ornatur lauro collega secunda.
plebeiae Deciorum animae, plebeia fuerunt
nomina; pro totis legionibus hi tamen et pro   255
omnibus auxiliis atque omni pube Latina
sufficiunt dis infernis Terraeque parenti.
pluris enim Decii quam quae seruantur ab illis.
ancilla natus trabeam et diadema Quirini
et fascis meruit, regum ultimus ille bonorum.   260
prodita laxabant portarum claustra tyrannis
exulibus iuuenes ipsius consulis et quos
magnum aliquid dubia pro libertate deceret,
quod miraretur cum Coclite Mucius et quae
imperii finis Tiberinum uirgo natauit.   265
occulta ad patres produxit crimina seruus
matronis lugendus; at illos uerbera iustis
adficiunt poenis et legum prima securis.
    malo pater tibi sit Thersites, dummodo tu sis
Aeacidae similis Volcaniaque arma capessas,   270

quam te Thersitae similem producat Achilles.
et tamen, ut longe repetas longeque reuoluas
nomen, ab infami gentem deducis asylo;
maiorum primus, quisquis fuit ille, tuorum
aut pastor fuit aut illud quod dicere nolo.   275

9

Scire uelim quare totiens mihi, Naeuole, tristis
occurras fronte obducta ceu Marsya uictus.
quid tibi cum uultu, qualem deprensus habebat
Rauola dum Rhodopes uda terit inguina barba?
nos colaphum incutimus lambenti crustula seruo.   5
non erit hac facie miserabilior Crepereius
Pollio, qui triplicem usuram praestare paratus
circumit et fatuos non inuenit. unde repente
tot rugae? certe modico contentus agebas
uernam equitem, conuiua ioco mordente facetus   10
et salibus uehemens intra pomeria natis.
omnia nunc contra, uultus grauis, horrida siccae
silua comae, nullus tota nitor in cute, qualem
Bruttia praestabat calidi tibi fascia uisci,
sed fruticante pilo neglecta et squalida crura.   15
quid macies aegri ueteris, quem tempore longo
torret quarta dies olimque domestica febris?
deprendas animi tormenta latentis in aegro
corpore, deprendas et gaudia; sumit utrumque
inde habitum facies. igitur flexisse uideris   20
propositum et uitae contrarius ire priori.
nuper enim, ut repeto, fanum Isidis et Ganymedem
Pacis et aductae secreta Palatia matris
et Cererem (nam quo non prostat femina templo?)
notior Aufidio moechus celebrare solebas,   25
quodque taces, ipsos etiam inclinare maritos.
'utile et hoc multis uitae genus, at mihi nullum
inde operae pretium. pingues aliquando lacernas,
munimenta togae, duri crassique coloris
et male percussas textoris pectine Galli   30
accipimus, tenue argentum uenaeque secundae.
fata regunt homines, fatum est et partibus illis

quas sinus abscondit. nam si tibi sidera cessant,
nil faciet longi mensura incognita nerui,
quamuis te nudum spumanti Virro labello   35
uiderit et blandae adsidue densaeque tabellae
sollicitent, αὐτὸς γὰρ ἐφέλκεται ἄνδρα κίναιδος.
quod tamen ulterius monstrum quam mollis auarus?
"haec tribui, deinde illa dedi, mox plura tulisti."
computat et ceuet. ponatur calculus, adsint   40
cum tabula pueri; numera sestertia quinque
omnibus in rebus, numerentur deinde labores.
an facile et pronum est agere intra uiscera penem
legitimum atque illic hesternae occurrere cenae?
seruus erit minus ille miser qui foderit agrum   45
quam dominum. sed tu sane tenerum et puerum te
et pulchrum et dignum cyatho caeloque putabas.
uos humili adseculae, uos indulgebitis umquam
cultori, iam nec morbo donare parati?
en cui tu uiridem umbellam, cui sucina mittas   50
grandia, natalis quotiens redit aut madidum uer
incipit et strata positus longaque cathedra
munera femineis tractat secreta kalendis.
dic, passer, cui tot montis, tot praedia seruas
Apula, tot miluos intra tua pascua lassas?   55
te Trifolinus ager fecundis uitibus implet
suspectumque iugum Cumis et Gaurus inanis
(nam quis plura linit uicturo dolia musto?),
quantum erat exhausti lumbos donare clientis
iugeribus paucis! meliusne hic rusticus infans   60
cum matre et casulis et conlusore catello
cymbala pulsantis legatum fiet amici?
"improbus es cum poscis" ait. sed pensio clamat
"posce," sed appellat puer unicus ut Polyphemi
lata acies per quam sollers euasit Vlixes.   65
alter emendus erit, namque hic non sufficit, ambo
pascendi. quid agam bruma spirante? quid, oro,
quid dicam scapulis puerorum aquilone Decembri
et pedibus? "durate atque expectate cicadas"?
uerum, ut dissimules, ut mittas cetera, quanto   70
metiris pretio quod, ni tibi deditus essem
deuotusque cliens, uxor tua uirgo maneret?

scis certe quibus ista modis, quam saepe rogaris
et quae pollicitus. fugientem saepe puellam
amplexu rapui; tabulas quoque ruperat et iam   75
migrabat; tota uix hoc ego nocte redemi
te plorante foris. testis mihi lectulus et tu,
ad quem peruenit lecti sonus et dominae uox.
instabile ac dirimi coeptum et iam paene solutum
coniugium in multis domibus seruauit adulter.   80
quo te circumagas? quae prima aut ultima ponas?
nullum ergo meritum est, ingrate ac perfide, nullum
quod tibi filiolus uel filia nascitur ex me?
tollis enim et libris actorum spargere gaudes
argumenta uiri. foribus suspende coronas: 85
iam pater es, dedimus quod famae opponere possis.
iura parentis habes, propter me scriberis heres,
legatum omne capis nec non et dulce caducum.
commoda praeterea iungentur multa caducis,
si numerum, si tres impleuero.' iusta doloris,   90
Naeuole, causa tui; contra tamen ille quid adfert?
    'neglegit atque alium bipedem sibi quaerit asellum.
haec soli commissa tibi celare memento
et tacitus nostras intra te fige querellas;
nam res mortifera est inimicus pumice leuis.   95
qui modo secretum commiserat, ardet et odit,
tamquam prodiderim quidquid scio. sumere ferrum,
fuste aperire caput, candelam adponere ualuis
non dubitat. nec contemnas aut despicias quod
his opibus numquam cara est annona ueneni.   100
ergo occulta teges ut curia Martis Athenis.'
    o Corydon, Corydon, secretum diuitis ullum
esse putas? serui ut taceant, iumenta loquentur
et canis et postes et marmora. claude fenestras,
uela tegant rimas, iunge ostia, tollite lumen,   105
e medio fac eant omnes, prope nemo recumbat;
quod tamen ad cantum galli facit ille secundi
proximus ante diem caupo sciet, audiet et quae
finxerunt pariter libarius, archimagiri,
carptores. quod enim dubitant componere crimen   110
in dominos, quotiens rumoribus ulciscuntur
baltea? nec derit qui te per compita quaerat

nolentem et miseram uinosus inebriet aurem.
illos ergo roges quidquid paulo ante petebas
a nobis, taceant illi. sed prodere malunt   115
arcanum quam subrepti potare Falerni
pro populo faciens quantum Saufeia bibebat.
uiuendum recte, cum propter plurima, tum est his
idcirco ut possis linguam contemnere serui.
[praecipue causis, ut linguas mancipiorum   120
contemnas; nam lingua mali pars pessima serui.
deterior tamen hic qui liber non erit illis
quorum animas et farre suo custodit et aere.]
   'utile consilium modo, sed commune, dedisti.
nunc mihi quid suades post damnum temporis et spes   125
deceptas? festinat enim decurrere uelox
flosculus angustae miseraeque breuissima uitae
portio; dum bibimus, dum serta, unguenta, puellas
poscimus, obrepit non intellecta senectus.'
   ne trepida, numquam pathicus tibi derit amicus   130
stantibus et saluis his collibus; undique ad illos
conuenient et carpentis et nauibus omnes
qui digito scalpunt uno caput. altera maior
spes superest, tu tantum erucis inprime dentem.
[gratus eris, tu tantum erucis inprime dentem.]   134A
   'haec exempla para felicibus; at mea Clotho   135
et Lachesis gaudent, si pascitur inguine uenter.
o parui nostrique Lares, quos ture minuto
aut farre et tenui soleo exorare corona,
quando ego figam aliquid quo sit mihi tuta senectus
a tegete et baculo? uiginti milia fenus   140
pigneribus positis, argenti uascula puri,
sed quae Fabricius censor notet, et duo fortes
de grege Moesorum, qui me ceruice locata
securum iubeant clamoso insistere circo;
sit mihi praeterea curuus caelator, et alter   145
qui multas facies pingit cito; sufficiunt haec.
quando ego pauper ero? uotum miserabile, nec spes
his saltem; nam cum pro me Fortuna uocatur,
adfixit ceras illa de naue petitas
quae Siculos cantus effugit remige surdo.'   150

BOOK FOUR

10

Omnibus in terris, quae sunt a Gadibus usque
Auroram et Gangen, pauci dinoscere possunt
uera bona atque illis multum diuersa, remota
erroris nebula. quid enim ratione timemus
aut cupimus? quid tam dextro pede concipis ut te   5
conatus non paeniteat uotique peracti?
euertere domos totas optantibus ipsis
di faciles. nocitura toga, nocitura petuntur
militia; torrens dicendi copia multis
et sua mortifera est facundia; uiribus ille   10
confisus periit admirandisque lacertis;
sed pluris nimia congesta pecunia cura
strangulat et cuncta exuperans patrimonia census
quanto delphinis ballaena Britannica maior.
temporibus diris igitur iussuque Neronis   15
Longinum et magnos Senecae praediuitis hortos
clausit et egregias Lateranorum obsidet aedes
tota cohors: rarus uenit in cenacula miles.
pauca licet portes argenti uascula puri
nocte iter ingressus, gladium contumque timebis   20
et mota ad lunam trepidabis harundinis umbra:
cantabit uacuus coram latrone uiator.
   prima fere uota et cunctis notissima templis
diuitiae, crescant ut opes, ut maxima toto
nostra sit arca foro. sed nulla aconita bibuntur   25
fictilibus; tunc illa time cum pocula sumes
gemmata et lato Setinum ardebit in auro.
   iamne igitur laudas quod de sapientibus alter
ridebat, quotiens a limine mouerat unum
protuleratque pedem, flebat contrarius auctor?   30
sed facilis cuiuis rigidi censura cachinni:
mirandum est unde ille oculis suffecerit umor.
perpetuo risu pulmonem agitare solebat
Democritus, quamquam non essent urbibus illis
praetextae, trabeae, fasces, lectica, tribunal.   35
quid si uidisset praetorem curribus altis

extantem et medii sublimem puluere circi
in tunica Iouis et pictae Sarrana ferentem
ex umeris aulaea togae magnaeque coronae
tantum orbem, quanto ceruix non sufficit ulla?   40
quippe tenet sudans hanc publicus et, sibi consul
ne placeat, curru seruus portatur eodem.
da nunc et uolucrem, sceptro quae surgit eburno,
illinc cornicines, hinc praecedentia longi
agminis officia et niueos ad frena Quirites,   45
defossa in loculos quos sportula fecit amicos.
tum quoque materiam risus inuenit ad omnis
occursus hominum, cuius prudentia monstrat
summos posse uiros et magna exempla daturos
ueruecum in patria crassoque sub aere nasci.   50
ridebat curas nec non et gaudia uolgi,
interdum et lacrimas, cum Fortunae ipse minaci
mandaret laqueum mediumque ostenderet unguem.
    ergo superuacua aut si perniciosa petuntur,
propter quae fas est genua incerare deorum?   55
    quosdam praecipitat subiecta potentia magnae
inuidiae, mergit longa atque insignis honorum
pagina. descendunt statuae restemque secuntur,
ipsas deinde rotas bigarum inpacta securis
caedit et inmeritis franguntur crura caballis.   60
iam strident ignes, iam follibus atque caminis
ardet adoratum populo caput et crepat ingens
Seianus, deinde ex facie toto orbe secunda
fiunt urceoli, pelues, sartago, matellae.
pone domi laurus, duc in Capitolia magnum   65
cretatumque bouem: Seianus ducitur unco
spectandus, gaudent omnes. 'quae labra, quis illi
uultus erat! numquam, si quid mihi credis, amaui
hunc hominem. sed quo cecidit sub crimine? quisnam
delator quibus indicibus, quo teste probauit?'   70
'nil horum; uerbosa et grandis epistula uenit
a Capreis. 'bene habet, nil plus interrogo.' sed quid
turba Remi? sequitur fortunam, ut semper, et odit
damnatos. idem populus, si Nortia Tusco
fauisset, si oppressa foret secura senectus   75
principis, hac ipsa Seianum diceret hora

Augustum. iam pridem, ex quo suffragia nulli
uendimus, effudit curas; nam qui dabat olim
imperium, fasces, legiones, omnia, nunc se
continet atque duas tantum res anxius optat,   80
panem et circenses. 'perituros audio multos.'
'nil dubium, magna est fornacula.' 'pallidulus mi
Bruttidius meus ad Martis fuit obuius aram;
quam timeo, uictus ne poenas exigat Aiax
ut male defensus. curramus praecipites et,   85
dum iacet in ripa, calcemus Caesaris hostem.
sed uideant serui, ne quis neget et pauidum in ius
ceruice obstricta dominum trahat.' hi sermones
tunc de Seiano, secreta haec murmura uolgi.
uisne salutari sicut Seianus, habere   90
tantundem atque illi summas donare curules,
illum exercitibus praeponere, tutor haberi
principis angusta Caprearum in rupe sedentis
cum grege Chaldaeo? uis certe pila, cohortis,
egregios equites et castra domestica; quidni   95
haec cupias? et qui nolunt occidere quemquam
posse uolunt. sed quae praeclara et prospera tanti,
ut rebus laetis par sit mensura malorum?
huius qui trahitur praetextam sumere mauis
an Fidenarum Gabiorumque esse potestas   100
et de mensura ius dicere, uasa minora
frangere pannosus uacuis aedilis Vlubris?
ergo quid optandum foret ignorasse fateris
Seianum; nam qui nimios optabat honores
et nimias poscebat opes, numerosa parabat   105
excelsae turris tabulata, unde altior esset
casus et inpulsae praeceps inmane ruinae.
quid Crassos, quid Pompeios euertit et illum,
ad sua qui domitos deduxit flagra Quirites?
summus nempe locus nulla non arte petitus   110
magnaque numinibus uota exaudita malignis.
ad generum Cereris sine caede ac uulnere pauci
descendunt reges et sicca morte tyranni.
    eloquium ac famam Demosthenis aut Ciceronis
incipit optare et totis quinquatribus optat   115
quisquis adhuc uno parcam colit asse Mineruam,

quem sequitur custos angustae uernula capsae.
eloquio sed uterque perit orator, utrumque
largus et exundans leto dedit ingenii fons.
ingenio manus est et ceruix caesa, nec umquam   120
sanguine causidici maduerunt rostra pusilli.
'o fortunatam natam me consule Romam:'
Antoni gladios potuit contemnere si sic
omnia dixisset. ridenda poemata malo
quam te, conspicuae diuina Philippica famae,   125
uolueris a prima quae proxima. saeuus et illum
exitus eripuit, quem mirabantur Athenae
torrentem et pleni moderantem frena theatri.
dis ille aduersis genitus fatoque sinistro,
quem pater ardentis massae fuligine lippus   130
a carbone et forcipibus gladiosque paranti
incude et luteo Volcano ad rhetora misit.

　　bellorum exuuiae, truncis adfixa tropaeis
lorica et fracta de casside buccula pendens
et curtum temone iugum uictaeque triremis   135
aplustre et summo tristis captiuos in arcu
humanis maiora bonis creduntur. ad hoc se
Romanus Graiusque et barbarus induperator
erexit, causas discriminis atque laboris
inde habuit: tanto maior famae sitis est quam   140
uirtutis. quis enim uirtutem amplectitur ipsam,
praemia si tollas? patriam tamen obruit olim
gloria paucorum et laudis titulique cupido
haesuri saxis cinerum custodibus, ad quae
discutienda ualent sterilis mala robora fici,   145
quandoquidem data sunt ipsis quoque fata sepulcris.
expende Hannibalem: quot libras in duce summo
inuenies? hic est quem non capit Africa Mauro
percussa oceano Niloque admota tepenti
rursus ad Aethiopum populos aliosque elephantos.   150
additur imperiis Hispania, Pyrenaeum
transilit. opposuit natura Alpemque niuemque:
diducit scopulos et montem rumpit aceto.
iam tenet Italiam, tamen ultra pergere tendit.
'acti' inquit 'nihil est, nisi Poeno milite portas   155
frangimus et media uexillum pono Subura.'

o qualis facies et quali digna tabella,
cum Gaetula ducem portaret belua luscum!
exitus ergo quis est? o gloria! uincitur idem
nempe et in exilium praeceps fugit atque ibi magnus   160
mirandusque cliens sedet ad praetoria regis,
donec Bithyno libeat uigilare tyranno.
finem animae, quae res humanas miscuit olim,
non gladii, non saxa dabunt nec tela, sed ille
Cannarum uindex et tanti sanguinis ultor   165
anulus. i, demens, et saeuas curre per Alpes
ut pueris placeas et declamatio fias.
unus Pellaeo iuueni non sufficit orbis,
aestuat infelix angusto limite mundi
ut Gyarae clausus scopulis paruaque Seripho;   170
cum tamen a figulis munitam intrauerit urbem,
sarcophago contentus erit. mors sola fatetur
quantula sint hominum corpuscula. creditur olim
uelificatus Athos et quidquid Graecia mendax
audet in historia; constratum classibus isdem   175
suppositumque rotis solidum mare credimus, altos
defecisse amnes epotaque flumina Medo
prandente et madidis cantat quae Sostratus alis.
ille tamen qualis rediit Salamine relicta,
in Corum atque Eurum solitus saeuire flagellis   180
barbarus Aeolio numquam hoc in carcere passos,
ipsum conpedibus qui uinxerat Ennosigaeum
(mitius id sane. quid? non et stigmate dignum
credidit? huic quisquam uellet seruire deorum?)—
sed qualis rediit? nempe una naue, cruentis   185
fluctibus ac tarda per densa cadauera prora.
has totiens optata exegit gloria poenas.
  'da spatium uitae, multos da, Iuppiter, annos.'
hoc recto uoltu, solum hoc et pallidus optas.
sed quam continuis et quantis longa senectus   190
plena malis! deformem et taetrum ante omnia uultum
dissimilemque sui, deformem pro cute pellem
pendentisque genas et talis aspice rugas
quales, umbriferos ubi pandit Thabraca saltus,
in uetula scalpit Garamantis simia bucca.   195
plurima sunt iuuenum discrimina, pulchrior ille

hoc atque ardalio multum hic robustior illo:
una senum facies, cum uoce trementia membra
et iam leue caput madidique infantia nasi;
frangendus misero gingiua panis inermi.   200
usque adeo grauis uxori natisque sibique,
ut captatori moueat fastidia Cosso.
non eadem uini atque cibi torpente palato
gaudia; nam coitus iam longa obliuio, uel si
coneris, iacet exiguus cum ramice neruus   205
et, quamuis tota palpetur nocte, iacebit.
anne aliquid sperare potest haec inguinis aegri
canities? quid quod merito suspecta libido est
quae uenerem adfectat sine uiribus? aspice partis
nunc damnum alterius. nam quae cantante uoluptas,   210
sit licet eximius, citharoedo siue Seleuco
et quibus aurata mos est fulgere lacerna?
quid refert, magni sedeat qua parte theatri
qui uix cornicines exaudiet atque tubarum
concentus? clamore opus est ut sentiat auris   215
quem dicat uenisse puer, quot nuntiet horas.
praeterea, minimus gelido iam in corpore sanguis
febre calet sola, circumsilit agmine facto
morborum omne genus, quorum si nomina quaeras,
promptius expediam quot amauerit Oppia moechos,   220
quot Themison aegros autumno occiderit uno,
quot Basilus socios, quot circumscripserit Hirrus
pupillos, quot longa uiros exorbeat uno
Maura die, quot discipulos inclinet Hamillus;
percurram citius quot uillas possideat nunc   225
quo tondente grauis iuueni mihi barba sonabat.
ille umero, hic lumbis, hic coxa debilis; ambos
perdidit ille oculos et luscis inuidet; huius
pallida labra cibum accipiunt digitis alienis,
ipse ad conspectum cenae diducere rictum   230
suetus hiat tantum ceu pullus hirundinis, ad quem
ore uolat pleno mater ieiuna. sed omni
membrorum damno maior dementia, quae nec
nomina seruorum nec uoltum agnoscit amici
cum quo praeterita cenauit nocte, nec illos   235
quos genuit, quos eduxit. nam codice saeuo

heredes uetat esse suos, bona tota feruntur
ad Phialen; tantum artificis ualet halitus oris,
quod steterat multis in carcere fornicis annis.
ut uigeant sensus animi, ducenda tamen sunt   240
funera natorum, rogus aspiciendus amatae
coniugis et 'fratris plenaeque sororibus urnae.
haec data poena diu uiuentibus, ut renouata
semper clade domus multis in luctibus inque
perpetuo maerore et nigra ueste senescant.   245
rex Pylius, magno si quicquam credis Homero,
exemplum uitae fuit a cornice secundae.
felix nimirum, qui tot per saecula mortem
distulit atque suos iam dextra conputat annos,
quique nouum totiens mustum bibit. oro parumper   250
attendas quantum de legibus ipse queratur
fatorum et nimio de stamine, cum uidet acris
Antilochi barbam ardentem, cum quaerit ab omni,
quisquis adest, socio cur haec in tempora duret,
quod facinus dignum tam longo admiserit aeuo.   255
haec eadem Peleus, raptum cum luget Achillem,
atque alius, cui fas Ithacum lugere natantem.
incolumi Troia Priamus uenisset ad umbras
Assaraci magnis sollemnibus Hectore funus
portante ac reliquis fratrum ceruicibus inter   260
Iliadum lacrimas, ut primos edere planctus
Cassandra inciperet scissaque Polyxena palla,
si foret extinctus diuerso tempore, quo non
coeperat audaces Paris aedificare carinas.
longa dies igitur quid contulit? omnia uidit   265
euersa et flammis Asiam ferroque cadentem.
tunc miles tremulus posita tulit arma tiara
et ruit ante aram summi Iouis ut uetulus bos,
qui domini cultris tenue et miserabile collum
praebet ab ingrato iam fastiditus aratro.   270
exitus ille utcumque hominis, sed torua canino
latrauit rictu quae post hunc uixerat uxor.
festino ad nostros et regem transeo Ponti
et Croesum, quem uox iusti facunda Solonis
respicere ad longae iussit spatia ultima uitae.   275
exilium et carcer Minturnarumque paludes

et mendicatus uicta Carthagine panis
hinc causas habuere; quid illo ciue tulisset
natura in terris, quid Roma beatius umquam,
si circumducto captiuorum agmine et omni   280
bellorum pompa animam exhalasset opimam,
cum de Teutonico uellet descendere curru?
prouida Pompeio dederat Campania febres
optandas, sed multae urbes et publica uota
uicerunt; igitur Fortuna ipsius et urbis   285
seruatum uicto caput abstulit. hoc cruciatu
Lentulus, hac poena caruit ceciditque Cethegus
integer et iacuit Catilina cadauere toto.

    formam optat modico pueris, maiore puellis
murmure, cum Veneris fanum uidet, anxia mater   290
usque ad delicias uotorum. ‘cur tamen’ inquit
‘corripias? pulchra gaudet Latona Diana.’
sed uetat optari faciem Lucretia qualem
ipsa habuit, cuperet Rutilae Verginia gibbum
accipere atque suum Rutilae dare. filius autem   295
corporis egregii miseros trepidosque parentes
semper habet: rara est adeo concordia formae
atque pudicitiae. sanctos licet horrida mores
tradiderit domus ac ueteres imitata Sabinos,
praeterea castum ingenium uoltumque modesto   300
sanguine feruentem tribuat natura benigna
larga manu (quid enim puero conferre potest plus
custode et cura natura potentior omni?),
non licet esse uiro; nam prodiga corruptoris
improbitas ipsos audet temptare parentes: 305
tanta in muneribus fiducia. nullus ephebum
deformem saeua castrauit in arce tyrannus,
nec praetextatum rapuit Nero loripedem nec
strumosum atque utero pariter gibboque tumentem.
i nunc et iuuenis specie laetare tui, quem   310
maiora expectant discrimina. fiet adulter
publicus et poenas metuet quascumque mariti
ex ira debet, nec erit felicior astro
Martis, ut in laqueos numquam incidat. exigit autem
interdum ille dolor plus quam lex ulla dolori   315
concessit: necat hic ferro, secat ille cruentis

uerberibus, quosdam moechos et mugilis intrat.
sed tuus Endymion dilectae fiet adulter
matronae. mox cum dederit Seruilia nummos
fiet, et illius quam non amat, exuet omnem   320
corporis ornatum; quid enim ulla negauerit udis
inguinibus, siue est haec Oppia siue Catulla?
deterior totos habet illic femina mores.
'sed casto quid forma nocet?' quid profuit immo
Hippolyto graue propositum, quid Bellerophonti?   325
erubuit nempe haec ceu fastidita repulso
nec Stheneboea minus quam Cressa excanduit, et se
concussere ambae. mulier saeuissima tunc est
cum stimulos odio pudor admouet. elige quidnam
suadendum esse putes cui nubere Caesaris uxor   330
destinat. optimus hic et formonsissimus idem
gentis patriciae rapitur miser extinguendus
Messalinae oculis; dudum sedet illa parato
flammeolo Tyriusque palam genialis in hortis
sternitur et ritu decies centena dabuntur   335
antiquo, ueniet cum signatoribus auspex.
haec tu secreta et paucis commissa putabas?
non nisi legitime uolt nubere. quid placeat dic.
ni parere uelis, pereundum erit ante lucernas;
si scelus admittas, dabitur mora paruula, dum res   340
nota urbi et populo contingat principis aurem.
dedecus ille domus sciet ultimus. interea tu
obsequere imperio, si tanti uita dierum
paucorum. quidquid leuius meliusque putaris,
praebenda est gladio pulchra haec et candida ceruix.   345
    nil ergo optabunt homines? si consilium uis,
permittes ipsis expendere numinibus quid
conueniat nobis rebusque sit utile nostris;
nam pro iucundis aptissima quaeque dabunt di.
carior est illis homo quam sibi. nos animorum   350
inpulsu et caeca magnaque cupidine ducti
coniugium petimus partumque uxoris, at illis
notum qui pueri qualisque futura sit uxor.
ut tamen et poscas aliquid uoueasque sacellis
exta et candiduli diuina tomacula porci,   355
orandum est ut sit mens sana in corpore sano.

fortem posce animum mortis terrore carentem,
qui spatium uitae extremum inter munera ponat
naturae, qui ferre queat quoscumque labores,
nesciat irasci, cupiat nihil et potiores   360
Herculis aerumnas credat saeuosque labores
et uenere et cenis et pluma Sardanapalli.
monstro quod ipse tibi possis dare; semita certe
tranquillae per uirtutem patet unica uitae.
nullum numen habes, si sit prudentia: nos te,   365
nos facimus, Fortuna, deam caeloque locamus.

11

Atticus eximie si cenat, lautus habetur,
si Rutilus, demens. quid enim maiore cachinno
excipitur uolgi quam pauper Apicius? omnis
conuictus, thermae, stationes, omne theatrum
de Rutilo. nam dum ualida ac iuuenalia membra   5
sufficiunt galeae dumque ardent sanguine, fertur
non cogente quidem sed nec prohibente tribuno
scripturus leges et regia uerba lanistae.
multos porro uides, quos saepe elusus ad ipsum
creditor introitum solet expectare macelli,   10
et quibus in solo uiuendi causa palato est.
egregius cenat meliusque miserrimus horum
et cito casurus iam perlucente ruina.
interea gustus elementa per omnia quaerunt
numquam animo pretiis obstantibus; interius si   15
attendas, magis illa iuuant quae pluris ementur.
ergo haut difficile est perituram arcessere summam
lancibus oppositis uel matris imagine fracta,
et quadringentis nummis condire gulosum
fictile; sic ueniunt ad miscellanea ludi.   20
refert ergo quis haec eadem paret; in Rutilo nam
luxuria est, in Ventidio laudabile nomen
sumptus et a censu famam trahit. illum ego iure
despiciam, qui scit quanto sublimior Atlas
omnibus in Libya sit montibus, hic tamen idem   25
ignorat quantum ferrata distet ab arca
sacculus. e caelo descendit γνῶθι σεαυτόν

figendum et memori tractandum pectore, siue
coniugium quaeras uel sacri in parte senatus
esse uelis; neque enim loricam poscit Achillis   30
Thersites, in qua se traducebat Vlixes;
ancipitem seu tu magno discrimine causam
protegere adfectas, te consule, dic tibi qui sis,
orator uehemens an Curtius et Matho buccae.
noscenda est mensura sui spectandaque rebus   35
in summis minimisque, etiam cum piscis emetur,
ne mullum cupias, cum sit tibi gobio tantum
in loculis. quis enim te deficiente crumina
et crescente gula manet exitus, aere paterno
ac rebus mersis in uentrem fenoris atque   40
argenti grauis et pecorum agrorumque capacem?
talibus a dominis post cuncta nouissimus exit
anulus, et digito mendicat Pollio nudo.
non praematuri cineres nec funus acerbum
luxuriae sed morte magis metuenda senectus.   45
hi plerumque gradus: conducta pecunia Romae
et coram dominis consumitur; inde, ubi paulum
nescio quid superest et pallet fenoris auctor,
qui uertere solum, Baias et ad ostrea currunt.
cedere namque foro iam non est deterius quam   50
Esquilias a feruenti migrare Subura.
ille dolor solus patriam fugientibus, illa
maestitia est, caruisse anno circensibus uno.
sanguinis in facie non haeret gutta, morantur
pauci ridiculum et fugientem ex urbe Pudorem.   55
    experiere hodie numquid pulcherrima dictu,
Persice, non praestem uita et moribus et re,
si laudem siliquas occultus ganeo, pultes
coram aliis dictem puero sed in aure placentas.
nam cum sis conuiua mihi promissus, habebis   60
Euandrum, uenies Tirynthius aut minor illo
hospes, et ipse tamen contingens sanguine caelum,
alter aquis, alter flammis ad sidera missus.
    fercula nunc audi nullis ornata macellis.
de Tiburtino ueniet pinguissimus agro   65
haedulus et toto grege mollior, inscius herbae
necdum ausus uirgas humilis mordere salicti,

qui plus lactis habet quam sanguinis, et montani
asparagi, posito quos legit uilica fuso.
grandia praeterea tortoque calentia feno   70
oua adsunt ipsis cum matribus, et seruatae
parte anni quales fuerant in uitibus uuae,
Signinum Syriumque pirum, de corbibus isdem
aemula Picenis et odoris mala recentis
nec metuenda tibi, siccatum frigore postquam   75
autumnum et crudi posuere pericula suci.
haec olim nostri iam luxuriosa senatus
cena fuit. Curius paruo quae legerat horto
ipse focis breuibus ponebat holuscula, quae nunc
squalidus in magna fastidit conpede fossor,   80
qui meminit calidae sapiat quid uolua popinae.
sicci terga suis rara pendentia crate
moris erat quondam festis seruare diebus
et natalicium cognatis ponere lardum
accedente noua, si quam dabat hostia, carne.   85
cognatorum aliquis titulo ter consulis atque
castrorum imperiis et dictatoris honore
functus ad has epulas solito maturius ibat
erectum domito referens a monte ligonem.
    cum tremerent autem Fabios durumque Catonem   90
et Scauros et Fabricium, rigidique seueros
censoris mores etiam collega timeret,
nemo inter curas et seria duxit habendum
qualis in Oceani fluctu testudo nataret,
clarum Troiugenis factura et nobile fulcrum;   95
sed nudo latere et paruis frons aerea lectis
uile coronati caput ostendebat aselli,
ad quod lasciui ludebant ruris alumni.
[tales ergo cibi qualis domus atque supellex.]
tunc rudis et Graias mirari nescius artes   100
urbibus euersis praedarum in parte reperta
magnorum artificum frangebat pocula miles,
ut phaleris gauderet ecus caelataque cassis
Romuleae simulacra ferae mansuescere iussae
imperii fato, geminos sub rupe Quirinos   105
ac nudam effigiem in clipeo uenientis et hasta
pendentisque dei perituro ostenderet hosti.

ponebant igitur Tusco farrata catino:
argenti quod erat solis fulgebat in armis.
omnia tunc quibus inuideas, si liuidulus sis.   110
templorum quoque maiestas praesentior, et uox
nocte fere media mediamque audita per urbem
litore ab Oceani Gallis uenientibus et dis
officium uatis peragentibus. his monuit nos,
hanc rebus Latiis curam praestare solebat   115
fictilis et nullo uiolatus Iuppiter auro.
illa domi natas nostraque ex arbore mensas
tempora uiderunt; hos lignum stabat ad usus,
annosam si forte nucem deiecerat eurus.
at nunc diuitibus cenandi nulla uoluptas,   120
nil rhombus, nil damma sapit, putere uidentur
unguenta atque rosae, latos nisi sustinet orbis
grande ebur et magno sublimis pardus hiatu
dentibus ex illis quos mittit porta Syenes
et Mauri celeres et Mauro obscurior Indus,   125
et quos deposuit Nabataeo belua saltu
iam nimios capitique graues. hinc surgit orexis,
hinc stomacho uires; nam pes argenteus illis,
anulus in digito quod ferreus. ergo superbum
conuiuam caueo, qui me sibi comparat et res   130
despicit exiguas. adeo nulla uncia nobis
est eboris, nec tessellae nec calculus ex hac
materia, quin ipsa manubria cultellorum
ossea. non tamen his ulla umquam obsonia fiunt
rancidula aut ideo peior gallina secatur.   135
    sed nec structor erit cui cedere debeat omnis
pergula, discipulus Trypheri doctoris, apud quem
sumine cum magno lepus atque aper et pygargus
et Scythicae uolucres et phoenicopterus ingens
et Gaetulus oryx hebeti lautissima ferro   140
caeditur et tota sonat ulmea cena Subura.
nec frustum capreae subducere nec latus Afrae
nouit auis noster, tirunculus ac rudis omni
tempore et exiguae furtis inbutus ofellae.
plebeios calices et paucis assibus emptos   145
porriget incultus puer atque a frigore tutus,
non Phryx aut Lycius, non a mangone petitus

quisquam erit et magno: cum posces, posce Latine.
idem habitus cunctis, tonsi rectique capilli
atque hodie tantum propter conuiuia pexi.   150
pastoris duri hic filius, ille bubulci.
suspirat longo non uisam tempore matrem
et casulam et notos tristis desiderat haedos
ingenui uoltus puer ingenuique pudoris,
qualis esse decet quos ardens purpura uestit,   155
nec pupillares defert in balnea draucus
testiculos, nec uellendas iam praebuit alas,
crassa nec opposito pauidus tegit inguina guto.
hic tibi uina dabit diffusa in montibus illis
a quibus ipse uenit, quorum sub uertice lusit.   160
namque una atque eadem est uini patria atque ministri.
    forsitan expectes ut Gaditana canoro
incipiant prurire choro plausuque probatae
ad terram tremulo descendant clune puellae,
[spectant hoc nuptae iuxta recubante marito   165
quod pudeat narrare aliquem praesentibus ipsis.]
inritamentum ueneris languentis et acres
diuitis urticae. maior tamen ista uoluptas
alterius sexus; magis ille extenditur, et mox
auribus atque oculis concepta urina mouetur.   170
non capit has nugas humilis domus. audiat ille
testarum crepitus cum uerbis, nudum olido stans
fornice mancipium quibus abstinet, ille fruatur
uocibus obscenis omnique libidinis arte,
qui Lacedaemonium pytismate lubricat orbem;   175
namque ibi fortunae ueniam damus. alea turpis,
turpe et adulterium mediocribus: haec eadem illi
omnia cum faciunt, hilares nitidique uocantur.
nostra dabunt alios hodie conuiuia ludos:
conditor Iliados cantabitur atque Maronis   180
altisoni dubiam facientia carmina palmam.
quid refert, tales uersus qua uoce legantur?
    sed nunc dilatis auerte negotia curis
et gratam requiem dona tibi, quando licebit
per totum cessare diem. non fenoris ulla   185
mentio nec, prima si luce egressa reuerti
nocte solet, tacito bilem tibi contrahat uxor

umida suspectis referens multicia rugis
uexatasque comas et uoltum auremque calentem.
protinus ante meum quidquid dolet exue limen,   190
pone domum et seruos et quidquid frangitur illis
aut perit, ingratos ante omnia pone sodalis.
interea Megalesiacae spectacula mappae
Idaeum sollemne colunt, similisque triumpho
praeda caballorum praetor sedet ac, mihi pace   195
inmensae nimiaeque licet si dicere plebis,
totam hodie Romam circus capit, et fragor aurem
percutit, euentum uiridis quo colligo panni.
nam si deficeret, maestam attonitamque uideres
hanc urbem ueluti Cannarum in puluere uictis   200
consulibus. spectent iuuenes, quos clamor et audax
sponsio, quos cultae decet adsedisse puellae:
nostra bibat uernum contracta cuticula solem
effugiatque togam. iam nunc in balnea salua
fronte licet uadas, quamquam solida hora supersit   205
ad sextam. facere hoc non possis quinque diebus
continuis, quia sunt talis quoque taedia uitae
magna: uoluptates commendat rarior usus.

12

Natali, Coruine, die mihi dulcior haec lux,
qua festus promissa deis animalia caespes
expectat. niueam Reginae ducimus agnam,
par uellus dabitur pugnanti Gorgone Maura;
sed procul extensum petulans quatit hostia funem   5
Tarpeio seruata Ioui frontemque coruscat,
quippe ferox uitulus templis maturus et arae
spargendusque mero, quem iam pudet ubera matris
ducere, qui uexat nascenti robora cornu.
si res ampla domi similisque adfectibus esset,   10
pinguior Hispulla traheretur taurus et ipsa
mole piger, nec finitima nutritus in herba,
laeta sed ostendens Clitumni pascua sanguis
iret et a grandi ceruix ferienda ministro
ob reditum trepidantis adhuc horrendaque passi   15
nuper et incolumem sese mirantis amici.

nam praeter pelagi casus et fulminis ictus
euasit. densae caelum abscondere tenebrae
nube una subitusque antemnas inpulit ignis,
cum se quisque illo percussum crederet et mox   20
attonitus nullum conferri posse putaret
naufragium uelis ardentibus. omnia fiunt
talia, tam grauiter, si quando poetica surgit
tempestas. genus ecce aliud discriminis audi
et miserere iterum, quamquam sint cetera sortis   25
eiusdem pars dira quidem sed cognita multis
et quam uotiua testantur fana tabella
plurima: pictores quis nescit ab Iside pasci?
accidit et nostro similis fortuna Catullo.
cum plenus fluctu medius foret alueus et iam   30
alternum puppis latus euertentibus undis
arboris incertae, nullam prudentia cani
rectoris cum ferret opem, decidere iactu
coepit cum uentis, imitatus castora, qui se
eunuchum ipse facit cupiens euadere damno   35
testiculi: adeo medicatum intellegit inguen.
'fundite quae mea sunt' dicebat 'cuncta' Catullus
praecipitare uolens etiam pulcherrima, uestem
purpuream teneris quoque Maecenatibus aptam,
atque alias quarum generosi graminis ipsum   40
infecit natura pecus, sed et egregius fons
uiribus occultis et Baeticus adiuuat aer.
ille nec argentum dubitabat mittere, lances
Parthenio factas, urnae cratera capacem
et dignum sitiente Pholo uel coniuge Fusci;   45
adde et bascaudas et mille escaria, multum
caelati, biberat quo callidus emptor Olynthi.
sed quis nunc alius, qua mundi parte quis audet
argento praeferre caput rebusque salutem?
non propter uitam faciunt patrimonia quidam,   50
sed uitio caeci propter patrimonia uiuunt.
iactatur rerum utilium pars maxima, sed nec
damna leuant. tunc aduersis urguentibus illuc
reccidit ut malum ferro summitteret, ac se
explicat angustum: discriminis ultima, quando   55
praesidia adferimus nauem factura minorem.

i nunc et uentis animam committe dolato
confisus ligno, digitis a morte remotus
quattuor aut septem, si sit latissima, taedae;
mox cum reticulis et pane et uentre lagonae   60
accipe sumendas in tempestate secures.
sed postquam iacuit planum mare, tempora postquam
prospera uectoris fatumque ualentius euro
et pelago, postquam Parcae meliora benigna
pensa manu ducunt hilares et staminis albi   65
lanificae, modica nec multum fortior aura
uentus adest, inopi miserabilis arte cucurrit
uestibus extentis et, quod superauerat unum,
uelo prora suo. iam deficientibus austris
spes uitae cum sole redit. tum gratus Iulo   70
atque nouercali sedes praelata Lauino
conspicitur sublimis apex, cui candida nomen
scrofa dedit, laetis Phrygibus mirabile sumen,
et numquam uisis triginta clara mamillis.
tandem intrat positas inclusa per aequora moles   75
Tyrrhenamque pharon porrectaque bracchia rursum
quae pelago occurrunt medio longeque relincunt
Italiam; non sic similis mirabere portus
quos natura dedit. sed trunca puppe magister
interiora petit Baianae peruia cumbae   80
tuti stagna sinus, gaudent ubi uertice raso
garrula securi narrare pericula nautae.
    ite igitur, pueri, linguis animisque fauentes
sertaque delubris et farra inponite cultris
ac mollis ornate focos glebamque uirentem.   85
iam sequar et sacro, quod praestat, rite peracto
inde domum repetam, graciles ubi parua coronas
accipiunt fragili simulacra nitentia cera.
hic nostrum placabo Iouem Laribusque paternis
tura dabo atque omnis uiolae iactabo colores.   90
cuncta nitent, longos erexit ianua ramos
et matutinis operatur festa lucernis.
neu suspecta tibi sint haec, Coruine, Catullus,
pro cuius reditu tot pono altaria, paruos
tres habet heredes. libet expectare quis aegram   95
et claudentem oculos gallinam inpendat amico

tam sterili; uerum haec nimia est inpensa, coturnix
nulla umquam pro patre cadet. sentire calorem
si coepit locuples Gallitta et Pacius orbi,
legitime fixis uestitur tota libellis   100
porticus, existunt qui promittant hecatomben,
quatenus hic non sunt nec uenales elephanti,
nec Latio aut usquam sub nostro sidere talis
belua concipitur, sed furua gente petita
arboribus Rutulis et Turni pascitur agro,   105
Caesaris armentum nulli seruire paratum
priuato, siquidem Tyrio parere solebant
Hannibali et nostris ducibus regique Molosso
horum maiores ac dorso ferre cohortis,
partem aliquam belli, et euntem in proelia turrem.   110
nulla igitur mora per Nouium, mora nulla per Histrum
Pacuuium, quin illud ebur ducatur ad aras
et cadat ante Lares Gallittae uictima sola
tantis digna deis et captatoribus horum.
alter enim, si concedas, mactare uouebit   115
de grege seruorum magna et pulcherrima quaeque
corpora, uel pueris et frontibus ancillarum
inponet uittas et, si qua est nubilis illi
Iphigenia domi, dabit hanc altaribus, etsi
non sperat tragicae furtiua piacula ceruae.   120
laudo meum ciuem, nec comparo testamento
mille rates; nam si Libitinam euaserit aeger,
delebit tabulas inclusus carcere nassae
post meritum sane mirandum atque omnia soli
forsan Pacuuio breuiter dabit, ille superbus   125
incedet uictis riualibus. ergo uides quam
grande operae pretium faciat iugulata Mycenis.
uiuat Pacuuius quaeso uel Nestora totum,
possideat quantum rapuit Nero, montibus aurum
exaequet, nec amet quemquam nec ametur ab ullo.   130

BOOK FIVE

13

Exemplo quodcumque malo committitur, ipsi
displicet auctori. prima est haec ultio, quod se
iudice nemo nocens absoluitur, improba quamuis
gratia fallaci praetoris uicerit urna.
quid sentire putas homines, Caluine, recenti   5
de scelere et fidei uiolatae crimine? sed nec
tam tenuis census tibi contigit, ut mediocris
iacturae te mergat onus, nec rara uidemus
quae pateris: casus multis hic cognitus ac iam
tritus et e medio Fortunae ductus aceruo.   10
ponamus nimios gemitus. flagrantior aequo
non debet dolor esse uiri nec uolnere maior.
  tu quamuis leuium minimam exiguamque malorum
particulam uix ferre potes spumantibus ardens
uisceribus, sacrum tibi quod non reddat amicus   15
depositum? stupet haec qui iam post terga reliquit
sexaginta annos Fonteio consule natus?
an nihil in melius tot rerum proficis usu?
magna quidem, sacris quae dat praecepta libellis,
uictrix fortunae sapientia, ducimus autem   20
hos quoque felices, qui ferre incommoda uitae
nec iactare iugum uita didicere magistra.
quae tam festa dies, ut cesset prodere furtum,
perfidiam, fraudes atque omni ex crimine lucrum
quaesitum et partos gladio uel puxide nummos?   25
rari quippe boni—numera—uix sunt totidem quot
Thebarum portae uel diuitis ostia Nili.
nona aetas agitur peioraque saecula ferri
temporibus, quorum sceleri non inuenit ipsa
nomen et a nullo posuit natura metallo.   30
nos hominum diuomque fidem clamore ciemus
quanto Faesidium laudat uocalis agentem
sportula? dic, senior bulla dignissime, nescis
quas habeat ueneres aliena pecunia? nescis
quem tua simplicitas risum uulgo moueat, cum   35
exigis a quoquam ne peieret et putet ullis

esse aliquod numen templis araeque rubenti?
quondam hoc indigenae uiuebant more, priusquam
sumeret agrestem posito diademate falcem
Saturnus fugiens, tunc cum uirguncula Iuno   40
et priuatus adhuc Idaeis Iuppiter antris;
nulla super nubes conuiuia caelicolarum
nec puer Iliacus formonsa nec Herculis uxor
ad cyathos et iam saccato nectare tergens
bracchia Volcanus Liparaea nigra taberna;   45
prandebat sibi quisque deus nec turba deorum
talis ut est hodie, contentaque sidera paucis
numinibus miserum urguebant Atlanta minori
pondere; nondum imi sortitus triste profundi
imperium Sicula toruos cum coniuge Pluton,   50
nec rota nec Furiae nec saxum aut uolturis atri
poena, sed infernis hilares sine regibus umbrae.
inprobitas illo fuit admirabilis aeuo,
credebant quo grande nefas et morte piandum
si iuuenis uetulo non adsurrexerat et si   55
barbato cuicumque puer, licet ipse uideret
plura domi fraga et maiores glandis aceruos;
tam uenerabile erat praecedere quattuor annis
primaque par adeo sacrae lanugo senectae.
nunc si depositum non infitietur amicus,   60
si reddat ueterem cum tota aerugine follem,
prodigiosa fides et Tuscis digna libellis
quaeque coronata lustrari debeat agna.
egregium sanctumque uirum si cerno, bimembri
hoc monstrum puero et miranti sub aratro   65
piscibus inuentis et fetae comparo mulae,
sollicitus, tamquam lapides effuderit imber
examenque apium longa consederit uua
culmine delubri, tamquam in mare fluxerit amnis
gurgitibus miris et lactis uertice torrens.   70
    intercepta decem quereris sestertia fraude
sacrilega. quid si bis centum perdidit alter
hoc arcana modo, maiorem tertius illa
summam, quam patulae uix ceperat angulus arcae?
tam facile et pronum est superos contemnere testes,   75
si mortalis idem nemo sciat. aspice quanta

uoce neget, quae sit ficti constantia uoltus.
per Solis radios Tarpeiaque fulmina iurat
et Martis frameam et Cirrhaei spicula uatis,
per calamos uenatricis pharetramque puellae   80
perque tuum, pater Aegaei Neptune, tridentem,
addit et Herculeos arcus hastamque Mineruae,
quidquid habent telorum armamentaria caeli.
si uero et pater est, 'comedam' inquit 'flebile nati
sinciput elixi Pharioque madentis aceto.'   85
    sunt in fortunae qui casibus omnia ponant
et nullo credant mundum rectore moueri
natura uoluente uices et lucis et anni,
atque ideo intrepidi quaecumque altaria tangunt.
[est alius metuens ne crimen poena sequatur.]   90
hic putat esse deos et peierat, atque ita secum:
'decernat quodcumque uolet de corpore nostro
Isis et irato feriat mea lumina sistro,
dummodo uel caecus teneam quos abnego nummos.
et pthisis et uomicae putres et dimidium crus   95
sunt tanti. pauper locupletem optare podagram
nec dubitet Ladas, si non eget Anticyra nec
Archigene; quid enim uelocis gloria plantae
praestat et esuriens Pisaeae ramus oliuae?
ut sit magna, tamen certe lenta ira deorum est;   100
si curant igitur cunctos punire nocentes,
quando ad me uenient? sed et exorabile numen
fortasse experiar; solet his ignoscere. multi
committunt eadem diuerso crimina fato:
ille crucem sceleris pretium tulit, hic diadema.'   105
sic animum dirae trepidum formidine culpae
confirmat, tunc te sacra ad delubra uocantem
praecedit, trahere immo ultro ac uectare paratus.
nam cum magna malae superest audacia causae,
creditur a multis fiducia. mimum agit ille,   110
urbani qualem fugituus scurra Catulli:
tu miser exclamas, ut Stentora uincere possis,
uel potius quantum Gradiuus Homericus, 'audis,
Iuppiter, haec nec labra moues, cum mittere uocem
debueris uel marmoreus uel aeneus? aut cur   115
in carbone tuo charta pia tura soluta

ponimus et sectum uituli iecur albaque porci
omenta? ut uideo, nullum discrimen habendum est
effigies inter uestras statuamque Vagelli.'
    accipe quae contra ualeat solacia ferre   120
et qui nec Cynicos nec Stoica dogmata legit
a Cynicis tunica distantia, non Epicurum
suspicit exigui laetum plantaribus horti.
curentur dubii medicis maioribus aegri:
tu uenam uel discipulo committe Philippi.   125
si nullum in terris tam detestabile factum
ostendis, taceo, nec pugnis caedere pectus
te ueto nec plana faciem contundere palma,
quandoquidem accepto claudenda est ianua damno,
et maiore domus gemitu, maiore tumultu   130
planguntur nummi quam funera; nemo dolorem
fingit in hoc casu, uestem diducere summam
contentus, uexare oculos umore coacto:
ploratur lacrimis amissa pecunia ueris.
sed si cuncta uides simili fora plena querella,   135
si deciens lectis diuersa parte tabellis
uana superuacui dicunt chirographa ligni,
arguit ipsorum quos littera gemmaque princeps
sardonychum, loculis quae custoditur eburnis,
ten, o delicias, extra communia censes   140
ponendum, quia tu gallinae filius albae,
nos uiles pulli nati infelicibus ouis?
rem pateris modicam et mediocri bile ferendam,
si flectas oculos maiora ad crimina. confer
conductum latronem, incendia sulpure coepta   145
atque dolo, primos cum ianua colligit ignes;
confer et hos, ueteris qui tollunt grandia templi
pocula adorandae robiginis et populorum
dona uel antiquo positas a rege coronas;
haec ibi si non sunt, minor exstat sacrilegus qui   150
radat inaurati femur Herculis et faciem ipsam
Neptuni, qui bratteolam de Castore ducat;
[an dubitet solitus totum conflare Tonantem?]
confer et artifices mercatoremque ueneni
et deducendum corio bouis in mare, cum quo   155
clauditur aduersis innoxia simia fatis.

haec quota pars scelerum, quae custos Gallicus urbis
usque a lucifero donec lux occidat audit?
humani generis mores tibi nosse uolenti
sufficit una domus; paucos consume dies et   160
dicere te miserum, postquam illinc ueneris, aude.
quis tumidum guttur miratur in Alpibus aut quis
in Meroe crasso maiorem infante mamillam?
caerula quis stupuit Germani lumina, flauam
caesariem et madido torquentem cornua cirro?   165
[nempe quod haec illis natura est omnibus una.]
ad subitas Thracum uolucres nubemque sonoram
Pygmaeus paruis currit bellator in armis,
mox inpar hosti raptusque per aera curuis
unguibus a saeva fertur grue. si uideas hoc   170
gentibus in nostris, risu quatiare; sed illic,
quamquam eadem adsidue spectentur proelia, ridet
nemo, ubi tota cohors pede non est altior uno.
    'nullane peiuri capitis fraudisque nefandae
poena erit?' abreptum crede hunc grauiore catena   175
protinus et nostro (quid plus uelit ira?) necari
arbitrio: manet illa tamen iactura nec umquam
depositum tibi sospes erit, sed corpore trunco
inuidiosa dabit nimius solacia sanguis.
'at uindicta bonum uita iucundius ipsa.'   180
nempe hoc indocti, quorum praecordia nullis
interdum aut leuibus uideas flagrantia causis:
quantulacumque adeo est occasio sufficit irae.
Chrysippus non dicet idem nec mite Thaletis
ingenium dulcique senex uicinus Hymetto,   185
qui partem acceptae saeua inter uincla cicutae
accusatori nollet dare. plurima felix
paulatim uitia atque errores exuit, omnes
prima docens rectum, sapientia. quippe minuti
semper et infirmi est animi exiguique uoluptas   190
ultio. continuo sic collige, quod uindicta
nemo magis gaudet quam femina. cur tamen hos tu
euasisse putes, quos diri conscia facti
mens habet attonitos et surdo uerbere caedit
occultum quatiente animo tortore flagellum?   195
poena autem uehemens ac multo saeuior illis

quas et Caedicius grauis inuenit et Rhadamanthus,
nocte dieque suum gestare in pectore testem.
Spartano cuidam respondit Pythia uates
haut inpunitum quondam fore quod dubitaret   200
depositum retinere et fraudem iure tueri
iurando. quaerebat enim quae numinis esset
mens et an hoc illi facinus suaderet Apollo.
reddidit ergo metu, non moribus, et tamen omnem
uocem adyti dignam templo ueramque probauit   205
extinctus tota pariter cum prole domoque
et quamuis longa deductis gente propinquis.
has patitur poenas peccandi sola uoluntas.
nam scelus intra se tacitum qui cogitat ullum
facti crimen habet. cedo si conata peregit.   210
perpetua anxietas nec mensae tempore cessat
faucibus ut morbo siccis interque molares
difficili crescente cibo, Setina misellus
expuit, Albani ueteris pretiosa senectus
displicet; ostendas melius, densissima ruga   215
cogitur in frontem uelut acri ducta Falerno.
nocte breuem si forte indulsit cura soporem
et toto uersata toro iam membra quiescunt,
continuo templum et uiolati numinis aras
et, quod praecipuis mentem sudoribus urguet,   220
te uidet in somnis; tua sacra et maior imago
humana turbat pauidum cogitque fateri.
hi sunt qui trepidant et ad omnia fulgura pallent,.
cum tonat, exanimes primo quoque murmure caeli,
non quasi fortuitus nec uentorum rabie sed   225
iratus cadat in terras et uindicet ignis.
illa nihil nocuit, cura grauiore timetur
proxima tempestas uelut hoc dilata sereno.
praeterea lateris uigili cum febre dolorem
si coepere pati, missum ad sua corpora morbum   230
infesto credunt a numine; saxa deorum
haec et tela putant. pecudem spondere sacello
balantem et Laribus cristam promittere galli
non audent; quid enim sperare nocentibus aegris
concessum? uel quae non dignior hostia uita?   235
mobilis et uaria est ferme natura malorum.

cum scelus admittunt, superest constantia; quod fas
atque nefas, tandem incipiunt sentire peractis
criminibus. tamen ad mores natura recurrit
damnatos fixa et mutari nescia. nam quis   240
peccandi finem posuit sibi? quando recepit
eiectum semel attrita de fronte ruborem?
quisnam hominum est quem tu contentum uideris uno
flagitio? dabit in laqueum uestigia noster
perfidus et nigri patietur carceris uncum   245
aut maris Aegaei rupem scopulosque frequentes
exulibus magnis. poena gaudebis amara
nominis inuisi tandemque fatebere laetus
nec Drusum nec Teresian quemquam esse deorum.

14

Plurima sunt, Fuscine, et fama digna sinistra
[et quod maiorum uitia sequiturque minores]   1A
et nitidis maculam haesuram figentia rebus,
quae monstrant ipsi pueris traduntque parentes.
si damnosa senem iuuat alea, ludit et heres
bullatus paruoque eadem mouet arma fritillo,   5
nec melius de se cuiquam sperare propinquo
concedet iuuenis: qui radere tubera terrae,
boletum condire et eodem iure natantis
mergere ficedulas didicit nebulone parente
et cana monstrante gula. cum septimus annus   10
transierit puerum, nondum omni dente renato,
barbatos licet admoueas mille inde magistros,
hinc totidem, cupiet lauto cenare paratu
semper et a magna non degenerare culina.
mitem animum et mores modicis erroribus aequos   15
praecipit atque animas seruorum et corpora nostra
materia constare putat paribusque elementis,
an saeuire docet Rutilus, qui gaudet acerbo
plagarum strepitu et nullam Sirena flagellis
conparat, Antiphates trepidi laris ac Polyphemus,   20
tunc felix, quotiens aliquis tortore uocato
uritur ardenti duo propter lintea ferro?
quid suadet iuueni laetus stridore catenae,

quem mire adficiunt inscripta, ergastula, carcer?
rusticus expectas ut non sit adultera Largae   25
filia, quae numquam maternos dicere moechos
tam cito nec tanto poterit contexere cursu
ut non ter deciens respiret? conscia matri
uirgo fuit, ceras nunc hac dictante pusillas
implet et ad moechum dat eisdem ferre cinaedis.   30
sic natura iubet: uelocius et citius nos
corrumpunt uitiorum exempla domestica, magnis
cum subeant animos auctoribus. unus et alter
forsitan haec spernant iuuenes, quibus arte benigna
et meliore luto finxit praecordia Titan,   35
sed reliquos fugienda patrum uestigia ducunt
et monstrata diu ueteris trahit orbita culpae.
    abstineas igitur damnandis. huius enim uel
una potens ratio est, ne crimina nostra sequantur
ex nobis geniti, quoniam dociles imitandis   40
turpibus ac prauis omnes sumus, et Catilinam
quocumque in populo uideas, quocumque sub axe,
sed nec Brutus erit Bruti nec auunculus usquam.
nil dictu foedum uisuque haec limina tangat
intra quae pater est. procul, a procul inde puellae   45
lenonum et cantus pernoctantis parasiti.
maxima debetur puero reuerentia, si quid
turpe paras, nec tu pueri contempseris annos,
sed peccaturo obstet tibi filius infans.
nam si quid dignum censoris fecerit ira   50
quandoque et similem tibi se non corpore tantum
nec uultu dederit, morum quoque filius et qui
omnia deterius tua per uestigia peccet,
corripies nimirum et castigabis acerbo
clamore ac post haec tabulas mutare parabis.   55
unde tibi frontem libertatemque parentis,
cum facias peiora senex uacuumque cerebro
iam pridem caput hoc uentosa cucurbita quaerat?
    hospite uenturo cessabit nemo tuorum.
'uerre pauimentum, nitidas ostende columnas,   60
arida cum tota descendat aranea tela,
hic leue argentum, uasa aspera tergeat alter.'
uox domini furit instantis uirgamque tenentis.

ergo miser trepidas, ne stercore foeda canino
atria displiceant oculis uenientis amici,   65
ne perfusa luto sit porticus, et tamen uno
semodio scobis haec emendat seruulus unus:
illud non agitàs, ut sanctam filius omni
aspiciat sine labe domum uitioque carentem?
gratum est quod patriae ciuem populoque dedisti,   70
si facis ut ciuis sit idoneus, utilis agris,
utilis et bellorum et pacis rebus agendis.
     plurimum enim intererit quibus artibus et quibus hunc tu
moribus instituas. serpente ciconia pullos
nutrit et inuenta per deuia rura lacerta: 75
illi eadem sumptis quaerunt animalia pinnis.
uoltur iumento et canibus crucibusque relictis
ad fetus properat partemque cadaueris adfert:
hic est ergo cibus magni quoque uolturis et se
pascentis, propria cum iam facit arbore nidos.   80
sed leporem aut capream famulae Iouis et generosae
in saltu uenantur aues, hinc praeda cubili
ponitur: inde autem cum se matura leuauit
progenies stimulante fame festinat ad illam
quam primum praedam rupto gustauerat ouo.   85
     aedificator erat Caetronius et modo curuo
litore Caietae, summa nunc Tiburis arce,
nunc Praenestinis in montibus alta parabat
culmina uillarum Graecis longeque petitis
marmoribus uincens Fortunae atque Herculis aedem,   90
ut spado uincebat Capitolia nostra Posides.
dum sic ergo habitat Caetronius, inminuit rem,
fregit opes, nec parua tamen mensura relictae
partis erat. totam hanc turbauit filius amens,
dum meliore nouas attollit marmore uillas.   95
     quidam sortiti metuentem sabbata patrem
nil praeter nubes et caeli numen adorant,
nec distare putant humana carne suillam,
qua pater abstinuit, mox et praeputia ponunt;
Romanas autem soliti contemnere leges   100
Iudaicum ediscunt et seruant ac metuunt ius,
tradidit arcano quodcumque uolumine Moyses:
non monstrare uias eadem nisi sacra colenti,

quaesitum ad fontem solos deducere uerpos.
sed pater in causa, cui septima quaeque fuit lux   105
ignaua et partem uitae non attigit ullam.
   sponte tamen iuuenes imitantur cetera, solam
inuiti quoque auaritiam exercere iubentur.
fallit enim uitium specie uirtutis et umbra,
cum sit triste habitu uultuque et ueste seuerum,   110
nec dubie tamquam frugi laudetur auarus,
tamquam parcus homo et rerum tutela suarum
certa magis quam si fortunas seruet easdem
Hesperidum serpens aut Ponticus. adde quod hunc de
quo loquor egregium populus putat adquirendi   115
artificem; quippe his crescunt patrimonia fabris
(sed crescunt quocumque modo maioraque fiunt)
incude adsidua semperque ardente camino.
[et pater ergo animi felices credit auaros]
qui miratur opes, qui nulla exempla beati   120
pauperis esse putat, iuuenes hortatur ut illa
ire uia pergant et eidem incumbere sectae.
sunt quaedam uitiorum elementa, his protinus illos
inbuit et cogit minimas ediscere sordes;
mox adquirendi docet insatiabile uotum.   125
seruorum uentres modio castigat iniquo
ipse quoque esuriens, neque enim omnia sustinet umquam
mucida caerulei panis consumere frusta,
hesternum solitus medio seruare minutal
Septembri nec non differre in tempora cenae   130
alterius conchem aestiuam cum parte lacerti
signatam uel dimidio putrique siluro
filaque sectiui numerata includere porri.
inuitatus ad haec aliquis de ponte negabit.
sed quo diuitias haec per tormenta coactas,   135
cum furor haut dubius, cum sit manifesta phrenesis,
ut locuples moriaris, egentis uiuere fato?
   interea, pleno cum turget sacculus ore,
crescit amor nummi quantum ipsa pecunia creuit,
et minus hanc optat qui non habet. ergo paratur   140
altera uilla tibi, cum rus non sufficit unum
et proferre libet finis maiorque uidetur
et melior uicina seges; mercaris et hanc et

arbusta et densa montem qui canet oliua.
quorum si pretio dominus non uincitur ullo,   145
nocte boues macri lassoque famelica collo
iumenta ad uiridis huius mittentur aristas
nec prius inde domum quam tota noualia saeuos
in uentres abeant, ut credas falcibus actum.
dicere uix possis quam multi talia plorent   150
et quot uenales iniuria fecerit agros.
sed qui sermones, quam foede bucina famae!
'quid nocet haec?' inquit 'tunicam mihi malo lupini
quam si me toto laudet uicinia pago
exigui ruris paucissima farra secantem.'   155
scilicet et morbis et debilitate carebis
et luctum et curam effugies, et tempora uitae
longa tibi posthac fato meliore dabuntur,
si tantum culti solus possederis agri
quantum sub Tatio populus Romanus arabat.   160
mox etiam fractis aetate ac Punica passis
proelia uel Pyrrhum inmanem gladiosque Molossos
tandem pro multis uix iugera bina dabantur
uulneribus; merces haec sanguinis atque laboris
nulli uisa umquam meritis minor aut ingratae   165
curta fides patriae. saturabat glebula talis
patrem ipsum turbamque casae, qua feta iacebat
uxor et infantes ludebant quattuor, unus
uernula, tres domini; sed magnis fratribus horum
a scrobe uel sulco redeuntibus altera cena   170
amplior et grandes fumabant pultibus ollae.
nunc modus hic agri nostro non sufficit horto.
    inde fere scelerum causae, nec plura uenena
miscuit aut ferro grassatur saepius ullum
humanae mentis uitium quam saeua cupido   175
inmodici census. nam diues qui fieri uolt,
et cito uolt fieri; sed quae reuerentia legum,
quis metus aut pudor est umquam properantis auari?
'uiuite contenti casulis et collibus istis,
o pueri,' Marsus dicebat et Hernicus olim   180
Vestinusque senex, 'panem quaeramus aratro,
qui satis est mensis: laudant hoc numina ruris,
quorum ope et auxilio gratae post munus aristae

contingunt homini ueteris fastidia quercus.
nil uetitum fecisse uolet, quem non pudet alto   185
per glaciem perone tegi, qui summouet euros
pellibus inuersis: peregrina ignotaque nobis
ad scelus atque nefas, quaecumque est, purpura ducit.'
    haec illi ueteres praecepta minoribus; at nunc
post finem autumni media de nocte supinum   190
clamosus iuuenem pater excitat: 'accipe ceras,
scribe, puer, uigila, causas age, perlege rubras
maiorum leges; aut uitem posce libello,
sed caput intactum buxo narisque pilosas
adnotet et grandes miretur Laelius alas;   195
dirue Maurorum attegias, castella Brigantum,
ut locupletem aquilam tibi sexagesimus annus
adferat; aut, longos castrorum ferre labores
si piget et trepidum soluunt tibi cornua uentrem
cum lituis audita, pares quod uendere possis   200
pluris dimidio, nec te fastidia mercis
ullius subeant ablegandae Tiberim ultra,
neu credas ponendum aliquid discriminis inter
unguenta et corium: lucri bonus est odor ex re
qualibet. illa tuo sententia semper in ore   205
uersetur dis atque ipso Ioue digna poeta:
"unde habeas quaerit nemo, sed oportet habere." '
hoc monstrant uetulae pueris repentibus assae,
hoc discunt omnes ante alpha et beta puellae.
talibus instantem monitis quemcumque parentem   210
sic possem adfari: 'dic, o uanissime, quis te
festinare iubet? meliorem praesto magistro
discipulum. securus abi: uinceris, ut Aiax
praeteriit Telamonem, ut Pelea uicit Achilles.
parcendum est teneris; nondum impleuere medullas   215
maturae mala nequitiae. cum pectere barbam
coeperit et longae mucronem admittere cultri,
falsus erit testis, uendet periuria summa
exigua et Cereris tangens aramque pedemque.
elatam iam crede nurum, si limina uestra   220
mortifera cum dote subit. quibus illa premetur
per somnum digitis! nam quae terraque marique
adquirenda putas breuior uia conferet illi;

nullus enim magni sceleris labor. "haec ego numquam
mandaui" dices olim "nec talia suasi."   225
mentis causa malae tamen est et origo penes te.
nam quisquis magni census praecepit amorem
et laeuo monitu pueros producit auaros
quippe et per fraudes patrimonia conduplicare
dat libertatem et totas effundit habenas   230
curriculo; quem si reuoces, subsistere nescit
et te contempto rapitur metisque relictis.
nemo satis credit tantum delinquere quantum
permittas: adeo indulgent sibi latius ipsi.
cum dicis iuueni stultum qui donet amico,   235
qui paupertatem leuet attollatque propinqui,
et spoliare doces et circumscribere et omni
crimine diuitias adquirere, quarum amor in te
quantus erat patriae Deciorum in pectore, quantum
dilexit Thebas, si Graecia uera, Menoeceus,   240
in quorum sulcis legiones dentibus anguis
cum clipeis nascuntur et horrida bella capessunt
continuo, tamquam et tubicen surrexerit una.
ergo ignem, cuius scintillas ipse dedisti,
flagrantem late et rapientem cuncta uidebis.   245
nec tibi parcetur misero, trepidumque magistrum
in cauea magno fremitu leo tollet alumnus.
nota mathematicis genesis tua, sed graue tardas
expectare colus: morieris stamine nondum
abrupto. iam nunc obstas et uota moraris,   250
iam torquet iuuenem longa et ceruina senectus.
ocius Archigenen quaere atque eme quod Mithridates
composuit: si uis aliam decerpere ficum
atque alias tractare rosas, medicamen habendum est,
sorbere ante cibum quod debeat et pater et rex.'   255
    monstro uoluptatem egregiam, cui nulla theatra,
nulla aequare queas praetoris pulpita lauti,
si spectes quanto capitis discrimine constent
incrementa domus, aerata multus in arca
fiscus et ad uigilem ponendi Castora nummi,   260
ex quo Mars Vltor galeam quoque perdidit et res
non potuit seruare suas. ergo omnia Florae
et Cereris licet et Cybeles aulaea relinquas:

tanto maiores humana negotia ludi.
an magis oblectant animum iactata petauro   265
corpora quique solet rectum descendere funem
quam tu, Corycia semper qui puppe moraris
atque habitas, coro semper tollendus et austro,
perditus adquirens sacci mercator olentis,
qui gaudes pingue antiquae de litore Cretae   270
passum et municipes Iouis aduexisse lagonas?
hic tamen ancipiti figens uestigia planta
uictum illa mercede parat, brumamque famemque
illa reste cauet: tu propter mille talenta
et centum uillas temerarius. aspice portus   275
et plenum magnis trabibus mare: plus hominum est iam
in pelago. ueniet classis quocumque uocarit
spes lucri, nec Carpathium Gaetulaque tantum
aequora transiliet, sed longe Calpe relicta
audiet Herculeo stridentem gurgite solem.   280
grande operae pretium est, ut tenso folle reuerti
inde domum possis tumidaque superbus aluta,
Oceani monstra et iuuenes uidisse marinos.
non unus mentes agitat furor. ille sororis
in manibus uoltu Eumenidum terretur et igni,   285
hic boue percusso mugire Agamemnona credit
aut Ithacum. parcat tunicis licet atque lacernis,
curatoris eget qui nauem mercibus implet
ad summum latus et tabula distinguitur unda,
cum sit causa mali tanti et discriminis huius   290
concisum argentum in titulos faciesque minutas.
occurrunt nubes et fulgura: 'soluite funem'
frumenti dominus clamat piperisue coempti,
'nil color hic caeli, nil fascia nigra minatur;
aestiuom tonat.' infelix hac forsitan ipsa   295
nocte cadet fractis trabibus fluctuque premetur
obrutus et zonam laeua morsuque tenebit.
sed cuius uotis modo non suffecerat aurum
quod Tagus et rutila uoluit Pactolus harena,
frigida sufficient uelantes inguina panni   300
exiguusque cibus, mersa rate naufragus assem
dum rogat et picta se tempestate tuetur.
    tantis parta malis cura maiore metuque

seruantur: misera est magni custodia census.
dispositis praediues amis uigilare cohortem   305
seruorum noctu Licinus iubet, attonitus pro
electro signisque suis Phrygiaque columna
atque ebore et lata testudine. dolia nudi
non ardent Cynici; si fregeris, altera fiet
cras domus atque eadem plumbo commissa manebit.   310
sensit Alexander, testa cum uidit in illa
magnum habitatorem, quanto felicior hic qui
nil cuperet quam qui totum sibi posceret orbem
passurus gestis aequanda pericula rebus.
nullum numen habes . . . [si sit prudentia: nos te,   315
nos facimus, Fortuna, deam.] mensura tamen quae
sufficiat census, si quis me consulat, edam:
in quantum sitis atque fames et frigora poscunt,
quantum, Epicure, tibi paruis suffecit in hortis,
quantum Socratici ceperunt ante penates;   320
numquam aliud natura, aliud sapientia dicit.
acribus exemplis uideor te cludere? misce
ergo aliquid nostris de moribus, effice summam
bis septem ordinibus quam lex dignatur Othonis.
haec quoque si rugam trahit extenditque labellum,   325
sume duos equites, fac tertia quadringenta.
si nondum impleui gremium, si panditur ultra,
nec Croesi fortuna umquam nec Persica regna
sufficient animo nec diuitiae Narcissi,
indulsit Caesar cui Claudius omnia, cuius   330
paruit imperiis uxorem occidere iussus.

15

Quis nescit, Volusi Bithynice, qualia demens
Aegyptos portenta colat? crocodilon adorat
pars haec, illa pauet saturam serpentibus ibin.
effigies sacri nitet aurea cercopitheci,
dimidio magicae resonant ubi Memnone chordae   5
atque uetus Thebe centum iacet,obruta portis.
illic aeluros, hic piscem fluminis, illic
oppida tota canem uenerantur, nemo Dianam.
porrum et caepe nefas uiolare et frangere morsu

(o sanctas gentes, quibus haec nascuntur in hortis   10
numina!), lanatis animalibus abstinet omnis
mensa, nefas illic fetum iugulare capellae:
carnibus humanis uesci licet. attonito cum
tale super cenam facinus narraret Vlixes
Alcinoo, bilem aut risum fortasse quibusdam   15
mouerat ut mendax aretalogus. 'in mare nemo
hunc abicit saeua dignum ueraque Charybdi,
fingentem inmanis Laestrygonas et Cyclopas?
nam citius Scyllam uel concurrentia saxa
Cyaneas plenos et tempestatibus utres   20
crediderim aut tenui percussum uerbere Circes
et cum remigibus grunnisse Elpenora porcis.
tam uacui capitis populum Phaeaca putauit?'
sic aliquis merito nondum ebrius et minimum qui
de Corcyraea temetum duxerat urna;   25
solus enim haec Ithacus nullo sub teste canebat.
nos miranda quidem sed nuper consule Iunco
gesta super calidae referemus moenia Copti,
nos uolgi scelus et cunctis grauiora coturnis;
nam scelus, a Pyrrha quamquam omnia syrmata uoluas,   30
nullus apud tragicos populus facit. accipe nostro
dira quod exemplum feritas produxerit aeuo.
    inter finitimos uetus atque antiqua simultas,
inmortale odium et numquam sanabile uulnus,
ardet adhuc Ombos et Tentura. summus utrimque   35
inde furor uolgo, quod numina uicinorum
odit uterque locus, cum solos credat habendos
esse deos quos ipse colit. sed tempore festo
alterius populi rapienda occasio cunctis
uisa inimicorum primoribus ac ducibus, ne   40
laetum hilaremque diem, ne magnae gaudia cenae
sentirent positis ad templa et compita mensis
peruigilique toro, quem nocte ac luce iacentem
septimus interdum sol inuenit. horrida sane
Aegyptos, sed luxuria, quantum ipse notaui,   45
barbara famoso non cedit turba Canopo.
adde quod et facilis uictoria de madidis et
blaesis atque mero titubantibus. inde uirorum
saltatus nigro tibicine, qualiacumque

unguenta et flores multaeque in fronte coronae: 50
hinc ieiunum odium. sed iurgia prima sonare
incipiunt; animis ardentibus haec tuba rixae.
dein clamore pari concurritur, et uice teli
saeuit nuda manus. paucae sine uolnere malae,
uix cuiquam aut nulli toto certamine nasus   55
integer. aspiceres iam cuncta per agmina uoltus
dimidios, alias facies et hiantia ruptis
ossa genis, plenos oculorum sanguine pugnos.
ludere se credunt ipsi tamen et puerilis
exercere acies quod nulla cadauera calcent.   60
et sane quo tot rixantis milia turbae,
si uiuunt omnes? ergo acrior impetus et iam
saxa inclinatis per humum quaesita lacertis
incipiunt torquere, domestica seditioni
tela, nec hunc lapidem, qualis et Turnus et Aiax,   65
uel quo Tydides percussit pondere coxam
Aeneae, sed quem ualeant emittere dextrae
illis dissimiles et nostro tempore natae.
nam genus hoc uiuo iam decrescebat Homero,
terra malos homines nunc educat atque pusillos;   70
ergo deus, quicumque aspexit, ridet et odit.
a deuerticulo repetatur fabula. postquam
subsidiis aucti, pars altera promere ferrum
audet et infestis pugnam instaurare sagittis.
terga fugae celeri praestant instantibus Ombis   75
qui uicina colunt umbrosae Tentura palmae.
labitur hic quidam nimia formidine cursum
praecipitans capiturque. ast illum in plurima sectum
frusta et particulas, ut multis mortuus unus
sufficeret, totum corrosis ossibus edit   80
uictrix turba, nec ardenti decoxit aeno
aut ueribus, longum usque adeo tardumque putauit
expectare focos, contenta cadauere crudo.
hic gaudere libet quod non uiolauerit ignem,
quem summa caeli raptum de parte, Prometheu,   85
donasti terris; elemento gratulor, et te
exultare reor. sed qui mordere cadauer
sustinuit nil umquam hac carne libentius edit;
nam scelere in tanto ne quaeras et dubites an

prima uoluptatem gula senserit, ultimus ante   90
qui stetit, absumpto iam toto corpore ductis
per terram digitis aliquid de sanguine gustat.
    Vascones, ut fama est, alimentis talibus usi
produxere animas, sed res diuersa, sed illic
fortunae inuidia est bellorumque ultima, casus   95
extremi, longae dira obsidionis egestas.
[huius enim, quod nunc agitur, miserabile debet
exemplum esse tibi, sicut modo dicta mihi gens.]
post omnis herbas, post cuncta animalia, quidquid
cogebat uacui uentris furor, hostibus ipsis   100
pallorem ac maciem et tenuis miserantibus artus,
membra aliena fame lacerabant, esse parati
et sua. quisnam hominum ueniam dare quisue deorum
uentribus abnueret dira atque inmania passis
et quibus illorum poterant ignoscere manes   105
quorum corporibus uescebantur? melius nos
Zenonis praecepta monent — nec enim omnia quidam
pro uita facienda putant — sed Cantaber unde
Stoicus, antiqui praesertim aetate Metelli?
nunc totus Graias nostrasque habet orbis Athenas,   110
Gallia causidicos docuit facunda Britannos,
de conducendo loquitur iam rhetore Thyle.
nobilis ille tamen populus, quem diximus, et par
uirtute atque fide sed maior clade Zacynthos
tale quid excusat: Maeotide saeuior ara   115
Aegyptos. quippe illa nefandi Taurica sacri
inuentrix homines, ut iam quae carmina tradunt
digna fide credas, tantum immolat; ulterius nil
aut grauius cultro timet hostia. quis modo casus
inpulit hos? quae tanta fames infestaque uallo   120
arma coegerunt tam detestabile monstrum
audere? anne aliam terra Memphitide sicca
inuidiam facerent nolenti surgere Nilo?
qua nec terribiles Cimbri nec Brittones umquam
Sauromataeque truces aut inmanes Agathyrsi,   125
hac saeuit rabie inbelle et inutile uolgus
paruula fictilibus solitum dare uela phaselis
et breuibus pictae remis incumbere testae.
nec poenam sceleri inuenies nec digna parabis

supplicia his populis, in quorum mente pares sunt   130
et similes ira atque fames. mollissima corda
humano generi dare se natura fatetur,
quae lacrimas dedit. haec nostri pars optima sensus.
plorare ergo iubet causam dicentis amici
squaloremque rei, pupillum ad iura uocantem   135
circumscriptorem, cuius manantia fletu
ora puellares faciunt incerta capilli.
naturae imperio gemimus, cum funus adultae
uirginis occurrit uel terra clauditur infans
et minor igne rogi. quis enim bonus et face dignus   140
arcana, qualem Cereris uolt esse sacerdos,
ulla aliena sibi credit mala? separat hoc nos
a grege mutorum, atque adeo uenerabile soli
sortiti ingenium diuinorumque capaces
atque exercendis pariendisque artibus apti   145
sensum a caelesti demissum traximus arce,
cuius egent prona et terram spectantia. mundi
principio indulsit communis conditor illis
tantum animas, nobis animum quoque, mutuus ut nos
adfectus petere auxilium et praestare iuberet,   150
dispersos trahere in populum, migrare uetusto
de nemore et proauis habitatas linquere siluas,
aedificare domos, laribus coniungere nostris
tectum aliud, tutos uicino limine somnos
ut conlata daret fiducia, protegere armis   155
lapsum aut ingenti nutantem uolnere ciuem,
communi dare signa tuba, defendier isdem
turribus atque una portarum claue teneri.
sed iam serpentum maior concordia. parcit
cognatis maculis similis fera. quando leoni   160
fortior eripuit uitam leo? quo nemore umquam
expirauit aper maioris dentibus apri?
Indica tigris agit rabida cum tigride pacem
perpetuam, saeuis inter se conuenit ursis.
ast homini ferrum letale incude nefanda   165
produxisse parum est, cum rastra et sarcula tantum
adsueti coquere et marris ac uomere lassi
nescierint primi gladios extendere fabri.
aspicimus populos quorum non sufficit irae

occidisse aliquem, sed pectora, bracchia, uoltum   170
crediderint genus esse cibi. quid diceret ergo
uel quo non fugeret, si nunc haec monstra uideret
Pythagoras, cunctis animalibus abstinuit qui
tamquam homine et uentri indulsit non omne legumen?

16

Quis numerare queat felicis praemia, Galli,
militiae? nam si subeuntur prospera castra
<   >
me pauidum excipiat tironem porta secundo
sidere. plus etenim fati ualet hora benigni
quam si nos Veneris commendet epistula Marti   5
et Samia genetrix quae delectatur harena.
    commoda tractemus primum communia, quorum
haut minimum illud erit, ne te pulsare togatus
audeat, immo, etsi pulsetur, dissimulet nec
audeat excussos praetori ostendere dentes   10
et nigram in facie tumidis liuoribus offam
atque oculum medico nil promittente relictum.
Bardaicus iudex datur haec punire uolenti
calceus et grandes magna ad subsellia surae
legibus antiquis castrorum et more Camilli   15
seruato, miles ne uallum litiget extra
et procul a signis. 'iustissima centurionum
cognitio exigitur de milite, nec mihi derit
ultio, si iustae defertur causa querellae.'
tota cohors tamen est inimica, omnesque manipli   20
consensu magno efficiunt curabilis ut sit
uindicta et grauior quam iniuria. dignum erit ergo
declamatoris mulino corde Vagelli,
cum duo crura habeas, offendere tot caligas, tot
milia clauorum. quis tam procul adsit ab urbe   25
praeterea, quis tam Pylades, molem aggeris ultra
ut ueniat? lacrimae siccentur protinus, et se
excusaturos non sollicitemus amicos.
'da testem' iudex cum dixerit, audeat ille
nescio quis, pugnos qui uidit, dicere 'uidi,'   30
et credam dignum barba dignumque capillis

maiorum. citius falsum producere testem
contra paganum possis quam uera loquentem
contra fortunam armati contraque pudorem.
    praemia nunc alia atque alia emolumenta notemus   35
sacramentorum. conuallem ruris auiti
improbus aut campum mihi si uicinus ademit
et sacrum effodit medio de limite saxum,
quod mea cum patulo coluit puls annua libo,
debitor aut sumptos pergit non reddere nummos   40
uana superuacui dicens chirographa ligni,
expectandus erit qui lites incohet annus
totius populi. sed tum quoque mille ferenda
taedia, mille morae; totiens subsellia tantum
sternuntur, iam facundo ponente lacernas   45
Caedicio et Fusco iam micturiente parati
digredimur, lentaque fori pugnamus harena.
ast illis quos arma tegunt et balteus ambit
quod placitum est ipsis praestatur tempus agendi,
nec res atteritur longo sufflamine litis.   50
    solis praeterea testandi militibus ius
uiuo patre datur. nam quae sunt parta labore
militiae placuit non esse in corpore census,
omne tenet cuius regimen pater. ergo Coranum
signorum comitem castrorumque aera merentem   55
quamuis iam tremulus captat pater; hunc fauor aequus
prouehit et pulchro reddit sua dona labori.
ipsius certe ducis hoc referre uidetur
ut, qui fortis erit, sit felicissimus idem,
ut laeti phaleris omnes et torquibus, omnes   60

Commentary

SATIRE 1

The first satire was probably not the first that Juvenal wrote. The first book comprises Satires 1-5, and we can suppose that he completed 2-5 and then added an introduction. The broad structure of this programmatic satire is as follows:

1-21   Introduction: reason for writing.
22-80   First exposition: objects of satire.
81-146   Second exposition, marked by a clear new beginning: the main vices isolated.
147-171   Conclusion: reasons for illustrations from the past.

The structure is thus roughly, though not precisely, symmetrical. The expositions are not tidy and systematic. There are three reasons for this. First, J's subject is life, and life is not tidy and systematic. Second, J knows well the reinforcement principle. He is a teacher. He makes the point covertly. He has suffered under others' poetry: he is going to inflict his on others: he has suffered education . . . . Good teachers know that you do not analyse your subject-matter into self-contained units, but you revert several times to the things you really want to see established, in different ways. This is what J does. Third, rhetoric is repetitive, and J is a rhetorical poet.

It should be said that some interpreters see the break, more symmetrically, at 86: 81-6 then sum up the previous section. But on the whole 80 seems an end and 81 a new start.

In 22-80 J depicts the kaleidoscope of suitable objects for satire whirling past as he stands at the street-corner. Some of these are examples of sexual perversion, but it is a mistake to isolate this, and it plays relatively little part in this satire. 37-147 deal with corruptions associated with wealth and position, *luxuria,* miserliness and extravagance. This is in pointed contrast to the condition of the poor, and the *patronus—cliens* relationship makes the point. Satires 2, 6, 9 will take up the theme of sexual perversion, Satires 5 and 9 (and, in part, 3) the relationship between the wealthy and their dependants. (Satire 1 is introductory to the first book, but J does not abandon his concerns). If we may judge from Lucilius, Horace and Persius, the satirist was expected modestly to acknowledge the majesty of epic (which he is not writing) — though some satirists, notably Persius, for this reason attack the pretensions of epic; to explain the moral urge which drives him to satire, and the style appropriate to this. J introduces all these themes, but treats them in an individual way. The programme is standard, not the treatment. In fact a basic pattern can be traced. A dissuading interlocutor advises prudence; other *genres* are safer. The satirist claims provocation, but makes some concession. The pattern may be traced with variations in Lucilius XXX; Horace *S* 2, 1; Persius 1; and later in Régnier xii; Boileau ix; Pope 'An Epistle to Dr Arbuthnot'; and (with strong irony) Swift 'Verses on the Death of Dr Swift'.

1-21   *I spend all my time listening to long, bad, irrelevant, mythological, pretentious doggerel from versifiers no better educated than I am. I'm going to have my revenge, and follow in Lucilius's footsteps.*

1   J begins his programmatic satire with a flurry of rhetorical questions.
Semper: answered by *numquam:* both are given emphasis by being at the beginning.
auditor: not *audiam:* it's not that he listens, but he's a professional listener. Supply *sim* or *ero.*
tantum: takes the main caesura from the third foot to the fourth: this infernal listening goes on: it is ambiguous between 'only' and 'to such an extent'.
reponam: could be pres. subj. (am I to to . . . ?) or fut. ind. (am I going to . . . ?): the difference is slight. We must invent an object: 'am I never to repay (the debt)?'
2   *Theseide*: i.e. an epic poem on the life of Theseus, the Athenian hero, as *Aeneis* is the epic of Aeneas. It would take several days to read. Note how the natural placing of the word between *rauci . . . Cordi* gives the effect of it coming up from the depth of his lungs. Cordus is unknown.

3 *recitaverit*: fut. pf: the action is past, the result future.

togatas (fabulas): comedies in Roman costume; our surviving Latin comedies are adaptations from Greek (*palliatae*).

4 *inpune*: note the repetition in a different metrical position. The word is strong and gives the opening blast its tone.

5 *Telephus, Orestes*: titles of plays, no doubt imitated from Euripides, who wrote tragedies on both themes. *Summi* etc., 'or an *Orestes* which, the margin at the end of the scroll being already full (abl. abs.) is written on the back as well (*et*) and still not finished'. The book (*uolumen* = roll) consists of sheets glued together at the margin. The author has got to the end of his scroll: he fills up the margin, as some letter-writers do, then turns over to the back of the thin papyrus, like airmail paper, designed for writing on one side only. Read the Latin aloud and note the breathless outpouring of words before we reach *Orestes*.

7 He knows the mythological references of the poets as well as you know your own home. Some of what follows relates to the story of Jason and his friends sailing to the Black Sea in the ship *Argo* to steal the Golden Fleece: Valerius Flaccus who wrote *The Story of the Argonauts* died about AD 90, and this may be a hit at him.

lucus Martis: the sacred grove of Mars, where the Fleece was kept. The cliffs of Aeolus (the Romans use an adjective) are rocky islands off the south of Italy, now called Lipari; the Argonauts called there. Aeolus: a wind-god. Vulcan's cave: the hollows under the volcano Stromboli. Vulcan (hence 'volcano'): the smith-god, god of fire. The winds are very important in Homer's *Odyssey*. Aeacus is an underworld god.

10-11 *alius*: Jason; the tone is satirical and contemptuous: note the diminutive *pelliculae. Monychus*: a Centaur, half man and half horse. King Peirithous of the Lapiths invited the Centaurs to his wedding. They assaulted the women present and a colossal brawl followed. If you find all this mythology obscure and tedious, you are right. J is saying 'Why bother with all this irrelevance, when real subjects are around you?'

Note in putting this long sentence into English: (a) as usual take the main sentence from 12 first, (b) use nouns in the first part where J uses verb-constructions: 'the movement (or activity) of the winds, the ghosts tortured by Aeacus, the land from which Mr X is liberating by theft that wretched (dimin.) gold sheepskin, the size

of the rowans used as javelins by Monychus.

12 *Fronto*: a rich man with a garden shaded with trees and a marble colonnade used for public recitals, perhaps T. Catius Fronto (Mart. 1, 55) who is named in *Acta Fratrum Arualium* with Q. Fulvius Gillo Bittius Proculus (cf 40). The gardens were perhaps in Praedia Quintanensia 24 km from Rome (A. Premerstein in *Herm.* 43 (1908) 322ff).

conuolsa . . . ruptae: a good example of hyperbole, the technical term in literary criticism for exaggeration. Servius on Verg. *G* 3, 328 draws attention to the parallel between this and Vergil's *rumpent arbusta cicadae*, which J may indeed be parodying.

13 *lectore*: no *a*: instrument not agent: 'through the reader's persistence' (note again: the Romans prefer adjectives, we prefer nouns).

14 *expectes*: 'you can expect'.

15 *et nos ergo*: 'Well, I too . . . '. Note how *et nos . . . et nos* frames the line; cf 1, 100; 2, 81; 2, 127; 6, 457; 14, 139. Final vowels of common words have a tendency to become short, as *ergo* here, cf *bene, male*.

ferulae: the Roman schoolmaster believed in corporal punishment. Horace (*Ep.* 2, 1, 70-71) calls a famous practitioner *plagosum . . . Orbilium*. Quintilian, the great educationalist — and teacher — of J's young days, was unusual in deprecating it. Roger Ascham in 1570 echoed him in condemning 'crueltie in scholemasters in beating away the love of learning from children'. Elementary education was the business of the *litterator*; next came the *grammaticus* for grammar and 'set book' literature.

16 *consilium dedimus Sullae*: the next stage was the rhetorical school. Exercises were of two kinds, *suasoriae*, speeches of advice to prominent historical figures, and *controuersiae*, speeches for the prosecution or defence in a fictitious lawsuit. The elder Seneca (whose son reacted away from his rhetoric into philosophy) preserved for us seven of the former, and thirty-five of the latter. They are sometimes dramatic and entertaining. A man rapes two girls on the same night. The penalty for rape was death, unless the victim elects marriage. One victim demands death, the other marriage. Which should win? A slave-owner, importing a slave, declares him to be free, to evade customs-duty. Can the slave claim his freedom? J returns to the teacher of rhetoric at 7, 150-77.

Sullae: L. Cornelius Sulla (138-78 BC), right-wing statesman and soldier, who attained sole power in Rome and then abdicated.

priuatus: tr. 'abdicate and'.

altum: acc. with *dormiret* 'sleep a deep (sleep)'.

17 *est: parcere* is subject and *stulta ... clementia* predicate.

cum: occurras is subjunctive, so tr. 'since'.

18 *periturae:* 'which will be ruined anyway': *perire* is used as passive of *perdere.* The phrase is taken from Martial (2,1,4).

19 *cur:* go first to *edam.*

decurrere: military, 'parade' or 'take the field'.

20 *equos ... flexit:* metaphor from chariot racing.

Auruncae ... alumnus: the great satirist C. Lucilius (c. 170-102 BC) who came from Suessa Aurunca in Campania, not far from J's home town. The elder Pliny (*NH* pref.) says that he was the first Roman with a critical nose for style. Horace thought him a slapdash writer but respected his position and admired his courage (*S* 1,10,3; 2,1,62). He was very popular in Juvenal's day (Quint. 10,1,93). J admired his outspokenness (1,151-4) and his aggressive temper (1,165-6). J mentions him here so as to place his own work in the invective traditions of the *satura.*

21 The courteous tone lulls us; the onslaught is the more shocking.

22-80 *Look at all the characters around us: a eunuch getting married; an Amazon of a woman; a millionaire ex-barber; Crispinus; a bloated lawyer; a government informer; gigolos; the gang of a man who's ruined his ward. Why stick to mythology with this subject-matter around? And the complaisant husband; the youngster who has lost all his money on horses; the forger; the woman-poisoner. Wealth comes from crime: honesty is left to freeze. Indignation would make me a poet, even if talent failed.*

22 The juxtaposition of this line with what has gone before is brilliant. We see side by side boring mythology, and present vice which makes the blood boil.

tener: usually used of a young boy or girl, appropriate to the effeminate eunuch. Note how *spado* comes unexpectedly; also how *tener ... spado* embraces *uxorem,* a type of effect common in Latin poetry. Eunuchs would marry to prove they were men, as did Eutropius, eunuch at the court of Arcadius (Claud. *In Eutrop.* 2,88-90).

Meuia: not otherwise known. We know from other sources (Suet. *Dom.* 4) that the emperor Domitian (81-96) encouraged women to fight in the arena. Maevius is normal Latin for a man of good family,

whether for good or bad (S. Lancel in *Hommages à Jean Bayet* Brussels 1964 pp. 355-64).

Tuscum: the forest-land housed boars.

23 *nuda ... mamma:* like the goddess Diana, or the Amazon Penthesilea in Vergil (*A* 1,492).

uenabula: plural for poetic convenience: tr. 'spear'.

24 Note the shape of the line, object-instrument-verb-subject, and the *omnis-unus* contrast. The line pivots on *opibus;* wealth outstrips birth (*patricios* emphasises birth). Stress is thrown on *unus.* The barber concerned was probably named Cinnamus (Mart. 6,17; 7,64).

25 *grauis:* ambiguous, and closely with *iuueni:* to him in his adolescence his beard was an unfamiliar weight (to be clipped) but one which gave him dignity. But Fletcher in *Latomus* 35 (1976) 110 points out also its relation to *sonabat* cf Sil. 2,545 *grauior sonuit per litora fluctus.* The line, repeated at 10,226 is a parody of Vergil (*Ecl.* 1,28 *candidior postquam tondenti barba cadebat*).

26 *uerna:* a native (cf Mart. 10,76,4).

Canopi: town of Egypt, some 24 kilometres from Alexandria.

27 *Crispinus:* Egyptian who came to Rome as a trader in fish, and lived to be a member of Domitian's Privy Council; cf *Sat.* 4. Note that *pars Niliacae plebis* gives no hint of what is to come: we focus down on the actual person. J reverses the usual method by which three phrases referring to the same object grow more expansive: he contracts and becomes more precise.

Tyrias: dyed with purple made from crushed shellfish found off the coast of Phoenicia; cf Mart. 8,48,1 *Tyriam Crispinus abollam.*

reuocante: 'hitching up'

28 *uentilet:* pulling it on and off the finger.

aestiuum: does this mean that he has a lighter 'summer-ring' which because it is gold is still too heavy, or is it just the equivalent of 'in summer'? (cf George Eliot *Daniel Deronda* c68: 'I understand why the Romans had summer rings — if they had them'). Housman took the former view (*CR* 17 (1903) 467). It was not a usual Roman practice, which is why J comments on it. So schol.: *per luxuriam anulos aestiuos et hiemales inuenerat.* Martial (11,37) suggests that someone's ring is too big for his finger and ought to be worn round the ankle (i.e. as a slave's fetter). Lord Petersham had a different snuffbox for each day of the year, and said of a Sèvres snuffbox that it was 'a nice summer box but it would not do for winter wear'.

aurum: i.e. gold ring.

29 *maioris:* 'the weight of a larger ring with a jewel', almost the same as 'the larger weight of a ring with a jewel' (transferred epithet).

gemmae: i.e. 'ring with a jewel' which would be larger than a plain gold band.

30 *saturam:* not our 'satire': see introduction. *Satura* is a medley, a discursive commentary. But by his reference to Lucilius, J has associated himself explicitly with the tradition of invective. The structure of the line should be closely examined. Notice the break after the fourth foot (the so-called 'bucolic diaeresis'); the internal rhyme, *saturam . . . nam,* both accented syllables; the alliterations, hissing at *saturam . . . scribere,* cutting at *quis . . . iniquae;* the stumbling, grumbling effect of *-am non . . . nam* (Quintilian calls *m* a 'moping' letter). David Worcester calls this epigram 'a brilliant stroke of rhetoric'. The labourer who has been exploited or the person injured by a drunken driver is not usually forced to satire. It is in fact perfectly easy to refrain. But J deludes us with his rhetoric. Skelton quotes the line in 'Why Come Ye Nat to Courte?'; cf Wither 'Satire to King James':' 'Tis a hard thing not to write Satyres now.'

iniquae: 'unjust', brought right forward for emphasis. We say 'the injustice of the capital'.

31 *urbis:* Rome. So regularly: compare our 'He works in the City', though that isolates the business centre, and J is concerned with the whole life of the capital.

ut teneat se: the broken rhythm at the end suggests the effort which must be made.

32 *Mathonis:* by 7,129 he has become bankrupt.

33 *plena ipso:* a splendid phrase: the elision helps the sense of the fat man cramming himself in. The *lectica* was large enough for two. The *lectica* is a symbol for J (on foot) of the power of the rich, almost like a Rolls-Royce: it recurs at 63-7 and 158-9.

magni: 'eminent'.

delator: 'informer'; cf 3,116; 4,48; 10,70. Augustus began the practice of rewarding informers against those who were in breach of his legislation on the family (Tac. *Ann.* 3.28; Suet. *Nero* 10). Tiberius, who was liable to follow some of Augustus's worse precedents, in reviving the law of treason greatly increased the scope of the informers, who received a quarter of the property of anyone condemned on information received from them (Tac. *Ann.* 4,20). Tiberius called them 'protectors of the laws'; Tacitus regarded them as *genus hominum publico exitio repertum* (*ib.* 4,30). We can only guess at the identity of this arch-informer. The most plausible guess is M. Aquilius Regulus: the younger Pliny (*Ep.* 1,5.14) describes him as the most villainous of all two-legged creatures — cultivated by many, feared by more. Herrmann has argued for a covert attack on Publicius Certus, for his part in the condemnation of Helvidius Priscus.

34 *rapturus:* i.e. 'the man who denounced . . . and is going to steal . . . '.

de: ambiguously placed, but must be taken with *superest* as well as *rapturus.*

comesa: a carcase ravaged by a wild beast.

35 *Massa:* Baebius Massa, a freedman who rose to senatorial rank: he was favoured for his work as an informer. He was procurator of Africa in AD 70 and proconsul of Baetica in AD 93, but was subsequently condemned for financial irregularities (Tac. *Hist.* 4,50; *Agr.* 45; Plin. *Ep.* 7,33; Mart. 12,29 *fur nummorum*).

palpat: strictly of quieting horses: exactly our 'curry favour'.

36 *Carus:* Mettius Carus, another notorious *delator* (Plin. *Ep.* 1,53; 7,19,5; Tac. *Agr.* 45; Mart. 12,25,5). Even the most vicious *delatores* tremble before their anonymous 'boss', like lesser devils before Lucifer.

Thymele summissa Latino: actors (Mart. 1,5,5 qua *Thymelen spectas, derisoremque Latinum;* 9,29 an epitaph on Latinus). Latinus was also an informer, and a dangerous one, who used to regale Domitian with the day's gossip. *Summissa* has a complex meaning: she is sent as a substitute; she is demeaned; she is sent to be a sexual object.

37 *cum:* continued from 32.

summoueant: 'supplant'.

merentur: note the ironic use of a commendatory word, an effect J likes; cf 38 *optima.*

38 *noctibus:* 'by the way they spend their nights'.

optima: see on 37.

39 *processus:* 'advancement'.

uetulae uesica beatae: uesica, 'bladder', used of the woman's sex-organ; *beatae* 'wealthy'. Lucian makes his *Teacher of Orators* (24) (perhaps a satirical attack on Pollux) describe the easiest road to advancement as sleeping with rich women; he submitted to the graveyard kisses of a 70-year-old with only four teeth (but gold-stopped), only to be pipped at the post.

40 *unciolam . . . deuncem:* 'one-twelfth . . . eleven-twelfths: Roman fractions were duodecimal.

Proculeius . . . Gillo: unknown. But Q. Fulvius Gillo Bittius Proculus was proconsul of Asia in 115-16 and a relative of the younger Pliny (*Ep.* 9,13,13), whom J had no cause to like: it would be quite amusing to use his name for a gigolo.

41 'every heir receives an inheritance proprotionate in size to his organ of sex!'

42 *sane:* 'by all means'

sanguinis: satirical: *sanguis* is used as a substitute for *semen.*

Note the assonance in the fifth foot. *inguinis — sanguinis,* echoed further by *calcibus anguem* in the next line.

43 The simile is from epic (Hom. *Il.* 3,33-5; Verg. *A* 2,329-80) and is gloriously incongruous.

44 At Lyons there were an altar and temple to Rome and Augustus, with an annual festival. In the winter of AD 39-40 Caligula held a competition there for public speaking in Greek or Latin. The winners received rewards: the losers had various penalties, such as licking away their unsuccessful writing, being publicly flogged and being ducked in the Rhône (Suet. *Cal.* 20).

45 *siccum iecur:* the liver was regarded as the seat of the passions, which is why Tityos, who failed to keep his passions under control, was condemned to having his liver eternally pecked out: the heat of anger has made it clay. Note the image of fire.

46 Read the sentence aloud and note the repetition of *-um* in three emphatic positions (and *-om* and *-em* unemphatic), an effect used for great scorn. There is scorn too in alliteration on *p.* The three successive words in the same rhythm, all accented on the first syllable, *populum gregibus comitum,* give an appropriately bumpy effect.

hic . . . hic: 'one man . . . another' the subject: tr. *spoliator* and *damnatus* 'who has ruined . . . who has been condemned'.

populum emphatic by position.

premit: 'jostles'.

spoliator: financially and perhaps also sexually.

47 *pupilli:* an orphan, under a guardian till the age of 14.

prostantis: prostare means 'to display goods for sale' and so 'to prostitute yourself'. Here it is proleptic: 'so that he becomes a prostitute'.

48 'What does loss of civil rights matter so long as your money is safe?'

49 *exul:* emphatic by position 'even in exile'.

octaua: sc. *hora:* about 2 p.m., as the Roman day ran from sunrise to sunset. Dinner normally started at the ninth hour.

Marius: Marius Priscus, who was prosecuted by Tacitus and the younger Pliny in AD 100 for his financial misappropriations as proconsul of Africa (Plin. *Ep.* 2,11), and condemned to banishment. The reference gives us clear evidence that J's first book of *Satires* was not published till at least four years after Domitian's death.

fruitur dis iratis: a kind of oxymoron, perhaps based on a phrase of Seneca (*HF* 34), where Juno says of Hercules *iraque nostra fruitur:* you do not normally 'enjoy' or 'profit from' the anger of the gods. The broken rhythm at the end of the line expresses effectively the dislocation of the natural order.

50 *tu:* apostrophe, a rhetorical switch to the second person, is a common poetical device.

uictrix: parallel to *exul* 'despite your victory'.

prouincia: i.e. Africa.

51 *credam:* 'am I not to believe?'

Venusina . . . lucerna: Horace was born at Venusia in 65 BC. Horace may have satirised real people, but more urbanely. *lucerna:* partly because (as we still say) he burned the midnight oil, partly because the satirist exposes his fellow-men by the light of his satire.

52 *agitem:* moving from 'assail' to 'write about': our 'deal with' has both meanings.

Heracleas aut Diomedeas: generalised plurals 'epics about Hercules or Diomedes' (*Odyssea,* our Odyssey, is an epic about Odysseus). Heracles or Hercules was the legendary son of Zeus (Jupiter) who underwent twelve heroic Labours: we know of numerous epics about him which have not survived. One Iulus Antonius wrote a twelve-book epic on Diomedes, a hero of the Trojan War, perhaps telling of his journeyings and settlement in Italy. Note the heavy spondaic ending *Heracleas,* appropriate to the weight of the subject. In general the rhetorical rhythmic effect of the line is a take-off of epic.

53 *mugitum labyrinthi:* Pasiphaë, queen of Crete, mated with a bull, and produced the Minotaur, a bull-man, who was killed by Theseus. The word *labyrinthus* seems to be connected with the double-axe, a symbol in Minoan Crete: the idea of the labyrinth or maze in which the Minotaur lived may simply arise from the complexity of the great palace of Cnossos, but the maze is a basic magical symbol, to 'lose' dangerous spirits, and was also associated with a dance-pattern (originally magical). A labyrinthine maze appears on later coins of Cnossos.

54 Daedalus, the great inventor, devised the hollow cow in which Pasiphaë hid for her unnatural mating: he invented wings with which he and his son Icarus could escape from Crete, but the boy flew too near the sun, the wax melted, the wings fell off and he plummeted into the sea, a scene powerfully portrayed by Breughel, where the tiny, helpless form is seen against a foreground of normal activity. *puero* instrumental ablative: the body is inert and unwilling. *fabrum:* sarcastic 'the flying joiner'. These are all epic themes. J structures his poem on the contrast between epic themes and present reality.

55 *leno:* the complaisant husband. The Lex Voconia of 169 BC forbade a citizen in the highest property-bracket to make a woman his heir. This could be evaded by a third party (in this case the husband) being the legal heir on behalf of the woman, who claims the inheritance as return for her favours. It is not certain that the law was still in force. Domitian (Suet. *Dom.* 8) ruled against women of bad character receiving an inheritance; J may rather be referring to an evasion of this.

56 *doctus spectare lacunar:* a splendid phrase, though it is not quite clear whether he is keeping his eyes fixed on the ceiling as in philosophical contemplation (Quint. 2,11,4; 10,3,15; 11,3,160), or as in admiration of its ornate beauties (Sen. *Ep.* 90,15 describes ceilings where the painted panels could be changed, like theatrical scenery).

57 Another splendid picture. The Romans had a proverb *non omnibus dormio.* Plutarch (*Mor.* 760A) has a good story of Gabba, Augustus's court jester, pretending to be asleep to allow Maecenas to carry on with his wife, but when a slave crept in to steal some wine calling out 'You damned fool, don't you realise that I'm only asleep for Maecenas?'; cf also *Plaut. MG* 821-2 – *eho/an dormit Sceledrus intus? – non naso quidem.*

58 *putet:* supply 'a young man' as subject.

curam . . . cohortis: 'the command of a cohort (of auxiliaries)'. The young man is an *eques*, not of senatorial rank; if the latter he would have held the office of *tribunatus legionis.* An *eques* passed through three stages: *praefectura cohortis sociorum, tribunatus legionis* and *praefectura alae.* After

this he was eligible for remunerative administrative posts. The army, as in nineteenth-century England, was an obvious career for restoring lost fortunes. But one who hopes for a military career should not be appearing on the racetrack.

59 *donauit . . . caret:* giving the past behaviour to account for his present need of a commission; *caret = perdidit.*

praesepibus: horse-racing was a passion with the Romans, and much money changed hands. At Carthage there was found a lead tablet crudely depicting a racetrack with nine competing chariots. Thirty-two horses are named under a curse. We may assume that the amateur magician had backed the remaining four-horse chariot (*CIL* VIII 12504).

61 *Flaminiam:* sc. *uiam* the main north road from Rome over the Pons Mulvius to Ariminum.

puer: not yet a *iuuenis* (which he must be to seek a commission). He lost his fortune as a 'teenager'.

Automedon: Achilles's charioteer in Homer. Ironical, since J is bringing the epic figures he rejects into the present.

62 *lacernatae:* the mistress is wearing a man's clothing. Some interpreters, perhaps rightly, see *lacernatae* as meaning that the person is male, and *amicae* as satirical of the homosexual factor.

63 J depicts himself standing at the street corner, filling the ancient equivalent of notebooks (wax tablets) with what he sees. The effect is that of 'I am a camera'.

64 *iam:* with *sexta.* He has six bearers already, and we can expect him, like Verres, to have eight at any moment. For the litter as a symbol, see on 33.

feratur: causal subjunctive: note how the subject (*signator*) is held up for surprise effect.

66 'putting you much in mind of Maecenas in his indolence'. Maecenas, Augustus's friend and minister, and patron of Vergil and Horace, was known for his extravagant tastes, his affectations and his laziness.

67 *signator falsi:* called as witness to someone else's will, he has introduced a forged document in his own favour, and affixed his seal to that.

lautum et beatum: again the contrast between words of approbation and the degrading reality.

68 *fecerit:* causal subjunctive again, linked with *feratur:* logically equivalent to *cum fecerit . . . et feratur.*

69 *Calenum:* a light wine from Cales in

Campania.

70 *rubeta:* poison from the bramble frog. Ancient tradition said that it had two livers; the first, pounded, squeezed and served in wine was a deadly poison, the second an antidote. Clausen reads *rubetam.* But *rubeta* is the reading of the better MSS; if it is right, *uiro* is dat., and *sitiente* = thirst-causing.

71 A line in which each word is enriched by its neighbour: *instituitque rudes, rudes melior, melior Lucusta, Lucusta propinquas.*

rudes . . . propinquas: 'her less expert neighbours'.

melior: ironical, like *optima* (1,38).

Lucusta: in apposition: a notorious poisoner from Gaul, responsible for Agrippina's poisoning of the emperor Claudius, and Nero's of Britannicus (Suet. *Nero* 33; Tac. *Ann.* 12,66; 13,15-6). She had been the subject of satiric attack by a satirist named Turnus (schol. ad loc.). Nero's brief successor Galba had her executed. But the anonymous lady is even more successful.

72 *per famam et populum:* 'through the crowds, through the wagging tongues'.

nigros: because of the poison.

73 *aude aliquid:* elision of a long vowel adds a certain bitter weight.

Gyaris: Gyara, a small, barren, waterless island in the Aegean (Tac. *Ann.* 4,30), used for deportations for serious crime: the ancient Botany Bay. In recent years it has again been used as a political prison.

carcere: the Romans did not use imprisonment as a basic punishment: 'the condemned cell'.

dignum: again a commendatory word ironically used.

74 *aliquid:* the Romans used masc. or neut. in this phrase, as do we: 'he thinks he is somebody', 'if you want to be anything at all'. There is an amusing parallel in Pliny *Ep.* 23,2 *cum tribunus essem, erraverim fortasse qui me aliquid putavi.*

probitas laudatur et alget: a splendid epigram. *Laudare* sometimes has the force of praising without practising, like the definition of a classic, 'a book more praised than read'. So Verg. *G* 2,413 *laudato ingentia rura,/ exiguum colito.* See also Massinger *Fatal Dowry* 2,1 '. . . in this partial avaricious age / what price bears honour, virtue? Long ago / it was but praised and freezed; but nowadays / 'Tis colder far, and has nor love nor praise.' (ref. from Prof. G. B. A. Fletcher)

75 *criminibus:* originally 'accusations', by now 'crimes'.

hortos: horti is a private estate or park, of which there were not a few in Rome.

praetoria: originally a military HQ, then the emperor's palace and so any large private house.

mensas: a common ground of extravagance especially with the tops a single slab of citruswood; the philosopher Seneca was said to have 200 of them (Dio Cass. 61,10,3).

76 *stantem extra:* i.e. in high relief, or possibly as a handle.

77-78 The image of the he-goat, notoriously lusty, leads on to sexual corruption, the extravagance of the wealthy is linked to the idea of bribery. Tr. 'How can anyone sleep when fathers-in-law seduce their daughters-in-law for money, when brides can't be trusted, when teenagers commit adultery?'

Corruptor implies bribery and seduction.

78 *praetextatus:* the *toga praetexta* or *praetexta* was a cloak with a purple fringe worn by officers of state and boys under the age of puberty (14); *praetextatus adulter:* this is a paradox implying rare precocity. The purple fringe was originally magical protection for those specially vulnerable.

79 One of the most famous, and most quotable lines in J. Victor Hugo imitates it in his 'Muse Indignation, viens.' Compare Pope 'Epilogue to the Satires: Dialogue II' 197, 'Ask you what Provocation I have had? /The strong Antipathy of Good to Bad.' So Swift spoke of his 'perfect rage and resentment' (F. E. Ball *The Correspondence of Jonathan Swift* IV 34).

uersum: a modest word.

80 The construction is not quite obvious: supply *facere* with *potest* and *facio* with *ego.* Cluvienus is not known, but is perhaps a very prosy prose-writer: even he might be driven to verse by the corruptions of the time. The name may be a cover for some other name of the same rhythm, Decianus, say (Mart. 1,61,10), or Cerialis (Mart. 11,52); or by allusion to Helvidius Priscus, who came from Cluviae. (See L. A. MacKay in *CP* 53 (1958) 236-40). The use of *uel Cluuienus* as climax is a piece of witty bathos, in some ways closer to the poet's real satiric technique than *indignatio.*

81-126 *My book is a mish-mash of human life — of vices — of love of money, greed and extravagance. The rich gamble their fortunes away and have nothing for the poor. They scrutinise all who claim their charity, and these include men in high office, though it is rich immigrants who claim and receive priority. No, money may not have a temple, but it is the real god. And the poor watch magistrates and women in litters — and sometimes absent women — receiving contributions.*

81 Note the shape of the sentence in Latin. We should perhaps translate 'The mish-mash of my little book *consists* of prayers, fears, . . ., all that men *have done* (and are still doing) from the time when . . .

Deucalion: the Greek Noah, both derived no doubt from the Mesopotamian myth of Utnapishtim, and folk-memories of a historical flood, identified in the strata of the ancient city of Ur by Sir Leonard Woolley. The story of Deucalion is told by Ovid (*Met.* 1,260). He and his wife Pyrrha alone were spared when the king of the gods destroyed the rest of mankind by flood. They took refuge in a boat, and were grounded on Mt. Parnassus. They were told by the goddess Themis to throw the bones of their mighty mother behind them. Deucalion surmised that this meant Mother Earth. They threw stones over their shoulders, which turned into men and women. J ironically starts the new section with a chunk of the mythology he has rejected. The new beginning of his theme is marked by the story of the new beginning of mankind and it is no better than the old.

nimbis tollentibus: abl. abs.

82 *nauigio montem ascendit:* a witty paradox.

sortes: 'oracles', strictly strips of wood with responses on them, drawn at random in the Italian manner of consultation.

83 *caluerunt:* the image of fire: heat gives life.

mollia: proleptic, 'grew warm and soft'.

84 The sex-theme. A very skilful line: *maribus* is separated as far as possible from *puellas,* and *Pyrrha* stands between them; but the position of *nudas* brings them together. The great mother of the race appears as a procuress. Is not J demythologising?

85-86 J's famous 'programme', brilliantly expressed. Does he live up to it? The Cambridge scholar, Ernest Harrison, said well: 'Not prayers, fear, anger, pleasure, joys and bustle are his theme, but selfish prayers, craven fear, wild anger, unwholesome pleasure, illicit joys, and feverish bustle.' It is just here that *satura* becomes satire. The analysis of basic human emotions into pleasure and pain in the present, and hope and fear about the future is due to Zeno and the Stoics (DL 7,110). J characteristically substitutes *ira* for *dolor.* Note the breathless asyndeton. Martial (from whom J borrows) has *hominem pagina nostra sapit* ('tastes of': 10,4,10).

86 *discursus:* a skilfully chosen word, 'hithering-and-thithering'.

farrago: from *far,* a kind of grain, mixed fodder for cattle, 'mish-mash', a variant on *satura,* and a satirical comment on theories of its origin.

est: agreeing naturally with the singular predicate *farrago* nearest it rather than with the strictly plural subject.

87 *uitiorum:* he picks out from the *farrago* what really concerns him.

88 *sinus:* tr. 'pocket', a fold of the toga used for that purpose.

Notice the personification in *auaritiae.* J does not single out lust or cruelty, but the love of money.

89 *hos animos:* 'such vitality': supply *sumpsit;* the phrase comes from Luc. 8,544.

neque enim: 'As a matter of fact, . . . not', or perhaps 'For example, . . . not.'

loculis: loculi is a small box or wallet with compartments ('small places').

itur: impersonal passive, 'there's no going'.

90 *casum:* 'the luck' from the *fall* of the dice.

posita: 'set at their side'.

91 *dispensatore:* a trusted slave who had charge of the finances. Tr. 'What battles you will see at the table with bank-manager as batman!'

92 *simplex:* 'ordinary'.

sestertia centum: the *sestertius* (from *semis-tertius* = 2½) was a small silver coin, 2½ asses (after 217 BC 4 asses), ¼ denarius. The neuter plural *sestertia* comes to be used for *milia sestertia,* with the distributive numerals (e.g. *centena*) or sometimes with the cardinal numerals (e.g. *centum,* as here). This then means '100 000 sesterces'. Further the genitive plural *sestertium* is used elliptically with a numeral adverb for (*centena milia*) *sestertium;* so *quater milies sestertium* = 400 000 000 sesterces. It is very hard to give any equivalent in modern currency. A highly skilled specialist slave for farmwork cost 8000 sesterces in Italy under the early Empire; a 25-year-old woman slave fetched the equivalent of 5000 sesterces in Egypt in AD 129 (*Pap. Oxy.* 1,95); but average prices were much lower. J suggests that an annual income of 20 000 sesterces is minimal for comfort (9,140-1), and that a wise man would limit his ambitions to a fortune of 400 000 sesterces (14,322-8).

93 *et:* 'and at the same time'.

horrenti: 'shivering'.

tunicam: a long linen shirt or dress, worn in different patterns by men and women, slipped over the head, fastened with a belt, and reaching to the knees.

reddere: 'give as his due', not 'give back'. Cato (*RR* 59) says that a slave should have a new shirt and new cloak-blanket every two years. J's satire retains its target in every generation.

94 *uillas:* 'mansions'; cf Mart. 7,73,6 *Quisquis ubique habitat, Maxime, nusquam habitat.*

fercula: tr. 'courses', lit. dishes or trays for carrying in *(ferre)* food.

95 *secreto:* 'in private', alone.

auus: with *quis:* but tr. 'in our grand-fathers' time.' Note how *auus? nunc* are placed together.

sportula: lit. 'a small basket'. The rich man had large numbers of dependants, *clientes,* to whom he was *patronus.* Originally he would entertain them to dinner; then it became more convenient to provide them with a basket of food; later money for buying food was substituted. The common tr. 'the dole' is misleading as implying public responsibility. Note how *sportula primo* echoes *fercula septem.*

primo: they are not allowed in.

turbae rapienda togatae: a vivid phrase: they are a mob, they are all grabbing — and they are all citizens; the dative of the agent is regular with the gerundive.

97 *ille:* the patron in person. Offbeat rhythm at the end of the line emphasises the fear.

99 *agnitus accipies:* 'you must be identified before receiving your rations'. Note the alliteration.

100 *Troiugenas:* J's name for the ancient aristocracy: the legendary foundation of Rome by Trojan refugees is familiar from *The Aeneid.* It corresponds to our 'those who came over with the Conqueror'.

ipsos . . . ipsi: very emphatic. For the shape of the line v. 1,15 n.

101 *praetori:* even those in office are subservient to wealth.

102 *libertinus:* in the first century AD, especially under Claudius, freedmen attained great wealth and influence in what we would today call 'civil service posts', senior administrative posts. According to the lives (see Introduction) J was himself the son of a wealthy freedman, but he does *not* align himself with this *libertinus.*

prior: rhetorical repetition.

ego adsum: three word-accents in the last two feet mean that *ego* has particular weight.

103 *timeam:* deliberative: 'Why should I . . . ?'

104 *Euphraten:* the great river of Mesopotamia is used as a general term for the East. J dislikes most things foreign: cf 3,58ff.

molles: 'effeminate'.

fenestrae: i.e. holes for ear-rings: an Asiatic practice.

105 *arguerint:* potential subjunctive, 'might prove'.

licet: 'even though'.

quinque tabernae: 'five business-premises bring me in 400 000 sesterces' (v.1,92 n). An *eques* ('knight'), a member of the 'middle class', needed property valued at this sum: the freedman in question has it as his income.

purpura maior: the broad purple stripe on the *tunica* which marked out the senator.

107 *Laurenti:* a town near the coast of Latium; Pliny *(Ep.* 2,17,3) describes the surrounding country as good grazing for sheep in winter.

108 *Coruinus:* a member of the *gens Valeria* now fallen on bad times; Nero gave a pension to one of the family 'in reduced circumstances' through no fault of his own (Tac. *Ann.* 13,34).

ego: tr. *'while* I'. J puts the two clauses in stark contrast: a Greek writer would have used . . . μέν . . . δέ . . . The broken rhythm at the end emphasises *plus.*

109 *Pallante:* an immensely able, rich and arrogant freedman who controlled the treasury under Claudius. An income of 400 000 sesterces would nowhere near out-match Pallas in fact.

Licinis: Licinus, a Gaul, captured by Julius Caesar, and seemingly emancipated by Augustus under Caesar's will. He was procurator of Gaul in 16-15 BC. The plural means 'Licinus and his like'. Note how J expresses the attitudinising of the freedman by exaggerated alliteration: *quinque . . . quadringenta . . . quid confert; parant . . . purpura . . . optandum; custodit . . . conductas Coruinus; possides plus Pallante.*

expectent: 'let them wait!'

110 *uincant divitiae:* a variant on Hor. *Ep.* 1,1,54 *uirtus post nummos.*

sacro . . . honori: 'sacrosanct office': tribunes of the plebs were sacrosanct.

111 *pedibus . . . albis:* foreign slaves had their feet marked with white chalk at the slave-market to distinguish them from those born locally *(uernae).*

112 *sanctissima diuitiarum/maiestas:* a weighty phrase enhanced by a five-syllable word at the line's end.

113 *Pecunia:* J has in mind Hor. *Ep.* 1,6,37 *regina Pecunia.* The Romans had a penchant for exalting abstract qualities into deities: see J. Ferguson *Religions of the Roman Empire* pp. 72-3; Cic. *ND* 2,61; Plin. *NH* 2,5, 14-5; Aug. *CD* 4,21. But Augustine and Arnobius (4,9) do speak of a *dea Pecunia.* Their source is Varro, as is J's.

J says they build temples to Pax, Fides, etc. but do not honour them; they do not build a temple to Money, but Money is their real god. Cf A. H. Clough *The Latest Decalogue* 'No graven images may be/Worshipped, except the currency.' It is a theme for satire that so many US banks are built in the form of classical temples. See also B.L. Ullmann in D.M. Robinson Festschrift II 1092-5.

115 *Pax:* Augustus dedicated the Ara Pacis in the Campus Martius: Vespasian a temple.

Fides: traditionally introduced by the legendary King Numa.

Victoria: Augustus dedicated an altar in the senate-house after Actium.

Virtus: honoured on 29 May, with her own priests; there was one temple in Rome to Virtus and two others to Virtus and Honos. *Virtus* is not, except in philosophical writing, our 'virtue'. It is rather 'toughness', 'courage', the quality of a *uir:* see J. Ferguson *Moral Values in the Ancient World* pp. 159-64. The temples were dedicated by military commanders.

116 *Concordia:* with a temple at the entrance to the Capitol. The line is obscure: probably 'Concord who gives a cackling reply when you greet her nest'. The idea seems to be that storks nested on the temple; the scholiast says that *nido* is used satirically for *templo;* the noise of the storks (*crepitare* is used elsewhere, e.g. Ov. *M* 6,97) is taken to be Concord's reply; and the harsh sound contrasts satirically with the idea of Concord.

117 *summus honor:* i.e. the consul: *honor* = office. Even the consul receives the *sportula.* Roman office was unpaid.

118 *rationibus:* 'bank balance'.

119 *comites:* the poorer *clientes* whose service is to go round with their patron, making an impressive *entourage,* acting as claqueurs, etc.

hinc: i.e. from the *sportula,* on which they depend for clothes, shoes, food and charcoal.

120-1 *densissima ... lectica:* sing. for pl. 'carriages in crowds'; a *lectica* was a litter in which you would lie down or recline while being carried.

centum quadrantes: the regular amount of the sportula: 25 asses = 6¼ sesterces.

122 *circumducitur:* from one house to another.

123 *hic:* 'one man asks (for a contribution) for his absent wife': dative of advantage.

nota ... arte: 'an old dodge': it is an amusing picture.

124 *clausam ... sellam:* the sedan would be curtained for a woman, and might be curtained for a man (3,242).

125-6 He addresses the man in charge, the fictitious wife, and the man in charge again. (*Galla mea est* = 'it is my wife Galla'). Some editors give *profer, Galla, caput* to the man in charge. *quiescet:* i.e. 'she must be asleep'.

127-46 *Dependants spend all day hanging round their patron, in the law-courts and elsewhere, and then have to go away without any dinner, and buy their own, while the patron dines alone on a meal fit for a banquet. Still, a hot bath on top of an over-stuffed belly may lead to a sudden and un-lamented demise.*

127 *ipse dies:* Martial has a good epigram (4,8,1-7)

Prima salutantes atque altera detinet hora:
exercet raucos tertia causidicos:
in quintam uarios extendit Roma labores:
sexta quies lassis: septima finis erit:
sufficit in nonam nitidis octaua palaestris:
imperat extractos frangere nona toros:
hora libellorum decuma est, Eupheme,
 meorum ...

('From six to eight the morning call: / From eight to nine the lawyers bawl: / Up to eleven the work extends: / An hour's break: at one it ends: / From one to two we exercise: / From two to three we close our eyes: / And three, my friend, 's the time for verse ...) J perhaps takes off from Martial, as often. But he doesn't go through the whole day: satiric purpose breaks through. The well-organised day is an ironic touch.

pulchro: sarcastic. Note how the line pivots on *distinguitur,* which does 'break up' *pulchro ... ordine.*

sportula: see 1,95. There is a problem here. Martial's evidence (e.g. 3,7,3; 10,70,13) is that the *sportula* was distributed in the evening. We cannot suppose that either J or Martial is wrong. Therefore either practice varied, or there was a change in the period between Martial's verses and this, or those who attended the *salutatio* but were not free later could collect in the morning, or *sportula* is loosely used for the *salutatio* which earned it.

128 *iurisque peritus Apollo:* there were many forums in Rome: this is the forum of Augustus, built, Suetonius tells us (*Aug.* 29) because the existing forums could not cope with the legal business, itself cramped because of the emperor's unwillingness to offend rich owners of property, lying at the foot of the Capitol to the north of the *Forum Romanum,* with a massive precinct

wall, and an interesting design employing two hemicycles. It contained the temple of Mars the Avenger, statues of military commanders, and a notable ivory statue of Apollo (Plin. *NH* 7,53,183), who naturally became *iuris peritus* with all the lawsuits. The idea is borrowed from Martial (2,64,8) who applies it to the statue of Marsyas in the *Forum Romanum.*

129 *triumphales:* sc. *statuas.*

130 *nescio quis:* contemptuous.

titulos: the formal inscription with family and distinctions.

Aegyptius atque Arabarches: the *arabarches* was originally a customs officer in the region east of the Nile; the word means literally 'ruler over Arabs'. Cicero applied it to Pompey, both for his eastern conquests and his operations in public finance (*Att.* 2,17,3). It is probably right to take it as implying great power in a region which the writer regards as 'primitive', 'emir' or 'nabob', but it may have overtones of 'get-rich-quick at the public expense'. The reference is undoubtedly to Tiberius Julius Alexander, whose father, Alexander Lysimachus, had been governor of the Thebaid. The family was Jewish, but the son abjured his religion, became a Roman *eques,* procurator of Judaea, and prefect of Egypt, perhaps also praetorian prefect (Pap. Hibeh 215; E. G. Turner in *JRS* 44 (1954) 54ff). There is an unsolved riddle whether *arabarches* is the same as *alabarches,* seemingly a collector of special taxes among the Jews (an appropriate reference here). For: J. Lesquier *L'Armée romaine d'Egypte* (1918) 432ff. Against: M. I. Rostovtzeff in *YCS* 2(1931) 50-1.

131 *non tantum:* sc. *sed etiam cacare.*

meiiere: an obvious token of contempt. But it was treasonable to piss against an emperor's statue (SHA *Caracalla* 5), sacrilegious against a god's (Plut. *Stoic. Repugn.* 22,1045).

132 The discontinuity led Housman, Knoche and Anderson to think that something has dropped out before this line.

133-4 *longissima cenae spes homini:* an excellent epigram.

134 *miseris:* dative of the agent with the gerundive.

ignis: charcoal. Remember the fire-theme: it is a basic need for life.

emendus: sc. *est:* the emphatic word held up till last. They had hoped to get it free: they have to pay for it.

135 *uorabit:* for the future; cf *quiescet* (1,126): we can say 'he will be consuming'.

136 *rex horum:* 'their lord and master',

common of the *patronus.*

iacebit: the Romans reclined at meals.

137 *de:* 'out of', almost 'despite'.

orbibus: round tables.

una: emphatic 'one single'.

mensa: 'table', not (as sometimes) 'course'. J is attacking not the luxury but the failure to share with those who have less.

139 *parasitus:* tr. 'There will soon be no such thing as a dinner-stooge.' The *parasitus,* also known tellingly as *umbra* ('shadow'), accompanied the *patronus* to dinner-parties, and had a free meal at the cost of feeding-in flattering remarks, making openings for the patron's jokes, and leading the laughter at them. He is a stock figure in comedy. G. K. Chesterton uses it as a suitable occupation for *The Club of Queer Trades.* Our word *parasite* is derived from these dinner-stooges.

quis ferat: 'who could stand . . . ?'

140 *luxuriae sordes:* oxymoron, bringing two conflicting ideas together into a convincing whole.

gula: lit. 'the gullet' and so by transference 'gluttony', but here retaining something of the literal meaning. *quanta est gula* comes from Mart. 5,70,5.

quae sibi totos: precisely echoing *quis ferat istas* in the previous line: the effect is to reinforce the unbearability of it. Both give a broken rhythm in the fifth foot, and the consecutive two-syllable words *sibi totos ponit apros* and *poena tamen praesens,* each with a stress-accent on the first syllable, come like hammer-blows: read the lines aloud.

141 *propter conuiuia:* behind these words is a proverbial sentiment *suillum pecus donatum a natura ad epulandum* (Varro *RR* 2,4,10 'Nature gave herds of pigs for parties'), and a philosophical view of the divine provision of animals for human use, common among the Stoics and traceable certainly to Socrates.

142 *tu:* note the change from third to second person. So the prophet Nathan tells King David (who has murdered Uriah the Hittite for his wife Bathsheba) a story of a rich man who stole a poor man's single lamb, and turns on him with the words 'You are the man' (2 Sam. 12:7).

143 *turgidus:* 'bloated', in an emphatic position. Mayor has collected many passages showing that the Romans believed that a hot bath immediately after dinner helped digestion, though they knew that it carried attendant dangers. J is here paying Persius (3,98-106) the tribute of imitation, but Persius is more brutally realistic.

crudum: the MSS are divided between *crudum* and *crudus.* The word can mean 'overstuffed' of the eater, or 'uncooked' of

the food: *crudum* makes a stronger line
(*pauonem* needs an adj.) and perhaps can be
extended to mean 'undigested': *crudus*
would also require *portans.*

pauonem: a luxury animal, first served in
a Roman banquet by the statesman and
lawyer Hortensius towards the end of the
Republic (Varro *RR* 3,6,6). They were
originally imported from the east (Masefield
was not wrong to put them on his 'Quin-
quereme of Nineveh from distant Ophir'),
but later bred on islands off the coast of
Italy. The medical writer Galen says that
the flesh is tough, stringy and indigestible.

144 *intestata:* 'unprecedented' 'never
found': neg. of *testatus* 'evident'. This
interpretation is due to Housman (*CR* 13
(1899) 432-3). It gives point to *senectus,*
and parallels Mart. 6,29,7 *immodicis breuis
est aetas et rara senectus.* This sentence
requires us to supply a verb, which is easily
done.

145 *nec tristis:* i.e. 'and laughable'.
fabula: 'gossip'.

146 *ducitur:* picks up *it* in a kind of
anaphora.

iratis plaudendum . . . amicis: dat. of the
agent with gerundive. Note how *iratis . . .
amicis* surround, almost throng round,
plaudendum funus. They are angry because
their expectations are frustrated. For *capta-
tores* see Petronius 124ff. J seems to take up
intestata in its more normal sense 'without
a will'; the estate would devolve on the next
of kin or as *bona uacantia* to the state (Gaius
3,1-7) J introduces a double twist: first
plaudendum where the normal response calls
for *plangendum;* this accepted, *amicis*
becomes incongruous, and gives a climactic
ending.

139-46 are very skilfully shaped. The main
caesura moves from 3½ to 2½ to 1½ to 2½;
in 143 if *crudum* is right the sense-break
comes after 1. The passage concludes with
three hammer-blow, end-stopped lines. The
last line is of a type the Romans liked,
though not truly 'golden', with two pairs of
noun + adj. and a verb. Read the passage
aloud.

147-71 *The moral degradation is as bad as
it can be. One push and it's over. So to satire.
But have you the ability, the openness?
Attack Tigellinus and you'll be burned alive.
Then are the crooks to go free and laugh at
us? Keep your mouth shut when you meet
them face to face. Epic is safe enough: to
follow Lucilius in convicting the conscience
is to turn fear to anger. Think before you
declare war. All right, I'll try attacking the
dead.*

147 The programme which follows is
indebted to Lucilius (bk 30) (see Griffith),
and falls into a standard pattern of satiric
apology (Kenney) — a statement of inten-
tion; warning by interlocutor; counter-
questions by satirist; warning renewed in
fresh terms; final rejoinder, giving scope for
an unusual twist; cf Hor. *Sat.* 2,1,57ff; Pers.
1,103-23.

quod . . . addat: tr. 'for posterity to add'.
moribus: 'behaviour', with the implication
that it is bad.

148 *minores:* 'generations to come' as
maiores = 'past generations'.

149 *omne in praecipiti uitium stetit:* a
vivid visual picture of a gang of vices stand-
ing on a high peak with a steep drop in front
of them, but what does J mean to convey by
it? (a) We should not lose altogether the idea
that vice has 'peaked'; it is implicit in the
picture. Future generations cannot go higher
(note the irony). (b) But *in praecipiti*
stresses the point that it has nowhere to go
but down. This in turn links two ideas:
(i) that vice leads to disaster (Sen. *Ep.* 23,6
has a similar phrase about pleasure), (ii) that
it is there for the satirist to push it over the
precipice. The picture is not quite a single
one (how would you paint it?), but it bridges
the inability of posterity to surpass the
present, with the rôle of the satirist. *Stetit* is
a true perfect, 'has taken its stand'.

utere uelis: the poet turns to address him-
self — or any other prospective satirist. There
is an abrupt change of metaphor — so abrupt
that it almost becomes an Irish bull, like Sir
Boyle Roche's famous alleged remark, 'Mr
Speaker, I smell a rat; I see him forming in
the air and darkening the sky; but I'll nip
him in the bud.' J's effect is not dissimilar:
note how it takes up *nauigio montem
ascendit* (1,82): the mood is that of J. A.
Symonds's 'These things shall be! A
loftier race/Than e'er the world hath known,
shall rise.'

150 *pande sinus:* a common enough
metaphor: so Cic. *TD* 4,5,9 *panderem uela
orationis.* J is in fact using rhetorical clichés
in a manner reminiscent of parody. So W. S.
Anderson: 'J implies that even indignation is
ridiculous when expended without control.'
But J uses *sinus,* and in so doing brings in
other overtones. *Sinus* is anything curved or
hollowed. So *pande sinus* ('spread your
sails') could mean 'Open up your hiding-
place — and come out to battle' or 'Turn
your pockets inside out' (as we would say)
'— you need all your resources' or 'Expose
your body' (an insult, linking with J's
sexual preoccupations).

dices: forsitan is normally found with the subjunctive, but the verb coming first makes the indicative easy to accept. J imagines himself objecting to his own commission: a kind of internal dialogue follows.

hic: at this point.

150-1 *unde ingenium par materiae?* a fine concise phrase: the verb must be supplied. Cf Ov. *P* 2,5,26 *materiae . . . sufficit ingenium.* Note that the last syllable of *materiae* is not elided. There are many other examples (e.g. 2,26; 3,70; 6,274, 468; 10,281; 12,110; 14,49; 15,126). They tend to coincide with a strong caesura in the third foot, which makes the break easier, especially when, as here, there is a strongly punctuated break. If you read with a pause you are hardly aware of the hiatus.

151-2 *priorum scribendi:* notice the two different genitives.

152 *flagrante:* the heat of anger gives life to the poetry.

153 *simplicitas:* held up till the end. We expect *libertas:* indeed Cicero has a similar phrase with that word (*Planc.* 13,33). *Simplicitas* gives J a double meaning: they were direct and open, but it would be disingenuous to behave so in his day.

153-4 *'cuius . . . an non?'* the structure is not certain. It is probably best to suppose J is paraphrasing Lucilius (see on 1,20): it is not a full verbal quotation since *audeo* could not scan as a dactyl in Lucilius's day, though Lucilius might have had *ausus.*

154 *Mucius:* P. Mucius Scaevola, a famous legal expert, consul in 133 BC, and a supporter of Tiberius Gracchus and opponent of Lucilius's patron Scipio Aemilianus, for which Lucilius pilloried him (Pers. 1,114-5). J has in mind Hor. *S* 2,1 where the same sort of question is asked.

155 *pone:* for *si pones* or *si ponis,* but we use the same construction: 'Put down Tigillinum and you'll burn for it.' *Tigillinum:* C. Ofonius Tigellinus, was an attractively handsome young man from Sicily, who was banished for adultery with Caligula's sister. He inherited a fortune, had his banishment rescinded, bought estates and bred horses. In AD 62 he became Nero's prefect of the praetorian guard. According to Philostratus (*V. Ap.* 4,43) his eyes and ears were everywhere. He is depicted as an extravagant voluptuary, sexual monster and bloodthirsty tyrant in all our sources. When Nero fell, he ratted, and was protected by Galba but forced to suicide by Otho in AD 69, more than thirty years before J is writing. *Tigillinum* seems to be a punning allusion to the sort of person he was,

together with *tigillum,* a log o. raggot.

155-7 *taeda . . . harena:* the reading (MSS are divided between *lucebis* and *lucebit, gutture* and *pectore,* and *deducit* and *deducis*) and meaning are quite uncertain. The best explanation is to suppose with A. E. Housman that a line has fallen out after 156, something like (following Sen. *Ira* 3,3,6) *quorum informe unco trahitur post fata cadauer.* Then 'you will burn in the coat of pitch in which men stand and blaze as they send out smoke, pinned by the throat, men whose dead body is dragged by a hook and bashed out of shape after execution, leaving a broad furrow in the middle of the sand.' *taeda* is the *tunica molesta* or 'robe of pain', a coating of pitch and other inflammable material (cf 8,235). Tacitus has a horrifying description of the execution of Christians by Nero and Tigellinus using these very methods: they were employed as street lamps (*Ann.* 15,44). *fixo gutture:* a curved hook was put through the underpart of the chin. *sulcum deducit harena:* there is a secondary meaning, since ploughing the sand was proverbial of useless activity (cf 7,48-9): J suggests that to attack directly the Tigillinuses of his own day would be labour wasted. The fire-theme is here both metaphorical and literal: the fire of anger is requited with the fire of the stake. (If the emendation is not accepted, *deducit* means that Tigillinus causes a furrow to be traced.)

158 If it's dangerous to attack living criminals are they to go scot-free?

tribus patruis: though the scholiast treats this as a generalisation, we may suspect a *cause célèbre* of some sort.

aconita: a particularly deadly poison, apparently undetectable in wine.

uehatur: delib. subj.

159 *pensilibus plumis:* note the alliteration: 'in a pillowed palanquin'. The symbol of the litter returns: see on 33.

despiciat nos: the offbeat rhythm expresses both the scorn and the protest.

160 *contra:* if J is keeping mum *when face to face* only, it follows that he is — indirectly — attacking present vices.

digito: we use the same gesture. The Egyptian god of silence, Harpocrates, is depicted with finger to lip.

161 The meaning of this line is quite uncertain. Probably 'To have said the one word "That's the man" will be regarded as an accusation'; possibly 'If a person says the one word "That's the man" there will be

someone to bring a charge against him.'
In the first supply *is*, in the second *ei*. The
point is complicated because the man bring-
ing the accusation is accusing an accuser.
uerbum idiomatically for *unum uerbum* —
even though there are two.

162   To write epic about the mythological
past is innocent enough, says J ironically.
Aeneas, the legendary founder of Rome, is
the hero of Vergil's *Aeneid,* the fierce
Rutulian, his opponent Turnus. But mytho-
logical themes may have contemporary
points of allusion. Euripides continually
used the Trojan War to refer to the contem-
porary war between Athens and Sparta, and
in the twentieth century Shakespeare's
Coriolanus sparked off a riot in Paris.

163   *nulli . . . Achilles:* 'no one is en-
dangered by the death of Achilles'. (This is
better than the alternative 'no one worries
about': J has in mind Ov. *Tr.* 2,411-2, where
the phrase is *nec nocet auctori. nulli* is
common in verse for *nemini,* which does not
fit the dactylic metres without elision. Note
the Latin idiom: *percussus Achilles* where
we say 'the death of Achilles'. Achilles is the
hero of Homer's *Iliad,* where his death is
foretold by Hector (H. *Il.* 10,359). But J has
in mind the fact that P. Papinius Statius
(AD 45-96) was able to write an *Achilleis*
under Domitian without losing the favour
of the court, though he died a natural death
before reaching the end of Achilles's life.
Notice how J uses 'ring-form': we are back
to the mythical poems of the beginning.
There they were irrelevant: here too.

164   *Hylas:* Heracles's page, one of the
Argonauts, whose good looks led the
nymphs of the river Ascanius to pull him in
when he was drawing water. The story is
exquisitely told by Theocritus (*Id.* 13):
Vergil (*Ecl.* 6,44) tells of the whole shore
echoing 'Hylas — Hylas' as the others hunt
for him. So also Val. Fl. 3,596-7. Tr. 'or by
the frantic hunt for Hylas when he took the
plunge after his pitcher.'

165   *ense uelut stricto:* a straightforward
simile, not original; Persius said *secuit
Lucilius urbem* (1,114). These three lines
stand in contrast to the last three; in Greek
they might have had μὲν · · · δὲ to point the
contrast.

Lucilius: see on 1,20.

ardens: note how skilfully this leads to
the next picture: Lucilius's heat (the basic
symbol) makes the man, whose conscience
is frozen with fear, blush outwardly and
sweat inwardly. Macrobius described
Lucilius as *acer et uiolentus poeta* (3,16,17).

166   *infremuit:* an animal metaphor

'roared': the word is poetic, and appears in
this form in Verg. *A* 10,711; Sil. 3,230.

frigida mens est: verbatim from Lucr.
3,299, in a passage which made an impres-
sion on several later writers: heat is
associated with anger, cold with fear.

167   *praecordia:* external, 'their bodies'
(Ov. *M* 7,559).

168   *inde ira et lacrimae:* a variant on the
proverbial *hinc illae lacrimae* (Ter. *Andr.*
126; Cic. *Cael.* 25,61; Hor. *Ep.* 1,19,41).
Even under the Republic poets might not
challenge politicians with impunity, as
Naevius found. *Ira* is the guilty man's,
lacrimae the poet's.

uoluta: epic parody cf. Verg. *A* 4,533
secumque ita corde uolutat; 6,157;6,185.

169   *ante tubas:* keeping the image of
ense . . . stricto in 1,165: the *tuba* sounded
the call to join battle — or to retreat. He has
also in mind Lucilius fr. 1017 *haec tu me
insimulas? nonne ante in corde uolutas?*

galeatum: on the march the Roman
soldier carried his helmet slung round his
neck by a strap, as we can see depicted on
Trajan's column. At Ruspina Caesar told his
troops to put on their helmets the moment
Labienus's forces came into sight (*Bell. Afr.*
12,3).

duelli: archaic for *belli* (so that war
originates as a 'duel'; cf *bis* from *duis*). But
why does J use the archaism here? Probably
to give his caution a kind of hieratic wisdom
and religious validity.

170   So he tells us explicitly that he is not
taking living targets. But we should not
regard the matter as thereby closed: J may
simply be covering himself. The Rome of
the third Satire was not a thing of the past,
even if individuals are not recognisable. And
is it not an attack on the present to suggest
that it is not safe to attack the present? What
did Trajan think of that? Further, the words
in context also mean that he is firmly taking
his *exempla* from the actualities of Rome,
not from Greek mythology.

171   *Flaminia:* sc. *Via* see on 1,61. *Via
Latina* was probably the most ancient of the
great Roman trunk roads, named after the
territory it passed through rather than its
builder. It ran south-east for 220 kilometres
through Cales to Casilinum, where it linked
up with *Via Appia.* All the main roads were
lined with tombs after leaving the city;
those along *Via Appia* are best known, but
Domitian was buried along *Via Latina* (Suet.
Dom. 17), and one suspects a concrete
reference involved with *Via Flaminia.*
Plainly only the upper classes afforded such
tombs, and they provide J with his chief

targets.

cinis: the last flicker of the fire-theme. The cold ashes of the dead will not requite the fire of his anger with the fire of the stake.

General comments

H. E. Butler said of this poem: 'No better preface has ever been written; it gives a perfect summary of the motives, the objects, and the methods of the poet's work in language which for vigour and brilliance he never surpassed.' His inspiration is Lucilius, as he makes clear. 'He has nothing of the almost pathetic philosophic detachment of Persius, nor of the easygoing compromise of Horace. He does not palter with problems of right and wrong, nor hesitate over his moral judgements; casuistry is wholly alien to his temper. It is indignation which makes the verse, and from this fact, together with his rhetorical training, his chief merits and his chief failings spring. He introduces no novelty into satire save the almost unvarying bitterness and ferocity of his tone.'

In actual fact, although most commentators treat the poem with respect, for many it is a half-puzzled respect. Butler may assert that no better preface has ever been written, but it is not the preface *they* would have written. They know that they could have written a theoretically better preface themselves; but they have a suspicion, amounting to near-certainty, that it would not have been half as effective.

Overt criticism concentrates on three points — looseness of structure, lack of moral proportion, and the final calculating refusal to attack the living, which accords ill with the claim of *indignatio*.

The structure is undoubtedly loose, illogical and repetitive. Nettleship called it 'a series of incoherent complaints', and 'ill-proportioned pieces' in which the pictures 'are hurried together in no intelligible order'. We have discussed this in the preliminary notes to the poem. The looseness is deliberate; there is a carefully structured freedom of structure. This (to repeat) is partly because J's theme is life, and life is not tidy; partly because J is operating on the reinforcement principle, and dips into his themes more than once; partly because he is rhetorical. It allows us a break in the middle, a new beginning, and so makes the fresh wave of attacks more powerful; there is an element of *reculer pour mieux sauter.* it adds verisimilitude to the assumption of anger; anger does not operate tidily. It is the greatest mistake to answer this criticism by suggesting that there are major differences

of analysis between the first and second parts of the poem, and imposing on the poem a neater framework than it possesses. J is a more conscious artist than some critics, who emphasise the torrent of his *indignatio,* allow. He was patently a slow writer: his satires were produced at the fastest at an average rate of one a year, and probably more slowly. But the *genre* within which he has chosen to work did not allow that sort of minute planning. His effects are conscious, but broad.

The charge of lack of moral proportion we shall meet again: see the General comments on Satires 3 and 4. It is a charge which could only be levelled by a critic sadly lacking in a sense of humour. It is almost true to say that satire depends on a lack of proportion — just as the cartoonist depends for his effects on getting some superficial trait, like General de Gaulle's nose, out of proportion. For this is funny in itself, just as it is funny in itself to think of the lecture hall smashed up by the voices of all those poets. But at the same time the disproportion takes you into a kind of Wonderland or Topsyturvydom in which you begin to wonder (shall we say?) whether perhaps the proportions of the nose are right and the policies wrong, or whether the actual policies are not as inflated as the caricatured nose.

The third charge is the most serious. It does not affect our response to the greater part of the satire, but for some it leaves a nasty taste at the end, which destroys the power of what has gone before. For some, not for all, since J's withdrawal is so vividly achieved that our admiration for his verse pictures blots out rational analysis.

experiar quid concedatur in illos
quorum Flaminia tegitur cinis atque Latina

is one of the most memorable and best remembered phrases in all J. But this is an evasion, not an answer. The urge to caution was not confined to J. Horace too shows it, as Niall Rudd has amply demonstrated (*The Satires of Horace* c.5). Tacitus (*Ann.* 4,33) suggests that even attacks on the dead might give offence. But this is not a full answer either. The answer is in fact patent; it has already been given; it is twofold. First J is certainly pillorying the present under the guise of the past; indeed he quite specifically says that the abuses are present, even if he clothes them in the bodies of the dead. For Rome is his theme, and the degeneration of Rome is continuous from past to present. But, second, it was in fact an exceedingly courageous assertion to make, that it was dangerous to attack the living. Pliny's *Panegyricus* is a flattering address suggesting that there has been a total change from the tyranny of Domitian. J says that Rome is still a police state, that the upper classes are still riddled with selfishness and perversion, that the poor are still neglected, and that Rome has still abandoned the traditional Roman values.

These criticisms have not worried the average reader, who is carried along by the poem as it is. We may single out five particular qualities which constitute a strong part of its appeal. The first is his insistence on the relevance of literature to life. This storms out through the tempestuous surge of his initial drive, through the sarcasm of epic allusion and epic parody, through the skilled and witty second birth of his poem in the hands of Deucalion and Pyrrha, by contrast with his true themes, *quidquid agunt homines, uotum, timor, ira, uoluptas,/gaudia, discursus* (85-6), and the unforgettable pictures of real humanity, Crispinus twirling the ring on his finger, or Matho bulging from his litter. Secondly, there is his fury, which drives on his verse like a forest-fire, destructive and consuming. Some of his other poems have moments of respite, the third has vignettes of country-life to contrast with urban degeneracy, the eleventh is a poem of some charm. The first is unrelieved; the only contrasts are where a bitter laugh supervenes on the anger. Ernest Harrison (see on 85-6) has made the point: J's subject-matter is not character, but bad character, not behaviour, but anti-social behaviour. It is a powerful, pessimistic view of humanity. Thirdly, J uses imagery with considerable skill, and this poem is sustained, almost unnoticeably, by the image of fire, essential to life (83,135, 171), stirring the satirist to life (45, 152, 165), kindling the hearer's conscience (166-7), but also in danger of kindling a counterfire (155-6). Fourthly, and most obviously, comes J's power of phrase, from *Semper ego auditor tantum?* (1) through *probitas laudatur et alget* (74) and *si natura negat, facit indignatio uersum* (79) and *ducitur iratis plaudendum funus amicis* (146) to the last words of all. Finally, and supremely, there is his gift for shaping verbal cameos in a few deft strokes, and the vivid scenes 'shot' as he lounged at the street-corner. Those who read this poem may not be able to offer a coherent analysis of its structure, but they will be unresponsive indeed if they do not have in their minds a whole series of pictures, of the woman fighting barebreasted in the arena, of Crispinus and Matho, of the young aristocrat driving furiously to impress his girl who is dressed as a man, of the litter with its six bearers, the poisoner, the chaos at the patron's as rich upstarts push past their seniors, the empty litter ('Ssh, she's asleep'), the aristocrat dining alone — yes and the cruel Tigellinus, and the guilty blush turning to anger, and at the last the great roads flanked with tombs. This is what we are intended to carry away and do carry away.

Bibliography

Anderson, W. S. 'Studies in Book I of Juvenal' *YCS* 15 (1957) 34-45

Baldwin, B. 'Cover-names and Dead Victims in Juvenal' *Ath.* 45 (1967) 304-12

Bertman, S. S. 'Fire Symbolism in Juvenal's First Satire' *CJ* 63 (1968) 265-6

Church, J. E. 'The Construction of Juvenal, Satire I' *TAPA* 35 (1904) lxxi-lxxiv

Consoli, S. *Giovenali: Satire prima* Rome 1911

Elmore, J. 'The Plan of Juvenal's First Satire' *CW* 18 (1924) 166-7

Griffith, J. G. 'The Ending of Juvenal's First Satire and Lucilius, Book xxx' *Hermes* 98 (1970) 56-72

Helmbold, W. C. 'The Structure of Juvenal I" *UCP* 14 (1951) 47-60

Herrmann, L. 'Cluviaenus' *Latomus* 25 (1966) 258-64

Kenney, E. J. 'The First Satire of Juvenal' *PCPhS* 8 (1962) 29-40

Knapp, Ch. 'A Brief Review of Juvenal Satire I' *CW* 19 (1925-6) 19-21

MacKay, L. A. 'Notes on Juvenal' *CP* 53 (1958) 236-9

Martyn, J. R. C. 'A New Approach to Juvenal's First *Satire' Antichthon* 4 (1970) 53-61

Rudd, N. and Courtney, E. *Juvenal: Satires I, III, X* Bristol 1977

Stero, L. R. 'The Satirist's Apologia' *Classical Studies II* (University of Wisconsin Studies) Madison 1922 pp. 148-67

Townend, G. B. 'Juvenal's Automedon' *Hommages à Marcel Renard* I (*Coll. Latomus* 101) Brussels 1969 pp. 725-7

Zorzi, E. *Giovenale: Satira prima* Milan 1966

SATIRE 2

There is some reason for thinking that this is the earliest of all Juvenal's satires. It attacks Domitian. It would hardly be published in his lifetime, but *nuper* (2,29) makes clear that it was produced as soon as possible afterwards, and a draft may have circulated privately earlier.

Its subject is homosexuality. Highet entitles his brief chapter on it 'The Faerie Queenes'. In the middle of the twentieth century a change of temper took place by which the satire almost passed from not being read because it *treated* homosexuality to not being read because it *attacked* homosexuality. But we must come to Juvenal on his own terms, not on those of Victorian prudery or gay lib.

Juvenal's attack is directed not against homosexuality as such, but against the particular perversion which leads a man to play a woman's rôle.

The structure is basically simple, though it has been the subject of some detailed discussion:

1-63 Hypocritical homosexuals
  1-35 Moralising immoralists
  36-63 Their exposure by Laronia
64-148 Aristocratic perversion
  64-81 Creticus and corruption in high office
  82-116 The secret society of transvestites
  117-48 Gracchus and open perversion
149-70 Conclusion. Once we conquered by military power. That is undone. But wait! We can still corrupt foreigners with our morals.

1-35 *It would be good to escape, even to the far north, from these preachers who play the moralist and practise sexual deviation. I prefer the open deviants: at least it isn't their fault. It's the hypocrisy of the thing, like the Gracchi complaining about revolutionaries. And what about the censorious emperor in incest with his niece? To such critics even extreme vice is justified in snapping back.*

1-3 J is indignant from the beginning. There is an important contrast with Martial 1,24 *aspicis incomptis illum, Deciane,/capillis,/cuius et ipse times triste supercilium,/qui loquitur Curios adsertoresque Camillos?/nolito fronti credere: nupsit heri.* Martial is simply amusing: a shaggy moralist

is denouncing vice, but he is himself a homosexual (*nupsit* is a favourite homosexual joke; it properly is used of bride not groom). J abjures the wit for anger.

1 *Ultra:* the word will be picked up in 159.

Sauromatas: otherwise the Sarmatae, a Slavic people, in the area from the Vistula to the Don. They appear again at 3,79; 15,125. Domitian won a victory over them (Suet. *Dom.* 6; Mart. 7,6,10); J wants to escape beyond them.

fugere: adumbration of a military metaphor recurring through the poem.

libet: note the impersonality.

2 *Oceanum:* the river which flows round the inhabited world, frozen in the north.

3 *Curios:* M'. Curius Dentatus, consul 290 and 275-4 and censor in 272, conqueror of Pyrrhus, was a standard of traditional virtue (cf 11,78; Val. Max. 4,3,5; 6,3,4). The Stoics tended to be republicans. The plural is generic.

Bacchanalia: the rites of Dionysus were celebrated by women.

4 *gypso:* i.e. a plaster cast.

5 *Chrysippi:* (c. 280-207 BC), third head of the Stoa, succeeding Cleanthes in 232. A voluminous writer and systematiser. Later generations said 'If there had been no Chrysippus there would have been no Stoa.' See Diog. Laert. 7,179-202; E. Bréhier *Chrysippe.*

perfectissimus: the Stoics believed that you were either perfectly wise or you were not wise at all.

6 *Aristotelen:* (384-322 BC), pupil of Plato, founder of the Lyceum, the greatest biological scientist of antiquity, nothing to do with the Stoics, but Juvenal does not mind. Note the Greek ending: J scorned the Greeks.

similem: 'a likeness of', a portrait, as in Martial 1,109,19.

Pittacon: (c. 650-570 BC), again with a Greek ending, statesman of Mytilene and one of the legendary seven sages, with no connection with the Stoics.

7 *archetypos:* the Greek word reinforces the scorn. These are 'originals'.

pluteum: 'bookcase': the busts stand on top.

Cleanthas: Cleanthes (331-232 BC), who succeeded Zeno as head of the Stoic school; a commoner, and something of a religious genius. The plural is generic.

8 *frontis nulla fides:* a striking epigram, prefixed to one of the satires in the early English *Time's Whistle* by R.C.

8-10 Strong alliteration and assonance.

9 *tristibus obscenis:* the antithesis between *tristis* and *turpis* is vital to the satire. *Tristis* is a technical term for Stoic solemnity. The two words do not form a natural oxymoron, but take on the meaning 'moralising immoralists'. J shows that it isn't an oxymoron after all. For a similar contrast see Quint. 1 proem 15 *uultum et tristitiam et dissentientem a ceteris habitum pessimis moribus praetendebant;* 12,3, 12 *in publico tristes, domi dissoluti.*

castigas: he addresses the moralist.

cum: 'although'.

10 *Socraticos . . . cinaedos:* the Stoics, like most later philosophical schools, claimed descent from Socrates. There is allusion to Socrates's undoubted affection for handsome boys (Plat. *Charm.* 155D; *Meno* 76C; *Phaed.* 893), though Plato goes to some trouble to indicate that he kept his physical impulses under strict control (*Symp.* 219B-C). There is an exceptionally judicious evaluation in W. K. C. Guthrie *A History of Greek Philosophy* III 390-8.

fossa: an obvious sexual metaphor.

12 *atrocem animum:* a traditional Stoic trait. The phrase is a take-off on Hor. *O* 2,1,24 *atrocem animum Catonis.*

leui: depilated.

13 *mariscae:* lit. 'figs'; here 'the piles'.

14 *rarus sermo:* characteristic of Stoics.

15 shaggy eyebrows and hair short. cf Pers. 3,54 *detonsa iuuentus.*

uerius ergo: bucolic diaeresis in two successive lines effectively picks out this sentence.

16 *Peribomius:* sc. 'does it'. The name is Greek in form, perhaps deriving from 'around the altar', i.e. a disreputable priest.

fatis: i.e. it isn't his own fault; he can't help it. They can. *Morbum* (17) and *furor* (18) have the same implication.

17 *incessu:* Cat. 42,8 *turpe incedere* of a prostitute's gait. So often, e.g. Tac. *Hist.* 1,30 of Otho.

18 *horum:* Peribomius and his like.

20 *Herculis:* a Stoic hero, and type of the perfect sage.

21 *Sexte:* a senatorial name, as the scholiast says.

22 *Varillus:* a diminutive: *uarus* means 'straddling'; varicose is from the same root.

quo deterior te?: a harsh rhythm for a harsh subject.

23 *Aethiopem albus:* there wasn't much colour-prejudice in Graeco-Roman antiquity. In Homer Ethiopians are favoured by the gods. Agatharchides (*Mar. Erythr.* 16) points to the Greek view that colour is irrelevant. At Carthage the black Olympius was a heroic figure (*Anth. Lat.* R 277 no. 353). Heliodorus takes an Ethiopian king as a model of wisdom and justice (*Aeth.* 9,21). There are plenty of records of mixed marriages, which are freely discussed by Aristotle (*Hist. An.* 7,586a; *Gen. An.* 1,722a) and Plutarch (*Mor.* 563). See in general Frank Snowden's excellent *Blacks in Antiquity* esp. c. 8.

24 *Gracchos:* Tib. Sempronius Gracchus and C. Sempronius Gracchus, sons of Tib. Sempronius Gracchus (consul in 177 BC and censor in 169) and Cornelia, grandsons of Scipio Africanus, reforming statesmen. Tiberius as tribune in 133 carried a land law designed to alleviate poverty. When he sought re-election he was lynched by a right-wing mob. Gaius, as tribune in 123 and 122, subsidised wheat, encouraged colonies, organised public works, weakened senatorial control of the law courts, and tried to extend Roman citizenship in Italy. He died in a riot after the proclamation of martial law (*senatus ultimum consultum*). The name leads up to the aristocratic pervert of 117.

25 Proverbial for a perturbation of nature, e.g. Liv. 4,3, 6; Lucr. 3,854; Verg. *A* 5,790.

26 *Verri:* the extortionate governor of Sicily whose prosecution by Cicero made the latter's name. Cicero in prosecuting him makes the point that you must be free from the offences you condemn (2 *Verr.* 3,2), which may have given J the idea of this passage.

Miloni: T. Annius Milo, tribune in 57 BC, political gangster who was exiled to Massilia for his murder of Clodius in 52. (He thanked Cicero for the failure of his defence; the mullets at Massilia were so good.) He was later executed for political violence in 48.

27 *Clodius:* P. Clodius Pulcher, radical member of the ancient Claudian family, tribune in 58 BC, killed by Milo in gang warfare on 18 Jan 52.

Catilina: L. Sergius Catilina, a patrician of distinction, praetor in 68 BC, unsuccessful candidate for the consulship in 63 and 62. He gathered round him bankrupt and discontented aristocrats with a programme of social reform. An organised conspiracy was frustrated by Cicero and Catiline was executed.

Cethegum: C. Cethegus, an accomplice of Catiline. These two are coupled again at 8,231; 10,287. The alliteration is full of scorn.

28 *in . . . dicant:* precisely 'speak against'.

tabulam: the proscription-list.

Sullae: L. Cornelius Sulla (c. 138-78 BC), brilliant soldier and right-wing statesman, who suppressed ruthlessly the radicals, and as dictator carried a programme of conservative reforms, subsequently abdicating his power and going into retirement.

discipuli tres: the second triumvirate of Antony, Octavian (later Augustus) and Lepidus, who drew up a formidable list of proscriptions, in which Cicero lost his life. Note the rhythm, and the alliteration.

29 *qualis:* all that has gone before leads up to this. It becomes clear that this is the emperor Domitian, who was alleged to have incestuous relations with his niece Julia, and as censor in 90 revived stringent laws to enforce morality, including ironically the *lex Iulia de adulteriis* (Mart. 6,2). Plin. *Ep.* 4,11 has a similar indictment of him.

nuper: an indication that this is one of the earliest, and probably the earliest of the satires.

tragico: incest was a tragic theme, as in *Oedipus.*

31 *atque:* almost 'including'.

Veneri Martique: Venus was married to the lame smith-god Vulcan (a Beauty-and-the-Beast myth) but had an affair with Mars, and was caught *in flagrante delicto* Hom. *Od.* 8,266-366; Ov. *M* 4,171-89).

timendas: note how rhyme holds the lines together.

32-3 Note the skill with which J deploys the hexameter: Green draws attention to the 'slow, sluggish heaves' of the first line, suggesting uterine contraction, followed by the explosive *solueret* of the delivery, and the panting *-ff-* in *effunderet offas.*

33 *offas:* shapeless bits, used here of an abortion: a vulgar word associated with sows.

34 *uitia ultima:* 'sinners': abstract for concrete.

35 *Scauros:* 'men like Scaurus'; cf 6,604; 11,91. So Hor. *O* 1,12,37. M. Aemilius Scaurus the elder (consul 115, censor 109) was a model of virtue (Cic. *Font.* 7; Val. Max. 5,8,4); his son hardly so. The family was extinct by J's time (Sen. Eld. *Suas.* 2,22).

36-69 *Laronia knew how to send them about their business. 'What a golden age,' she cried, 'with such a censor! If we are citing laws, what about those against deviancy? The men are worse than the women. They do women's work; they bribe their wives to tolerate their male lovers.'*

36 *ex illis: uitia ultima.*

toruum: another Stoic term.

Laronia: Also at Mart. 2,32,5. She is delightfully portrayed, the representative of natural as opposed to unnatural vice. The name itself is respectable: a Q. Laronius was suffect consul in 33 BC.

37 *lex Iulia: de adulteriis et stupro et pudicitia,* enacted by Augustus in 18 BC, which took jurisdiction from private into public hands. A woman, however, could not initiate proceedings for adultery. *Stuprum* included male homosexuality, and liaison with a widow or free unmarried girl who was not a recognised concubine or prostitute.

dormis: Fletcher quotes Shakespeare *MM* 2,2,90 'the law hath not been dead though it hath slept.'

39 *opponunt:* continuing the military metaphor.

40 *tertius . . . Cato:* Domitian, the censor of morals. The first Cato was M. Porcius Cato the Censor (234-149 BC), a traditionalist, who taxed luxury, opposed Greek influence, wrote in support of agriculture (cf 11,90). The second was his great-grandson, M. Porcius Cato Uticensis (95-46 BC), also a traditionalist and a Stoic moralist as well, who was inflexibly opposed to Caesar, and who committed suicide after the battle of Thapsus.

41 *opobalsama:* the juice of the balsam, used in embalming, and in general for perfume. cf. Mart. 11,8; 14,59.

44 *Scantinia:* the *lex Scantinia de nefanda uenere,* of uncertain date, condemning sodomy, was ruthlessly enforced by Domitian (Suet. *Dom.* 8). Note the bucolic diaeresis.

45 *peiora:* Bücheler for *nam plura.*

46 Military metaphors all through, as the scholiast comments.

47 *molles:* the effeminate, queans.

49 The names do not seem especially significant. (But see R. A. Lafleur in *Rev. Phil* 48 (1974) 71-4.) The passage is, however, slightly odd, as lesbians were known at Rome, cf. Mart. 7,67; J in adapting the passage removes the charge (6,418-33), which plays no part in the sixth satire.

50 *Hispo:* the fem. is Hispulla, who appears as unchaste (6,74) and fat (12,11). The names are rare, but note Ti. Caepio Hispo, proconsul of Asia 117-8, and Pliny's relatives Calpurnia Hispulla and Corellia Hispulla.

utroque: Schol.: *inguina lambentis et stuprum patientis.*

· 51 Men may try to behave as women, but women do not ape men. When it suits him J takes another view, e.g. 1,22.

53 *luctantur:* i.e. fight for show, cf 1,22.

coloephia: the athlete's meat ration, but also slang for the penis, a strong double meaning; they were also phallic-shaped rolls; Martial's Philaenis, with similar double meaning, consumes sixteen of these (7,67,12).

54 *uos:* you men.

56 *Penelope . . . Arachne:* abl. A beautifully-shaped line. Penelope the wife of Ulysses, wove a tapestry in his absence, unweaving it by night to hold off her suitors. Arachne was a Lydian who challenged Athene to a spinning contest and was turned into a spider.

57 *codice:* a block of wood to which slaves were chained. The reference is to Antiope in a play by Pacuvius, who was chained to a log by Dirce, cf Prop. 3,15,11.

58 *tabulas:* his will.

Hister: he appears in 12,111 as a legacy-hunter.

59 *puellae:* to keep her quiet about his double-life.

60 *tertia:* tolerating the male lover. The Second Sex has become the Third.

61 *tu nube:* addressed to the girl.

cylindros: a jewel ground into this shape.

62 *tristis:* the verdict of guilty, but with pointed allusion to Stoic *tristitia.*

63 *coruis . . . columbas:* the scholiast points out that the proverbial difference between raven and dove, black and white, aggressive and peaceable, hoarse and mellifluous, involves sexual behaviour. There is strong alliteration.

censura: with allusion to Domitian, who was censor in 85, cf 29.

64-81 *Laronia routed the fake Stoics, but there are still the aristocrats, like Creticus, wearing women's clothes. Not the most suitable attire for the administrators of law. And the thing is contagious.*

64 *fugerunt:* picking up 1 and continuing the military metaphor.

uera ac manifesta canentem: Laronia is characterised as a Sibyl.

65 *Stoicidae:* coined by J for these pseudo-Stoics.

66 *multicia:* gauze (n. pl.).

67 *Cretice:* again at 8,38 of an aristocrat. The name belonged to the Caecilii Metelli, being awarded to the conqueror of Crete. The use of the name would not be wounding, as the Metelli were extinct.

hanc uestem: obj. of *mirante.*

68 *Proculas et Pollittas:* Proculus was an ancient Roman name (Liv. 1,16); Procula is found again at 3,203: the schol. glosses *in criminosas.* Pollitta is a perhaps Etruscan

termination: we find Gallitta, Iulitta, Livilitta. Polla is found, e.g. a sister of Vipsanius Agrippa or in the poems of Statius (*S* 2,2,10 etc.); Pollucia was d. of L. Vetus (Tac. *Ann.* 16,10). Creticus's moralising forms a bridge with the first section.

Fabulla: not otherwise known: the name appears often enough in Martial (1,64 etc.). The names Fabullus or Fabulla are found associated with the Valerii and the Fabii among the great families.

69 *Carfinia:* not otherwise known.

talem: picked out by the punctuation: 'as diaphanous as his'.

70 *Iulius: double entendre* 'the month of July' but also the proper name Julius, associated with the imperial house. So *ardet* and *aestuo* have the double meaning of hot and afire with love: *ardenti* recurs of love at 165.

71 *turpis:* part of the contrast, cf 9.

72 *habitum:* acc. of exclamation. 'What a costume for the people to hear you in!'

leges ac iura ferentem: this is an attack on the power élite.

73 *uulneribus crudis:* 'with their wounds unhealed'. The military theme.

76 *testem:* J has been preparing for this pun: a formal witness and the male sex-organ.

77 *acer et indomitus:* from Lucan's description of Caesar (1,146).

78 *perluces:* i.e. wearing see-through clothes: brilliantly expressed. Seneca is always moralising about such outfits (*Ben.* 7,9; *Const. Sap.* 18; *Cons. Helv.* 16; *Ep.* 90).

78-81 After the staccato phrases of the previous lines J passes to four lines of smooth structure reminiscent of Vergil. He is in fact alluding to Vergil's description of infection spreading among sheep (*G* 3,440-566), and spreading through contaminated clothing to man. The parallel is clear, but where Vergil looks on the animals with human pity, J sees the humans as bestial. J's lines were quoted time and again in the Middle Ages and Renaissance.

81 A proverbial phrase *uua uuam uidendo uaria fit.* Compare the Persian 'One plum gets colour by looking at another'. It is uncertain whether we should read *conspecta* with the proverb, or *contacta* from Vergil with allusion to *contagio.* A third reading *confecta* has little to commend it.

82-116 *There is a steady degeneration. If you go this far you will be accepted into the secret society of transvestites, worshipping the Good Goddess, putting on make-up and ornaments, carrying a mirror that once*

belonged to the illustrious pervert Otho,
who bothered about his complexion on
campaign, unlike the real women-com-
manders, Semiramis and Cleopatra. They
have a shrill-voiced priest. The next logical
stage is self-castration.

83 A brilliant epigram, marked off by
the bucolic diaeresis, and the harsh writing
at the end of the line with the broken
rhythm and the biting *-cc-* and *-tt-*. *Turpis*
remains a keyword. Humphries' version is
tempting: 'No one hits bottom at once.'
J improves on Sen. *Ag.* 153 *extrema nemo*
primo tentauit loco.

86-7 *bonam . . . deam:* the Good God-
dess, from whose worship men were strictly
excluded. It was a major scandal when P.
Clodius in 62 BC intruded on the rites,
disguised as a woman (6,335-41).

87 *more sinistro:* 'it's all cack-handed'.

88 *exagitata:* Hooker in his *Ecclesias-*
tical Polity says of the Scottish Kirk, 'We
must not exagitate them.'

89 *ite, profanae:* normally, of course,
ite, profani.

92 The scholiast says that *The Dippers*
(Baptae) is the title of a work in which
shameless people are portrayed by Eupolis
(the contemporary of Aristophanes), who
introduces Athenian citizens dancing like
women to proposition a music-girl. Lucian
(Indoct. 27) thought it a shocking play.
Cotys or Cotyto was a Thracian goddess,
whose orgiastic worship was introduced
into Athens from Corinth in the fifth
century BC: hence *Cecropiam,* from the
mythical Athenian king Cecrops.

93 *ille:* 'one of them'.

94 *trementis:* proleptic, 'till they flutter
like a girl's'.

95 *ille:* 'another'.

priapo: Priapus was son of Dionysus and
Aphrodite, both fertility powers; his birth-
place was Lampsacus in Mysia. His statue,
with erect phallus, stood in gardens to en-
sure their prosperity. One common form
shows his phallus supporting a lap full of
fruit. The phallus was a good-luck symbol,
found on the walls of houses, and we have
plenty of lamps and bells and statuettes
based on the form. At Herculaneum there
was found a drinking vessel in the form of
a grotesque jester *(morio)* with extended
phallus. So the elder Pliny writes 'It is the
fashion to protray lust on cups and to
drink from objects of an obscene shape.'
(NH 33,1).

97 *indutus:* the construction is variously
explained. *Induere* can be used with acc.
of costume + dat. of person or acc. of

person + abl. of costume. Here the passive
or middle is used with a retained accusative
of the costume.

scutulata: checks or plaids, from Gaul
(Plin. *NH* 8,48).

98 *per Iunonem:* a woman's oath: the
servant is as perverted as the owner. Juno,
who became identified with the Greek god-
dess Hera, was originally the power of
fertility in woman, corresponding to the
male Genius.

99 *pathici gestamen Othonis:* a parody
of Verg. *A* 3,286 *magni gestamen Abantis.*
The heroic allusions make of Otho a
counter-hero or anti-hero. M. Salvius Otho
(AD 32-69), Poppaea's husband, was
reputedly Nero's lover (Suet. *Otho* 2; Mart.
6,32,2). He was briefly emperor in 69, oust-
ing Galba and being ousted by Vitellius,
preferring death to more bloodshed.

A sustained military image starts here.
Otho carried a mirror instead of a shield, a
love-gift *(spolium).*

100 *Actoris Aurunci spolium:* a direct
quotation from Verg. *A* 12,94. Lelièvre
argues an allusion to Nero as Otho's lover,
with a punning reference in *actor* (perform-
ing artist). It is worth noting that Vergil's
Turnus was in Nero's histrionic repertoire
(Suet. *Nero* 54).

102-3 *annalibus . . . historia:* allusion to
Tacitus. J seems to say 'Why did Tacitus not
include this?' The poem, itself early, was
presumably revised for publication c. 110.

104 *nimirum summi:* four ms and one n
in 12 letters: the effect is carried on in the
next line. *summi ducis:* 'it is the sign of a
supreme commander.'

Galbam: Serv. Sulpicius Galba (c. 3 BC-
AD 69), an elderly statesman of high repu-
tation, invited disastrously to succeed Nero.
Tacitus assessed him in a brilliant epigram
omnium consensu capax imperii nisi
imperasset (Hist. 1,49). J is not unfavour-
able to Galba (6,559; 8,222).

105 A line of cutting alliteration: note
in the previous line *duCis, oCCidere,* and
the cognate *Galbam.* For *constantia* see Tac.
Hist. 2,47,3.

106 *Bebriaci:* Bebriacum, between
Verona and Cremona, site of the decisive
battle between Otho and Vitellius.

107 Otho used a dough pack as a mud-
pack is used in beauty parlours today.

108 *Sameramis:* mythical and sensuous
queen, founder of Babylon (Ov. *Am.*
1,5,11), lover, soldier and builder, perhaps
the historical Sammuramat, regent of
Assyria 810-805 BC.

109 *Actiaca:* the battle of Actium in 31

BC saw the defeat of Cleopatra and Antony by Octavian (the future Augustus).

Cleopatra: Cleopatra VII (69-30 BC), the brilliant Egyptian queen, lover of Caesar and Antony, with the ambition to be a world-ruler; her association with Antony strengthened Octavian's propaganda; driven to suicide on 10 Aug., 30 BC.

111 *turpis:* the key-word again.

Cybeles: the Great Mother of Asia Minor, brought from Pessinus to Rome in 204 BC in the form of a black betyl; her priests were eunuchs. Catullus 63 is a powerful poetic treatment of the theme. There is a kind of zeugma: 'the freedom of Cybele and of speaking in a cracked voice'. The sentence is further complicated by the linking together of abstract and concrete in the subject.

113-4 A succession of *m* and *n*, giving a stammering effect in contrast to the apparent meaning.

114 *conducendusque magister:* 'a teacher worth hiring': sarcastic. Note the sonorous four-word line.

115 *Phrygio:* the cult of Cybele was prominent in Phrygia.

116 *abrumpere:* the MSS vary between this, *abscindere, abscidere* and *excidere.*

117-48 *Worst of all is the noble Gracchus, who openly flaunted his behaviour and appeared as a bride in a ceremonial wedding. How can Romulus or Mars put up with this behaviour of their citizens? The very concept of social duty is perverted. Their one regret is that they can't bear children. Gracchus goes one worse, and appears in the arena as a gladiator.*

117 *quadringenta:* a sum with which Juvenal was obsessed, because it was the capital qualification for an *eques* cf. 1,106; 5,132-3; 14,322-4.

Gracchus: a well-known name of the Sempronii, cf. 2,24.

119 *feliciter:* 'Good luck!'; cf Phaedr. 5,1 *'feliciter' subclamant,* etc.

121 *proceres . . . nobis:* J here both associates himself with and dissociates himself from the aristocracy. They should be all Romans, but the aristocrats have betrayed all that is Roman.

censore: with allusion to Domitian: see on 29.

haruspice: because unnatural occurrences were portents to be interpreted.

123 *ederet:* 'were to give birth to': impf. subj. for an 'impossible' condition.

124 *segmenta:* strips of brocade.

125-6 The *ancilia* were archaic figure-of-

eight shields sacred to Mars. The sacred priests of Mars, the Salii, carried them through the city on the first of March at the ceremonial start of the campaigning season.

126 *pater urbis:* Romulus.

127 *pastoribus:* contrasting the simple rural life of the founding fathers with the perils and problems of urbanisation.

128 *Gradive:* cult-title of Mars, 'Infantry-man', from the same root as *gradior.*

urtica: lit. 'stinging-nettle'; J uses it here and at 11,158 for the itch of lust.

129 The honorific titles are belied by the rhythm at the end.

131 *patri:* Jupiter, father of gods and man.

uade: 'Clear off'.

132 *campi:* the Campus Martius where the armies traditionally mustered outside the city boundary.

132-42 There is an important relation with Mart. 12,42. Martial has *barbatus rigido nupsit Callistratus Afro* in his first line. A bearded moralist (only Stoic—Cynics wore beards at this time) is in homosexual marriage (see on 2,1-3). Martial's climax is addressed to Rome *expectas numquid ut et pariat?* The joke is there for its own sake. J holds up *nubit,* and puts it in the mouth of a wedding guest, leaving himself free for denunciation, with the one redeeming mercy — no children will result. We might think that J abjures wit for anger, but it is a little more subtle: to an audience familiar with Martial's poem the wit is there, and it is taken up and embraced in the anger.

132 *officium cras:* a new speaker. The words are picked out by the bucolic diaeresis and by the harsh rhythm: note also the rhyming effect in 130-3.

133 *ualle Quirini:* The phrase does not occur elsewhere; it seems to refer to the forum.

135 *liceat:* 'if we live long enough'. The condition is mixed, the remoter subjunctive of the if-clause being taken up by a vigorous future indicative.

135-6 *fient, fient:* rhetorical repetition or *geminatio;* cf 5,112-3; 6,116-7; 6,279-80; 8,147-8.

136 *cupient:* *ista* is subj., a vivid person-ification.

acta: the official records.

137 Excellent hyperbole.

139 *iuris:* 'authority' or 'power'; for the extra-legal use, cf Cic. *De Or.* 1,70; Ov. *M* 8,730 *in plures ius est transire figuras;* Sen. *Oed.* 447; *QN* 2,11,2; Luc. 1,406-7; 8,636; 9,887-8; 10,262; Plin. *NH* 18,337; Quint. 1,4,4 *uerba quae frequenter ius ab*

auctoribus sumunt (refs from Prof. G. B. A. Fletcher).

141 *Lyde:* a Greek name: there may be a side-reference to the practices of the Etruscans, who were believed to come from Lydia.

142 At the *Lupercalia* on 15 Feb. young men ran round the city-boundaries striking any they met, women especially, with strips of goatskin to promote fertility. Cf Shakespeare *Julius Caesar* 1,2,7 'Our elders say/The barren touched in this holy chase/Shake off their sterile curse.' There is an account of it in Dion. Hal. *Ant. Rom.* 1,80,1; and Ov. *F* 2,19-37. For the interpretation see J. G. Frazer on Ovid ad loc,; W. W. Fowler *The Roman Festivals* pp. 310-21; A. K. Michels 'The Topography and Interpretation of the Lupercalia' *TAPA* 84 (1953) 35-59.

143-8 These lines cut across the theme of homosexuality. We must not expect logic from a satirist: it is another example of un-Roman behaviour (cf 8,199-210). We may think that J was wiser than he knew: such overt violence is itself a sexual perversion. Seneca also links homosexuality and the arena (*QN* 7,31).

143 *monstrum:* portent.

tunicati fuscina Gracchi: Gracchus has the trident and costume of the *retiarius* who fought with a net: part of the disgrace is the display of the person (Dio Cass. 73,17,4 of Commodus). Other gladiators found the *retiarii* to be *turpes* (6,0 9).

144 *gladiator:* a slave's profession: J is scornful of free men who descend to it. Seneca has a fine indictment of the games though his presence at them somewhat belies his sentiments (Ep. 7).

145 A sonorous, majestic line with its two five-syllable words and spondaic ending.

Capitolinis: family name of several aristocratic *gentes:* it is found among the Claudii, Cornelii, Flavii, Iulii, Mamilii and Manlii.

Marcelli: plebeian family of the *gens Claudia.*

146 Catuli: family of *gens Lutatia,* see 8,253.

Pauli: of *gens Aemilia.*

Fabii: one of the most powerful patrician houses, traditionally of Sabine origin.

minoribus: descendants.

et Fabiis et: a deliberate take-down from the previous line.

ipsum: the patron who has paid for the games.

149-70 *No one believes in a life after death, but if there were one, the heroes of old*

would be ashamed of such people. So we've come to this. Our armies have reached the Orkneys, but our vices are worse than those of our subjects. An Armenian hostage has been involved in the corruption. Keep them in Rome, they'll find plenty of lovers, give up their masculine prowess and take our Roman practices back home.

149-52 An Epicurean sentiment but cf. also Cic. *TD* 1,5; 1,21; *ND* 2,2; *Div.* 2,15; *Cluent.* 61,171; Sen. *Ep.* 24 *nemo tam puer est ut Cerberum timeat et tenebras;* Ps-Q. 10,16 *negat ullos esse manes.*

149 *manes:* spirits of the dead, cf Propertius's assertion *sunt aliquid manes* (4,7,1).

150 *Cocytum:* the river of wailing, one of the waters of Hades, which form the hexameter *Styx, Acheron, Lethe, Phlegethon, Cocytus, Avernus.*

Stygio ranas: as in Aristophanes's play *The Frogs.* The Styx was the river encircling Hades.

151 *cumba:* the ferry-boat of Charon.

152 *nondum aere lauantur:* who are not yet old enough to be charged for a bath; the charge was a *quadrans.*

153 *sed tu uera puta:* 'But just suppose it *were* true.' What follows is a satirical inversion of the vision in Verg. *A* 6.

Curius: cf 2,3. There the name stood for ethical *uirtus* in the broader sense, here for *uirtus* shown in battle.

154 *Scipiadae:* Scipio Africanus the elder and younger, the first victor over Hannibal at Zama in 202 BC, the second the annihilator of Carthage in 146. The word, archaic in form, is taken from Lucr. 3,1034; Verg. *A* 6,843. Note the contrast with *Stoicidae* (65), at the same point in the line.

Fabricius: C. Fabricius Luscinus (consul 282, 278 BC, censor 275, the opponent of Pyrrhus, with a reputation for austere incorruptibility). Cicero (e.g. *Par. Stoic.* 50) uses him as the type of Roman virtue.

Camilli: M. Furius Camillus, the general who captured Veii in 396 BC, and saved Rome from the Gauls in 387-6.

155 *Cremerae legio:* a platoon of 300 members of the Fabian clan, annihilated by Veii in 477 BC (Liv. 2,48-50).

Cannis: the scene of Hannibal's great victory over the Romans in 216 BC.

156 *tot bellorum animae:* a fine phrase. The point of the military image is now clear: it reinforces the masculine—feminine dichotomy. Note the contrast between *animae* and *umbra.*

157 *lustrari:* purification either by sprink-

ling water, often with a branch of laurel or olive, or by burning sulphur or pine torches.

159 *traducimur:* 'So we've been brought to this.' The satire is coming full circle. Notice how *ultra* picks up the first word of all. But the impersonal *libet* has become intensely personal.

arma quidem ultra: here the bucolic diaeresis combines with the triple accent and the elision to pick these words out bitterly. They drive home the point of the military image.

160 *Iuuernae:* Ireland, which the Romans did not reach. The word is the same as Hibernia. References to Britain are based on Tacitus *Agricola.*

161 *Orcadas:* the Orkneys, reached by Agricola fairly recently in AD 84 (Tac. *Agr.* 10).

163 *et tamen unus:* picked out for emphasis by bucolic diaeresis and offbeat rhythm. J ends with a case-study.

164 *Armenius Zalaces:* the name is not, I think, known, though presumably genuine. Zalace is named as a city of Media by Ptolemy (6,2,10). Armenia had a convoluted history: it was a buffer-state between Rome and Parthia. Armenia Maior, east of the Euphrates, played them off against one another till its annexation by Trajan; Armenia Minor, to the west, was incorporated by Vespasian into Cappadocia.

ephebis: a Greek term for a young man of age for military call-up. The Greek should make us suspicious, but only when we reach *mollior* do we find the construction.

165 *tribuno:* Michel tried to make this young Trajan (trib. 71-81; in Armenia 84 or later), a lover of boys and wine. Not very likely.

166 Rolfe Humphries' translation is irresistible: 'This, I suppose, could be called The Intercourse between Nations.' Again the bucolic diaeresis picks out alike what goes before and after.

167 *hic fiunt homines:* what does J mean? It is *homo* not *uir.* Perhaps 'all too human'. Or perhaps 'not males but unsexed humans'. It is thus a variant on Mart. 9,56, 11-2 *dum puer es, redeas, dum uultu lubricus, et te/non Libye faciat, sed tua Roma uirum.*

168 The reading and meaning are quite uncertain. The MSS have *indulsit:* this, as Housman showed, is a solecism. Clausen proposed *indulget.* (At 140 V has *indulsit* for *indulget.*)

169 *mittentur:* 'will be laid aside'.

bracae: quite literally. But this is only an incidental effect. These are all the accoutre-

ments of the foreign male, a soldier and a cavalryman. He has become Roman and feminine. The line is beautifully shaped with its four words in asyndeton, its internal 'rhyme' (*cultelli . . . flagellum*), its alliteration (*frena, flagellum*).

170 *praetextatos:* i.e. Roman, from the *toga praetexta. referunt:* 'bear back in triumph', a final fling for the military metaphor.

Artaxata: Ardaschan, the capital of Armenia. Hannibal in exile helped to build it, it was rased by Corbulo, and rebuilt by Tiridates.

Another carefully-shaped line to end the poem, with its heavily spondaic beginning. The conclusion is of course bitterly ironical. The Romans have lost the capacity to win battles, but maintain their power by infecting others with their effeminacy. It makes an excellent climax for the military image.

General comments
This is not one of the better-known satires, because of its subject matter, but it is strong, vivid and single-minded. The object of attack is homosexuality, though this is not clear till later. J is original as a satirist in choosing this for a full-size target. It was a commonplace for attack by moralists; J gives this a twist by placing the moralists under attack. In the first part the people concerned are moralistic preachers. The incongruity lies in the contrast between their profession and practice, and it is a stroke of some genius to place their exposure in the mouth of an honestly outspoken whore. Up to this point the theme might be hypocrisy. We might be listening to a bitter version of a Horatian sermon on the pot calling the kettle black. The medieval scribes actually entitled it *De Fictis Moribus Institutis.* Now we find the continuing theme in the homosexuals. In the second part the people are Roman aristocrats. The incongruity lies in the contrast between the virile traditions of Rome (*uirtus* means toughness in battle) and the effeminacy of the perverts. Three *exempla* are taken. Creticus with his combination of high office and private corruption forms a bridge with the hypocrites. Worse is the secret society of transvestites. Worse still is the open perversion of Gracchus: at the end of the *exemplum* J digresses to Gracchus's fighting in the arena — another example of overt aristocratic perversion. The conclusion contrasts the military record of the ancestors with the present effeminacy. But J offers an

ironical twist. All is not lost. If the Romans can no longer defeat foreigners in battle, they can corrupt their morals.

The poem is held together by five structural factors. The first is a simple device of ring-form. The word *ultra* in 2,1 is taken up in 2,159. The idea of *retreating* to the distant north is taken up in the recollection that the Roman soldiers once *advanced* to the distant north. The impersonality of the beginning has become intensely personal. At the beginning the old *mores* (2,2) are insincerely preached and to be escaped from; at the end the new *mores* are to be exported (2,170: the last word).

Secondly, the emperor Domitian holds together the idea of the censorious deviant and the high-society deviant. References to his censorship recur at 30, 40, 63, 121, that is in the first section of the first part, in the middle, and in the last section of the second part. Domitian is a favourite target, notably in Satire 4, both in himself and as a symbol.

Thirdly, as Stegemann has well shown, Laronia's speech anticipates the detailed descriptions which follow, or, if you like, the detailed descriptions echo and confirm Laronia's speech. Note especially her assault on effeminate attire (41), homosexual practices (50), feminine activities (54). This balance holds the two main parts of the poem together.

Fourthly, as Anderson has demonstrated, military imagery holds the poem together from first to last.

Fifthly, as Anderson has again shown, the word *turpis* is a key word, which contrasts with the professions of the Stoics and the traditions of Rome, and forms a kind of thread on which the *exempla* are strung as beads. Note it at 9, 71, 83, 111. Where the word does not appear the idea is sometimes implicit or represented by a synonym.

There is fine writing in the satire. The rhetorical list of the villains blaming their own villainy (24-8) is wittily and excellently done; *perluces* (78) is an excellent touch; the description of infection has been admired, quoted, and imitated (78-81); *nemo repente fuit turpissimus* (83) is one of J's best epigrams. There are sonorous lines (114, 145), forming a contrast with other deliberately harsher effects round about. The climax of the last two lines is contrived with careful skill.

So too the visual pictures on which J depends so much. We *see* the frowning Stoics; we *see* Laronia laughing at them. We see the queans making up their brows and eyes till they flutter; we see Otho in his general's tent with a mudpack on his face; we see Gracchus at his shameful 'marriage'.

And the final ironical twist is brilliant.

Bibliography

Anderson, W. S. 'Studies in Book I of Juvenal' *YCS* 15 (1957) 45-55

Consoli, S. 'La satira II di Giovenali nella tradizione della cultura sino alla fine del medio evo' *RFIC* 42 (1914) 209-48.

Ercole, P. *Studi Giovenaliani* Lanciano 1935 pp. 185-221

Lelièvre, P. J. 'Juvenal: Two Possible Examples of Word-Play' *CP* 53 (1958) 241-2

Martyn, J. R. C. 'Juvenal 2, 78-81 and Virgil's Plague' *CP* 55 (1970) 49-50

Michel, A. 'Juvénal, Héliodore et le tribun d'Arménie' *REL* 41 (1963) 315-27

Stegemann, W. *De Juvenalis dispositione* Weyda 1913

SATIRE 3

Samuel Johnson entitled his masterly imitation 'London', Boileau less concisely, and in two separate satires, turned the city into Paris, and if we were to give the original a title it would surely be 'Rome'. It is an indictment of urban life, especially as it affects the poor but freeborn Roman, put into the mouth of one Umbricius.

The structure is loose, but is something as follows:

But of course J is not a tidy writer, and he is continually reverting to a theme once stated. For example, the rich–poor contrast returns at 212, 239, by implication 260 (*uolgi*), 284.

1-20 *My friend is right to leave Rome for the deserted countryside. Anything is better than the danger from jerry-built houses — and poets. Even the sacred spot where he left the city is taken over by immigrants or made artificial.*

1 *digressu:* an interesting beginning to a satire on Rome. J makes his prime point immediately. The only way to be a Roman is to leave Rome. Motto and Clark (*TAPA* 96 (1965) 269) say well that Umbricius is in essence Rome itself; it is not he who is abandoning the City but the City which abandons its true people.

ueteris: like our 'old', either 'old in years' or 'of long-standing'.

confusus: 'upset'.

amici: at 3,21 J calls him Umbricius. He is J's mouthpiece, but J could hardly put into his own mouth overwhelming reasons for leaving Rome — and then stay. Martial did leave, and wrote J his praises of country life (12,18). It is a mistake to identify Umbricius with the *haruspex* of Pliny (*NH* 10,6,19) and Tacitus (*Hist.* 1,27).

2 *uacuis:* emphatic in position. There had been a drift from country to town, much as is happening in parts of Africa today: the satirist exaggerates it. But J is early making one of his main points: the city is too crowded.

sedem figere: the words fit appropriately in the middle of *uacuis . . . Cumis.*

Cumis: Cumae stands on the bay of Naples: it was the oldest Greek colony in Italy, being settled in the eighth century BC, and Naples (Nea-polis, the new city) was founded from there. The citadel is very impressive.

3 *destinet:* 'he intends', causal subj. In Russian *stany* = I intend.

unum: implying that she has no others.

Sibyllae: the Sibyl was a prophetess, whose ecstatic utterances were believed to be inspired. Sibyls were found in several parts of the Mediterranean — Varro lists ten (Lact. *Inst.* 1,6,8-12). The Sibyl of Cumae was probably the most famous: there is a splendid description of a consultation in Verg. *A* 6,77-102. The grotto of the Sibyl with its long cavernous corridors and places for lustration is still numinous and awesome.

4 *ianua:* we too use 'door' metaphorically.

Baiarum: Baiae was a famous bathing resort on the bay west of Naples. Duff calls it 'the Roman Brighton'.

4-5 *amoeni secessus:* genitive of quality; cf 15,76; Hor. *S* 1,1,33 *paruola . . . magni formica laboris.*

5 *Prochytam:* a barren island off the coast not far from Baiae.

Suburae: valley between the Viminal and Esquiline hills in Rome notorious for noise, filth and crime. Martial, in retirement in Spain, pictures J wandering restlessly through the shouting streets of Subura (12,18,1-2).

6 *miserum . . . solum:* strong irony here. J will show that the vileness and loneliness in Rome are far worse than in Cumae.

7 'that you do not think it worse to be scared of fires, the continual collapse of buildings, etc.' Fires were not infrequent, as the buildings were of wood, and pack-a-jam together; Augustus built up a fire-brigade of 7000, but this did not avert the disastrous fire of Nero's reign, and another under Titus.

lapsus: he develops this at 3,190-6.

8 *saeuae:* note the personification of Rome, a brutal mistress, like the matron of 6,474ff.

9 *Augusto:* swelteringly hot.

recitantes . . . poetas: the *recitatio* was introduced by Asinius Pollio under Augustus. It was a formal presentation of a poem or poems before an audience. It served for fairly unobtrusive censorship. It could be the occasion for valuable critical judgement; it could also lead to an excess of rhetoric, a parade of learning, a melodramatic desire to shock, brilliant epigrams and the like. Many of the virtues and vices of 'silver' Latin are due to the *recitatio* — including J's. Attending the *recitatio* might be part of a dependant's duty to his *patronus.* J brings in the poets fairly early in this satire: they appear right at the beginning of the first satire. Here they form a humorous, bathetic climax to the perils of the capital.

10 *tota . . . una:* contrasting words at beginning and end: the possessions are not large.

raeda: a four-wheeled wagon, waiting at the city-gate for the goods to be brought down by hand, since wheeled traffic, except for contractors' lorries and ceremonial processions, was not allowed within the city in daylight, a regulation towards which urban centres seem to be returning.

11 *ueteres arcus:* the arches of the *aqua Marcia* (144 BC), the first of the aqueducts to make extensive use of arches.

madidam Capenam: the *porta Capena* was a southern gate for *Via Appia* to leave for Capua: *madidam* because of the dripping from the aqueduct. So Martial (whom J may, as often, have in mind) *Capena grandi porta qua pluit gutta* (3,47,1).

12 *nocturnae:* note the Roman idiom: we say 'by night'.

Numa: the legendary second king of Rome, noted for his piety. He stands for the ancient Roman virtues, whose loss J deplores.

constituebat: 'dated'. J is taking off traditional history in the manner of Sellar and Yeatman or Richard Armour.

amicae: 'his girlfriend'. This is the nymph Egeria, Numa's inspiration, and in some traditions his consort. Livy in telling the story characteristically confounds two versions. In one Numa invents his meeting with the nymph to back up his reforms (1,19); in the other she is his wife and he invents meetings between her and the Camenae, goddesses of inspiration (1,21).

13 *fontis:* apparently a spring in the valley outside the walls, Plutarch (*Numa* 13) says that Numa consecrated the meadows to the Muses (i.e. the Camenae), and set the spring apart as holy water for the Vestal Virgins.

nemus: a glade or grove, an open space surrounded by trees, often regarded as the abode of a divinity. We have to remember that the countryside was replete with divine powers: when Vergil speaks of *divini gloria ruris* (G. 1,165) he means 'the majesty of the gods' own countryside'. Diana's sacred grove at Aricia is a good example; Lucan has a horrific account of one in Germany (3,399-452). Roman authors continually refer to the sense of divine presence suddenly assailing them in a grove (e.g. Verg. A 8,352; Ov. *Am.* 3,1,1; 3,13,7); travellers walking through the African 'bush' have experienced the same sensation.

14 *Iudaeis:* the first indication of the nationalism and xenophobia which form a part of J's satire. The Jews were expelled from the capital under Claudius, but there must have been a major incursion after the fall of Jerusalem in AD 70, and despite punitive taxation by the Flavians the community remained strong. They were unpopular, partly because of their different customs, the refusal to eat pork, circumcision and Sabbath-observance, partly because of their refusal to participate in Roman religious observance, partly because of political tensions. They hire this sacred grove for a place of prayer (*proseucha* cf 3,296). The synagogues are often called *proseuchae*; if there was no building the faithful met in the open near

running water (Acts 16:13).

quorum . . . supellex: 'whose worldly wealth amounts to a basket and some straw'. J's use of a Greek word is deliberate: he wants the thing to sound alien. He uses *cophinus* and *fenum* of the Jews again at 6,542. *Cophinus* was a basket for collecting scraps (Matthew 16:9); our words 'coffin' and 'coffer' both come from it. Some interpreters think that *cophinus* and *fenum* should be taken closely together to mean a picnic basket packed with hay to keep the food warm on the Sabbath when cooking was not permitted; it scarcely sounds effective, but apparently is (R. L. Dunbabin in *CR* 39 (1925) 112). Better is the idea that they sell eggs at the gate: straw was used to protect eggs (11,70-1) and by sellers at this very gate (Mart. 3,47,14).

15-6 'Every tree is under strict orders to pay rent to the Roman people; the Camenae have been thrown out; the whole forest's turned beggar.' The general sense is clear, less so the precise import. An implicit pun between *fenum* and *fenus* forms a link with the money-theme. The Jews had to pay for the use of the grove; they included anyway numbers of beggars. The trees were identified with their former occupants, the Camenae, now with the Jews. Notice that words like *caudex, stipes, truncus* were terms of abuse like our 'blockhead'. For the Camenae see on 3,12.

17-8 *speluncas dissimiles ueris:* 'obviously artificial grottoes', creating a 'sacro-idyllic' scene, such as we see in wall-paintings.

18 *praesentius: praesens ades* was a standard prayer.

esset: the imperfect subjunctive means 'it would be if grass channelled the waters' (but it doesn't).

20 *ingenuum:* 'natural'.

21-57 *Umbricius said 'There's no room for integrity in Rome. So I'm off to Cumae while I've still some life left in me, and leave Rome to the crooks, liars, flatterers, go-betweens, conspirators, and blackmailers.*

21 *quando:* 'since'.

artibus: 'skills'. *Ars* is seldom to be translated 'art'; it is closer to 'science', 'craft', 'expertise'.

honestis: the *venue* is significant. The city stretches its tentacles a little outside the walls, but from this point Umbricius will get free: In the city things are not straightforward: Jewish beggars replace the Camenae; a place naturally numinous has been urbanised, sophisticated and spoiled.

23 *res:* assets, money, resources.

here: the form *heri* was by now obsolete, as we learn from Quintilian (1,7,22).

eadem: i.e. *res* 'and those same assets will wear away something tomorrow from the scanty residue.' The expression seems strained, and it is hard to be certain that the manuscripts are right; *res* is an awkward subject to *deteret,* and at 16,50 *res atteritur,* which is more natural. The offbeat rhythm at the end of the line expresses something of the harshness of Umbricius's feelings.

24   *deteret:* i.e. *deteri patietur.*

25   *Daedalus:* the legendary inventor of 1,54. He invented wings to enable himself and his son Icarus to escape from Crete. Icarus crashed. Daedalus landed safely in Cumae. J likes these allusive, riddling descriptions of places; cf 3,117 Tarsus.

26-8   four clauses of increasing weight and baroque effect: Highet compares 1,22-9. Umbricius leaves, J writes satire.

27   *Lachesi:* with Clotho and Atropos one of the three Fates, Moirai or Parcae, who determine, spin and sever the thread of each individual's destiny.

torqueat: 'for her to spin'.

29-30   *Artorius et Catulus:* unknown as individuals, but their characters are clear enough. The indictment which follows is at first sight surprising; business enterprises associated with temple-building, river-control, harbour-construction, cleaning out the sewers, and public funerals, do not seem so highly reprehensible. But (a) J is taking the line of traditional Roman upper-class moralism. Senators were legally debarred from trading. To old Cato gentleman-farming was the only occupation worthy of a gentleman, trade and business were dubious, and moneylending as bad as murder (Cato *Agr.* pref.; Cic. *Off.* 2,25,89). So the landed aristocracy in Britain looked down on the manufacturers. (b) No doubt there were profiteers, and this led to a general revulsion from the whole profession; there was a similar revulsion from building speculators in the 1970s in England. Responsibility for public works was formerly in the hands of aediles, but under the Empire *curatores* were appointed from the senate, who passed the actual work on to contractors.

nigrum in candida: a proverbial expression (Ov. *M* 11,314).

32   *siccandam eluuiem:* i.e. cleaning out the sewers, for which the contractors employed convict labour. Trajan (Plin. *Ep.* 10,32,2) includes this in *ministeria quae non longe a poena sunt.*

33   'and to offer their own persons for sale at an ownership auction'. The *hasta,*

spear, a relic of sales of war-booty, marked the auction, and was the sign that *dominium* was officially transferred. What were these city-slickers up to? Either they were selling themselves, investing the money, and then buying back their freedom with a profit, or they were selling themselves and subsequently showing some legal flaw in the transaction, or they were going through a fraudulent bankruptcy deal, when they had plenty of resources stashed away to recover their independence.

34-8   'These people who once played in the band at gladiatorial displays and were always there at the arena in the country-towns, and were familiar for their puffed-out cheeks in all the centres of population, now put on shows themselves, and kill a man democratically when the crowd turn their thumbs inward and give the order; and then go back and buy up the right to claim the takings from the public lavatories.' There are some problems. The *cornicines* seem to have played incidental music to accompany the 'entertainment'. *Arena* is the sand and so the arena. The construction of *buccae* is not certain; rather than accept a change of construction ('and their puffed-out cheeks are familiar') it is probably better to suppose that *bucca* was a nickname; they are the well-known 'cheeks' or well-known (gender attracted) as 'cheeks'. Only *equites* had the right to present shows; Martial (3,16) also attacks parvenus who aspire to social position in this way. The crowd gave their verdict on a beaten gladiator by a gesture of the thumb: *premere pollicem* for life, *vertere pollicem* for death. But just what the gestures were is not clear. Probably *premere pollicem* is to press the thumb forward and upward, *vertere* to turn it down and towards the body.

populariter: generally taken as meaning 'to gain popularity', but the meaning is not paralleled, and it seems more likely that J is suggesting that the sponsor of the spectacle is in fact just one of the common mob himself. For the 'shows' see Sen. *Ep.* 95,33 *homo, res sacra homini, iam per lusum et iocum occiditur.*

38   *foricas:* small public lavatories by the roadside, at which you could 'spend a penny'. He collected the pennies.

cur non omnia?: sc *faciant.* Why should they not be as indifferent to real value as Fortune?

39   *magna ad fastigia rerum:* high rhetoric, for purposes of deflation.

40   *Fortuna:* a goddess at Rome, often portrayed unstably standing on a wheel. She

was originally a fertility goddess (from *ferre*); at Praeneste and Antium she had oracular power; she became assimilated to the Greek Tyche, basically Chance, Luck. J is sarcastic about her: *nos te,/nos facimus, Fortuna, deam* (14,315).

41 The climax of this part of the satire, and one of J's finest effects. The whole section which follows has been much admired. It appealed to the Renaissance rhetoricians; it finds an echo in Rostand's *Cyrano de Bergerac* (2,8). The succession of lines ending in two-syllable words, the first two after a heavy pause, is especially compelling: we have a sense of 'What? Another?' Note that Umbricius does not think beyond dependence. J is obsessed by the *patronus-cliens* relationship, and his satiric point is 'There is no honest independent work to be had in Rome.'

faciam: 'am I to do', deliberative subjunctive. J takes this from Mart. 3,38,13-4: *'quid faciam? suade: nam certum est uiuere Romae.'* / *si bonus es, casu uiuere, Sexte, potes.*

mentiri nescio: we say 'I don't know how to tell lies.' The inf., being a verb-noun, can be the direct object of *nescio.*

librum: the ultimate danger for J; cf 1,1;3,9.

42 *motus astrorum:* for astrological purposes; cf 6,553-71; 14,248. The words *funus promittere patris* (note the alliteration) explain this.

44 *ranarum uiscera:* not poisoning but for magic or divination.

45 *quae mittit:* 'the presents'.

46 *quae mandat:* 'the messages'. The asyndeton between the two phrases is effective.

47 *comes:* a member of the staff of a provincial governor; *exeo* is also a technical term.

48 'like a cripple with a paralysed right hand, a useless body.' We must supply *homo. Extinctae dextrae* is genitive of quality, parallel to *mancus; corpus non utile* is probably best taken in apposition with the subject. His moral scruples are as debilitating as physical injuries for the governor's purposes. We have plenty of evidence from the end of the Republic (e.g. Catullus) that the staff were expected both to help feather the governor's nest and to feather their own.

49 *diligitur:* 'wins confidence'.

conscius: 'party to crime': Mart. 6,50,5 *uis fieri diues, Bithynice? conscius esto.*

cui: two short syllables as at 7,211; Mart. 1,104,22; 8,52,3; 11,72,2; 12,49,3; Sen. *Tro.* 852; *Ag.* 146.

feruens aestuat: a common metaphor, consistently extended.

52 *secreti:* noun.

53 *carus erit Verri:* a cynical judgement. C. Verres was the notorious propraetor of Sicily 73-70 BC, brilliantly prosecuted by Cicero and exiled to Massilia, to be proscribed in 43 BC by Antony who was after the fruits of his earlier thefts. He became the type of the corrupt governor; still, it is interesting that J does not pick on someone nearer his own day. The repetition *Verri . . . Verrem* is an example of the rhetorical device of *uariatio.*

54 *tanti:* genitive of value (Woodcock 86-7): 'do not value wealth so highly as to lose your sleep over it.' Duff well says that the subject of *tanti est* is the prize we wish to gain, and the *ut*-clause the price we have to pay; but that in a later form of the construction the two are precisely reversed (as 13,95). Montaigne (17) quotes this passage and adds 'I am of a humour that, life and health apart, there is nothing for which I will beat my brains at the price of vexation and constraint.'

opaci: usually 'shady' 'wooded' but here surely 'turbid'.

55 *Tagi:* river of Spain and Portugal, the modern *Tajo* or *Tejo,* celebrated as one of the rivers where you could pan for gold.

56 *ponenda:* gerundive 'which you will later have to part with'.

57 *tristis:* take with what follows: 'and be troubled because you are an object of fear . . . '. For postponed *et* see 1,57;6,422; 9,108;15,20.

amico: amicitia was part of the formal language of political alliance, a fact vital to the understanding of Catullus's poems.

58-125 *'Principally I want to get away from the Greeks. They flood our country and everybody apes them. They come from all over the place, and will take on any job for the price of a meal. They oust the true-born Roman. They are consummate flatterers, actors off the stage. They are over-sexed and hold no one sacred. They are philosophers and informers. Roman dependants are simply pushed out.'*

58 *gens:* 'nationality'

60 *pudor:* 'politeness' conveys the sense reasonably well; J has in mind the obligation of *hospitium,* the welcome to strangers.

Quirites: 'citizens of Rome', ironical, and in sharp contrast to *Graecam.*

61 *Graecam:* there were many Greeks in Rome. Some of them had, as freedmen, risen to positions of considerable power, e.g.

Pallas and Narcissus under Claudius. Some
were professional men, doctors and artists.
Some were no doubt, as J suggests, among
the unemployed, and ready to turn their
hand to anything. See N. K. Petrocheilou
Roman Attitudes to the Greeks Athens
1974; A. Wardman *Rome's Debt to Greece*
London 1976.

quamuis . . . Achaei?: 'And yet what a
small section of our dregs are Greeks!'
Achaei (sc. *sunt*) is nom. pl.: Achaea was the
official name for the province of Greece. So
Lucan describes Rome as *mundi faece
repletam* (7,405), and Tacitus says that
everything shameful and abominable crowds
into Rome from all sides (*Ann.* 15,44). This
then was a standard upper-class view. The
fact of foreign settlement is amply attested
elsewhere. Athenaeus even says that there
are more cities in Rome than days in the
year — complete tribes have settled there *en
masse;* he instances Cappadocians, Scythians,
and peoples from Pontus (1,20c). But
although J goes on to the Syrian element the
ultimate point of the satire is that the
Romans themselves are un-Roman, and we
should not forget that Cicero calls the
indigenous city-mob *faex Romuli* (*Att.*
2,1,8;cf. 1,16,11. *QF* 2,9,5). Note how
Achaei and *Orontes* echo rhythmically
Quirites, with which they contrast.

62   A magnificent image. The Orontes
(today Nahrel-Asi) is the river on which the
great cosmopolitan city of Antioch stood; it
is used here to convey the Near East gener-
ally. The author of the commendatory
verses 'The Church Militant' prefixed to
George Herbert's 'The Temple' had J in
mind when he wrote 'Now *Seine* is swallow-
ing *Tiber;* if the *Thames,*/By letting in them
both pollute her streams.' Elsewhere J
speaks of Syrian litter-bearers (6,351) and
innkeepers (8,159).

63   *tibicine:* Horace (*S* 1,2,1) calls the
flute-girls *ambubaiae:* they probably began
to come to Rome after Rome's first mili-
tary incursions into the East in the early
second century BC, and no doubt appeared
in larger numbers after Pompey's settlement.

chordas obliquas: the *sambuca,* much like
our harp.

64   *gentilia tympana:* tambourines, used
in the worship of Cybele, 'native'.

65   *circum:* the Circus Maximus, a well-
known haunt of prostitutes (6,582-91;
Cyprian *Spect.* 5).

iussas: by their owners, who got the pro-
ceeds of their prostitution.

prostare: cf 1,47.

66   *ite:* to the racecourse.

picta: 'embroidered'.

lupa: lit. a she-wolf, applied to a prosti-
tute. Lactantius (1,19) says *lupa, id est
meretrix.* The brothel is called *lupanar* (the
wolves' den).

mitra: 'turban' or 'head-tie', associated by
the Romans with Lydians and Phrygians. In
Verg. *A* 4,216 it is applied scornfully by
Iarbas to the Trojan Aeneas's clothes;
Servius, commenting on the passage says
*multa enim lectio mitras proprie meretricum
esse docet.* Our word 'mitre' comes from it.
Note the pattern of long and short *a* in this
line.

67   *rusticus:* even the conservative country
folk.

trechedipna: from two Greek words
τρέχειν, δεῖπνον, 'run (to) dinner', either
the ancient equivalent of evening shoes
or of a tuxedo. The word is applied to
a parasite (cf 1,139) by Plutarch (*Symp.*
8,6,1). The ridiculous Greek words are used
for their alien effect.

Quirine: the very Roman name contrasts.
Quirinus was an ancient god worshipped on
the Quirinal, in early Rome third in the
pantheon after Jupiter and Mars, and later
identified with Romulus. The word is per-
haps Sabine (D. Hal. 2,48). The name
Quirites (3,60) of the Roman citizens in
their peaceable capacity is cognate. Note
the sequence of endings *Quirites: Achaei:
Orontes: . . . : Quirine.*

68   A beautifully-shaped line with the
short Latin words interspersed with the two
long alien Greek words. *Niceteria* are prizes
for victory: but these were normally crowns
for the head, sacrificial animals, or monetary
rewards, and unless he is referring to gar-
lands of some kind it is more likely that J is
confused and means *nicetica,* which are
charms to ensure victory, and might well be
worn round the neck. *Ceroma* is a com-
pound of wax with oil and earth, with which
athletes rubbed their bodies before wrestling:
all such sports were of course performed
naked. Reinmuth in *Phoenix* 21 (1967)
191-5 argued that *ceroma* is a special wrest-
ling-surface. *Ceromaticus* is rare.

69   *alta Sicyone:* a well-known town in
the Peloponnese. The main residential area
was in the plain, but Demetrius Poliorcetes
at the end of the fourth century BC razed
the residential area to the ground and re-
moved the citizens to the acropolis (DS 20,
102)

Amydone: a town in Macedonia,
mentioned in Homer.

70   *Andro:* an island in the Aegean.

ille: there is no distinction here between

the use of *hic* and *ille:* different Greeks are flocking from all over Greece.

Samo: an island of major importance off the coast of Asia Minor. Note the hiatus at *Samo, hic,* made easy by the punctuation break: see on 1,151. But the point here is a burlesque of Verg. *A* 1,16 where exactly the same hiatus occurs.

Trallibus . . . Alabandis: towns of Asia Minor (Tralles, Alabanda). Ironically, Tralles was a field for immigrants from Italy under the early Empire. By J's time there was a Christian church there.

71 *Esquilias: Esquiliae* = Mons Esquilinus, one of the 'seven hills' to the east of the city. Early, there was a burial ground for the lower classes there. Claudius executed immigrants who tried to pass as Roman citizens on the hill, presumably outside the walls (Suet. *Claud.* 25); there may be a touch of irony in J's reference. Later it became a very fashionable area, but not in J's time, though the Gardens of Maecenas on the site of the old cemetery, added tone to the area.

uimine: Viminalis Collis, another of the seven hills, on the north-east side, named after a willow-copse. *Viminalis* ($- \cup - \cup$) will not fit into a dactylic line. The Viminal is not much mentioned in our sources, and was presumably a lower-class area of settlement. There is a contrast between the ghettoes in which they settle, and their achievement (in the next line).

72 *uiscera:* lit. the internal organs, so the child born from them. The Greeks get themselves adopted into noble families.

domuum: a keyword for Romans: in more aristocratic days the word 'house' carried the same connotation.

domini: nom. pl. 'heads of the houses'.

73 *ingenium:* lit. 'something inborn', here 'native wit'. Supply *est illi* 'The Greek possesses'.

perdita: 'lost'; here in a moral sense, 'criminal'.

74 *Isaeo:* not the great Athenian fourth-century orator, but an Assyrian who came to Rome in AD 97 in his sixties. Pliny says that he surpassed his reputation; he was impressed by his capacity to speak impromptu and by the fullness of his delivery (Plin. *Ep.* 2,3; Philostrat. V. *Soph.* 1,20,1; Suidas ad nom.).

ede: 'Say': Dr Ede, Dean of Worcester at the end of Elizabeth's reign, has a punning epitaph using this word, his own name, and *(a)ede* ('church'): *'Ede quis es.' 'Ede.' 'Ede cur hic.' 'Quia praefuit aedi.'* Note the sharp break before the fifth foot ('bucolic diaeresis').

illum: 'the Greek', generalised.

75 *secum:* he brings along with him anyone you like', i.e. 'in his own person' but it spoils the point so to translate it. Dryden had this passage in mind in his characterisation of Buckingham: 'A man so various that he seem'd to be/Not one, but all mankind's epitome:/Stiff in opinions, always in the wrong,/Was everything by starts and nothing long;/But in the course of one revolving moon,/Was chymist, fiddler, statesman, and buffoon.' ('Absalom and Achitophel' 545)

76-7 One of J's most famous passages, a breathless catalogue of professions. The insertion of one or two Latin words (*pictor, augur, medicus:* note how they alternate) is far more effective than a string of pure Greek: the Greeks are infiltrating into Latin. The sound patterns are carefully contrived: notice among others *grammaticus . . . geometres; rhetor . . . pictor; pictor . . . aliptes; geometres . . . aliptes . . . schoenobates; medicus magus.*

grammaticus: roughly 'secondary school teacher'.

rhetor: roughly 'college lecturer'.

geometres: probably in the lit. sense of 'land surveyor' but perhaps 'mathematician': three syllables — gĕōmetres, though Friedländer argues for $\cup \cup - -$.

pictor: 'painter'. It certainly seems that the vast majority of artists in Rome were Greek.

aliptes: from a Greek word meaning 'to anoint the skin with oil'. The athletics coach who saw that this was done, and so applied also the humbler office of bath-attendant or masseur; he reappears at 6,422.

77 *augur:* from *auis* 'bird', a seer or diviner who used the observation of birds, and so any prophet or fortune-teller.

schoenobates: 'tightrope walker', acrobats who danced on a tightrope. There is a Latin word *funambulus,* but J does not want to imply that it is a Roman thing to do.

medicus: the Romans depended on immigrant physicians even more than the British. J names Themison (10,221) and Archigenes (13,98); Martial names Baccara (11,74), and we can add from other sources Alcon, Hermocrates, Herocles, Sotas.

magus: originally a Persian sage, but with our sense of magician, wonder-worker.

78 *Graeculus:* the diminutive (also used by Cicero) is a splendid touch, cutting him down to size. Amusingly, and presumably because of this passage, the emperor Hadrian, and admirer of all things Greek,

was nicknamed Graeculus *politus disciplinis canendi, psallendi, medendique scientia, musicus, geometra, pictor, fictorque ex aere uel marmore* (Aur. Vict. *Epit.* 14,2).

esuriens: the climax 'for a meal'.

in caelum iusseris ibit: J caps his climax with this superbly concise epigram. Peter Green translates 'Tell him to fly — he's airborne.' (Supply *si* with *iusseris* to understand the strict form of the sentence.)

79 *in summa:* 'in fact', driving home the point. So Plin. *Ep.* 1,12,12; 5,6,42; cf 8,4,8 (refs from Prof. G. B. A. Fletcher).

Maurus: strictly a Moor from Mauretania, but general for African.

Sarmata: from the region between the Vistula and the Don in Poland and southwest Russia. For the form cf ποιητής *poeta;* ναύτης, *nauta.*

Thrax: Thrace was just outside the Greek world.

80 *qui sumpsit pinnas:* an ingenious justification of *in caelum iusseris ibit.* Daedalus (3,25)', the pioneer of human flight, was in myth the great-grandson of the Athenian hero Erechtheus (DS 4,76). There is a punning reference to gladiators: see on 158 *pinnirapi.*

81 *conchylia:* bright purple clothes, again at 8,101. J is reacting against the spectacle of exotic dress, especially when showy and expensive, and in fact officially limited by 'sumptuary' laws. The Greek word drives the point home.

me prior ille: three word-accents in the last two feet slow up the end of the line, and emphasise the indignation.

82 *signabit:* witnesses to legal documents, such as wills, marriage-contracts and the manumission of slaves, affixed their seals in order of seniority.

toro meliore: the Romans did not sit at table; they *reclined* at full length on the left elbow, and ate with their right hand. In the classical dinner-party there was a square or nearly square table, with one side open for service, and couches along the other three sides, each with three places separated by cushions, There was a conventional order of precedence. The middle couch had precedence, then the top, then the bottom. As numbered on the diagram the order of precedence on each couch was 1,2,3, except on the middle couch, where the place of honour was 3. The host normally reclined at 1 on the bottom couch, to be next to the guest of honour. But by J's time the tables were often round, and there was a semicircular couch called *sigma* after the Greek letter, whose capital form was C (Mart.

2,60,9; 10,48,6; 14,87,1). The diners need not be nine, and the places of honour were now the two ends (*cornua*, 'horns'). We have literary evidence of six, seven, eight at a party. A fresco at Pompeii shows the sigma and round table.

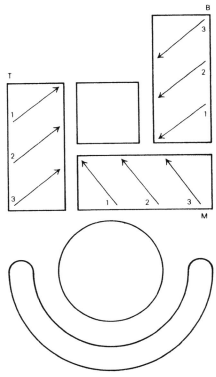

83 *pruna et cottana:* sc. *aduecta sunt. Pruna* are plums from Damascus: our word 'damson' has that derivation: *cottana* are identified by the elder Pliny (13,10,51) as figs from the same region. J's blurring of Greeks and Syrians is a little like the average European's failure to distinguish Chinese from Japanese ('they're all Easterners'), though it should be remembered that there were many Greeks settled in Syria.

84 *usque adeo nihil est:* a loose phrase. J likes *usque adeo* (5,129; 6,182; 10,201; 15,82) with an adj.; here with nihil. 'Is it so negligible . . . ?'

nostra: ambiguous between 'my' (J was not Roman-born, but Umbricius was), and 'our', generally of the indigenous but indigent.

caelum hausit: a vivid conflation of 'drank in the air' and 'looked up at the sky'.

85 *Auentini:* the most southerly of the seven hills.

baca . . . Sabina: the olive, a staple part of ancient diet. The Sabines were traditionally tough and simple-living.

86 *quid quod:* 'What of the fact that . . . ?' tr. 'What's more . . . '

adulandi . . . prüdentissima: they have a genius for flattery. The thought is taken from Martial's account of one Menogenes (12,82). The genitive is not easy to define, but definition follows usage, not the other way round. It has been explained as 'objective' (*prudens = sciens*), or as representing the field within which they show their expertise. The phrase is witty in its unexpectedness.

87 *amici:* with both *indocti* and *deformis:* a political term cf 3,57. A key word in this section: ending ll. 87, 101, 107, 112, 121.

88 *ceruicibus:* the pl. to mean 'neck' is common, but there may be an implication there that there is rather more of it with Hercules. We get the effect if we tr. 'shoulders'. There is a juxtaposition of the natural and the heroic.

89 Antaeus was a giant, son of Earth and Neptune, a champion wrestler, who lived in North Africa, and who challenged all comers, and, after defeating them, killed them. He was said to be invincible as long as he was in contact with his Mother Earth, so that throwing him strengthened him. Hercules defeated him by lifting him off the ground, and crushing him to death while in mid-air. The scene was a favourite with sculptors both in the classical era and the Renaissance.

90-1 A clumsy clause, harsh and riddling: lit. 'than which not even the male sounds worse by whom as husband the hen is being pecked.' Note that until we reach *gallina* we have not the slightest idea what he is talking about. The sudden restoration of personification at *marito* has the force of a double twist. *gallina marito* is from Mart. 13,64,1. In addition there may be an allusion to the high-pitched tones of the eunuch-priests of Cybele (*galli*), such as Martial makes in the same passage. The effect is certainly of ridicule.

92-3 An excellent epigram: 'We can offer flattery, too; they are believed.' The great satirist is always liable suddenly to look ruefully at himself — no more honest, only less efficiently dishonest.

93 The Greeks are excellent actors on stage: it is not surprising that they can play a part in real life. Male actors played female rôles in the ancient theatre.

melior: sc. *est Graecus.* Words of approba-

tion in J are often two-edged. The Greek is a better actor but not a better man. Plato's criticism of drama in *The Republic* was that it encouraged people to be for ever playing a part, instead of being consistently themselves. The perfidy of the Greeks was as proverbial as of perfidious Albion. Seventy-five expressions for it have been counted. A character in Plautus (*Asin.* 199) simply speaks of *Graeca fides;* Polybius himself (6,56) says that Greeks are not to be trusted, and Cicero (*Flacc.* 9,12) that an oath was a joke to them.

Thaida: in the *fabulae palliatae,* Latin plays derived from Greek New Comedy, named after the *pallium* or Greek cloak, characters tended to be standardised. There were three stock women's rôles, *meretrices* or whores (Thais appeared in a famous play by Menander, and in Terence *The Eunuch*), *matronae* or *uxores,* respectable wives, and *ancillae* or servants (Doris is a stock name here).

95 *palliolo:* she has taken it off to do housework.

96 *persona:* the mask, *through* which the actor's voice *sounded*

96-7 'Under that slim belly you'd say it was all smooth with nothing there except a divide with a narrow opening.'

98 *illic:* 'in Greece'.

98-9 Antiochus, Stratocles, Demetrius and Haemus were all Greek actors performing in Rome. Demetrius was noted for serious parts, gods, kindly old men, respectable elderly women, as well as young men and slaves: he had an attractive voice. Stratocles liked restless parts in which he used his voice to comic effect, old grouches, tricky slaves, parasites and pimps. Demetrius was famous for his use of gesture (*iactare manus;* cf 3,106) and expressive movement, Stratocles for his laughter, speed, and Pooh-Bah-like disappearance of his neck. (Q. 11,3,178)

99 *mollis:* the range of meaning extends from 'effeminate' to 'passionate'.

100 *natio comoeda est:* we may, perhaps, must, translate 'they are a nation of actors', but the Latin is neater.

rides: a more mannered version would be *si rides,* but subordinate clauses are a sophisticated form of simpler, more direct constructions. We may tr. 'Laugh — and . . . '

cachinno concutitur: note the alliteration, expressing the cackling, tittering laughter. The whole picture recalls Theophrastus's portrait of the flatterer who responds to a stale joke by stuffing his cloak in his mouth as if he can't hold back his laughter.

101 *amici:* cf 3,87.

102 *nec dolet:* a punch to end the phrase.
poscas: the first two have been everyday
occurrences, J now raises suppositions, 'if
you were to ask' — but the conclusion is
certain, and the main clause is indicative.

103 *endromidem:* a thick woollen
sweater: the Greek word is deliberate. It is
also used by Martial (4,19,4; 14,126). One
recalls Harpo Marx shivering in a shower of
feathers which look like snow.

104 *sumus ergo pares:* also in Mart.
2,18,2, who has also *omni/et nocte utitur
et die* at 9,62,1-2.
melior: double-edged as usual.

106 *iactare manus:* a gesture of admira-
tion, used with an actor's skill: see on 3,98-9.

107 *rectum:* adverbially, 'straight', but as
with *melior* (3,104); tinged with irony.
amicus: as on 3,87.

108 'if the golden cup turned bottom
uppermost gives a drumming sound.' The
idea seems to be that he turns his cup up-
side down and uses the hollow base as a
jerry, showing off his capacity to strike
the target. The gold is contrasted with the
use to which it is put. Martial has an epigram
(1,37) about a man who uses crystal goblets
and a gold chamber-pot so that crapping is
more expensive than eating. Others have
separated 108 from 107 and take *crepitum*
as the gurgling sound of the last drop ('No
heeltaps, chum!').

109 The exact reading is uncertain, the
meaning clear. Most of the MSS have *aut,*
which does not scan.

110 Mayor says well that the words
matrona, laris, uirgo all speak of the purity
of a Roman home, hallowed by domestic
religion.

111 *sponsus:* her fiancé.
leuis: lēuis, of chin and buttocks.

112 *horum si nihil est:* 'if none of these
is available'.
auiam resupinat amici: 'he lays his friend's
grandmother', taken from Mart. 4,5,6
where it is dropped in casually: J uses it for
a climax.

113 A weak gloss, with an awkward
change from sing. to pl., probably written
in from 3,57.

114-8 Some scholars think that this too
is an addition by an 'improver', partly
because the transition is awkward, partly
because it might seem indebted to Tacitus's
account of the events in *Ann.* 16,21-33,
which was not yet written.

114 *transi:* 'pass over', 'leave on one
side', as always in J (6,602; 7,190; 10,273).
gymnasia: lit. 'places of nakedness' since

the Greeks wore no clothes for athletic
sports. The typical mark of Greek culture
(cf Cat. 63,60), one of the chief features of
the Hellenisation of Judaea by Greek over-
lords. Trajan says to Pliny *gymnasiis indul-
gent Graeculi* (Plin. *Ep.* 10,40,2), where the
language is contemptuous. Plutarch (*Q.
Rom.* 40) says that the Romans viewed with
scorn the Greek predilection for athletics
instead of real military training. Seneca
(*Brev. Vit.* 12,2) evidently regards watching
athletics as morally corrupting, presumably
as encouraging homosexual practices.

115 *maioris abollae:* the scholiast says
that this was a proverb, but no one else
quotes it. The general effect is of our 'big-
wig'. *Abolla* was a thick cloak, worn by
philosophers (Mart. 4,53,5), soldiers (Varro
apud Nonius s.v.), royalty (Suet. *Calig.* 35),
dandies (Mart. 8,48), high officials (J 4,76
though this may be satirical). Presumably
therefore, like our 'overcoat', the term
itself is beyond class distinctions and the
man *maioris abollae,* here called *maior
abolla,* was the man who could afford the
more expensive sort. Some interpreters
would translate 'crime of a thicker texture'.
Either way it is a vivid metaphor.

116 *Stoicus:* P. Egnatius Celer was born
at Berytus and educated at Tarsus, a great
Stoic centre. He became a Stoic professor
himself. He came to Rome and became a
cliens and *amicus* of Barea Soranus. He
denounced Soranus and his daughter
Servilia for high treason and magic (Schol.
ad J 6,552) in AD 66. Tacitus has a full
account of the events (see on 3,114-8). The
informer was widely execrated, and his
condemnation under Vespasian four years
later was popular. But J is certainly here
pillorying the dead (1,171).
occidit: indirectly.
delator: the granting of rewards to in-
formers is typical of a police state. It was
started by Augustus and encouraged by
Tiberius. Titus, Nerva, and later Trajan, did
something to discourage the practice. For
another comment on the informers see 4,48.

117 *discipulumque senex:* there is a
slight problem as Barea Soranus seems to
have been older than Celer, and F. Ritter
proposed *discipulam* in reference to
Servilia. But J may not have known their
relative ages; we normally think of a teacher
as older than a student. The chiasmus and
contrasts in *delator amicum/discipulumque
senex* are excellently contrived.

118 A riddling description of Tarsus:
such periphrases are introduced for variety,
interest, and a little parade of learning.

Pegasus, the winged horse, emerged from
the blood of the Gorgon Medusa after
Perseus cut off her head. Tarsus, on the river
Cydnus, was said to be named from the
horse's hoof (ταρσός). But ταρσός can
mean feather, and J plays on that meaning.
caballi ('nag') is a piece of bathos, of
demythologising, at the end of the preten-
tious phrase.

119 *regnat: rex* was a smear-word to the
Romans, as deadly as 'communist' to the
Americans, or 'capitalist' to the Russians.
There were two reasons for this: first, the
association with the tyrannical monarchy of
the legendary Tarquins, and, second, the
association with Oriental potentates. Caesar
was murdered because he was believed to be
aspiring to *regnum;* Cleopatra was suspect as
regina (a fact to be remembered every time
Dido is called *regina* in Vergil's *Aeneid*).

120 *Protogenes:* Caligula had a lackey of
that name (D. Cass. 59,26), but it is not at
all certain that there is any reference, and
they are perhaps just general names, like our
'Smith, Brown and Robinson'.

122 *solus habet:* the isolation of these
words at the beginning of the line, and the
sharp asyndeton, are highly effective: 'he
refuses to share his patron with anyone; he
monopolises him.' In Lucan (1,290) Curio
says to Caesar (see on *regnat* 3,119) *partiri
non potes orbem,/solus habere potes.* But J
may also have in mind an epigram in which
Martial makes repeated play with the refrain
solus habes (Mart. 3,26).

122 *facilem:* note how the indictment of
the plausible Greek includes an indictment
of the gullible Roman aristocrat.

124 *summoueor:* used of the lictors
('police') 'moving the crowd along'. There is
an element of jealousy in J's attack.
perierunt: 'are wasted'.
longi seruitii: from Hor. *S* 2,5,99.

125 *nusquam:* than in Rome: 'nowhere is
a dependent dropped with less to-do', an
excellent epigram to conclude the section.

126-89 *'But this apart, the poor are in a
bad way at Rome. The rich beat us to all the
perquisites. Money talks, not good character;
it's your income they're interested in. And
the worst thing about poverty is the way
they laugh at you. You get pushed about by
children of low class who've made good.
Poverty obstructs the emergence of quality
everywhere, but it's tougher at Rome. In the
countryside you can live the simple life and
be proud of it, and you don't have to keep
up appearances, and aren't looked down on
by your neighbours. At Rome we all live*

*beyond our means, and there's a price
attached to everything.'*

126 We now leave the Greeks (*porro*),
and come to the real point. The Greeks are
not Romans — but neither are the Romans.
officium: Cic. *Fam.* 11,17 contrasts
officia, services, with *merita,* services which
establish a claim on the recipient.

127 *hic:* in Rome.
togatus: cf 1,96; the toga was worn for
official duties.

128 *lictorem:* the praetor goes in state
with his formal attendants.

129 *dudum:* from its position, with both
iubeat and *uigilantibus,* a common form of
ambiguity.
orbis: abl. pl. fem. from *orbus.* The
captatores, seeking to become adopted as
heirs of the rich, are a constant object of
satirical attack. See also 1,146; 4,19. The
words here represent the praetor's 'fevered
imagination' (G. B. A. Fletcher).

130 *Albinam et Modiam:* the *orbae,* other-
wise unknown.
salutet: the *salutatio* was the formal duty
of *cliens* to *patronus.*

131 *diuitis hic:* contrasting with *pauperis
hic* (3,127): in Rome money talks.
cludit latus: originally of the squire or bat-
man protecting the soldier's left flank, so
simply 'respectfully accompanies'.

132 *alter:* i.e. the slave.
quantum: the pay at this period is not
known, but the elder Pliny notes it as high
(*NH* 34,11); in the third century AD it was
25 000 sesterces.

133 *accipiunt donat:* pointed collocation
Caluinae uel Catienae: aristocratic names.
There was a well-known Junia Calvina in
the first century AD (Tac. *Ann.* 12, 4; Suet.
Vesp. 23; Anon. *Ludus de Morte Claudii* 8),
who was *sane decora et procax;* another
Calvina was related to the younger Pliny
(*Ep.* 2,4). The contrast between the aristo-
cratic mistresses and the city tarts is taken
from Horace (*S* 1,2,28ff).

135 *uestiti:* 'dolled up'.
136 *Chionen:* 'Snow-White', the name
of a prostitute in a number of Martial's
epigrams (1,34; 1,92; 3,30; 3,34; 3,83; 3,87;
3,97; 11,60). The name, while descriptive
of a kind of beauty, is ironical.
sella: seemingly some kind of couch
associated with brothels and prostitution
(Plaut. *Poen.* 268); the emperor Tiberius is
said to have developed *sellaria* (Suet. *Tib.*
43; Tac. *Ann.* 6,1), his own version of the
harem.
137 The corruptions of the law courts.
da: 'produce'. J likes to use an imperative

where more formal writing might use an if-clause; cf 3,78 *in caelum iusseris ibit.*

hospes: Publius Cornelius Scipio Nasica chosen by the senate as the *uir optimus* in 204 BC to escort the black betyl, which was the visible presence of the Mother of the Gods, from Pessinus to Rome (Liv. 29,11; 29,14).

138 *numinis Idaei:* 'the deity of Ida', a mountain in Phrygia, not far from Troy, where the Great Mother was worshipped.

Numa: one of the legendary kings, the type of piety: there is a pun with *numinis.* (For puns with vowel-sounds of different lengths see *Rhet. ad Herenn.* 4,29.)

139 When the Temple of Vesta caught fire in 241 BC L. Caecilius Metellus, as *pontifex maximus,* rescued the Palladium (the image of Athene—Minerva, believed to have fallen from heaven to Troy, a symbol of invulnerability). He lost his sight in the rescue (6,265).

140 Another brilliant epigram: note the chiastic shape. Supply *itur* with *ad censum.*

141 *pascit seruos:* a standard expression; cf 9,67; Sen. *Ep.* 17,3; 20,7.

142 *paropside:* lit. 'side-plate', but here generally 'plate' or 'dish'. As it is here used collectively we can simply tr. 'How large is his dinner-service?' The Greek word is deliberate: the Romans are behaving in un-Roman ways.

144 *fidei:* an unexpected parallel with *nummorum:* see on 1,113.

Samothracum: sc. *deorum.* The island of Samothrace in the north-east Aegean had a famous mystery-cult, focusing on some obscure divinities, who were identified with Castor and Pollux, or with the Cabeiri of Asia Minor. See S. Cole *The Samothracian Mysteries* (1975). The cult stood in respect second only to Eleusis at this period. The point here is that the initiates were scrupulously bound not to perjure themselves.

145 *nostrorum:* the gods of Rome. Jupiter was particularly hot on perjury.

fulmina: the sign of Jupiter's anger: *fulmina atque deos* can be taken as a hendiadys ('divine wrath').

146 A neatly-shaped line (*deos dis*), but the meaning is, perhaps deliberately, not clear. The abl. abs. at the end should have strong point. The pauper is believed to flout thunderbolts and gods — *because* the gods forgive him? *Although* the gods forgive him? The first implies 'with the connivance of the gods'; the second 'though the gods have nothing to condemn'. The second has more point, and plays on the

root-meaning of *in-gnoscere.* But there is some ambiguity.

147 *quid quod...?:* 'What of the fact that...?' i.e. Furthermore...' cf 88.

148 *hic idem:* i.e. the poor man.

149 *sordidula:* the diminutive (cf Plaut. *Poen.* 137) is an excellent touch. It was an expensive matter to keep the toga spotlessly white: the streets were muddy in winter and dusty in summer.

150 *uolnere:* we may tr. 'tear' or 'rent' but there is a metaphor, and it is a double metaphor, for the poor man, like his clothes, is wounded and scarred within.

151 *non una:* i.e. several.

152-3 One of J's most famous epigrams, alike for its direct expression, its unexpectedness and its insight. The sentiment seems derived from Crantor of Soli (Stob. *Flor.* 96,13): 'In your whole life no misfortune can fall/more pitiful than poverty. However brilliantly/endowed by nature, if poor you'll be laughed at.' cf Lucian *Nigrinus* 21.

153 *inquit:* 'says someone'. We are now in the theatre. The first fourteen rows were reserved for the *equites.* But to be an *eques* was a matter not of birth but of property: the qualification being 400 000 sesterces. So the well-born but indigent are ousted by the *nouveaux riches.*

154 *si pudor est:* 'if he's any sense of decency.' The real indecency is the expulsion of good people for want of money.

puluino ... equestri: only found here; they were normally called just *equestria* or *quattuordecim ordines.*

155 *legi:* Lex Roscia Theatralis of BC 67, reaffirmed by Domitian (Suet. *Dom.* 8). Full references in H. Hill *The Roman Middle Class* Oxford 1952 p.160.

et sedeant hic: the broken rhythm for the chucking-out. Note that *hic* retains an ambiguity: 'in this seat' but also 'in Rome'.

156 *fornice:* lit. 'arch' or 'vault', and so the brothels 'underneath the arches'.

157 *nitidus:* 'la-di-da'.

praeconis: the auctioneers might be very rich: witness Arruntius Euarestus (Jos. *Ant.* 19,1,18).

158 *pinnirapi:* the word is perhaps coined by J, lit. 'plume-snatcher'. The gladiator known as the Samnite wore a plumed helmet; his opponent would cut off the plume as a sign of victory.

iuuenes: 'sons', for the unmetrical *filios* (cf 6,262). Gladiators themselves were forbidden by law to sit in the fourteen rows.

lanistae: a contractor who specialised in training and hiring out teams of gladiators: the word was associated, perhaps rightly, with the Etruscan for 'butcher'; cf *lanius.*

159 *uano:* a slightly unexpected word. Of people it usually means 'deceitful'. The point is perhaps that Otho was trying to make a differentiation by merit but it worked out differently. So something like 'wrong-headed'.

distinxit: 'put up the barriers between us'.

Othoni: L. Roscius Otho who moved the original bill: see on 3, 155. But there is innuendo against Domitian. As often Martial has a parallel (5, 8), where it is *edictum domini deique nostri,* i.e. Domitian.

160 *gener:* predicative, 'as a prospective son-in-law'.

hic: again 'at Rome', regularly at this point in the line.

161 *sarcinulis:* 'bags and baggage', 'goods and chattels'. Mayor and Duff suggest that it is a regular term for dowry; the point is rather that it is not. J uses it here and at 6, 146. The diminutive adds to the point — 'however small'.

162 *in consilio . . . aedilibus:* the aediles, in early time superintendents of public works, came to exercise a wider jurisdiction, over the water supply, traffic, and some aspects of public order. They had therefore the right to impose fines, and might invite friends to join them as advisers in such cases. J suggests that it was a remunerative office. It is not likely to have been officially paid, though a *patronus* might give extra benefit to a *cliens* for services rendered. It is not unlikely that those acquitted or given low fines might show their gratitude.

163 *olim:* 'long ago', not a Ciceronian use. Again at 6, 346, etc.

tenues: 'of slender means'.

migrasse: J has in mind the 'secessions' of the *plebs,* who are recorded as withdrawing from the city on five occasions between 494 and 287 BC. After the Great Fire, when Nero's Golden House was spreading its tentacles over Rome, the underground press produced the epigram *Roma domus fiet: Veios migrate, Quirites — si non et Veios occupat ista domus* (Suet. *Nero* 39, 2).

Quirites: emphasising their Romanness, and contrasting with *agmine* as civilian with military display.

165 *res angusta domi:* a neat enough phrase for J to repeat (6, 357).

166 *magno:* sc. *constat.* Green (ingeniously): 'Inflation hits the rental/Of your miserable apartment'. The sentence is carefully shaped with *magno* at beginning and end.

167 *frugi cenula:* the diminutive is meaningful. *Frugi* is the dative of *frux* or

frugis, used as an indeclinable adjective 'frugal'. The dactylic *cenula* and the whole phrase contrast with the swelling long syllables of *seruorum uentres* (repeated at 14,126).

168 *fictilibus:* 'earthenware'.

quod: 'a thing which'; the antecedent is *cenare.*

169 *Marsos:* a people of Latium noted for tough, simple living. The whole phrase is an echo of and tribute to Vergil (*G* 2, 167 *Marsos pubemque Sabellum*).

Sabellam: the Sabines were hardy mountaineers living in the Apennines to the north-east of Rome. The word *Sabelli* is cognate, but used more loosely and widely. Martial describes Munatius Gallus as *simplicior priscis . . . Sabinis* (10, 33). He also has an excellent contrast between dining in Rome and in the country; *hic pretiosa fames* (it costs a lot to go hungry) *conturbatorque macellus* (the butcher bankrupts you)/*mensa ibi diuitiis ruris operta sui* (10, 96, 9-10).

170 *Veneto:* of the sort worn by the Veneti, another tribe from the countryside around Venice, but including Vergil's home town of Mantua; the Vergilian allusion in the previous line may have suggested the reference. Some editors read *ueneto,* 'bluish-green', perhaps from the colour of the northern Adriatic. The scholiast says *a colore aut a prouincia.*

cucullo: it was not normal for men to wear a hat of any kind in the city — except for disguise (6, 117).

172 *togam:* J repeatedly adverts to the inconvenience and expense of constantly wearing the *toga* at Rome. Augustus insisted on its being worn in the forum or circus (Suet. *Aug.* 40). So Martial (10, 96, 11-2), in an epigram J has here in mind, complains that he gets through four a year in the city, while one lasts four years in the country. In the country the *tunica* (our T-shirt is a reasonable parallel) was worn. Hence Martial's *tunicata quies* (10, 51, 6), who also classifies among the real blessings of life *lis numquam, toga rara, mens quieta* (10, 47, 5). The younger Pliny finds one of the charms of his villa in *nulla necessitas togae* (*Ep.* 5, 6, 45) and contrasts *togati et urbani* with *duri et agrestes* (*Ep.* 6, 30, 4).

nisi mortuus: the free Roman was dressed in the toga for his funeral. Martial (9, 57, 8) speaks of the *pallens toga mortui tribulis* ('the shiny toga of the dead down-and-out'). Magistrates were buried in the *toga praetexta* appropriate to their office (Liv. 34, 7).

ipsa: with *maiestas,* which is held up for effect; we can translate 'even'.

173 *herboso*: stone theatres were not uncommon outside Rome by now: Pompeii had two. Friedländer therefore took this to mean that the theatre was insufficiently used and grass grew between the cracks of the stones. But J is talking of the real countryside, and the old explanation that the plays were put on in a grassy dell is probably best.

quando: performances were infrequent. By contrast in Rome at the time of Claudius 159 days of the year were public holidays: on most of these there would be spectacles in the circus, theatre or amphitheatre. See J. Carcopino *Daily Life in Ancient Rome* London 1941 pp. 202-47. The country farmers had to work more solidly. So also *tandem:* they look forward to the holiday for a long time.

174 *redit:* pf., contracted from *rediit.* They do not mind the familiar play returning.

pulpita: 'stage'. Our 'pulpit' suggests a relationship between preaching and acting.

175 *exodium:* Gk ἐξόδιον, a going-out piece, a farce which followed the serious plays. It is odd that J should use a Greek term: he may not have consciously realised that it was Greek: words become easily acclimatised.

personae: the mask (lit. the thing the actor sounds through), regularly worn in ancient drama, enabling an actor to double rôles, and suggesting a connection of the origins of drama with ancestral masquerades.

pallentis: the reference is probably to the mask of Lamia, a spooky monster who would threaten to swallow children, and would be white as a death-spirit. See M. Bieber *History of the Greek and Roman Theatre* (Princeton ²1961) p. 248.

hiatum: the mask anyway had a wide mouth for the sound to emerge, but in the Lamia mask it would be very wide ('All the better to swallow you with').

176 *matris:* note the presence of women in the audience.

177 *illic:* 'in the country', by contrast with *hic.*

orchestram: the *orchestra,* the circular or semi-circular space between the stage and the audience, was the dancing-floor where the chorus performed. The Romans did not use the chorus, and therefore the orchestra was used for the seats of honour, in the capital for the senators, in the provinces for the local town council.

178 *uelamen:* an exquisitely ironical phrase: it does not veil, but reveal.

honoris: 'office'.

179 *aedilibus:* magistrates in country districts bore various titles. We know of aediles at Arpinum (Cic. *Fam.* 13, 11, 3) and Arretium (Pers. 1, 30). At Fundi they were praetors (Hor. *S* 1, 5, 34). Often they are simply referred to as *duumuiri.*

180 *hic:* back to Rome. Note the rhythm at the end of the line: three word-accents in the last two feet gives a laboured feeling: it is *aliquid plus.*

181 *aliena sumitur arca:* i.e. 'borrowed'.

182-3 *ambitiosa paupertate:* the two long words express the pretentiousness. But *ambitiosa* has a double meaning, 'pretentious' but also that they have to go round canvassing loans to keep it up. J is girding at what we call 'keeping up with the Joneses'.

183 *quid te moror?:* 'to cut a long story short' (Green).

183-4 *omnia Romae cum pretio:* 'Everything at Rome has a price attached': one of J's most brilliant epigrams. Jugurtha, a couple of centuries before, called Rome *urbem uenalem et mature perituram si emptorem inuenerit* (Sall. *Jug.* 35, 10). It is worth noting how J has refined and condensed the idea, taking *omnia cum pretio* from another part of Sallust (*ib.* 86, 3).

184 *das:* 'pay', in bribes to a string of servants.

Cossum: the scholiast, guessing, simply says 'a noble'. It would seem so at 8, 21, but at 10, 202 we meet a *captator* of that name, and J may be referring to a jumped-up flatterer who has taken his patron's name as his heir. The family belonged to the *Gens Cornelia.* The thought is from Martial 10, 10, 5.

185 *Veiiento:* we meet him again at 4, 113; 6, 113. A. Didius Gallus Fabricius Veiiento was a notorious character, as Pliny implies (*Ep.* 4, 22, 4). He was praetor in AD 55. He ran dogs instead of horses in the circus to defeat the monopoly of the contractors (DC 61, 6). Nero banished him for slander and selling offices (Tac. *Ann.* 14, 50). He was recalled and became consul under Vespasian (*CIL* 16, 158). Domitian made him consul again in 80, and a third time in 82 or 83, and an *amicus principis.* He was a notorious *delator* (Aur. Vict. *Epit.* 12). He was still in favour under Nerva. We have an inscription set up jointly with his wife in honour of a Gallic goddess (*CIL* 13, 7253; *ILS* 1010): *A. DIDIVS GALLVS/ FABRICIVS VEIENTO COS/III XVVIR SACRIS FACIEND/SODALIS AVGVSTAL SOD FLAVIAL/SOD TITIALIS ET ATTICA EIVS/NEMENTON VSLM.* It

suggests a certain religiosity in old age.

clauso . . . labello: He does not reciprocate the greeting, but at least he has noticed you.

186   *ille . . . hic:* 'one . . . another'. These are the slaves who have to be bribed. There is a nice contrast, one having his own hair cut, the next gloating over his boyfriend's curls.

deponit: as a sacrifice, no doubt to Venus. For a similar sacrifice of the hair in war see Tac. *Hist.* 4, 61; for the boyfriend handsome in the offering of his hair Mart. 7, 29, 3.

187   *libis uenalibus:* if the reading is right this must mean that little cakes have to be offered to the patron's *genius* — at a price of course.

'accipe . . . habe': with Duff I have put these words in quotation marks, addressed by the poor *cliens* to the slave: 'Take your money and keep your lump of dough.' Michael Coffey suggests to me a further implication in *fermentum:* ' — and I hope it blows you up!' Without the quotation marks we must understand a play of words in *fermentum:* 'Take and keep all for yourself the yeast of anger'.

189   *cultis:* 'fashion-conscious'.

peculia: legally slaves could not own property, but in practice they might accumulate savings with which to buy their freedom.

190-231   *'In country towns there is no fear of collapsing houses or death by fire. And when you do lose all you have in a disaster, the poor man has no redress, but the rich man gets back in voluntary contributions more than he has lost; he even sets his own house on fire for the purpose. Go to the small country towns — if you can tear yourself away from the races. You'll buy a house for less than a year's rent of a city slum; you'll grow your own vegetables. You'll be master of your property — even if it's only a single lizard.'*

190   *timet aut timuit:* a neat expression; cf 8, 70 *damus ac dedimus.*

Praeneste: In Latium, 32 km from Rome, high on a hillside, so *gelida;* Horace (*O* 3, 4, 22) calls it *frigidum* (the name is sometimes treated as neut., sometimes fem.); the modern Palestrina, from which the composer came.

ruinam: falling houses.

191   *Volsiniis:* Volsinii in Etruria, 130 km north-west of Rome, the modern Bolsena. The broken rhythm is interesting: it reminds us of the insecure buildings in Rome.

192   *Gabiis:* Gabii in Latium, about half-way to Praeneste, the modern Castiglione. It was much depopulated by the end of the

first century BC (Cic. *Planc.* 9, 23); Dionysius of Halicarnassus (4, 53) in Augustus's reign says that only the sections along the main road were inhabited. No over-crowded slums there!

proni Tiburis: also in Latium, 30 km east-north-east of Rome, on a notable hill-site, the modern Tivoli. Horace (*O.* 3, 4, 23) calls it *supinum;* whether face-down or face-up it is sun-bathing on its hilltop. As Duff says, a city on a hill may be thought of as leaning forward or backward.

193   *tenui tibicine fultam:* 'inadequately shored up'. Note the alliteration reinforcing the hyperbole.

194   *labentibus:* the buildings, occupants, or both.

195   *uilicus:* the landlord's agent.

texit hiatum: exactly as we say 'papering over the cracks'.

196   *pendente . . . ruina:* 'with collapse hanging over our heads', literally and metaphorically.

197   *incendia:* a new danger. Most of the poorer housing was of wood and close-packed. There were serious fires under Augustus in 23 BC and AD 6. There were two disastrous fires in Tiberius's reign, one on the Caelian in AD 27, and one on the Aventine in AD 37; the Great Fire of AD 64 under Nero; another under Titus around the Campus Martius, which took three days to extinguish. Later in the second century, under Commodus in AD 193, there was another devastating outbreak. After the fire of 23 BC Augustus established a fire brigade of 600 slaves. This was inadequate, and in AD 6 he replaced them by 7000 freedmen, known as *uigiles,* under the *Praefectus Vigilum;* they were organised in seven cohorts each responsible for two regions of the city, with a main station and a sub-station.

198   *nocte metus:* picks up incendia, but includes floods (Tac. *Hist.* 1, 86; Suet. *Otho* 8; Mart. 10, 85) and burglars.

poscit aquam: Our idiom is 'shouts FIRE!': *'aquam!'* was the Roman alarm.

friuola: 'bits and pieces', 'odds and ends'.

199   *Vcalegon:* your neighbour. As Aeneas watches the sack of Troy in Vergil (*A* 2, 311), *iam proximus ardet Vcalegon.* The name means 'not caring' and comes from Homer (*Il.* 3, 148). J knows that the Vergilian allusion will be recognised. You — the ordinary Roman — are the modern Aeneas, descendant of the founder — only *you* won't be able to escape. The use of proper names in this whole passage is a good example of his technique.

tabulata tibi iam tertia: strong alliteration on *t*; the teeth chattering with fear. Note too how *tertia fumant* inverts the verbal pattern of *friuola transfert. Insulae* seem to have risen to five storeys (R. Meiggs *Roman Ostia* ²1973 pp 240-1) and perhaps higher. Paupers were at the top: *tibi* does not mean that the second floor is his, but that the fire endangers him. See A. Hudson-Williams *GR* 24 (1977) 29-30.

200 *trepidatur:* impersonal passive: 'the alarm is raised'.

202 *reddunt:* 'lay'. The *us* and *os* represent the cooing of the doves. The point however is not their maddening noise: it is that there are no human voices, only the sound of rain and birds — and they are leading a normal domestic life.

203 A fresh point. The poor do not receive compensation for their losses, the rich do.

Cordo: a poor man.

Procula: presumably a dwarf.

minor: 'too small for'.

urceoli sex: the broken rhythm as usual brings in an element of contempt or bitter emphasis: the diminutive suggests that the jugs are of no value.

204 *ornamentum:* in apposition to *urceoli.*

abaci: a marble tabletop, usually used to display silver, which Cordus does not possess.

nec non: 'oh yes, and'.

paruulus: again the diminutive. The *cantharus* was a large cup; it is almost an oxymoron to speak of a tiny little one. It is pushed out of sight under the table, not on display.

205 *recubans:* 'lying on its back', i.e. with the pedestal smashed.

Chiron: the wise Centaur who tutored Achilles. J is referring to a statue.

206 *iam:* with *uetus,* almost 'pretty old'.

Graecos . . . libellos: Cordus had some culture. He could not afford long texts, but acquired and prized a few papyrus rolls. The normal form of the ancient book consisted of sheets of papyrus glued together at the margins with a rod affixed to both ends; on one of which the scroll was rolled: the scroll could then be unwound from one rod on to the other exposing one sheet at a time.

cista: the rolls were stored in a box: the technical word was *scrinium* or *capsa:* the implication is that Cordus used any old box.

207 *opici:* 'Philistine'. The Greeks called non-Greek-speakers βάρβαροι, *barbari,* or barbarians, lit. those who go 'bar-bar-bar'. Ὀπικοί was their name for the non-Greek-

speakers of central Italy, and used disparagingly in the same way. Pliny (*NH* 29, 7) quotes Cato to the effect that the Greeks called Romans both *barbari* and *opici.*

mures: 'rats'.

208 *enim:* 'surely'.

208-9 An excellent epigram, curiously reminiscent of Matthew 13:12 'the man who has not will forfeit even what he has'. Had J caught an echo of that somewhere? Or were both repeating a lost proverb? Or was it a feature of the times which two purveyors of epigrammatic wisdom expressed similarly for different purposes? Ter. *Andr.* 314 has *id aliquid nihil est.* J's variant *nil-nihil* helps to point the phrase.

211 *hospitio tectoque:* we say 'with the welcome of a roof'.

212 *Asturici:* a nobleman. The form of the name denotes the military conqueror of a region, as Trajan was called Dacicus. The Metelli went in for such names. Asturia was a province of Spain.

horrida mater: 'noble ladies tear their hair': supply *est,* and note singular for plural.

213 *pullati proceres:* 'the top brass are in mourning'. Note the scornful alliteration.

differt uadimonia: i.e. 'closes the courts'.

214 *tum:* 'then', not when the poor suffer. The use of the first person pl. at *gemimus* is ironical.

215 *ardet:* sc. *domus.*

accurrit . . . donet: 'someone is rushing up to make him a present': subj. of purpose.

216 *inpensas:* not monetary contributions, which the word does not mean, but building materials.

nuda et candida signa: marble statues of nudes.

217 *Euphranoris:* sculptor and painter of the fourth century BC, notable for works of monumental proportions. Nothing of his survives.

Polycliti: Argive sculptor of the fifth century BC, who worked in bronze and marble. A number of his works exist in later copies, including the famous *Man with a Spear,* known as the canon because of its perfect proportions. A four-syllable word at the line's end is not infrequent with foreign names.

218 *haec:* 'a lady', regarded as particularly prone to fall for eastern religions. A weighty line with internal rhyme on the accented syllables. Such lines, known as 'leonine' (probably from a forgotten poet named Leo) were very popular in medieval poetry. The reading is not certain. Housman read *praedarum* for *praeclarum,* and *aera,* for

haec, taking *ornamenta* in apposition, which could be right. Some editors on the basis of other manuscripts read *phaecasianorum* or *phaecasiatorum* in 218, referring to Greek gods wearing Greek-style shoes.

deorum: 'gods' for their temples, as in Mart. 6, 4, 4.

219 A contrast with Cordus. The poor man loses *libelli,* a *cista,* and a broken statue of Chiron; the rich man receives *libri, foruli* (shelves for several bookboxes), and a statue of Minerva to stand in the middle.

220 *modium:* strictly a corn-measure, but slangily applied to money, the idea being that the rich measured their money instead of counting it (cf Xen. *Hell.* 3,2,27; Plaut. *Stich.* 587; Hor. *S* 1, 1, 96; Petr. *Sat.* 37). This makes it probable that the reference is to money rather than silver plate.

221 *Persicus:* another aristocratic name like Asturicus (3, 212). But the two seem to be the same person. J is being sarcastic: the noble has a title of some kind — was it from Spain? or Persia? — it doesn't matter — the result is the same.

orborum: double meaning: not only 'childless' (which is why he receives help) but generally 'destitute', with bitter irony.

et merito iam: the offbeat accent reinforces the bitterness, and throws extra weight on *suspectus. iam* with *suspectus:* see on 206.

222 *tamquam:* regularly in Silver Latin for the actual grounds for suspicion.

suas incenderit aedes: taken from Mart. 3, 52 where the fraud, whose name is Tongilianus, recoups five times the cost of the house. The whole passage 212-22 is a careful elaboration of Martial.

223 *circensibus:* the chariot-races in the Circus Maximus, which accommodated a quarter of a million spectators, immensely popular, as later in Constantinople. Plays were available in the countryside, not chariot-racing. J later suggests that the man in the street wants only two things, *panem et circenses* (10, 81), and that the chief penalty of exile is to miss the races for a year (11, 53).

223-4 *Sorae ... Fabrateriae ... Frusinone:* all small towns in Latium. For the annual rent of a single dark, filthy attic in Rome you can buy a cottage in the country.

226 *hic:* 'in the countryside': at this point J wants his hearers to identify with the positive not the negative. The other will strike home harder when he returns to it with another *hic* at 232.

breuis: it is not deep, because the countryside is well-watered and the water lies near the surface: so there is no need to wind the bucket up and down.

227 *tenuis:* delicate because recently planted. But there is a double meaning in the implication that plants and people, however *tenuis* (humble, poor), can flourish in the countryside.

228 *bidentis:* objective gen.

uilicus: i.e. the man in charge.

229 *Pythagoreis:* vegetarians. Pythagoras of Samos, a shadowy figure of the sixth century BC, emigrated to southern Italy where he founded a religious community dedicated to the study of mathematics, the fostering of political moralism, and a religious mysticism centring on the immortality of the soul and its transmigration into other humans and animals in successive incarnations. (So in Shakespeare's *Twelfth Night* 4, 2, 54 'What is the opinion of Pythagoras concerning wildfowl?' 'That the soul of our grandam might haply inhabit a bird.') Hence vegetarianism. The line is a real climax, pointed by the five-syllable word at the end.

231 *unius ... lacertae:* editors rightly quote Boswell's *Life of Johnson* year 1778: 'One of the company asked him the meaning of the expression in Juvenal, *unius lacertae.* JOHNSON: "I think it clear enough; as much ground as one may have a chance to find a lizard upon." ' As lizards are all over the place in Italy, the reference is to a very small plot. Note how the two words frame the line, a stylistic device (sometimes called 'overarching word-order') much used by Catullus (e.g. 64, 5). The allusions to animals in this section are worth consideration — *columbae* (202), *mures* (207), *lacertae* (231), none unsympathetic. Only man is vile. A carefully constructed five-word line forms an artistic climax to the section.

232-67 'The noise at nights is terrible. In the morning the streets are packed. The rich man is carried comfortably in his litter while you are fighting your way through the crowds. At lunchtime you get caught up in a picnic-party — all the slaves with kitchen stoves on their heads, trotting to keep them burning. Then in the afternoon there are builders' wagons. If one collapses the load crushes the poor man. His body disappears completely. His servants are preparing for his return, but he is wandering disconsolately on the shores of Styx.'

232 This (as indicated) begins a swift run through the day: the following section moves to the period after dark.

plurimus aeger: singular, as in 1, 120.

uigilando: last syllable short. There seems to have been a tendency (easily understood) to clip the final *o* short at this period; Seneca often does it in his tragedies. J does not do it with the ablative elsewhere, though he does with *ergo* (as 1, 3), *octo* and the present ind. of verbs.

233 *inperfectus:* 'undigested', an unusual meaning.

234 *meritoria:* 'lodgings','digs'.

235 *magnis opibus:* probably instrumental ablative. For the thought see Mart. 12, 57, 3 *nec quiescendi in urbe locus est pauperi.*

dormitur: impersonal passive.

236 *inde caput morbi:* a vivid, compact phrase: *caput* is metaphorical, *morbi* both literal and metaphorical.

raedarum: a kind of four-wheeled stage-coach drawn by two or four horses. No wheeled traffic except building contractors' lorries being allowed in the city in the day-time, the nights were naturally noisy.

237 *mandrae:* a stall or pen for keeping animals. J uses it wittily to refer to the animals, held up so long (*stantis*) that they might be in their stalls, and bleating or lowing their indignation (*conuicia*): others refer *conuicia* to the herdsman.

238 *Druso:* the emperor Claudius (Ti. Claudius Drusus Caesar) who was alleged to sleep through the law-suits he was judging (Suet. *Claud.* 8; 33).

uitulisque marinis: seals. The elder Pliny (*NH* 9, 15) says *nullum animal grauiore somno premitur.* The implication is that Claudius was a dumb brute too.

239 *si uocat officium:* precisely 'if duty calls'.

240 *Liburna:* a battle-cruiser used by the Liburni who lived in what is now Yugoslavia, used by J as a hyperbolic image of a litter. The image is helped by the fact that Liburnian slaves might be used on litters, but *Liburna* for a litter is an original conceit.

241 The elder Pliny always employed his journeys in this way, and criticised his nephew for wasting time by walking (Plin. *Ep.* 3, 5, 15-6).

242 *clausa... fenestra:* window-glass was known but not much used. There were shutters of talc (*lapis specularis* cf *specularibus* 4, 21). But heavy curtains would be enough to produce a fug.

243 *tamen:* probably taking up the last point: 'even asleep he'll race us'.

244 *unda:* an obvious but good image: walking through a crowd is rather like wading in deepish water.

prior: 'in front'.

245 *assere:* the pole of a litter.

246 *at:* 'worse still'; it is used to add a climactic horror.

metretam: a barrel holding about forty litres.

247 *luto:* Only the main thoroughfares were paved, and they would accumulate a lot of mud, horse dung, slops and rubbish; the side streets must have been terrible. In Pompeii there are stepping-stones to cross the roads.

planta: sing. for pl., but it's as if the crowd has a collective foot.

248 *digito:* 'toe'.

clauus: soldiers wore nailed boots.

249 *sportula:* not, seemingly, despite the scholiast, the dole offered by *patronus* to *cliens,* which makes no sense here, but a kind of picnic (Suet. *Claud.* 21).

251 *Corbulo:* Cn. Domitius Corbulo, consul, and son of a consul, an able military commander and stern disciplinarian, who served with notable success in Germany and the East before being driven to suicide by Nero in AD 67. He was a great bull of a man, *corpore ingens* (Tac. *Ann.* 13, 8).

253 *cursu uentilat ignem:* a vivid picture. The fuel would be charcoal.

254 *coruscat:* 'judders', but the Latin is more vivid. As in 1, the effect is cinematographic, a swift succession of short animated sequences. The whole picture parodies Vergil's picture of a falling tree (*A* 2,626-9).

255 *serraco:* 'cart', not a literary word (Quint. 8, 3, 21). Builders' wagons were allowed in Rome in daytime.

altera... plaustra: 'a second wagon'; the plural is a poetic convenience.

257 *saxa Ligustica:* marble from Luna, on the borders of Etruria and Liguria, near Carrara: this was the best Italian marble.

258 *montem:* a striking image. Note the 'moaning' of the *ms* and *ns* in *agmina montem.*

259 *ossa:* involving a pun with *montem,* since Ossa was one of the mountains the Titans piled up to scale the sky.

260 *uolgi:* No one bothers about the bodies of the poor.

261 *more animae:* in Homer the soul vanishes like a dream (Hom. *Od.* 11, 222). With the poor man involved in an accident the body does too.

domus: his household. Again a succession of photographic images, But it comes as a shock to find that J's poor downtrodden Roman none the less has his own slaves.

Horace, who lived simply, had three to wait on him at dinner (*S* 1, 6, 116).

secura: derived from *sine cura.*

262-3 *sonat unctis striglibus:* it was normal practice to take a bath before dinner. The Greeks and Romans used olive oil for soap and scraped it off with a strigil of wood, bone or metal. Here they are of metal (*sonat*). It looks as if the servants have only just got round to cleaning the scrapes from the previous day's bath. The shortened form *striglibus* is another example of language change; there is a tendency to eliminate central short vowels. Mayor draws attention to *angulus,* angle; *frigidus, froid; calidus, chaud.*

263 *lintea:* linen towels.

guto: a small narrow-necked flask for the oil.

264 *at ille:* the standard position to emphasise this phrase in a hexameter.

265 *in ripa:* of the Styx, the river encircling the world of the dead: there are echoes of Vergil's picture of the scene in *Aen.* 6.

nouicius: as a new slave. We have just seen his old slaves. He, recently free, is now the slave of death.

266 *porthmea:* a Greek form, acc. sing. masc., 'ferryman', Charon, the mythical ferryman of the dead.

nec sperat: the unburied were not permitted to enter the world of the dead, and left wandering on the nearer shore, and haunting the earth as ghosts.

caenosi: ancient sources make much of the muddy approaches to the underworld, e.g. Ar. *Frogs* 273.

alnum: the alder tree was used for shipbuilding.

267 *porrigat:* 'to proffer', subj. of purpose.

trientem: the fare for the ferry, placed between the teeth at burial. J did not take these myths seriously (2, 149-54). But others did, and it is a mistake to see a whimsical irony here. There is deadly pathos.

268-314 *'There are other dangers: falling tiles, objects thrown from watching windows. Then there's the restless young drunkard who can't sleep unless he's bashed someone. He avoids the rich man with his train of attendants, and picks on you, abuses you and beats you up. The poor man's freedom is to pray to get away with a few teeth left. Even when you've reached home there are armed burglars. When they are driven from their country refuges they come to prey on the city. We need so many fetters that it looks as if there's no iron for agricultural implements! How much better it was in the old*

days when Rome needed only one prison.

269 The physical dangers from accidents form a bridge to the gangsters: there is no special reason for tiles falling by night, though they might be more dangerous because unseen.

quod spatium: sc. *sit:* 'consider how large is the distance to the towering roofs from which a tile bashes your head in'. Augustus limited the height to twenty-one metres (Strab. 5,235).

270 *testa:* originally *tosta* from *torrere,* baked clay, so a tile; then metaphorically of the top of the head, giving Italian *testa* and French *tête.*

fenestris: there were no ground-floor windows on the street side for fear of burglars, but the upper storeys might have such apertures, as we can see at Herculaneum. There were laws to restrain people from throwing things like broken crockery into the street (*Dig.* 9, 3), but in the dark they were ignored.

272 *silicem:* the pavement.

ignauus: 'unbusinesslike' (Duff), the opposite of *(g)nauus.*

273 *casus:* objective genitive with *inprouidus.*

ad cenam si: spondaic fifth foot with off beat rhythm, admirably expressing the way the thud of the falling object knocks him off balance.

274 *intestatus:* pun on 270.

adeo: 'in fact', a Silver Latin usage. Supply *sunt* with *tot fata.*

275 *uigiles:* a superb touch. The windows seem to be watching for him to pass. It forms a link between the falling objects and the hoods. Note the visual image of the lights in the darkness.

276 *optes:* 'you should pray'.

tecum: the prayer is regarded as a kind of guardian-spirit.

277 *contentae:* the windows.

patulas . . . pelues: 'shallow basins', no doubt jerries.

278 The *grassator* (cf 305), as the Romans called the hood or mugger. Dissolute emperors like Nero and (in his younger days) Otho were known to play the part (Tac. *Ann.* 13, 25; Suet. *Ner.* 26; *Oth.* 2).

cecidit: from *caedere,* as the long *i* shows.

280 *Pelidae:* Achilles, Peleus's son, whose grief for Patroclus left him tossing and turning all night: *cubat in faciem, mox deinde supinus* is virtually a translation from Homer (*Il.* 24, 10-1 cf Sen. *Dial.* 9, 2, 12 who describes him as *modo pronus, modo supinus*). There is strong irony in the comparison of a crude bully with an epic hero.

281 Housman said that this verse 'of all interpolations in Juvenal, is the most ruinous and evident: it is triply condemned by sense, by diction, and by metre.'

282 *somnum rixa facit:* an excellent concise statement. Treat as a generalisation: 'a fight's a good sleeping-draught'.

inprobus: not of the approved standard, whether excessive or deficient. Here probably 'arrogant', 'cocky', impetuous', like the Greek νεανίας. Notice the chiasmus *inprobus annis . . . mero feruens; annis* of course refers to his youth.

283 *hunc quem:* note how the two mono-syllables have the effect of checking the movement of the young tough.

coccina laena: a thick scarlet cloak: both the quality of the wool and the bright expensive dye show a rich man who will be well-attended. Aeneas had such a cloak *Tyrio ardebat murice laena* (Verg. *A* 4, 262); so too the anonymous man of fashion in Persius (1, 32) with his *hyacinthina laena.*

284 *comitum:* in one sense just those with him, but the word was regularly used of the imperial courtiers, and lesser aristo-crats had their own 'courts'.

285 *multum . . . flammarum:* partitive genitive, 'a quantity of torches'. A succession of *m* (and *n*) often indicates a kind of stammering hesitation, here inculcated in the bully, as in *linquens multa metu cunctantem et multa parantem* (Aeneas in Verg. *A* 4, 390) and indeed the pull of emotion against reason in *mens immota manet, lacrimae uoluuntur inanes* (*ibid.* 449).

aenea lampas: singular for plural, as often. The rich villas of Pompeii and Herculaneum produced excellent examples of showy bronze candelabra. These were carried by special slaves called *lampadarii* or *lanternarii.* A flash of light passes across J's dark canvas, as at 275.

286 Eight word-accents in the line as he cautiously picks his way.

breue: 'weak'.

287 *candelae:* a taper, often home-made. Martial (14,40) calls it *ancillam . . . lucernae,* the lamp's skivvy or maidservant, suggesting that in richer households it was used to light the lamp. The succession of visual effects is highly cinematographic.

dispenso et tempero: Latin likes to express an idea through two parallel verbs or nouns; we more often use an adverb: 'sparingly regulate'.

288 *contemnit:* note the long hold-up after *me* before the verb is reached; also

the cutting *cs, candelae, cuius . . . contemnit . . . cognosce,* going on to *contra . . . que . . . quid . . . cum . . . cogat . . . cuius aceto, cuius conche,* and interspersed with pummell-ing *ps.*

prohoemia: a Greek word, originally the instrumental introduction to a song, then the exordium of a speech, then (like our 'prelude') used generally. A number of MSS have *praemia;* one wonders if there is not a pun. The outcome is contained in the prelude. The *h* is intrusive.

289 *uapulo:* used as passive of *pulso.*

290 *contra:* 'in my path'.

starique iubet: 'orders a halt', impers. passive.

291 *quid agas cum:* also at 4, 14 'what are you to do . . .?'

et idem: 'and stronger as well'.

292 *aceto:* sour wine, the cheapest drink available.

293 *conche:* a cheap bean (14,131; Mart. 5, 39, 10; 7, 78, 2; 13, 7, 1).

tumes: beans cause wind and flatulence: 'are you bursting with'.

sectile porrum: 'spring leeks' (Green) conveys it well. Leeks were eaten either young when individual blades were cut (*sectile* or *sectivum*), or fully-grown when the whole head was pulled (*capitatum*). The implication is that his breath stinks of it. Horace confirms that this was cheap market-produce eaten by the lower classes (*S* 1, 6, 114).

294 *sutor:* apparently cobbling was regarded as a typical lower-class occupation (Cic. *Flacc.* 7, 17).

elixi ueruecis labra: probably just the head (part for whole) of a boiled sheep, but with underlying innuendo. For *ueruex* is an old ram, tough and tasteless, and the head was the giveaway part of that (Plaut. *Capt.* 820). It also means a blockhead (mutton-head), and there is an implication that the victim of the hold-up is like his food. So *labra* is pointed; he shows his blockheaded-ness in his failure to speak. And *elixus* appears twice in Plautus in contexts which suggest a double meaning (*Poen.* 278; *Most.* 1115).

296 *ubi consistas:* 'where's your pitch' for begging or selling cheap goods.

quaero: 'am I to seek?': indic. in a rhetori-cal delib. question.

proseucha: a Greek word for a Jewish prayer-meeting: after all Umbricius has said before, the crowning insult.

298 *feriunt:* the toughs, but one has a sense of the sinister 'they' who form a back-cloth to Lear's limericks.

uadimonia . . . faciunt: 'lay a charge against you': *uas* or *uadimonium* is a bail or security forfeited if the person concerned fails to appear in court.

299 *haec:* looking forward, 'the following', attracted into the gender of *libertas* cf. Verg. *A* 6, 129 *hoc opus, hic labor est.*

300 The second part of the line is a rhetorical elaboration of the first.

302 *metuas:* 'you should (not) fear'; the same use as at 276. We now move on to burglars.

qui spoliet te: 'to rob you'. The broken rhythm for bitter emphasis; the poor victim is really staggering.

304 A piece of consciously fine writing, a five-word line of 'golden' type, with two adjectives separated from their two nouns by a single verb. The shops had folding shutters (*compago*) across, secured by a bar fastened in place with a chain. Shutting up shop was a noisy operation.

305 *grassator agit rem:* a skilful effect. Like Macbeth the gangster 'is about it' (*agit rem*). The offbeat *rem* at the end of the line represents the thud as the victim falls, as in Vergil's *procumbit humi bos* (*A* 5, 481). The succession of three syllables, two syllables, one syllable trails away into the nothingness of death, as in the same Vergil passage, or Catullus *occidit breuis lux* (5, 5).

306 *armato . . . custode:* singular for plural, as often. We might expect *a* or *ab*, but the effect is 'occupied by the weapons of the police', instrumental.

307 *Pomptina palus:* the Pomptine marshes, south-east of Rome between the hills and the sea, a desolate, malarial region successfully drained only in the twentieth century, an area therefore for criminals, refugees and outlaws.

Gallinaria pinus: a pine-forest on the road to Cumae, and near that town, another haunt of outlaws, the headquarters of Sextus Pompeius for his piratical exploits in the 30s BC. When the military made a move to clean up these areas the criminal hid in the slums of the city. But it is slightly odd to be reminded that there are holdup-men near Cumae, where Umbricius is going for peace and quiet.

308 *huc:* to Rome.

uiuaria: 'a game-park'. The *uiuarium* was a preserve, game-park or fishpond where animals were bred and fattened against future consumption: J is not thinking of them as the animals being preserved, but as predators let loose in such a place. We would say 'like

foxes into a chicken-run'. Umbricius and his like are the victims.

309 *non:* with both parts.

310-1 'The largest amount of iron goes on fetters, with the result that you are afraid that ploughshares, bill-hooks and hoes may run short.' An excellent example of satiric hyperbole. *Marra* (fem. sing.) was a mattock used for cutting out weeds, *sarcula* (n.pl.) were hoes. See K. D. White *Agricultural Implements of the Roman World* Cambridge 1967 pp. 40-7.

312 The idealisation of a Golden Age in the past is a commonplace (cf 13, 38). See the authoritative work by Arthur Lovejoy and George Boas *A Documentary History of Primitivism and Related Ideas in Antiquity* (Baltimore 1935). Only the Epicureans stood out against it.

proauorum atauos: Plaut *Pers.* 57 gives the genealogical table: *pater, auos, proauos, abauos, atauos, tritauos:* it was clever to note that the words fit a free iambic trimeter. J means no more than remote ancestors.

313 *regibus:* Rome was traditionally ruled by seven kings, from its foundation by Romulus (753 BC being only one of many legendary dates for this) to 509 BC (the traditional date of the deposition of the last king). There was a tendency to idealise them all except Tarquinius Superbus, and particularly the first four, well exemplified by Cic. *De Republica II.*

tribunis: representing the early Republican régime. Military tribunes with consular power were appointed in place of consuls in 445 BC.

314 *uno . . . carcere:* the *carcer Mamertinus,* traditionally ascribed to the fourth king, Ancus Martius (Liv. 1, 33). Imprisonment was not a normal punishment, but a temporary captivity pending banishment, execution or some other penalty.

315-22 *'I could add other reasons, but the driver is calling and it's time to go. If you similarly decide to retire to Aquinum send for me. I'll be prepared to enlist in your army there as a listener.'*

315 *causas:* for leaving Rome.

316 An ironic use of a convention of pastoral poetry (Verg. *Ecl.* 1,83; 6,86; 10,77). But with evening Umbricius is not breaking off a competition, or folding his sheep; he is leaving Rome for ever.

317 *mulio:* with the final *o* shortened as often in J.

318 *ergo:* here too.

319 *Aquinum:* in Latium on Via Latina, J's home town.

320 *Heluinam Cererem:* the famous inscription (see the Introduction) is a dedication, perhaps of a shrine or altar, to Ceres by [D. Iu]nius Iuuenalis, who may be our Juvenal (*CIL* 10, 5382). The cult title is not otherwise recorded, but it probably means that she was the patron-goddess of the wealthy Helvii, a well-known family in the locality (*CIL* 10, 5477; 5585). Ceres (cf *creare*) was a corn-goddess identified with the Greek Demeter.

uestram: tr. 'your people's Diana': *noster* is regularly used with singular reference, *uester* rarely if ever.

Dianam: a goddess of the wildwood, identified with the Greek Artemis, and exquisitely hymned by Catullus (35). We may reasonably assume that the two goddesses had the two main temples in Aquinum. They are associated in *CIL* 3,7260.

321 *conuerte:* 'bring me to join you'.

ni pudet illas: the satires are personified as girls. Umbricius modestly suggests that they are worthy of a better audience; what that says for J's modesty is another matter.

322 *auditor:* the wheel has come full circle from 1, 1. But J was an unwilling *auditor,* and Umbricius comes willingly. The reading *adiutor* is much inferior.

caligatus: a difficulty at the end in a word which we expect to be pointedly climactic. Most scholars take it to mean simply 'with thick boots', against the cold. But *caligatus* always refers to the footwear of the private soldier (*gregarius*), and the line is a parody of Lucan 1, 382 *Hesperios audax ueniam metator in agros* where Laelius, a chief centurion, is promising to follow Caesar in war against Pompey, even in Rome. So Umbricius is saying, 'I'll join your army as a private soldier — but not in Rome — and help you fight your satiric battles by swelling your audience.' But there is also a touch of a pun *gelidos — calidus — caligatus.* Cumae might well be warmer than Aquinum; it is 80 km further south, and on the coast, wheras Aquinum is inland, and at the foot of the Apennines.

agros: the last word is of the countryside.

Highet says well: 'There is no reply. Umbricius turns his back on the city for ever. Juvenal drifts away under the dripping arch of the gate, to merge in the smoke, the wealth, the noise of Rome.' (Hor. *O* 3,29,12).

General comments

Highet writes well: 'This is one of the finest satires ever written. It deals with an important theme; it is full of variety; it is well arranged; it is alive with brilliant epigrams; and, unlike many stirring satires, it is very largely true. It was true in Juvenal's day; it has been true in several different periods and places since he died; and it is true today.'

'The theme is the power and vileness of the big city', Highet continues, and reminds us of De Quincey's London, 'the stony-hearted stepmother', and Cobbett's Great Wen, and Balzac's Rastignac declaring war on Paris. It is Spengler's Megalopolis. It is the urban society which spreads its tentacles over the twentieth century; look at the end of J's satire, substitute 'high' for *ebrius* (278) and think of New York after dark in the 1970s.

We shall expect to find two themes: denunciation of city life and idealisation of the countryside; it is significant that pastoral poetry developed in the first great conurbation of the ancient world, Alexandria. The denunciation is obvious: it permeates the whole poem; every time Rome is named it is rejected (41, 83, 119, 137, 165, 183, 314). It is important to see it not only in the actual facts but in what they symbolise. The very person of Umbricius is a case in point. He is in one sense shadowy, as his name implies. A mass-society like Rome kills individualism. In another he is an heroically isolated figure, seeking to find his individuality, not in the solitary life of an eremite, but in the community of a small country-town. His departure symbolises despair of the city, as (for example) the gimcrack buildings symbolise the collapse of moral standards. But there is an ambiguity about the poem, since Umbricius abandons the city, but J does not; he has a love-hate relationship with it.

The idealisation of the countryside is clear enough too, and J brings it in now and again for purposes of contrast. It is there implicitly in the opening lines: somewhere there must be streams which are not harnessed to artificial grottoes (16-20). It recurs in the delightful account of the country festival (172-9), in the security of Praeneste and the country towns (190-3), in the cheapness and independence of a country cottage (223-31); and in Umbricius's final thrust (318-22).

At the beginning J does not idealise the countryside. On the contrary, he calls it *miserum* and *solum,* vile and lonely. As W. S. Anderson has shown, this is deliberate. Cumae may be vile and lonely — but Rome is even worse. J points this by his repeated use of *miserabile* (166, 276) and *miserae*

(288) of life in the city; the judgement of the vileness shouts at us from every paragraph. Vile then — but lonely? It would seem to be an absurd paradox, among the *turba* (239), the *magno populus . . . agmine* (244), the feet everywhere (247); J gives us an unforgettable picture of a mass society. But this is the point. There may be few people in the countryside, but there is fellowship (172-9), and at the end Umbricius's willingness to join J (322). There may be masses of people in Rome, but the poor man is in isolation. It's a society of 'each for himself and the devil take the hindmost'. J never depicts the poor man with family or friends; he is alone against the world, alone in his garret as the smoke climbs higher, alone except for the doves or rats, alone as he lies awake at night, alone pushing against the crowd, alone in death (the picture of the servants waiting his return, introduced for pathos, is a shock precisely because it runs counter to this isolation), alone as he walks under the dangerous windows, alone face to face with a mugger.

The satire, even more than the rest of J, is indebted to Martial. The basic city— country antithesis had been made a theme for satire by Horace (*S* 2, 6; cf *Ep.* 2, 2, 65-80), and was something of a rhetorical and philosophical commonplace. Martial too treated it (1, 49; 10, 70; 12, 18; 12, 57), and 12, 18 is actually addressed to J, and though it would be a mistake to identify Martial with Umbricius, we may well suppose that this gave J the idea of elaborating the theme. Similarly the contrast between rich and poor, the other main polarity of the satire, was an established satiric theme, but J's main debt is not to his predecessors in satire but to Martial's epigrams (3, 38; 4, 5). The point is shown by detailed borrowings: see the notes on 5, 11, 34-8, 49, 86, 104, 108, 136, 159, 172, 222 for a few examples.

J has been criticised for two defects in this satire. The first is the racism of 58-125. J certainly does write like a racist; he is similarly contemptuous of the Jews (14; 296). But this section is not merely or even primarily a piece of jingoistic racism. Its point lies in quite another direction. J is establishing that Rome is no place for the Romans. He argues it first in a — in the strict sense of the word — superficial way. Rome has become a Greek city. He goes on to argue it at a more profound moral level. The Roman aristocrats have lost any moral claim to be Roman either. This is the point of the juxtaposition of 58-125

and 126-89. J may attack the Greeks as un-Roman, but not half as hard as he attacks the Romans as un-Roman. For Umbricius, and J behind him, lay store by the ancient Roman values: look at the reference to Numa (12), Scipio, Metellus and Numa (137-9), the days of remote ancestors, of kings and tribunes (313-4). The only way in which Umbricius can find a society which lives by the ancient Roman values, and himself live by those values is by leaving Rome, not because of non-Roman Greeks, but because of un-Roman Romans. This is the irony of the poem.

The other point for which J is criticised is a lack of proportion. 7-9 are a typical example: fire, collapse of buildings, mortal perils and poets reciting in August. We can find similar examples: flattery of an author does not seem a crime commensurate with being a party to large-scale corruption (41-57); and it is probably better to be laughed at (152-3) than crushed to death (259). The criticism is misguided. There are two points here. One is that J is a satirist, who makes his point through laughter, even if that laughter has an echo which is grim. The bathos at 7-9, for example, is carefully calculated, and so far from showing that J suffers from lack of proportion, it demonstrates his masterful sense of proportion. But there is a serious point as well. It is that the small things are truly symptomatic of the large. Those who keep you listening to dull epics in the heat, are the same people who keep you living in cold, noisy, dangerous attics; in both cases they care nothing for you. The man who tells lies about his patron's books will end by telling lies about his patron's crimes. The point is a valid one, and by stating it extremely, J makes it effectively.

In two ways the satire is by any standards outstanding. One is in J's gift of coining a striking phrase, often by its concise summing up and by its unexpectedness driving home some major point. Consider *quid Romae faciam? mentiri nescio* (45) *in caelum iusseris ibit* (78) *si dixeris 'aestuo', sudat* (103) *nusquam minor est iactura clientis* (125) *nil habet infelix paupertas durius in se/quam quod ridiculos homines facit* (152-3) *omnia Romae/cum pretio* (183-4) *et tamen illud/perdidit infelix totum nihil* (208-9) *unius sese dominum fecisse lacertae* (231) *si rixa est ubi tu pulsas, ego uapulo tantum* (289) *maximus in uinclis ferri modus* (310), to name but a few, every one encapsulating memorably some point which J wishes to establish.

The other dominant quality is J's capacity to convey visual impressions through words. We have encountered it in the first satire, and shall encounter it constantly. From the scene at the gate with the water dripping from the aqueduct, and the integrity of wood and spring and natural rock marred by artificial grottoes and marble borders, we receive a succession of unforgettable visual, almost cinematographic impressions. Consider for example the picture of the fire spreading, the neighbour moving out his things, the doves cooing in the eaves, the poor man lying asleep as wisps of smoke begin to seep up through the floor (197-202); Cordus's bare room with a short bed, a chipped slab of marble with six small pots proudly displayed on it, and a small cup and broken statue underneath, and the rats scurrying away from a broken book box (203-7); the street scene, the rich man moving easily in his litter, the poor man struggling against the crowd (there was a similar scene — though with a different point — at the end of *Les Enfants du Paradis*), every detail closely observed, the resistance in front, the pressure behind, the jabbing elbow, the litter-pole, the beam, the barrel, the mud, the trampling feet, the soldier's nailed boot (238-48). Or consider the street-accident: first the swaying carts with fir-trunks, viewed from underneath (the details are precise), then the slow-moving wagon loaded with marble, a close-up of the axle-shaft cracking or wheel working loose, a view from underneath of a mountain of marble descending — and the body is not to be seen; next a series of shots of the slaves cheerfully busy at home, each job precisely identified; then a misty, silent scene by the river, as the dead man sits, the boat with its grim ferryman appears, he comes forward but is waved back, the boat disappears again churning up the mud as it goes (257-67). Or again the hold-up: the pitchy blackness, the poor man moving through the dark, a tile crashing on the pavement, lighted windows like eyes in the darkness, a broken pot narrowly missing him, the slops from a piss-pot hitting him fair and square; next the mugger, tossing and turning on his bed, suddenly sitting up, draining a cup of wine, throwing on a shirt and going out into the darkness; next his aggressive advance into a broader street, the darkness broken by a brilliant flash of light, a scarlet cloak, a mass of torches and bronze candelabra, as he hastily slinks back into the darkness; then a tiny light appearing, a taper in a cupped hand, and the young tough stepping out to confront the bearer (268-89).

So J puts pungent phraseology and masterly word-painting at the service of the most bitter indictment of urbanisation ever penned.

Bibliography

Adamietz, J. *Untersuchungen zu Juvenal* (*Hermes* Einzelschriften Heft 26) Wiesbaden 1972

Anderson, W. S. 'Studies in Book I of Juvenal' *YCS* 15 (1957) 55-68

Colton, R. E. 'Echoes of Martial in Juvenal's Third Satire' *Traditio* 22 (1966) 403-19

Fredericks, S. C. 'Daedalus in Juvenal's Third Satire' *CB* 49 (1972) 11-3

Fredericks, S. C. 'The Function of the Prologue (1-20) in the Organisation of Juvenal's Third Satire' *Phoenix* 27 (1973) 62-7

Giri, G. 'Una satira di Giovenale e gli effetti delle letture pubbliche' *La Cultura* 1 (1921-2) 539

Labriolle, P. de 'La troisième satire de Juvenal' *Humanités* (Cl. de lettres) 6 (1930) 219-326

Lafleur, R. A. 'Artorius and Catulus in Juvenal 3' *Riv. Stud. Class.* 22 (1974) 3-7

Lelièvre, F. J. 'Virgil and Juvenal's Third Satire' *Euphrosyne* 5 (1972) 457-62

Lutz, C. 'Democritus and Heraclitus' *CJ* 49 (1953-4) 309-14

Magariños, G. *Juvenal y su Tercera Satira* Madrid 1956

Marache, R. *Juvénal: Saturae III, IV, V* Paris 1965

Motto, A. L. and Clark, J. R. *'Per iter tenebricosum:* The Mythos of Juvenal 3' *TAPA* 96 (1965) 267-76

Rudd, N. and Courtney, E. *Juvenal: Satires I, III, X* Bristol 1977

Sherwin-White, A. N. *Racial Prejudice in Imperial Rome* Cambridge 1967.

Witke, E. C. 'Juvenal 3, an Eclogue for the Urban Poor' *Hermes* 90 (1962) 244-8

SATIRE 4

This poem falls into two uneven sections.

1-27 Crispinus
28-36 Bridge passage
37-154 Domitian

The two sections are loosely held together by the theme of the principal characters' behaviour over an exceptionally large fish.

The second section is of particular interest, as it portrays a meeting of the *consilium principis,* Domitian's Privy Council or inner Cabinet. It is one of the earliest such accounts; it is of course satirical, but it would be a pointless satire were it not formally correct. The Council seems to have consisted of twelve in all, the emperor in the chair, the two praetorian prefects, Crispinus and Fuscus, and nine statesmen, mostly of consular rank and some very decidedly senior, giving continuity with previous reigns. J.A. Crook writes in *Consilium Principis* (51): 'Juvenal's Satire is of the utmost importance in the understanding both of the consilium and of Flavian politics. Here are jurists, soldiers, diplomats, aged and venerable counsellors — a most respectable and capable body, once we have penetrated behind the screen of prejudice with which their careers have been overlaid. The mere *delator* with no public service to his name, the Sura or Armillatus, finds no place here, for these are statesmen. Of the eleven, the only *equites* seem to be the praetorian prefects, and one of the senators is *praefectus urbi. Ex officio* is not an appropriate term in dealing with men who appear on a body as loosely constituted as these political councils, but the praetorian and urban prefects were naturally and necessarily in the closest confidence of the emperor and unlikely to be left out when anything serious was afoot.' Juvenal does not impugn their effectiveness in dealing with the great problems of government, only their effectiveness in dealing with Domitian.

1-27 *My theme is again Crispinus in all his immorality. He actually paid 6000 sesterces for a mullet — and kept it all to himself.*

1 *Ecce:* giving the satire a strongly dramatic tinge; frequent in comedy for the entry of a character. In earlier Latin it tends to be accompanied by the acc. (expressing the object of thought or emotion, the so-called acc. of exclamation,

e.g. Plaut. *Epid.* 680 *ecce me!* 'Here I am'), in classical Latin by the nom., as here.

iterum: this simple word creates large problems. (a) It may refer to 1, 26. If so, either (i) the first satire was not written programmatically after the others, or (ii) the opening of this satire was altered for publication in book form. (b) It may indicate that Juvenal wrote a lost satire pillorying Crispinus: on the whole this does not seem likely. (c) It may be part of the dramatic *mise-en-scène:* in real life Crispinus was always turning up. 'God! here's Crispinus *again!*' (d) Most probably it is a reference to the traditions of satire. Horace (*S* 1, 4, 13-4; cf 1, 1, 120), referring to an *aretalogus* (see on 15, 16) of his own day, has *ecce/Crispinus.* J simply says 'Here's Crispinus again!'

Crispinus: one of Domitian's favourites: see on 1, 27. The point is that he came to Rome as a fishmonger.

saepe: he does not in fact appear again.

2 *ad partes:* continuing the image of the theatre: 'to play his rôle': we might tr. 'on to the stage'.

monstrum: not quite our 'monster'; it means a prodigy portending evil.

4 *deliciae:* a word found only in the plural: the sense of delight, so that which causes delight, so a person who causes delight, a beloved, mistress or lover, so, as here, a voluptuary.

uiduas . . . adulter: 'in his sexual excesses draws the line only at unmarried girls.' This is not to his credit; he gets more kick out of poaching on others' preserves. *Adulter* of sex-crime generally, not just adultery.

5 Some scholars think that a passage has dropped out between 4 and 5, describing how Crispinus came to a sticky end, and giving point to *igitur.* Others take *igitur* as moralising: 'He's a villain: so in the end his wealth gets him nowhere.'

5-6 *quantis . . . porticibus:* 'the length of the covered ways in which . . .'. Nero's Golden House had three drives protected from the weather, each nearly half a kilometre long (Suet. *Ner.* 31). J has taken his cue from Martial, who has two epigrams about such indoor riding (1, 12; 12, 50). Normally, even with the extravagance of the mansions with covered ways included, these would be for walking or being carried in a litter, and the reference to driving may be satiric hyperbole, or reference to some notorious exploit. See also 7, 178ff.

6 *nemorum:* Roman houses regularly enclosed open courtyards, which were sometimes planted as gardens, and might contain trees if they were large enough.

7 *uicina foro:* as in London today the price of land soared near the centre of the city. When Julius Caesar laid out his forum the cost of the land exceeded 100 000 000 sesterces (Suet. *Jul.* 26).

aedes: also *uicinas foro.*

8 Jahn proposed deleting this moralising sentiment, which may have been inserted by a Christian scribe thinking of Isaiah 57: 21 'There is no peace for the wicked.' The continuity is better without it.

9 *incestus:* 'irreligious' or 'sacrilegious'. Isid. *Orig.* 5, 26, 24 *incesti iudicium in uirgines sacratas uel propinquas sanguine constitutum est.*

cum quo: cf 87: *quocum* is the usual form: it is not easy to see why J has varied it.

9-10 'a man with whom not long ago a priestess, set apart by her sacred headdress, slept, and was doomed to be buried under the earth with her blood still living.' The reference is probably to the notorious case of Cornelia, the senior Vestal Virgin (*vittata sacerdos*), who was convicted in AD 91 of breaking her vows of chastity (Suet. *Dom.* 8; Plin. *Ep.* 4, 11). She had many lovers, all of whom Domitian executed, except for an ex-praetor named Valerius Licinianus, whom he banished. Domitian revived the ancient punishment for Vestals who broke their vows: Cornelia was laid on a bier, and covered with a pall, and carried through the streets to an underground cell near the Colline Gate, where she was immured alive: so no one except the gods had the responsibility for the actual death of the sacred though polluted person. None of our other sources associate Crispinus with this offence. Juvenal either alleges that he was not found out, or that Domitian protected him, or is referring to some later intrigue with another Vestal, in which case (as there is no record of any other execution) *subitura* means 'deserving to be buried'. There is irony in the *uiduas tantum aspernatus adulter* seducing a Vestal, but J's point is that Crispinus always looks for an added dimension of criminality to give spice to sex. *uittata* is pointed: 'despite her sacro-sanctity marked out by her dress.' *nuper* goes primarily with the whole episode, but has a second point of reference in

uittata: she takes off her headband to sleep with him.

11 *sed nunc:* sc. *agendum est.*

12 *fecisset . . . caderet:* technical legal terms, 'had been guilty of . . . would be suffering sentence'. The change of tense shows the continuing condemnation for a past act.

idem: neut. acc.

iudice morum: i.e. Domitian, who took on himself the office of censor in AD 84. Sources hostile to Domitian make much of his combination of personal immorality and censorship of immoral behaviour in others, a psychologically interesting combination.

13 *quod turpe . . . decebat:* a similar phrase at 8, 181.

Titio Seioque: standard names for citizens in Roman law, like our John Doe or Richard Roe.

14 *quid agas . . . ?:* exactly our 'What are you to do . . . ?'; cf 3, 291.

15 *crimine:* 'charge'.

persona: here our 'a person', a late use of the word.

mullum sex milibus emit: deliberate bathos, of course: yet at the same time, the small items are symptomatic of the large (see General Comments on Satire 3). It is also a pointed reference. Tiberius introduced sumptuary laws, controlling extravagance, precisely because of the sale of three mullets for 30 000 sesterces (Suet. *Tib.* 34). The weight of a mullet seldom exceeded 9½ kg (Plin. *NH* 9, 30, 64); larger ones were therefore valued, though Horace is sarcastic about the idea that flavour improves with weight (Hor. *S* 2, 7, 33). The rich liked to show off their large mullets and would even bring them in to be cooked alive in the presence of their guests (Plin. *NH* 9, 66). Strictly *mullus* is the red mullet or surmullet. See A.C. Andrews 'The Roman craze for surmullets' *CW* 42 (1948-9) 186-8.

16 *sane:* 'of course' – sarcastic.

sestertia: 'thousands of sesterces': see on 1, 92. It weighed 2.4 kg.

17 'as people say who can't resist laying on a thick subject still thicker': there is a dig at court-flattery.

18 *laudo:* we expect impf. subj. 'I would approve if he had'. Juvenal makes it more direct: 'I always approve a scheme if the inventor has gained by it.' Strongly ironic.

munere tanto: 'by a gift on that scale'.

19 *praecipuam . . . ceram:* a will was written on wax tablets; the principal

inheritors appeared on the first of these. The scholiast glosses: *primam, in qua heredes primi scribuntur*. But *praecipuum* is a legal term referring to specific bequests carried out before the general bequests (Suet. *Galba* 5).

orbi: for the practice of *captatio* see on 1, 146; 3, 129.

20 *ratio ulterior:* 'a deeper motive'.

21 *specularibus:* the Romans used talc (*lapis specularis*) for the windows of carriages, and sometimes of houses: see Mayor ad loc. It came from all over the Mediterranean, the best from Spain and Cappadocia (Plin. *NH* 36, 160-2). See 3,242.

antro: J is referring to her sedan. But he says 'grotto' or 'cave', and the fantastic image should be kept.

22 *sibi:* dat. of advantage!

miser et frugi: in comparison to Crispinus: sarcastic. *frugi* is used as an indeclinable adj.; cf 3, 167.

23 *Apicius:* M. Gavius Apicius, millionaire gourmet early in first century AD (Plin. *NH* 10, 13; Tac. *Ann.* 4, 1), author of an early cookery-book (Schol. ad loc; Sen. *Cons. Helv.* 10, 3), though the one which survives under his name is a later compilation. In a famous episode, Tiberius was given a 2 kg mullet. With his mordant sense of humour, he had it put up for sale, to see whether Apicius or P. Octavius (another rich gourmet) would buy it. Octavius secured it for 5000 sesterces (Sen. *Ep.* 95, 42). Apicius ran through something between 60 and 100 million sesterces on good living: when his fortune was down to 10 000 000 he committed suicide, as he had too little to live in the style to which he was accustomed (Mart. 3, 22, from whom Juvenal probably took it; cf Sen. *Cons. Helv.* 10, 3).

hoc tu: sc. *fecisti.* The two monosyllables are given extra weight by the punctuation.

24 *succinctus:* i.e. with clothes tucked up into the belt to free the limbs for action, like our 'with sleeves rolled up'. The innuendo is that Crispinus was once a slave employed in manual work.

patria: from *patrius:* papyrus grew in Egypt.

papyrus: a rush which grew in profusion in Egypt, used of course for paper, but also, as Pliny tells us (*NH* 13, 22, 72) for a kind of cloth, and incidentally, as chewing-gum.

25 *squamae:* sc; *emptae sunt:* very sarcastic.

minoris: genitive of price.

26 *provincia:* the part of Gaul bordering on the Mediterranean to the south and Italy to the east, called *Gallia provincia* by Caesar (*BG* 1, 19), and widely known as 'the province', generally called Narbonensis in imperial times, and still called Provence.

tanti: genitive of price.

27 *sed:* 'yes and', an idiomatic usage intensifying rather than contradicting.

Apulia: the modern Puglia in south-east Italy, its wide plains hot and oppressive and raked by a burning wind in summer which drove the cattle to the hills. Cicero (*Att.* 8, 3, 4) calls it the most sparsely populated part of Italy, and Seneca (*Ep.* 87, 6) comments on its uninhabited tracts: so land was cheap.

28-36 *When the palace buffoon throws away so much money on extravagant eating, what are we to expect of the emperor? Tell the true story, Muses.*

28 *qualis:* acc. pl.

gluttisse: a splendidly evocative word, onomatopoeic of liquid being gulped down, and giving us our 'glutton': both *t*s and both *s*s must of course be sounded.

putamus: 'are we to imagine': the pres. indic. is often used where we might expect a deliberative subj.; cf Cat. 1, 1 *cui dono lepidum meum libellum . . . ?* 'To whom am I to dedicate my booklet of wit?'

29 *induperatorem:* archaic for *imperatorem*, originally the commander-in-chief, but by this time closely equivalent to our 'emperor' which is derived from it. The transition to Domitian, neatly enough carried out. J may be making a virtue of necessity (Duff) in using the archaic form, as *imperatorem* will not fit dactylic verse, but he could have used many other phrases. The archaism following the vulgarism points the irony.

30 *modicae:* ironical: our 'modest' conveys it precisely.

margine: the mullet was a mere incidental.

31 *purpureus:* the colour of his dress (1, 27) applied to him.

ructarit: i.e. *ructaverit.*

scurra: what Jack Point calls 'a private buffoon', but the word originally means a fop, and then a high-society debauchee, and J intends something of all these.

Palati: the Palatium or Palatine was one of the seven hills of Rome. Augustus had his residence there, and subsequent emperors also built there, and from there the imperial administration was conducted: it was conveniently adjacent to the Forum

Romanum. Domitian was the most
extravagant of the imperial builders on
the Palatine (Nero operated elsewhere),
which makes the reference pointed. We
may translate 'palace', but there is a
bit more to it than that. Duff well says
that *scurra Palati* 'is contemptuous for
amicus principis'.

32 *princeps equitum:* not an official
title, but the prefect of the praetorian
guard was known as *princeps equestris
ordinis* (Vell. Pat. 2, 127, 47).

33 *municipes:* the fish are his fellow-
citizens.

fracta de merce: if the reading is right
this must mean 'from a damaged cargo',
i.e. he bought cheap and sold 'as good
as new'. But the language is awkward.
Some MSS have *facta,* and it is possible
that the right reading is *faria,* i.e. *Pharia*
'Egyptian'.

siluros: the so-called 'sheath-fish'.

34-6 These lines must clearly be a parody
of Statius.

34 *Calliope:* one of the nine Muses, not
originally distinguished in function, but
by Roman times the inspirer of heroic epic,
a satirical touch like *induperatorem.*

considere: this brings us down with a
bump. The scene is dramatised. The Muse
leaps to her feet to begin the sing-song
declamation, but this is historical fact,
not an exercise of the creative imagination,
to be spoken, not poetically delivered.
J has in mind invitations to the Muse to
rise and sing, as Verg. *A* I, 525-8;
Stat. *Theb.* 4, 34-8.

35 The line falls into three strongly
marked sections: note how the breaks are
varied from those in 34.

cantandum: not 'to be sung', but 'to be
delivered in the poetic manner'.

puellae: a mild joke. Mayor: 'Amid the
general profligacy, and when many poets
speak of Orpheus as son of Calliope, and
of other Muses as mothers, it is no slight
compliment to call you *virgins'*. But it may
be no more than flattery of their youthful
looks. If we had Statius's poem we might find
a sharper point.

36 *Pierides:* from Pieria in Thessaly
where the Muses had their home.

37-71 *When Domitian was persecuting
the world, a humble fisherman from
Ancona caught a huge turbot; he rushed
across Italy to present it to the emperor,
won admission while senators were
excluded, and made his presentation in
a flattering address.*

37 *semianimum:* four syllables. The

sound-effect of the first two-and-a-half feet
is grotesque, especially if you recall that
the Romans did not differentiate in
pronunciation between long *a* and short *a*
(*iam* and *-ian-*); every syllable ends with
m or *n*.

laceraret: like a wild animal; the image
is established before the subject is
named. This is the first mention of
brutality, in the first line of the emperor's
section.

Flavius . . . ultimus: T. Flavius Vespasianus
achieved imperial power with the help of
the armies of the east in AD 69, after
a year of chaos following Nero's suicide.
His house is known from his *nomen* as the
Flavian dynasty. He was succeeded by his elder
son Titus (AD 79-81), and he in turn by
his younger brother T. Flavius Domitianus.
Domitian was able and ambitious, and
would brook no rivals. His repression
of the senate and his executions for
alleged conspiracy eventually caused his
assassination in AD 96; he left no heir, and
was thus the last of the Flavians. He was
succeeded by the weak but worthy Nerva.
The scholiast cites an epigram by Martial
not otherwise known: *Flavia gens, quantum
tibi tertius abstulit heres!/paene fuit tanti
non habuisse duos:* implying that the third
and last totally undid the work of the first
two.

orbem: a key-word for the understanding
of this satire; it recurs at the end of 1,132
where it is the fish. The macrocosm and
the microcosm — the emperor treats them
both alike.

38 *caluo:* Domitian was, like Caesar,
bald, and sensitive about it, indeed violent
in his reactions (Suet. *Dom.* 18). The
scholiast says that J was banished to Egypt
for writing this passage: see Introduction.

seruiret: 'was a slave to'.

Neroni: the type of tyranny, the last
Julio-Claudian, as Domitian was the last
Flavian, but handsome (though he went
to seed with indulgence) where Domitian
was ugly.

39 *incidit:* 'there turned up'.

Hadriaci spatium admirabile rhombi: a
splendid parody of high-flown epic writing.
The Romans, because their writing is
usually concrete, like to vary it with this
type of expression and write 'an
extraordinary size of a turbot' where we
say 'a turbot of extraordinary size'
cf 4, 81 *Crispi iucunda senectus.* The
long space *Hadriaci . . . rhombi* expresses
well the fisherman's hands getting wider and
wider as he describes his catch. Note how

J uses the adj. *Hadriaci* where we say 'in the Adriatic' and link the thought with the verb.

rhombi: the turbot was valued next to the mullet and the sea eel (*murena*): the best were caught off Ravenna. See 11, 121. Ancona is a little further south down the Adriatic coast.

40 Ancon, the modern Ancona, was named from the curving promontory on which it is situated: the name means 'elbow'. It was founded by refugees from the dictatorship of Dionysius in the Dorian city of Syracuse in the early fourth century BC. Aphrodite (Venus) was the city's patron goddess and appears on the coins, but the mention of the temple is not mere decorative detail, but a reminder of the goddess whom the emperor both scorned and served, as he stamped out sexual immorality in others and practised it himself. The language continues to parody epic.

41 *impleuitque sinus:* beautiful writing: the folds of the net, but we think at first that it filled the whole bay.

neque enim: 'and indeed . . . not'.

haeserat: tr. 'as it lay there it was . . .'.

illis: probably turbot, but some would refer it to tunny, in which case 'those fish'.

42 *operit:* the idea is that hibernation makes them fat.

glacies Maeotica: the ice on the Sea of Azov.

43 *torrentis:* double meaning: the Black Sea has a strong current, and it is warm by comparison with the Sea of Azov.

45 *monstrum:* see on 1.2; but the use of the same word for Crispinus (who dominates the first fish) and the second fish is significant: Crispinus is to the emperor as a fish is to him.

cumbae linique magister: another epic expression.

46 *pontifici summo:* all the emperors held the office of *pontifex maximus,* the supreme religious official. What else do you do with a unique portent than have it interpreted by the highest authority? The point is ironical. There is an additional allusion to the gormandising at *pontificum dapes* (Mart. 12, 48, 12; cf Hor. *O* 2, 14, 28).

proponere: 'offer for sale'.

47 *auderet:* 'Who would have the nerve?'

et: 'even'.

48 *delatore:* see on 3, 115, and note the use of the sing., like our 'many a'. We receive a vivid visual picture of a seemingly desolate beach with informers lying in wait behind a breakwater or crouching behind a rock. It is a vignette of the police-state.

algae inquisitores: there seem to be three points: (a) *inquisitor* is a technical term for a person looking for evidence to support a charge; (b) *alga,* seaweed, is proverbially of little value (Verg. *Ecl.* 7, 42; Hor. *S* 2, 5, 8), so that there is an implication that nothing is too trivial for these snoopers; (c) the whole phrase has a literal meaning; the inspectors will turn the very seaweed upside down, and it would be no use trying to hide the catch away.

49 *agerent cum:* technical phrase: 'would lay a charge against', 'would have the law on'.

nudo: he is naked because he is fishing, like Peter in John 21:7; he is naked because he has no money from which to pay a fine; he is naked because he is defenceless against tyrannical bureaucracy.

50 *non dubitaturi:* tr. 'and they would not hesitate'.

51 *uiuaria Caesaris:* rich men, and supremely the emperor, kept parks and fishponds from which to stock their table. The reference is pointed. Domitian was liable (in the opinion of the suffering senators) to claim anything as his preserve (Plin. *Paneg.* 50, 1; Mart. 4, 30).

52 *ueterem:* ambiguous, primarily 'its former master', but also 'its aging master' and 'in old age to its master'.

53 *si quid . . . credimus:* 'if we have any confidence in', with both parts.

Palfurio: the scholiast identifies him as Palfurius Sura (cf Suet. *Dom.* 13), son of a consular, in Vespasian's disfavour, converted to Stoicism, something of a poet and orator, under Domitian restored to favour as a leading *delator.* Armillatus was evidently a man of the same kidney.

55 *fisci:* 'the imperial treasury'. Sen. *Ben.* 7, 6, 3 *Caesar omnia habet, fiscus eius priuata tantum ac sua.* Domitian's advisers evidently suggested that he interpret the second statement in the light of the first. The two lines seem to parody a legal formula.

56 *ne pereat:* a beautiful ambiguity 'to save his skin' and 'so that the fish may not go for nothing'.

letifero: again the epic touch. But epic and commonplace phrases alternate.

57 *quartanam:* the quartan fever, so-called because its attacks come at three-day intervals (the Romans counted inclusively), and therefore relatively mild. Cicero writes in sympathy to Tiro on an

illness that now that the fever has changed
to a quartan he should get stronger
(*Fam.* 16, 11, 1). Martial, writing of a
doctor who died of fever, says that he
ought rather to have caught his own
specialism, the quartan (10, 77). The
medical writer Celsus (3, 15) says *quartana
neminem iugulat*. After the fatal fevers
associated with the autumn sirocco, the
colder weather with its milder attacks is
welcome.

58   *recentem:* predicate, just as we say
'kept it fresh'.

59   *auster:* the hot sirocco, which would
soon turn the fish bad.

60   *ut:* 'when'. The word opens a
passage of epic parody.

lacus: Domitian had a luxury villa in
the Alban hills outside Rome (cf 1, 145).
It was so big that Septimius Severus
transformed it into a legionary camp, which
in turn became the basis of the modern
town. The lakes are *lacus Albanus (lago
Albano)* and *lacus Nemorensis (lago di
Nemi).*The journey from Ancona to Rome
is about 135 km as the crow flies,
and over difficult mountain territory.
The poor fisherman would expect to
find the emperor in Rome, and still have to
toil some distance southwards along Via
Appia.

quamquam: common in Silver Latin
(though not in Cicero) with an adj., part.,
adv., or adverbial phrase.

61   Alba Longa, the site of the later
Castel Gandolfo, was traditionally
founded by Aeneas's son Ascanius; archaeo-
logists have found a necropolis going back
to the second millennium BC. It was at
one time head of a league of cities. Rome
destroyed it in the time of the kings,
traditionally under Tullus Hostilius; the
inhabitants were deported to Bovillae.
But a temple of Vesta remained, incorpora-
ting the fire which Aeneas was believed
to have brought from Troy. It was not on
the scale of the temple in the Forum
Romanum (*minorem*). Inscriptions tell of
Vesta Albana (Orelli 1393) and *Virgo
Vestalis maxima arcis Albanae* (ibid 2240 n),
and there was still a college of Vestals
there under the Christian emperors of the
fourth century AD (Symm. *Ep.* 10, 118-9).

62   Another line of mock-epic grandeur.

63   *facili . . . cardine:* ironical, used by
Horace of the readiness of the door to
open for young lovers to meet (*0* 1, 25, 5).

64   A splendid line. *Exclusi . . . patres*
surround the gates, the fisherman and the
fish, like the spectators in a Greek theatre.

Admissa is a technical word; we might say
'granted an audience'. Pliny compares the
accessibility of Trajan with the suspicious
aloofness of Domitian (*Paneg.* 47); more,
under Domitian, *par metus admissis et
exclusis* (48). There is a vivid visual
picture, and the irony of the gates opening
'easily' for the fish while the senators are
shut out.

65   *itur:* impersonal passive.

Atriden: mock-epic. Agamemnon, son of
Atreus, was commander-in-chief (*imperator*)
of the Greek forces at Troy. There is a
double antonomasia, the patronymic for the
name, and the mythological for the real
person.

Picens: Ancona is in the territory of
Picenum. The name is not just journalism:
it reminds us of his journey and suggests
a provincial accent.

66   *maiora:* 'things too great for'.

genialis agatur ista dies: 'make today a
holiday'. The *genius,* originally the spirit
of fertility in the male, residing in the head,
came to be regarded as a kind of guardian-
angel, the Greek δαίμων, the deity within.
So that there is a touch of ambiguity in
the concept, cf Hor. *0* 3, 17, 14 *cras Genium
mero/curabis* 'tomorrow you will look
after your Spirit with wine.' (cf *Ep.* 2, 1,
144.) So phrases like *genio indulgere* are
ambiguous between a divine libation and
self-indulgence (cf Pers. 2, 3 *funde merum
genio*). It is particularly apposite to the
emperor, since, from Augustus onwards,
those emperors who refused to be deified
in their lifetime (of whom Domitian was
not one), permitted offering to be made
to their genius. 'Holiday' with its root
in 'holy day' has something of the same
ambiguity. The root *gen-* is an interesting
one. It is involved with birth, cf genetics,
genocide (cf also kindergarten, kin); it
also gives us words like general (cf kind)
from the family or group; also gentle (cf
kind) from the behaviour of the truly
well-born; and through the loss of the g
produces (g)natal, (g)nature, and co-gnate
words. This passage helps us to understand
the scope of 'genial'.

67   *propera . . . sagina:* 'Hurry up and
have a good blow-out'; lit. 'to distend your
stomach by cramming'. The language,
from a fisherman to an emperor, is
decidedly odd. The artificial structure of
the line (two dissyllables, followed by
four trisyllables) gives the impression of a
prepared speech, and the combination of
blunt sentiment and semi-sophisticated
vocabulary is delightfully incongruous.

Martial (4, 8, 9) says *laxatur nectare Caesar* of Domitian where *laxatur* rather means 'relaxes'.

68 *tua . . . in saecula:* with *seruatum.* The sentiments are high-flown, and redolent of the return of the Golden Age.

69 *ipse capi uoluit:* the idea is taken from an epigram of Martial, also in flattery of Domitian: *ipse suas anser properauit laetus ad aras* (9, 31, 5). cf Ov. *F* 4,269 *ipse peti uolui.* J's concision is masterly.

quid apertius?: 'What could be more blatant?' Note the bucolic diaeresis (strong break after the fourth foot), laying emphasis on the last two feet. This is satire against poems (like Mart. 4, 30) which depicted Domitian as having miraculous power over animals.

illi: Domitian.

70 *surgebant cristae:* the image from a cock. Our English word 'coxcomb' uses the image differently. This is the cock who 'stoutly struts his Dames before' (Milton *L'Allegro* 52). The phrase was presumably proverbial, though paralleled only in Jul. Val. *De gestis Alex.* 1, 37.

71 *dis aequa potestas:* strictly, 'equal to that of the gods', but the ellipsis is easy. Domitian claimed the titles *dominus et deus* (Suet. *Dom.* 13); Martial is careful to accord it to him (5, 8, 1 *edictum domini deique nostri;* cf 10, 72, 3); Statius (*Silv.* 4, 3, 128) has *en hic est deus.* A Christian writer of the period provides a counter-assertion that Jesus not Domitian is *dominus et deus* (John 20:28). The pattern fostered by Augustus, and followed by the wiser emperors, was to refuse deification during life, but to proclaim themselves (like Hercules) the son of a divine father, and to expect that, if they served mankind well, their labours (like those of Hercules) would be rewarded after death by a kind of co-option to the heavenly senate. This is the point of Tiberius's rebuke to a courtier who referred to *sacras eius occupationes— pro sacris laboriosas dicere coegit* (Suet. *Tib.* 27). *potestas* is subj. of *possit* as well as *laudatur:* we can say 'Power is capable of believing anything of itself'.

72-122 *There being no dish large enough, the Privy Council are summoned for consultation. The statesmen hurry in one after another.*

72 *patinae mensura:* 'a dish of the right size': for the shape of the phrase cf 39. Martial (13, 81) has a couplet:

Quamuis lata gerat patella rhombum, rhombus latior est tamen patella:

Highet quotes a story of the gourmet Brillat-Savarin, who faced with the same problem used a laundry-boiler as a cooking-pot (*Physiologie du Goût* Paris 1865 pp 330-4).

73 *proceres:* the Privy Council, *amici Caesaris.*

quos oderat ille: a splendid touch, showing Domitian's character rather than theirs, and suggesting the way they speak of him just as 'he'.

74 *miserae magnaeque:* a kind of oxymoron, unexpected in combination: the alliteration on *m* is a mournful effect.

75 *pallor:* a splendid touch showing us the emperor through the courtiers, *sedet pallor* is epic (Ov. *Met.* 2, 775), but note the relation to 76: the emperor, and pallor, are in session.

amicitiae: not personal friendship — J has just said that their relationship was hate and fear — but political association, and in relation to the emperor public responsibility: see on 73.

Liburno: the majordomo, an Illyrian slave of suitable physique to be a bouncer or chucker-out. The scholiast says *qui admissionibus praeerat.* Martial praises life in Spain by saying *procul horridus Liburnus et querulus cliens* (1, 49, 33).

76 *sedit:* 'is in session'.

abolla: see on 3, 115. But note that this is the only suggestion that it was worn by high officials, and the reference may be satirical.

77 *Pegasus:* According to the scholiast his father was a ship's captain who named him after the ship's figurehead, the legendary winged horse of Bellerophon. The son became a learned jurist, so that the people said 'He's not a man, he's a book'. He also attained the posts of *consul suffectus* and *praefectus urbi* with responsibility for order in the capital, according to the *Digest* (1, 2, 2, 47) under Vespasian. The dramatic date is early in Domitian's reign: hence *modo.*

attonitae: lit. 'thunderstruck' with the implication that their divine master has thundered; also 'paralysed' like a bird before a snake. The point of reference is rather Domitian than Pegasus.

positus: i.e. *praepositus.*

uilicus: tr. 'slave-driver'. Domitian treats his subjects as slaves: this is the implication of *dominus.* Pegasus is seen as a senior slave (like the manager of an estate) charged with keeping the other slaves in order.

78 *praefecti:* the other important posts

were *praefectus annonae* (Minister of Food), *praefectus praetorio* (Commander of the Praetorian Guard), and *praefectus uigilum* (Head of Police and Fire Brigade).

atque: linking *optimus . . . sanctissimus.*

79 Punctuation from Green.

80 *inermi:* J espouses military 'realism' against pacifist 'idealism'.

81 *Crispi:* Q. Vibius Crispus, born at Vercellae about AD 10, *consul suffectus* probably about the age of 50, *curator aquarum* from 68-71 (Frontinus *Aq.* 102), some time later governor of Africa (Plin. *NH* 19 proem 4). He was an unflappable advocate, better however in civil cases than on public affairs. He was immensely rich; Martial implies the unlikelihood of being *diuitior Crispo* (4, 54, 7); the scholiast put his fortune at 200 000 000 sesterces. He appears as a kind of Vicar of Bray, holding office under Nero, one of Vitellius's drinking-companions (DC 65, 2, 3), still in favour under Vespasian (Tac. *Dial.* 8); Statius calls him *Nestorei.* Tacitus has an ambivalent account of him, *pecunia potentia ingenio inter claros magis quam inter bonos* (*Hist.* 2, 10; cf 4, 41-3; *Ann.* 14, 28). Quintilian is more favourable and calls him *compositus et iucundus et delectationi natus* (10, 1, 119; cf 5, 13, 48; 12, 10, 11). He was a man of wit. Domitian had a nasty way of killing flies; Crispus, asked if anyone was with the emperor, answered *ne musca quidem* (Suet. *Dom.* 3). The description which follows accords with Quintilian's picture. For the abstract expression *Crispi senectus* see on 39.

84 *clade et peste:* Domitian was a pestilential disaster.

illa: like *ille* (73).

85 *saeuitiam:* a key theme: see on 37.

honestum: 'moral', 'ethically sound'.

liceret: J uses the impf. in unreal past conditions to stress the continuance of the action or state; cf 6, 388; 7, 69; 7, 212; 8, 263.

86 *uiolentius:* 'more arbitrary'.

87 *cum quo:* as in 9.

aut nimboso: except with foreign words and proper names there are only eighteen lines with fifth-foot spondees. Here it has the effect of slowing up the line as if the *amicus* suddenly realises that it is dangerous to say anything at all. The weather ('what a wet spring it is!') would normally be as innocuous a conversational topic in Rome as in England.

88 *pendebat:* 'hung in the balance'.

89 *ille:* Crispus.

derexit bracchia: 'struck out against'.

J may have in mind a Stoic image. We are all swept down by the irresistible torrent of Fate. It makes no difference whether we swim with the stream or against it — except to our peace of mind.

90 *ciuis:* 'subject' in relation to a monarch (Cic. *Rep.* 3, 25, 37).

posset: consec. subj. 'the sort of subject to . . .'.

91 *uitam inpendere uero:* 'expend his life for the truth'.

92 *sic:* 'That is how . . .'.

93 *armis:* a tinge of sarcasm in the metaphor.

illa: the same oblique reference to the emperor.

94 *proximus:* next (to Crispus).

properabat: a vivid picture: he is in his eighties.

Acilius: the Acilii Glabriones were a plebeian family, though claiming descent from Aeneas, and some of the more distinguished held the office of *tribunus plebis.* They appear in the lists of consuls from 191 BC to AD 438. We know little of the father here mentioned; he may (with changed name) be M. Acilius Aviola, consul in AD 54. The son was consul with Trajan in AD 91. The auguries are said to have portended supreme power for the one and death for the other. A curious story tells how he fought in the arena at the Juvenalia while consul, and killed a lion; J implies that this was directed to winning the emperor's favour or lulling his suspicions. He fell under Domitian's displeasure, and was exiled and subsequently executed in AD 95. The hostile sources charge Domitian with jealousy of his prowess in the arena. The official accusation was based on alleged revolutionary activities. But Cassius Dio mentions him in connection with Flavius Clemens, husband of Flavia Domitilla, who was charged with atheism (i.e. subverting the state religion), 'a charge preferred against many who drifted towards Jewish practices'. The catacomb of Domitilla was associated with the Christians, and the name Acilius Glabrio is similarly found in the catacomb of Priscilla. It is therefore a reasonable deduction that the younger Acilius was a Christian convert, though clearly not at the time of his consulship. One has only to read Revelation, written during persecution at this very period, to see how this accords with the charge of political subversion.

95 *iuuene:* a standard equivalent for *filio* in dactylic verse; cf 3, 158.

indigno . . . maneret: consecutive subj. is regular and natural with *(in)dignus qui. saeua:* see on 85.

96 *domini:* see on 11.71, 77.

olim . . . est: 'has long been' (and still is — hence the present): Cicero would use *iamdudum.* The whole sentence is a memorable epigram.

98 *fraterculus:* not a common word: the diminutive is effective here.

gigantis: there is a complex point. The giants were sons of Earth. In Greek γηγενής sometimes means a country bumpkin. In Latin *terrae filius* is used of someone whose parentage is unknown (Cic. *Att.* 1, 13; Pers. 6, 57-9). But also the giants tried to challenge the Olympian gods, and were annihilated by Jupiter's thunderbolt. Their *fraterculi,* not strong enough to shift mountains, too insignificant to be noticed, may be supposed to have escaped. The aristocrats arouse the suspicion of their *dominus et deus* and he annihilates them; even the *fraterculi* fear. Safer with Jupiter than Domitian!

100 *Numidas:* African. The word originally means 'nomad' and is then applied to the tribes of the Kabylie, from where it is used generically for African. The Latin masculine noun *numida* is used adjectivally without changing the termination to the more common masculine forms. There was some controversy in antiquity as to whether bears really came from Africa (Plin. *NH* 8, 131; Serv. in Verg. *A* 5, 37), which seems odd, if they were actually being imported for the arena, and it is odd that Augustine tells us that only in his day were they introduced into Carthage (c. *Acad.* 1, 2), but there is enough ancient and modern evidence to justify it (see Mayor ad loc.). Martial has *Libyci . . . ursi* (1, 104, 5).

Albana . . . harena: 'in the amphitheatre at Alba': Latin uses an adjective where we use a noun; cf Cic. *Fam.* 7, 37, 1. *dicta . . . Sestiana* 'Sestius's words'. Domitian had a private amphitheatre attached to his villa (Suet. *Dom.* 19).

nudus: not completely: 'stripped for action'.

101 *uenator:* the technical word for the gladiator who faced wild animals in the arena. For a full account of the *uenationes* see L. Friedländer *Roman Life and Manners under the Early Empire* vol. II Eng. tr. (London nd) pp. 62-90. M. Grant *Gladiators* (London 1967) is slight and has little to the point. For a well-illustrated popular account see J. Pearson *Arena*

London 1973 pp 115-29.

intellegat: note the distinctive emphasis of the subj. ('Who could fail to detect . . .?') and indic. *miratur* ('Who in fact raises his eyebrows at . . .?').

103 *Brute:* L. Junius, nephew of Tarquinius Superbus, escaped death by pretending to be mad, and received the cognomen Brutus ('the idiot') in consequence, living to be the liberator of Rome from the autocracy of Tarquin. Note how 101-3 all have a strong punctuation-break after the first syllable of foot 2. Juvenal usually seeks variety (Vergil is supremely skilful in this); he is clearly therefore producing a special effect, intensifying his point by rhythmic repetition.

barbato: barbers were introduced into Rome from Sicily about 300 BC and beards did not again come into fashion till Hadrian — except for philosophers. The beard was thus the sign of a simpler, less sophisticated age. Those who are interested in this fascinating topic should consult Reginald Reynolds's discursive but not unscholarly *Beards* (London 1950).

104 *melior uultu:* 'more cheerful', from Martial 4, 1, 4 *semper et hoc uoltu uel meliore nite.* The point is that of 98. He is not quite out of the top drawer (*ignobilis*) but looks no happier for all that.

105 *Rubrius:* Rubrius Gallus managed to survive changes at the top. He was sent by Nero against Galba but turned coat (DC 63, 27); under Otho he was in command at Brixellum, and represented the troops in negotiations (Tac. *Hist.* 2, 51); he was one of Caecina's advisers against Vitellius and we again find him acting as a go-between (*ib.* 99); under Vespasian he held a successful command against the Sarmatians (Jos. *Bell. Iud.* 7, 4, 3). C. Rubrius Gallus, *consul suffectus* in AD 101, may have been his son.

offensae: according to the scholiast the seduction of the empress Domitia Longina in her youth.

106 'and even so with no more sense of decency than a queer writing about others'.

107 *Montani:* not known for certain. There was a Curtius Montanus who was suspended for an alleged libel of Nero, and subsequently restored and prominent in the senate in the early days of Vespasian (Tac. *Ann.* 16, 28-9, 33; *Hist.* 4, 40-3). Our man here goes back to Nero's days (l. 137), but if it be he, he has evidently gone to seed, as he was *probae iuuentae.* Perhaps our man is the father; Highet refers to the familiar combination of the soft

self-indulgent father and the excitable,
high-principled revolutionary son. We
know also of T. Junius Montanus, *consul
suffectus* in AD 81. Pliny the younger
writes to an otherwise unidentified
Montanus (*Ep.* 7, 29; 8, 6).

uenter: for the shape of the phrase see
39, 81. J uses the circumlocution so
much in this satire that we suspect a satire
on the statesmen's refusal to speak directly.

abdomine tardus: 'slow by reason of his
paunch': the abl. gives the origin of the
slowness. The word is a coarse one, applied
to pig's bellies (Plaut. *Curc.* 323; Plin.
NH 8, 77, 209).

108   *Crispinus:* cf 1.

matutino . . . amomo: the effect of the
word-order is that he is in the middle,
bathed in scent. The whole line is mock-
epic. Perfumes were widely used by the
male Roman aristocrat, but only at evening
parties. *Amomum* is cardamom; it comes
from nothern India, via Mesopotamia; the
Romans were vague about origins and
called it *Assyrium;* the perfume was prepared
from the leaves.

109   *funera:* 'corpses'. The other main
occasion for perfumes. Persius describes
a dead man as *crassisque lutatus amomis*
'plastered with perfume' (3, 104); Martial
wittily has

qui non cenat et ungitur, Fabulle,
hic uere mihi mortuus uidetur   (3, 12, 4-5).

J's phrase is a good example of satiric
hyperbole carefully handled and not
overdone.

110   *Pompeius:* a *delator* not mentioned
elsewhere. We know of a Cn. Pompeius
Ferox Licinianus who was *consul
suffectus* under Trajan; he was perhaps too
junior at this stage. Cn. Pompeius Collega,
legate of Cappadocia in AD 75 or
M. Larcius Magnus Pompeius Silo, *consul
suffectus* in 82 or 83 is more likely.

susurro: another stock device of ancient
humour, the substitution of the unexpected
word, sometimes called paraprosdokian
(Greek 'contrary to the expected'). We
expect *machaera*, a sword or something
such, but a whisper is even more deadly.
Note how *tenui* sets up the ambiguity;
of the blade it is slender and so sharp;
of the whisper, almost inaudible.

111   A baroque, military, mock-epic
line.

112   *Fuscus:* Cornelius Fuscus. A man of
high birth who under Nero renounced
senatorial rank *quietis cupidine,* pre-
sumably under Epicurean influence. But

he could not throw off the attractions of
public life, and came out actively on behalf
of Galba, who made him governor of
Pannonia, and later (commanding the
Ravenna fleet) on behalf of Vespasian,
who gave him the rank of praetor. Under
Domitian he became praetorian prefect.
In AD 86 war broke out between Rome
and Dacia (roughly the modern Rumania).
Fuscus was given the command, failed
disastrously, was killed, his army
annihilated and their standards captured.
In AD 103 Trajan recovered one of these
(Tac. *Hist.* 2, 86; 3, 4; 12; 42; 66; 4, 44;
Suet. *Dom.* 6; DC 68, 9). Martial wrote
an epitaph for Fuscus (6, 76). J's line is
very biting: it's all very well dreaming about
battles in marble luxury; the real thing
is different. It will be noted that the
presence of Fuscus gives a dramatic date
for the episode early in Domitian's reign —
if J was bothered about chronological
consistency (see also on 147).

113   *prudens:* 'the trimmer' (Green).
Statius nicknames him Fabius, with
allusion to the famous general who pros-
pered by doing nothing.

Veiiento: a notorious *delator:* see on 3,
185.

Catullo: L. Valerius Catullus Messalinus,
consul with Domitian in AD 73. Pliny
(*Ep.* 4, 22) describes him . . . *qui luminibus
orbatus ingenio saeuo mala caecitatis
addiderat, non uerebatur, non erubescebat,
non miserebatur.* In Pliny's story,
Catullus being dead, Domitian asked one
day at dinner, 'What would have happened
to him, if he were alive today?' 'He would
be dining with us,' said one of the others.

114   *numquam uisae:* a single phrase:
the thought is based on an epigram of
Martial (8, 51).

flagrabat amore: parodying Cat. 67,
25 *siue quod impia mens caeco flagrabat
amore.*

115   A portentous line to suit its
subject. We are meant to think of Vergil's
description of the blinded Cyclops,
*monstrum horrendum, informe, ingens,
cui lumen ademptum* (*A* 3, 658). For
monstrum see on 2.

116   *caecus:* nearly always with more
than one dimension of meaning in Latin
poetry. He is physically blind; he is morally
blind; and his flattery blinds its recipient.

dirus: precisely 'abominable', except
that we have lost the association with bad
omens.

a ponte: beggars took their stand on
bridges (cf 14, 134 *aliquis de ponte*),

where the flow of people concentrated; blind men were often beggars; Catullus depended on Domitian's favour as the beggar on the bridge depended on the passers-by. The phrase could mean that he is still a beggar, or that he has risen from being a beggar to his present position. There is no doubt, as Green suggests, a parody of the offices of the senior civil servants, *ab epistulis, a libellis* and so on. Catullus is the Minister for Begging.

satelles: a subordinate accomplice in crime.

117 *Aricinos . . . ad axes:* 'at carriage-wheels outside Aricia'. Aricia was on Via Appia about 32 km from Rome; a steep hill meant that the carriages were moving slowly and made it a good pitch for beggars (Mart. 2, 19, 3 *Aricino . . . cliuo*).

mendicaret: for the construction see on 95.

118 A well-shaped line, with its two adjectives and two nouns separated by the verb: it gives a vivid picture with the beggar showering kisses although the carriage has moved on down the slope.

basia: J has introduced an amusing little joke. Catullus bears the same cognomen as the Republican poet. J plays on this. The poet introduced the word *basia* into Latin poetry. Further he liked to introduce *-ll-* words, especially at the end of a line. So here, of 109-16, five end in such a word. The point is particularly strong in 113-4; *basia* clinches it.

119 *stupuit:* a naturally intr. vb. which comes, like *mirari*, to mean 'wonder at' something. But there is a double meaning, for it also carries the sense 'be bemused', which he is, turning the wrong way.

120 There is an innuendo that he'd got his life similarly wrong.

at: ironical: 'unfortunately' (Duff).

illi: Catullus, not the emperor.

121 *Cilicis:* seemingly a gladiator, though the word is not otherwise attested in this sense. The Cilicians were notorious pirates, and might well be sent to the gladiatorial schools when captured.

122 *pegma:* a structure of wood, mounted on wheels and sometimes elaborately decorated, with upper storeys which could be raised into position or lowered by a system of weights as part of a spectacle. It was a considerable technological achievement, not without danger of accident (Phaedr. 5, 7, 7). We derive our word 'pageant' from it.

uelaria: the awnings spread above the seats: we can see them billowing over the

Pompeii amphitheatre in a wall-painting now in Naples: M. Bieber *A History of the Greek and Roman Theater* Princeton ²1961 Fig. 624.

123-135 *Veiiento gives his judgement that the fish is an omen. Montanus proposes that a dish should be specially made.*

123 *fanaticus:* strictly, one associated with a *fanum*, so a visionary prophet under divine inspiration.

oestro: lit. 'gadfly' *Tabanus bovinus*, and so (from the behaviour of cattle when stung) any form of frenzy or 'enthusiasm' or religious ecstasy.

124 *Bellona:* the ancient Roman war-goddess, later identified with the Cappadocian mother-goddess Ma, and served by ecstatic priests. Martial (12, 57, 11) speaks of *turba . . . entheata Bellonae* ('Bellona's god-inspired mob') in the streets of Rome. Notice the use of apostrophe, lit. 'a turning-away', breaking the narrative to address a person or thing, present or absent, directly. It is a rhetorical device adding variety and vividness.

126 *temone Britanno:* the British scythed chariot (*esseda*). *Temo*, strictly the shaft, is a little more than 'part for whole', as the British *essedarii* would run on to the shaft if it gave them an advantage (Caes. *BG* 4, 33). The early part of Domitian's reign saw the culmination of Agricola's campaigns.

127 *Aruiragus:* presumably a British chief, but otherwise unknown: the name of Joseph of Arimathea's legendary convert, and the character in Shakespeare's *Cymbeline* are later derivatives from this passage (Geoffrey of Monmouth 4, 16).

sudes: 'defences' or 'stakes'; he is referring to the dorsal fins, but it misses the point to tr. 'fins'. His image of armoured defence suggests to Veiiento his foreignness. The turbot does not have such a dorsal fin, but J was not an ichthyologist.

129 *Fabricio:* i.e. Veiiento.

130 The emperor as chairman puts the question.

conciditur?: the indic. is found, as well as the subj., in deliberative questions. The satire is very biting. J implies that this question, with a slightly different meaning ('Is he to be cut down?' rather than 'Is it to be cut up?') was regularly asked at the Council.

illo: the fish, ironically enough referred to as allusively as the emperor. In Brillat-Savarin's story (see on 72) the hostess cries,

'Oserais-tu bien deshonorer ainsi cette pauvre créature?' Montanus's language is high-flown.

131 *alta:* deep enough to hold the juices.

132 *tenui muro:* 'in its finely-worked wall'. He means the side of the casserole, but we must keep the metaphor, as J has throughout the poem the analogy of Domitian's political tyranny.

colligat: subj. of purpose: 'which is designed to hold'.

orbem: this establishes the point of the satire. Here it means the rounded bulk of the fish. But Domitian treats the world in the same way (see on 37).

133 *Prometheus:* the semi-divine being who made the human race out of clay in one version of the origins of mankind: used here humorously as the prototype of all potters: schol. *saturice figulus.*

135 *citius properate:* 'pretty quick', a regular use of the comparative. The plural shows that the order is addressed to the attendants.

castra: 'fortress'. Duff suggests 'court', but the meaning is unattested, and it misses the point of Domitian as a military autocrat, whose villa, as we have seen, is a fortress with access barred.

136-154 *The decision was taken, the Council dismissed. They had thought they were summoned to face a major crisis. It was a mere triviality. But better such a triviality than the slaughter of the Roman aristocracy.*

136 *uicit . . . sententia:* the formal phrase, and its normal word order (Liv. 2, 4, 3; Plin. *Paneg.* 76).

nouerat ille: note the 'bucolic diaeresis' isolating the last two feet. *ille* is here Montanus.

137 *noctesque Neronis:* cf Suet. *Ner.* 27 *epulas e medio die ad mediam noctem protrahebat.* The reference to Nero is pointed. J sees Domitian as the disastrous end of the Flavian dynasty as Nero was of the Julio-Claudian; cf 38.

138 *aliamque famem:* 'the second wind of appetite'; prose would have *alteram.* Martial (5, 78, 17-8) comments on the function of wine in renewing the appetite.

Falerno: sc. *uino,* one of the most famous Italian wines, grown in the *ager Falernus* in Campania.

140 *tempestate mea:* 'in my time', but we cannot wholly escape in the context of this poem the implication that the times were stormy.

Circeis: on the Campanian coast, famous

for oysters. 'He was expert in grasping at the first bite whether . . .'.

141 *Lucrinum ad saxum:* the *lacus Lucrinus (Lago Lucrino)* was and is near Baiae by the bay of Naples. I do not know of any other reference to the rock or rocks. The oysters were so famous that Martial simply calls them *Lucrina* (6, 11, 5; 12, 48, 4).

Rutupino . . . fundo: Richborough on the Kent coast, where there are impressive remains of a Saxon shore fort and the base of a signal-tower. Discarded oyster-shells have been discovered on Roman sites in Britain.

143 *echini:* a sea-urchin, also a delicacy.

144 *surgitur:* impersonal pass.: 'the court rises'. The line could come from epic.

misso . . . consilio: 'the Council is dismissed': *concilium* and *consilium* are both used in this sense. The dismissal is summary; they are not invited to dinner.

145 *Albanam . . . in arcem:* see on 60, 61, 135.

dux magnus: ironical, like the other titles in this poem: it is used by Statius of Domitian (*Silv.* 3, 1, 62). Note the word-order: the great commander is in the middle of the fortress.

146 *attonitos:* see on 77.

147 *Chattis:* a tribe from the Rhineland, against whom Domitian campaigned in AD 83, taking the title Germanicus in consequence. This (cf on 112) is another reason for a dramatic date of AD 82-3.

Sygambris: another Rhineland tribe, feared and noted as soldiers: we have no other indication that Domitian was involved with them.

148 *orbis:* reinforcing the double meaning: see on 37, 132.

149 *anxia:* the letter is animated, and depicted as frightened.

pinna: this completes the image, of a frightened bird. We have one or two earlier examples of arbitrary emperors summoning the Council for a triviality. Caligula is said to have called them to watch him dance (DC 59, 5, 5), Nero to announce a musical invention (DC 63, 26, 4).

150 A serious conclusion.

151 *saeuitiae:* the third occurrence of a key word (or root); cf 85, 95.

151-2 Suetonius gives an account of the senators executed by Domitian: Civica Cerealis, a proconsul; Salvidienus Orfitus; Acilius Glabrio (95); Aelius Lamia for jokes against him; Salvius Cocceianus, for celebrating Otho's birthday; Mettius

Pompusianus, for casting the emperor's horoscope and other offences; Sallustius Lucullus, governor of Britain; Junius Rusticus for honouring critics of the empire; Helvidius Priscus, jr, for a possible personal satire in a play; Flavius Sabinus, one of the royal family, as a possible rival emperor. It was not only the nobility who suffered (Suet. *Dom.* 10). We can see why J would be cautious about publishing contemporary satire in Domitian's reign, but his continued caution implies that the situation has not essentially changed.

152 *uindice:* Vindex was a liberation-leader against Nero: there are some indications of a pun (cf 38) and see on 54.

153 *cerdonibus:* schol. *ignobilibus; cerdo est proprie turpis lucri cupidus.* The word is derived from the Greek κέρδος, 'profit', i.e. those who work for money. In the *Digest* it is used as a proper name for slaves (i.e. those engaged in manual work). Those who assassinated Domitian included his niece's business manager, a junior officer, a freedman, the chief valet-de-chambre, and a professional gladiator (Suet. *Dom.* 17). J is engaging in bitter irony at the expense of the pusillanimous aristocrats from whom the tyrant had nothing to fear. But the assassins were not typical working-class; they were the agents of a palace revolution, and Domitian's wife was behind it. See M.P. Charlesworth in *JRS* 27 (1937) 60-2.

154 *nocuit:* 'destroyed'.

Lamiarum caede madenti: 'the man who was dripping with the blood of Lamiae'. Domitian executed Aelius Lamia (see on 151-2), and J uses him to personify the senatorial class. The whole of these last five lines seem based on traditional anti-Nero rhetoric, and are closely parallel to an attack on Nero's tyranny by the elder Pliny, ending *saeuius sic nos repleuit umbris (NH* 30, 15).

General comments
The primary theme is clear. It is *luxuria,* luxury, extravagance, associated with a strong sense of disproportion. It has been argued in a well-known essay by William Arrowsmith, 'Luxury and Death in the Satyricon" *Arion* 5 (1966) 304-31, that *luxuria* was the satiric target of Petronius, and it is not surprising to find it here and elsewhere in J (e.g. 6, 293) as an object of attack. A second theme is bestial savagery or cruelty: it is a thought which continually recurs, especially in the second section of the poem from the opening (4, 37

laceraret) onwards: *saeuus* or *saeuitia* appears three times explicitly (85, 95, 151). A third subject is Domitian's pretensions, whether as a military genius, or as an autocrat who treated citizens as slaves, or as a power equal to the gods (4, 71) and a god incarnate himself. For this last, J parodies those poets who have prostituted their Muse to courtly flattery, and particularly Statius and his *Bellum Germanicum.* This explains the continual parodies of epic style (e.g. 29, 39-40, 44-5, 60-9, 81, 107-8, 112, 123-4, 130-5, 144-5). It seems likely that some of these are detailed parodies of Statius. Valla in his commentary quotes from some lost scholiast Statius's lines:

lumina, Nestorei mitis prudentia Crispi,
et Fabius Veiiento — potentem signat
    utrumque
purpura, ter memores implerunt nomine
    fastos —
et prope Caesareae confinis Acilius aulae.

J's *Crispi iucunda senectus* is clear parody of the first line. This parodic element also explains, at least in part, the military allusions (e.g. 111-2, 124-8, 135, 146-9), though it is important to see this as part of J's satire on the emperor and not just as a skit on his lackey-poet.

In this poem the hangers-on of the emperor are an incidental not an essential target, as they have been in the third satire. They are there as a backcloth to the emperor, not the other way round. J delights to show them excluded while the fisherman and his fish are admitted, as he delights to show them dismissed without any share in the spoils, and at the end he makes the point directly: the *cerdones* do something about the situation, the *nobiles* allow themselves to be extinguished. But the extinguisher, not the extinguished, is central to this satire.

Three questions thrust themselves forward as we reflect on this poem. What is the connection between the two parts of the poem? Why is there such a difference of length between them? Why satirise a ruthless tyrant through such a trivial episode?

We can discuss the first two questions together. There is no agreed answer to them. A number of critics have castigated the poem for this lack of proportion; some have even suggested that the attack on Crispinus is a fragment of a lost satire against him, which has been cobbled on to an integral satire against Domitian; others, more sympathetic to the poem as it stands, admit the lack of proportion, but suggest that in satire this is irrelevant. Three constructive points may be made: (i) Both parts are an attack on *luxuria* and on pretension. The first is the attack of direct anger: it is naturally bitter and concise. The second is presented in mock-epic: it is naturally urbane and leisured. They are thus complementary to one another, and together they add up to a powerful offensive on two fronts. (ii) Crispinus in the first section parallels Domitian in the second. Both men are overconcerned with a fish, trivial in their perversions, vicious in their characters. It is as if we get the vivid picture of Crispinus; the mask is stripped away, and there to be contemplated at leisure is the emperor. Further, the contemptibility of Crispinus infects the view we take of Domitian. (iii) The two parts are structured in chiasmus or cross-formation. The movement of the first passes from crime to triviality, the second from triviality to crime.

The third question is given an excellent partial answer by Gilbert Highet in *Juvenal the Satirist* (78): 'Juvenal remembers what some of his critics forget: that ridicule is as powerful a weapon as invective, and that it is more properly the arm of satire. Many a great scoundrel will be unmoved if he is called a villain, and some impressionable people will try to emulate him. But if he is shown to be a fool, he will wince, and those who might have admired him will turn away with a grin. When Napoleon asked Talleyrand what he thought of the execution of the Duc d'Enghien, Talleyrand replied, "It was worse than a crime. It was a blunder." In the same way, Juvenal shows that his worst-hated butts were not merely knaves; they were also fools.'

But there is another point, which we have encountered in earlier satires. It is that the trivial action reveals the inner character and in some sense represents the world-shattering crime. It happens that we can illustrate this from the life of Domitian in another way. Suetonius gives us a picture of a man who at the beginning of his reign displayed considerable virtues both as a human being and as an emperor. But he used to spend hours in solitude catching flies and stabbing them with a sharp pin (Suet. *Dom.* 3). Before long he was stabbing senators. The flies in Suetonius's narrative and the fish in J's satire perform the same function. In the

end there is nothing trivial. J emphasises the point verbally. 4, 37 and 4, 132 both end with the word *orbem*. In the first it means 'world', which Domitian was flaying. In the second it is the 'circumference' of the fish, which the emperor proposes should be cut up: indeed the magnificent ambiguity of *conciditur?* (130) makes the point in its own way. The political reference of the satire is clear. The emperor treats the fish like the world and the world like the fish.

Perhaps the most brilliant aspect of the satire is the technique J uses for building up the picture of Domitian (a picture somewhat indebted to Seneca's of Caligula: *Const. Sap.* 18; *Ben.* 2, 2). There is very little directly about him. J's technique is indirect: we see the emperor largely through his effect on others. Directly, he is described at 38 as a bald-headed Nero: this is the only reference to his looks. We are told that he was open to flattery (69-71), and that he hated his 'friends' (72). He speaks only once (130), four words in Latin, and innocent words on the surface, though we have noted the sinister overtones in *conciditur?* And that is all — directly.

But our indirect picture is built up from the first line. The introduction of Crispinus is meant as an introduction to Domitian, a monster of evil without one small redeeming virtue, contriving to be at once vicious and trivial. Our second indirect view of the emperor is through the fisherman, surrounded by informers, believing that the emperor claims everything, fearful, rushing to the palace, unctuous in flattery: this is the effect of Domitian's rule on a commoner. The crowd outside the villa, excluded senators among them, are part of this picture: they are worse off than this terrorised, bumbling countryman. Next the Council, summoned over a triviality, the pallor on their faces just because they are *amici principis,* the hasty snatching of official robes, the two most honourable men, old age notwithstanding, taking care to be there first, and swimming with the tide, the latecomers hurrying in terrified, the last to come speaking first, as if to assure the emperor of their conscientious concern. Each of them is characterised in turn, compromising, weak, hypocritical, criminal, gluttonous, vicious, murderous, lustful. They speak flattery and disband. And at the end J shows us dead bodies and terror.

If I were filming this I should not show Domitian at all — at least not his face.

I might use a shot from above showing a
bald pate and a wreath as the fisherman
kneels before the throne, and I might
show feet and toga as the emperor enters the
Council-chamber, and perhaps a movement
of a jewelled finger. But I would show the
emperor reflected in the fear and viciousness
of the faces around, and in the state of
country and city. This is what, in words,
J achieves.

Bibliography

Anderson, W.S. 'Studies in Book I of
Juvenal' *YCS* 15 (1957) 68-80

Birt, Th. 'Der Aufbau der 6ten und 4ten
Satire Juvenals' *Rh M* 70 (1915)
524-50

Colton, R.E. 'Cabinet Meeting: Juvenal's
Fourth Satire' *CB* 40 (1964) 1-4

Crook, J.A. *Consilium Principis* Cambridge
1955

Cuq, E. 'Mémoire sur le *consilium
principis* d'Auguste à Dioclétien'
*Mémoires présentés à l'Acad. des
Inscriptions* Ie série, 9 (1884) 2, 311-504

Ercole, P. *Studi Giovenaliani* Lanciano
1935 pp. 161-83

Griffith, J.G. 'Juvenal, Statius, and the
Flavian Establishment' *GR* 16 (1969)
134-50

Heilmann, W. 'Zur composition der

vierten Satire und des ersten Satiren-
busches Juvenals' *Rh M* 110 (1967)
358-70

Helmbold, W.C. and O'Neil, E.N. 'The
Structure of Juvenal IV' *AJP* 77
(1951) 68-73

Kilpatrick, R.L. 'Juvenal's "Patchwork"
Satires: 4 and 7' *YCS* 23 (1973)
229-41

Lafleur, R.A. 'Juvenal's "Friendly
Fingernails" ' *Wiener Studien* NS 9
(1975) 230-5

Marache, R. *Juvénal: Saturae III, IV, V*
Paris 1965

Mispoulet, J.B. 'Le Turbot' *Rev. Phil.*
13 (1889) 32-44

Nägelsbach, C.F. 'Ueber die Composition
der vierten und sechsten Satire
Juvenals' *Philol.* 3 (1848) 469-82

Scivoletto, N. 'Plinio il Giovane e
Giovenale' *Giorn. ital. di filol.* 10
(1957) 133-46

Scott, I.G. *The Grand Style in the Satires of
Juvenal* (Smith Coll. Class. Stud. 8)
Northampton, Mass. 1927

Stegemann, W. *De Juvenalis dispositione*
Weyda 1913

Thomson, J.O. 'Juvenal's Big-Fish Satire'
GR 21 (1952) 86-7

Townend, G.B. 'The Literary Substrata to
Juvenal's Satires' *JRS* 63 (1973) 148-60

Weinreich, O. 'Juvenals IV. Satire und
Martial' *Studien zu Martial* Stuttgart 1928

SATIRE 5

A dinner party. Highet heads his account
of it 'Snobs and snubs'. Rhetorically it is a
*suasoria: an cena diuitis pauperi ferenda
sit.* It is comparatively brief, and decidedly
vivid and vigorous. The structure is
basically logical and straightforward, and
the variations from the basic structure are
carefully controlled.

1-11   Introduction
12-155 The Dinner Party
  12-23   The invitation
  24-79   Wine, service, bread (inferior
            for guests)
  80-106   Fish (inferior for guests)
  107-13   Digression in which J attacks
            Virro
  114-24   Game and truffles (of which
            the guests get none)
  125-45   *Amicitia*
  146-8   Mushrooms (inferior for guests)
  149-55   Dessert (inferior for guests)

156-73   Conclusion

The attack on the host, Virro (108-13), is
seemingly renewed at 156-60, but turns to
an attack on the guest, Trebius, for his
pusillanimity. 125-45 is a bridge between
the two, and breaks the account of the main
course. The normal Roman dinner menu
passed through *gustus* or *promulsis* (hors
d'oeuvres); *fercula* (main course); *mensae
secundae* (dessert). The *fercula* here is
symmetrically divided between fish (inferior
for guests), game and truffles (which the
guests do not share), mushrooms (inferior
for guests). No *gustus* is mentioned; J's
account of the dessert is balanced by the
wine and bread.

Hall (S.2) imitates the satire closely
even to the names.

1-11 *If you're not ashamed to be a
parasite at another man's table, suffering his*

insults, I'd never trust you even on oath.
Better be a street-beggar than that.

1   J (like Horace) likes to give us the
impression that we're breaking into a
conversation already started. For life is
like that. It flows: it hasn't neat beginnings
and ends. So it takes us a line or two to
find out what is happening, and it isn't till
19 that we learn the hanger-on's name.

propositi: 'your way of life', a philosophi-
cal term, like *mens: pudet* (impersonal)
takes the genitive of the field within which
the shame is felt (Woodcock 73(4)).

atque eadem est mens: the first of three
harsh line-endings in eight lines. This is
especially harsh with two elisions and four
word-stresses in the last two feet.

2   'with the result that you think the
supreme good consists in living from
another man's crusts' (or possibly the *ut-*
clause depends on *mens* and defines the
intention). Supply *esse: uiuere* (a verb-
noun) is subject (or predicate) of *esse.*

bona summa: hardly more than *summum
bonum,* the technical philosophical term
for the ultimate goal of life. The poets use
singular and plural interchangeably; if we
want to make more of it, it becomes 'all
the goals of all the philosophies'.

aliena . . . quadra: abl. of the source
from which life is obtained. The Roman
bap (*placenta*) was designed to be broken
into quarters, like scofa bread.

3   *Sarmentus:* seemingly a freedman of
Maecenas, who was in Augustus's favour
for his table-wit, and who rose to wealth
only to fall into poverty again. (Schol. ad
loc.; Plut. *Ant.* 52; Hor. *S* 1, 5, 52).

iniquas: because it accepts the rich and
patronises the poor.

4   *Caesaris:* i.e. Augustus.

Gabba: a wit of the same period, *ille suo
felix Caesare Gabba uetus* (Mart. 10, 101,
2; cf 1, 41, 16).

5   *quamuis:* with *iurato.*

iurato: from *iurari,* a deponent form
occasionally found.

credere: inf. after *metuere* is poetic: but
the inf. as a verb-noun can be the object
of fear.

noui: from *noscere:* the pf. has a
present meaning, 'I have recognised' and
so, 'I know'.

hoc tamen ipsum: very emphatic: three
word-accents after a bucolic diaeresis.

7   *puta:* 'suppose', 'imagine'. The first
of four lines with a strong third-foot
caesura; the rhythmic repetition hammers
home the point rhetorically.

8   *crepido:* any raised platform: *crepido*

semitae is the sidewalk or pavement, but
probably J is thinking of the steps of
temples (where money was deposited), a
natural pitch for beggars.

pons: see on 4, 116.

et tegetis pars: broken rhythm again; the
rush-mat was an emblem of poverty.
Martial (11, 56) tells of a Stoic philosopher
who sleeps on a mat and a bedbug.

9   *dimidia breuior:* sc. *parte:* 'too short
by half', ablative of the measure of
difference, a variety of the instrumental
abl. (Woodcock 82).

tanti: 'worth so much', sc. *est:* see on 3,
54.

iniuria cenae: 'the insult of a dinner', a
startling phrase: *cenae* is gen. of definition,
'the insult consisting in the dinner'
(Woodcock 72(5)).

10   *cum:* 'although'.

possit: sc. *fames.*

honestius: ironic, since it strictly refers
to aristocrats and holders of high office like
the host.

illic: on the beggar's pitch.

11   *tremere:* two-edged: better to shiver
with cold as a beggar than to tremble with
other emotions at the millionaire's table.

sordes farris: i.e. *sordidum far:* the
expression is typical of J; cf 4, 81
Crispi . . . senectus.

canini: 'thrown to the dogs', a vigorous
end to the introduction.

12-23   *An invitation to dinner is reckoned
full payment for all your services, and it
comes only once every two months or
more. And poor Trebius is overjoyed to
receive it, although he's earned it by short
nights.*

12   *fige:* 'impress on yourself' (cf 9,
94; 11, 28): the exact usage is not easy to
parallel elsewhere, and perhaps we should
treat it as strong slang 'get this straight'.

13   The shape of the line is noteworthy.
J has not intertwined his two adj.-noun
pairs (*solidam — ueterum* are rhythmically
interchangeable). The effect is of a series
of heavy phrases delivered with pointed
breaks: *discumbere iussus — mercedem
solidam — ueterum (capis) officiorum.*
But there is also an effective chiasmus, and
irony in the juxtaposition of *solidam
ueterum,* and the five-syllable word at the
end lends ironic weight.

14   *fructus:* sc. *est.*

amicitiae magnae: i.e. with an *amicus
magnus:* J used this phrase more than once
and always ironically (1, 33; 3, 51).
Strictly the *sportula* was a substitute for

the dinner invitation and discharged the obligation.

inputat hunc rex: the bucolic diaeresis and the two accents in the last foot mark these words out for ironic emphasis, as does the repetition of *inputat. Inputat* is a metaphor from business practice, 'charges to your account', another ironic hit at the 'Protestant ethic'. *Rex* is the patron; it held for the Romans overtones of oriental splendour and tyranny (1, 136).

15 *ergo duos post:* a second bucolic diaeresis followed again by broken rhythm in the last two feet puts bitter weight on the words.

17 *tertia:* i.e. the place of lowest dignity on the couch of lowest dignity: see on 3, 82.

culcita: the cushion or bolster placed between guests on the same couch and offering support for the elbow.

18 Note the abrupt writing; the sentence ending at the weak caesura in the fifth foot; the offbeat accent on *quid.*

19 *Trebius:* the name is found in inscriptions from J's home town of Aquinum (*CIL* 10, 5528-9).

rumpere somnum: so *nocte* (3, 127). The early-morning duty-call was a ground for complaint by the *clientes, officia antelucana* (Plin. *Ep.* 3, 12, 2; cf Mart. 3, 36, 3; 10, 82, 2; 12, 18, 13, etc.).

20 *ligulas dimittere:* 'trailing his shoelaces in all directions' i.e. in his hurry he has not tied them. The word probably comes from *ligare* ('tie') though some ancients took it as diminutive (*lingula*) from *lingua* ('tongue').

21 *salutatrix:* in Mart. 7, 87, 6 of a magpie.

orbem: the round of visits.

22 *dubiis:* i.e. they are beginning to disappear.

23 *serraca Bootae:* i.e. the Great Bear, sometimes called the Plough or Charles's Wain (*serraca*) in England. Bootes is the ploughman or ox-driver: *frigida* because it is a northern constellation, pointing to the north star: *pigri* because it appears almost stationary.

24-79 *And what a dinner! You get cheap wine which makes you quarrelsome; he has an old vintage. He drinks from jewelled chalices, you from a cup with four spouts, and cracked at that. Even your water is inferior to his. You have an African stableboy as waiter, he has a handsome expensive boy from Asia; and at that your waiter gives you no service. You eat a hard rye-bread; he has pure white; and if you forget yourself and take from the wrong dish you are firmly told off. Was it for this that you toiled uphill in all weathers?*

24-5 *sucida . . . lana:* three passages explain this. Varro *RR* 2 11, 6 explains that sheep begin to sweat in spring, and wool greasy with sweat is called *sucida;* Pliny (*NH* 29, 9) that this wool was steeped in oil, wine or vinegar for use as a poultice; the medical writer Celsus (2, 33) *lana sucida ex aceto uel uino.* Plainly only a cheap wine would be so used, but the wine served to the guests would be rejected even by the wool — an excellent hyperbole.

25 *Corybanta:* acc. sing., a Greek form. The corybant was an ecstatic follower of the Mother of the Gods; 'out of a guest you'll see a charismatic'. The scholiast comments *uinum malum mentem turbat.*

26 *iurgia proludunt:* 'insults form the preliminary exhibition'. The metaphor is from the gladiatorial displays, where (as in fencing) there were no doubt standard exercises before the serious contest begins. There is an implication that the host is putting on a show for himself rather than a meal for his hangers-on.

torques: an excellent word, meaning to whirl or brandish, as with a sling or spear, but expressive also of the whirl he is in himself.

27 *saucius:* a notable and presumably deliberate ambiguity; the meaning passes from 'reeling' or 'drunk' (Mart. 3, 68, 6), going with the preceding words, to 'injured', going with what follows.

28 *libertorum:* the home-team, hostile to the intruder.

cohortem: military metaphor.

29 A carefully constructed line with two noun-adj. combinations interlocking and centring on a verb.

Saguntina: with *lagona.* Saguntum in Spain was famous for cheap, coarse earthenware. But there is a double allusion, since Hannibal's capture of Saguntum sparked off the Second Punic War.

lagona: instrumental abl.: the jugs are the weapons.

30 *ipse:* the host: his name, we learn later, is Virro.

capillato: see on 4, 103. The Romans dated their years (and therefore their vintages) by the consul's name.

diffusum: sc. *uinum.* This is the process corresponding to our bottling, the transfer of the wine from the original *dolia* into *amphorae,* and implies a vintage wine.

31 *bellis socialibus:* 'the wars with the allies' (91-88 BC): the Romans use an adj. where we use a noun-phrase. We do in fact know of 200-year-old vintages (Plin. *NH* 14, 55).

32 *cardiaco:* 'dyspeptic'.

cyathum: the ladle used to transfer the wine from mixing-bowl to cup: tr. 'spoonful'.

missurus: there is an implied conditional: 'he, who *would* never present a spoonful of wine to a friend even *if* he were dyspeptic.'

33 *Albanis:* in Latium (cf 4, 61), not far from Rome. Dionysius of Halicarnassus (1, 66, 3) ranks the wine of Alba second only to Falernian. It is a stock feature of the *cena* (Hor. *S* 2, 8, 16).

de: J allows monosyllabic preps at the end of a line; cf 6, 58; 8, 255; 14, 114; 14, 306.

34 *Setinis:* Setia, the modern Sezza, is also in Latium; its wine was a favourite with Augustus. Pliny (*NH* 14, 8, 59ff) ranks the Setine as 1er *grand cru,* Falernian as 2^e, the wines of Alba and Sorrento as 3^e, and the Mamertine vintages of Sicily as 4^e.

patriam titulumque: a slight zeugma since the name of the place of origin is on the label.

35 *fuligine:* the amphoras were stored in a smoky atmosphere to help the wine to mature (Mart. 10, 36, 1, to which the whole passage is indebted).

testae: anything made of earthenware, here the jar.

36 *coronati:* it was normal to wear garlands at parties or on special occasions.

Thrasea: P. Clodius Thrasea Paetus, *consul suffectus* in AD 56, a rare example of a man of integrity in politics, though some charged him with being more interested in flaunting his conscience than in useful service, a Stoic who made pointed protests (unlike his fellow-Stoic Seneca) at Nero's outrages, and was driven to suicide in AD 66. Thrasea and Seneca both offered bitterly satirical vows to Jupiter Liberator at their deaths (Tac. *Ann.* 15, 64, 4; 16, 35, 2; DC 62, 21, 4; H. Mattingly in *JRS* 10 (1920) 38). But Thrasea was no organiser of coups, a Socrates not a Brutus.

Heluidius: Helvidius Priscus, another political Stoic, son-in-law to Thrasea, exiled in AD 66, recalled in 68, executed by Vespasian, perhaps in 75. There is

some evidence that radical Stoics at this time did not object to the existence of an emperor, but wanted him to be the best man possible, and so stood against tyrannical or immoral behaviour, and also against hereditary succession. But, however radical, they enjoyed good wine.

Brutorum et Cassi: M. Brutus, Dec. Brutus, and C. Cassius Longinus, leaders of the conspiracy against Julius Caesar. The name of Brutus always conjured up also L. Junius Brutus, who established the Republic.

natalibus: celebration of the birthdays of the dead was a normal feature of Roman society (Mayor ad loc.).

37 *ipse:* the host. Note again the bucolic diaeresis throwing weight on what follows.

38 *Heliadum crustas:* 'embossments of the daughters of the Sun', a typically allusive Silver Latinism, i.e. cups chased in amber. The Heliades were sisters of the ill-fated Phaethon, and were turned into trees and wept tears of amber.

inaequales berullo: the only line in J which ends with three spondees: *inaequales* because the jewels make the surface uneven, but of course the cup is *different,* and *unfairly* different from those given to the guests.

39 *Virro:* the name, like that of Trebius, is long held up. It is a rarish but genuine name. Vibidius Virro was expelled from the senate in AD 17 for immoral behaviour. J brings the name back at 9, 35 for a queer. The name (*uir-ro*) is ironical. Syme in *JRS* 39 (1949) 17 suggests that the family was Paelignian, making Virro and Trebius neighbours in origin.

41 *numeret ... obseruet:* purpose: 'to count'.

ungues ... acutos: schol. *ne ex ipsa aut gemmam rapias aut unguibus aurum radas.*

42 *praeclara:* predicate: 'as outstanding'.

iaspis: three syllables.

44 *in uaginae fronte:* a neat ambiguity: 'on the front of his scabbard' but also 'in front of his mistress', with some contrast to the homosexual Virro.

45 *iuuenis praelatus Iarbae:* a characteristically allusive periphrasis. The reference is to Aeneas, whom Dido preferred to the African chief Iarbas. Epic parody is never far from J's intent.

46 *Beneuentani sutoris:* Vatinius (Tac. *Ann.* 15, 34) was a shoemaker from Beneventum, a favourite of Nero, and a man rich enough to offer the public a

gladiatorial show in AD 62. He had a long
nose, and in consequence a cup with four
long nose-like spouts was named after
him. The passage is based on Mart. 14, 96
*uilia sutoris calicem monumenta Vatini/
accipe: sed nasus longior ille fuit.*

47 *siccabis calicem:* from Hor. *S* 2, 6,
68 *siccat inaequalis calices conuiua.*

48 *rupto . . . uitro:* either abl. abs. or
dat. ('for its broken glass'): the sulphur
was used as cement.

50 *Geticis:* the Getae were a Thracian
tribe on the Danube, enjoying proverbially
cold winters.

decocta: water purified by boiling and
iced with snow, an invention of Nero's;
cf Sen. *QN* 4, 13, 5; Plin. *NH* 31, 23, 40.

51 *modo:* 'just now' with *querebar.*

52 *cursor:* not one of the professional
house-servants, but one of the stableboys
dragged in to wait at table.

53 *Gaetulus:* a Berber from the Sahara.
Mauri: strictly from Mauretania, i.e.
western Algeria and Morocco, so any
Negro.

et: placing the rel. clause parallel to
nigri.

54 *per mediam . . . noctem:* an
encounter with any black creature by night
was portentous (Plut. *Brut.* 48; [Sen.]
Ludus 13, 3): we still have superstitions
about black cats. But J may mean no more
than that it would give you a shock to meet
him.

55 *Latinae:* the natural route for
Trebius between Rome and Aquinum. For
the tombs along the road see on 1, 171.
J after extending the description of the
Moor through one line uses another to add a
picturesque digression.

56 *flos Asiae:* sc. *stat.* The homosexual
atmosphere is overpowering: so is the
contrast of beauty and ugliness. For the
metaphor cf Ter. *Eun.* 319 (of a girl)
CH. anni? sedecim/PA. flos ipsus; Cat. 24,
1 (of a boy) *O qui flosculus es Iuuentiorum.*
The province of Asia covered western Asia
Minor. Miletus was particularly famed for
such slaves.

57 *Tulli:* Tullus Hostilius, one of the
more military of the early kings of Rome.
Anci: Ancus Martius, another of the
early kings. Horace (*O* 4, 7, 15) couples
them as *diues Tullus et Ancus:* there
may be an allusion, and if so it is a
reminder that death is round the corner.

58 *ne te teneam:* a throwaway phrase,
adding a conversational touch. The line is
remarkable for its sound, first *nē tĕ tĕnĕ,*

then the rolling *rs* and the succession of
m and *n.*

59 *friuola:* 'bits and pieces' (cf 3, 198),
satirical.

quod cum ita sit: another throwaway
conversational phrase.

Gaetulum Ganymedem: a striking phrase,
bringing 'barbarian' Africa alongside Greek
mythology, pointed by alliteration, and
sharpened by the four-syllable final word
creating an offbeat rhythm. Ganymede was
a handsome boy from Asia, kidnapped by
Jupiter for his good looks to be a decora-
tive adjunct to Olympian banquets as
drinks-waiter.

62 *digna supercilio:* 'excuse his air of
superiority'.

ille: your own waiter: even he doesn't
bother.

63 *calidae gelidaeque:* sc. *aquae:* for
mixing with the wine.

64 *quippe:* our 'as a matter of fact',
explaining what has gone before.

indignatur: 'he thinks it beneath him'.

ueteri: ambiguous between 'doddering'
(the view of the slave) and 'faithful',
'of long standing' (the view of the *cliens*).

65 *poscas . . . recumbas:* subj. because
in the thoughts of the slave. The psycholo-
gical analysis is excellent.

stante: the technical term for waiting
at table, but in formal antithesis to
recumbas. It is tempting to translate 'be-
cause you are lying in wait while he is
standing and waiting'.

66 Heinrich proposed the deletion of
this line, which adds nothing and weakens
what has gone before.

67 *porrexit:* i.e. in *canistris* (74).

murmure: 'grumbling'.

68 *uix fractum:* 'which has been broken
with difficulty' like the rock-cakes in the
Punch cartoon (Hostess: 'Take your pick.'
Another guest *sotto voce:* 'You'll need
it.').

frusta farinae: note the alliteration.

69 *quae genuinum agitent:* 'designed
to give your grinders work to do': note
the subj.

70 *niueus:* There is a curious contrast
between Teutons and Latins across the
ages. Goethe's remark (24.9.1792) is
irresistible: 'White and black bread is the
true shibboleth that parts German and
Frenchman. Where the girls are blonde,
the bread is black, and where the girls are
dark, the bread is white.'

siligine: the highest-quality flour.

72 *salua . . . reuerentia:* 'Show a proper
respect for the *boîte à pain*'. The Greek

word is very sarcastic; cf 3, 67-8, 76-7.
The bread was sometimes served directly
from the pan.

73 *inprobulum:* 'naughty': the dimin.
does not occur elsewhere.

superest: 'there is someone to keep an
eye on you'.

cogat: 'to force you': subj. of purpose.

74 *uis tu:* a sharp order, couched in
pseudo-polite language: 'Kindly . . .'.

75 *colorem:* a beautiful touch, literally
'the colour', but in Silver Latin also 'the
quality'.

76 *scilicet:* very sarcastic: 'so it was for
this'. Trebius is talking to himself, but the
language is mock-epic.

77 *cucurri:* cf 19-23.

78 *Esquilias:* the Esquiline, one of the
Seven Hills, to the east of the Forum, an
area of fashionable housing.

79 *Iuppiter:* Often of the sky or the
weather, but the use of the name creates
a different world from ours, and should be
retained.

paenula: a cloak used for protection
against the weather.

nimbo: a cloudburst, rainstorm or
cataract.

80-106 *The patron has a lordly lobster;
you have a shrimp garnished with half an
egg. He has oil from Venafrum; you have
old lamp-oil. He has mullet and lamprey;
you have eel and pike fed on sewage.*

80-2 The meaning is clear, the syntax
contorted. 'See how the lobster which is
being carried in for the patron identifies
his dish by means of its long body, and how
its tail looks down on the dinner-party,
buttressed as it is with asparagus on every
side.' There are a number of awkward-
nesses: (a) *quam* might be absolute, or
with *longo,* or (though probably not) with
lancem; (b) *quae fertur domino* might be
taken with *lancem* or with *squilla,* and is
perhaps deliberately ambiguous; (c) either
quibus or *qua* is otiose (but we can see the
shape, clumsily in English, 'with what
asparagus being buttressed how . . .');
(d) the change from *quam,* or even *quam
longo,* to *qua* is clumsy. We may suspect
that J is conveying that the magnificence
of the patron's meal (and its contrast with
the client's) lead to a kind of stammering
incoherence.

81 *squilla:* part of the satirist's stock-in-
trade (Lucil. 1240).

82 *despiciat:* a nice touch, literally
because carried in by a tall butler, and
metaphorically, at least in the minds of
the diners.

84 *dimidio . . . ouo:* 'a shrimp squeezed
in by half an egg': presumably half a hard-
boiled egg stuffed with a shrimp. Martial
(2, 43) has an epigram on a Painful Dinner-
Party with similar contrasts: the patron
eats mullet, but *concolor in nostra,
cammare, lance rubes.* The similarities
suggest that J is expanding Martial's idea.

85 *feralis cena:* the *cena nouendialis,*
offered at the tomb eight days after the
funeral, included eggs. Presumably the egg,
which is often found in tombs, carries
with it, like seeds (which are similarly
found) the promise of new life.

86 *ipse: dominus.*

Venafrano: sc. *oleo.* Venafrum was on the
borders of Samnium and Campania and
produced olive oil of high quality. Another
stock theme (Hor. *S* 2, 8, 45; cf 2, 4, 69).

perfundit: 'soaks'.

at hic qui: the three monosyllables make
a brilliant ending. The guest's mouth is
watering, and then he can't believe his
eyes *at — hic - qui.*

87 *pallidus . . . caulis:* Martial too (13,
17, 1) disapproves of *pallentes . . . caules.*

olebit lanternam: 'will smell of the lamp'.
Olive oil was a staple product, for butter
and sauces, for soap, and for lamp-oil: only
poor-quality oil was used for the latter —
and J suggests that Virro has scraped out
his lamps to provide oil for his guests. The
joke is derived from Horace (*S* 1, 6, 123
*ungor oliuo,/non quo fraudatis immundus
Natta lucernis*).

88 'The oil placed on your sauces was
brought up the Tiber by some sharp-
prowed reed-boat of the kings of Africa;
it explains the fact that no one at Rome
occupies the same bath-room as Boccar;
it protects its users from venomous snakes.'
An excellent example of J's hyperbole, and
his amusing indifference to 'foreign parts'.

alueolis quod: note the offbeat rhythm:
the word implies miniature dishes.

89 *canna:* a reed, and so presumably a
barge constructed of reeds which was used
for local work on the Nile, like that
described by Pliny (*NH* 7, 206). It is of
course (despite Kon-Tiki) unthinkable
that such a boat should be used on the open
sea; that is part of the humour. A scholiast
suggests that J is referring to an African
merchantman called *gandeia.* This is other-
wise unattested, but if it existed, it merely
adds to the complexity of the joke.

Micipsarum: there was a Micipsa, king of
Numidia, father of Hiempsal and Adherbal,
and uncle of Jugurtha. J is not worried about
the fact that he had been dead for 200

years or that he lived 1600 km from the Nile. The plural is 'generic': 'kings like Micipsa'.

prora . . . acuta: the barge, or merchant-man, has now become a warship with a battle-prow, moving up the Tiber to the heart of Rome.

subuexit: 'carried *upriver*'.

90 *Boccare:* Boccar, Bocchar ,or Bocchor, was an even earlier king of Mauretania, in Hannibal's day: the name is applied to any African.

91 The line is suspect, being absent from P and ignored by the scholiasts.

92 *mullus:* see on 4, 15.

uel quem: the ending here is hardly doing more than contrast with the next line.

93 *Tauromenitanae:* a really heavy beginning. Tauromenium, on the eastern coast of Sicily is the modern Taormina, a selfconsciously attractive resort built on a cliff, with a spectacular ancient theatre commanding a spectacular view of Etna. The passage which follows might have come from a late twentieth-century concern for the environment.

95 *scrutante macello:* abl. abs: we too can say 'the market looks in every corner of the areas close by', but we should recognise it as a striking phrase.

96 *Tyrrhenum:* i.e. in the *mare Tyrrhenum,* the roughly triangular portion of the Mediterranean bounded by Sardinia and Corsica, the western coast of Italy and Sicily.

97 *prouincia:* the provinces, not Italy; often, though not here, specifically of the area we still call Provence; they 'supply the cooking-fires'.

98 The scenario is that Aurelia is a wealthy widow, Laenas a fortune-hunter. He tries to win her favours by bringing her rare delicacies; she — sells them. For the *captatores* see on 3,129. The younger Pliny (*Ep.* 2, 20, 10) has a story about a fortune-hunter named Regulus persuading one Aurelia to leave him her best dress! The name is common enough, but that particular story may have suggested its use here to J. The chiasmus *emat Laenas, Aurelia uendat* leads admirably to the unexpected final word, the humorous device known, from Greek, as paraprosdokian. We expect 'eats' not 'sells'. The effect is taken from Mart. 7, 20, 22, with the same word and point.

99 *muraena:* 'lamprey', a great delicacy; cf Hor. *S* 2, 8, 47. The best came from Tartessus, Messana, and the *mare Carpathium;* rich men kept a stock in a salt-water tank, and the notorious Vedius Pollio threw in slaves as food for his.

100 *gurgite de Siculo:* the flooding current in the straits of Messina, which gave birth to the stories of Charybdis. For Sicilian lampreys see Plin. *NH* 9, 79, 169, Varro *RR* 2, 6, 2: Mart. 13, 80; Macrob. 3, 15, 7.

100-1 Mock-epic, perhaps in direct parody of a passage in Ovid (*M* 11, 432) descriptive of Aeolus *qui carcere fortes/ contineat uentos.*

se continet: 'jails himself.'

101 *madidas:* so Verg. *G* 1, 462 *umidus Auster.*

pinnas: the winds are depicted with wings.

102 *lina:* nets made of flax.

Charybdim: see on 100. Charybdis is represented as a maelstrom (Hom. *Od.* 10, 421ff), though there is none in the Straits.

103 *anguilla:* 'eel': the name (cf *anguis*) suggests to J a snake.

104 *glacie aspersus:* the text has been impugned on three grounds: (a) the syntax is clumsy; (b) Tiberinus is not the name of a fish; (c) fish are not made spotty by ice or cold. Clausen therefore proposed *glaucis sparsus (AJP* 76 (1955) 58-60). But Bradshaw has given good reasons why the text may stand: (a) the double ablative is not very common, but equally not exceptionally difficult, especially as *aspersus maculis* virtually = *maculatus;* (b) Galen certainly thought *Tiberinus* was the name of a fish; (c) it does not matter whether the fish is damaged by cold, but whether J thought it was. Vergil (*G* 3, 298-9, 440-3) and Columella (7, 5, 5) attribute disease among flocks to the cold. The fish are suffering from *saprolegnia,* which causes white spots or patches, and would be liable to appear after a hard winter among fish which have been swimming in polluted water (which encourages the fungus). In these conditions the fish become sluggish and easily caught, and would be a glut on the market: the blotchiness would be naturally explained by the ice on the river rather than an undiagnosed fungus.

Tiberinus: a fish from the Tiber, otherwise unknown. Bradshaw follows the common view that it is the sea-bass, *lupus (Morone labrax* or *Labrax lupus).* This was normally a delicacy, and the suggestion is more likely that it was a pike, a notorious scavenger. The pike is not *lupus,* but neither, necessarily, is *Tiberinus.*

et ipse: not clear. Does this connect it with the eel (which seems pointless)?

Or with the client? This would give point —
except that Trebius seems to be a name
from Aquinum, not a Roman born and
bred. But this may be right: we need not
expect complete consistency, and J always
seeks to identify his sufferers as true
Romans.

105 *cloaca: cloaca maxima,* an
astonishingly enlightened contribution
to hygiene, running underground through
the main part of Rome under the Forum
and out into the Tiber, where it created
pollution — another modern problem.

106 *cryptam:* another underground
drain linking with *cloaca maxima.*

Subura: see on 3, 5.

107-13 *No one asks you to give as
generously as patrons in the past; they
considered liberality its own reward. We
are asking you to treat us as fellow-
citizens; then be as miserly as you like.*

107 *ipsi:* Virro.

pauca uelim: sc. *dicere.* The ellipsis is
conversational and easy. Ter. *Andr.* 29 has
the variant *paucis te uolo.* J at this point
pushes himself into the scene in a burst of
indignation. The passage (107-13) takes
us momentarily away from the actual scene,
only to plunge us back.

praebeat aurem: our cliché is 'lend an
ear'.

109 *a Seneca:* J has inverted this clause,
with the result that we have repeated long
a, a kind of nostalgic sigh. L.Annaeus
Seneca (c. 4 BC-AD 65), the millionaire
Stoic, and regent at the start of Nero's
reign. For his character see J. Ferguson
'Seneca the Man' in D.R. Dudley *Neronians
and Flavians: Silver Latin I* London 1972
pp 1-23. Seneca's work *De Beneficiis* shows
sensitivity on this subject, e.g. 1, 1, 7 *gratus
adversus eum esse quisquam potest, qui
beneficium aut superbe abiecit aut
iratus impegit aut fatigatus, ut molestia
careret, dedit?*

Piso: C. Calpurnius Piso, leader of a
conspiracy against Nero in AD 65.
Tacitus (*Ann.* 15, 48) says of him
*exercebat largitionem aduersus amicos et
ignotis quoque comi sermone et congressu.*
Martial couples Seneca and Piso nostalgi-
cally together as patrons: *Pisones
Senecasque Memmiosque/et Crispos mihi
redde — sed priores* (12, 36, 8-9; cf 4,
40, 1-2).

bonus: a seemingly simple word with
many implications. Piso was *bonus* because
he performed *benefacta;* he was an aristo-
crat; he also lived up to the moral element

in *bonus;* he was courteous (a common
meaning); and he was a *bonus ciuis,* both
in trying to get rid of the tyrant and in
behaving *ciuiliter.*

Cotta: presumably Ovid's patron, Cotta
Maximus, though he accords oddly with
two of a later generation. He was son
of M. Valerius Messalla Corvinus. Ovid
repeatedly refers to his merits as a patron,
e.g. *Pont.* 1, 7, 83 *is me nec comitem nec
dedignatus amicum est.* J's general
indebtedness to Ovid makes the reference
probable. There was a later Cotta Messalinus
who appears in Tacitus, but he seems to
have been an unsavoury character. Cotta
reappears at 7, 95.

110 *titulis:* the list of offices held such
as appears on many inscriptions (cf 1, 130).

fascibus: the bundle of rods containing
an axe, carried by lictors in front of the
senior magistrates, emblematic of the
powers of corporal and capital punishment.

111 *solum:* given great weight by the
punctuation, a rare point for so decisive a
break (cf 3, 134), and by the near-rhyme
with (*fascibu)s olim.*

112 *ciuiliter:* i.e. as a citizen with
fellow-citizens, not as a *dominus.*

hoc face et esto: close to *si hoc facis,
esse licet.* The words are light and conversa-
tional, but the bucolic diaeresis, and the
intrusive word-accent in *face* pick them
out.

113 *esto:* the rhetorical repetition is a
simple but effective means of conveying
intensity.

diues tibi, pauper amicis: a splendid
and typical climactic epigram, but what
exactly does J mean? For (a) on the
face of it J is saying, 'Be courteous and
we don't mind your being stingy,' but the
stinginess is in fact central to the discour-
tesy; (b) if this is right, the meaning is
'Treat yourself as if you were a millionaire,
and your friends as if you were a pauper';
cf Mart. 9, 2, 1 *pauper amicitiae cum
sis, Lupe, non es amicae;* (c) but there seems
also an innuendo that for all his riches
he becomes poor in respect of friends.

114-55 *He has goose's liver, fattened
fowl, boar, truffles. The carver is
expected to perform fantastic convolutions.
You will be thrown out if you open your
mouth. You wouldn't dare to toast your
patron. Of course if you had a fortune he'd
be all over you — provided you were
childless. As it is, he takes a patronising
interest if you have three children, and
gives them, cheap presents. He has mush-*

COMMENTARY   181

rooms fit for an emperor. He has apples
which might have come from the Garden
of the Hesperides. You have a rotten apple
fit only for a performing monkey.

114   *anseris . . . iecur:* Athenaeus
(13, 384c) comments on the extravagant
enthusiasm of Romans for this delicacy.
The geese were fattened on figs (Hor. *S*
2, 8, 88; Pollux 6, 49); the liver was further
distended after removal by adding milk and
honey (Plin. *NH* 10, 27, 52). Martial depicts
the result (13, 58): *Aspice quam tumeat*
magno iecur ansere maius:/miratus dices
'Hoc, rogo, creuit ubi?' In our own time
foie gras made into *pâté* has also been
accounted a delicacy.

anseribus par: the return to the dinner
party is marked by harshly broken rhythm.

115   *altilis:* sc. *auis* (from *alere*), a fowl
specially fattened in cold cramped dark
conditions: the modern 'animal machines'
are not new in principle.

flaui . . . Meleagri: a translation of
Homer's ξανθὸς Μελέαγρος (*Il* 2, 642)
who killed the famous boar of Calydon:
the mythological allusion is all but auto-
matic. The four-syllable final word, creating
an offbeat rhythm, is not infrequent with
foreign names, but it also helps to
continue the mood.

ferro: his spear.

116   *spumat:* the better reading; inferior
MSS have *fumat.* The word is a cliché for the
boar (Mart. 11, 69, 9; 14, 70, 2); the head
looks as if he is still alive. Martial (14, 221,
2) has *spumeus in longa cuspide fumet aper.*

aper: it will be noted that in this course
the guests do not receive inferior fare,
they receive nothing, although the boar is
animal propter conuiuia natum (1, 141).

tubera: 'truffles', also called *terrae*
tubera (Mart. 13, 50), another special
delicacy.

uer: Plin. *NH* 19, 13, 37 *tenerrima autem*
uerno esse.

117   *tonitrua:* Pliny in the same passage
claims that thunderstorms encourage their
growth.

118   *frumentum:* Rome was increasingly
dependent on grain imported from North
Africa.

Alledius: an otherwise unknown epicure,
who may be identical with an *eques* named   .
Alledius Severus who was alive in mid-
first century (Tac. *Ann.* 12, 7), or perhaps
a descendant.

119   *Libye:* three syllables (υυ -), a
Greek form. Libya was the general name
for Africa west of Egypt.

dum: 'provided that'.

120   *structorem:* cf 11, 136: strictly
the butler in charge, or head-waiter, who
makes all the 'arrangements'; here also the
carver (*carptor, scissor, diribitor*).

121   *chironomunta: jouant des mains:*
the Greek (acc. m. of the pres. part.
precisely parallel to *saltantem*) is pointed:
the carver's over-elaborate movements
of legs and hands are compared to those of
a ballet dancer or pantomime. At
Trimalchio's feast the carver performs to
music (Petr. *Sat.* 36).

uolanti cultello: 'with air-borne knife'.

123   'and it is of course a matter for
the most careful distinction': ironic.

124   *lepores:* a stock theme: cf 167;
11, 136; Hor. *S* 2, 8, 89 (cf 1, 5, 72;
2, 5, 10; Pers. 1, 24)

gallina secetur: cf 11, 135.

125   *ab Hercule Cacus:* a bandit who
stole Hercules's cattle. Hercules forced
his way into the cave from which Cacus
operated and strangled him: *pedibusque*
informe cadauer/protrahitur (Verg. *A* 8,
264). J's line and a half are a splendid
description of a 'bounce'.

127   *hiscere:* 'to open your mouth'.

tria nomina: Quint. 7, 3, 27 *propria liberi*
quae nemo habet nisi liber, praenomen,
nomen, cognomen, tribus; Sen. *Ben.* 4, 8,
3 *si quod a Seneca accepisses, Annaeo te*
debere diceres, uel Lucio, non creditorem
mutares, sed nomen, quoniam siue praenomen
eius siue nomen dixisses siue cognomen,
idem tamen ille est. The *praenomen* was the
given name of the individual; the *nomen*
belonged to the *gens;* the *cognomen*
(sometimes in the form of a nickname
originally fitting an individual, e.g. P.
Ovidius Naso, 'the nose', given to one of his
ancestors) a branch of the *gens.* Occasionally
a fourth, individual, name was adopted,
e.g. P. Cornelius Scipio Africanus. Slaves
had only a single name: freedmen regularly
made this their *cognomen* and added their
patron's *praenomen* and *nomen,* e.g.
M. Tullius Tiro, Cicero's freedman. The
irony consists in the fact that Trebius *is*
free.

propinat: the first syllable varies in
quantity. The custom survives in some
circles of one diner rising with the words
'I wish to take a glass of wine with X', who
then rises and drinks simultaneously.
In the ancient world the proposer drank and
passed the same cup to his toast.
Theramenes, condemned by the tyrannical
Critias to drink hemlock (in the Latin

version), *propino, inquit, hoc pulchro Critiae* (Cic. *TD* 1, 40, 96).

128 *contacta:* double meaning, 'touched', 'polluted'.

129 *usque adeo, quis:* note the broken rhythm, especially the weight put on the last syllable.

130 *perditus:* double meaning: you would be shameless to say it, and doomed in saying it.

regi: 'his majesty' the patron, as often.

131 *laena:* see on 3, 283.

132 *quadringenta:* 400 000 sesterces, the fortune of an *eques:* see on 1, 106. The passage raises historical problems as it seems to refer to the emperor giving a man the money for equestrian rank; other examples relate to the replenishment of the numbers with provincials by Caligula and Vespasian, the *equus publicus* or ceremonial parade, and enrolment in jury panels (*decuriae iudicum*). See Fergus Millar *The Emperor in the Roman World* p. 280.

aut similis dis: the broken rhythm again for bitter expostulation, with weight on *dis.*

133 *melior:* nearly always ambiguous in J.

fatis: there is perhaps a suggestion that (as in Homer) the gods cannot go against the fates, but (as against the Stoics) men can.

donaret: technically, and properly, called an unfulfilled condition.

homuncio: 'manikin', 'mere man'. J may have in mind a passage in Seneca voicing an anti-Stoic sentiment: *nos homunciones sumus, omnia nobis negare non possumus* (*Ep.* 116, 7).

134 *ex nihilo:* 'from being a mere nothing': Lucr. 1, 150 *nullam rem ex nilo gigni diuinitus umquam.*

quantus . . . amicus: a form of J's favourite *magnus amicus* (1, 33, etc.): the *amicitia* is a form of social and political alliance.

136 *ilibus:* the best cut of boar (cf Mart. 10, 45, 4).

The apostrophe to cash is a witty parody of the grand manner.

137 *uos estis frater:* a splendid touch.

et domini rex: the roles inverted: again the offbeat rhythm gives a touch of harshness with emphasis on *rex.*

138-9 A parody of Dido's words in Verg. *A* 4, 328 *si quis mihi paruulus aula/luderet Aeneas.* Even if you have money you won't receive Virro's *amicitia* unless he has a chance of becoming your

heir: another hit at the *captatores.*

139 *luserit:* a prohibition (whether second or third person) is regularly expressed by *ne* + pf subj., the pf. here corresponding to the Greek aorist, for momentary action (Woodcock 128-9).

Aeneas: i.e. son and heir.

nec: 'nor even': its use in prohibitions (for *neu*) is not very common, but eased here by the antecedent being *nullus.*

illo: Virro.

140 *iucundum et carum:* predicative. Jahn proposed the deletion of this line, which certainly adds nothing, though it is not unworthy of J. It is well-shaped, with the adjectives and nouns grouped chiastically round the verb.

141 *nunc:* 'as things are'. Friedländer must be wrong in continuing the fantasy, and supposing that Mycale is a concubine, and therefore does not endanger Virro's inheritance of Trebius's imagined wealth: *nunc* brings us back to stern reality.

Mycale: Trebius's wife, presumably a freedwoman. The name is perhaps the Jewish Michal, Greek Μιχάλη.

et pueros tres: offbeat rhythm again The *ius trium liberorum,* stressed by Augustus, gave special privileges to those with three children, which makes it worth Virro's retaining Trebius as a *cliens,* however he treats him.

142 *ipse:* Virro: note the bucolic diaeresis.

143 *nido:* 'brood': the depersonalisation is pointed. The phrase parodies Verg. *A* 12, 475 *nidisque loquacibus escas.*

uiridem thoraca: the point is uncertain: Schol. *armilausiam* (a piece of military costume) *prasinam, ut simiae.* The point is plainly that Virro is getting off as cheaply as he can. *Thorax* is a Greek word, and likely to be sarcastic; *uiridem* perhaps means 'green with age', as would happen with a piece of uncared-for bronze. See also H.J. Rose in *HSCP* 47 (1938) 12-3.

144 *minimas:* still on the cheap.

nuces: both to play with (like knucklebones) and to eat: *nuces relinquere* = 'to put away childish things'.

assemque rogatum: a small coin, and they have to beg for that.

145 *parasitus:* the children going the way of the father.

146 The contrast is taken from Mart. 3, 60, 5 (*sunt tibi boleti, fungos ego sumo suillos*); the whole satire is indebted to this poem.

ancipites: notoriously, even today: cf

Plin. *NH* 22, 47, 96 *quae uoluptas tanta tam ancipitis cibi?*

147   *Claudius:* the emperor, who was removed by some poisoned mushrooms administered by his wife Agrippina, with the help of Lucusta (cf 1, 71; 6, 620). Claudius attained deity through death, and Nero called mushrooms *deorum cibum*, 'the food of the Gods' (Suet. *Ner.* 33). See also Tac. *Ann.* 12, 67; Suet. *Claud.* 44; DC 60, 34. The passage is based on Mart. 1, 20, 4 *boletum qualem Claudius edit, edas.*

148   *edit:* the repetition is effective.

149   *reliquis Virronibus:* i.e. all those whom he treats as equals.

150   *quorum . . . odore:* double meaning: 'whose scent alone is enough for a feast', 'whose scent is all you 'll get to eat'. See Mart. 1, 92, 9 *pasceris et nigrae solo nidore culinae.*

151   *Phaeacum:* the mythical people of Homer's *Odyssey* (7, 114ff), who enjoy a Utopian natural climate with fruit growing all the year round.

autumnus: as Homer says that the crops do not fail in summer or winter we should perhaps translate 'apple-picking time' rather than 'autumn'. The word was derived by the Romans (perhaps wrongly) from *augere.*

152   Hercules's twelfth Labour was to secure the golden apples of the Hesperides, the daughters of Evening, who were located to the far west on the banks of Oceanus, or in north-west Africa (as here). J draws a satirical contrast between the golden fruit, and their black-skinned guardians.

153   *scabie mali:* a rotten apple: for the form of phrase see on 4, 39 *spatium . . . rhombi.*

aggere: the Agger Tarquini near the Porta San Lorenzo, an early defensive earthwork, a favourite place for a stroll, and therefore for fortune-tellers and other street-entertainers (6, 588; 8, 43): 'the Embankment'.

154-5   A rather mysterious roundabout description. The most plausible explanation is of a performing monkey trained to ride a goat dressed as a cavalryman. See Mart. 14, 202, 1.

flagelli: objective gen., giving *metuens* the force of an ordinary adjective ('fearful') rather than a verb ('fearing') cf 7, 210 *metuens uirgae.*

156-73   *Virro is not stingy: he is making an exhibition of you. You cannot claim to be a free man and treat him as a king. You are a* slave to the smell from his kitchen. You're led astray by the hope of a good dinner. He knows what he's about. You get what you deserve — and if you carry on that way there's worse in store.

157   Picking up the point implied at 26. The Romans did put on performances to accompany meals.

158   *melior:* ironic.

plorante gula: 'than a greed with a grievance': Trebius does not emerge free from J's lash. The hiatus after *gula* gives the effect of the gulp as he swallows his pride.

159   *si nescis:* 'in case you don't realise it'.

160   *diu:* ambiguously placed with both *presso* and *stridere.* Part of the point is that his teeth are clenched because there is nothing for him to eat.

161   Mart. 2, 53, 3 *liber eris, cenare foris si, Maxime, nolis;* 9, 10, 4 *liber non potes et gulosus esse.* J points the way in that a *liber* cannot be the subject of a *rex.*

162   *captum:* contrast with *liber.*

nidore culinae: from Mart. 1, 92, 9: see on 150; but in Martial it is the poor man's own kitchen, which points the way here.

163   *nec male:* effective understatement.

nudus: complex in meaning: lacking even the *bulla* or *nodus* to wear, destitute, defenceless. There is a kind of word-play between *nidor, nudus, nodus.* J is giving his poem ring-form by reverting to the theme of lines 6-11.

illum: Virro.

164   *Etruscum . . . aurum:* the gold phallic amulet (*bulla*) worn round the neck by the freeborn, to avert the powers of evil, adopted from Etruscan practice.

165   Those who could not afford gold, and the sons of freedmen, wore a leather amulet, *bulla scortea,* J's *signum de paupere loro;* the *nodus* is the thong from which it hung. The circumlocution is typical of J.

166   *ecce dabit iam:* the hopeful aside of the guest: bucolic diaeresis and offbeat rhythm point the satire and emphasise *iam* ('any minute now'), which is repeated two lines later.

168   *minor:* 'smaller than his' (or perhaps 'too small for him'), but a tolerable meal.

altilis: see on 115.

169   *inde:* 'and so': bucolic diaeresis. We must read the words which follow as a Roman would: 'with at the ready (?some weapon), untouched (?unblooded as yet) — all of you are the same, drawn (plainly

a sword!) — bread: an excellent example
of paraprosdokian, the unexpected climax.

170 *sapit:* double meaning, exactly our
'has taste'.

omnia ferre: bucolic diaeresis to
emphasise the words.

171 *si potes, et debes:* the climactic
epigram: the satire has turned from Virro
to Trebius.

uertice raso: the standard guise of the
morio or buffoon; cf Arnob. 7, 33
*dii . . . delectantur stupidorum capitibus
rasis.* The reference back to lines 3-4
clinches the ring form (see on 163).

172 *quandoque:* 'sooner or later'.

173 *flagra:* 'the lash': he will not be
afraid of it because he will be used to it.

amico: the last word, with its double
meaning, points the satire.

General comments

This is the final climactic satire to the first
book. Like 1 and 3, it deals with the polarity
between rich and poor: the intermediate
satires are portraits of the upper crust. It is
precise and brilliant: J is like a film director,
who uses exact details and minute
particulars to make his point. These recur
throughout: the unfastened shoelaces
flying in all directions (20), the blood-stained
napkin (27), the jewelled cups (38), the
tough bread (68) the haughty lobster-tail
leering down from the couch of asparagus
(81), the snake-like eel (103) and blotchy
fish (104), the ballet-dancing carver (121),
the hopeful presenting of the children
and the cheap gifts they receive (141-5).

The poem is rhetorical in structure. It is
in fact, as Highet shows, a *suasoria,*
designed to persuade someone to do some-
thing. 1-11 forms the *propositio* (the point
is emphasised in contrast to Trebius's own
propositum; 12-155 the *tractatio;* 156-73
the *conclusio.*

This apart, the poem falls into the well-
known *genre* of pieces about dinner parties,
and, in particular, the Horrid or Painful
Dinner-Party. The theme goes back to
Lucilius (30, 1060-1). The most famous
example is Trimalchio's dinner party in
Petronius. But closer to J are a number of
epigrams by Martial, to which he is
undoubtedly indebted. We may note 2, 14
(the passion to receive a dinner invitation);
2, 43 (contrast of clothes, menu, service:
a principal source); 2, 53 (diners-out have
no freedom); 3, 49 (contrast between
host's and guest's wine); 3, 60 (extended
contrast of course after course: a principal
source); 4, 68 (*ut cenam inuitor, Sexte,*

an ut inuideam?); 4, 85 (contrast of cups
and of their contents); 6, 11 (contrast of
menu); 9, 2 (mistress treated better than
clients); 9, 48 (Garricus takes all the boar
and does not even invite the poet). That
the Painful Dinner-Party is not just an
invention of the satirists may be seen from
the younger Pliny *Ep.* 2, 6, in which he
describes dining out with a host who *sibi
et paucis optima quaedam, ceteris uilia et
minuta ponebat.* Pliny prides himself
because *eadem omnibus pono* — though he
takes off a little of the lustre by explaining
that it isn't that his guests are served with
the best, but that he for such occasions
shares what he serves them.

The theme remained an important one.
It recurs in Lucian, and in post-
Renaissance satire, where it takes off
from J. Berni in Italy, Régnier and Boileau
in France, Hall, Oldham and Addison in
England all have admirable works on the
theme.

The contrast of the menus is drawn
with all J's gift of creating an atmosphere
by allusions and associations. Virro's wine
was bottled in the historic past when
consuls wore beards; it would have graced
the table of Republican-minded Stoics like
Thrasea and Helvidius. The amber on his
cup recalls the tears of the Daughters of the
Sun, the jewels have links with Aeneas, the
legendary founder of Rome. His cup-bearer
comes from the exotic east, but is associated
with the ancient kings. His mullet brings
up all the romance of *Tauromenitanae
rupes,* his lamprey all the mythology of
Charybdis. His boar was worthy of
Meleager's hunting, his mushrooms of an
emperor's eating. Trebius's produces a
very different series of associations. His
wine recalls orgiastic religion and the
brawls of Centaurs and Lapiths. The type
of cup assigned to him bears the name of
a cobbler from Beneventum. His waiter
comes from the African desert, and would
appear on a dark night like an apparition
from beyond the grave. The oil which
garnishes his fish stinks of the lamp and
recalls the dark continent and poisonous
snakes; the fish itself comes from the
sewers. Any bright remark and he is
treated as Hercules treated a gangster.
The climactic contrast, beautifully drawn,
is between the apples (149-55). J, whose
capacity for detailed observation would
have allowed two direct pictures, but who
prefers to work allusively, associated
the one with the gardens of Alcinous and
of the Hesperides (not without a touch of

satire), and the other with the reward of a performing monkey. He implies that Trebius is treated as such, and, in allowing himself to be so treated, is little more than that.

The point of J's *satire* is the switch from Virro to Trebius. In some sense there is no switch. The proem is directed against Trebius. But we are used to J's obsessive attacks on the upper classes: in the long central section our indignation is directed against Virro, and J by his personal incursion (107-13) creates in us the sense that this is what he is on about. It is a shock when the wheel comes full circle (pointed by explicit allusion: see on 163, 171), and the satire is suddenly pointed away from Virro for inflicting these humiliations to Trebius for inviting them. *ille sapit, qui te sic utitur. omnia ferre/ si potes, et debes* (170-1). One sometimes feels that J's circumlocutions are designed

to set off the merciless lucidity of such a climax. And the last three words lump tormentor and victim together — *tali dignus amico* (173).

Bibliography

Adamietz, J. *Untersuchungen zu Juvenal* (*Hermes* Einzelschriften Heft 26) Wiesbaden 1972

Anderson, W.S. 'Studies in Book I of Juvenal' *YCS* 15 (1957) 80-6

Bradshaw, A.T. von S. *'Glacie Aspersus Maculis:* Juvenal 5, 104' *CQ* 15 (1965) 121-5

Marache, R. *Juvénal: Saturae III, IV, V* Paris 1965

Robertson, D.S. 'Juvenal V 103-6' *CR* 60 (1946) 19-20

Shero, L.S. 'The *cena* in Roman Satire' *CP* 18 (1923) 126-43

SATIRE 6

This is by far the longest Latin poetical satire to survive, and is in fact nearly twice as long as any other. It fills a whole *uolumen* on its own; all the other books of J have at least three satires.

Two major problems relate to its theme and its structure. It has often been called something like 'A Legend of Bad Women'. Highet, however, claimed that the whole poem was a satire on marriage, and suggested (after *Punch*): 'Advice to those About to Marry: Don't.' This is, however, too simple. J starts from Postumus, and his hope of marriage. But we lose Postumus after 377, and he is somewhat dragged in there. It is true that the husband appears from time to time in the last 300 lines or so, but only incidentally: he is not central to what is going on. If there is a single personal theme it is Woman; if we are seeking a comprehensive title, the appropriate one would be 'Woman'. It would not be 'A Legend of Bad Women'. J's misogyny does not allow any but bad women.

Our view of the subject matter will affect our view of the structure. Highet suggests four sections:

1-132 Woman's unchastity makes marriage absurd
136-285 Married love is an illusion

(133-5 are displaced in his view)
286-351 Roman women have been ruined by luxury
352-661 The follies and crimes of women make marriage impossible.

These four sections produce a climax: wives deceive their husbands — tyrannise over their husbands — despise and ignore their husbands — torment and kill their husbands. It is, however, an unbalanced structure, dividing (with the displacement) 132:150:66:313. It does not really account for 184-99 and 242-67. Further, if anything is certain about this poem, it is that it has a beginning, a middle and an end. These are clearly marked:

1-20 Prologue
286-300 Epilogue to Part I and Prologue to Part II
643-61 Epilogue.

This gives us a first section broadly concerned with marriage, and a second dealing with the corruptions of women generally. This pattern corresponds closely with that proposed by C.F. Nägelsbach as long ago as 1848. Other schemes have been propounded.

Another preliminary point. J is as always attacking the upper classes. He occasionally puts in an aside to say that the lower classes are just as bad, or would be if they could, but this is designed to reinforce his offensive against upper-class women: if we do not grasp this we shall not grasp the point and structure of 582ff, for instance.

Our understanding of this satire is complicated by uncertainties about the text. The most notorious complication is the discovery by Winstedt of some thirty-six additional lines in a MS in Oxford. It is impossible to be certain whether these are genuine (though they are fully worthy of J), or if so whether the passage of thirty-four consecutive lines should be filled in where they appear (after 364) or after 345. Their discovery leads us to think that there may be other lost passages which might even turn up.

In his first book J showed little interest in women. There is the murderous wife of Satire 1, 69-72; 2 deals with male homo-sexuality, and references to women are strictly incidental (2, 60-1; 68-9); 3 has a swift sketch of prostitution (3, 132-6). That is about all. He now makes up for lost time.

1-20 *In Saturn's reign, Chastity lingered on earth, when men and women lived unsophisticated lives, close to Nature, born of the soil. Once Jupiter grew up all changed. Justice and Chastity departed together.*

1 *Pudicitiam:* the theme asserted at once. Note the personification, such as the Romans readily adopted. Pudicitia Patricia and Pudicitia Plebeia had separate cults (Liv. 10, 23). The poem begins with a twist. Normally it is Justice who characterises the Golden Age; cf 19.

Saturno rege: Saturn, perhaps originally the *numen* of sowing, was an archaic Italian divine power, before Jupiter became dominant. He became identified with the Greek Cronos. For those who saw history as a decline and fall, the reign of Saturn was the Golden Age of primal innocence; cf 13, 38-40. Vergil's 'Messianic' Eclogue sees the birth of the child as restoring that age: *redeunt Saturnia regna* (*Ecl.* 4, 5).

3 *spelunca:* the thought is taken from Lucretius 5, 955 *sed nemora atque cauos montes siluasque colebant,* though the Epicureans saw civilisation as a climb up from the state of nature.

laremque: the household god.

5 *uxor:* the theme reintroduced.

6 *frondibus:* also from Lucr. 5, 970.

uicinarum: the wild animals are near; men have not isolated themselves in cities.

7 *Cynthia:* Propertius's mistress, whose real name was Hostia, a *femme de société.* His first poem begins *Cynthia prima suis miserum me cepit ocellis* (Prop. 1, 1). Note how J uses apostrophe to avoid the unmetrical dative. The line has an odd rhythm, very jerky, with a strong stop at the end of every foot except the second.

8 *passer:* Lesbia, otherwise Clodia, Catullus's mistress and sister to the Clodius who will appear later (345) had a tame bird which died: *o miselle passer,/ tua nunc opera meae puellae/flendo turgiduli rubent ocelli* (Cat. 3, 16-8). In Saturn's reign the women had less style, but more morality.

9 *ubera:* a double implication: the fertility contrasted with the sterility we shall meet later: but also a primarily animal term.

10 *horridior:* 'shaggier'.

glandem: again from Lucr. 5, 939; cf 13, 57.

11 From Lucr. 5, 907 *tellure noua caeloque recenti.*

12 *rupe et robore:* an emendation by Scholte of the MS *rupto robore.* It was a proverbial expression going back to Homer *Od.* 19, 163; cf Stat. *Theb.* 3, 559; 4, 340 *saxis nimirum et robore nati.*

13 The alternative myth, that Prometheus fashioned men out of earth and water (Ov. *M* 1, 82-3). The absence of parents means that there is no room for *pietas.* The Golden Age is not untarnished. The simple life is an animal life.

14 *ueteris uestigia:* a wicked parody of Verg. *A* 4, 23 where Dido recognises the traces of an ancient fire within herself, i.e. love. The phrase also appears in Cat. 64,295; Ov. *Am.* 3, 8, 49.

15 *Ioue:* Jupiter in the myth ousted Saturn. But J suggests that once Jupiter became adolescent, sexual corruption set in, a conclusion which might be strongly supported by the myths of his amours, but a bold one none the less.

16 *Graecis:* J's *bêtes noires,* as in the third satire.

17 *alterius:* an unexpected twist: normally you swear on your own head, so that you suffer if you are forsworn. Pliny tells a story of Regulus perjuring himself in swearing on his son's head (*Ep.* 2, 20, 6).

timeret: timere + acc. of the person feared is common, + dat. of the thing on whose behalf fear is felt is good, idiomatic Latin; the combination is rare.

18 *aperto:* 'unwalled'.

uiueret: there is an easy transition from 'no one' (i.e. everyone felt no fear) to 'everyone'.

19 *Astraea:* the daughter of Zeus, personification of justice, the last of the immortals to leave (Aratus *Phaen.* 101-36; Ov. *M* 1, 150 *ultima caelestum, terras Astraea reliquit*). She became the constellation Virgo. Her return would mark the restoration of *Saturnia regna* (Verg. *Ecl.* 4, 5).

20 *hac: Pudicitia;* In Hesiod (*WD* 199-201) Aidos (= Pudicitia) and Nemesis (= Astraea) abandoned mankind in the degenerate Iron Age.

21-37 *Postumus, sexual immorality's a long-established practice. Are you really thinking about taking a wife in our day? Commit suicide. Or sleep with a pretty boy: he'll be less demanding.*

21 *Postume:* Postumus Ursidius, to whom the satire is addressed.

22 *sacri genium contemnere fulcri:* 'to ignore the divine power of the sanctity of the bed'. The word *genius* is well-chosen, for its root has to do with birth, and it is the *numen* of the family, the power of male fertility, conceived of as in the head of the *paterfamilias;* it comes to mean a spiritual power generally, like the Greek *daemon*. The *fulcrum* is the head of the bed; as W. C. F. Anderson showed (*CR* 3 (1889) 322-4): an image of one of the gods might stand there.

23 *ferrea . . . aetas:* in Hesiod's account there are five ages — golden, silver, bronze, heroic (a temporary improvement emphasising the final degeneracy), and iron (Hes. *WD* 109-201).

24 *argentea saecula:* other vices are recent; sexual promiscuity is a long-established pastime. The plural *saecula* is simply for metrical reasons.

25 *sponsalia:* the written contract was called *tabulae sponsales;* the word comes from the promise made on the bride's behalf *'sponden ergo?' 'spondeo.'* (Plaut. *Aul.* 256).

nostra: abl. with *tempestate.*

28 *eras:* 'you used to be'.

29 *Tisiphone:* one of the three Furies with snakes in their hair. Normally the agent with a passive verb has *a* or *ab,* but the ablative itself expresses the origin of the action, and in any case the word hardly means more than 'madness'.

30 *saluis tot restibus:* for hanging

himself.

32 *Aemilius pons:* the first stone bridge over the Tiber, begun in 179 BC, later known as the Ponte Rotto; one arch remains. J recommends it for suicide. This is the first line in this satire with offbeat rhythm at the end. It expresses the thud of the body on the water, like Vergil's *procumbit humi bos* (*A* 5, 481).

33-7 These lines suggest J's antipathy to heterosexual love, and sympathy for some form of active homosexuality; this is reinforced by Mart. 12, 18, 22-3, addressed to J: *ille quem tu/. . . cupias.*

36 Note the cutting alliteration.

37 *lateri:* D.W.T. Vessey in *Liv. Cl. M.* 1 (1976) 39-40 shows the reference to a normative copulatory position (Ov. *AA* 3, 781-8).

38-59 *Ursidius wants an heir, even though it means doing without the gifts of legacy-hunters — Ursidius, once famed for his adulteries. He wants a moral wife. If he finds one he can thank the gods. Even isolated country-girls would succumb even in small towns — and do, in caves and mountains.*

38 *lex Iulia: de maritandis ordinibus* passed by Augustus in 18 BC and amended and completed by lex Papia Poppaea in AD 9. The law limited the rights of the unmarried to receive inheritances, and offered privileges in public life to the fathers of large families. See *Cambridge Ancient History* 10, 448-52.

tollere: to take up from the ground in acknowledgement of paternity. Note how the bucolic diaeresis picks out the words.

39 *cariturus:* 'though he will have to give up'. The luxuries are gifts from the *captatores* or legacy-hunters, who are satirised in 12, and in Petronius 124ff.

turture: for it as a luxury food see Mart. 3, 60, 7. *Tur* four times in three lines.

40 *mullorum:* the red mullet. There were two kinds *Mullus barbatus,* which Cicero (*Par. Stoic.* 5, 2) calls *mullulus barbatulus (iubis* here), fr. *vrai rouget,* and *Mullus surmiletus* (Plin. *NH* 9, 64), fr. *rouget-barbet.* It is a shore-fish. Galen (6,715) describes it as superior to all the rest for pleasure in eating. Two-pounders (0.9 kg) were rare (Mart. 3, 45, 5; 11, 49, 9). A four-pounder (1.8 kg) was phenomenal. Calliodorus paid 1300 sesterces, the price of a slave, for one. Martial (10, 31) comments *non est hic, improbe, non est/ piscis; homo est.* Seneca (*Ep.* 95) tells of a 4½-pounder (2 kg) given to Tiberius;

Octavius outbid Apicius for it at 5000
sesterces. J (4, 15) cites a price of 6000
sest.; Pliny (*NH* 9, 67) tells of Asinius
Celer buying one for 8000 The highest
point of this mad luxury-buying was in
Tiberius's reign when three mullets
fetched 30 000 between them, and led
Tiberius to impose a sumptuary tax on
fish. Some owners tried to develop them
in fishponds (Mart. 10, 30), but they were
inferior in these conditions (Plin. *NH*
9, 64). It was fashionable to have the mullet
brought in alive and cooked at table,
gradually changing colour (Plin. *NH* 9, 66;
Sen. *QN* 3, 18).

macello: the market where the luxuries
are bought is said to be legacy-hunting.

44 *perituri cista Latini:* Latinus was an
actor (1, 36). The scene is a typical
bedroom-comedy scene from any age.
He hides in a closet to escape imminent
destruction at the jealous husband's hands.

46 *nimiam pertundite uenam:* blood-
letting was normal medical relief for mad-
ness.

47 *delicias hominis:* acc. of exclamation.

Tarpeium: the sanctuary of Jupiter
Capitolinus: the Tarpeian rock was a crag
on the Capitol.

48 *auratam:* to gild the horns of the
offering made it a special sacrifice (cf
Liv. 25, 12, 13).

Iunoni: Juno Pronuba, with Jupiter
the guardian of marriage.

49 *capitis:* the power of sex was believed
to reside in the head: see R.B. Onians *The
Origins of European Thought.*

pudici: the key-word in this section.

50 *Cereris uictus:* the goddess of the
harvest (her name has the same root as
creare). Her festival in August involved a
ceremonial, white-clad procession of women
carrying the first-fruits. Participation
involved nine days without sexual inter-
course. Giangrande (*Eranos* 63 (1965)
26-41) proposed *uictus* for *uittas*.

dignae: i.e. *pudicae*.

51 *timeat . . . oscula:* the scholiast
comments *quia et irrumantur mulieres,
dicit.*

52 *corymbos:* clusters of ivy-berries, used
as a religious symbol.

53 *Hiberinae:* i.e. a woman from Spain.

56-7 *Gabiis . . . Fidenis:* sleepy country-
towns, coupled again at 10, 100. cf Hor.
Ep. 1, 11, 8 who conjoins them as remote
backwaters. At 3, 192 Gabii is contrasted
with Rome, J's point is that even in the
backwoods they fall. He is as cynical as
Ovid: *cunctas/posse capi* (*AA* 1, 269-70);

casta est quam nemo rogauit (*Am.* 1, 8, 43).

57 *agello cedo paterno:* 'I'll believe
in that innocent paternal estate': note
the force of the diminutive. There is an
implication that she is in more danger
from her father than at Gabii or Fidenae.

58 *aut in:* a very odd ending to a line,
since the preposition was taken so closely
with the following word as to form a
single phrase: the effect is to run the lines
together; cf 5, 33.

59 *Iuppiter et Mars:* note the weight
flung on the name of Mars, which is
offbeat. The countryside was the scene of
their amorous exploits.

60-113 *Can't you find a reliable wife?
No; they are all struck on dancers,
singers and actors — and gladiators.
Eppia, wife of a senator, eloped without a
qualm to Alexandria with a gladiator. He
was no beauty either. It's the violence
they like: let him retire, and he'll become
as dull as her senator-husband.*

60 *porticibus:* almost 'shopping-centres';
they were covered walks, often with shops
behind.

61 *cuneis:* the oval amphitheatres and
semicircular theatres had their seats
naturally divided into wedge-shaped blocks.

63 *chironomon:* nom.: the *pantomimus*,
from his use of gesture, but J affects the
Greek word in scorn; we can translate it as
if it were *chironomo*.

Ledam: seduced by Jupiter in the form
of a swan; we too can say that Bathyllus
dances Leda.

molli: it is hard to choose between
'effeminate' and 'passionate' here.

Bathyllo: the great dancer of this name
lived under Augustus. It looks as if the
name, once famous, was adopted by
others: this seems to be a handsome
pantomimus under Domitian.

64 'Tuccia has no authority over her
bladder.' We may think of teenyboppers
confronted with a pop star. The point is
that J is not here talking of the domineering
women — their turn will come. Here the
husbands can't control the women, but
they can't control themselves; they are
slaves to their physical impulses. The
names do not seem significant: these women,
unlike Eppia and Messalina, are not.

66 *rustica discit:* Humphries has a
Shakespearian pun: 'She's a country-girl,
but learning her country matters.'

67 'the curtain is packed away and
ceases to function.'

69 'the long period till the games in

honour of Cybele from the plebeian games'.
The Ludi Megalenses were held on 4-10
April at the temple of Magna Mater on
the Palatine from 191 BC and centred on
theatrical entertainment. The Ludi
Plebeii were first recorded in 216 BC,
and lasted from 4-17 Nov. In between came
the games in honour of Ceres (12-9 Apr.),
Flora (28 Apr.-3 May), Apollo (6-13 July)
and the Ludi Romani (5-19 Sept.). The
winter quarter must have seemed dull by
comparison.

tristes: depressed by the absence of ballet.
70 *personam:* the actor's mask.

thyrsum: staff sacred to Dionysus, god
of the theatre, wreathed with ivy and
tipped with a pine cone.

subligar: scholiast *tragoedi uestem,* the
Greek perizoma.
71 *Vrbicus:* an actor.

Atellanae: sc. *fabulae;* cf Liv. 7, 2:
primitive drama named from Atella in
Campania.
72 *Autonoes:* daughter of Cadmus and
mother of Actaeon.
73 *fibula:* large circular ornament
performing the equivalent male office
of a chastity belt. cf Mart. 7, 81 where the
evidence of the *fibula* is impressive until
it falls off.
74 *Chrysogonum:* a Greek singer:
love-making was thought to be bad for the
vocal chords.

Hispulla: the aunt of the younger Pliny's
wife was Calpurnia Hispulla (*Ep.* 4, 19;
8, 11): two others of the name were in
his circle (*Ep.* 1, 12, 9; 3, 3). Highet
(*J the Satirist* 291-3) suggests that no love
was lost between Pliny and J. See also
2, 50; 12, 11.
75 *Quintilianus:* the great orator,
perhaps J's teacher, whom Martial called
gloria Romanae, Quintiliane, togae (2, 90,
2). Here the representative of serious
reading. Compare Sidney Carter's song
'Plato in a paperback/I have never read./
Murder, sex and mystery,/That is what I
like instead./First of all there's Thunder-
ball/And then there's Fanny Hill./So
Plato in a paperback/Is waiting for me
still.' But there may be another point of
reference. Quintilian (6 pref. 6) at the
age of perhaps 50 married a girl who bore
him two children before the age of 19
and then died. He speaks of her with
fulsome praise: but one wonders what sort
of life she had, and whether she would have
resisted a sexy actor. Quintilian is himself
an example of the Roman craze for
marriage.

76-7 The names of musicians: pop
stars. Note the use of Greek terms, adding
to J's contempt. *Glaphyrus* means 'elegant'.
78-81 Mock epic. Note the religious
celebration for the illegitimate child,
an important juxtaposition in the poem.
80 *conopeo:* spondaic fifth foot, 'a
mosquito-net'. The adj. is puzzling. I take
it to refer to the *testudo* of interlocking
shields used in siege-warfare, an allusion to the
fighting father: 'for defence'. Others render
'a tortoiseshell cradle', an odd meaning for
conopeo. Another view is 'a tortoiseshell
cradle with mosquito-net'. But I know no
evidence for cradles of tortoiseshell.
81 *nobilis:* 'high-born' (Lentulus is a name
from the senatorial class), but also 'plain
for all to see'. The combination *nobilis
Euryalum* creates a kind of oxymoron,
especially as *Euryalum* (an epic name) is
defined by *murmillonem.* (The scholiast
glosses with *nomina lanistae et gladiatorum.*)

Murmillo: also *mirmillo* and *myrmillo*
(by assimilation to Achilles's Myrmidons):
named from the crest on his helmet in
fish-shape; cf 8, 200. The elaborate
preparations match a triumphal procession,
with the victor's bays and the stands —
except that it's only in narrow side streets:
it turns out to be for the arrival of a midget
murmillo.
82. *senatori:* perhaps Fabricius
Veiiento (113): it must have been a
notable scandal.

ludum: a school of gladiators to which
Sergius, with whom she was eloping,
belonged.
83 *Pharon:* the island with the famous
lighthouse marking the harbour of
Alexandria.

Nilum: the river of Egypt.

Lagi: the father of Ptolemy Soter,
founder of the Ptolemaic dynasty whose
capital was Alexandria.
84 *urbis:* Rome. J has no love for
Egypt, so it is an extreme statement that
Egypt rejects Roman depravity: contrast
2, 170.

Canopo: a city on the Nile delta; cf 1, 26;
15, 46.
85 *Pietas* is shown within the family and
nation. Eppia is *impia.*
87 A deliberately bathetic climax. *Ludi*
include festivals, race-meetings, theatre
and music-hall. Paris was a famous
pantomimus under Domitian, put to death
in AD 85 for an affair with the empress;
cf 7, 87. Martial wrote an epitaph for him
(11, 13) saying that all joy, wit, delight
and love were buried in his grave.

88-91 Eppia is in contrast with the *montana uxor* of 5.

89 *segmentatis:* with a luxurious patch-work quilt. A heavily spondaic line.

91 *molles:* cushioned of the chairs, passionate of their occupants.

92 *Tyrrhenos:* the Etruscan sea was off the west coast of Italy. She sailed from Ostia or Puteoli.

93 *pertulit . . . constanti:* tough, military words.
Ionium: sc. *fluctum:* the sea east of the straits of Messina.

94 On the long journey she passes through one sea after another.

94-102 Gertrude Hirst draws attention to the triple contrast: the wife terrified, the mistress bold; the wife faint, the mistress fit; the wife a nuisance, the mistress a good sport. J espouses this triplicity.

95 *timent:* sc. *mulieres.*

97 An excellent, and startling, rhetorical epigram.

98 A good example of a mixed conditional, the protasis remote (subjunctive), the apodosis immediate (indicative).

99 *summus uertitur aer:* 'the sky is spinning': she has a convenient attack of dizziness.

100 *illa maritum:* the woman of 98, as opposed to *haec:* 'the former' and 'the latter'. The bucolic diaeresis picks out the epigram in the first four feet (which is further pointed by cutting alliteration on *q* and *c*), and stresses what follows, which is grotesque and brilliant: she is (literally) sick of her husband.

101 *prandet:* she is not suffering from *mal de mer.*

104 *uidit:* 'did she see in him'.
ludia: again at 266; cf Mart. 5, 24, 10 *Hermes, cura laborque ludiarum.* It is not found elsewhere.

105 *sustinuit:* 'she put up with'.
Sergiolus: an affectionate diminutive; her pet name for him.
radere guttur: to shave, a practice not affected before the age of 40.

107 *sulcus:* 'a furrow' made on the face by the metal edge; suggested by Nisbet for the MS *sicut.*

108 *gibbus:* 'a wart'.

110 *facit . . . Hyacinthos:* 'their profession turns them into Valentinos' — or whoever is the current image of the handsome male. Hyacinthus was Apollo's darling. The irregular rhythm at the end is not uncommon with foreign names, though

here J seems to use it for added contempt.

111 Note how J inverts the order of 85-6: *coniugis . . . sororis . . . patriae . . . natos . . . pueris . . . patriae . . . sorori . . . uiro.*

112 *ferrum est quod amant:* J discerns the connection between a taste for violence and a misdirected sex-instinct.

113 *accepta rude:* 'once pensioned-off': a retired gladiator was called *rudiarius.*
Veiiento: presumably her husband: v 82 n.

114-35 *Eppia is a private individual. What of royalty? Claudius's wife would steal out from the palace once he was asleep, disguise her hair with a wig and occupy a room in a brothel, taking on all comers for cash, last to leave, tired but never satisfied. No point in mentioning love-charms. Women do anything for lust.*

114 *curas:* vb 'do you care?'

115 *riuales diuorum:* a commonplace of those in supreme power, but with particular allusion to the deification of Claudius and other emperors.
Claudius: (10 BC-AD 54), s. of Drusus and Antonia, a scholar and recluse, who succeeded his nephew Gaius in 41, and proved a sane and wise ruler. He is the subject of two vivid novels by Robert Graves: it has to be remembered that they are fiction not history.

116 *uxor:* Messalina (c. AD 25-48), grand-daughter of Octavia, m. Claudius in AD 39 or 40: he was thirty-four years her elder. Her promiscuity was notorious, though no other source gives J's extreme account. She was exposed in 48 and executed (10, 329-45 and notes there).

118 *meretrix Augusta:* a splendid phrase, indebted to Prop. 3, 11, 39 *meretrix regina* of Cleopatra. Messalina acting the prostitute appears in other sources (Plin. *NH* 10, 83, 172; Dio Cass. 60, 31, 1). 118 and 117 were rightly reversed by Hermann.

117 *Palatino:* the imperial palace was on the Palatine Hill.
tegetem: 'an old blanket'. The juxta-position is pointed.

119 *linquebat:* sc. *Palatinum cubile.*
non amplius una: 'not more than one': the idiom is obvious, though not strictly grammatical.

120 *galero:* generally a bonnet, here a wig.

123 *Lyciscae:* 'the Wolf-girl', appropriate in a *lupanar.*

124 *Britannice:* Claudius's son, named after his conquest of Britain. After

Messalina's exposure, Claudius married
Agrippina who persuaded him to adopt her
own son L. Domitius (Nero), who
succeeded in AD 54. Britannicus was
murdered the following year.

125 *intrantis:* 'the man who came in to
her'.

130 A marvellous phrase.

131 A strongly visual picture, such as
J likes. Some of the details are from the
rhetorical schools (Sen. Eld. *Contr.* 1, 2,
1, 7 and 21).

133 *hippomanes:* a growth on the
forehead of a newly-born foal, from which a
love-philtre might be distilled giving its
recipient the amatory violence of mares.
See Verg. *A* 4, 515-6 and A. S. Pease's
learned note. cf 616 below.

uenenum: not 'poison' but 'a magic
potion'.

134 *priuigno:* the stepmother in love
with her stepson is found in the Phaedra-
Hippolytus myth, as well as in the law
courts.

135 *summum:* Courtney: the MS
minimum gives the diametrically wrong
meaning.

136-60 *'What about Caesennia?' Her
dowry was a million sesterces, enough to
persuade her husband to call her chaste.
He's on fire with money not love; she's
bought her freedom. 'Bibula then?' Her
husband loves her face, not her. Once her
beauty fades she'll be packed off. Till
then, she's in the saddle, and as extravagant
as they come.*

136 *optima:* the word marks a change.

Caesennia: the Caesennii were a well-
known *gens:* L. Caesennius Paetus was
consul in AD 61.

137 *bis quingena:* 'a million sesterces',
the amount qualifying a person for senator-
ial status, and a rich woman's dowry
(10, 335; Mart. 11, 23, 3).

tanti: gen. of price or value: the gen. is
always used in *tanti, quanti, pluris,
minoris:* it is probably an extended use of
a gen. of description; cf *haud magni pretii.*

139-40 Two neat lines arranged
chiastically. The fire and wound of love are
common metaphor, controlling for instance
the imagery of Vergil *A* 4: v. J. Ferguson
in *Proc. Verg. Soc.* 10 (1970-1) 57-63.

140 *libertas emitur:* she pays for
freedom to do as she likes; she may
legitimately make eyes at others (*innuat*)
or write love-letters while he is about.
Lucilius (1223) had an account of a
complaisant husband saying however *non*

omnibus dormio. cf also Sen. *Ben.* 1, 9, 3;
Jerom. *Ep.* 127, 3.

141 *uidua:* 'unmarried' (to all intents
and purposes).

142 *Bibulae:* the name Bibulus is found
among the Calpurnii and Publicii. It
means 'drunkard', and this is enough to
explain its use here.

Sertorius: a *gens* of Sabine origin, of
whom the best-known is Q. Sertorius, an
attractive adventurer of the first century
BC.

143 *excutias:* 'shake out': changing the
image we might say 'winkle out'.

144 *tres rugae subeant:* 'just let three
wrinkles appear unexpectedly': *tres* of a
small number.

arida: proleptic 'and becomes dry'.

146-7 It is a rare, and clearly deliberate
device for two successive lines to end with
the same word. The repetition is emphasised
by the break before the second *exi.*

147 Take as one phrase: 'you're getting
on our nerves with your eternal snivelling.'

149 *calet:* lit. 'she's hot', clearly 'she's
got it good'; the use is not exactly paralleled,
but *frigere* means 'to be a flop'.

150 *Canusinam:* Canusium in Apulia
was noted for its dark wool.

ulmosque Falernas: elms were used to
train the vines, so *ulmos* means
'vineyards'. Falernian was one of the most
famous Italian wines.

151 *quantulum in hoc!:* compared with
what's to come. The elision is rare in J;
cf 14, 73 *plurimum enim.*

153 *mense quidem brumae:* sc.
December. At the Saturnalia, 17-9 Dec.,
there was a public holiday: canvas stalls
(*casa candida*) were set up in the Campus
Martius, blocking the *porticus Agrippae*
with its fresco of Jason and the Argonauts.

mercator Iason: the leader of the
expedition to fetch the Golden Fleece
from Colchis, from where he returned via
the Danube, Rhine or Elbe, and North
Sea: see J. R. Bacon *The Voyage of the
Argonauts.* J debunks the myth: Jason
was not an epic hero but a money-
grubbing merchant.

155 *crystallina:* vases of rock-crystal.

156 *murrina:* perhaps vases of agate:
murra is unidentified, but it was a natural
mineral (Plin. *NH* 37, 204).

adamas: 'diamond'.

Beronices: a Jewish princess, sister to
Herod Agrippa, with whom she was
reputed to have incestuous relations
(*incestae* at 158 has thus a double
allusion); she and Agrippa encountered

Paul as a prisoner at Caesarea (Acts
25-6). The future emperor Titus was in
love with her, and she spent some time
in Rome, but Rome was suspicious of
another Cleopatra.

158 *barbarus incestae:* the scholiast is
somewhat muddled. He has *barbarum
Ptolomaeum significat et Beronicem
sororem eius.* Rose (*HSCP* 47 (1936) 14)
has argued that it passed from Ptolemy
XIII to his sister and queen Cleopatra
VII (*incestae*), then to Herod Agrippa, from
him to Berenice, from her to Titus, and
from his estate to the open market.

gestare: Housman for *dedit hunc:
gestare* dropped out by haplography after
cestae, and *dedit hunc* was inserted from
the previous line. For the construction
see 14, 30 cf Verg. *A* 12, 211 *patribusque
dedit gestare Latinis.*

159 *mero pede:* 'barefoot' *Corp. Glos.
Lat.* 5, 657, 54 *me* [*t*] *ro pede id est
nudo pede; Prud. Pers.* 6, 91 *stabat calce
mera.* Josephus has an account of Berenice
making offerings at Jerusalem barefoot
(*BJ* 2, 314).

sabbata: the Jewish Day of Rest.

160 *uetus:* 'traditional': Tacitus (*Hist.*
5, 4) records the Jewish tabu on pork.

senibus: proleptic, 'allowing them to live
to a ripe old age'.

161-83 *'Is there not one up to your
standards?' Well, they're rare birds, and
insufferable when they turn up. I'd rather
marry a nobody like Vetustina than
Cornelia, Mother of the Gracchi, bringing
me her father's exploits. Niobe's boast-
fulness was the death of her children.
A faultless wife has more bitterness than
sweetness.*

162 Effective asyndeton, as reading
aloud reveals.

163 *auos:* probably statues, as the
imagines or masks were not displayed in the
walks.

164 The story is told in Liv. 1, 13.
The Romans had adjusted a shortage of
women by raiding the Sabines. The Sabines
retaliated by invading Rome. The women
intervened (as Mary Slessor stood between
two armed tribes in Calabar, or Belfast
housewives between Catholic and
Protestant mobs in 1970) between their
brothers and husbands. The scene has
often been painted: there are notable
versions by Poussin in the Louvre (Paris)
and the Metropolitan (New York). Sabine
women had a reputation for chastity
(10, 299; cf Mart. 1, 62, 1).

165 *rara auis:* one of J's most famous
phrases, though not of his coining, since
Seneca describes a good wife as *rara auis*
(*De Matr.* 56).

nigroque . . . cycno: a kind of oxymoron,
almost a contradiction in terms, though
black swans are found: *albus coruus* (7,
202) is similarly used.

166 *cui constant omnia:* 'in whom
everything adds up': the image is from
accounting. J has shifted his ground from
saying 'No woman is virtuous' to 'They're
unlivable with when they are.' Tennyson,
from the women's viewpoint, makes
Guinevere say: 'to me/He is all fault
who has no fault at all./For who loves
me must have a touch of earth;/The low
sun makes the colour.' (*Lancelot and
Elaine* 131-4). cf also Wilde's remark 'he
hasn't a single redeeming vice'.

166-7 *malo, malo:* an effect J uses on a
number of occasions; cf 279-80; 2, 135-6.
It is called *geminatio.*

167 *Vetustinam:* Mart. 2, 28, 4. The MS
reading is *Venusinam,* which does not
scan (cf 1, 51); *Venustinam* is also found.
We need a name of a woman of no
importance: considering J's dependence on
Martial it is best to look in Martial's
poems.

Cornelia: daughter of Scipio Africanus,
mother of Tiberius and Gaius Gracchus
and the model of motherhood (Val. Max.
4, 4, proem.). CORNELIA MATER
GRACCHORVM was inscribed on a statue
in her honour. Her sons were both
assassinated, so that the introduction of
Niobe is apt, but J deflates it by the
further comparison to the sow. Mart. also
takes Cornelia to deflate her (11, 104, 17).

169 *supercilium:* 'haughtiness'.

170-1 The exploits of her father Scipio,
who defeated Hannibal's ally Syphax in
203 BC, and Hannibal himself at Zama in
202, conquering Carthage and ending
the Second Punic War.

171 *migra:* 'get lost' (Green),

172-7 The legend of Niobe, who boasted
her superiority in having seven sons and
seven daughters to Latona, who had but
one of each. But Latona's were Apollo
and Diana, who shot up Niobe's
children in a kind of gangster raid. Niobe
herself was turned to stone, but this
would not help J's argument.

172 Note the stammering effect
achieved by the broken syntax combined
with alliteration on *p.*

Paean: title of Apollo as god of healing.

174 *Amphion:* Niobe's husband, who

committed suicide in grief. However, the gallant husband does not offer his own life but his wife's. A spondaic line.

177 *scrofa... alba:* the white sow with its litter of thirty, a portent of the founding of Alba Longa (12, 70-4; Verg. *A* 3, 389; 8, 43), here a deflating comparison.

178 *tanti:* gen. of value: 'worth so much'.

grauitas: with *pietas* (a sense of duty), one of the basic Roman virtues, well exemplified by the familiar 'He nothing common did or mean/Upon that memorable scene' (Marvell on King Charles). See J. Ferguson *Moral Values in the Ancient World* c. ix.

178-9 *se... inputet:* 'to be always thrusting itself in your teeth'.

179-80 'There is no delight in this rare and supreme blessing.' Philosophically the *summum bonum,* the highest good, is the thing for which you live, your 'end'.

181 *plus aloes quam mellis habet:* sc. 'she'. We still use honey as an image of sweetness and aloes (the juice of a plant of the Liliaceae) of bitterness.

182 *horreat:* Green inverts the sentence and renders 'doesn't give him cold shivers'.

septenis... horis: the abl. is often used in Latin even though duration of time is involved; cf 10, 239. The implication of the phrase is simply 'more than half the day'.

184-99 *Some trivialities are quite insufferable. One is the aping of Greek ways and Greek speech by Italian women. They even make love in Greek. It's all right for the young, but what about an 82-year-old? Greek endearments may work the men up — but your face is the index of your years.*

185 *nam:* 'for example'.

186 *Tusca:* an Italian girl from Tuscany. Note the effective juxtaposition.

Graecula: J cannot resist hitting at the Greek dominance over Roman culture (which was an actual fact); cf 3, 58-125. Note the diminutive, contemptuous, as at 3, 78, but mocking the affectation of society airs. Martial's Laelia (10, 68) was another Etruscan become Greek.

187 *Sulmonensi:* Sulmo was a county-town in the territory of the Paeligni: it was the birthplace of Ovid, cynical poet of love, which gives the allusion added piquancy.

Cecropis: Cecrops was a mythical king of Athens; cf 2, 92; so Cecropis means an Athenian woman.

omnia Graece: emphasised by the bucolic diaeresis.

189 The whole line is ironically reminiscent of J's own satiric programme: 1, 85-6.

191 *concumbunt Graece:* there are analogies in the conventional British view of the French. J moves subtly backwards and forwards between language and behaviour. (Harriet Wimsey, waking after her wedding-night, lay speculating whether Peter's first words would be in French or English: Dorothy Sayers *Busman's Honeymoon.*)

dones... puellis: 'You can allow that to young girls.'

195 ζωὴ καὶ ψυχή: 'my life, my soul': terms of endearment.

ferendis: Housman for the MS *relictis,* which is inappropriate to *uerba lasciua.*

197 *digitos habet:* to arouse physical passion. An excellent personification, picked out by the bucolic diaeresis.

197-8 *ut... pinnae:* i.e. 'to reduce you to impotence': the voice encourages passion; the face quenches it.

198 *mollius:* as often, ambiguous between 'gentle', 'effeminate' and 'passionate'.

198-9 *Haemo... Carpophoro:* actors; cf 3, 99 *molli... Haemo.*

200-30 *If you are not intending to love your wife it seems a pity to go through the expense of a ceremony. If you're in love, then you're simply going to be under the yoke. She'll determine your actions, emotions, friendships. She'll set you to put her lovers in your will. She'll order you about. And they don't stay with one subject-husband. Eight in five years. It should be on the gravestone.*

200 *legitimis... tabellis:* 'a legal document'. Roman marriage had three forms. *Coemptio* was a legal fiction of purchase from the father; *usus* was cohabitation with a declaration of intention, valid only after a year's continuous cohabitation; *confarreatio* was a picturesque religious sacrificial ceremony, difficult of annulment. In all the wife passed into the husband's *potestas,* and from the third century BC free marital association was increasingly found among the upper classes, the wife retaining authority over her property.

202 *cenam:* 'the wedding-breakfast', as vital a part of the ceremony then as now.

mustacea: dessert in the form of gâteaux.

203 *labente officio:* 'when the company is breaking up': *officio,* the obligation to attend, the ceremony itself, or (as here) the people attending.

crudis: 'to them when they're stuffed'.

205 The present consists of gold coins with the emperor's titles Dacicus and Germanicus, commemorating victories in Dacia (Rumania) and Germany. Martial (8 ded.) gives both titles to Domitian, but *DACICVS* is not found on coins. The reference must therefore be to Trajan, who took the title Germanicus in 97 and Dacicus in late 102 or early 103. There is no other reference to such a wedding-present, but it was a normal gift to gladiators (Mart. *Epig. Lib.* 29, 6), and we may suppose that J is satirically referring to marriage as a battle between man and woman.

206 *simplicitas:* 'single-mindedness' but with an innuendo of 'simple-mindedness'.

207-8 The animal image is vital; cf 43; also 270.

209 *ardeat ipsa licet:* 'even if she's in love herself'. The phrase is borrowed from Mart. 8, 59, 12: in Martial it is literal, J turns it into a metaphor.

210 *spoliis:* the military metaphor again; cf 232.

igitur: Quintilian.(1, 5, 39) raises the question whether this should appear as the first word of a sentence and admits that the practice of good authors differs.

utilis: a utilitarian standard, espoused among others by Epicureans. The more good-natured the husband, the more advantage will be taken of him.

214 *haec dabit affectus:* 'she'll arrange your likes and dislikes'.

ille: antecedent of *cuius.*

215 *barbam:* the Romans grew beards up to the age of 40 and then shaved them off.

216 *cum:* although'.

217 *iuris idem:* 'the same point of right'.

harenae: gladiators; cf 3, 115 *abollae.*

218 'you will be dictatorially forced to include more than one of her lovers among your inheritors.'

219-23 A dialogue with the wife speaking first.

219 *crucem:* the punishment for slaves and rebels. In Petron. 53 Trimalchio's slave is subject to crucifixion for cursing his master. In Plaut. *Bacch.* 362 Chrysalus is afraid of becoming Crucisalus; cf *Asin.* 548-51.

220 *audi:* 'hear the case first'.

222 *homo:* Aristotle had called a slave 'a living tool' (*Pol.* 1, 4, 2, 1253 b). This is echoed by Varro *RR* 1, 17, 1 *instrumenti genus uocale.* Epicureans and Stoics alike had a more humane view; cf Petron. 71 *et serui homines sunt et aeque unum lactem biberunt:* Sen. *Ep.* 47, 1 *'serui sunt.' immo humiles amici.* The early Empire saw a remarkable growth in humane legislation over the condition of slaves: for example, legislation of Claudius gave freedom to a sick slave abandoned by his owner (Suet. *Claud.* 25; *Dig.* 40, 8, 2), Domitian banned castration (Suet. *Dom.* 7) and Hadrian curtailed the owner's traditional power of life and death (SHA *Hadr.* 18, 7). Conditions in the mines were appalling (Strab. 12, 3, 40; Diod. Sic. 3, 12-4; 5, 38); equally, some slaves achieved positions of distinction like the doctor, surgeon and oculist Merula (*ILS* 7812).

nil fecerit, esto: 'All right: let's accept that he's done nothing.'

223 Legally by Roman tradition, the owner had absolute rights, even of life and death. Plut. *Cato Maior* 25 records cooks flogged for preparing an unsatisfactory dinner. See also on 219.

224 *regna:* for the Romans an abhorred régime, an eastern autocracy, here recalling Cleopatra.

225 *permutat:* 'keeps changing'.

flammea conterit: 'wears out her wedding-veil'.

226 *repetit:* one thinks in the 1970s of Richard Burton and Elizabeth Taylor, or of an early Hollywood marriage in which the same couple was divorced twice and each time reunited.

227 *ornatas:* with laurels for the wedding.

uela: awnings leading to the door.

229 *octo:* eight in five years would be good going even in Hollywood. Africans are known to refer to the 'western practice of consecutive polygamy'. Pompey was married five times, Caesar and Antony each four. cf Sen. *Ben.* 3, 16, 2 *numquid iam ulla repudio erubescit, postquam illustres quaedam ac nobiles feminae non consulum numero sed maritorum annos suos computant, et exeunt matrimonii causa, nubunt repudii?*

230 *sepulcri:* ironical, as the great distinction, recorded on tombstones, was to have had one husband only.

231-45 *There'll be no peace while your mother-in-law is alive. She knows every trick to corrupt her daughter. All women are litigious, and have made themselves expert lawyers.*

231 *concordia:* ironical.

socru: the mother-in-law joke is part of the human condition.

232 *spoliis:* cf 210 for the military image.

nudi: ambiguous: it is her power when they are *naked* which renders him defenceless, so that she may (proleptic) *strip him of his possessions.*

233 *illa docet:* the anaphora underlines the irony.

234 *rude:* 'obvious': these words recall the *montana uxor* of 5.

nec simplex: by contrast with the husband's *simplicitas* (205).

235 *corpore sano:* 'although she's perfectly fit'.

236 *Archigenen:* a well-known doctor, who appears again at 13, 98; 14, 252. A Syrian from Apamea, he was of the Eclectic school, author of a pharmacology and other works, and was prominent at Rome in Trajan's reign.

pallia: 'bedclothes'. It should perhaps be emphasised that it is the mother-in-law who pretends to be ill, so that her daughter may have an excuse for visiting her house for her assignations.

240 *habet:* sc. herself. The bucolic diaeresis emphasises the epigram.

241 *turpi . . . turpem:* 'whore'.

242 *femina litem:* a juxtaposition of things which ought to be incompatible.

243 *Manilia:* not otherwise known.

244 *libellos:* 'formal pleas'.

245 *principium:* the opening of the case, otherwise the *exordium,* in Greek *prooemion* (Quint. 4, 1, 1).

locos: divisions of a speech, or perhaps purple passages.

Celso: probably A. Cornelius Celsus, who wrote on medicine and rhetoric; possibly Iuventius Celsus, jurist.

246-67 *Some women prefer violence even to men, and practise as gladiators (though they wouldn't want a sex-change: they'd have less fun). He's a lucky man who sees his wife's fighting equipment up for sale. So upper-class women go through all the motions of the gladiator. Gladiators' wives don't!*

246 *endromidas:* cf 3, 103; thick suits, usually of cheap material, though here dyed a fashionable purple. The word is Greek. Mart. 4, 19, 4-5 couples *endromida* and *ceroma.*

Tyrias: 'purple': the dye came from the

murex, a shellfish found off the coast of Palestine.

femineum ceroma: 'women wrestling': *ceroma,* another Greek word, is the ointment of oil and wax rubbed on the skin before wrestling to make the skin slippery: so the actual wrestling. The Greek word justifies the spondaic fifth foot and the offbeat rhythm, but J is also using it to express his indignation at this break in the natural order.

247 *pali:* a dummy opponent in the form of a stump of wood.

248 *rudibus:* wooden swords used in practice.

lacessit: 'challenges'.

249 *numeros:* we could almost say 'the exercises by number'.

dignissima: ironic; cf 50.

250 *Florali . . . tuba:* the festival of Flora, goddess of flowers, the Floralia, lasted from 28 April to 3 May. It was instituted as an annual festival in 173 BC (Ov. *F* 5, 329ff.). It was a fertility ritual in which prostitutes played an important part, and there was a good deal of sexual licence. The trumpet was generally used to inaugurate public activities.

matrona: for the expected *meretrix.*

251-2 Alliteration on *p,* as often, expresses scornful rejection.

253 *sexu:* her sex.

uires: 'violence', even more than *uiros,* men: the word-play was recognised by the ancients although the first syllable varies in quantity (3, 138; *Rhet. ad Her.* 4, 29). Note how the bucolic diaeresis helps to isolate the preceding words.

254 *nollet:* 'she would not wish' sc. even if she could.

256-7 The armour of the gladiator known as the Samnite, sword-belt, armlet (protecting the right arm: the left having a shield), crested helmet, and greave (normally *ocrea,* worn on the left leg only, as some cricketers prefer a pad only on the left or advanced leg; cf Liv. 9, 40, 3). Note the extraordinary sound of 256 with alliteration on *cr* and repeated *-is-.*

257 *diuersa:* as a Thracian, with greaves on both legs.

259 *cyclade:* a blouse of light material with an embroidered fringe. The letter -*y*- here and in *bombycinus* shows Greek words, and forms part of J's indignation.

260 *bombycinus:* the whole story of Roman silk is much trammeled. The Chinese jealously kept the secret of the

true silkworm, till it was smuggled out
in the reign of Justinian in the sixth
century AD. Chinese silk (*serica*) was a
luxury import. One strange aspect of
the story is that it was coarsely woven:. the
Romans with superior technology unwove
it, rewove it more finely and exported it
back to China! *Bombycina* was said to
come from Mesopotamia, but this may be
just the middlemen with a monopoly of
one kind of Chinese weave. *Coae uestes*
from the island of Cos were woven from
the product of some insect resembling a
silkworm, but otherwise unknown; they
were different from and inferior to
Chinese silk, superior to anything else
available in the Greek world. See J.
Ferguson 'China and Rome' in H.
Temporini (ed.) *Aufstieg und Niedergang der
Römischen Welt* II 9,2 pp. 581-603.

261   *monstratos:* 'prescribed'; cf 249
numeros.

262-3   *quanta ... quam denso:* there is a
double construction: 'see what huge
puttees, of what thick fibre, sit tight on her
hams', 'see the size of her puttees and the
thickness of their padding'.

264   *scaphium:* 'potty': so Mart. 11,
11, 6. It is derived from a Greek word
for boat.

265   *neptes:* grand-daughters,
descendants.

Lepidi: the Aemilii Lepidi were among
the *crème de la crème* of the aristocracy.

caeciue Metelli: L. Caecilius Metellus
lost his sight in saving a statue from a
temple fire in 241 BC and took the name
Caecus; cf 3, 139; Plin. *NH* 7, 34; Ov.
F 6, 437ff.

266   *Gurgitis aut Fabii:* Q. Fabius
Maximus, consul in 292, 276 and 265
BC, and *princeps senatus,* was nicknamed
Gurges ('The Maw') because of his
youthful extravagance (Macr. *Sat.* 3, 13,
6); he was grandfather of Hannibal's
opponent.

ludia: cf 104.

267   *Asyli:* schol. *nomen gladiatoris:*
for the *-y-* in the name, see on 259.

268-85   *Your wife will nag you in bed.
Conscious of her own guilt she'll assail
your love-affairs, real or imaginary. Poor
fool, you think it's a sign of her love.
If only you could read her own love-
letters! But catch her in the act, she'll have
a defence: 'What's good enough for you is
good enough for me.' Guilt breeds
shamelessness.*

270   *orba tigride:* an excellent

hyperbole. Martial (3, 44, 6) has the
same image, with equal but different
hyperbole, of a poet eager to recite his
verses. Note the emphasis on barrenness,
which will be important later. The animal
comparison goes back at least to some
vicious verses of Semonides.

272   *pueros:* as objects of homosexual
affection.

paelice: abl. of cause.

uberibus: ironic, for its literal meaning
is associated with the breast and the
rejected fertility.

273-5   The sentence is an unusual shape,
with ablative absolutes strung along at
the end. Begin a fresh sentence in English.
'She has always plenty of tears ...'.

274   *statione:* a military metaphor 'on
duty'.

275   *amorem:* 'you think it's love.'

276   *tu tibi tunc:* sarcastic alliteration.

uruca: 'you miserable worm'.

tabellas: forming a scornful near-rhyme
with *labellis.*

277   *exorbes:* from *ex-sorbere:* 'kiss
away'.

quae scripta: object of *lecture.*

278   *zelotypae:* 'jealous', also at
5, 45, a Greek word which had passed into
currency.

279   *sed iacet:* 'But suppose you catch
her lying'. The situation is ironical —
the husband a slave, the slave a husband.

aut equitis. 'dic: the broken rhythm
expresses the horror of the discovery.
The repetition *dic/dic* from the last word
of one line to the first of the next
(*geminatio*) is espoused occasionally by J
(cf 166-7; 2, 135-6). '*dic ... colorem*' is
addressed by the woman to Quintilian.

280   *Quintiliane:* the teacher of
rhetoric: see on 75.

colorem: 'line of defence'.

281   '*haeremus. dic ipsa.*': 'I'm stuck
have a go yourself': Quintilian's answer.
Her *color* follows, and it is devastating.
J. G. Griffith (*Hermes* 98 (1970) 63) says
well: 'The lady's *color* is as impudent as
it is unanswerable: "what's sauce for the
gander is sauce for the goose", to invert a
familiar English adage.' In Menander's
Epitrepontes 693-707 Charisius realises he
is wrong to condemn his wife for the sort
of sexual behaviour he takes for granted
in himself. This is the ground of Jesus's
words 'Let him that is without sin among
you cast the first stone' (John 8:7). The
double standard is the theme of Mozart's
opera *Le Nozze di Figaro.*

283   *mare caelo confundas:* proverbial

of 'the world turned upside down': see
on 2, 25.

284 *homo sum:* Duff rightly identifies
three levels of meaning: (a) I have the
feelings of a human being: Ter. *Haut.* 77
homo sum; humani nihil a me alienum puto;
(b) I have the weaknesses of a human being:
Petron. 75 *nemo, inquit, nostrum non
peccat. homines sumus, non dei;* (c) I have
the rights of a human being, and am not to
be treated as an animal or a slave (cf 222).
Note that she denies this humanity to the
slave with whom she is lying.

285 *animos:* the pl. means a disposition,
here an arrogant and violent high-spiritedness.

286-300 *In the old days poverty, hard
work and danger kept women chaste. The
rot set in with peace and prosperity. Excess
of all kinds, foreign customs spread. A
woman drunk loses all standards.*
Augustine *Ep.* 138, 8 uses this passage as
evidence that wealth and indolence, not
Christianity, were the undoing of Rome:
audiant satiricum suum. cf also Victor
Hugo *L'Armée Terrible* Jan 1871 II
Lettre à une femme: 'Ce qui fit la
beauté des Romaines antiques/C'étaient
leurs humbles toits, leurs vertus
domestiques,/Leurs doigts que l'âpre laine
avait faits noirs et durs,/Leurs courts
sommeils, leur calme, Annibal près des
murs/Et leurs maris debout sur la porte
Colline.'

286 *monstra:* 'abnormal portents'.

288 *contingi:* 'to be infected'.
uellere Tusco: Etruria was an area of
sheep-farming, and spinning wool was a
traditional woman's occupation. It is
found in their epitaphs, as in the well-
known *domum seruauit. lanam fecit.*
(*Remains of Old Latin* (Loeb) 4, 12).

291 *Hannibal:* in 211 BC he marched
within sight of the walls of Rome, creating
panic (Liv. 26, 10). After his retreat the
Romans offered thanks to a curious
godling, Rediculus Tutanus, who turned
back and kept safe, and whose effective
existence was confined to this one occasion.
Collina turre: the Roman army took up
position before the walls between the
Esquiline and Colline gates. The latter
stood on the Collis Quirinalis: hence the
name. The *turris* probably refers to the
agger, a defensive earthwork built by
Servius Tullius.

292 Duff well quotes Shakespeare 1
Hen. IV 4, 2 'the cankers of a calm world
and a long peace'. See also Vell. Pat.
2, 110, 2 *Pannonia, insolens longae pacis
bonis;* Tacitus uses the phrase often and

abusively; cf R. Syme *Tacitus,* p. 218. There
have however been two world wars since
Duff wrote, and J might have taken a
different view in the third century.

293 *luxuria:* a target of the satirists,
Petronius and Juvenal in particular.
It is wider than our 'luxury' and includes
excess of all kinds. This will be the theme
of the rest of the satire. The description
saeuior armis sets the context of a key image.

294 Compare Sall. *Cat.* 10 *qui labores,
pericula, dubias atque asperas res facile
tolerauerant, eis otium, diuitiae, optanda
alias, oneri miseriaeque fuere.* Moralists
who so express themselves are usually
comfortably off and in no great danger.
ex quo: 'ever since'.

295 *fluxit:* cf 3, 62 *in Tiberim defluxit
Orontes.*

296 *Sybaris:* a Greek settlement in
southern Italy, proverbial for luxury.
Typical stories told of a Sybarite getting
backache from hearing about men digging,
or finding that his bed of roses blistered
him.
colles: the seven hills of Rome.
Rhodos: the wealthiest island of the
eastern Mediterranean: note the Greek
termination, pointed by the anti-Greek J.
Miletos: great city of Asia Minor: again
the Greek termination. Milesian tales
were tales of sexual excess. Miletus was
the entrepôt for much of the caravan
trade from the East. Spondee in fifth foot.

297 *Tarentum* is another Greek settle-
ment in southern Italy. The reference is
to an event in 281 BC. A Roman delega-
tion was visiting Tarentum. There was a
festival of Dionysus: hence *coronatum*
and *madidum.* In the theatre a drunk
insulted L. Postumius (*petulans*
represents the Greek *hybris*) by defaecating
over his clothing. The crowd roared their
applause, but Postumius replied, 'Laugh,
laugh while you can. You'll have a long
time for tears when you have to wash my
clothes clean with your blood.' (Dio Cass.
9 fr.; cf Zonaras 8, 2).

298 *obscena pecunia:* 'filthy lucre'.

300 *uenus:* by metonymy for the
person. But note that there is ambiguity.
There is no difference in the Latin between
Venus and *uenus.* We can't escape the
image of Venus drunk.

301-13 *Women when drunk don't know
what's happening. Look how Tullia and
Maura actually relieve themselves over the
statue of Chastity and ride each other
beneath it.*

Roman tradition was severe against women drinking. There was an old story of one Egnatius Maetennus acquitted by Romulus of guilt although he beat his wife to death for drinking. Another old story told of a woman forced t'o death by her family for so much as opening the drawer containing the keys of the wine-cellar. A woman found guilty of drinking excessively without her husband's know-ledge was stripped of her dowry. The traditionalist Cato says that the explanation of the custom of greeting women with a kiss is to see if their breath smells of drink (Plin. *NH* 14, 14, 89-90; cf Polyb. 6, 11a, 4; Plut. *QR* 6, 265 B; Dion. Hal. *Ant. Rom.* 2, 25, 6; Cic. *Rep.* 4, 6; Val. Max. 2, 1, 5; 6, 3, 9; Aul Gell. 10, 23, 1; Tert. *Apol.* 6).

303 *Falerno:* the celebrated Campanian wine. Perfumes are mixed in instead of water in Petron. 70.

304 *concha:* a shell-shaped bowl for perfumes; cf Hor. *O* 2, 7, 22 *funde capacibus/unguenta de conchis.* J's revellers pour the wine into the perfume bowl.

304-5 A good description of drunkenness; cf Petron. 64 *et sane iam lucernae mihi plures uidebantur ardere totumque triclinium esse mutatum.*

306 *sanna:* a grimace (a Greek word).

308 *Maura:* the obvious meaning of this proper name is the African girl. *Pudicitiae:* her shrine was in the *forum Boarium.* The allusion takes us back to the first line.

307 *Tullia:* the gens Tullia was an ancient patrician house which became extinct: Cicero belonged to a plebeian family of the same name.

309 *micturiunt hic:* their action to the statue of Chastity parallels the action of the Tarentine to the Roman ambassador. Note the harsh offbeat rhythm.

311 *equitant:* sc. one another.

314-45 *It is notorious what goes on in the rites of the Good Goddess, when the women are aroused by music and wine. The ladies beat lower-class women in any competition in impropriety. When they are worked up they call in the men, and will use slaves or animals if need be. Once no one would dare such profanation — but the scandals are well-known.*

314 *nota ... secreta:* a paradox: the secret rites are notorious.

bonae ... deae: the Good Goddess, who had a shrine in a grotto on the Aventine and whose festival, a fertility-cult, was celebrated on 4 Dec. by selected *matronae,*

guided by the Vestals, in the house of one of the senior magistrates (who had to sleep out) and conduced to the well-being of the people of Rome (Dio Cassius 37, 35, 4; Plut. *Cic.* 19-20). Abstention from sexual intercourse was an important aspect of preparation for the festival. Profanation by a male was a serious offence (cf 331, 345; 2, 86). The goddess's name was not known: she was associated with the god Faunus.

315 *cornu:* a horn-shaped Phrygian pipe.

uino: this is right: there was an amphora of wine called euphemistically 'honeypot' or 'milk'. The vine was prominent in the floral decorations.

316-7 *Priapi maenades:* a brilliant phrase. The maenads or Bacchants were the wild women-worshippers of Bacchus-Dionysus; Euripides's play insists on their chastity. Priapus was the ithyphallic garden-god of the Romans. Neither is appropriate to a gathering of Roman matrons honouring the Good Goddess.

318 Tertullian (*Apol.* 9, 18) has *libido, cuius ... saltus* (pl.).

319 *madentia:* 'tipsy'.

320 *lenonum ancillas:* 'the call-girls'.

Saufeia: we meet her again drinking at 9,117: it is an aristocratic name.

321 *pendentis ... coxae:* 'a supple hip', like Apuleius's Fotis (*Met.* 2, 8).

322 *Medullinae:* another high-class name of the gens Furia. Claudius was at one point engaged to a Livia Medullina Camilla.

fluctum: i.e. supple movement.

323 *palma:* the symbol of victory.

dominas: the aristocratic ladies.

uirtus: supply *est* with both clauses: 'the victory is with the ladies, their quality matches their birth'. The satire is mordant for (a) *uirtus* is appropriate to a *uir*, male, (b) philosophically it has come to mean 'virtue', of a kind they do not possess, (c) if their 'virtue' matches their birth, and this is their virtue, what does that tell us of their birth? Their behaviour damns the Roman upper classes.

326 *Laomedontiades:* mock-epic. Priam, the long-lived king of Troy, was son of Laomedon.

Nestor: the long-lived elder statesman of the Greeks in the Trojan War, ruler of sandy Pylos, where Carl Blegen has excitingly unearthed his palace.

327 *tum femina simplex:* 'then they become women pure and simple'. There is a reference back to 253-4. *Simplex* is ironically ambiguous: they are neither pure nor simple.

328 *antro:* the grotto: see on 314.

329 *fas:* a religious term: the moment was perhaps dawn.

331 *si nihil est:* 'if there's nothing doing'.

incurritur: impersonal 'they run'. The bucolic diaeresis picks out the words.

abstuleris spem: the offbeat rhythm as the behaviour becomes more unnatural.

332 *uenit:* 'comes': the *e* is short.

et: 'even'.

conductus: the young men come of their own accord, the slaves are under orders. They have to pay the water-carrier.

aquarius: not the inspector of the water-supply, but a water-carrier, a job regarded as menial drudgery; cf *Gloss.* 5, 652, 23 *aquarius melastinus,* i.e. *mediastinus.*

334 *summittat asello:* the three double consonants express well their stammering urgency. The final degradation of the 'golden ass', the man in ass's form, was to be to lie openly with a woman. Apuleius gives the idea a further twist: it is degrading to the donkey (*Met.* 10). Shakespeare's *A Midsummer Night's Dream* contains a fantasy on the theme.

337 *Mauri atque Indi:* i.e. the news of the scandal has spread through Africa and Asia.

psaltria: we do not know the identity of this musical 'lady': it was presumably a genuine scandal.

penem maiorem: the 'longstanding fallacies' of the Freudian limerick.

338 *duo Caesaris Anticatones:* M. Porcius Cato Uticensis was an implacable opponent of Julius Caesar. After the battle of Thapsus in 46 BC he took the Stoic path of suicide. Cicero wrote a pamphlet in his praise. Caesar charged Hirtius with replying to it (Cic. *Att.* 12, 40, 1), but himself wrote first one and then a second Anticato broadsheet. The two brought together in a single volume will have been unusually long for such political squibs.

339 *conscius . . . mus:* even a male mouse hesitates to profane the rites. (Conversely female animals are not permitted on Mount Athos, which is given over to male monastic communities.) The broken rhythm at the end of the line here is not scornful, but expresses the quick darting movement of the mouse.

340 *intulerit:* cf Cic. *Leg.* 2, 36 *ille qui in sacrificium cogitatam libidinem intulit.*

342 *tunc:* 'in days gone by'.

hominum: with *quis.*

numinis: 'divine power'. The word means literally a 'nodding'. The power of fertility was believed to reside in the head, the testes being the mere channels of emission, so that to move the head was to stir up the power of life. In Homer when Zeus nods Olympus quakes (*Il.* 1, 524ff). In the earliest stages of Roman religion there were powers, not personified, presiding over the operations of home and farm, one for ploughing and another for harrowing and another for sowing, and so on. These are usually called *numina.* In general *numen* simply means divinity or divine power.

343 *Numae:* Numa Pompilius, second king of Rome (traditionally 715-673 BC), a ruler of renowned piety, who built the Regia (later the seat of the *pontifex maximus*), reformed the calendar of festivals, and organised the priestly colleges.

344 *Vaticano . . . de monte:* the clay was dug out *in situ,* long before it was built over.

345 *Clodius:* P. Clodius Pulcher, loose-living, radical aristocrat, who was having an affair with Caesar's wife Pompeia, and attended the sacred rites disguised as a flute-girl in 62 BC when they were being held in Caesar's house. There was a major scandal. Clodius was brought to trial but got off by bribing the jury. Note the link with the reference to his sister at 8.

01-34, 346-51 *Houses with a professed queer are the worst; these pollute the cups they drink from. Even in the gladiatorial schools they are segregated. The women use them as their intimate advisers. And they can't be trusted: their get-up is feminine, but they're masculine in bed. It's no use setting a guard on your wife; she'll corrupt the guard. And poor and rich are equally lustful.*

In 1899 E. O. Winstedt, then quite a young student, was examining an eleventh-century MS of J in the Bodleian and found that it contained thirty-six lines not in any other MS. Thirty-four of these followed 365, and two followed 373. The lines are both obscure and obscene. Housman sorted out their meaning. Their authenticity has been a matter of intense debate. If J did not write them we have to postulate another satirist of like temper and equal genius. It is better to suppose them genuine, and to wonder how many similar passages we may have lost. More recently, J. G. Griffith has shown good reason for taking them after 345 rather than 365.

01-2 *professus obscenum:* i.e. a *cinaedus* (cf 03).

03 *inuenies:* indefinite 'you'. Note *es, is.*

05 *permittunt:* the owners of the house: at this stage vague, but in 014 it becomes clear that the women are responsible, as in the context of this satire we may already suspect.

06 *colocyntha:* a gourd, a word that was used with sexual innuendo; here a nickname.

chelidon: lit. 'a swallow'. Sen. *Ep.* 87, 16 *unus ex Cleopatrae mollibus.* J treats the word as fem.

07 *laribus:* the household gods, and so the establishment.

lanista: the manager of a troupe of gladiators.

09 *psyllus:* cf Charis (*Gramm. Lat.* 1, 110 K) *inde effeminati hodieque in ludo syllae dicuntur, quos uulgo inprudenter psyllos appellant.* The ψιλός was a light-armed soldier, and the Romans allowed a kind of pun with vowels of different quantity, *lĕuis* (light) and *lēuis* smooth) (Q. 9, 3, 70).

Euhoplo: 'well-armed', a reasonable name for a gladiator. More, ὅπλον is used of the phallus (Ar. *Ach.* 592; Thesm. 232; Hesych. s.v.). The MS *eupholio* is meaningless. Housman proposed *euphono,* Leo *Euhoplio,* a wrong form. But Housman was wrong to object that Roman satirists do not coin names of this kind; they are frequent in Petronius.

retia: i.e. the *retiarii,* the net-fighters, regarded as the dregs of the gladiators.

010 *tunicae:* as the *retiarius* is referred to by his weapon, the homosexual is also referred to by his dress. Others take the *retiarius tunicatus* as a condemned criminal. To admit a *cinaedus* to your household is like admitting a condemned criminal to your troops.

ponit: the subject is the antecedent of *qui.*

011 *munimenta umeri:* 'shoulder-pads', not part of his armour since he fights *nudus:* corresponding to *turpi . . . tunicae,* part of the dress of the queer.

pulsatoremque: 'which strikes down his opponent': Leo for MS *pulsatamque arma.*

tridentem: the weapon of the *retiarius,* with strong sexual reference.

012 *pars ultima:* 'the remote corners'.

013 *has animas:* 'these washed-out creatures' like shades of the dead.

neruos: 'prison-cell': the word means sinew, so cord, so fetter. But it also means the male sex-organ (9, 34; 10, 205).

015 *Albanum Surrentinumque:* good wines, from Alba Longa near Rome, and Surrentum in Campania (the modern Sorrento).

016 *sepulchri:* for the use of tombs (often of course quite elaborately built and equipped) by prostitutes see Mart. 1, 34, 8.

018 *seruant:* this is the MS reading: 'for them they reserve their languors and their serious moments.' Housman would reverse this sense and read *soluunt* or *releuant.* Axelson's *reserant* ('unlock the secrets of') is tempting.

019 Compare the hostess in the Vergilian *Copa* 2 *crispum sub crotalo docta mouere latus* or Fotis in Apuleius *Met.* 2, 7 *lumbis sensim uibrantibus, spinam mobilem quatiens placide decenter undabat.*

020-2 A vivid visual picture, characteristic of J, with the eye-shadow, orange robe and hairnet; cf 2, 93-5.

025 *fortissimus:* for all his effeminate style, he is masculine enough in bed. Again the bucolic diaeresis isolates and emphasises what precedes it.

026 *Thais:* the name is taken from the celebrated Athenian courtesan of the time of Alexander, mistress of Ptolemy I.

Triphallo: the title of a play by Naevius, from its strongly sexual main character: *docili* is not easy: perhaps 'expert'.

027 *hunc mimum:* sc. *putas.*

sponsio fiat: 'let's bet on it'.

028 *purum:* i.e. *purum putum* (Varr. *RR* 2, 2, 10).

contendo: 'I bet' sc. *in quoduis pignus.* This is an exchange between husband and gigolo.

029 *uocat:* indic. used deliberatively, 'is to call'; cf 3, 296 *in qua te quaero proseucha?;* 4, 130 *conciditur?* Slaves might be tortured to give evidence in Roman law. Note the three successive lines with strong breaks near the end.

031 *seram:* a bolt or crossbow.

031-2 *quis custodiet ipsos custodes:* one of the most famous of all epigrams; it is hard to think that it is not authentic J. 030-4 appear in a slightly different form in the other MSS as 346-8; it is hard to choose between *custodiet* there and O's *custodiat.* Kipling used the quotation as the climax of 'In Ambush' in *Stalky and Co.*

032 *lasciuae furta puellae:* recalling love-elegy.

033 *hac mercede:* 'at the same price', i.e. they receive her favours too.

crimen: 'crime' as at 285.

034 *prospicit hoc prudens:* ironical, since these are the qualities normally looked

for in a wife: the alliteration points the irony.

346-8 These lines virtually repeat 030-4, and if that is restored these should be omitted.

350 *silicem:* the Romans used volcanic basalt for paving-stones. The woman who has to walk is no better than the lady who can afford a carriage. One fashionable British church had a women's meeting on Monday and a ladies' meeting on Tuesday. J would have been equally suspicious of both.

351 *longorum:* 'tall'.

ceruice: 'shoulder'.

Syrorum: as litter-bearers Syrians, Cappadocians and Liburnians were in most demand. Mart. 9, 22, 9 *ut canusinatus nostro Syrus assere sudet.*

352-65 *Ogulnia hires a whole train of people to escort her to the games. She gives the remains of her family silver down to the last plate away to athletes. Women never come to terms with limited resources. Men sometimes do look forward. Women expect their resources to be renewed by a process of natural growth.*

352 *Ogulnia:* the name is from an old plebeian family: Q. Ogulnius Gallus was consul in 269 BC.

353 Asyndeton is common in such catalogues.

354 *nutricem:* to add respectability.

flauam: 'blonde', so presumably a slave captured from a northern tribe. Sir Ronald Storrs in *Ad Pyrrham* wrote at length on the cult of the unfamiliar beauty, the dark lady in the north, the *bella biondina* or *chioma dorata* in the south. One French version of 'I am black but comely' (Song of Solomon 1:5) has 'je suis brunette mais blonde'.

355 *argenti:* partitive genitive: 'the family plate'.

356 *leuibus:* 'smooth' (long *e*), probably from their practice of anointing their bodies with oil, but possibly 'beardless', i.e. young; cf Mart. 14, 205, 1 *sit nobis aetate puer, non pumice, leuis.*

et uasa nouissima: 'including the very last plate'.

357 *res angusta domi:* also at 3, 165.

358 *haec:* either *res angusta* or *paupertas.*

360 *prospiciunt:* picking up 034.

frigusque famemque: the alliteration gets well the effect of panting with cold and hunger.

361 *formica:* the stock-in-trade of moralists. 'Go to the ant, you sluggard'

(Proverbs 6:6-8); Babrius 140; Verg. *G* 1, 186 *inopi metuens formica senectae; A* 4, 402; Hor. *S* 1, 1, 32-5. Ogden Nash protested: 'The ant has made himself illustrious/Through constant industry industrious./So what? Would you be calm and placid/If you were full of formic acid?'

362 *pereuntem . . . censum:* acc. + part., a Greek usage.

363 *uelut:* as often for *uelut si.*

pullulet: a vivid metaphor from living growth.

364 From Hor. *S* 1, 1, 51 *at suaue est ex magno tollere aceruo.*

365 *quanti:* gen. of price or value: see on 137.

gaudia: ironically of perverted pleasure; cf 379; 420; 597; 602; also 367 *delectent.*

366-78 *Some women like eunuchs — no danger of an abortion! They're best if they're fully mature before the operation. The poor slave-dealers' kids, done when young, are utterly miserable. Some eunuchs are fine figures of men: let them sleep with your wife, but not with your boy.*

366 *eunuchi:* castration was an oriental practice, by tradition originating in Mesopotamia (Amm. Marc. 14, 6, 17); it had only recently been legally proscribed in Rome (Suet. *Dom.* 7; Dio Cass. 67, 2; 68, 2; *Dig.* 48, 8, 4, 2 *nemo liberum seruumue inuitum sinentemue castrare debet*), though Roman opinion looked askance at it. The practice was governed by a number of factors: (a) it was sometimes, as in Egypt, a punishment for adultery; (b) it was practised by priests, e.g. of Cybele, Artemis of Ephesus, Atargatis, Hecate at Lagina, who preserved their fertility for the Mother-goddess; (c) it was used on slaves to make them tractable, and to fit them to be guardians of the womenfolk.

368 As usual the bucolic diaeresis isolates the previous words.

370 *pectine nigro:* of the pubic hair.

372 *tonsoris:* the barber is the only loser.

Heliodorus: the Greek surgeon who performs the operation.

373AB Also from O, Winstedt's MS.

373B *ciceris:* lit. 'chickpea', an expression for the male sex-organ, as the scholiast on Aristophanes *Fr.* 545 tells us.

375 *custodem uitis et horti:* Priapus whose ithyphallic statue protected gardens.

378 *tondendum:* i.e. his beard has begun to grow; he has reached adolescence.

Bromium: the name is a title of Dionysus,

the divine child, which is presumably the idea behind its use here, though the literal meaning 'noisy' may have something to do with it.

379-97   A musical wife has the musicians at her beck and call. They drool over their instruments. One noble lady was making offerings for her protégé's victory — just as if for the illness of husband or son. Do the gods really listen to such prayers? They can't have much to do.

379 *cantu:* 'music', not just singing.

fibula: see on 73.

380 *uocem uendentis praetoribus:* i.e. who sings for pay at public events.

organa: Humphries: 'she holds their instruments in her hands'. The bucolic diaeresis points it.

381 *testudine tota:* the tortoiseshell sounding-board of the lyre. The *ts* give the effect of plucked strings.

382 *sardonyches:* rings of sardonyx, fem. at 7, 144.

crispo: curly-haired, and so vibrating, transferred from the string to the plectrum.

numerantur: a Silver Latin usage, 'are sounded one after the other'. cf Mart. 8, 28, 7; 8, 65, 9.

pectine: the plectrum, but there is a strong innuendo and double meaning; cf 370.

383 *Hedymeles:* a fictitious Greek name for a virtuoso: it means 'sweet singer'.

operas dedit: 'gave a performance'.

hunc tenet, hoc se: bucolic diaeresis, and four word-stresses in the last two feet emphasise her obsession. The language is sexual throughout.

385 *quaedam:* clearly a genuine and recognisable incident.

de numero Lamiarum: of the aristocracy. Aelius Lamia was a well-known patrician; cf 4, 154.

nominis Appi: i.e. of the gens Claudia.

386 *farre et uino:* a normal sacrifice: offerings of grain were common enough at Rome, e.g. millet cakes at the Parilia in April, and in general there was a movement away from blood sacrifices during the Republican period. Wine was poured on the sacrificial fire as a surrogate for the blood.

Ianum Vestamque: i.e. all the gods, for Janus, the god of opening (*ianua* = a door, January the first month, the Kalends his holy day), came first in prayers, and Vesta, we are told, last (Cic. *ND* 2, 67 *in ea dea, quod est rerum custos intumarum, omnis et precatio et sacrificatio extrema est*).

387 *Capitolinam quercum:* Domitian inaugurated a Greek festival, *agon Capitolinus,* in AD 86 to celebrate his restoration of the Capitoline temple (Suet. *Dom.* 4); there were three competitive sections, music, horse-racing and athletics. The prizes were wreaths of oak-leaves: Mart. 4, 54, 1 speaks of *Tarpeiae . . . quercus.* The festival, held every five years, lasted into the fifth century.

Pollio: a famous *citharoedus* (7, 176; Mart. 4, 61, 9).

388 *fidibus promittere:* 'lay it before his lyre'.

quid faceret plus: the bucolic diaeresis and offbeat rhythm express J's contempt. For the tense, see on 4, 85.

faceret: 'could she do'.

391 *cithara:* most edd. take this as standing for *citharoedus,* as *arena* for gladiators at 217. In one sense this is right, but so to translate it loses the ambiguities of 380-4.

uelare caput: the Romans (unlike the Greeks) covered their heads while praying.

dictataque uerba: 'the prescribed formula'. The elder Pliny (28, 3, 10-3) tells us of the importance of set prayers to the Romans. No word must be omitted or out of turn. Mistakes in the prayers were believed to lead to alterations in the liver or heart of the sacrificial victim.

392 *mos:* the *mos maiorum,* essential to the Romans.

aperta palluit agna: in her anxiety she almost faints when the victim is inspected. The favour or disfavour of the gods was revealed by the state of the victim's liver and other vital organs.

394 *his:* 'people like her'.

Iane pater: Herodian (1, 16, 1) calls him 'the most archaic indigenous god in Italy'; Procopius (*Bell. Goth.* 1, 25) calls him 'the first of those ancient gods whom the Romans in their own language call Penates' (a puzzling sentiment). According to Varro (Aug. *CD* 7, 28), some thought him the sky, others the universe. Gavius Bassus (Lyd. *Mens.* 4, 2) made him the air; some (Ov. *F* 103 *me Chaos antiqui — nam' sum res prisca — uocabant*) made him Chaos, the original gulf or void. Speculators inevitably identified him with the sun (e.g. Macrob. *Sat.* 1, 9, 9). He certainly seems to have some seniority even over Jupiter. His head appears on the *as* from the mid-fourth century BC, Jupiter's on the *semis.* Third-century silver coins from Capua have Janus on the obverse, Jupiter on the reverse. He was invoked — however we precisely reconstruct the text — in a very ancient hymn of the Salii cited by Varro (*LL* 7, 26). At Aquileia (*CIL* 5, 783) there was an inscription to Jupiter Dianus. The title *pater* here suggests seniority.

Janus was a god of the gate or door (*ianua*). He was a god of opening and closing (Patulcus and Clusius), portrayed looking both ways. He was the god of the opening year (January was his month), and the opening month (honoured on the Kalends).

His origin remains uncertain. A. B. Cook in his great *Zeus* made him a sky-god. Zas or Zan is a form of Zeus; the *di*-root suggests a sky-god; the links with Jupiter are strong. Frazer made him an oak-god, impressed by the parallel with Diana, a spirit of the wildwood. Others would simply have him the *numen* of the *ianua*.

magna otia caeli: a good epigram; they can't have much on hand if they've time to bother with trivialities. *Otium* is incidentally exactly what the Epicureans postulated of the gods, except that the Epicurean gods had no truck with human prayers either.

395 *quod uideo:* 'as far as I can see'.

396 So J. C. Squire wrote in 1915, 'God heard the embattled nations sing and shout/"Gott strafe England!" and "God save the King!"/God this, God that and God the other thing;/"Good God!" said God, "I've got my work cut out." ' Lucian *Icaromenippus* 25 has an amusing picture of Zeus coping with trivial prayers.

397 *uaricosus:* with standing.

398-412 *Worse still is the woman who sets up as an expert on world affairs, among men too. She knows the news from the ends of the earth and the details of the latest sex-scandal from the city. If not, she makes them up — disasters especially.*

398 *cantet:* sc. *uxor.*

399 *coetus ... uirorum:* cf Stat. *Theb.* 9, 825-7 *nonne hanc, Gradiue, proteruam/ uirginitate uides mediam se ferre uirorum/ coetibus.* There was a deal of male chauvinism about in Rome, despite, or because of, the relative social freedom of upper-class Roman women.

400 *paludatis:* the *paludamentum* was the purple cloak which signified a commander's *imperium.*

401 *siccisque mamillis:* a symbol of her failure in femininity: we might almost say 'straight-faced and straight-chested'.

402 *eadem:* 'as well'.

403 The Chinese and Thracians represent the lands beyond the imperial frontiers to the east and north.

secreta nouercae: we soon get away from high policy to her real interests.

404 *diripiatur:* 'is being mobbed (by the girls)'.

406 *modis quot:* the inverted order and broken rhythm are alike harsh.

407 *cometen:* a Greek word with Greek termination; it indicates a heavenly body with a tress of hair streaming behind, in Lat. *stella crinita.* Comets, comparatively rare in appearance, have in many cultures been thought to presage major upheavals affecting the destiny of nations; cf Tac. *Ann.* 14, 22; Suet. *Claud.* 46; *Nero* 36 *stella crinita, quae summis potestatibus exitium portendere uulgo putatur; Vesp.* 23. Trajan was campaigning in Armenia in 113 and 114, and began his campaign against Parthia in 115 or 116. By correlation with the observations of Chinese astronomers, we know that there was a large comet visible in Rome in November 115. This gives us a firm point of reference for this satire. See further on 411.

409 *ad portas:* ac. *urbis.*

quosdam facit: 'makes up her own', pointed by the bucolic diaeresis.

Niphaten: a mountain-range in Armenia, as Horace knew (*O* 2, 9, 20). J treats it as a river, either in ignorance (Lucan 3, 245 does the same) or satirically, to show that Mrs Know-All doesn't know all. J probably took his reference from Verg. *G* 3, 30 *pulsumque Niphaten,* where Armenia and Parthia are also combined.

411 There was an earthquake in Antioch in Dec. 115 in which Trajan had a narrow escape (Dio Cass. 68, 24-5: he does not mention floods). Human nature does not change. Then, as now, it was the disasters which 'hit the headlines'.

412 *quocumque* is indef., *cuicumque* relative.

413-33 *Worse is the utterly self-centred woman who orders her neighbours to be beaten up if they incommode her, goes late to the baths, enjoys some stimulation from the masseur, keeps her dinner-guests waiting, then drinks too much on an empty stomach and throws it up, to her husband's disgust.*

415 *experrecta:* the MSS have *exortata* or *exorata: experrecta* appears in the scholium to 417, and Duff tentatively proposed restoring it here, suggesting that it was glossed by *exorta,* which was then corrected *metri causa* to *exorata.*

417 *dominum:* 'the owner'.

418 *canem:* watchdogs were relatively
common in Roman society. A cast of a
chained housedog with heavy collar was
taken from the ashes of Pompeii. A mosaic
at the entrance to a Pompeian house
proclaims (with a picture) *CAVE CANEM;*
cf Petron. 29; Verg. *Ecl.* 8, 107 *Hylaxin
limine latrat.* Shopkeepers used them also.
Molossian hounds were most favoured
(Lucr. 5, 1063-72). See J. M. C. Toynbee
Animals in Roman Life and Art.
   grauis: ironical, for *grauitas* was an ancient
Roman virtue; cf 178.

419 *balnea nocte subit:* the use of the
public baths before dinner was usual,
but it was normally at the eighth or ninth
hour, which we would call early afternoon,
though baths were open after dark (*ILS*
6891; cf lamps found in the Pompeii baths).
Women, if there was only one public baths
establishment, used it in the morning
(*ILS* 6891), but separate women's baths
developed adjacent to the men's, using
one heating system (Vitr. 5, 10, 1;
ILS 5683-4). Mixed bathing was practised,
probably at less reputable establishments;
it must have been known at this period,
as Hadrian banned it (SHA *Hadr.* 18, 10).
   conchas: for oil, cf 304.
   castra moueri: by now this was becoming
a faded metaphor (Prop. 5, 8, 28; Sen.
Ep. 83, 5; Mart. 5, 14, 3, etc.) but it
serves a double purpose here, indicating
that she makes a visit to the baths a
major upheaval (almost as if she were
moving house and settling in), and main-
taining the sexual-military psychological
link.

420 *sudare:* in the Laconicum or
Turkish bath.

421 She has a work-out with dumb-
bells (*halteres*) till her arms can take no
more.

422 *cristae:* lit. a cock's comb, used
also of a tuft of leaves: here only, the
clitoris.
   aliptes: the man whose job was to see oil
was available for the body, a Greek word:
we may tr. 'masseur'.

424 *fameque:* the *e* is usually
lengthened in verse; cf 14, 84; Lucr. 3,
732; Verg. *A* 6, 421; Ov. *M* 5, 165;
8, 846; 11, 369; Luc. 3, 352; Mart. 1, 99,
18. The invitation was usually for the ninth
hour or at latest the tenth, so they will
have been getting really hungry.

425 *rubicundula:* from the Turkish
bath, a visual touch.

426 *oenophorum:* the object of her
thirst.
   plena . . . urna: we use a similar phrase:
it holds 'a full three litres'.

427 *sextarius alter:* her aperitif is a
couple of pints.

428 *orexim:* 'appetite', Greek for
esuritionem.

429 *dum redit:* 'until it returns': a
clever phrase, for it varies a stock phrase
such as *delibera hoc dum ego redeo* (Ter.
Ad. 196): we use 'return' in the same
way.
   loto . . . intestino: a vividly ugly phrase,
given weight by the spondaic fifth foot.

430 *Falernum:* see on 150; 303.

431 *peluis:* the jerry.

431-2 There must be some fable here
we have lost, though the simile expresses
her writhing movements, and contains a
strong sexual reference.

432 *bibit et uomit:* direct and shocking:
the bucolic diaeresis picks it out.

434-56 *Even worse is the bluestocking
with her learned conversation. Once she
starts, no one else has a chance. Moderation
in all things. If she wants to play the man,
why not do it properly, clothes and all?
Don't have a wife who is always correcting
your grammar and quoting poets you've
never heard of. A husband should be allowed
his solecisms in peace.*

434 J's attack on the bluestocking.

435 *Vergilium:* P. Vergilius Maro
(70-19 BC), author of *The Aeneid.*
   Elissae: Dido, whose love for Aeneas
leads to her death. The fourth book of
The Aeneid shows Aeneas torn between
love and duty. The views (neither
uncommon) which say 'Of course it was
monstrous of Aeneas to abandon her' or
'Of course Aeneas was right to go' both
undervalue Vergil. It is interesting that J's
bluestocking, a woman like Dido, and
Augustine (*Conf.* 1, 13), an African like
Dido, have sympathy for her. The tempta-
tion Dido offered was precisely the *luxuria*
to which Rome had now in J's view
succumbed.

436 *committit:* 'ranks'.

437 *Homerum:* the greatest Greek epic
poet, author of *The Iliad* and putative
author of *The Odyssey.* Comparisons
between Homer and Vergil date back to
Vergil's own day; cf Prop. 3, 26, 66
nescio quid maius nascitur Iliade. Domitius
Afer (Quint. 10, 1, 86) said *secundus est
Vergilius, propior tamen primo quam
tertio.* In truth the comparison is idle,

for though they are both writers of epic, they are so different that it is almost like asking whether Rembrandt is a greater painter than Beethoven a musician; cf 11, 180.

438 *grammatici:* secondary teachers, to whom a child went from about 10 to 14. Literary texts were used as a grounding in grammar and syntax; a certain amount of other matters will have rubbed off in the course of reading. Greek and Latin were both taught.

rhetores: Greek ending with short *e* (cf Mart. 2, 64,5). Boys went to the rhetor at about 13 or 14 to be educated in the principles of advocacy, fluent speech and ingenious argument. The course would include, though incidentally, some history.

440 *tanta cadit uis:* the broken rhythm, giving three word-accents where we expect only two, expresses well both the unnatural talk and the impossibility of getting a word in edgeways.

441 Onomatopoeia of pots and bells.

443 *laboranti ... Lunae:* the regular phrase for an eclipse of the moon. It was believed that this was caused by witch-craft: Hecate, the witches' divinity, was associated with the moon. The power of the witches was countered by clanging gongs and trumpet-blasts; cf Liv. 26, 5, 9 *cum aeris crepitu, qualis in defectu lunae silenti nocte cieri solet.* These served a double purpose — to scare away evil spirits and to drown the witches' spells. The clattering tongue of J's bluestocking serves both purposes. See further Tac. *Ann.* 1, 28; Mart. 12, 57,16-7.

444 'The philosopher puts a limit even on virtue.' The allusion is to Aristotle (384-322 BC) who said that virtue is a mean between two extremes, one of defect and the other of excess, e.g. courage is a mean between cowardice and rashness. Or there may be a reference to μηδὲν ἄγαν, 'avoid excess', which was attributed to Chilo, one of the Seven Sages (Arist. *Rhet.* 1389b4).

446 *tunicas:* men's wear which only reached to the knee; women's dress covered the ankles.

447 *Siluano:* a power of the wildwood (*silua*), associated and even identified with Mars, worshipped in the countryside with sacrifice offered by men only (so too with Heracles).

quadrante: the charge paid by men for admission to the baths. Women evidently either paid more or nothing at all; we have no other evidence either way.

448 *tibi:* Postumus, or any other man.

recumbit: at dinner.

449 *dicendi genus:* cf Quint. 12, 10: he recognises three styles, Attic, Asiatic, Rhodian — straightforward, grandiloquent and between the two respectively.

curuum ... enthymema: 'don't let her load up her speech and fire off her rounded argument'. The *enthymema* is defined as (a) a proposition sustained by reason, (b) a conclusion drawn by a process of deduction, positive or negative; cf Quint. 5, 10, 1-2. Aristotle insists that the *enthymema* is a kind of syllogism in which you argue positively or negatively from a premiss to a conclusion (*Rhet.* 2, 22, 1395b-7a). The whole image is military from the twisting of the ropes to give the artillery catapult the power to fire rounded cannonballs. Note rhythm in 450.

451 Duff well quotes Quint. 1, 8, 21 *mihi inter uirtutes grammatici habebitur aliqua nescire.* R. L. Stevenson has an excellent Fable (12) ' "Look round you," said the citizen. "This is the largest market in the world." "O, surely not," said the traveller. "Well, perhaps not the largest," said the citizen, "but much the best." "You are certainly wrong there," said the traveller. "I can tell you ..." They buried the traveller at the dusk.'

452 *uoluit:* 'reads', the ancient book being a roll formed of papyrus sheet glued margin to margin.

Palaemonis: Q. Remmius Palaemon, outstanding *grammaticus;* cf Suet *Gramm.* 23 *docuit Romae ac principem locum inter grammaticos tenuit.*

artem: a technical treatise.

453 The formal rules of language were stringent; it was for the *grammaticus* to give a grounding in them: he taught *ratio loquendi et enarratio auctorum* (Quint. 1, 9, 1).

454 In the second century there emerged an interest in the usage of pre-Ciceronian authors, which we can follow in Fronto (tutor to Marcus Aurelius) and Aulus Gellius. Gellius (19, 10) has a vivid picture of Fronto tracking down the phrase *praeter propter* ('there or thereabouts') in Ennius.

455 *opicae:* see 3,207; it refers to Roman ignorance of Greek culture.

456 *soloecismus:* Suet. *Verb. Diff.* s.v. says *soloecismus in sensu fit, barbarismus in uoce,* i.e. the one is in syntax, the other in accidence. Sinnius Capito (Aul. Gell. 5, 20) defined it *soloecismus est impar atque inconueniens compositura partium orationis.* The word is derived from the

unsophisticated usages at Soli on the coast
of Cilicia (Diog. Laert. 1, 2, 4; Aul. Gell.
1, 7, 3; Strabo 683; Suid. s.v.) — odd for
the town which produced Chrysippus,
Philemon and Aratus. J is alluding to
Mart. 11, 19 quaeris cur nolim te ducere,
Galla? diserta es/saepe soloecismum
mentula nostra facit.

457-73 Jewels transform a woman for bad.
How she loves piling on the make-up!
Her husband gets stuck in the cosmetic
pack she's using for her lover. Some of her
cosmetics come from India — and she must
have she-asses with her wherever she goes.
What needs such treatment — a face or a sore?

457 turpe putat nil: the offbeat rhythm
as usual to help to shock us.

459 elenchos: pearls, of pear shape
(Plin. NH 9, 113), used in ear-rings or
finger-rings.

460 A weak line which reads like a
marginal comment by a copyist who
could turn a hexameter.

462 Poppeana: some cosmetic devised
by Poppaea, the beautiful wife first of
Otho, then of Nero. Spondaic fifth foot.

463 hinc . . . uiscantur: his lips get
stuck in the make-up.

464 quando uideri: the bucolic
diaeresis divides two equally pungent
epigrams.

465 foliata: Plin. NH 13, 2, 15 tells us
that this perfume contained seven ingred-
ients: nardinum siue foliatum constat
omphacio aut balanino, iunco, costo, nardo,
amomo, murra, balsamo.

466 Indi: much of the trade with
India was in luxury goods: here there is
special reference to nard. See in general
M. P. Charlesworth Trade-Routes of the
Roman Empire; R. E. M. Wheeler Rome
Beyond the Imperial Frontiers.

467 tectoria prima reponit: 'takes off
the final layer of stucco': the metaphor is
(excellently) from plastering a building.

469 asellas: imitating Poppaea, who
bathed in asses' milk for her complexion
(Plin. NH 11, 238).

470 Hyperboreum: lit. 'beyond the North
wind', the home of a mysterious people
associated with Apollo.

471 quae: the Latin language works
both precisely and ambiguously. When
we reach it the 'antecedent' (really
'postcedent') is facies. At present we keep
in our minds the meaning 'she', and this
half remains with us — 'is it/she a face
or an ulcer?'

472 medicaminibus: just 'concoctions',

but it prepares us for ulcus.
siliginis: i.e. a bread poultice.

474-507 If her husband's been uncoopera-
tive at night, the servants get beaten.
She pays the public floggers an annual
salary, unmoved herself during the
beatings. Her lady's maid is beaten if her
mistress's hair won't stay in position in
an out-of-date hairstyle. She looks a
sight too, different front from back,
worst of all if she's short.

474-5 toto . . . die: note how this
embraces the activities. But J does not
fulfil this programme.

476 libraria: the servant who weighs
out the wool for the workers, only here
in literature, elsewhere called lanipendia.

476-7 ponunt . . . tunicas: for a beating.

477 cosmetae: men charged with their
patroness's appearance. J uses the word
symbolically, ridiculing the mania for
things Greek, and with some confusion of
sex-rôle.
Liburnus: the litter-bearer: Liburnians
from Dalmatia, like the Moesi (9, 143),
were liked in this rôle.

478 alieni: suffering not for his own
but her husband's sound sleep.

478-9 The lines are held together by
their first words; cf 483-4.

479-80 ferula is a cane, flagellum a
knotted rope, scutica a strap.

480 tortoribus annua: these would be
public slaves, normally paid at piecework
rates: she pays a retainer.

481 uerberat: not personally, as the
context makes clear.

482 pictae: 'embroidered'.

483 et caedit: note the chiastic
structure: uerberat atque . . . linit, audit
. . . et caedit. Also the way the repetition
et caedit holds 483-4 together; cf 478-9.
transuersa diurni: the acta diurna
(cf 2, 136; 7, 104), consisting not, like a
book, of pages glued side by side, but,
being appreciably shorter, written right
across the page. Some interpreters,
however, take diurnum to be a ledger or
account-book.

485 cognitione: a formal trial properly
before the praetor or other official.

486 praefectura: another formal term;
the two great prefects were praefectus
urbi and praefectus praetorio. But her
investigation and exercise of authority
are unconstitutional.
Sicula . . . aula: Sicilian dictators (the
term implies unconstitutional autocrats)
had a notorious record of cruelty, Phalaris
above all; cf 8, 81.

non mitior: = *grauior:* see 418 n.

487 *si constituit:* 'if she's made a date'.

488 *hortis: horti* were private parks; cf 1, 75. Platner and Ashby list over sixty, with some overlap. Some, however, became public: *horti Agrippae* and *horti Caesaris* were left by will to the people of Rome, and there seems to have been some right of access to the imperial *horti Sallustiani* (Ps.-Sen. *Ep. ad Paul.* 1).

489 *Isiacae . . . lenae:* the temple of Isis was notorious for assignations; cf 9, 22.

490 *umeros:* acc. of respect, a Greek construction, not uncommon in verse; cf Ov. *M* 9, 307 *flaua comas.*

Psecas: the name of the lady's maid, who is Greek: the name is that of one of Diana's nymphs in Ov. *Met.* 3, 172. The savage treatment of maids by their mistresses is often alluded to; cf Mart. 2, 66, 4 *et cecidit saeuis icta Plecusa comis;* it is hard to say how widespread it was. Here the mistress has pulled Psecas's hair and torn her dress.

492 *altior . . . cincinnus:* the hair-style (cf 496, 502), as Gertrude Hirst shows, is Flavian, with a high dressing, curled in ringlets on a wire-frame, as in the statues usually but wrongly called Julia, daughter of Titus. The style lingered on in the provinces, but by the time of Trajan was unfashionable at Rome. It is hard to say why J makes her use an out-of-date style: he may perhaps be making an additional point: she doesn't really even know what the fashion is. There is a strong point, as the bucolic diaeresis shows.

taurea: a *scutica* (480) of bull-hide.

494 *admisit:* 'committed'.

hic: 'in this'.

495 *si . . . nasus tuus:* an excellent epigram, picked out by the bucolic diaeresis.

laeuum: sc. *crinem.*

497 *consilio:* the business is as serious as that in the *consilium principis* (cf *Sat.* 4).

materna: one of her mother's servants, as some *amici principis* served more than one emperor.

498 *emerita:* of a discharged veteran soldier: she has served well in the hairpin regiment and been transferred to the woolworkers.

sententia prima: sententia is the formal term for political discussion (4, 136); cf Plin. *Paneg.* 76 *uicit sententia non prima sed melior.* The senior consular spoke first.

499 *censebunt:* another formal political

term (4, 130).

502-3 These lines are adapted by Paulinus of Nola (25, 86) to the theme that Christian brides should not be overadorned.

502 *adhuc:* 'in addition'.

altum: proleptic: 'to make it high'.

503 *Andromache:* wife of Hector, prince of Troy, herself of heroic stature (Ov. *AA* 2, 645 *spatiosior aequo*). J has in mind Martial's epigram on a dwarf (14, 212) *si solum spectes hominis caput, Hectora credas:/si stantem uideas, Astyanacta putes.*

504 *cedo si:* 'what if' (cf 13, 210). It is an odd phrase, an old imperative form of *dare,* with the intensive *ce.* We must supply *consilium* (cf Ter. *Haut.* 2, 3, 9).

505 *Pygmaea:* the African pygmies were known from Egypt (Hdt. 2, 32, 6; Arist. *Hist. An.* 8, 12, 597a) and appear in Nile landscapes: a mythology grew round them. The authentic Pygmies are central African hunters, about a metre and a half tall, ranging in companies of about 100. There are perhaps 150 000 left.

506 *coturnis:* originally an actor's boot which could be worn on either foot (so a nickname of the crossbench politician Theramenes), later a high boot, also used on stage, but with a thick sole like our platform shoes, giving added stature and dignity.

507 *leuis:* 'light' (short *e*) i.e. 'as if airborne'.

erecta . . . planta: 'on tiptoe'.

508-41 *She ignores her husband; she might be a neighbour not a wife, apart from her effect on his bank-balance. And the superstition! The eunuch priests of Cybele offering banal advice for gifts. The expiatory acts, bathing in the river and crawling up the Campus Martius. For Isis, she'll even go to Meroe to fetch holy water. Then a jackal-headed god intercedes for her — at a price.*

508 *mentio:* there is a strong tendency to shorten final *o* in Silver Latin; cf 1, 3 *ergo,* 3, 232 *uigilando.*

511 *rationibus:* 'to his account-book'. The following bucolic caesura marks a violent break from extravagance to superstition. But there is a sequence of thought, and J continually returns to the material demands of her religious instructors (518, 541, 543, 546, 585).

512 *Bellonae:* one form of the great Asiatic mother-goddess. This is the Cappadocian goddess Ma, identified by the Romans with their war-*numen* Bellona.

matrisque deum: Cybele, another of her forms. For her entry into Rome see on

3, 137; also 2, 111.

513 *semiuir:* the priests of Cybele were
eunuchs. The apposition of *facies* is as
natural in Latin as in English, 'a face to
be viewed with awe by his juniors in
obscenity': *minori* is treated as a noun.

515 *tympana:* 'tambourines', an
authentic touch.

516 *plebeia:* with *bucca: et* is
displaced.

tiara: a high pointed cap with cheek-flaps,
much favoured in Asia Minor.

517 *Septembris et austri:* the late
summer sirocco, a kind of hendiadys.
His advice is platitudinous.

519 *xerampelinas:* sc. *uestes.* The
Greek word, lit. 'like dried vine-leaves',
i.e. russet-coloured, as usual expresses J's
contempt.

521-2 A well-expressed piece of
scepticism, such as an Epicurean might
produce. It was normal religious practice to
lay your offences on a *piaculum,* which was
then offered up in sacrifice or driven out
like a scapegoat — but not handed over
for ready wear.

522 The scholiast says that this was a
purification after sexual intercourse. Water
is an obvious instrument of purification:
before the Eleusinian Mysteries, initiates
bathed in the sea. Christian ascetics
followed similar practices.

523 *ter:* a mystical number: 3 and 7
were regarded as specially potent. Vergil
says *numero deus impare gaudet (Ecl.*
8, 75).

matutino: agreeing with *Tiberi,* but
effectively an adverb 'in the morning'.

524 *uerticibus:* 'eddies'.

524-5 *superbi totum regis agrum:* the
Campus Martius, outside the *pomerium,*
where the temple of Isis stood (528); it was
once the estate of Tarquinius Superbus, the
last king, who was ousted, traditionally
in 509 BC.

525 *tremibunda:* alike with cold and
superstition.

526 *candida . . . Io:* Io in Graeco-Roman
mythology was daughter of the river-god
Inachus; Jupiter fell in love with her, but
turned her into a cow to protect her from
Juno's jealousy. In this form she wandered
through many lands, ending in Egypt,
where she gave birth (Ov. *M* 568-747).
She was identified with the Egyptian Isis
(Hdt. 2, 41), who also wandered far
after the death of Osiris, and being, in one
aspect, a moon-goddess, was depicted with
crescent horns.

527 This pilgrimage took place, as we

know from an inscription (*CIL* 3, 83).
The temple of Isis at Meroe was found on
excavation to contain many Graeco-Roman
offerings.

528 *Meroe:* an island and kingdom of the
Upper Nile, well studied by Peter Shinnie.
J may possibly have known it at first
hand; cf. 13, 163 and Introduction.

528-9 *in aede Isidis:* in the Campus
Martius; cf 9, 22. Isis was a fertility
goddess, whose worship spread widely in
the Roman Empire: Domitian gave it support.
Isis claimed to be the one true divinity, all
the other gods and goddesses being manifes-
tations of her power, as we know from her
hymns and aretalogies (cf Apul. *Met.* 11, 4:
*summa numinum, regina manium, prima
caelitum, deorum dearumque facies
uniformis*). Her image, with the child
Horus on her knee, passed into Christian
art (R. E. Witt *Isis in the Graeco-Roman
World* pls 55-6, 69).

ouili: lit. 'sheepfold', an enclosed area
in the Campus Martius where the *comitia
centuriata* gathered to vote, also called
saepta. The scholiast takes it literally
*ouilia quia ibi Romulus et pastores
adsueuerunt pecora pascere:* it is more
probably metaphorical from the shape and
function of assembling.

530 The practice of sleeping in holy
places (*incubatio*) in the hope of a divine
revelation was common in the healing
sanctuaries of Aesculapius; there is no
other indication of its use in connection
with Isis. In the healing sanctuaries the
priests were responsible for helpful mani-
festations associated with mental and
physical healing; there was probably
some drug or hypnosis, the god would
appear and give advice or even perform an
operation. Something similar may have
happened here.

dominae: cf Apul. *Met.* 11, 5, 1
elementorum omnium domina.

532 The priests bald and in white linen
can be seen in a wall-painting from
Herculaneum (R. E. Witt pl. 23; cf
528-9 n).

534 *plangentis populi:* for Osiris,
consort of Isis, killed by the wicked
Set, but resurrected. The myth is
connected with the land of Egypt
alternately shrivelled by drought (Set)
and fertilised by the waters of the Nile;
it is also a promise of life beyond death,
and a dead man was addressed as Osiris.

Anubis: the dog-headed or jackal-headed
Egyptian god, who helped Isis to embalm
the dead Osiris (Plut. *Is. et Os.* 14),

often identified with Hermes or Mercury (R. E. Witt pl. 46; cf 528-9 n).

535 She does penance for being a proper wife.

537 *cadurco:* the Cadurci lived in Gallia Narbonensis, and wove excellent quilts (7, 221); here the bed itself.

538 *argentea serpens:* the sacred asp, the mark of divine majesty in Egypt, which Cleopatra VII used for her suicide.

540 *ansere:* the goose was sacred to Isis.

541 *popano:* the ritual cake, carried in procession in a basket by women called *canephoroi.*

corruptus: again a piece of Epicurean-type scepticism. The gods are not moved by bribes (though the priests may be).

Osiris: cf 534. He had his own mysteries alongside those of Isis (cf Apul. *Met.* 11, 27).

542-68 *Or it's fortune-telling. An old Jewish woman interpreting dreams. An eastern diviner promising a lover or an inheritance, sometimes using a human victim and informing against his client. Greatest faith attaches to the astrologers, especially if they've been in exile or prison. Your aristocratic wife consults them about her mother's death (yours long before that), or her lover's life: marvellous subjects for the gods!*

542 *cophino fenoque:* see on 3, 14.

543 *tremens:* 'palsied'.

544 *legum:* the Torah, the Mosaic code, the precious inheritance of the Jews.

Solymarum: of Jerusalem, more properly Hierosolyma: the adjectival form is found here only.

545 *arboris:* the meaning is not clear. The Jews were allowed to squat among the trees outside the Porta Capena; cf 3, 16 *arbor,* and there may be no more to it than that. But the tree of life is a fundamental religious concept, and trees play some part in eastern cults, e.g. the ceremonial *arbor intrat* in the festival of Cybele: J is not above mixing his cults. It is not likely that he is referring to Christian reverence for the cross, though *infelix arbor* means a 'gibbet', and there was confusion at the period between Jews and Christians.

summi . . . caeli: cf 14, 97: the Jews often spoke of 'heaven'. The god of the Jews was respected for his power, and associated by the Greeks with the title Hypsistos, All-Highest. His power was sought by magicians, often under the name IAO.

547 *somnia:* i.e. the interpretation of

dreams: oneiromancy was a cardinal part of natural divination.

548 *spondet:* a new interpreter will appear by the end of the sentence.

amatorem: he is speaking to a married woman.

549 *calidae:* 'before the warmth has left the body'.

columbae: the victim indicates that the wife came to ask about love.

550 *Armenius uel Commagenus:* for Armenia see on 2, 164. Commagene lay in northern Syria, and enjoyed independence or quasi-independence from 162 BC to AD 17 and again from AD 38 to 72 when it was incorporated into Syria. The inhabitants of these regions had no special reputation in these matters. J is using any Easterner as a whipping-boy.

haruspex: artificial or inductive divination consisted in the observation of animals, plants or inanimate meteorological occurrences. Augury was the observation of birds: *extispicium* consisted in observing the size, shape, colour and markings of the vital organs of a sacrificial victim, especially the liver and gallbladder of a sheep, a practice developed among the Etruscans. Model livers carefully marked out have been found at Piacenza and elsewhere; they were no doubt used in training.

552 *pueri:* cf Cic. *Vat.* 6, 14 *cum puerorum extis deos manis mactare soleas.* Many cultures have used human sacrifice for particularly momentous occasions.

deferat: the process of *delatio,* or informing against someone for reward, was a regular but unpopular practice; cf 3, 116. Here the *haruspex* commits the crime himself but informs against the women; cf Sen. *Dial 4, 7, 3 alius delator uenit eius criminis cuius manifestior reus est.*

553 *Chaldaeis:* observation of the stars for religious purposes goes back a long way in Mesopotamia, and their ziggurats, or pyramidal temple-structures were, among other things, observatories. The system was expounded by a Babylonian priest named Berosus in the third century BC, and the combination of determinism and pantheism in Stoic philosophy supported the view that observation of the stars might lead to information about human destiny. The emperors had a love-hate relation with the *mathematici,* sometimes patronising them, sometimes expelling them; it was of course a dangerous matter to cast an emperor's horoscope, especially if it involved prophesying his death. See further 9, 33; 10, 94.

553-4 *fonte Hammonis:* at the oasis of
Siwa in Egypt, near the Libyan border,
was a spring of water, warm by night and
cool by day, and an oracle sacred to the
ram-horned god Ammon, whom the
Greeks identified with Zeus. Consultation
with this oracle involved Alexander
the Great in a substantial detour but left
him with a mystical certainty of his divine
destiny as Zeus's son. Lucan has a splendid
passage about Cato's refusal to consult
this oracle (9, 564-86).

555 *Delphis:* the greatest of Greek
oracles, originally a shrine of Earth, but
later sacred to Apollo, whose priestess, the
Pythia, gave oracular responses, which
the priests tidied up, generally into
hexameters. In addition to the great
political consultations there were more
ordinary questions about family and
economic problems (Eur. *Ion* 303). The
oracle had not ceased to exist; indeed
Plutarch was proud to be one of its
priests at this very time; it thrived in the
middle of the century and survived till
the fourth. See also Mart. 9, 42, 4. But
of course there were fewer state-consulta-
tions. Two hundred years later the oracle
did reply to Julian: 'Tell the emperor the
well-built hall has fallen to the ground./
Phoebus has no shelter, no prophetic
laurel,/no speaking spring. The speaking
water is quenched.' This, as Prudentius
said in his *Apotheosis* (438), and Milton
in his 'Ode on the Morning of Christ's
Nativity', was due to the spread of
Christianity. See in general H. W. Parke
and D. E. W. Wormell *The Delphic Oracle*
Oxford 1956.

557-9 These lines are puzzling. 558-9
are not in all the MSS and were not
known to the scholiast, but they seem
authentic. The astrologer was named
Ptolomaeus (Tac. *Hist.* 1, 22) or Seleucus
(Suet. *Oth.* 4). The great citizen was
Galba, Nero's successor (see on 2, 104);
Otho was his immediate successor in AD 69
(see on 2, 99). It is odd to say that Otho
was afraid of Galba, though he did use
danger to his own life as a pretext for
treachery. The *tabella* is a horoscope. The
Year of the Four Emperors gave plenty of
scope to Vicars of Bray.

559 *Othoni:* dat. of the agent.
560 *inde:* antecedent to *si.*
ferro: 'handcuffs'.
561 *castrorum in carcere:* it looks as if
there was a prison associated with the
barracks of the praetorian guard; cf
Trajan in Plin. *Ep.* 10, 57 *uinctus mitti ad*
praefectos praetorii mei debet.
562 *genium:* i.e. *ingenium.*
habebit: sc. in the opinion of others.
563 *Cyclada:* exile or deportation,
often to an island, was one of the severer
punishments, equivalent to a long period
of imprisonment today (cf 1, 73; 10,
170). The Cyclades are the Aegean islands
in a circle round Delos; the form here is a
Greek acc. sing.
564 *Seriphos:* one of the Cyclades.
The names of islands are generally feminine.
It was here that Danae and the infant
Perseus were washed ashore. For its use as a
place of banishment cf 10, 170; Tac.
Ann. 2, 85; 4, 21.
565 *ictericae:* 'suffering from jaundice'.
lento: 'long-delayed'.
566 *Tanaquil:* wife of Tarquinius
Priscus, a woman of implacable ambition
whose skill in divination enabled her to
foretell and secure the greatness of
Servius Tullius, her son-in-law (Liv. 1, 34);
both make the name apt to J's aristocrat.
567 *adulter:* 'her lover': J holds up the
final *post ipsam*, which clinches the phrase,
he is applying the attitudes expected within
marriage to adultery.
568 Again J girds at the triviality of
the prayers (cf 394-7); again we think of
the Epicurean *quod super nos nihil est ad*
nos (Tert. *Ad Nat.* 2, 4).

569-91 *She at least leaves it to others.*
Avoid like the plague the woman who
studies the almanacks for herself, and
gives rather than seeks advice. Poor
women go off to the palmists and fortune-
teller; the rich import Asiatics and pay
state officials; poor women go in their
finery to the circus to ask about their
marital affairs.

570 *Saturni:* Saturn was believed to
have a baleful influence; cf Luc. 1, 652
stella nocens . . . Saturni. Our 'saturnine'
is not a favourable word.
quo . . . astro: 'in which constellation':
the part of the sky in which the planet
appears helps to determine the interpreta-
tion.
Venus: a bringer of joy and blessing;
cf Luc. 1, 661 *Venerisque salubre sidus.*
573 *sucina:* balls of amber held in the
hand for their fragrance.
574 *ephemeridas:* 'almanacks,', a
Greek word, used as usual satirically.
575 She won't go with him on an
overseas posting, she won't even come back
with him from an overseas posting, unless . . .
576 *numeris:* volumes of astrology:

mathematics was developed in the service of astrology.

Thrasylli: leading astrologer and intimate of Tiberius (Tac. *Ann.* 6, 21; Dio Cass. 55, 11; Suet. *Tib.* 14); he died in AD 36. His son Balbillus, another astrologer, was a leading figure at Rome: see on 9, 32.

577 *ad primum lapidem:* i.e. a very short journey, only 1½ km from the *aureum miliarium* in the forum.

579 *inspecta genesi:* 'only when she has consulted her horoscope'.

580 *licet:* 'even if'.

581 *Petosiris:* an Egyptian (as his name implies) who with one Nechepso published a treatise on astrology in the middle of the second century BC (Plin. *NH* 2, 21, 88; 7, 49, 60). Note offbeat rhythm.

582-91 *Women of lower rank go down to the racecourse to consult the fortune-tellers there about their sex-problems. (The rich have a tame astrologer in their house.)*

582 *mediocris:* 'not upper-class'. 457-609 are on rich women. It is characteristic of J to divert for a moment to poorer women (just as bad) and then return.

582-3 *spatium . . . metarum:* 'she will cover the space on either side of the turning-posts.' The gen. is not easy to parallel in Latin (but cf Cael. Aurel. *De morb. acut.* 2, 194 *utrimque orarum:* ref. from G.B.A. Fletcher), but it is not difficult in Greek: Thuc. 3, 6 ἑκατέρωθεν τῆς πόλεως. The Circus Maximus where the chariot-racing took place lay in the Vallis Murcia between the Aventine and the Palatine. The outer arcade was the place to find fortune-tellers (Cic. *Div.* 1, 132 *de circo astrologos*). The *metae,* marking the turn, were sets of three conical pillars.

583 *frontemque manumque:* they practise palmistry and the like.

584 *poppysma:* a sound with the lips to avert evil; Green cites a similar sound made by Greek peasant-women today on hearing unexpected news. Cf. Plin. *NH* 28, 25; Mart. 7, 18, 11.

585 *Phryx:* as in 550 J is happy to bring in any Easterner for blame.

augur: strictly one who observes omens from birds, but here just 'prophets'.

et inde: he's actually been paid to come all the way from Phrygia.

586 *astrorum mundique peritus:* gen. of the field within which he is skilled. cf. Ter. *Ad.* 695 *ceterarum rerum socordem.*

587 *publica fulgura condit:* strictly *publice,* 'on behalf of the people', but the transition is an easy one. For an object to be struck by lightning was a portent, which called for official action. The *pontifex* or his representative would ceremonially bury any scorched material, and put a wall round the spot to consecrate it as a *bidental* (cf *CIL* 9 1047, etc.).

588 *aggere:* a defensive earthwork between the Esquiline and Colline Gates; cf 291; 8, 43. It was a pleasant walk, apart from the strolling players, fortune-tellers and the like. See on 5, 153.

589 *aurum:* a difficulty, since this is the poor woman: still she is not destitute, she is perhaps wearing her one good ornament to go out.

590 *falas:* wooden towers or columns. Servius on Verg. *A* 9, 706 says that they were movable towers used in mock battles.

delphinorumque columnas: on the *spina,* the low marble plinth which ran up the middle of the Circus, were seven columns, set up by Agrippa in 33 BC, each with a bronze dolphin: the race was of seven laps, and the number of dolphins visible indicated the number of laps completed (Dio Cass. 49, 43, 2). It is not clear how this was done, as they must have been too heavy to move: perhaps a cloth covering was removed. An alternative system had wooden eggs (*oua*) visible on columns at either end of the *spina;* these were removed lap by lap.

591 'whether she should give the barman the push and marry the old-clothes dealer' — an indication of her social position.

592-609 *They do at least become mothers. The rich take measures to avoid children (just as well: there'd be some of mixed blood!), and introduce foundlings, favourites of Fortune.*

592 *hae:* the poorer women.

discrimen: we sometimes forget the perils in a less sterilised age. Euripides makes his Medea say that she would rather stand three times in the front line of battle than bear one child (Eur. *Med.* 250-1).

594 A highly allusive reference to abortion.

595 *huius:* antecedent to *quae,* the female abortionist.

597 *infelix:* the husband: *gaude, infelix* is a kind of oxymoron. For *gaude* see 365 n.

598 *uellet:* sc. 'your wife'.

600 *Aethiopis:* lit. 'burnt-face', a general term for the dark-skinned peoples

without close geographical reference.
J shows a little colour-prejudice (cf 2, 23).
Here it is perhaps class-prejudice, since a
Negro would be encountered only as a
slave.

decolor: neither black nor white,
'coffee-coloured' we might say.

601 *numquam . . . uidendus:* 'you'd
prefer not to see by daylight.'

602 *transeo:* 'I pass over'.

suppositos: children left to die, and
picked up by others wanting a family and
brought up as their own. Exposure of
unwanted children was a regular practice
of the Graeco-Roman world: a papyrus
letter from a soldier named Hilarion to
his wife Alis, full of love, tells her, when the
baby is born, to keep it if a boy, expose it if
a girl. Exposure did not lay the taint of
homicide on the parents.

604 *ad spurcos . . . lacus:* the reservoirs
which received the water for the aqueducts.
People came there for water first thing in
the morning, so there was some hope that
the exposed child might be picked up.
The reservoirs are filthy, partly because
churned up by the buckets (Sen. *Ep.*
36, 2), partly because of the scenes they
witness.

salios: the leaping priests of Mars.

Scauri: aristocrats of the gens Aemilia
(cf 2, 35).

605 *Fortuna:* see on 3, 140; 9, 148.
She is a power of moral relativism.

inproba: 'shameless'.

606 Bucolic caesura and broken rhythm
here and in 608 point J's scorn.

608 She produces a private entertain-
ment for herself; cf Plin. *Ep.* 4, 11, 2
quos tibi, Fortuna, ludos facis!

610-26 *Wives administer charms and
potions to their husbands, which drive
them crazy. See how Caesonia's love-
philtre to Caligula set the world by the
ears. Agrippina's poisoning of Claudius was
beneficial by comparison.*

610 *cantus:* 'spells': so also *carmina*
(our 'charms').

Thessala: Thessaly was famed for its
witches: the sixth book of Lucan gives a
lurid picture of them at work.

612 His wits are so addled that he lets
her spank him with a slipper.

desipis: the change to second person is
startling. This is not directed to Postumus,
who is not yet married, but to the married
male reader ('How's your memory?'). But
note the link between the thought that it
is insane to marry (28) and the wife

driving the husband insane.

inde: 'due to drugs'.

614ABC These lines are not in the best
or the majority of MSS; when they do appear
they are in different places, and twice in
the margin. G. Valla, the 1486 editor, says
of them *sed hi tres uersiculi in multis non
sunt codicibus, quos in antiquissimo
legunt codice et Probus etiam refert.*

614A-B A reference to the daughters
of Danaus who, for killing their husbands,
were forced in Hades to carry water in leaky
containers which would not hold their
contents.

614C *Phalarim:* tyrant of Acragas in
Sicily, notorious for his cruelty; cf 486;
one of his more unpleasant practices was
to roast his victims alive in a brazen bull;
their screams became the bull bellowing.
Hor. *Ep.* 1, 2, 58-9 has *Siculi . . . tyranni
. . . tormentum.*

615 *auunculus ille Neronis:* C. Caligula,
emperor AD 37-41, who was said to be
driven mad by a love-potion from his
wife Caesonia (Suet. *Cal.* 50), whom he
married in 39 and who was killed with him.

616 Pliny the Elder gives an account of
this (*NH* 8, 66, 165): *equis amoris
innascitur ueneficium, hippomanes
appellatum, in fronte, caricae magnitudine,
colore nigro:* it was a growth on the
forehead of a new-born foal which the
mother would bite off if it were not
immediately seized (so Verg. *A* 4, 516
matri praereptus amor), very potent as a
love-charm. cf 133.

617 Note how this links back to the
Messalina passage.

618 *cuncta:* 'the whole world went up
in flames'. The power of the emperor is
compared with that of Jupiter.

620 *Agrippinae:* mother of Nero and
fourth wife of Claudius. Note the spondaic
fifth foot.

621 *boletus:* she was said to have assassi-
nated him with a dish of poisoned mush-
rooms. Claudius was deified, and Nero
thereafter referred to mushrooms as the
food of the gods (Suet. *Claud.* 44; *Nero*
33; Dio Cass. 60, 35). cf 5,147.

622-3 Claudius was a careful and sane
administrator, whose measures bear the
stamp of his personality, but his exaltation
of freedmen into positions of responsibility
was unpopular, and his grotesque,
slobbering, tremulous appearance was
against him: Suet. *Claud.* 30 *risus
indecens, ira turpior spumante rictu,
umentibus naribus, praeterea linguae
titubantia caputque cum semper tum in*

quantulocumque actu uel maxime tremulum.

descendere in caelum: a brilliantly paradoxical phrase. Claudius's apotheosis was the occasion of much ribaldry. There survives a scandalously amusing anonymous *Ludus de Morte Claudii,* and we know that Seneca wrote an *Apocolocyntosis* ('Pumpkinification' — though other and obscener interpretations have been given): there is no good reason for equating the two.

624 *haec:* going back to Caesonia's love-charm. J means that Caligula's madness decimated the upper classes (it is odd that he regards that as disastrous), but that the death of Claudius was beneficial. This is an unsatisfactory judgement. Caligula's megalomania is doubtfully attributable to drugs, though it was worse after his illness in Oct. 37, and Drusilla's death in June 38 (Josephus *Ant.* 18, 256 says that he was corrupted by absolute power); and the reign of Claudius's successor Nero ended in unmitigated disaster. J is hawking a paradox. Caesonia was attempting a good act (to win Caligula's love) and that was deleterious. Agrippina was committing a crime, and that was a blessing.

626 *tanti:* gen. of price.

627-42 *Murder of a stepson is normal practice these days. Adopted children must learn to watch for poisoned food. This isn't dramatic fiction. It's real. Remember Pontia, who killed her two sons — at one meal too.*

627 *oderunt:* sc. *uxores diuites.*

628 *iam iam:* 'at this very instant': some translators take 'now for a long time' but this is wrong.

629 *pupilli:* adopted sons, orphans: for a case involving just such an attempted poisoning see Stat. *S* 5, 2, 76-97.

631 'Those pies are steaming black with poison supplied by mother.' J produces a line of golden shape (adj. 1, adj. 2, verb, noun 1, noun 2) for these sinister words.

632 *mordeat ante aliquis:* the taster, a common feature of courts, is not expected in a private house. According to some, the taster connived at Claudius's death (Suet. *Claud.* 44).

633 *papas:* elsewhere only in inscriptions: it is clearly our 'papa', equally clearly not the *paterfamilias:* perhaps then a familiar address for the 'tutor' or *paedagogus.* J really lays on a stammering of *p.*

634-7 Some critics have taken this as a serious avowal that J is extending the scope of satire. This shows an unbelievable lack of humour. Corruption in high places and society crimes had been the stuff of satire since Lucilius. J does not mean more than our 'Perhaps you think that I'm making up a novel.'

634 *altum ... coturnum:* see on 506: *altum* is both literal and figurative.

635 *finem ... legemque:* ancient theory insisted that a particular poetic *genre* should be expressed in the appropriate verse-medium. Thus the hexameter was for epic, didactic and satire; the elegiac couplet for love and sorrow; the iambic trimeter for tragic dialogue, the 'limping' iambic for lampoons; and so on. Catullus is not classified among lyric poets by Quintilian, because he did not write in lyric metres.

636 *Sophocleo:* Sophocles (496-406 BC) is taken as representative of tragic drama.

bacchamur: an appropriate word, since Bacchus-Dionysus was the god of the theatre, but the implication is that he is drunk or out of his mind (both results of the god's action).

hiatu: probably 'rhetoric', or (less politely) 'claptrap' is the best we can do; the dramatic masks had unnaturally wide mouth-apertures.

637 *Rutulis:* an ancient people on the coast of Latium; their hero Turnus opposes Aeneas in Vergil's *Aeneid.*

Latino: here 'of Latium': the area south of the Tiber, from the mountains to the sea.

638 *uani:* sc. *essemus:* 'I wish I were being nonsensical.'

Pontia: Petronius's daughter (so the scholiast). After Petronius's death she poisoned her children and on condemnation committed suicide — first enjoying an extravagant dinner — her father's daughter. The case was naturally sensational. Martial refers to it three times: 2, 34, 6; 4, 43, 5; 6, 75.

639 *aconita:* cf 1, 158.

641 *duos una:* there is a kind of oxymoron in putting these words together: the build-up is deflated when we find that the indignation is that she killed two children at one *meal* (we need to supply *sustulisti*): this is part of J's satirical method.

uipera: an obvious term of abuse, particularly apposite to the poisoner. In Ter. *Eun.* 5, 1, 8 a character says

quid ais, uenefica? Donatus comments
aptum conuicium et comicum in ancillas,
uenefica, lupa, uipera et sacrilega.

643-61 *They murdered in the old stories —*
but not for money. A hot-blooded crime's
understandable, but not cold-blooded
murder. No husband is safe. It's like the
old stories of Clytemnestra and others,
only methods today are subtler — though
cold steel comes in if needed.

643 *Colchide:* Medea, princess of
Colchis and a sorceress, who fell in love
with the adventurer Jason, helped him
secure the Golden Fleece, and later when
he abandoned her, took revenge by killing
their children. The story is told with
great power by Euripides.

644 *Procne:* wife of Tereus, king of
Thrace: he raped her sister Philomela,
and in revenge she killed their son Itys.
They were turned into birds in the myth,
Tereus into a hoopoe, Procne into a
nightingale and Philomela into a swallow
(there are variant versions). No dramatisa-
tion of the story survives, but Sophocles
wrote a play called *Tereus,* and we know of
other dramatic treatments by Philocles
and Carcinus

645-6 The absence of a word-accent
on the first syllable of the sixth foot puts
us off beat, and helps to put a crashing
weight on the following climax.

646 *admiratio:* 'surprise' not 'admira-
tion'.

647 *nocentes:* with *hunc sexum,* an
easy sense-construction.

649-50 A vivid simile, made more vivid
by J's making the mountain withdraw
from the boulders: the boulders' falling
is then, so to speak, not their fault. It is
meant to recall Vergil's Turnus (*A* 12,
684-7).

649 *iugis . . . quibus:* both are the so-
called dat. of disadvantage: the basic use
of the dat. is for the person or thing
indirectly concerned in an action.

652 *spectant:* sc. in a play.

653 *Alcestim:* Admetus, king of Thessaly,
was doomed to die unless a surrogate
could be found. His parents refused to
save him; his noble wife Alcestis died in
his place. Later, Hercules rescued her from
death. Euripides wrote a tragi-comedy
around her, portraying her with sensitive
sympathy.

654 The aristocratic ladies of Rome
would not save their husbands at the
cost of their own lives; they'd save their
pet dogs at the cost of their husbands'

lives. Duff rightly quotes Pope (a good
classical scholar): 'Not louder shrieks to
pitying heaven are cast,/When husbands or
when lap-dogs breathe their last.'
('Rape of the Lock' 3, 157-8).

655 *Belides:* forty-nine of the fifty
daughters of Danaus killed their husbands
on their wedding-night. The story was
told dramatically by Aeschylus. Belus was
father to Danaus.

Eriphyle: wife of the saintly Amphiaraus,
she was bribed to induce her husband to
take part in the campaign of the Seven
against Thebes in which he lost his life;
she in turn was killed by her son Alcmaeon.
Sophocles wrote a tragedy *Eriphyle:* so did
the Roman Accius.

656 *Clytaemestram:* wife of Agamemnon,
leader of the Greek forces in the Trojan
War, who with her lover Aegisthus killed
him with an axe on his return because he
sacrificed their child Iphigeneia to secure
a favourable wind. The story is portrayed
with great dramatic power in Aeschylus
Agamemnon.

657 *Tyndaris:* Clytemnestra, d. of
Tyndareus.

658 Fancy using a clumsy instrument
requiring both hands when you could use
the minute lung of a toad! Notice the
transferred epithets.

659 The wheel of the poem comes full
circle, for Clodia (8) was accused
of poisoning her husband Metellus.

660 *Atrides:* Agamemnon, s. of Atreus.

661 Mithradates VI, king of Pontus
(c. 120-63 BC) was a serious toxicologist,
who immunised himself against assassina-
tion by accustoming himself to poison in
small doses. See A. E. Housman 'A
Shropshire Lad' 62, ending, 'I tell the
tale that I heard told./Mithridates, he
died old.' Also for a detective story on
the theme, Dorothy L. Sayers *Strong*
Poison.

General comments
Henry Nettleship was scathing about the
bad composition of this piece, calling it 'a
mere chamber of horrors'. Yet its power
remains, beyond the morbid fascination
of its subject and J's treatment of it.
The structure is loose, but controlled.

The first satire begins with a flurry of
questions, it is angry and impatient. The
prologue to the sixth is suave, calm,
deliberate, almost epic in its approach.
The key-word is Chastity (*Pudicitia*). The
point is contrast with what follows. The
introduction is smooth; what follows is

violent. This careful planning may lead us
to distrust the spontaneity, though not the
intensity, of the violence which follows.
But J has no unqualified admiration for
the simple life: he speaks to and for
civilisation.

The introduction over, J moves into
his mise-en-scène. He is dissuading Postumus
from marriage; to do so he piles on the
examples of unchastity. But we might say
that he is using the dramatic situation of
the dissuasive in order to pile on the
examples; Postumus's marriage is the
pretext, not the reason. The theme of this
long section is expressed in four words,
unus uir Hiberinae sufficit? (53). The
pin-up boys are actors, musicians and
gladiators, and it would not be difficult
for a modern satirist to find modern
parallels.

Between 60 and 135 there is a carefully
controlled build-up. In the first section
the women are nobodies: Thymele is a
country-bumpkin. J is making the point
(as he does also at 55-9) that the rustic
simplicity which he pictures with favour
in the prologue is no longer there. We
cannot recover that primitive chastity.
It is no use Postumus following Umbricius
into the countryside. Corruption has
spread there. Nor is J concerned to depict
a marital situation where the wife rules
and the husband obeys. The husbands
can't control their wives but *Tuccia
uesicae non imperat* (64); she too is a
slave — to her physical impulses. From
these weeny-boppers we pass to Eppia,
a rung up the ladder, a senator's wife.
J reinforces the point already made; she
goes to the simple life from the life of
luxury — but does not thereby become
chaste. J uses this section to establish the
relationship between sex and violence,
ferrum est quod amant (112). Then from
the senator's wife we pass to the top of
the social ladder, the empress Messalina.
But as we progress up the social ladder
so we plunge deeper into unchastity. The
girls in the first section each go for a
single idol; they deceive their husbands
but don't abandon them. Eppia sets her
sights on a single man, though he is
portrayed as almost subhuman, and
abandons her husband. But Messalina, in
two marvellous phrases, *excepit blanda
intrantis atque aera poposcit* (125) *et
lassata uiris necdum satiata recessit* (130).

We turn to look at married love: the
word *optima* (136) points a new theme.
Caesennia is no example of true married

love because her husband married her
for her money, not for herself. Bibula's
husband married her for her looks, not
for herself. At 161 J switches the theme
slightly and identifies some qualities in
women which may be praised in themselves
but don't make for a happy marriage: these
are, successively, pride (161-71) and
delight in childbearing (172-83). The
third quality he condemns: it is the aping
of foreign, and particularly Greek habits
(184-99). J cannot resist an attack on the
hated Greeks. But although this passage
is hostile, he does not here say that
there is nothing to learn from the Greeks.
This too is a positive quality carried to
excess. The fault is *omnia Graece* (187);
J honours the old Roman virtues, though
not the pride to which they lead. These
Graeculae have not even grounds for
superbia.

J comes back to Postumus (200 *tibi*).
Now the theme is that of the wife who
'wears the trousers'. The relation of wife
to husband is described under three
images — overlord and slave (219ff),
litigation (242-5, picked up at 268 and
280-5), and war between the sexes (246-
67, also picked up in what follows). Two
vital animal metaphors frame the whole
passage. At the outset the husband is
described as putting his neck in the yoke,
like any dumb ox (207-8; cf 43); towards
the end the wife is described as a tigress
(270). This section is untidy: the bit
about the mother-in-law is dragged-in by
any standards: but this is the nature of the
lanx satura. Its climax is the guilty wife's
final defence: *homo sum* (284): brilliant
for it is a wholly justified plea — against
the average husband's treatment of his
wife, but not in defence of her present
behaviour.

286-300 then, as we have suggested,
forms a bridge passage. J returns to the
introductory theme of past chastity,
but now gives it a historic rather than a
prehistoric context. But as he does this
he deftly changes the theme. Chastity was
a theme of the past; he now identifies the
theme of the present, *luxuria,* which
includes all forms of extravagance, including
extravagant sexual behaviour. J brings
the two themes together in a single
brilliant symbol — Venus drunk (300):
we may write *uenus* with or without a
capital as we choose. The rest of his poem
will be about *luxuria:* it is now an attack
on high-society women. The description

of *luxuria* as *saeuior armis* fixes the sustained military metaphor of the poem.

J first establishes the indifference to Chastity in the picture of Tullia and her companion's scandalous behaviour by the very statue of the goddess, then turns to the use of religion to cover lust: the example, from the rites of the Good Goddess, has to do solely with upper-class women. The Oxford fragment, if it rightly belongs here, takes the odd fascination which men who are both homosexual and heterosexual exercise on some women; the gladiatorial theme is introduced, in seeming irrelevance, but reinforcing much that has gone before. J attacks the rich, but throws in that the poor are as bad. He then takes up again Tuccia and her group, and Eppia's infatuation for a gladiator, in the picture of Ogulnia selling her family plate for the latest star, and brings out a generalisation about women's improvidence.

From here till the end there is a succession of follies and crimes of society women, brilliant cameos, loosely strung together, but recurring to points already made, till the whole effect is overwhelming. First, some women like making love to eunuchs: sex has for them become a sterile pursuit of titillation (366-78). Some use music as a cover or substitute, and pay for their protégé's success (379-97): this takes up the girls' pursuit of musicians, and the use of religion as a cloak. Then come sketches of the politically-minded gossip (398-412); the domineering dictatress (somewhat diverted by an ugly picture of her over-indulgence at a feast) (413-33); the bluestocking (a wickedly amusing caricature) (434-56); and the extravagantly made-up society woman (457-73).

Next J turns to ask how an upper-class woman spends her day. We expect a varied account, like the day of a *cliens* in 1, 127ff. We don't get it. We receive instead, spelt out in pictorial form, a one-word answer: 'Cruelty'. J uses an image from political autocracy (486), and links the passage with the earlier comparison to a slave-owner (219ff), the domineering dictatress (413ff), and, incidentally, with the passage on extravagant attention to cosmetics (457ff).

A long subsection takes up the theme of superstition (508-91), which we might call the abuse of religion. At the end J adverts to the superstitions of the poor. J does this from time to time. The satire

is on women. The poor are no better than the rich, but the rich are worse than the poor, because they can afford *luxuria*.

Reference to the poor allows him to hit straight back at the rich. The poor at least have children, where the rich seek abortions: again sex is nullified in sterility, as in the eunuch passage. This is important. J is not wholly anti-sex. J now follows a line of thought which again links the abuse of sex, and with it the indifference to embryonic life, to violence and the indifference to all life. He sketches the abortions of unwanted children (and the provision of substitute children for the deluded husband); the combination of hypersexuality with superstition leading to the use of love-potions; love-potions leading to poison.

So finally to the epilogue (643-61), which has interesting links with the introduction to the first poem. Note the poisoner-wife (6, 659; 1, 69-72), the theme of *ira* (6, 647; 1, 85), the image of the cliff (6, 649-50; 1, 147). This poem too brilliantly comes full-circle. For Clodia, the unchaste society lady (8), was sister of Clodius who broke the rites of the Good Goddess (345), and was herself allegedly her husband's poisoner (659). The burden is that real life is far grimmer than anything in mythology.

It is of course a mistake to try to fit every subsection into a prearranged plan. But this sketch may show that this satire has one primary theme — Women. It focuses attention on two qualities — Chastity in its absence, Luxury in its presence. Its attack is concentrated upon upper-class women, as J usually concentrates his satire upon the upper classes. They set the tone for society. As they have more privileges, so they have more responsibilities. But others are not exempt. J holds his satire together by subsidiary themes and images which recur throughout — the gladiatorial shows, superstition, sterility, cruelty, dictatorship, for example.

It is a picture of sustained grimness. He sweeps us on by four qualities.

First, there is the very intensity of his indictment.

Second, he succeeds with great skill in titillating as he condemns. There is perhaps an ambiguity in J, a combination of rejection and fascination. He certainly plays on such an ambiguity in his reader.

Third, there is the brilliance of his epigrams. The bucolic diaeresis tends to pick out a phrase epigrammatically. There are only two strong breaks before the fifth foot in the fourth satire: here there are perhaps twenty (depending on the punctuation offered). We owe to the sixth satire *unus Hiberinae uir sufficit?* (53) *facit hoc illos Hyacinthos* (110) *et lassata uiris necdum satiata recessit* (130) *rara auis in terris nigroque simillima cycno* (165) *concumbunt Graece* (191) *minimum dormitur in illo* (269) *homo sum* (284) *uenus ebria* (300) *iam fas est, admitte uiros* (329) *sed nunc ad quas non Clodius aras?* (345) *quis custodiet ipsos/custodes* (0 31-2) *crimen commune tacetur* (0 33) *bibit et uomit* (452) *soloecismum liceat fecisse marito* (456) *facies dicetur an ulcus?* (473) *ante tamen de te Tanaquil tua* (566) *Fortuna inproba* (605) *quae non faciet quod principis uxor?* (617) *nos utinam uani* (638) *septem, si septem forte fuissent* (641) and many more.

Finally, there are his cameo portraits. One after another they come — Tuccia unable to control her sexual excitement; Apula crying out at the show as in an orgasm; Thymele up from the country at the fashionable shows; Eppia standing with her gross he-man;regardless of the tossing seas; Messalina in the brothel wanting more; the proud Cornelia with her Scipionic lineage; the girls with a passion for Greek ways; Tullia and Maura at the statue of Chastity; the scene at the Bona Dea rites; Ogulnia off to the show; the political gossip; the bluestocking; the girl with the bread-poultice on her face as her husband kisses her; the woman beating and shaking her maid because her own hair won't fall into an out-of-date style; Caesonia with her love-philtre; Pontia with her poison. We see them as we read, and once we see, we cannot forget. That is J's power.

Bibliography

Anderson, W. S. 'Juvenal 6: A Problem in Structure' *CP* 51 (1956) 73-94

Axelson, B. ΔΡΑΓΜΑ Lund 1939

Birt, T. 'Der Aufbau der sechsten und vierten Satire Juvenals' *Rh. Mus.* 70 (1915) 524-50

Colin J. 'Juvénal, les baladins et les rétiaires d'après le manuscrit d'Oxford' *Atti della Acc. delle Scienze de Torino* 87 (1952-3)

Ercole, P. *Studi Giovenaliani* Lanciano 1935 pp. 185ff

Gallo, C. 'Fonti ed imitazioni della sesta satira di Giovenale' *Orpheus* 2 (1955) 76-82

Griffith, J. G. 'The Oxford Fragments of Juvenal's Sixth Satire' *Hermes* 91 (1963) 104-14

Harris, C. F. *Juvenal's Sixth Satire* Columbia University thesis 1949

Hirst, G. *Collected Classical Papers* Oxford 1938

Labriolle, P. de 'La sixième satire de Juvénal: Les femmes romaines' *RCC* 32 (1931) 385-98, 531-45, 690-706

Luck, G. 'The textual history of Juvenal and the Oxford lines' *HSCP* 76 (1972) 217-32

Madia, S. *Il fantasma della donna nella poesia di Giovenale* Messina 1957

Morford, M. 'A note on Juvenal, 6, 627-61' *CP* 67 (1972) 198

Nägelsbach, C. F. 'Ueber die Composition der vierten und sechsten Satire Juvenals' *Phil.* 3 (1848) 469-82

Nardo, D. *La sesta satira di Giovenale e la tradizione erotico-elegiaca latina* Padua 1973

Quartana, M. 'Giovenale, la sua satira e le donne' *Atene e Roma* 22 (1919) 198-214

Reeve, M. D. 'Gladiators in Juvenal's Sixth Satire' *CR* 23 (1973) 124-5

Singleton, D. 'Juvenal VI, 1-20 and some Ancient Attitudes to the Golden Age' *GR* 19 (1972) 151-64

Vianello, N. 'La sesta satira di Giovenale' *Historia* 4 (1930) 747-75

SATIRE 7

The theme of the seventh satire is literary patronage, and it is a bitter attack on the upper classes for their failure in supporting men of letters. The date is relatively simple to fix. A new emperor has come to power with some pretensions as a literary patron. This must be Hadrian (see Introduction); this alone makes any sense of the succession of J's satires. Other views have been held, but they are virtually impossible: for evidence of date see on 41. Hadrian succeeded in 117: he reached Rome in 118, and shortly after that is the likely date of the satire.

The structure is straightforward.

1-35 *The only hope of men of letters lies in the emperor. Otherwise we're driven to be bath-attendants, bakers or auctioneers — selling our friends' plays too. Still better this than perjury — leave that to get-rich-quick foreign ex-slaves. The emperor is looking for talent. If not, you might as well burn your works and smash your pen. Rich patrons do not go beyond praise; time passes, the poet has missed the chance of other professions and lives to curse his Muse.*

1 A direct statement. But which is the emperor? Almost certainly Hadrian, presumably not long after his accession in 117; he reached Rome in Aug 118. Hadrian was himself a poet and patron of the arts, *facundissimus Latino sermone, Graeco eruditissimus* (Eutrop. 8, 7, 2), *eloquio togaeque studiis accommodatior* (Aur. Vict. *Caes.* 14, 1), a man of restless curiosity, founder of the Athenaeum (Aur. Vict. *Caes.* 14, 3).

spes: almost a technical term; cf Calp. Sic. 4, 31 *spes magis arridet* of Nero's accession.

ratio studiorum: 'inducement to literature'. Writing was an *ars*, a matter of professional expertise, to be developed by disciplined practice (*studium*).

tantum: 'only'.

2 *tempestate:* not, with most edd., 'time' but 'storm'.

Camenas: ancient Italian divine powers (cf 3, 16), perhaps water-spirits, equated with the Greek Muses from the time of Livius Andronicus (*Od.* 1).

3 *respexit:* exactly our 'has shown any respect for', from the idea of looking twice at something. Often used of the gods, e.g. Cic. *Att.* 1, 16, 6 *nisi quis deus nos respexerit.* See also Calp. Sic. 4, 87-8 of Nero *me quoque . . . Caesar respiciat.*

4 *Gabiis:* see on 3, 192: a one-horse town. *conducere:* J does not approve; cf 3, 31; 3, 38.

furnos: bakehouses: we can see them at Pompeii, Herculaneum and Ostia with millstones, ovens and counters.

6 *praecones:* auctioneers were looked down on (3, 157): they were inevitably loud-mouthed. But there was money in the business: Euarestius Arruntius made his fortune at it (Jos. *Ant.* 19, 1, 18); cf Mart. 6, 8.

Aganippes: spring of the Muses on Mount Helicon. A stately phrase contrasting with the low professional alternatives.

7 *atria:* 'auction-rooms'; cf Cic. Quinct. 12 *ab atriis Liciniis atque a praeconum consessa.*

Clio: one of the Nine Muses; cf 4, 34; 7, 35; not necessarily the Muse of history: the Muses are originally non-specialists. There is wit in bringing her in: all J is saying is that poets become auctioneers.

8 *Pieria . . . in umbra:* 'in the poet's secluded retreat'. For *umbra* see Hor. *Ep.* 2, 2, 77-8. Pieria is the strip of coastland between Mount Olympus and the sea, the legendary burial-place of Orpheus, and one of the earliest centres of the worship of the Muses. Another stately phrase adding to the ambiguities of tone.

9 *ames:* 'you must put up with': the Greek *agapan*, which the Christians adopted for Christian love, has the same sense.

Machaerae: clearly the name of an auctioneer. J indulges his prejudices by making it Greek. The name means 'sword' or 'dagger', and may refer to *sectio*, the division and auctioneering of confiscation goods, a highly unpopular practice.

10 *commissa . . . auctio:* we would say 'the battle of the sale-room'.

11 Effective asyndeton as the goods disappear one after another. Traces of similar equipment were found in Herculaneum, and may be seen in the Cupids frieze in House of Vettii, Pompeii.

12 A paraprosdokian: the list of furniture ends in copies of plays which he is also selling off. Alcithoe, daughter of Minyas; she and her sisters Leucippe and Arsippe were turned into bats for their refusal to follow Dionysus (Ov. *Met.* 4, 1-40, 390-415; Ael. *VH* 3, 42; Plut. *QG* 38). *Thebes* is likely to refer to the stories of Laius, Oedipus and the Seven against Thebes, of which Aeschylus made a trilogy. *Tereus* (cf 6, 644) was the theme of tragedies by Sophocles, Livius Andronicus

and Accius. Paccius and Faustus are unknown. The last syll. of *Terea* is shortened; cf 3, 266; 8, 133; 14, 214.

13 i.e. it's a better life than perjury.

14 *faciant:* Lat. was a living, changing language. Cicero used the indic. with *quamquam;* cf 12, 25.

equites Asiani: he is referring to former slaves from the East who have become successful businessmen. Tiberius's law requiring three generations of freedom before being granted the *anulus* of the *eques* was ignored in practice, and *dominae munere factus eques* (Mart. 7, 64, 2) was common enough. Asia is the Roman province, not our continent.

15 Some edd. treat this line as a gloss: elsewhere *Bithyni* has a long first syllable (10, 162; 15, 1) but this is not quite determinative, as other similar words — e.g. Cyrene, Orion, Hymettus, Diana — are scanned both ways. Postponed *quamquam* is in J's style; cf 6, 198-9 (see J. G. Griffith in *CR* 1 (1951) 140-2). Cappadocia and Bithynia were not included in Roman Asia. See Mart. 10, 76, 3 *de Cappadocis eques catastis.*

16 *altera . . . Gallia:* 'a new Gaul', i.e. Galatia: the Galatians, as Griffith shows, acted as escorts for the slave-trains of Asia Minor; cf Claud. *In Eutrop.* 1, 59. It is difficult to make sense of the alternative reading *gallica.*

17-9 These lines are exceptionally assonant. In the first, *m* and *n* predominate with *t* and *d* cutting across the first part. In the second the cutting sounds of *c(q)* and *t* are dominant, but *m* and *n* assert themselves at the end of the line. The third is a humming sequence of *m* and *n.*

19 *laurum:* the Pythia at Delphi, Apollo's servant in prophecy, chewed laurel-leaves to achieve ecstasy; so it is used of Apollo's poetic inspiration; cf Tib. 2, 5, 63 *sic usque sacras innoxia laurus/uescar.* We are told that Prof. Oesterreich once chewed a large number of laurel-leaves as a scientific experiment, but that the results were uninspiring. J intends *laurumque momordit* as bathetic after the highflown description of the poet.

20 *hoc agite:* a ritual phrase; cf Sen. *Ben.* 3, 36, 2 *hoc agite, optimi iuuenes.*

et stimulat uos: the offbeat rhythm drives home the urgency.

21 *ducis indulgentia:* a technical phrase recurring twenty times in Pliny's letters to Trajan; cf Stat. *S* 1, 2, 174; Suet. *Caes.* 19; *Vit.* 5. Here it seems almost as if *indulgentia* is personified rather than an abstract form of *indulgens dux.*

22 *speranda:* Housman for MS *spectanda* or *expectanda.*

23 *croceae membrana tabellae:* 'the parchment of the yellow tablet', i.e. 'the tablet with its yellow parchment'. Parchment (*pergamene*) was invented at Pergamum when the Egyptians placed an embargo on papyrus export. It was a sheepskin preparation, more expensive than papyrus, but thick enough to be written on both sides, and the sheets were not glued on to one another in a roll (as with papyrus) but bound much as in our books. Here however the reference seems to be to the tablets which were used for notes and rough drafts. Usually these were of wax enclosed in wood; they could be smoothed and reused. But parchment stretched over wood was also used; the writing could be erased and the surface reused (as we know from palimpsest MSS, which have been used more than once) cf. Quint. 10, 3, 31; Mart. 14, 7.

25 *dona:* J's phrase is witty: there is a presentation, as to a patron, and Vulcan will give no more in return than any other.

Veneris . . . marito: Vulcan, the ugly, lame fire-god married to Venus in a beauty-and-the-beast myth expressing the union of beauty and craftsmanship. So Plato burnt his poetry on meeting with Socrates.

Telesine: not otherwise known. There was a Lucceius Telesinus, consul in 66, banished by Domitian for his philosophy (Tac. *Ann.* 16, 14; Dio Cass. 63, 1; Philostr. *V. Ap.* 4, 40; 7, 11; 8, 12).

26 *tinea pertunde:* 'perforate with the bookworm', i.e. 'let the bookworm riddle them with holes' — but the direct is more vivid.

27 *frange miser calamum:* Ben Jonson has the passage in mind in the Apologeticall Dialogue at the end of *The Poetaster:* 'O, this would make a learn'd and liberal soul/To rive his stained quill up to the back/And damn his long-watch'd labours to the fire.' The phrase has a curious history. J took it from Mart. 9, 73, 9 *frange leues calamos* ('pens' as here); Martial took it from Calp. 4, 23 *frange puer calamos* (where it means 'pipes'); Calpurnius from Verg. *Ecl.* 3, 12-3 *Daphnidis arcum/fregisti et calamos* ('arrows'). So we have the same phrase with three different meanings (see Rudd pp. 93-4).

uigilataque proelia: 'battles over which you have burned the midnight oil'; cf Stat. *Theb.* 12, 811 *o mihi bis senos*

multum uigilata per annos/Thebai.
29 *hederis:* ivy was sacred to Bacchus;
cf Ov. *Tr.* 1, 7, 2 *hederas, Bacchica
serta:* so of successful poetic inspiration.
There is a kind of hendiadys: 'a bust,
crowned with ivy'.
  macra: because of his poverty, a
sardonic touch.
30 *spes nulla ulterior:* 'it's no use
hoping for more'.
  diues: used as a noun; cf 3, 240.
31 *laudare:* cf 1, 74 *probitas laudatur
et alget.*
32 *Iunonis auem:* the peacock. Hadrian
dedicated a splendidly-bejewelled peacock
of gold to Hera (= Juno) (Paus. 2, 17, 6).
Ancient writers explain its association with
the queen of heaven by reference to its
starry tail (e.g. Ov. *M* 15, 385). Its first
Greek home seems to have been Samos,
Hera's island.
33 *pelagi:* objective genitive.
34 Note the play of the cutting *t* and
hissing *s*.
35 *Terpsichoren:* one of the Muses,
certainly not here specially associated with
dancing; cf 7.
  facunda et nuda: not quite an oxymoron,
but an effectively unexpected combination.

36-97 *The private patron is useless; he's often
a poet himself. If you want to give a public
performance he offers you a ramshackle
distant house; you have to supply the
seating yourself. Yet we have an incurable
itch to write. Real, independent genius
can't flourish like that. Horace needed a
good meal for his poetry. If Vergil had
been destitute, his writing would have
fallen flat. The rich can look after a
mistress, not a poet. Lucan was all right
with his independent income. Statius was
dependent on the favour of a dancer like
Paris. Indeed it is the Parises who control
promotion. The patrons of the Augustan age
have no successors.*

36 *accipe nunc artes:* 'Just listen to their
tricks.' *ars* = practical skill; *scientia* =
theoretical knowledge.
37 *et Musarum et Apollinis aede:* one
of Apollo's functions was patron of culture,
and one of his titles was Musagetes, leader
of the Muses. There is reference to the
libraries established by Augustus in
association with the temple of Apollo
Palatinus, and by Livia close by on the
Palatine in honour of the Muses: the
libraries were independent but administered
jointly.
38 *Homero:* see 6, 437.

39 *mille:* a round figure: in Aul. Gell.
17, 21, 3 Homer is set 160 years before the
foundation of Rome. Modern scholarship
places *The Iliad*'s 'composition' most
probably to the eighth century BC. Rudd
terms these 1½ lines 'a crescendo of
absurdity'.
40 *recites:* for the *recitatio* see on 3, 9.
The form of mixed conditional is common,
a more remote if-clause followed by a vivid
main clause: 'if you were to . . . that's
what he does'.
41 This whole description of hiring a
hall for a literary performance seems
indebted to Tac. *Dial.* 9.
  longe: 'at a distance'.
42 *sollicitas . . . porcas:* 'a herd of
frightened pigs': *porcas* is an emendation
(Jessen in *Phil.* 1 (1889) 320-7): the MS
portas was suggested by *ianua.*
43 *scit dare:* 'he knows how to give
you': in Greek this might be a μὲθ-
clause, with δὲ two lines later.
44 *comitum:* nicknamed 'Sophocles',
for their shouts of *sophos* ('well done'),
or *Laudiceni*, a pun between Laodiceans
and praisers.
45 *regum:* 'patrons'; cf 1, 136. Supply
tantum as obj. to *dabit.*
45-7 There are three types of seating.
Nearest to the stage are hired armchairs
(*cathedris*) for the distinguished guests;
behind these are benches (*subsellia*), and at
the back a scaffolding (*tigillo*) to support a
'gallery' (*anabathra*). It was quite an
expensive business.
48-9 A proverbially sterile operation
(Verg. *A* 4, 212; Ov. *H* 5, 115; *Tr.* 5, 4,
48; *Pont.* 4, 2, 16; Sen. *Ben.* 4, 9, 2, etc.).
Note *uersamus:* J includes himself: he too
is governed by this pathological obsession
with a fruitless activity.
50 *ambitiosum:* sc. *te.*
51 Surely a gloss. So Jahn. It is missing
from the Leiden MS.
52 *scribendi cacoethes:* a splendid
phrase: the thought is borrowed from Hor.
Ep. 2, 1, 108-9 *calet uno/scribendi
studio.* The natural tr. is 'itch', though it
is technically a non-malignant growth. Pope
liked to render it 'itch'; cf Prol. Sat. 224
'the itch of verse and praise'.
53 *uatem:* the poet as seer or prophet
is a commonplace, but the sense of a
religious calling is not to be dismissed as
merely conventional, e.g. Prop. 3, 1, 3
sacerdos; Cat. 16, 5 *pium poetam* (poetry
a patriotic and religious duty). The Muses
are not just a poetic ornament.
  publica uena: he does not draw from

the common stream: for the literal meaning see Ov. *Tr.* 3, 7, 16; Mart. 10, 30, 10: Ovid talks of his verse metaphorically as flowing from such a 'vein' (*Pont.* 2, 5, 21; 4, 2, 20); cf also Donatus *Vit. Verg.* 41 *non communi uena editos.*

54 *expositum:* 'which has been treated before'.

55 *feriat ... moneta:* metaphor from coining. The temple of Juno Moneta (the Warner) was associated with the state coinage: hence our word 'mint'.

55 *triuiale:* lit. 'found at the crossroads': so, 'commonplace'.

56 *sentio tantum:* 'I just feel he exists'.

57 *acerbi:* obj. gen.; cf 33.

59 *Aonidum:* the Aones were an ancient people of Boeotia, who traced their descent back to a son of Poseidon. Aganippe and Mount Helicon (6) were in Aonia, so Aonides = Muses.

59-60 *antro Pierio:* the phrase is borrowed appropriately from Horace (*O* 3, 4, 40). For Pieria see 8.

60 *thyrsum:* the staff sacred to Bacchus, tipped with a pine-cone and wreathed with ivy, symbol of ecstasy and inspiration, probably with side-reference to Hor. 2, 19, 8 (see on 62).

61 *aeris inops:* the gen. is used with words of fullness and emptiness, an extension of the partitive use.

62 *satur:* i.e. he's had a decent meal: but there is a cross-reference to *satura.*

Horatius: Q. Horatius Flaccus (65-8 BC), the amiable, bonhomous satirist and lyric poet of the Augustan age.

euhoe: the cry of the Bacchants; cf Hor. *O* 2, 19, 5-7: note again the religious context; cf 53. This evidently formed a bridge in J's mind to lead him to Vergil: the only occurrence of *euhoe* in Vergil is associated with the Fury Allecto who drives Amata to the hills in Bacchic frenzy (*A* 7, 389).

64 *dominis Cirrhae Nysaeque:* Apollo and Bacchus. Cirrha was the port for Delphi, Apollo's oracular shrine; cf 13, 79; Mart. 1, 76, 11 *quid tibi cum Cirrha?* Nysa was the legendary Asian scene of Bacchus's upbringing; cf Verg. *A* 6, 805 *Liber agens celso Nysae de uertice tigris.* The dat. 'of the agent' is not uncommon with passive verbs.

67 *attonitae:* the poet ought to be *attonitus,* awestruck, divinely inspired by visions, but not *attonitus,* 'intent on' hiring halls: for this usage see Sen. *Ep.* 72, 8; 118, 3; Luc. 5, 476: Apul. *Met.* 4, 22 *huic me operi attonitum* (Fletcher

in *Latomus* 35 (1976) 113 following Mayor).

68 *Rutulum:* Turnus, Aeneas's opponent; cf 1, 162. The ref. is to Verg. *A* 7, 445-66.

Erinys: the Fury Allecto, with snakes hissing in her hair, and monstrous *facies* (cf 67).

69 *Vergilio:* cf 6, 435: his reputation had begun in his lifetime; cf Prop. 2, 34, 65-6 *cedite Romani scriptores, cedite Grai!/nescio quid maius nascitur Iliade.*

puer: J is making two points. The word means 'slave', the old colonial 'boy' (cf 9, 64). But there was also a story that Asinius Pollio presented Vergil with a handsome boy named Alexander, who is the Alexis of *Ecl.* 2 (Suet. *Verg.* 9). Martial reverts to this several times. He makes Maecenas say to Vergil: *accipe diuitias et uatum maximus esto:/tu licet et nostrum, dixit, Alexin ames* (8, 55, 11-2; cf 5, 16, 11-2; 8, 73, 10). By using *puer* J alludes to the story without letting it obtrude (Rudd pp. 98-9).

tolerabile: a nice touch, since Vergil often used a word of this formation at this point of the line; cf *A* 4, 53 *cum tractabile caelum;* 94 *memorabile numen;* 569 *mutabile semper* and often.

desset: for the tense see on 4, 85.

70 *caderent ... hydri:* i.e. his description of Allecto would fall flat.

71 *surda ... bucina:* a beautifully-shaped phrase pointed by the bucolic diaeresis.

72 *Rubrenus Lappa:* an unknown writer.

coturno: strictly the high boot of the tragic actor; cf 6, 634. But it is loosely applied to epic, and Martial writes of *coturnatus Maro* (5, 5, 8; 7, 63, 5).

73 *Atreus:* f. of Agamemnon; he killed the children of his brother Thyestes and served them up to him for dinner; cf 8, 228. He is more obviously a theme for drama (e.g. Seneca *Thyestes*), but might have fitted into an epic. Note how Atreus is said to do the pawning, rather than Lappa to write his *Atreus.*

74 *Numitor:* cf 30 *diues auarus:* the name is taken from the ancient king of Alba (Liv. 1, 3, 10): it is used by Verg. *A* 6, 768.

quod mittat: 'to give'; cf 3, 45.

75 *Quintillae:* his mistress. Note the elaborate chiasmus from *non habet* to *habet.*

76 *leonem:* Syphax in North Africa used to keep lion-cubs (Sil. *It.* 16, 235-6). Domitian had a tame lion (Stat.

Silv. 2, 5). For Pliny's account of lions see
NH 8, 17-42-21, 58. They were brought
to the arena by Q. Scaevola, consul in
95 BC; Pompey had a sensational show
with 600. See also Martial 1, 14. Gibbon
wrote of this passage: 'If wit consist in
the discovery of relations natural without
being obvious, that of the poet and the
lion is one of the wittiest possible.'

77   *iam domitum:* so more expensive.

79   *Lucanus:* M. Annaeus Lucanus (AD
39-65), author of the unfinished epic
Bellum Ciuile, whose reputation in the
sixteenth century rivalled Vergil's
Aeneid; he lost his life for complicity in
the conspiracy of Piso against Nero; he
belonged to a wealthy family from Spain,
and had an independent income.

78-80   *hortis marmoreis:* a brilliantly
ironical phrase — all marble, no green.

80   *Serranus:* an epic poet mentioned
by Quintilian (10, 1, 89).

tenui: 'with slender resources'.

Saleiio: Saleiius Bassus, another epic
writer, who received a grant from
Vespasian (Quint. 10, 1, 90; Tac. *Dial.*
5; 9-10). Both died young.

81   An excellent epigram.

82   *curritur:* impersonal passive:
'people flock'.

amicae: there is a double-take; we
expect it to mean his mistress, and it turns
out to be his popular poem. The erotic
imagery is maintained in what follows.

83   *Thebaidos:* an epic poem narrating
the expedition of the Seven against Thebes
and the quarrel between the sons of
Oedipus, in twelve books, which took
twelve years to write, being finished in
AD 94.

Statius: P. Papinius Statius (AD 45-96),
author of *Thebais,* the unfinished
Achilleis, and short poems collected
under the title *Silvae.* He was not as poorly
off as this implies. J's picture of him is not
wholly sympathetic: among other things
Statius was one of Domitian's bootlickers.

84   *diem:* for the performance, as a
girl might promise a night for love.

84-5   *dulcedine . . . libidine:* erotic
imagery.

captos adficit: i.e. *capit et adficit,* as
commonly.

86   *fregit:* i.e. he has brought down
the house.

87   *intactam:* 'virgin' with double
meaning; cf. Mart. 1, 66, 7 *uirginis pater
chartae.*

Paridi: the famous actor and dancer:
see on 6, 87: here under the image of a

brothel-keeper exploiting a virgin.

uendit: this is the only evidence from
the imperial period of poets selling their
plays, but cf Ter. *Hec.* prol. 6-7.

Agauen: d. of Cadmus and Harmonia,
wife of Echion, mother of Pentheus, whom
she tore limb from limb in a Bacchic fury;
the story was presented in Euripides
Bacchae and Iophon *Pentheus* (lost), as
well as by Pacuvius and Accius. We have
no other evidence of Statius as a dramatist,
but Paris may be dancing to accompany a
narrative or lyric poem. Such would be an
obvious by-product of *Thebais.*

88   *ille:* sc. Paris.

militiae: all *tribuni* were given the rank
of *equites* (marked by a gold ring) after
six months' service: hence *semenstri . . .
auro.* Claudius instituted titular appoint-
ments as a means of promotion to the
rank of *eques* (Suet. *Claud.* 25). Such
appointments were made by the emperor, but
Paris is a court favourite and can influence
them; cf Plin. *Ep.* 4, 4 *hunc rogo semestri
tribunatu splendidiorem . . . facias.* Martial
passed upwards by the same route (3, 95,
9 *uidit me Roma tribunum*).

89   *semenstri . . . auro:* note how the
words symbolically encircle *digitos uatum;*
cf 53 n.

90   *histrio: pantomimus* will not fit a
dactylic hexameter. Note how the bucolic
diaeresis picks out the preceding scornful
epigram. The scorn is directed both at
the power of the Greek actor, and at the
impotence of the aristocracy.

Camerinos: a patrician family of the
gens Sulpicia, one of whom was put to
death by Nero (Dio Cass. 62, 18); cf 8, 38.

91   *Baream:* Barea Soranus, also an
aristocrat executed by Nero; cf 3, 116.
Tacitus (*Ann.* 16, 21) says Nero *uirtutem
ipsam exscindere concupiuit.*

tu: sarcastic anaphora.

magna atria: taken from Martial 3, 38,
11 *atria magna colam.*

92   A beautifully-turned line. Pelopea
was d. of Thyestes who incestuously raped
her, and mother of Aegisthus (others of
the name are also found in myth: see
Hyg. 87; 88; Apollod. 2, 14; Lucian
Salt. 43). For Philomela see on 6, 644: both
were parts danced by the *pantomimus.*
For the *praefectura* see 1, 58 n. The schol.
comments on this line *propter hunc
uersum missus est in exilio a Claudio
Nerone:* see Introduction on J's life.

93   *pulpita pascunt:* scornful alliteration,
continued from 92. Horace scorned to pay
court to the *pulpita* (*Ep.* 1, 19, 39-40):

J bitterly says that in his day one has to.

94 *Maecenas:* patron of Horace and Vergil: see 1, 68 and cf Mart. 8, 56, 5 *sint Maecenates, non derunt, Flacce, Marones* (oddly misquoted by Duff).

Proculeius: C. Proculeius, brother-in-law to Maecenas: we do not know him as a patron of literature, but he was liberal to his family (Hor. *O* 2, 2, 5-8).

95 *Fabius:* Paulus Fabius Maximus, patron of Ovid.

Cotta: M. Aurelius Cotta Maximus Messallinus, patron of Ovid, s. of M. Valerius Messalla Corvinus adopted into the gens Aurelia.

Lentulus: unknown for certain: there were many Cornelii Lentuli.

96 *tum . . . tunc:* bitterly sarcastic anaphora.

97 *toto . . . Decembri:* with particular reference to the Saturnalia, which began on 17 Dec. *Saturnalibus, optimo dierum* (Cat. 14, 15), and was extended as far as 23 Dec.; gifts were exchanged, social distinctions dropped, slavery relaxed (Hor. *S* 2, 7), dicing for money authorised, and a good time had by all. J's point is that poets used to be pleased to work at that time (it was a popular season for disseminating light verse): now they cannot afford to enjoy themselves.

98-104 *What about historians? They're no better off. They work harder, burn more midnight oil, spend more on paper. What do they get for it? The patron's more likely to pay his slave for reading the news.*

99 *atque olei plus:* a harsh offbeat ending. The oil is the 'midnight oil' in the lamps. For the phrase *oleum et operam perdere* see Plaut. *Poen.* 332; Cic. *Att.* 2, 17, 1.

100 *modo:* 'limit'.

millensima: there were about 200 pages to a roll: so this implies five books. Livy's history ran to 142!

101 *omnibus:* dat. 'for all of you'.

damnosa: 'costly', with a strong additional innuendo of 'prodigal'.

102 *atque operum lex:* again offbeat rhythm, harshly insistent.

103 A straightforward image from agriculture.

104 *acta:* the *acta diurna,* the official gazette; cf 2, 136; 6, 483. Most of us spend more time on the newspapers than on the study of history.

legenti: this would be done by a slave, who would not therefore be paid: the

implication (cf *daret*) is that he would be more likely to pay the slave (which he does not do) than the historian. Petr. *Sat.* 53 parodies the reading.

105-49 *'Men of letters are a lazy lot.' Then what of lawyers? They seem busy enough and pretend to large incomes; in fact a charioteer gets a hundred times their pay. The lawyer bursts himself — for a palm branch at his garret door. His reward is cheap food and poor wine. A nobleman, with his ancestral triumphs and his own broken-down equestrian statue, may do all right, however badly he pleads. Your run-of-the-day lawyer has to bankrupt himself with a show of being well-off. You are judged by your ring, and attendants. Eloquence in rags wins no recognition: you'd be better off in Gaul or Africa.*

105 *genus ignauum:* a popular view of all writers.

lecto: the Romans used a couch for reading and writing.

umbra: our 'ivory tower'; cf 8.

106 *ciuilia:* in contrast to *umbra: ciuilia officia* is a stock phrase (e.g. Sen. *Tranq.* 3, 1).

107 *comites:* a good personification: the *libelli* are to them what *clientes* are to a *patronus.*

libelli: note the dimin.: exactly our 'briefs'.

108 *magna sonant:* 'talk big'.

sed: not adversative: we can say 'but especially'.

110 'who comes with a large ledger for a difficult case of debt': *nomen* is the entry. A client with a big business and a difficult case implies a good fee.

111 *folles:* bellows as a metaphor for lungs was used in English nineteenth-century slang: in J's time the metaphor was not yet dead: it is taken from Hor. *S* 1, 4, 19.

112 *conspuiturque sinus:* the schol. gives two explanations (a) he is spluttering in his eagerness; (b) he is spitting to avert the evil eye. The latter is certainly right: spitting is an apotropaic measure. One aim was to avert the jealousy of Nemesis; cf Plin. *NH* 28, 7, 36 *ueniam a diis spei alicuius audacioris petimus in sinum spuendo.*

messem: reverting to the image of 103-4.

113 A line of interesting shape, with four short words in the first part, and two five-syllable words in the second: the

effect is to make the latter inflated and
pompous.

patrimonia: 'fortunes', not necessarily
inherited.

114 *russati:* in the races in the Circus
there were four firms, stables, *factiones,*
each with its own colour: originally two,
red and white, then blue and green in
addition: Domitian tried unsuccessfully to
add gold and purple. The partisan passions
make the Manchester United supporters of
the 1970s seem tame: in Constantinople in
AD 532 30 000 lives were lost in riots
over the races. The reds were an
unfashionable stable at this point.

Lacertae: the name of a charioteer: it
has been found against a charioteer's
figure on a lamp. Martial (10, 74, 5-6) says
grudgingly that a charioteer named Scorpus
received fifteen bags of gold in one hour.

115 *consedere:* a technical term. J is
parodying Ov. *Met.* 13, 1-2 *consedere
duces, et uulgi stante corona/surgit ad hos
clipei dominus septenplicis Ajax.* After
Achilles's death there was a formal debate
to decide who should inherit his armour.
Ajax, the leading fighter, lost to the
subtler Ulysses. Reconstruction of the
debate was a stock rhetorical exercise.

pallidus: R. Burton *Anatomy of
Melancholy* (with J in mind): 'Why do we
take such pains? Why the insane desire to
turn pallid over more paper?'

116 *pro libertate:* this was a common
case, *assertio in libertatem,* the claim of a
man that he is not subject to slavery.

116-7 *bubulco iudice:* note the ablative
absolute at the end, giving the effect ' —
and before a jury of clodhoppers too.' For
jurymen from the wilds of the country see
Quint. 4, 2, 45; 11, 1, 45; 12, 10, 53. The
common word *bubulco* breaks the high-
flown language. Cf. Sen. Eld. *Contr.* 11, 15,
1.

118 *scalarum:* he lives in a garret.

palmae: palm-branches on the door
indicated a successful plea; cf Mart. 7,
28, 6 *excolat et geminas plurima palma
fores.*

119 *pretium:* see Quint. 12, 7, 8-12.
for lawyers' charges. Mart. 4, 46 gives a
similar picture of a lawyer named Sabellus
fobbed off with oddments. By the Lex
Cincia of 204 BC the Roman lawyer was
not allowed to charge a fee: he depended
on the generosity of his clients. Claudius
however allowed a maximum fee of
10 000 sesterces (Tac. *Ann.* 11, 5, 7).

petasunculus et uas: the diminutive and
the broken rhythm at the end pile on the

contempt.

120 *Maurorum epimenia:* the Greek
adds to the contempt: the Latin
menstrua (a month's rations) is available.
African *bulbi* were regarded as inferior.

121 *Tiberi deuectum:* the good wines
from Campania were brought *up* the Tiber
from Ostia.

lagonae: wine-jugs with wide mouths.

122 *egisti:* 'have pleaded'.

123 *pragmaticorum:* Greek again.
These are lawyers who lacked skill in
pleading and became researchers and
advisers, somewhere between a solicitor
and a law-clerk. By contrast, the advocates
in J's day were trained in rhetoric not law.

124 *Aemilio:* the name reflects his aristo-
cratic standing: it belongs to one of the
great *gentes.* J did not think much of
patrician lawyers; cf 8, 47-50.

quantum licet: see on 119.

et melius nos: the indignation comes out
in the broken rhythm: note the use of *et*
where we would say 'yet'; cf 1,74; 1,93;13,91.

126 *quadriiuges:* an antique going back to
Republican times, celebrating some an-
cestor, since under the Empire triumphs
were reserved for the emperor alone.

127-8 *curuatum . . . lusca:* the contem-
porary statue is in poor repair, the spear is
bent, and one of the eyes (coloured stones
inserted into the bronze) has dropped out.
This is the best explanation of an other-
wise curious description: it is sarcastic. In
any case it is a ludicrous statue of a lawyer
— though they liked equestrian statues
(Mart. 9,68,6). For other views see J.G.
Griffith (*CQ* 19 (1969) 382-3); J.F. Killen
(*Glotta* 67 (1969) 265-6).

meditatur: 'is practising for'.

129 *sic:* i.e. by trying to show off on a
similar scale. Pedo, Matho and Tongilius
are lawyers who lack Aemilius's wealth and
position. For Matho see 1, 32; 11, 34.

conturbat: sc. *rationes* 'goes bankrupt'.

130 *rhinocerote:* an oil-flask of rhino-
ceros horn: the oil was used where we use
soap: the language and flask are extravagant.

131 *lutulenta . . . turba:* his claqueurs,
muddy from going round with him.

132 *longo:* i.e. requiring six or eight
bearers.

Maedos: a Thracian people.

133 Note the asyndeton. They are none
of them cheap articles, and seem to be
arranged in ascending order.

134 *spondet.* 'wins him credit'.

Tyrio: purple, cf 1, 27; 6, 246.

stlattaria: seemingly derived from
stlatta, 'a pirate-ship' (Aul. Gell. 10,
25, 5). Quint. 12, 7, 11 calls bargaining for

fees *ille piraticus mos:* so Tongilius's purple cloak is 'extorted by piracy'. (See J.G. Griffith in *CQ* 19 (1969) 381-2.)

135 *illis:* Tongilius and all such.

135-6 The bucolic diaereses point the epigram between them. Supply *uestimenta.* The amethyst colour is a variant on the purple: Plin. *NH* 9, 62, 135 *amethysti colos eximius ille;* Mart. 1, 96, 7 *amethystinasque mulierum uocat uestes.* It was achieved by mixing two crushed shellfish. These colourful costumes were disapproved by moralists.

138 A typical J epigram, the climax in the final word.

139 *Ciceroni:* M. Tullius Cicero (106-43 BC), the great Republican lawyer and statesman, a *nouus homo* from Arpinum. See 10, 114. In his day fees were not allowed, but he did well enough from his clients: see J. Carcopino *The Secrets of Cicero's Correspondence* I pp. 43-140, an unfavourable verdict, but the evidence is there.

140 *dederit . . . fulserit:* pf. subj., which represents ' a hypothetical condition more vividly by not excluding the idea of fulfilment' (Woodcock), more frequent in verse than prose.

143 *Paulus:* this could well be the Aemilius of 124; even he has to take trouble to hire his effects.

144 *sardonyche:* Duff well quotes W.S. Gilbert *Trial by Jury* where the successful judge started as an impecunious barrister with 'a ring that looked like a ruby'.

144-5 *Gallus . . Basilus:* less successful lawyers. The cognomen Gallus is found in about forty Roman families. Basilus appears as a dishonest businessman at 10, 222; the name is rare. We may deduce a point from the combination: 'familiar or unknown, you have to be out of the very top drawer.'

145 *rara . . panno:* another scintillating epigram. Not of course 'seldom found' but 'seldom acknowledged'.

146 *flentem . . matrem:* alike in Greek and Roman courts it was normal in the peroration to bring on the defendant's family howling with grief. Quint. 6, 1, 41 has a good story of an advocate bringing on a weeping boy and asking him why he was weeping, to receive the reply 'I've been spanked by my tutor.'

147 *accipiat te:* bucolic diaeresis and offbeat rhythm.

148 *Gallia:* Lucian *Apol.* 15 speaks of the rewards open to oratory there. It was only later, in the fourth and fifth centuries, that writers from Gaul came to dominate Roman letters.

nutricula causidicorum: a vivid but unexpected phrase to describe Africa. It is true that in the second and third centuries Africa was the dominant force in Roman literature with Fronto (tutor to Marcus Aurelius) and Apuleius (both lawyers), as well as the Christians Tertullian, Minucius Felix, Cyprian, Arnobius, Lactantius; it is probable that the Bible was translated into Latin first in Africa. What is surprising is to find such a description so early in the century.

150-214 *Teachers of rhetoric are no better off, having the same old diet served up to them again and again, and great difficulty in securing their fees without a lawsuit. Music teachers do better. The rich pay heavily for their luxuries, not for their children's education. Quintilian is only the exception who proves the rule, blessed with all Destiny's gifts. Fortune exalts — and demotes. In the old days teachers did not spare the rod: now pupils use it on their teachers.*

150 *declamare:* speaking in the schools as against the courts; cf Mart. 2, 71, 1 *declamas belle, causas agis, Attice, belle.* This was part of the training of an orator, and we have records of the practice in the works of the elder Seneca. But it was also used as an adult recreation, somewhat as a debating society. The main division was between *suasoriae,* in which the pupil advised a historical character how to act in a given situation, and *controuersiae,* in which he had to determine the rights and wrongs in a fictitious narrative. These last were full of adventure, piracy, love and murder, and provided the Romans with their 'thrillers'.

o ferrea pectora: epic parody.

Vetti: plainly a teacher of rhetoric, otherwise unknown.

151 *numerosa:* 'sing-song' (see D.S. Wiesen in *CQ* 21 (1971) 506-8) and also 'crowded': the Latin can bear both meanings and we do not have to choose. Quintilian (1, 8, 2) has a good story of Caesar rebuking a sing-song style: *si cantas, male cantas: si legis, cantas.*

152 A passage in *Hermeneumata pseudodositheana (Corp. Gloss. Lat.* 3, 381, 20-57) suggests that secondary schoolboys delivered these compositions twice, once sitting, once standing. The subj. of *legerat* and *perferet* is then not Vettius, but the class or the individual student. The teacher might *prolegere* (Suet. *Gram.* 16; Mart. 1, 35, 2; 8, 3, 15). See W. Allen in *TAPA* 103 (1972) 1-14.

153 *cantabit:* of the sing-song declamation. *uersibus:* 'lines' whether of verse or prose.

154 *crambe repitita*: 'rehashed bubble-and-squeak' (from Green). The line is a justly famed hyperbolic epigram.

155 *color* 'argument for the defence'; see on 6, 280.

causae genus: Quint. 3, 9, 6 *sed ante omnia intueri oportet, quod sit genus causae:* they are *iudiciale* (law courts) *deliberatiuum* (an advisory opinion) and *demonstratiuum* (like Pericles's Funeral Speech or Pliny's Panegyric).

summa quaestio: the point on which the case turns: also *causae cardo* (Quint. 5, 12, 3; 12, 8, 2).

156 *sagittae*: shafts of argument, an easy metaphor.

157 A memorable line.

158 *appellas*: the regular word for demanding money; cf 9, 64; Cic. 2 *Phil.* 29, 71 *appellatus es de pecunia.*

scio: 'have I learned'.

159 *laeuae . . . mamillae*: for the heart as the seat of thinking see R.B. Onians *The Origins of European Thought:* Cic. *TD* 19, 19 *alii in corde, alii in cerebro dixerunt animi esse sedem et locum.*

160 *Arcadico*: i.e. country bumpkins: Pers. 3, 6 *Arcadiae pecuaria rudere dicas.* Arcadia is a rural area of southern Greece.

cuius mihi sexta: to end a line with three dissyllables changes the rhythm from a smooth flow to a harsh insistence. Note that we are here identified with the teacher.

161 *dirus*: Hannibal was fearsome to the Romans of his day — and is now to the teachers of J's time.

Hannibal: see 10, 147; and, for his use as a topic in the schools, 10, 165.

162 *deliberat*: a technical term of the schools; cf Quint. 3, 8, 19 *deliberat C. Caesar, an perseueret in Germaniam ire.*

163 *Cannis*: Hannibal's great victory in 216 BC (cf 2, 155): his failure to clinch it by an immediate march on Rome was as disastrous to his cause as Hitler's failure to invade Britain in 1941 was to the German army.

post nimbos: this refers to the occasion when he did come within sight of Rome in 211BC (cf 6, 290-1). The Roman army confronted him in front of the Colline Gate. Two days of violent rain and hail made battle impossible. What should he now do?

164 *a*: with *madidas* 'as a result of'.

165 'Name any sum you please: I'll pay without argument: what am I to pay . . .?'

quid do is conversational; cf 3, 184 *quid das ut Cossum aliquando salutes?* The indic. is idiomatically used in deliberative questions. The idiom is carefully examined by C.J. Morse in *CR* 6 (1956) 196-8. The two monosyllables in the sixth foot add weight.

166 *haec alii sex*: the bucolic diaeresis emphasises the point which precedes it; the offbeat rhythm helps the sense of disgust at the situation.

167 *sophistae*: not to be confused with the sophists of classical Greece, who were teachers of various subjects in higher education, properly distinguished from rhetors. The Second Sophistic was a movement spanning the second century AD, and consisted of orators. The greatest of them, Dio of Prusa, nicknamed Chrysostomus ('golden-mouthed), had been a leading figure in Trajan's reign.

168 *ueras . . . lites*: for the recovery of their fees, no longer make-believe situations.

raptore relicto: 'and leave the rapist in the lurch': the abl. abs. at the end, combined with alliteration, is very pointed. The theme of rape was a common feature of the storybook cases of Seneca the Elder *Contr.* 1, 5; 2, 3; 3, 5; 4, 3; 5, 6; 7, 3.

169 *fusa uenena silent*: 'the poison is poured away and silent'. Many of the stories turned on poison: Seneca the Elder *Contr.* 3, 7; 3, 9; 6, 4; 6, 6; 7, 3; 9, 5-6; Ps-Quint. 319; 321; 350; Quint. 7, 2, 11. Libanius calls it a commonplace (4, 739-70, 908-15 R; 7, 647-99; 8, 182-94 F).

malus ingratusque maritus: we have the case. Sen. Eld. *Contr* 2, 5 *torta a tyranno uxor numquid de uiri tyrannicidio sciret perseuerauit negare. postea maritus eius tyrannum occidit: illam sterilitatis nomine dimisit intra quinquennium non parientem. agit illa ingrati.* 9, 1 is another *ingrati actio.*

170 *ueteres*: used here as a noun; cf 30 *diues.* The healing of the seemingly incurable was another part of this world of melodrama and magic.

171 'he will discharge himself'; cf 6, 113.

172 *consilia*: ironical, since so much of his time is spent in listening to *suasoriae.*

173 *umbra*: cf 8; 105: the ivory tower of the schools contrasted with political or forensic speaking. Petron. 2 calls a rhetor *umbraticus doctor.* Stat. *S* 5, 2, 103-9 has exactly the same contrast of one who *tacita studiorum occultus in umbra* emerged to face the *tela* of real life.

174 *summula*: 'the little sum': the phrase itself is almost paradoxical.

tessera: sc. *frumentaria*: a voucher for free grain, given to the poor, and sometimes available for purchase.

uenit: 'is sold'.

176 *Chrysogonus*: a musician; cf 6, 74 and note the contrast there with Quintilian.

quanti: gen. of price.

Pollio: a musician; cf 6, 387; Mart. 3, 20, 18; 4, 61, 9.

177 *lautorum*: the upper classes compared with 'the unwashed poor'.

artem: usually taken as a treatise on the science of Rhetoric: only such a work is not given either by Quint. 3, 1, 18 or *The Suda* sv. Theodorus. So, just 'Theodorus's science'.

scindens: the reading of most MSS, confirmed by the gloss *diuidens*. What these musical specialists did was to subdivide the unitary science of rhetoric, and earn fees by teaching melodious delivery in isolation from all the regular teachers had to contend with. Most edd. read *scindes* with Jahn and one or two MSS: but see J.G. Griffith in *CQ* 19 (1969) 583-5.

Theodori: from Gadara in the Decapolis, which produced a surprising number of distinguished people: he had a college at Rhodes: the emperor Tiberius went to him for instruction.

178 *sescentis*: sc. *parantur*. L. Herrmann *REA* 42 (1940) 448-9 suggests that this is a hit at Pliny's villa (Plin. *Ep.* 2, 17). Pliny was a pupil of Quintilian (*Ep.* 2, 14, 9), and, as Highet has shown, no favourite of J. But the allusion is doubtful.

porticus: cf Mart. 12, 57, 23 *intraque limen clusus essedo cursus*.

179 *anne serenum*: here the pause picks out these words.

180 *que*: 'and still'.

181 *hic*: i.e. under cover.

182 *Numidarum*: a yellowish marble; cf Hor. *O* 2, 18, 3-6 where it is also a luxury. It is known as *giallo antico*.

183 *rapiat*: a strong word: almost it is to kidnap the winter sun.

184 *quanticumque*: gen. of price or value sc. *paratur*.

186 *Quintiliano*: most famous of all teachers of rhetoric, cf 6, 75; 6, 280. By a typical twist J takes him first as typical, then as atypical.

187 *ut multum*: 'at most'; cf Mart. 10, 11, 6; Jer. *Ep.* 133, 13 *unum aut ut multum tres homunculos*.

188 *filius*: the younger Pliny tried to encourage his fellow-townsmen to spend less money on luxuries and more on their children's education (Plin. *Ep.* 4, 13, 5).

unde igitur tot: the combination of bucolic diaeresis and offbeat rhythm make clear that J, contrary to what is generally said, was not an unequivocal admirer of Quintilian, who had an official salary of 100000 sesterces a year as State Professor of Rhetoric, and a practice as well.

189-90 *nouorum fatorum*: not so much 'unexpected good luck' as ' a status transformed by destiny'. Either way it is 'the exception which proves the rule'. *Fatum* is a Stoic concept (important for example in Lucan's epic) which is here used satirically, as we can see: J goes on to characterise the *felix* (a much chancier character) with all the qualities of the Stoic *sapiens*. It was a Stoic paradox that he who possesses one virtue possesses all. Cicero expounds some of these implications in *Paradoxa Stoicorum*, and teases Cato with them in *Pro Murena* 29, 61 *solos sapientes esse si distortissimi sint formosos, si mendicissimi diuites, si seruitudinem seruiant reges;* cf the description of Cato at 28, 58. Also Hor. *Ep.* 1, 1, 106-7 *sapiens uno minor est Ioue, diues/liber, honoratus, pulcher, rex denique regum*.

192 'He wears a crescent fastened to the black leather (strap of his shoe)': this was an amulet of ivory worn by the upper classes.

194 *si perfrixit*: 'even if he's suffering from a cold', but there is a double meaning, for *frigus* is used of a performance which is a flop.

distat enim quae: bucolic diaeresis and offbeat rhythm, picking out the poet's disgust.

195 *sidera*: Stoic belief in predestination of all except the will to accept one's destiny and in pantheism went easily along with astrology, which is effectively the theme of Manilius's poem in the previous century.

195-6 *incipientem . . . rubentem*: jingling rhyme again expressing contempt.

197 *Fortuna*: in Lucan's poem a personal lucky star, distinguished from and almost independent of *fatum*. See also 3, 40; 6, 605; 9, 148, etc. A century or so later the Aristotelian Alexander of Aphrodisias noted the contradiction in those who maintain that all is predestined by Fate — but still call upon Fortune (*An. Mant.* 182, 18).

de rhetore consul: Quintilian received the consular decorations. Two and a half centuries later Julian made this a systematic policy.

198 *de consule rhetor*: Cicero (*Fam.* 9, 16, 7; 9, 18, 1) gave lessons in rhetoric to Hirtius and Dolabella after his fall. But J has in mind Valerius Licinianus, who was in fact praetor not consul, who was banished by Domitian for an affair with a Vestal, and set up a school of rhetoric in Sicily, beginning one of his classes with the words *quos tibi, Fortuna, ludos facis! facis enim ex senatoribus professores, ex professoribus senatores* (Plin. *Ep.* 4, 11, 1).

199 *Ventidius*: P. Ventidius Bassus, prisoner in the triumph of Cn. Pompeius

Strabo in 89 BC, consul in 43, awarded a
triumph for a victory over the Parthians in
38. He had been a mule-driver: Aul. Gell.
15, 4 *mulas qui fricabat consul factus est.*

Tullius: Servius Tullius, born of a slave,
later king of Rome (Ramsay, Humphries and
Green are wrong to refer to Cicero; cf.
201).

201   Note the chiastic arrangement with
199.

202   *coruo . . . albo*: cf 6, 165 *nigroque
simillima cycno.*

203   *sterilesque cathedrae*: much as we
speak of a professorial chair. The phrase is
taken from Mart. 1, 73, 13-4 *at circum
pulpita nostra/et steriles cathedras basia sola
crepant.*

204   *Tharsimachi*: schol. *rhetoris apud
Athenas qui suspendio perit:* not the great
sophist, who also made contributions to
rhetorical theory.

204-5   *Secundi Carrinatis*: Roman
rhetor banished by Caligula for a rhetorical
exercise in dispraise of tyrants (Dio Cass.
59, 20, 7): as this was a regular theme of
the schools there must have been plenty
of shaking shoes. The schol. has *ueneno perit
cum fugeret paupertatem.*

205   *et hunc*: the Roman Secundus as well.

206   *gelidas*: creating the chill of death.

ausae: not having the courage to offend
the emperor by honouring him.

cicutas: hemlock, *conium maculatum,* was
a poison used in classical Athens for execu-
tions, e.g. that of Socrates.

207   A prayer of some beauty and irony:
we must supply *dent.* The thought first
appears in Eur. *Alc.* 477-8. See also Prop.
1, 17, 24 *ut mihi non ullo pondere terra
foret;* Ov. *Am.* 3, 1, 68 *et sit humus cineri
non onerosa tuo*; Pers. 1, 37. The thought
was common enough to be abbreviated on
tombstones STTL = *sit tibi terra leuis.*

208   The contradictions here become
acute. There may be perpetual spring in
Elysium; we might by extension ask for
perpetual spring in the tomb, the house of
the dead; but hardly in the urn. The off-
beat rhythm at *perpetuum uer* runs counter
to the gentleness of the surface meaning.

209   *sancti: sacer* means set apart by being
consecrated, *sanctus* is naturally inviolable:
all that is *sacer* is *sanctus*, all that is *sanctus*
is not *sacer.* Respect to parents is an integral
part of *pietas*: the *paterfamilias* is the
religious focus of the family.

210   *uirgae*: obj. gen. see on 5,154: the
ancient schoolmaster did not spare the rod;
cf Hor. *Ep.* 2, 1, 70-1 *plagosum Orbilium.*

Achilles: the Greek hero, son of Peleus and

Thetis, whose education was entrusted to
the centaur Chiron (cf 3, 205).

211   *cantabat*: 'went to music-school'.

et cui non tunc: the rhythm is broken,
perhaps like Achilles's immature playing:
in any case J is debunking: *cui* is dissyllabic:
the dat. is of 'disadvantage': the general effect
'(so respectful) that his master's tail could not
wring a giggle from him'.

212   But the succession of *c, t, d* and *g*
gives the line a kind of tittering sound. What-
ever Achilles did, we are meant to laugh. For
the tense of *eliceret* see on 4, 85.

213   *Rufus*: not otherwise known, pre-
sumably a Gaul. Cicero in an earlier generation
writes *magister ut discipulos metuat et iis
blandiatur spernantque discipuli magistros
(Rep.* 1, 43, 67).

214   *Ciceronem Allobroga*: by no means a
compliment: 'a backwoods Churchill': worse,
because the Allobroges were a Gallic tribe
intriguing with Catiline, and Cicero claimed
to have saved Rome from a new Gaulish
invasion.

215-43   *The secondary schoolmaster is
worse off still, with others taking their cut.
He'd better bargain so that his work doesn't
go for nothing. Parents pay reluctantly, but
expect teachers to know the impossible. He's
responsible for the boy's morale, and at the
end of it, receives in a year what a winning
charioteer gets for a single race.*

215   *gremio*: 'pocket', a fold of the toga
used for money.

Celadi: a *grammaticus*, not known.

Palaemonis: Q. Remmius Palaemon, a
teacher of the mid-first century AD, who
taught both Persius and Quintilian: *docuit
Romae ac principem locum inter grammaticos
tenuit* (Suet. *Gram.* 23): in fact his income
came to 400000 sesterces, but this was al-
together exceptional. He was also notoriously
extravagant.

216   *grammaticus . . . labor*: the secondary
teacher's stock-in-trade was the Greek and
Latin poets, Homer in Greek and Vergil and
Horace in Latin above all. Grammar and
diction were all or almost all that mattered.
Cicero says (*De orat.* 1, 42, 187) *in gram-
maticis poetarum pertractatio, historiarum
cognitio, uerborum interpretatio, pronuntiandi
quidam sonus.*

et tamen ex hoc: the line is deflated.

218   *discipuli custos*: the *paedagogus,* the
slave whose job was to escort the boy to
and from school and supervise his behaviour.

acoenonoetus: the Greek as usual indicates
disgust. The schol. glosses *communi carens
sensu* 'with no fellow-feeling', but the

more probable meaning is 'nitwit'; cf Aul.
Gell. 12, 12, 4.

219 *qui dispensat*: the *dispensator* or
cashier.

cede, Palaemon: the preceding break
isolates and strengthens this.

220 *inde*: 'from your fee'. He is to
bargain like a petty trader and allows him-
self to be beaten down.

222 *pereat*: 'go for nothing'.

quod: 'the fact that'.

mediae . . . *noctis*: this is hyperbole, but
classes did begin before dawn (cf Mart. 9,
68).

224 *ferro*: the weavers' comb, also
called *pecten* or *carmen*. The carders are
caritores, carminatores, pectinarii or
pectinatores.

225 *lucernas*: each pupil had his own.

227 *Flaccus . . . Maroni*: books rather
than busts. Horace and Vergil soon became
'set-books': there is some irony in this
fact; cf Hor. *Ep.* 1.20.17 *hoc quoque te
manet, ut pueros elementa docentem/
occupet extremis in uicis balba senectus.*

228 *cognitione tribuni*: 'a court order'.
The legal authority of the *tribunus plebis*
is not quite clear. His basic right was to veto
processes initiated by others. 11, 7 suggests
his right to sanction a contract. Tac. *Ann.*
13, 28 suggests that tribunes have *de facto*
been usurping the functions of consuls and
praetors. According to *Digest* 1, 2, 2, 34
under Hadrian tribunes had similar judicial
authority to consuls, praetors and aediles:
this has been questioned, but this passage
might be taken in confirmation.

229 *uos*: 'parents'.

230 *uerborum regula constet*: 'insist that
his usage of words is precise' (Humphries).

232 *digitos*: 'And have all authors at
their fingers' end' (Gifford).

233 *thermas*: there were three public
baths at this period: those of Agrippa (built
in 25 BC, destroyed by fire in AD 80 and
restored), Nero (AD 62 or 64, near the
Pantheon), and Titus (built hastily for AD
80). The great surviving baths of Caracalla
and Diocletian are later.

Phoebi balnea: a small, cheap private baths.
There were 856 of them in Rome (so the
Notitia). Phoebus is most probably the
owner of the baths (cf Mart. 1, 59, 3 *redde
Lupi nobis tenebrosaque balnea Grylli*),
though it is possible also that Apollo gave his
name to it.

234-5 These are all questions based on
Vergil, but not answerable from the text
of *The Aeneid*. Aeneas's nurse was Caieta
(*A* 7, 1-2) but we do not know Anchises's.

Anchemolus's incestuous relations with
his stepmother come at *A* 10, 389, but
the details are not supplied. Acestes, king of
Sicily, was *aeui maturus* (*A* 5, 73): what was
his exact age? He gave the Trojans (*Phrygibus*)
wine on their departure (*A* 1, 195): how
much? How many children did Lady Mac-
beth have? The Romans loved such
questions: the emperor Tiberius quizzed
the teachers about the name of Hecuba's
mother, the name Achilles took when dis-
guised as a girl, the subject of the Sirens'
song (Suet. *Tib.* 70). Sir Thomas Browne
picked up this last: 'What songs the *Syrens*
sang, or what name *Achilles* assumed when
he hid himself among women, though
puzzling questions are not beyond all con-
jecture.' (*Hydrotaphia* c. 5). There is an
entertaining story from antiquity about an
ignorant schoolmaster who was asked
'What was Priam's mother called?' and
answered, 'Your Majesty'.

237 *pollice ducat*: from moulding clay
or wax, the sculptor's art (cf Pers. 5, 40).
Duff quotes Ascham's *Scholemaster* 'for the
pure cleane witte of a sweete young babe is
like the newest wax, most hable to receive
the best and fayrest printing'. By contrast
Socrates claimed in his dealings with the
young to follow not his father's profession of
sculptor, moulding them to his will, but
his mother's profession of midwife, enabling
them to give birth to the thoughts that
were in them (Plat. *Theaet.* 149 A).

238 *cera*: wax was used for portrait-
busts; cf Mart. 7, 44, 2 *cuius adhuc uultum
uiuida cera tenet.* Ovid's advice on how to
fall out of love includes *ceras remoue (RA*
723).

239 *pater*: it seems noble, but is deflated
by what follows.

240 *uicibus*: 'reciprocally'.

241 *oculos in fine trementis*: an ancient
work on physiognomy (in V. Rose *Anecdota*
1 Berlin 1864) has fifteen pages on informa-
tion to be drawn from the eyes: *oculi
trementes* mean *uoracitatem et intemperan-
tiam uini cum intemperantia ueneris* (p. 119)
nihil non audebunt quod iniquum improbum
(p. 123). See also Servius on Verg. *Ecl.* 3, 8;
schol. in Pers. 1, 18. *in fine*: at the orgasm
(cf Mart. 9, 69, 1). Boys' behaviour was
regarded with suspicion (Hor. *S* 1, 6, 82;
Quint. 2, 2, 14).

243 The meaning of the punch-line is not
wholly clear. The schol. refers it to actors,
but Roman performances were not competi-
tive, so *uictor* has no obvious meaning. M.L.
Clarke (*CR* 98 (1973) 12) suggests that a
winning gladiator received 5 *aurei*, and this

was what the parent offered. F Davey (*CR* 85 (1971) 11) makes the teacher victor in the law-courts: 'take the gold the people request for you when you've won your case.' The most obvious reference is to the races. The charioteer's winnings were far more than a schoolmaster's pay. Probably the point is that if the schoolmaster is persistent he will be paid for a year's work as much as the charioteer receives for one winning race.

General comments

The theme of patrons and men of letters recurs throughout the story of literature. Best-known is Dr Johnson's *Letter to the Earl of Chesterfield.*

> Is not a patron, my lord, one who looks with unconcern on a man struggling for life in the water, and when he has reached ground, cumbers him with help? The notice which you have been pleased to take of my labours, had it been early, had been kind; but it has been delayed until I am indifferent, and cannot enjoy it, till I am solitary and cannot impart it, till I am known and do not want it. I hope it is no very cynical asperity not to confess obligations where no benefit has been received, or to be unwilling that the Publick should consider me as owing that to a Patron which Providence has enabled me to do for myself.

That is less volatile, less scintillating than J, but it has a solid and devastating dignity.

At Rome there was no book-trade — or not on a scale sufficient to give a writer an adequate income. A writer had to have an independent income, like Lucan (79), or the unnamed aristocrat (38): this was true of authors of the senatorial order, Silius Italicus, Tacitus or Pliny. Otherwise they were dependent on patronage. Sometimes this might come from the emperor. In an earlier generation Vespasian gave Quintilian a salaried post (189), and made a grant to Saleiius Bassus (80). Hadrian gave employment to Suetonius, Florus, Favorinus. What of the aristocracy? They are the target of J's attacks, and of Martial's.

Martial and J look back with nostalgia to the Augustan age. They are primarily aware of Maecenas as the ideal patron. Maecenas had indeed a nose for genius: he would not otherwise have picked out Vergil and Horace: but there were no Vergils or Horaces apparent a century and a half later. Martial says that they are mute and inglorious for want of a patron, but it is at least arguable that patronage was not forth-coming for lack of genius. Maecenas was in fact a canny and selective patron. There were others of course: Fabius and Cotta (95) or Asinius Pollio. But later ages had their patrons. Statius is not perhaps a specially good example as he seems to have moved in a rather small Epicurean circle: still, he has about twenty wealthy people to whom he shows deference: Martial has more like a hundred. And Statius and Martial pulled through: so did J. Furthermore, the continual *recitationes* of which they complain (e.g. 1, 1; 3, 9) do not suggest a total neglect of literature. Pliny was diligent in attendance at these (*Ep.* 1, 13, 5-6) and mentions as performers, himself apart, Silius Proculus, Sentius Augurinus, Calpurnius Piso, Passennus Paulus, Vergilius, Romanus, Maximus, Titinius Capito, Regulus, Saturninus, and others unnamed. This is not to say that men of letters were not in difficulty. Pliny, who had no financial axe to grind, asserts it (*Ep.* 8, 12, 1); so does Statius, who had (*Silv.* 1 pref.).

J's satire has a number of distinctive points.

First, it is an attack on the aristocracy. It is not an appeal for help: one of the differences with Johnson is that he is personally involved with an individual patron. J would not withdraw any point of his attack if he received 500 000 sesterces: *exempla nouorum fatorum transi* (189-90). Indeed one has the feeling that if the emperor suddenly eased the situation for a large number of writers, J would intensify his satire, not modify it, for he is less concerned with the fate of writers than with the sins of the aristocracy. Even if a significant number of noblemen had changed colour on this point, he would have felt disappointed, because disarmed of a powerful weapon. Literary patronage is a particular example of the wider *patronus-cliens* relationship. The *patronus-cliens* relationship is a particular example of the wider irresponsibility of the Roman aristocracy.

Secondly, J is unusual in coupling the condition of writers with the condition of teachers. There is, after all, no obvious affinity, apart from the fact that both are *studia.* The teacher, whether primary or secondary, has a more or less guaranteed source of income, even if it is small and he has to be litigious about it (168; 228); the writer does not. The point becomes clear if we see it in relation to the aristocracy. The aristocracy neglect writers, but they have nothing to gain by supporting writers, apart from some prestige. But, worse, they neglect teachers, and that is a sign that they care nothing for their own children; in other words they are failing in *pietas*, one of the essential Roman virtues. This is why J treats the *rhetor* before the *grammaticus*. The *rhetor* is concerned with technical training: the boys and their parents prefer to have this partially and flashily done (177-9) and have no sense of thoroughness. The *grammaticus* also has technical skills to impart, which the parents debase into triviality (229-36); but he is also something more important, a moral tutor (237-41) (J characteristically deflates the impact of morality to keeping an eye open for masturbation). As an attack on the aristocracy the structure of the satire leads to a climax.

Thirdly, J does not exempt the victims from his satire: he seldom does. The rich are the more guilty because they have more power, but poor and rich are alike involved in a corrupting system. One of the best examples of this is the way he describes Statius the poet and Paris the upstart patron as together involved in the business of literary prostitution (87). Writers suffer from a pathological disease (52), and J does not exempt himself from the charge (48-9 *nos tamen hoc agimus*). The poem, whether it deals with writers or teachers, is full of the concept of waste, of unprofitable occupation, of ploughing the sand (49), and eating rehashed bubble-and-squeak (154), waste not only imposed by the aristocracy, but springing from the inner futility of the men of letters themselves.

Fourthly, then, does this embrace the emperor too? Helmbold and O'Neil made an eloquent attempt to prove that it did, and that the emperor was Domitian. Anderson (*CP* 57 (1962) 158 n 17) and Rudd have refuted this. The *exempla* of this poem do not concentrate on the age of Domitian: they extend from the Republic, through the Augustan age and the Julio-Claudians as well. Further the language of 20-1, on which Helmbold and O'Neil rely, is by no means necessarily adversative: all the words can be, and are, used both unfavourably and favourably: it is at worst ambiguous. If we accept, as we surely must, that the emperor is Hadrian (and even if we don't), it is hardly likely that J would publish anything which could be interpreted as an assault on the emperor. This said, J does not seem very optimistic about help from the emperor, and his references have a cautious ambiguity. We have only to compare them with Statius's fulsome flattery of Domitian to see that. After all, Hadrian was not a member of some *diuina domus*: up till his very late adoption by Trajan he had been one of the senatorial aristocracy whom J had persistently attacked. Further, for all his interest in literature, his attitude to writers was ambiguous; he might humiliate them (SHA *Hadr.* 15, 10) or honour them (SHA *Hadr.* 16, 8). His favourite, Antinous, stood very much in the position of J's Paris (87). But the emperor is not really in point. The introduction is not about the emperor, but about the plight of men of letters. The point of the striking first line is not *in Caesare*, but *tantum*. J reinforces this *spes nulla ulterior* (30): it leads him to the *diues auarus* who is his theme.

One of J's most effective devices in this satire is his use of personification. Sometimes it is almost whimsical. The poet taking up auctioneering is described as Clio abandoning Aganippe's dales (6-7). To put his compositions on the fire is to present them to Venus's husband, as to a patron (24-5) (some bitterness here). Atreus pawns the poet's property (73). It is Pelopea and Philomela who create army officers (96). Hannibal is as fearful to the teacher of the second century AD as to the soldier of the third century BC (161). Horace and Vergil become blackened with soot (227). Some of J's images are of vivid power: notable here are *facunda et nuda senectus* (35) and *rara in tenui facundia panno* (145). There is some effective use of sustained imagery: we may instance the sustained erotic language in the passage about Statius (82-7), or the account of the professor of rhetoric abandoning the rapist, pouring out his poisons and leaving them speechless, together with the ungrateful husband and the cures for blindness (168-70); or the vision of the successful professor as the Stoic sage (190-202).

As always, the epigrams are masterly. We may pick out *scribendi cacoethes* (52); *satur est cum dicit Horatius 'euhoe'* (62); *gloria quantalibet quid erit, si gloria tantum est?* (81); *sed finem inpensae non seruat prodiga Roma* (138); *rara in tenui facundia panno* (145); *quis bene dicentem Basilum ferat?* (147); *nosse uolunt omnes, mercedem soluere nemo* (157) as only a few among many others.

Above all what distinguishes this satire is its tone: this has been the subject of a masterly study by Niall Rudd. He points for example to the introduction. It begins with a ringing assertion *Et spes et ratio studiorum in Caesare tantum* (1). But as soon as we turn to the behaviour of poets the tone changes. High-flown language is mixed in with the mention of backwoods places like Gabii and low professions like auctioneering, and the auctioneer's catalogue of secondhand junk ends with lofty tragedies. A poet is described as *nectit quicumque canoris/eloquium uocale modis laurumque momordit* (18-9): the language is overblown and at the end debunking. The poet is to present his poems to Vulcan, the fire, who will prove an ungrateful patron. He is to destroy the works he is writing in the hope of a starving bust. Every phrase is pointed, satirical, sardonic. It is the tone which tells.

He passes to the patron who writes verses, allows no superior but Homer — and him only for antiquity (a carefully controlled climax). A versified passage from Tacitus descants on the difficulties of performance. Then comes the famous *scribendi cacoethes*: poets must be diseased. A great poet needs food. The tone of the pictures of Horace and Vergil is worth careful examination: wry, affectionate, with a touch of whimsy — Horace, bald and pot-bellied, in a Bacchic rout; Vergil, without a boy to serve him, with his snakes falling flat. A malicious glimpse of Lucan, who had an independent income, follows, and an ambiguous picture of Statius, clothed in erotic imagery, which seems to sympathise with his poverty, and regards him as meretricious. Each of these vignettes has its characteristic tone: it will not do to confuse them or to ignore the ambiguity.

The tone remains similarly ambiguous through the rest of the satire. Historians are underpaid — but J has no great sympathy with them as they pile on their thousands of pages, and dismisses them curtly. The picture of lawyers is no more favourable, with their equestrian statues which they can't afford to keep up, their pirated and piratical purple, their petty lies and deceits. Teachers of rhetoric are served over and over again with the same diet of rechauffé bubble-and-squeak; they have themselves to thank for the tedium of their lives. The rich cannot be expected to wait for a fine day, or to allow their ponies' feet to be muddied, but is the professor any better? The successful professor is ironically described as a Stoic sage: he is only a child of fortune. There is a blessing on past generations who encouraged respect for teachers, but even that blessing is ambiguous, and by encouraging his reader to laugh where his Achilles did not, J makes his point (210-2). As for the elementary teacher, the prey of sharks, teaching in the dark by smoky lamplight, expected to be an infallible source of useless information — even his highest

parental role is debunked. As Rudd wisely says, 'if we leave out the wit and double vision, and talk only in terms of protest and compassion, we are bound to give a sentimental reading of the poem.'

For the poem is controlled by a dominant image: it is that of sterility, and this links it with the previous poem. Indeed many MSS head it *DE STERILITATE STUD-IORVM*. Images from farming recur (48; 103; 112), and the repeated use of *labor* and *merces* normally would reflect physical labour, and is ironical of the intellectual's *umbra*. The world of the Muses is a world of natural growth (6; 58). The rich man can control nature in his own interests. Lucan turns his gardens to marble (and incidentally to death) (79-80); the millionaire captures the sun (183); Quintilian has his *saltus* by the gift of Fortune (189). J ironically prays for flowers for the ashes of the upper classes of old (208). The turn of the year brings no spring to the teacher (242). Writers and teachers alike are workers in sterility, and the rich who can turn nature to their own advantage will not help them to bear fruit.

Bibliography

Colton, R.E. 'Juvenal and Martial on literacy and professional men' *CB* 39 (1963) 49-52

Ercole, R. 'Stazio e Giovenale' *Riv, indo-greco-ital. di filologia, lingua, antichita* 15 (1931) 43-50

Hartmann, A. *Aufbau und Erfindung der siebenten Satiren Juvenals* Basle 1912

Helmbold, W.C. and O'Neil, E.N. 'The Form and Purpose of Juvenal's Seventh *Satire*' *CP* 54 (1959) 100-8

Hild, J.A. *D Iunii Iuvenalis Satira Septima* Paris 1890

Kilpatrick, R.S. 'Juvenal's "Patchwork" Satires: 4 and 7' *YCS* 23 (1973) 229-41

Labriolle, P. de 'La 7e satire de Juvénal' *Humanités* (Cl. de Lettres) 7 (1931) 367-74, 419-27

Radermacher, L. 'Zur siebenten Satire Juvenals' *Rh.M.* 59 (1904) 525-31

Rudd, N. *Lines of Enquiry* Cambridge 1976 pp. 84-118

Tandoi V. 'Il ricordo di Stazio dolce poeta nella Sat. VII di Giovenale' *Omaggio a Ed. Fraenkel* Rome 1968 pp. 248-70

Townend, G.B. 'The Literary Substrata to Juvenal's Satires' *JRS* 63 (1973) 148-60

Wiesen, D.S. 'Juvenal and the Intellectuals' *Hermes* 101 (1973) 464-83

SATIRE 8

This is a rhetorical poem which sets its theme firmly in the first three words: *Stemmata quid faciunt?* It is addressed to a nobleman named Ponticus, who from the context hopes for the consulship and a provincial governorship. J's total theme is that character not ancestry makes for good repute, and he pursues the theme unremittingly. There are no digressions or loose ends in this satire.

The poem is rhetorically structured and I cannot do better than reproduce Highet's analysis, with one small variant.

1-38 *exordium*:
    general statement of theme
39-145 *propositio*:
    particular application:
      negative (Rubellius) 39-70
      positive (Ponticus) 71-145
146-268 *confirmatio*:
    exempla mala (146-235)
    exempla bona (236-60)
    exempla mala (261-8)
269-75 *conclusio*

It will be noted that this gives a nicely proportioned poem, the better because not balanced with precise symmetry. It will be noted also that the treatment is pessimistic: examples of vice enfold and outweigh the examples of virtue. The conclusion is powerful in its very brevity.

Hall 4, 3 is a paraphrase of this poem.

1-38 *What is the use of family trees and ancestral masks, if the present holder of the family name is a gambler, vicious, empty and effeminate? Virtue is the only true nobility. Take heroes from the past, let them be your models. Be an honorary gentleman for your virtues, rare enough to be enthusiastically greeted. Beware that your noble names are not relevant 'by opposites'.*

1 *stemmata*: 'family trees': a matter of Roman pride. The Romans had two traditional ways of recording their ancestry, one wax portrait-busts (*imagines*), the other a chart (*stemma* or *generis tabula*) in which the names were painted in a circlet of leaves precisely in a family tree: the stained-glass-window tree of Jesse gives something of the idea. For the distinction see Plin. *NH* 35, 6; Sen. *Ben.* 3, 28, 2. It is slightly odd to find a Greek word for such a Roman institution, but not odd to find J using it with disapprobation; cf also Mart. 4, 40, 1 *atria Pisonum stabant cum stemmate toto*. The satire begins

with a pointed question, and, as no other, announces its subject with the very first word.

faciunt: strong: action v. profession.

Pontice: not known: the dedicatee seems to have had hopes of the consulate (23). It is slightly odd that the name is not found among the old aristocracy. The only Ponticus known of this period is a crook of Nero's reign (Tac. *Ann* 14, 41). Martial uses the name in no complimentary way (cf Mart. 3, 60; 4, 85; 9, 19).

2 *sanguine*: 'pedigree'.

3 *Aemilianos*: J introduces almost all the great *gentes* into this satire. The termination -*anus* shows a member of the Aemilii adopted into another family, like P. Cornelius Scipio Aemilianus. The name thus shows the interaction between the great families — and the fact that their members were not necessarily 'pure-bred'. Prudentius uses this passage to rebuke pride of ancestry in his own day (*Symm.* 2, 556).

4 *Curios*: an ancient patrician family, including M'. Curius Dentatus; cf 2, 3.

iam dimidios: 'broken off in process of time'; cf 15, 5 *dimidio . . . Memnone*. J is debunking the whole process, while castigating the present incumbent for his neglect.

5 *Coruinum*: a branch of the gens Valeria.

Galbam: the emperor Galba boasted his descent from Jupiter and Pasiphae (Suet. *Galb.* 2). He belonged to the gens Sulpicia.

auriculis: the diminutive helps the sense of crumbling decay.

6 *generis tabula*: = *stemmate*.

7 *pontifices posse ac*: Housman for the repetitive *Coruinum posthac*.

multa . . . uirga: branches of the family tree, not with the schol. *multis fascibus*.

8 *equitum . . . magistros*: the dictator's second-in-command in time of crisis, originally commander of the cavalry, but later with more general functions.

dictatore: a temporary extraordinary magistrate, appointed by senate and consul at a time of crisis to hold authority for a maximum of six months.

9 *coram Lepidis*: a branch of the gens Aemilia, prominent in the late Republic through the consul of 79 BC and the triumvir who ineffectively held the balance between Antony and Octavian. His son held high office in the early Empire. The Lepidi retained their standing: hence their mention here.

uiuitur: impersonal passive. The bucolic

diaeresis points the words.

quo: 'what's the point of'. Broken rhythm.

11 *Numantinos*: the masks, conceived as the watching ancestors. Numantinus was a name conferred on Scipio Aemilianus after his capture of Numantia in Spain in 133 BC after an eight months' siege.

12 *duces*: 'they as generals'.

mouebant: idiomatic impf. 'used to break camp'.

13 *Allobrogicis*: Q. Fabius Maximus received the title Allobrogicus for his conquest of the Gallic Allobroges in 121 BC. There were other better-known military Fabii, including the famous negative strategist of the war with Hannibal. Allobrogicus was chosen, partly because his father was an Aemilius by birth and Fabius by adoption (cf 3), and because his son was a worthless profligate (Cic. *TD* 1, 33, 81). But J may have in mind Seneca's reference to the degenerate Paullus Fabius Persicus, cos AD 34 (*Ben.* 4, 30, 2; cf 2, 21, 5).

magna . . . ara: the *ara maxima Herculis* in the *forum boarium*, traditionally dedicated by the legendary Evander: the Fabii claimed descent from Hercules and Evander's daughter Vinduna.

14 *in Herculeo . . . lare*: 'in Hercules's household'.

si cupidus, si: broken rhythm as we come on the degenerate descendants.

15 *Euganea*: the Euganei lived in the hills south of Padua till driven out by the Veneti (Liv. 1, 1). The wool of their sheep was prized: Plin. *NH* 8, 73, 190 *alba Circumpadanis nulla praefertur*. Mart. 14, 155 preferred Apulia and Parma fleeces.

mollior agna: 'softer', 'more effeminate': Mart. 5, 37, 2 has the words seriously of a girl, here they are bitterly of a man.

16 *Catinensi*: Catina or Catana at the foot of Etna, famed for its pumice.

pumice: see Plin. *NH* 36, 42, 154-6 for pumice and its uses, which, as well as a depilatory, was powdered into eye-salves and tooth-powders.

lumbum: this is sometimes called a retained accusative with the passive *attritus*. It is really a blurring of the constructions *atterere eum* and *atterere lumbum*, put into the passive.

17 *traducit*: 'caricatures', 'exposes to ridicule'; cf 11, 31.

18 *frangenda . . . imagine*: the portrait-mask of a disgraced member of the family was removed and destroyed (cf Tac. *Ann.* 2, 32, 2).

funestat: used in its literal meaning of 'pollute through murder'. The whole line is a remarkable combination of sounds.

20 A memorably expressed sentiment: *nobilitas,* lit. that which makes a person worth knowing, but like our 'nobility' coming to mean 'blue-bloodedness': *uirtus,* lit. 'being a *uir*', i.e. courage and toughness, but through the philosophers also meaning 'moral goodness' more generally. There are Stoic overtones in the line, which owes something to Persius. It has been much quoted across the ages.

21 *Paulus*: 'a Paulus': L. Aemilius Paulus Macedonicus defeated Perseus of Macedon at the battle of Pydna in 168 BC.

Cossus: probably with reference to Cn. Cornelius Lentulus Cossus who received the title Gaetulicus for his victories in Africa in AD 6. Patient in poverty, he was not corrupted by wealth (Tac. *Ann.* 4, 44), and served with distinction under both Augustus and Tiberius. An earlier Cossus of the fifth century BC fought heroically against Fidenae.

Drusus: Nero Claudius Drusus (38-9 BC), brother of the emperor Tiberius, father of Germanicus and Claudius, he campaigned with Tiberius in Raetia and Germany. His nephew, another Drusus, was with Cossus in Pannonia, but was a man of less admirable character. A heavy spondaic line, cf 23.

22 *hos*: not *mores*, but 'these people'.

uirgas: the *fasces*, a bundle of rods, with an axe, carried before a consul by his attendant lictors to symbolise his powers of corporal and capital punishment.

24 *mihi*: the so-called 'ethic' dative: not 'you owe me' but 'in my view you owe': the dat. is used to bring a person or thing in indirect relation to the sentence.

animi bona: a technical term of philosophy: note how the bucolic diaeresis emphasises the preceding phrase.

25 *iustitiaeque tenax*: obj. gen.; cf Hor. *O* 3, 3, 1 *iustum et tenacem propositi uirum*.

26 *agnosco*: sc. *te*.

Gaetulice: see on 21.

27 *Silanus*: the Iunii Silani were prominent in the early Empire.

29-30 *quod clamet Osiri inuento*: the cry was 'we've found him; we rejoice together': εὑρήκαμεν, συγαίρομεν (schol.; cf [Sen.] *Apocol.* 13, 4 when Claudius reaches the underworld). Osiris was an Egyptian divine king, consort of the goddess Isis; he was killed and dismembered by his enemy Set; the joy has to do with the discovery and restoration of his body and his resurrection:the original myth relates to the annual return of the Nile waters over the land of Egypt. J elsewhere uses the myth of departing gods for the departure of virtue (e.g. 6, 19-20); here the myth is reversed!

31-2 *indignus . . . insignis*: an extra-ordinary near-rhyme such as J contrives only for scorn.

32-4 So we may call a six-footer 'Tich', and there was a day when a Black might be 'Snowball'.

32 *nanum*: the Romans kept dwarfs for their amusement; cf Quint. 2, 5, 1; Plin. *Ep.* 9, 17.

Atlanta: the legendary giant who held up the sky.

33 *Cycnum*: the name means 'Swan'; it was held by various mythological characters, including a handsome son of Apollo, who was turned into a swan.

prauam: 'ugly'.

extortamque: 'misshapen': more usually *distortam*, but cf Sen. *Ep.* 66, 43; 104, 18; Plin. *Ep.* 8, 18, 9 *extortus et fractus*.

34 *Europa*: Ovid (*M* 2, 833-75) oddly does not expatiate on her beauty: still, she attracted Jupiter.

36 *Tigris*: one of Actaeon's hounds (Ov. *M* 3, 217).

si quid adhuc est: offbeat rhythm for scorn.

37 *ergo cauebis*: here the bucolic diaeresis is more important for separating out these words, and so stressing the moral. A person who bears an ancient name had better watch out that he doesn't earn it 'by opposites'.

38 *ne tu sic Creticus aut Camerinus*: the three monosyllables throw great weight on the names, appropriately by contrast. Creticus was a name in the Caecilii Metelli earned through victories in Crete in 68-7 BC. The Camerini belonged to the gens Sulpicia; cf 7, 90.

39-70 *I'm directing my words at you, Rubellius Blandus. You boast your blue blood. But if you want eloquence, legal skill, or the military virtues it's among the commons that you'll find them. You are nothing but an emasculated patronymic. No one values a horse unless it wins races. Unless it does that its pedigree counts for nothing: it's up for sale and on to hauling carriages. Give us something of your very own to admire.*

39 *his*: instrumental 'by these examples'.

sermo: 'a chat': but remember that Horace called his satires *Sermones,* and note the movement to our 'sermon'.

39-40 *Rubelli Blande*: Tiberius's grand-daughter Julia married C. Rubellius Blandus (consul suff. AD 18) in AD 33 (Tac. *Ann.* 6, 27, 1); his son, C. Rubellius Plautus, was a Stoic and a political quietist, a man of high character, executed by Nero in AD 62.

Plainly, despite some interpreters, neither of these is meant. J is addressing a man whose name is his only claim to fame, presumably a later descendant or collateral (though one now dead; cf 71-2).

40 *Drusorum*: cf 21: Tiberius's son was Drusus Caesar.

41 *feceris*: a strong word; cf 1: the anti-thesis between word and action is a common-place.

42 *Iuli*: s. of Aeneas, and legendary ancestor of the gens Iulia, to which the imperial family of the Julio-Claudians was attached.

43 *aggere*: see on 5, 153; 6, 588.

44 *uolgi*: Cicero, himself a *nouus homo*, called them *faex Romuli (Att.* 2, 1, 8).

46 *Cecropides*: mock-epic: Cecrops was a mythical king of Athens: with J's views on the Greeks this preference for allusion is a damning degeneracy on the part of a Roman aristocrat.

47 *Quiritem*: oftener in the pl. of the Roman citizens organised for peace: the *numen* of this activity is Quirinus, later identified with the founding father Romulus.

48 *facundum*: one of the three familiar paths to power; cf Liv. 39, 40, 5 *ad summos honores alios scientia iuris, alios eloquentia, alios gloria militaris prouexit.* J says the commoners of his day outstrip the aristocracy in all three.

hic: 'another'.

plebe togata: ironic contrast with *Cecropides.*

49 *nobilis*: here a noun; cf, 7, 30; 7, 170.

50 *nodos*: exactly our 'knotty points'.

51 *hinc*: i.e. *de plebe.*

Euphraten: with reference to Trajan's campaigns in Mesopotamia.

iuuenis: 'as a soldier'.

Bataui: a people of Rhineland, subjugated by the Romans in AD 69.

52 *aquilas*: i.e. the legions, the eagle being the legionary standard.

at tu: very pointed in its detachment and emphasis.

53 *Hermae*: Hermes was originally the power of the cairn, a heap of stones sup-porting a tall vertical stone to guide travellers in mountainous country. He became the protector of messengers, travellers and brigands, a popular and friendly god, and ousted Iris as the gods' herald and ambassador. He protected roads, streets, and boundaries. He became the god of traders, perhaps because the boundary was the point of barter, perhaps because traders travelled, perhaps because he was the god of the

lucky find. A row of his images was found in the agora, the business-centre of Athens. These herms were vertical columns, squared off, with the god's head and a phallus for good luck: it was a major blasphemy when in 415 BC these last were broken off one night: *trunco* thus alludes to the latterday aristocrat's lack of spunk; cf 15 *mollior.*

55 *tua uiuit imago*: 'yours, though empty, is living' (Humphries).

56 *Teucrorum proles*: mock-epic: the Roman aristocrats claimed their descent from Aeneas and his fellow-Trojans; cf 1,100 *Troiugenas.*

animalia: cf Sen. *Dial.* 4, 16, 1 *animalia generosissima habentur quibus multum inest irae.*

57 *nempe uolucrem*: as usual the bucolic diaeresis emphasises the previous point. Pegasus was the legendary winged horse.

58 *sic*: referring to what follows.

facili: i.e. an easy victor.

cui: 'for whom'.

59 *feruet*: the spectators' hands grow warm with clapping; or perhaps the sound of their clapping surges up (Plin. *NH* 2, 82, 193 has *feruere* of sound).

uictoria: i.e. the shout of victory.

61 *clara fuga*: a neat oxymoron, indeed a paradox, for the *fortis* is not expected to run away, but in a race the horse in front is indeed trying to get away from the others.

aequore: 'the racecourse': *aequor* is a level tract of land or water.

puluis: the dust thrown up by his hooves. The Mediterranean lands have long dry periods: armies were visible at a distance as a cloud of dust.

62 *uenale pecus*: this is very scathing: horses are valued by their achievement not by their pedigree: if they do not achieve they are put up for sale as animals. The implication is that an aristocrat who does not achieve is no better than an animal, and merits selling as a slave.

62-3 *Coryphaei . . . Hirpini*: famous racehorses. Coryphaeus (the reading is uncertain) is not otherwise known. For Hirpinus, cf Mart. 3, 63, 12 *Hirpini ueteres qui bene nouit auos*: an inscription, cited by Mayor, says that he won first place 131 times, second 56, third 36. *HIRPINVS N. AQVILONIS VICIT CXXXI SECVNDAS TVLIT LVI TERT. TVL. XXXVI (N = Nepos).*

posteritas et: a very harsh ending to the line.

63 *rara*: we would say 'infrequently'.

65 *iubentur*: however degenerate, the blue-blooded humans still give orders: not the horses: the subj. is *nepotes.*

66 *epiraedia*: a variant on the Gaulish *eporedium*, taken as a hybrid compounded of *epi* (Greek) and *raeda* (Celtic), as Quintilian says (1, 5, 68). The schol. takes it to mean ornaments on a coach: if so they stand here for the coach itself.

67 *segnipedes*: hapax legomenon: Fredericks calls it a 'striking satiric epicism'.

molam uersare: usually the work of donkeys: also a punishment for slaves.

68 *ut miremur te, non tua*: excellently put.

priuum aliquid da: the rhythm drives the point home: *priuum* is a sure emendation by Salmasius of the MS *primum.*

69 *titulis*: the inscription on statue base or tomb recording achievements.

70 The striking alliteration shapes and points the line. For *damus ac dedimus*, cf 3, 190 *timet aut timuit.*

71-145 *Aristocrats like Rubellius lack feeling for others. What about you, Ponticus? Don't you rely on others' reputation. Show yourself a man of integrity. Don't place even life above honour. Eventually you may become a provincial governor. Avoid temptation. Retribution falls — but that doesn't help the provincials. Past generations have rapaciously seized their works of art: now they've little left. And don't forget that the Greeks may be soft, but they're tough in Spain, France and Illyria. And don't damage the African corn-supply. Victims still have weapons. If you govern justly, then I'll let you claim a lineage — back to Prometheus, if you like. If you abuse your authority, your ancestors' renown will expose you. Privilege breeds responsibility. What's the good of a nobleman being a forger or adulterer?*

72 *Nerone*: cf Tac. *Ann.* 13, 19, 3 *Rubellium Plautum, per maternam originem pari ac Nero gradu a diuo Augusto.*

73 *sensus communis*: a phrase with various meanings, 'common sense', 'ordinary sensitivity', ' the human faculty of perception', 'social conscience': here the primary meaning is 'feeling for others', *noblesse oblige*, but we should not forget the alternatives.

74 *fortuna*: 'class' or 'rank': we should not forget 7, 197-8.

76 *laudis*: part. gen. with *nihil.*

77 An excellent image: we should translate by three paratactic clauses, abl. abs. first, then the part., then *ruant.*

78 Vines were trained on elms: the elm is pictured as the wife in the vine's embrace, widowed if the vine falls and trails on the ground.

81 *Phalaris*: see on 6, 614c.

83 *pudori*: 'honour'.

84 A magnificent line. Pliny identifies

uiuendi causas as *optimam conscientiam, optimam famam, maximam auctoritatem,* family and friends (*Ep.* 1, 12, 3; cf 5, 5, 4).

85 *perit*: 'is already dead'.

86 *Gaurana*: cf 9, 57 Mons Gaurus (now Monte Barbaro) overlooks the oyster-beds of the Lacus Lucrinus in Campania.

Cosmi: the Coty of ancient Rome; cf Mart. 1, 87, 2; 3, 55, 1; 9, 26, 2; 11, 8, 9; 11, 49, 6; 12, 65, 4; 14, 110, 1; who also applies his name to a scent (11, 15, 6; 12, 55, 7) and to a special jar (3, 82, 26).

toto: idiomatically transferred epithet: we might tr. 'wholly'.

87 *prouincia*: the administrative regions of the Empire: at this period those administered by the senate were Sicily, Hispania Ulterior, Gallia Narbonensis, Macedonia, Achaea, Asia, Bithynia and Pontus, Cyprus, Cyrene and Crete, Africa and Numidia: by the emperor Hispania Citerior, Lusitania, Aquitania, Lugdunensis, Belgica, Germania Superior, Germania Inferior, Britannia, Alpes Maritimae, Alpes Cottiae, Raetia, Noricum, Pannonia Superior, Pannonia Inferior, Illyricum, Moesia Superior, Moesia Inferior, Dacia, Thracia, Epirus, Galatia, Cappadocia, Pamphylia and Lycia, Cilicia, Syria, Judaea, Arabia, Armenia, Egypt, Mauretania Caesariensis, Mauretania Tingitana. Hadrian was prompt to withdraw from Trajan's new provinces of Assyria and Mesopotamia.

88 *rectorem*: a loose term, chosen because of its associations with 'straightness'. The senatorial governors were styled proconsuls. The emperor usually administered through a *legatus propraetore,* but in some instances appointed a procurator or (as in Egypt) a prefect.

irae: dat.

89 *et*: 'above all'.

inopum sociorum. the offbeat rhythm adds to the point.

90 *ossa*: Cic. *Brut.* 17, 68 has the metaphorical use cf Mart. 5, 44, 11.

rerum: 'of their state' (with the same ambiguity in Latin). Under the Republic, running for office was an expensive business involving demonstrative extravagance to impress and win the voters: it was normal to recoup one's losses as propraetor or proconsul. Cicero made his reputation by his prosecution of C. Verres for extortion in Sicily. Extortion continued under the Empire, though successive emperors tried to stamp it out.

92 *fulmine*: the emperor is compared to Jupiter in his punitive wrath.

93 *Capito*: Cossutianus Capito, governor of Cilicia who was condemned for extortion

in AD 57 through the persistent integrity of the Stoic Thrasea Paetus on whom he was revenged after his return from banishment.

Tutor: unknown: a rare name: C. Vellaeus Tutor was cos. in AD 27 (*PIR* iii V 233). (The alternative reading *Numitor* is the error of a copyist who recalled Verg. *A* 6, 768 *et Capys et Numitor.*

94 *piratae Cilicum*: the Cilicians had been notorious for piracy, but the governors outpirated them.

quid damnatio confert?: the condemnation of the governor does not restore what he has extorted.

95 *Chaerippe*: a provincial, possibly one involved in the charges against Capito, which would involve the expense of a journey to Rome (Quint, 6, 1, 14 mentions a Greek quip from the prosecution). J, with typical hyperbole, suggests that he's down to rags and has to sell those.

96 *Pansa . . . Natta*: if there are definite allusions we have lost them. The names are quite minor. C. Vibius Pansa was one of Caesar's protégés. Natta is a name found in an obscure branch of the gens Pinaria: it is the name of a mean, dirty character in Horace (*Sat.* 1, 6, 124).

97 *naulum*: there is a neat double point: it may refer to the cost of the journey to Rome (cf 95 n) or the coin placed in a dead man's mouth to pay his ferry across the Styx (3, 167).

98 *erat par*: the offbeat rhythm suggesting that the present state is *impar.*

100 *aceruos*: Greek termination, nom. sing.

101 *Spartana*: Hor. *O* 2, 18, 7 *Laconicas . . . purpuras.*

Coa: Cos is an attractive island in the eastern Aegean: it was famous in antiquity for its healing sanctuary (the great doctor Hippocrates practised there) and for a form of silk, *Coae uestes,* cf 6, 260 n.

102 *Parrhasii*: fifth-century painter, born in Ephesus, later Athenian, noted for his careful outlines, and for psychological depictions.

Myronis: the greatest sculptor of the first half of the fifth century, interested in symmetry: among his masterworks were an Athene and Marsyas, and the Discobolus or Discus-thrower, which Samuel Butler extolled in a well-known hate poem.

103 *Phidiacum*: Phidias was the greatest of the fifth-century Athenian sculptors, noted above all for his gold-and-ivory statues of Zeus at Olympia (which Quintilian claimed added to revealed religion, and Dio Chrysostom exalted in a speech) and Athene for the Parth-

enon. These are lost, but he designed and supervised the Parthenon frieze (part of which is in the British Museum: the Elgin Marbles). His workshop at Olympia has recently been found.

Polycliti: Argive sculptor working in the second half of the fifth century. His *Doryphorus* or *Spearbearer* became the canon of proportion for subsequent artists.

104   *Mentore*: of unknown date but before 356 BC, the Cellini of antiquity, the greatest of silversmiths. Crassus paid 100 000 sesterces for two of his cups. Martial often mentions him (3, 40, 1, etc.).

105   *Dolabellae*: the reading is uncertain: note the hiatus, which gives a pause after the name, and a kind of appalled gasp. Cn. Cornelius Dolabella, governor of Cilicia in 80-79 BC, was condemned the following year for extortion: a second member of the clan was arraigned by Caesar for extortion in Macedonia and condemned in 77: a third, P. Cornelius Dolabella, Cicero's son-in-law, most extortionate of them all, was driven to suicide in 43 BC.

Antonius: C. Antonius Hybrida, uncle of the triumvir, arraigned by Caesar in 77 BC for extortion in Greece, continued his malpractices as governor of Macedonia in 62, and was banished for them three years later.

106   *sacrilegus Verres*: C. Verres, legate with Dolabella in Cilicia, propraetor of Sicily 73-70 BC, plundering temples and private individuals with proud disregard; cf 2, 26.

altis: deep in the water with the weight of plunder.

107   *occulta spolia*: it is rare for a short final *a* to be found in a long syllable.

plures de pace triumphos: an ironical collocation: triumphs were for victory in war and the spoils were openly displayed. 'Triumphs' in peacetime – *de pace* almost means '*over* peace' – were more lucrative.

109   *pater armenti*: a stud-horse.

agello: the dimin. indicates the poverty with a touch of pity from the poet.

110   *Lares*: the household gods, kept in a *lararium* or alcove such as may be seen in villas in Pompeii. They were in origin possibly powers of the farmland, possibly ancestral spirits, possibly both.

112   *despicias tu*: contemptuous offbeat rhythm, with bucolic diaeresis.

113   *imbellis Rhodios*: for Rhodes as a symbol of luxury, cf 6, 296. They were not always so unwarlike: it survived a siege by Demetrius in 305-304 BC and another by Mithradates in 88 BC.

unctamque Corinthon: the adj. ('scented')

and the Greek acc. alike suggest scorn. Corinth, the great commercial town advantageously sited on the Isthmus, was sacked by the Romans in 146 BC but soon reverted to prosperity, as Paul found out and as the extensive remains show.

115   *leuia*: J is back to the charge of effeminacy.

116   *horrida*: wild, bristly and masculine. Martial, a Spaniard, makes the same comparison between Spaniards and Corinthians (10, 65, 6-9), which is no doubt J's source.

axis: the diameter of the sphere of the universe, running through the earth to the sky: hence the sky itself: here almost 'the atmosphere'.

117   *Illyricumque latus*: 'the shore of Illyria' – Yugoslavia and Albania, a well-known recruiting ground for fighters, which was to give to Rome in the next century some of its soldier-emperors. See J.J. Wilkes *Dalmatia*.

118   *messoribus*: i.e. the north Africans, who provided Rome's grain supply.

circo et scenae: the circus and the theatre, the two main recreations of the people. The thought is much that of the better-known *panem et circenses* (10, 81).

uacantem: 'so that they can be free', proleptic. In the time of Augustus there were sixty-six public holidays a year for spectacles; in the time of Marcus Aurelius, 135 (SHA *M. Aur.* 10). This apart from special occasions: Trajan celebrated his Dacian triumphs with 123 days of spectacles (Dio Cass. 68, 15). It should be remembered that the Romans had no weekend.

119   *dirae*: because it might damage the corn supply.

120   *tenuis*: acc. pl. with *Afros*: proleptic, at least in part: they were poor before and are poorer after.

Marius: Marius Priscus, prosecuted by Pliny and Tacitus in AD 100 for his extortions. See 1, 49.

discinxerit: a vivid word, for money was carried in the belt, while at the same time we have the effect of stripping down to the loincloth. There is a play on Verg. *A* 8, 724 *discinctos Afros*.

124   *spoliatis arma supersunt*: quoted by Burke on 22 Mar. 1775 against a proposal to starve out the Americans. But the line is a gloss.

125   *sententia*: 'an epigram'.

126   *folium . . . Sibyllae*: the Romans had a legend that an old woman came to Tarquinius Priscus with nine books and asked an exorbitant price for them. When he refused she destroyed three, and asked the same price for the remaining six. He refused again, and she

destroyed three more, and he paid the original price for the last three. These were guarded carefully in the Capitoline temple under a special *collegium* of the *quindecimuiri,* who consulted them in national emergency on the instructions of the senate. They were said to be written on palm-leaves: Serv. ad. Verg. *A* 3, 444 *in foliis autem palmarum Sibyllam scribere solere testatur Varro.* They were destroyed in the fire of 83 BC, reconstituted and revised by Augustus, and placed in the temple of Palatine Apollo. The Sibyls were ancient female prophetic figures: one had her shrine at Cumae, where it remains impressively. J is giving his words — not without irony — the status of prophetic truth.

127 *cohors comitum*: a governor's retinue. *tribunal*: i.e. the judicial verdict.

128 *acersecomes*: ' a long-haired nancy-boy', a bitter Graecism, especially as it is a title of Apollo: the normal Latin was *puer capillatus.*

129 *cuncta*: with both nouns: see on 14, 276.

130 *Celaeno*: 'like a harpy' from Verg. *A.* 3, 211.

131 *tum licet*: this marks the beginning of the main sentence 'then I allow you to'. *Pico*: mythical king of Latium, s. of Saturnus and f. of Faunus; cf Verg. *A* 7, 48: The name means 'Woodpecker': it looks as if one of Mars's attendant animals became anthropomorphised.

132 *omnem Titanida pugnam*: i.e. 'all the warrior Titans'. The Titans were seemingly pre-Greek gods (Hes. *Theog.* 424), children of Earth: in the myth they challenge the power of Zeus who has ousted them (Cronos is one of their number), suffer defeat and are banished. Note the Greek acc.

133 *Promethea*: another Greek acc., with the final *a* shortened as often in Latin; cf 3, 266; 7, 12; 14, 214. Prometheus was one of the Titans, a fire-spirit in origin. Here the reference is to the legend that he made men of clay (the scene is splendidly portrayed on a sarcophagus in Naples; cf Paus. 10, 4, 4; Hor. *O* 1, 16, 13): it would be logically impossible for any human to trace his genealogy back to Prometheus.

134 *libro*: e.g. Hesiod's *Theogony.*

136 *uirgas*: cf 22.

137 *hebetes*: with use. *lasso lictore*: abl. abs., with employing them.

138 *ipsorum . . . parentum*: the sense that the ancestors are actually watching their descendants is strong today in Africa and other parts of the world, and was strong in ancient Rome; cf Sall. *Jug.* 85, 23 *maiorum*

gloria posteris quasi lumen est, neque bona neque mala eorum in occulto patitur. It should not be dismissed as a mere metaphor.

139 'and to shed the bright light of a torch on your shame'.

140-1 A careful epigram. J perhaps elaborated it because Sallust had put it with brilliant brevity: *in maxuma fortuna minuma licentia est (Cat.* 51, 13). JR 'Satire to Sir Nicholas Smith' (sometimes attributed to Donne) has 'And by their place more noted, if they err.'

142 *quo*: 'what's the point of . . .?': it is regularly followed by the acc., some verb being understood; cf Hor. *Ep.* 1, 5, 12 *quo mihi fortunam?*; Cato *Dist.* 4, 16 *quo tibi diuitias? mihi*: the so-called ethic dative, equivalent to 'tell me' or 'I ask you'. cf 8, 24.

143 *in templis: sc. uersantem.*

145 *Santonico*: the Santones were a tribe of Aquitania, north of the Garonne (cf the modern Saintes), from whom clothing was imported; cf Mart. 14, 128, 1 *Gallia Santonico uestit te bardo cucullo.*

146-82 *Lateranus as consul drives his own gig past his ancestral tombs — by night, but once his year of office is over he will do so openly. He worships Epona while sacrificing to Jupiter. He visits low haunts. We sow our wild oats, but he has never put his behind him. At his age he should have been commanding a frontier force, not reclining in low company. You'd punish a slave for such behaviour, but the nobility forgive in themselves conduct which the lower classes would scorn.*

146 Along the *Via Appia* or one of the other main roads out of Rome (cf 1, 171).

147 *carpento*: a covered carriage with two wheels, a gig: it can be seen on contemporary coins of Hadrian's wife Sabina. *Lateranus*: T. Sextius Lateranus, cos. AD 94: the reference to Nero (170) does not invalidate, since J so refers to Domitian (4, 38; cf Mart. 11, 33). Plautius Lateranus, consul designate when executed in the Pisonian conspiracy of AD 65, is less likely, because he was never consul, and because J is less likely to gird at an opponent of Nero, and because it is longer ago for a relative triviality to be remembered.

147-8 *ipse, ipse*: rhetorical *geminatio*; cf 2, 135-6; 6, 166-7; 6, 279-80. Here it emphasises Lateranus's crime in driving himself; cf 1, 61. It is the satirist's device to use triviality to point his attack, cf (with a difference) H. Belloc 'Lord Finchley tried to mend the Electric Light/Himself. It struck him dead; And serve him right./It is the business of the wealthy man/To give employment to the artisan.' People still look with surprise at someone in high position driving his own car.

mulio consul: a striking collocation: it prepares the way for 198 *citharoedo principe.*

149 *Luna*: not just a poeticism: a very real divinity to the ancient world, identified with Diana.

testes: acc with *oculos.*

150 *honoris*: 'office'.

153 *iam senis*: and so a stickler for tradition and eminently shockable.

maniplos: by syncope or contraction from *manipulos*, 'bundles of hay': he is groom as well as chauffeur.

154 *hordea*: 'barleys': purists and pedants disapproved of the plural (Quint. 1, 5, 15). Vergil used it (*G* 1, 210), and Bavius and Maevius, whom he had scorned, rejoined *hordea qui dixit superest ut tritica dicat* (Serv. ad loc.).

155 *interea*: sc. *ante finitum tempus honoris.*

lanatas: a traditional archaic religious formula; cf 15, 11, though it is here used as a noun.

robum: schol. *robustum, rufum: unde Hercules robus dictus est*: Festus p. 134 Lind. *robum rubro colore et quasi rufo significari, ut bouem quoque rustici appellant, manifestum est.* Plainly 'red' is right.

156 *more Numae*: the pietistic early king to whom much ritual was attributed.

Iouis ante altaria: at the *feriae Latinae* the consuls offered sacrifice to Jupiter Latiaris.

157 *Eponam*: a Gallic nature goddess associated with horses: see R. Magnen and E. Thévenot *Epona, déesse gauloise.* The cult spread from the area between Seine and Saône as far as the Balkans, Spain and north Britain. The schol. *dea mulionum est* is a guess.

facies: it is not quite clear what J means. Pictures of Epona on the stable walls? Pictures of other divinities J refers to by innuendo? Pictures of the ancestors of his horses, parodying his own *imagines?*

praesepia pictas: pointedly rejective alliteration, continued in the next line.

158-62 Something is wrong with the text here: I have accepted the addition of *et* to 161, with *iam* for *et* in 162 (Helmbold in *Mnem.* 4-5 (1952) 226-7) and left the rest, but there may be a graver disorder.

158 *popinas: peruigiles* and *instaurare* are both appropriate to the religious festival (cf Cic. *QF* 2, 4, 4 *Latinae instaurantur):* *popinas* is paraprosdokian, the twist in the

tail: tr. 'decides to celebrate in all-night festival — at the low taverns'.

159 *Syrophoenix*: Syrophoenicia (cf Mark 7: 26) here means the coastland of Syria with Tyre as its administrative centre. Hadrian however included the areas round Damascus and Palmyra, making it administratively separate from Syria Major in the north with its capital at Antioch, and Syria Palaestina. J is as usual showing his dislike of Easterners. Housman points out that the *repetitio* does not conform to Latin usage, which does not change the verb, and suspects that a line has fallen out.

160 *Idymaeae... portae*: the phrase does not recur: the schol. has *tabernarius qui prope portam manet. Idymaeus* sometimes is used for 'Jewish': so perhaps the *porta Capena*, the gate by the Jewish quarter (cf 3, 14). Other explanations seem less likely.

161 *regem*: of the aristocratic patron at 1, 136, here with a sideblow at oriental obeisance to oriental monarchy: see also on 179.

162 *uenali... lagona*: 'with her bottle for sale': there is a double meaning, for any such container may symbolise the *uulua.*

Cyane: 'Blue (-eyes)', a Greek name, no doubt a Syrian Greek, like Vergil's *copa Syrisca (Copa* 1).

succincta: for the better performance of her duties, as Duff ambiguously comments: waiting, dancing, and lovemaking.

164 *iuuenes*: the thought may come from Mart. 4, 78, 9 *haec faciant sane iuuenes.*

165 *turpiter audes*: cf 6, 97: *audere* is often strongly condemnatory: 'dare' is a weak tr.

166 *cum... prima barba*: the first shave was a ceremonial occasion, representing the end of boyhood: it sometimes coincided with putting on the *toga uirilis*: after the initial *barbae depositio* a neatly trimmed beard was affected till the age of 40 (cf 6, 105).

168 *thermarum calices*: there were refreshment-sellers at the baths: for the *thermae* see on 7, 233.

linteu: schol. *hoc est pictis uelis popinae succedit, aut linteis capsariciis tergitur*: the figured towels or bathrobes are less likely than linen awnings advertising the attractions inside.

169-70 *Armeniae Syriae... amnibus*: i.e. the Tigris and Euphrates (where Trajan had been campaigning recently).

170 *Rheno*: the Rhine formed a natural, and well-fortified, boundary: attempts to extend Roman territory to the Elbe had been a disastrous failure.

Histro: the Danube: Trajan had recently extended the boundary beyond the Danube,

but in Domitian's (or Nero's: see on 147) reign
it was still a frontier.

Neronem: Domitian apparently: see on 147.

171 *mitte*: 'send a message'; cf Cic.
Fam. 5, 20, 1, etc.

Ostia: 'to Ostia' (acc. pl. n.), the port of
Rome, from where he would sail for service
overseas.

172 *mitte*: the rhetorical device of
repetitio.

legatum: provincial governor: see on 88.
Note how *legatum* is verbally in *magna . . .
popina.*

popina: schol. *pro castris*: J has dared, and
triumphantly got away with a paraprosdokian
use of the same word twice (cf 158).

173 *percussore*: 'murderer'.
iacentem: 'at table'.

175 *sandapilarum*: a cheap bier for those
who could not afford a coffin; cf Suet. *Dom.*
17 *cadauer eius populari sandapila per
uespillones exportatum*: Mart. 2, 81, 2; 8,
75, 14 *angusta . . . sandapila*; 9, 2, 12.

176 'and the silent tambourines of a
eunuch priest of Cybele who is lying on his
back', i.e. he's in a drunken sleep: the
change from the people to the tambourines
is particularly effective.

177 *aequa . . . libertas*: the two great catch-
words of Greek democracy. J is not a democrat
or a revolutionary.

communia pocula: as Green says, this looks
like a sideswipe at Stoic egalitarianism. Seneca
in later life had a common board with his
slaves.

lectus: there is a mischievous double
meaning between *lectus tricliniaris* and *lectus
cubicularis,* common board and common
bed.

178 *alius*: 'different'.

179 *sortitus*: sc. *si sortitus sis.*

seruum: here the Stoic reference is ex-
plicit. To the Stoics the wise man is a king,
no matter if a slave; every one else is a slave,
no matter if a king. Lateranus is treated as a
king (161), but he is patently in Stoic
terms a *seruus.*

180 *Lucanos*: your estate in Lucania in
Southern Italy.

Tusca: the large chain-gangs started in
Etruria.

ergastula: slave-compounds or barracoons.
Hard labour in the chain-gangs on the estates
was a familiar punishment for slaves.

181 *Troiugenae*: cf. note on 1,100.

182 *turpia . . . decebunt*: there is a similar
phrase at 4, 13.

cerdoni: cf 4, 153. Originally a Greek
proper name (Herond. *Mim.* 6, 47-8; 7 passim;
Petron. 60; Mart. 3, 16; 3, 59, 1) common

among slaves or petty tradesmen such as
cobblers: in Latin a nickname for the latter
(cf Pers. 4, 51).

Volesos: Volesus Valerius traditionally
came to Rome with Tatius, and was ancestor
to the Valerii: Marcus Aurelius (4,33) uses
the name as an example of the once-famed,
now forgotten.

Brutum: L. Junius Brutus established the
Republic. J is panning their latterday des-
cendants not the forebears: the names
symbolise blue blood.

183-210 *This is bad enough, but there is
worse to come. Our nobles have actually
appeared in slapstick comedy — for money —
without being compelled by an autocrat.
What can you expect when the emperor
appears as a musician? There's nothing
beyond — except for Gracchus to appear in
the arena — and as a retiarius, without even
a helmet to disguise him, but with his
priest's cap and a gold ribbon.*

185 *Damasippe*: an odd name for J to
take, as it is obviously not that of any of the
old Roman nobility, and is in fact borrowed
from a bankrupt in Hor. *S* 2, 3. It comes
ultimately from Greek legend (a brother of
Penelope) and history (one of Philip II's
generals).

186 *sipario*: schol. *uelum sub quo latent
paradoxi cum in scenam prodeant*: it is not
to be confused with the *aulaeum*, which was
hoisted from under the stage: the *siparia*
were hung from above and used to divide
the set (Apul. *Met.* 1, 8; 10, 20): see M.
Bieber *History of the Greek and Roman
Theater* ed. 2 p. 180; we may tr. 'curtain'.
Seneca (*Tranq. An.* 11, 8) contrasts *cothur-
nus* (tragedy) with *siparium* (farce or mime)
which was played in front of such a curtain:
a relief in the Louvre (Bieber fig. 831)
shows just this.

clamosum: presumably the characters
screamed at the appearance of the ghost.

Phasma: The Ghost: title of plays by
Philemon, Theognetus and Menander, the
last tr. into Latin by Lavinius Luscus (Ter.
Eun. prol. 10). Plautus *Mostellaria* is an
adaptation, perhaps of Philemon's.

Catulli: not the lyric poet of the Republic,
but a writer of mimes under Nero, cf 13,
111; Mart. 5, 30, 3 *facundi scena Catulli.*

187 *Laureolum*: a play, presumably melo-
dramatic, also by Catullus (Tert. *Valent.* 14),
on the life and execution of a bandit of this
name (Jos. *Ant.* 19, 1, 13), which became
popular in Caligula's reign (Suet. *Cal.* 57).
Apparently the robber was caught and
crucified, escaped somehow from the cross,
but died of his wounds. This is the only way

to reconcile the accounts. It was a gory
piece, with much blood flowing. Martial
gives an account of an actual criminal playing
the role and being crucified at the end (*Epig.
Lib.* 7, 4 *non falsa pendens in cruce Laur-
eolus*). The melodrama enjoyed a good run:
we should not now remember, say, *Maria
Marten* except through revivals.

uelox: perhaps because Laureolus was a
fugitiuus; cf. 13, 111.

Lentulus: one of the distinguished family
of the Lentuli Cornelii.

188 *cruce*: the punishment for slaves,
bandits and revolutionaries. Note how the
bucolic diaeresis picks out the previous
words.

189 *ignoscas*: 'should you pardon'.

populo: i.e. the spectators.

durior: 'pretty brazen', an idiomatic use
of the comp.

190 *triscurria patricionum*: a resounding
phrase: *tri-* is intensive; cf. Plaut. *Rud.* 735
trifurcifer.

191 *planipedes*: 'flatfoot': actors in mime
wore no shoe. This is the normal word for
them; cf Atta *Aedilicia* fr. 1 *exultat planipes*;
Aul. Gell 1, 11, 12 *planipedi saltanti*; Auson.
Ep. 11. Plautus has the same meaning.

Fabios: cf 2, 146.

ridere potest qui: the offbeat rhythm
stresses the lack of decorum.

192 *Mamercorum*: a branch of the gens
Aemilia, tracing their ancestry back to a
Mamercus, son of king Numa. Grammatically
they may be at the giving or receiving end,
but plainly the sense is the latter.

alapas: i.e. knockabout slapstick.

quanti: 'for how much', gen. of price.

sua funera: a beautiful ambiguity, which
has exercised commentators because they
insist on choosing between meanings and
forget the poetical function of ambiguity
(see William Empson's classic *Seven Types
of Ambiguity*, and for an analysis based on
a classical play J. Ferguson 'Ambiguity in
Ajax' *Dioniso* 44 (1970) 12-29). The
primary meaning is no doubt their stage-
deaths, but it also refers to their moral
degradation, and it forms an easy transition
to the arena (200-1). I am less certain of the
suggested meaning 'their distinguished dead',
'their ancestry', but this may be an additional
layer of meaning. The one thing they do not
offer is their real death (195).

193 *Nerone*: see Tac. *Ann.* 14, 14, 8-10
where Nero uses their poverty as a lever to
bring down-and-out aristocrats on to the
stage.

194 *celsi*: because he appeared on a high
tribunal; cf 10, 37 *sublimem*. Later *celsitudo*

became an honorific title, precisely 'your
eminence'.

ludis: abl. 'at the shows'. Augustus in 22
BC transferred responsibility for public
entertainment from the aediles to the
praetors (Dio Cass. 54, 2).

195 *gladios*: 'execution'.

196 *quid* 'which?'.

sit. i.e. *esse uelit*.

197 *zelotypus*: the jealous husband, a
stock character, like Ford in Shakespeare's
Merry Wives of Windsor.

Thymeles: actress, cf 1, 36.

stupidi: the buffoon, another stock
character.

collega: 'partner', ironical.

Corinthi: actor.

198 *citharoedo principe*: cf 148
mulio consul. Nero was proud of his musician-
ship, though his voice was seemingly some-
what thin. He performed at the Ludi
Iuuenales in AD 59, and in the Theatre of
Pompey in AD 65 (Tac. *Ann.* 16, 4; cf 14,
15), and subsequently in Greece where he
carried off all the prizes (see on 226). He
was hurt by the lampoon *dum tendit citharam
noster, dum cornua Parthus* (Suet. *Nero* 39)
and by Vindex calling him *citharoedum
malum* (*ib.* 41). His dying words were
qualis artifex pereo 'What an artist the world
is losing!' (*ib.* 49). But what of Hadrian
(SHA 14)?

199 *ludus*: gladiatorial training-school.

200 *murmillonis*: a gladiator in Gaulish
armour, named from a fish on his visored
helmet, often opposed to the *retiarius* with
his net and trident; cf 6, 81.

201 *clipeo*: the shield, characteristic of
the Threx, another highly-armed gladiator.

Gracchum: we have met him at 2, 117.

et: Nisbet for *aut*.

falce supina. a scimitar, a curved sword
(here called a 'sickle') also characteristic of
the Threx, and a Thracian invention, called
harpe (Clem. Al. *Strom.* 1, 16, 75).

202-3 Omission proposed by Hermann:
if we retain it, it means 'he not merely speaks
against them: he positively dislikes them'.

203 *tridentem*: the weapon of the
retiarius, cf 6, 011: he tried to entangle
his opponent in his net and finish him off
with spear or dagger.

205 *spectacula*: i.e. the spectators.

207-8 *aurea . . . spira*: 'a ribbon of gold':
he retains a show of being different.

208 *galero*: the mitre worn by the Salii
(priests of Mars), which Gracchus dares to
wear in the arena to give him Mars's pro-
tection (see J. Colin in *Les études class.* 23
(1955) 409-15).

210 *secutor*: the heavily-armed opponent of the *retiarius*. J suggests that he is ashamed to be pitted against such a mountebank.

211-30 *Anyone with a free vote would opt for Seneca rather than Nero. He was a multiple murderer. Orestes killed his mother, but with good cause, and without killing his sister or wife, or poisoning his relatives, or singing on the stage. Nero prostituted himself in Greece. He can offer his musical trophies to his ancestors.*

212 *Senecam*: L. Annaeus Seneca (c. 2 BC - AD 65), a millionaire Stoic, had been Nero's tutor and was effectively regent at the beginning of his reign. He was unpopular because of his wealth and power, and because his behaviour did not seem fully to accord with his professions. (See J. Ferguson 'Seneca the Man' in D.R. Dudley (ed.) *Neronians and Flavians: Silver Latin I* pp. 1-23). His *Letters* (really essays on ethical subjects), always sententious, often noble, scintillatingly but tiresomely epigrammatic, are his greatest legacy, together with the rhetorical tragedies which deeply influenced Renaissance drama. He was driven to suicide after the conspiracy of Piso: it is unlikely that he was involved, but he was an obvious candidate for the succession (Tac. *Ann.* 15, 65). Some have seen a covert allusion to the death of the Stoic consular C. Avidius Nigrinus under Hadrian.

213 *non ... una*. i.e. 'more than one'.

214 The traditional penalty for parricide was to be scourged, sewn up in a leather sack with a dog, cock, snake and monkey (supposedly parricidal animals: like with like), and thrown into the sea (Dig. 48, 9, 9). For a full account see Cic. *Rosc. Am.* 22, 62-26, 73. Nero had been responsible for the death of his adoptive father Claudius, his adoptive brother Britannicus, his adoptive sister Antonia, his mother Agrippina (who muttered *occidat dum imperet*), his aunt Domitia Lepida, another aunt Domitia, his wife Octavia, and his second wife Poppaea, all of which would fall within *parricidium*.

215 *Agamemnonidae*: a sonorous patronymic for Orestes, whose mother Clytemnestra had killed his father Agamemnon: Orestes had the authority of the Delphic Oracle (*deis auctoribus*) urging him to revenge his father's murder even though it meant killing his mother. To Aeschylus the story created a theological and social problem, a justified action which extended the spiral of violence still further; to Sophocles it provided a moving drama with high dramatic irony; to Euripides it was a crime and the murderers were pathological; each produced a differently

powerful play.

217 *media inter pocula*: so Hom. *Od.* 11, 409-11; in Aeschylus he is killed in his bath.

218 *Electrae*: his sister: Nero killed Antonia. Two heavy names frame the line.

218-9 *Spartani ... coniugii*: 'his Spartan wife' impersonal for personal, as often. Orestes m. Hermione, d. of Menelaus and Helen. Nero killed his wives.

219 *aconita*: Claudius and Britannicus were poisoned.

220 *Oresten*: an excellent emendation by C.P. Jones (*CR* 23(1972) 313); cf Suet. *Nero* 21 *inter cetera cantauit ... Oresten matricidam*. It is an effective thought that Orestes was Orestes in real life and did not play Orestes on the stage. The MS *Orestes* is very weak in view of the preceding *ille*.

221 *Troica*: an epic (Dio Cass. 62, 29). Suetonius (*Nero* 52) had seen an autograph of some of Nero's poetry. See also Tac. *Ann.* 13, 3; 14, 16 for Nero's verse. A flattering contemporary ranked him above Vergil (*Einsied. Ecl.* 1, 48-9); Martial called him *doctus* (8, 70, 8). Only four lines survive, three on the source of R. Tigris (schol. in Lucan 3, 261), one about doves' feathers ruffled in the wind (Sen. *QN* 1, 5, 6 *colla Cytheriacae splendent agitata columbae*). His poem on the Trojan War had Paris as hero (Serv. on Verg. *A* 5, 770). We cannot judge his verse; he had genuine merit as a singer. Serious-minded moralists have accused J of a lack of proportion. Orestes was unlike Nero in that (a) his motive in killing his mother was different: he had divine authority for avenging his father, (b) he did not murder his sister or wife, (c) he did not use poison (d) he did not perform on the stage or write poetry. It is a marvellous satirical climax, at once funny and biting.

Verginius: L. Verginius Rufus, one of the more impressive men of the century, was governor of Germania Superior. In 68 Julius Vindex, governor of Gallia Lugdunensis, rose against Nero. Verginius in fact suppressed that revolt: he also refused to be nominated emperor himself (see *CIL* 5, 5702 *IOVI O M PRO SALVTE ET VICTORIA L. VERGINI RVFI.*) But he did not oppose Galba's principate (see on 2, 104) He lived through till 97; his funeral panegyric was given by Tacitus (Plin. *Ep.* 2, 1, 6). He left his own epitaph *hic situs est Rufus, pulso qui Vindice quondam/imperium asseruit non sibi sed patriae (ib.* 6, 10, 4).

222 *cum Vindice Galba*: see previous note.

224 *generosi*: back to the theme of blue blood.

artes: a beautifully ambiguous term

'accomplishments'.

225 *peregrina ad pulpita*: he travelled in Greece in AD 67-8, performing as he went.

226 *prostitui*: 'to prostitute himself': the sexual parallelism is explicit.

apium: a wreath of parsley was the victor's reward at the Nemean games (Plin.*NH* 19, 46, 158), and at the Isthmian (Plut. *Q. Conv.* 5, 676C): it is here taken of all such prizes: J is being contemptuous. Nero brought back 1808 prizes: he said that that Greeks were the only knowledgeable audience (Suet. *Ner.* 22 *solos scire audire Graecos*).

227-30 A brilliant ending to the section, bringing us right back to the theme of the ancestors.

228 *Domiti*: Nero was born into the gens Domitia: before his adoption by Claudius his name was L. Domitius Ahenobarbus. This Domitius is presumably the originator of the clan.

Thyestae: a tragic part performed by Nero (Dio. Cass. 63, 23, 6); cf 7, 73.

229 *syrma*: the tragic actor's robe with a long train; cf 15, 30; Hor. *AP* 215 *traxitque uagus per pulpita uestem.*

Antigones: note the Greek gen.: d. of Oedipus and Jocasta, and heroine of Sophocles *Antigone* where she confronts her uncle king Creon with the irreligion of his decree to refuse burial to Polynices. Nero himself wrote a tragedy on the theme (Philostr. *V. Ap.* 4, 39, 2).

Melanippe: d. of Aeolus and Eurydice, she had two children by Poseidon. Euripides wrote two lost plays about her, *Melanippe the Wise* (which Ennius adapted) and *Melanippe in Chains.*

230 *colosso*: Nero had a colossal statue of himself thirty-six metres tall, in the Domus Aurea but it was of bronze (Suet. *Ner.* 31; Plin. *NH* 34, 18, 45). J may have been confused, or may just be girding at Nero's megalomania. Nero did make such offerings (Suet. *Ner.* 12).

231-68 *Catiline and Cethegus were nobly-born criminals: Cicero, from Arpinum, not a noble, saved Rome and won the title 'father of his country'. Another from Arpinum, Marius, saved Rome from the Cimbri, and won more glory than his noble colleague. The Decii were plebeians: Servius Tullius was born of a slave. But the consul's sons tried to betray Rome - and it was a slave who saved Rome by informing against them.*

231 *Catilina*: the profligate and revolutionary: see on 2, 27: he was a member of the gens Sergia.

Cethegus: of the gens Cornelia: coupled with Catiline at 2, 27.

232 *arma tamen uos*: the bucolic diaeresis and offbeat rhythm add stress to these words.

234 *ut*: 'like'.

bracatorum: the toga-wearing Romans looked as askance at the trousered Gauls as trousered Europeans do at kilted Scots. Gallia Narbonensis was actually known as Gallia Bracata.

Senonum: the Gallic tribe which sacked Rome in 390 BC. The point is intensified by the fact that Catiline and Cethegus allied themselves to the Gallic Allobroges.

235 *tunica . . . molesta*: a shift soaked in pitch and worn by a condemned criminal who was tied to a stake and set on fire as a human torch: first used against the Christians charged with arson in AD 64 (Tac. *Ann.* 15, 44): see also 1, 155. See further Sen. *Ep.* 14, 5; Mart. 4, 86, 8 (of a wrapping for fried fish); 10, 25, 5; Tert. *Mart.* 5 (*tunica ardente*). There is a Mikado-like thought that this is an appropriate penalty for arson.

236 *uigilat consul*: Cicero, consul in 63 BC: he uses the verb himself (*Cat.* 1, 8). There is a contrast with Lateranus, awake for frivolity.

237 *nouus*: a *nouus homo* was the first of his family to attain curule office: Cic. was proud of this (*Leg. Agr.* 2 ,3 and often), though it was frequently thrown in his face. (*Sull.* 7, 22; *Att.* 1, 16, 10). The historian Velleius Paterculus called him in an excellent oxymoron *uir nouitatis nobilissimae* (2, 34, 3). This is J's point: Cicero was noble; Catiline, the nobly-born, was not. Coffey (*Roman Satire* 138) regards J's treatment of the *nouus homo* as a 'suspect sentimentality': he refers to Tac. *Ann.* 3, 53 for the imperial reality, and Val. Max 3, 4; Sen. Eld. *Contr.*2, 4, 13 for rhetorical *exempla.* See also J. Vogt *Homo Novus* (Stuttgart 1926) and Paully-Wissowa sv. *Novus Homo.*

Arpinas: he was born, like C. Marius, at Arpinum, somewhat to the east of Rome. He is in fact called *homo nouus Arpinas* in the attack on him by Pseudo-Sallust (3, 4), as also *Romule Arpinas* (ib. 4, 7; Quint. 9, 3, 89).

ignobilis: i.e. not accepted by the nobiles.

238 *muncipalis*: a small-town man trying to make good in the big city. J could claim the same.

eques: belonging to the second property group by birth, with a qualification of 400 000 sesterces, and being not less than the third generation of freeborn citizens. Cicero is proud to call himself *equitis Romani filio consule* (*Mur.* 8, 17). Pliny the Elder dates the revival of this class to Cicero's consulate (*NH* 33, 8, 34).

239 *attonitis*: 'the Romans in their terror'.

omni monte: the seven hills of Rome.

laborat: this takes up and develops *uigilat* (236): there is an implicit comparison with Hercules, whose labours were undertaken for the service of mankind, to rid them of pests.

240 *toga*: statesmanship, opp, to military skill, though Cicero depended on military action for his triumph. J has in mind Cicero's own words in his poem on his consulship *cedant arma togae, concedat laurea laudi* (*Pis.* 30, 73; *Off.* 1, 22, 77).

241 *nominis ac tituli*: 'partitive' gen. with *tantum*.

sibi: Jahn for MS *in*: the schol. read *sub*.

Leucade: an island off the west coast of Greece. It is in fact some 45 km south of Actium, the promontory sacred to Apollo off which the future emperor Augustus secured his power by defeating the navies of Antony and Cleopatra in 31 BC.

242 *Thessaliae campis*: J is referring to the battle of Philippi, on the Macedonian coast, where in 42 BC Octavian and Antony defeated the 'liberators' Brutus and Cassius. Thessaly was the scene of the earlier battle of Pharsalia, the decisive encounter between Julius Caesar and Pompey in 48 BC: Roman geography tends to be vague at best of times: this particular muddle is due to Vergil *G* 1, 489-92. The Romans are not alone in such confusion: an Englishman who asked a Canadian friend to meet his daughter at Montreal received the reply 'Meet her yourself: you're nearer.'

Octavius: C. Octavius, on adoption by Caesar became C. Julius Caesar Octavianus, and was in fact known as Caesar: Antony remarked bitterly that he owed everything to his name. He received the name Augustus in 27 BC. J takes him down by the name: even the greatest of emperors is not spared.

abstulit: neatly contrasted with *contulit* (240).

243 *caedibus . . . gladio*: there is an awkward·collocation of datives and ablatives. I take *sibi* dat. of advantage 'for himself', *Leucade* and *campis* locative, *gladio* instrumental, *caedibus* abl. of source or origin depending on *udo*.

243-4 *sed*: a strong contrast: 'but Rome was free when she called Cicero her parent — yes, the father of his country.' Note the rhetorical *repetitio*. For *parentem* see Cic. *Att.* 9, 10; for *patrem patriae*, accorded him by Q. Catulus, see Plut. *Cic.* 23; App. *BC* 2, 7; Cic. *Fam.* 15, 4, 2; *Sest.* 57, 121; *Pis.* 3, 6. (Despite Plutarch he was not the first to be so called, and it was not moved by Cato.) Cicero gave both titles to C. Marius, so that

they form an effective point of transition (*Pro Rab.* 10, 27). Augustus received the title on 5 Feb. 2 BC (*Res Gestae* 35; cf Ov. *F* 2, 127 *sancte pater patriae, tibi plebs tibi curia nomen/hoc dedit*). But J's point is that Augustus was an autocrat, and controlled the senate.

245 *Arpinas alius*: C. Marius (157-86 BC), tribune 119, praetor 115, consul in 107 (the first of seven times). He defeated the invading Cimbri and Teutones at Aquae Sextiae in 102 and Vercellae in 101. He was a tough self-made countryman, who became a radical leader, the instrument of reform, and the tool of less scrupulous politicians.

Volscorum: Arpinum is in Volscian territory.

247 *frangebat . . . uitem*: we would say 'had the baton broken': he rose from the ranks: the centurion carried a baton of vine-wood.

249 *Cimbros*: see on 245: there is a kind of hendiadys: 'he faced danger to the state from the Cimbri'.

251 *Cimbros stragemque*: again hendiadys 'the piles of dead Cimbri'.

252 *maiora cadauera*: the Germanic peoples were appreciably taller than the Italians: the Romans spoke of them as giants (Plut. *Mar.* 11; Diod. Sic. 37, 1, 5; Sen. *Ira* 1, 11, 1-2; Tac. *Germ.* 20).

253 *nobilis . . . collega*: his aristocratic fellow-consul Q. Lutatius Catulus, who was pushed into the background, partly by Marius's unusual personality and ability, partly by the desire for democratic reforms. J's point is that in those days achievement counted for more than birth. In actual fact the soldiers refused to let Marius have his triumph unless Catulus shared in it (Plut. *Mar.* 27; Cic. *TD* 5, 19, 56).

254 *Deciorum*: in 340 BC Rome was fighting the Latins. The two consuls were warned in a dream that one of them was claimed by the gods of the dead and the Earth Mother. In a ceremony known as *devotio* P. Decius Mus offered himself with a long formula invoking Janus, Jupiter, Father Mars, Quirinus, Bellona, Lares, Divi Novensiles, Di Indigetes, unnamed gods (a common precaution) and finally Di Manes, and ending *pro republica populi Romani Quiritium, exercitu, legionibus, auxiliis populi Romani Quiritium, legiones auxiliaque hostium mecum Dis Manibus Tellurique deuoueo* (Liv. 8, 9, 8). He then plunged into the thick of battle oblivious to danger. His son performed the same act in the battle of Sentinum in 295 during the Samnite wars (Liv. 10, 28, 15). They were

(obviously) a plebeian family.

255 *pro*: for the final prep. cf 5, 33; 6, 58.

257 *dis infernis*: the Di Manes, the collective power of the dead, honoured at the Feralia, Parentalia and Lemuria (Cic. *Laws* 2, 9, 22 *deorum maniurh iura sacra sunto*); later applied to the ancestral gods of a family, and later still to the divine power of a dead individual.

Terraeque parenti: the Roman Earth Mother worshipped as Tellus or Terra Mater, honoured at the *feriae sementivae* (the movable festival of sowing) and at the Fordicidia on 15 April, powerfully represented on the Ara Pacis Augustae. See in general F. Altheim *Terra Mater*.

258 *pluris*: gen. of value 'worth more'. Many editors delete the line.

259 *ancilla natus*: Servius Tullius, the sixth king of Rome, who is perhaps more authentic than this story of his birth; cf 7, 201; Liv 1, 39.

trabeam: the royal toga: Servius on Verg. *A* 7, 612 distinguishes this, *quod est purpureum, habet tamen album aliquid,* from two other forms of *trabea.*

Quirini: the divine power of the Romans in peaceful assembly (*Quirites*), forming a trinity with Jupiter and Mars, later as here identified with the founding father Romulus.

260 *bonorum*: early Roman history was viewed simplistically in the mood satirised by the authors of *1066 and All That*: kings were Good or Bad.

261 *prodita laxabant*: 'intended to betray and open': note the force of the impf.

tyrannis: Tarquinius Superbus, ousted traditionally in 509 BC, and his family.

262 *iuuenes*: 'sons'; cf 3, 158: *filii* does not fit into a dactylic hexameter.

consulis: Brutus, the Liberator and first consul, whose sons were executed on his authority for plotting to restore the Tarquins (Liv. 2, 3-6). There is a fine painting of his decision by David in the Louvre dating from 1789, a piece of revolutionary rationalism.

263 *dubia*: not yet safely established.

deceret: vivid for *decuisset*: see on 4, 85.

264 *Coclite*: Horatius Cocles whose 'keeping the bridge' against Lars Porsenna's attempt to reinstate the Tarquins was stirringly narrated by Lord Macaulay in *Lays of Ancient Rome* (Liv. 2, 10).

Mucius: C. Mucius made an unsuccessful foray to assassinate Lars Porsenna: on being captured he voluntarily put his right hand into the fire to show that torture would not shake him: he and his descendants took the cognomen Scaevola ('Lefty') (Liv. 2, 12-3).

265 *imperii finis*: acc. pl. in apposition t' *Tiberinum.*

Tiberinum: sc. *amnem* but we can tr. 'the Tiber': the Romans, like us, say 'swam the Tiber'.

uirgo: Cloelia, a hostage, who led a mass-escape by swimming the Tiber (Liv. 2, 13).

266 *seruus*: Vindicius, who informed against Brutus's sons (Liv. 2, 5).

267 *matronis lugendus*: as they ceremonially mourned Brutus and Valerius.

268 *legum prima*: the first constitutional execution: previously executions had been at the sovereign's whim.

269-75 *Better to be an Achilles born of Thersites than a Thersites born of Achilles. In any case, trace your ancestry right back, you'll find either shepherds or the unmentionable to whom Romulus gave sanctuary.*

269 *malo . . . Thersites*: a good epigram, picked out by the break at the end of the fourth foot. Thersites is the foul-mouthed butt of the Homeric heroes (Hom. *Il.* 2, 216): the contrast with Achilles recurs at 7, 30-1.

270 *Aeacidae*; patronymic applied to Achilles, Aeacus's grandson (Hom. *Il.* 18,221): Achilles was the swiftest-footed and finest fighter among the Greeks at Troy.

Volcania: Patroclus, Achilles's friend, was killed while wearing Achilles's armour: his mother Thetis got him new armour from Hephaestus (= Volcanus), the fire-god (Hom. *Il.* 18, 369-616). The phrase *Volcania arma* is taken from Verg. *A* 8,535; 12, 739; cf Cic. *TD* 2, 14, 33.

272 *ut*: 'although'; *tamen* is placed in an anticipatory position, and goes with *deducis,* picking up the clause.

273 *ab infami . . . asylo*: to fill his new city Romulus proclaimed a sanctuary on the Capitoline hill, and that gang was the first step to Rome's future greatness (Liv. 1, 8-9).

275 *pastor*: like Romulus.

illud quod dicere nolo: schol. with less reticence and less imagination *seruus aut infamis uel latro*: Highet thinks the unspoken word is 'thief' and links this to the thought that provincial governors should not be rapacious (89-134). No doubt this is part of the meaning, but J leaves the total enormity to us and to Ponticus to envisage. J's is a superbly debunking conclusion.

General comments

The eighth seems different from the other satires. It is more deliberate, more sustained, more consistent. It is a piece of persuasive oratory, unremitting and effective. The initial statement of theme – *stemmata quid faciunt?* – is immediate and direct. No other satire begins like it. The theme is consistently held.

The idea that nobility consists in virtue not birth is a philosophical theme of the Hellenistic period, found particularly among Cynics and Stoics (see e.g. Diog. Laert. 4, 46-7; Sen *Ep.* 44. J certainly knew and may be using the latter). From them it made its way into the Roman schools of rhetoric as a standard topic for show speeches (Sen. Eld. *Contr.* 1, 6; Val. Max. 3, 4-5). Horace had dealt with it in *Epode* 4 in which he criticises those who rank idiots with a family tree above intelligent nobodies. J develops it rhetorically, yet at the same time with mordant and pessimistic satire. His originality may be seen in the way in which the staring presence of the ancestral masks is seen not as an incitement to virtue, but as a frowning condemnation of vice.

The poem is meticulously constructed: we have noted the rhetorical structure, and the interplay between favourable and unfavourable *exempla*. But the individual sections are also carefully composed. A good example may be seen in the series of *exempla mala*. J begins from Lateranus, whose fondness for horses and low haunts is treated at length. Lateranus, at least in office, operates under cover of darkness. Damasippus appears on the stage openly to recoup the money he has wasted. Gracchus goes one stage lower, appearing as a gladiator, flaunting his priest's cap and gold ribbon, showing his face to all. (These last two are treated at equal length.) Nero combines exhibitionism with murder: he receives as much as Damasippus and Gracchus put together. The climax is treachery – mass murder against the state. It is represented by Catiline and Cethegus, and again by the sons of Brutus, both briefly and summarily treated, since there is no need for elaboration.

Effects are carefully prepared. Nero is mentioned in the context of Damasippus, preparing us for the indictment of the emperor himself. Catiline leads us to Cicero, Cicero to Marius (also from Arpinum), Marius, who rose from the ranks, to the plebeian Decii, and so by going back in time we are able unobtrusively to reach the end of the monarchy and the beginning of the Republic and renew the theme of treachery with Brutus's sons. Even this last has been prepared by the earlier mention of Brutus (182). Similar links between different parts of the poem are achieved by the repetition of poison (17; 219) and of *uirgas* (22;

136; 153), and by the use of *generosi* of Nero (224) reminding us that the theme is consistent.

In the light of this deliberate structure those who have charged J with a lack of proportion in the stress he lays on Lateranus's horsy activities and Nero's musical showmanship are accusing him not of carelessness but of a false sense of values. Some would answer that J is merely showing wit, and has no serious intention. I do not think that that is right. But a satirist operates through trivialities. In Satire 4 Domitian deliberates about the cutting up of a big fish: he thought nothing of cutting up the world: the word *orbem* underlines the point. Here the climax of Nero's crimes is that he sang the part of Orestes. There is a double point. It *is* witty to say 'He was worse than a murderer: he was a mountebank.' But there is a second point as well. Just as Domitian deliberated over the fish and thought nothing of what he did to the world, so Nero put all his effort and enthusiasm into playing Orestes on the stage, and thought nothing of killing his mother in real life.

It has often been pointed out that J succeeds in introducing into this satire a large number of the great families of Rome. We have the Aemilii (3; 9), Curii (4), Sulpicii (5), Valerii (5), Fabii (14), Cornelii (21; 105; 231), Claudii (21), Iunii (27), Antonii (38; 105), Domitii (228), Sergii (231), Iulii (242). This is deliberately and carefully contrived. J is exposing the whole aristocracy including the imperial house. That the majority of his examples come from the past does not weaken the present force of his indictment. He intends to focus attention on Nero for obvious reasons: it is equally natural that some of his examples will cluster round Nero. But there are some unsolved problems in his treatment. The very name Ponticus is one. We do not know whether he is real or imaginary. He *could* be real: the name existed. The odd thing is that it is not an ancient aristocratic name. Perhaps this is part of the point. Ponticus doesn't need to invent ancestors. Then the movement from Ponticus to Rubellius Blandus is unexpected. It might be effective if we knew more about this Rubellius Blandus, but J's account doesn't fit the only Rubellius Blandus we know. Again the name does not belong to the purest of the blue-blooded: the family tree rose from the *equites*. A third puzzle relates to Damasippus (185), which is a Greek name, not from the Roman aristocracy at all. Presumably it conceals a real person, whom J's readers would recognise: there may be a connection with Lateranus, since the name means 'Horse-Tamer' or something like it: perhaps J is for once going at one of his contemporaries under a pseudonym, a son of Lateranus, who has sunk lower than his father.

Highet comments on J's serious interest in the Roman aristocracy in this poem: he regards it as a constructive attempt to raise the standards of provincial government. I do not so see it. Certainly J has a serious purpose and a positive message, as he has in 10, doubtfully in 7, and certainly not in 6 or 9. This is *nobilitas sola est atque unica uirtus* (20). But the poem, like others, is an indictment, and if Ponticus is an invention, he is merely a peg on which to hang an indictment. The *bona exempla* are not the blue-blooded aristocracy: they are equites, plebeians, even slaves. Fredericks is surely right in terming the satire humorously cynical, but not morally hopeful.

The poem has fewer visual pictures than some, but the section on Lateranus is full of them — the man himself driving by moonlight, or acknowledging an elderly acquaintance with a flick of his whip; the greasy Syrian welcoming him subserviently; the eunuch sprawling on his back among his tambourines. The epigrams are less scintillating and more elaborate than sometimes. This is partly because the indictment is more elaborate: there is epigrammatic irony in his desire not to have his point dismissed as an epigram (125). So 140-1 or 227-30 are extended not concise. But there are brilliances. We do not forget *stemmata quid faciunt?* (1) or *nobilitas sola est atque unica uirtus* (20) or *et propter uitam uiuendi perdere causas* (84) or *mulio consul* (148: I suspect that some of the anger against's J's 'triviality' comes from a sense of being conned by his epigram) or *malo pater tibi sit Thersites, dummodo tu sis/ Aeacidae similis* 269-70); and to achieve a paraprosdokian twice on *popina* is a masterly double twist (158; 172). But on the whole it is the thought in this piece which we value: the expression does not carry him away: it remains secondary to the thought. In this light the conclusion may well appear the most brilliant in any of the satires.

Bibliography
Fredericks, S.C. 'Rhetoric and Morality in Juvenal's 8th Satire' *TAPA* 102 (1971) 111-32

SATIRE 9

This is the only one of J's satires to fall into the form of a dialogue. In theme it is close to Satire 2, and treats homosexuality: this led Highet to suppose that it was an early satire held back and pulled out again to complete the third book. This may be right. But the writing bears no signs of immaturity or uncertainty, and H.A. Mason has argued that in this satire we have quintessential Juvenal.

J meets a pervert named Naevolus, who has been living as 'husband' of an aristocratic pervert named Virro. It is an ugly, sordid subject and J presents it without moralising, and lets the stench of corruption speak for itself. This is indeed one of the most powerful of the satires.

The dialogue creates the structure, which is clear in its broad outlines, though there is a passage about a third of the way through where it is hard to be certain who is addressing whom.

1-26   Juvenal questions Naevolus about his unhappiness.
27-90a   Naevolus explains his patron's meanness.

90b-91   Juvenal interjects, asking Virro's answer.
92-101   Naevolus says that with his secret his life in in danger.
102-23   Juvenal says (a little sententiously) that servants will always gossip.
124-9   Naevolus reasserts his own concern about the future.
130-4   Juvenal replies that he needn't worry: there'll always be perverts.
135-50   Naevolus expresses his hope to retire with a small business.

There is no obvious symmetricality about this, as the following table shows:

J	26	1½	22(18)	5
N	64½	10	6	16

Basically Juvenal sets the scene: for the rest Naevolus makes the running. But Juvenal has a sententious comment about the exposure of the rich to their servants' gossip, and a mordant comment on the corruption of Rome which is the real climax of the piece.

1-26   *Why are you so grim, Naevolus, like*

Marsyas, or a sex-maniac caught in the act, or a spendthrift without a taker? You used to be a regular man-about-town. Now you've lost your sparkle and trimness. You used to be always hanging round temples to pick up women — or their husbands.

1 *Scire uelim*: a direct personal beginning 'I should like to know'.

Naeuole: the name occurs several times in Martial (1, 97; 2, 46; 3, 71; 3, 95; 4, 83) but none corresponds: the character in book 3 is a passive pervert.

tristis: like the pseudo-Stoics of Satire 2, but for a different reason.

2 *occurras*: 'bump into'.

Marsya: a satyr who claimed to be a better musician than Apollo. Apollo defeated him, and then flayed him alive. The scene was noted in art. There was a version in the forum at Rome (Hor. *S* 1, 6, 120; Mart. 2, 64, 8). See further on 12-5. Rev. Prof. Charles Raven was similarly described as looking like St Sebastian just after the first arrow had struck him. The scholiast identifies Marsyas with a contemporary lawyer; if so there is also direct innuendo.

3 *quid tibi*: idiomatic: Ov. *F* 1, 253 *nil mihi cum bello*; Mart 1, 77 *quid tibi cum Cyrrha?*

4 *Rauola*: the name (as the scholiast indicates) is derived from *rauulus* 'hoarse'.

Rhodopes: a Greek name; clearly a prostitute. The name is taken from Aesop's fellow-slave, Rhodopis, a Thracian, who was ransomed from slavery by Sappho's brother Charaxus, and acquired a large fortune in Egypt through her charms.

5 Jachmann argued that this was an attempt to replace what has gone before by a more respectable expression. Cf. Lucil. fr. 23, 1; Hor. *S* 1, 3, 81. Humphries, ingeniously: 'If a slave takes a lick at a tart, we always give him a licking.' Green's version is almost identical.

6-7 *Crepereius Pollio*: a spendthrift, offering three times the normal interest rate for a loan; cf. 11, 43. The normal rate was 1% per month.

8-9 *unde repente tot rugae?*: the bucolic diaeresis, and the three long syllables at the start of the next line, emphasise these words.

9-10 *agebas uernam equitem*: 'You played the part of a provincial squire.' Martial has *equitibus uernis* at 1, 85.

11 *pomerium*: the religious boundary marking off the city (Liv. 1, 44; Aul. Gell. 13, 14) originally ploughed ceremonially with a bullock and heifer yoked, the sods falling inwards. The implication is that

Naevolus was a provincial; cf 13, 111

urbani . . . Catulli. Cicero speaks of 'urban wit'.

12-5 Apuleius *Flor.* 1, 3, 12 describes Marsyas *barbarus, uultu ferino trux, hispidus, illutibarbus, spinis et pilis obsitus,.*

12-3 *siccae . . . comae*: Theocritus 14, 4 has 'dried-up curls' as a sign of depression.

14 *Bruttia*: pitch from Bruttium, from the pine-trees of Calabria, was well-known (Plin. *NH* 14, 20; 16, 11, etc.). Here it is a depilatory.

16-7 The style is mock-epic.

quarta: with reference to quartan fever, which recurs every three days; cf 4, 57.

18 J has Lucilius fr. 26, 55 in mind *animo qui aegrotat, uidemus corpore hunc signum dare.*

19 *sumit utrumque*: bucolic diaeresis picks out the epigram.

21 *propositum*: ironical, since it is often favourable.

22 *fanum Isidis*: in the Campus Martius outside the pomerium. The date is uncertain. A temple was voted in 43 BC, and one existed in Augustus's reign; this may have been rebuilt. The temple appears on a coin of Vespasian; it was destroyed by fire in AD 80 and restored by Domitian. The temple of Isis was notorious for assignations (cf 6, 489; Ov. *AA* 1, 77-8).

Ganymedem: four-syllable Greek name to end the line. He was Zeus's cupbearer, kidnapped to Olympus for his beauty, and his statue was an appropriate rendezvous for male homosexuals. The statue is not mentioned elsewhere.

23 *Pacis*: the Temple of Peace, built by Vespasian after the Jewish War, with famous statues (Plin. *NH* 34, 84; 36, 27).

aduectae . . . matris: Cybele, the Great Mother, whose worship was introduced in 204 BC (2, 111). Her religion was a mystery, requiring initiation. She had a grotto on the Palatine. The religion was for women only, and therefore an obvious place for wolvish men to watch.

24 *Cererem*: i.e. the temple of Ceres. On the slopes of the Aventine; the exact site has not been found. It traditionally dates to 493 BC: Liber and Libera were coupled with Ceres. It was destroyed by fire in 31 BC, restored and rededicated in AD 17.

25 *Aufidio*: A jurist Aufidius Chius is mentioned by Martial (5, 61, 16).

27-69 *'I'm getting nothing out of my profession. Pansies may be proverbially attractive, but they're no use if they don't pay. Virro keeps telling me he's paid me.*

*It's hard work, and we have to give him
Ladies' Day presents. He's got huge estates —
but none to spare for us — tells me off for
asking. It's my rent, my slave's keep that do
the asking! I need another slave; when they
shiver in winter, have I to tell them to wait
for the spring?'*

27   *utile*: an ironically Epicurean term.
It shows where Naevolus's real interests
lie: in his purse.

at mihi nullum: the bucolic diaeresis picks
out these words and gives them weight.

28   *pingues*: 'greasy'; *pinguis* of a cloak
usually means thick-woven (Mart. 4, 19, 1;
6, 11, 7); there is a double meaning.

lacernas: the perquisite of the *cliens* (Hor.
Ep. 1, 19, 38 *tritae munere uestis;* Pers. 1,
54; Mart. 12, 74, 4; all are 'worn'.)

30   *Galli*: French weaves were rough and
coarse (Mart. 4, 19, 1).

31   The silver he receives is wafer-thin and
of poor quality.

32   *fata*: Epicurean utilitarianism hasn't
paid him; the only answer can be Stoic
determinism. Note how this accords with
tristis (9, 1).

32-3   *partibus illis quas sinus abscondit*: a
nice touch. Naevolus's behaviour is frank,
his language circumlocutory. *Sinus* are the
front folds of the cloak; cf Petron. 24.

sidera: astrology was popular at this
period, and the Stoics fostered it. There
was some ambiguity in the official attitude.
Astrologers (*Chaldaei, mathematici*) were
expelled from Rome in AD 16, 52, 69 and
93, but Thrasyllus enjoyed the confidence of
Tiberius, and his son Balbillus was an *amicus*
of Claudius, and Prefect of Egypt under
Nero; cf 6, 553; 10, 94.

33-7   There is a parallel to this repellent
picture in Petronius 92, 7-10.

34   cf 1, 41. *Incognita* = 'unparalleled'.

35   *Virro*: the name of the stingy host in
the fifth satire. The name is provincial from
Juvenal's home district.

36   *tabellae*: 'love-letters': the assonant
endings of the words in this line express
the importunacy.

37   *αὐτὸς ... κίναιδος*: 'a man is drawn
forward by — a pansy', a parody of Hom.
Od. 16, 294; 19, 13; the device of the twisted
ending, the original last word being 'a sword',
naked steel as it were.

38   *monstrum*: an unnatural portent:
the word does not occur in the seventh or
eighth satires.

mollis auarus: both are strictly adjectives,
so the senses 'perverted miser' and 'miserly
pervert' jostle one another.

39   The miser's grouse. For the shape of

the line, cf Hor. *S* 1, 2, 120 *illam 'post paulo'
'sed pluris' 'si exierit uir'.*

40   *computat et ceuet*: a brilliant touch.
Alliteration on *c* is usually scornful.

43   An example of unconcealed verbal
obscenity.

45   The agricultural metaphor is common
of sex (Plaut. *Asin.* 5, 2, 24; Lucr. 4, 1272-
3; Mart. 1, 92, 12, etc.), but in agriculture,
as in normal sexual relations, ploughing
looks forward to harvesting.

46   Harsh rhythm at the end of the line.
Who is *tu*? Who is addressing whom?
Naevolus Virro? Naevolus himself? Virro
Naevolus? Or Juvenal Naevolus? It is hard
to be sure, harder because Ganymede was the
servant (Naevolus) but also the passive (Virro).
On the whole I take it to be Naevolus addres-
sing himself.

47   i.e. a Ganymede; cf 22.

48   *uos*: this clearly refers to Virro and his
kind, and is a thrust by Naevolus.

50   *tu*: this is Naevolus addressing himself.

umbellam: a rare word (Mart. 11, 73, 6,
otherwise medieval).

sucina: balls of amber, scented, which
ladies like to hold (6, 573).

51   *aut madidum uer*: offbeat rhythm.

cathedra: a woman's chair; cf 1, 65;
6, 91 *molles ... cathedras*; Mart. 3, 63, 7
femineas ... cathedras.

53   *femineis ... kalendis*: the Matronalia,
a festival on March 1, honouring Juno as a
women's goddess. The line is golden in form
with a verb and two pairs of noun + adj.

54   *passer*: the sparrow was sacred to
Venus, and had the reputation of being over-
sexed (Plin, *NH* 10, 107). So Chaucer of the
Somnour: 'As hoot he was and lecherous as a
sparwe.' Compare the sparrow in Catullus 2; 3.

55   *Apula*: Martial (10, 74, 8) similarly
commends the rich fields of Apulia.

miluos: some such association is proverbial
for large estates; cf Petr. 37; Pers. 4, 26.

56   *Trifolinus*: Trifolium in Campania
(Plin. *NH* 14, 8, 69). Martial did not think
much of the wine (13, 114).

57   *Cumis*: the earliest Greek colony in
Italy, near Naples (which it founded), home
of the Sibyl.

Gaurus: a mountain in Campania, now
Monte Barbaro; cf 8, 86. Statius (*S* 3, 5, 99)
writes of *Bacchei uineta madentia Gauri.*
Why *inanis*? Perhaps 'hollow', an extinct
volcano.

58   *uicturo*: that will live (vintage) or that
will conquer (strong).

59   *clientis*: an important word, for J is
attacking the *patronus—cliens* relationship.

62   *cymbala pulsantis*: the scholiast refers

this to a priest of Cybele (cf 6, 515; 8, 176).

legatum: 'a thing bequeathed', 'a bequest'.

63 *pensio*: 'rent'.

64 *puer*: slave, servant: the old colonial
'boy'. He can afford one only, and fears
that he soon won't be able to afford that;
cf 7, 69.

Polyphemi: the giant Polyphemus, the
Cyclops, had one eye, which Ulysses put
out (Hom. *Od.* 9, 106ff.).

68 *scapulis*: Seneca (*Ep.* 17, 10) has
uentri et scapulis as the parts that need
looking after, inside and out.

69 *durate*: parody of Verg. *A* 1, 207
durate et uosmet rebus seruate secundis.

cicadas: the cicada makes quite a startling
noise by rubbing its legs together, as is
familiar in Mediterrenean and tropical
countries. For the cicada as a sign of
summer, cf Ov. *AA* 1, 271.

69-91 *'Virro's wife would still be virgin
if it wasn't for me. He's a treacherous ingrate;
he owes me his son and daughter, and I'll
make it three if he wants.' You seem to have
a case. What's his answer?*

70 *ut*: 'although'.

76 *migrabat*: Highet in *CR* 2 (1972)
70-1 for MS *signabat.*

79-80 A cynical observation.

82 *ergo*: the *o* is long in J only here and
at 3, 281.

ingrate ac perfide: here is the brunt of
Naevolus's complaint.

84 *libris actorum*: the official records, the
acta diurna.

85 *argumenta uiri*: evidence of your
manhood.

90 *tres*: the Lex Papia Poppaea of AD
9 gave special privileges to those with a
family of three or more.

90-1 *iusta . . . tui*: ironical.

91-101 *'He doesn't care; another two-
legged ass will serve his turn. Don't breathe
a word of this; it's bad enough just to know
his secret. He's quite capable of having me
done in.'*

92 *alium . . . asellum*: he is frank about
his own bestialisation. *Asellus* is similarly
used in Petronius 24.

94 This passage harks back to the
perils of free speech at the end of the
first satire.

95 *pumice leuis*: 'smoothed with
pumice'.

96 An echo of *Lucr.* 3, 1069 *haeret et
odit.*

97 The bucolic diaeresis lays weight on
the charge of murder.

candelam: cf 13, 145-6.

100 *annona ueneni*: 'the price of poison':
an oxymoron. *Annona* means the corn-
supply; so the price of corn; and the market-
price generally; cf Horace's cynical *uilis
amicorum est annona (Ep.* 1, 12, 24).

101 *curia Martis*: the Areopagus, which
met in secret session.

102-23 *My dear Corydon, a rich man has
no secrets. Even if his slaves keep his
confidences, it gets about soon enough.
It's the best reason for decent living to
rise above servants' gossip.*

102 *o Corydon, Corydon*: a parody of
Verg. *Ecl.* 2, 69; Corydon, homosexually
attracted to Alexis, is addressing himself:
'What madness has overtaken you?' The
homosexual atmosphere in Vergil makes it
an appropriate echo. Further, Vergil's
conclusion is that there are plenty of good
fish in the sea. The allusion thus anticipates
J's climax at 9, 130.

103 *ut*: 'even though'. Seneca (*Ben.* 3,
27) has a good story of a senator who drunk-
enly wished for Caesar's death. One of his
slaves warned him in the morning of what
he had said, and advised him to make his
peace before Caesar heard. cf Ecclesiastes
10:20 'Do not speak ill of the king in your
ease, or of a rich man in your bedroom; for
a bird may carry your voice, and a winged
messenger may repeat what you say.'

107 The cock was expected to crow three
times before dawn.

109 *libarius*: a pastry-cook; cf Sen. *Ep.*
56, 3.

archimagiri: 'chefs', a Greek word, not
elsewhere in Latin.

110 *carptores*: 'carvers', also called
scissores; cf Trimalchio's pun *Carpe, carpe*
('Carver, carve 'er') (Petron. 36; 40).

113 *inebriet aurem*: a vivid, indeed
startling phrase, though ears are described as
thirsty (Cic. *Att.* 2, 14).

116 *Falerni*: the famous Falernian wine
came from the slopes of Mount Massicus in
Campania (Hor. *O* 1, 27, 10, etc.).

117 *Saufeia*: see 6, 320. The expiatory
sacrifice for the Roman people was offered
by the Roman matrons at the festival of
Bona Dea, held in the house of a consul or
praetor, and accompanied by libations.

118-9 'There are many reasons for a
moral life, but the greatest is to be able to
ignore servants' gossip.' A brilliant epigram
with its cynical twist. A similar effect is
found at 14, 47-8. *Tum est his* is
Housman's emendation of the MS *tunc est.*

120-3 These lines are clearly interpolated.
They do not seem to have been known to

the ancient commentators. 120-1 are mere repetition, 122-3 intolerably weak.

124-50 'Fair enough. But it doesn't help me. Life's speeding away; old age is coming.' Don't worry; as long as Rome stands there'll be pathics, careful not to disarrange their coiffures. Keep on with the aphrodisiacs. 'Tell that to men with luck. I live from hand to mouth. I'd like a regular income, a bit of silver, a couple of attendants, and an art business with a couple of skilled employees. That's all; it would bring me up to the poverty line. But Fortune passes me by.'

124   utile: again the Epicurean term; cf 27. The whole speech is redolent of popular Epicureanism: 'eat, drink and be merry, for tomorrow we die'. Needless to say this was not the philosophy of the authentic Epicurus. These seven lines have some of J's best writing, powerfully ironic in view of the repulsive character who speaks them.

126-7   decurrere uelox flosculus: J mocks his own purple passage in this mixed metaphor. Cicero (Leg. Agr. 1, 8, 24) has a voice shining in the darkness. We may also recall Sir Boyle Roche (cited on 1, 149) (Nisbet, following Ruperti, prefers to regard uelox . . . breuissima as interpolated.)

129   Ausonius imitated this line (Epig. 13, 3): obrepsit non intellecta senectus/nec reuocare potes qui periere dies.

130   J's bitter answer.

131   his collibus: the Seven Hills of Rome. The bucolic diaeresis emphasises the point, before and after.

133   The scholiast says that the use of one finger is a feminine movement in care not to disarrange the hair; cf Calvus fr. 18 Magnus, quem metuunt omnes, digito caput uno/scalpit. quid credas hunc sibi uelle? uirum. Green takes it as part of a private language, but the use is more general.

134   Two MSS add another line gratus eris, tu tantum erucis inprime dentem. erucis: an aphrodisiac.

135-6   Clotho et Lachesis: two of the Moirai or Fates, who spin the thread of human destiny. Clotho means Spinner, Lachesis Allocation, Atropos (the third) Inflexible. See Hesiod Theog. 904-6; Plato Rep. 10, 617b-21a.

136   pascitur inguine uenter: a clever phrase, 'my pecker provides for my stomach'.

137   Lares: see on 8, 110.

137-8   parui . . . minuto . . . tenui: he really lays his poverty on thick.

139   figam: a metaphor from hunting (cf

1, 23), but with obscene innuendo.

140   a tegete et baculo: marks of a beggar (and therefore affected by Cynic preachers).

141   puri: ironical.

142   Fabricius censor: C. Fabricius Luscinus, censor in 275 BC and P. Cornelius Rufinus ejected from the senate for illegal possession of silver plate in excess of 4½ kg in weight (Liv. Epit. 14).

143   de grege Moesorum: the Moesi lived in modern Bulgaria and Serbia; they were defeated by the Romans in 29 BC and made a province probably right at the beginning of the first century AD. Like the Liburni of Dalmatia (6, 477) they were in demand as litter-bearers.

144   clamoso . . . circo: from Mart. 10, 53, 1.

145   curuus: 'stooped', from bending over his work.

146   sufficiunt haec: the bucolic diaeresis and the offbeat rhythm combine to pick out these words with bitter stress. But why does Naevolus want such artists? Verres had them (Cic. 2 Verr.4, 24, 54) but Verres was not a poor man. Presumably Naevolus wants to go straight and set up in business.

147   pauper: a step up from being indigent. The point comes from Martial: a man who has nothing can't be called pauper.

148   Fortuna: Italian oracular goddess, bringer (ferre) of prosperity, worshipped at Praeneste, later identified with the Greek Tyche, our Fortune. She had an ancient temple in the Forum Boarium.

149   It is rare to have a hexameter line with less than thirty letters; cf Hor. S 2, 8, 39 inuertunt Allifanis uinaria tota; Hom. Il. 18, 136. The allusion is to Ulysses having himself tied to the mast and stopping his sailors' ears with wax as they sailed past Sicily, so that they could not hear the fatal attraction of the Sirens' song and he could do nothing about it (Hom. Od. 12, 173ff.). Seneca uses the same image (Ep. 31, 2). See a Hadrianic terracotta relief in the Louvre, or the red-figure bell-krater from Paestum, formerly in the Berlin State Museum.

150   J's phrase is taken from Prop. 3, 12, 34 Sirenum surdo remige adisse lacus. It is a fine ending; the irony lies in the character of the speaker.

General comments

It may well seem perverse to praise this satire. The sheer sordidness of the subject has left it unread by many (Duff censored this and the second), and it has been little imitated, though Boileau and Diderot took material from it. But though a satirist may exaggerate the grimmer realities of life, he can hardly ignore them and remain a satirist, and the repulsiveness of the theme is no index of the skill of the treatment. It *is* brilliantly treated, which is why the poem is so frequently cited in the Middle Ages.

Dialogue, as Hirzel showed in his book of that title, is one of the central traditions of satire. Horace uses it in *S* 2, 3; 2, 5; 2, 7; Persius in his third and fourth poems. This is the only occasion that J uses it. He does not employ it philosophically, to develop an argument or to present antithetical views dialectically. Rather he uses it dramatically, to spotlight his central character. There is a parallel in Terence *Phormio* 326-45, where a character similarly reveals his true nature. But the closest parallel is not with comedy but with mime, and the technique and characterisation of mime is somewhere behind J. In satire this sort of self-revelation is found in Ennius (of a parasite), and in Horace (*S* 1, 9).

Naevolus exposes himself through his own words: this is the point. The whole satire is an exposition of a *propositum uitae* (21). J likes to frame his satires so. But this might seem almost a bitter parody of his own more serious purposes. J's opening words do not really give us a picture of the inner Naevolus. We have external, visual images: an image of hanging Marsyas, a stock image (also used by Martial) of the look of a man caught in a particularly crude act of sexual deviation; and the look of a spendthrift who can't find a taker. For the rest we have the picture of a man who has something of a reputation of a man-about-town and a wit.

It is Naevolus who shows what he really is, a professional male prostitute with no enjoyment and no shame, wholly on the make, and interested only in his reward. We might call it the bitterest possible satire on the Puritan ethic. It all comes out. Naevolus has not merely served his pathic master directly — hard work too; he has got him the children on his wife the un-manned husband could not get for himself. Naevolus's values come out. Virro, the master-mistress, is thankless and treacherous (*ingrate ac perfide*). His perversions and weakness would be nothing — if he'd pay. Naevolus is afraid of his enmity and dare not go too far in challenging his meanness. Naevolus is grasping in his own way. He has one slave, as unique as the Cyclops's eye, and is afraid of losing that one; yet he immediately says that he must have two. So at the end; he'd like to have independence; he wants a couple of sturdy attendants from the Balkans, and a couple of skilled craftsmen in his employment. They do not seem modest demands.

But if Naevolus exposes himself, he exposes also the shifty, shadowy, paltry figure of Virro behind him. He is a contemptible pathic, slobbering with desire (35). He is himself impotent, a particular degradation in Roman eyes; he lacks *uirtus* in its most literal sense; he blubbers outside the door while his tool consummates his marriage for him (77). He is vindictive and cruel, caring for neither life nor limb (92-101). He is devious and secretive, treacherous and unreliable. He has no gratitude; he has no positive inner feelings, for his love is only physical desire. He is mean and stingy; Highet appropriately cites Macaulay's description of Marlborough, 'thrifty in his vices'. It is a damning indictment.

For what gives this satire its strength is the interweaving of two themes. There is the obvious theme of sexual perversion. But underlying it and going beyond it is the whole attitude of the aristocratic *patronus* to his lowly dependents. J makes this clear by Naevolus's explicit use of the word *cliens* (59). But it is the satirist's own comments which strike home here. At first (1-26; 90-1), he is content to feed Naevolus with lead lines. But his last two interjections are substantial. One (102-23) is an indictment of a society dominated by men like Virro. If those at the top are *perfidi*, society will be permeated with *perfidia*, and however secretive the rich may hope to be, their secrets will never be kept. His final comment (130-4) is pointed in its brevity. It brings the two themes together. As long as the seven hills stand, Naevolus will find a perverted employer in the aristocracy. The disease is now endemic. J presents his picture urbanely; herein lies the satire's power. The vicious obscenity in the fourth line is only a passing illustration; in society it is taken for granted, just as it is taken for granted that women go to temples to prostitute them-selves (23). Naevolus takes his life for granted, and Virro takes Naevolus for granted. There is no reforming zeal in this satire, only a detached record of total corruption. The sexual perversion which individuals affect, and the social perversion of the exploitation of one class by another are part of the same pattern of life. It is a profound observation.

Bibliography
Consoli, S. 'La satira IX di Giovenali nella
    tradizione della cultura sino alla fine del
    medio evo' *RFIC* 49 (1921) 79-97

Mason, H.A. 'Is Juvenal a Classic?' *Arion* I
    (1962) 8-44; 2 (1962) 39-79 repr.
    in Sullivan, J.P. *Satire* London 1963

SATIRE 10

Johnson called his justly famous imitation of
this, one of J's finest satires, 'The Vanity
of Human Wishes'. The phrase has become
proverbial, but as an account of J's satire
it is misleading, and something like 'False
and True Objects of Prayer' is more to J's
purpose. Highet entitled it 'From Hope and
Fear Set Free'.

The poem is more clearly structured than
any of the other satires.

1-22   Introduction (leading straight into)
23-7   Wealth
    28-53   Democritus and Heraclitus
54-113   Power
114-32   Eloquence
133-87   Military Ambition
188-288   Old Age
289-345   Good Looks
346-66   Conclusion

The digression on Democritus and Heraclitus
forms a break in the structure, and is obvious-
ly important. J, surely rightly, exemplifies
his theme before making the digression.
Democritus and Heraclitus stand for two
ways of life: involvement in a spirit of
satirical criticism or withdrawal in a
spirit of sorrow. This is precisely the
choice J has put before us in the third
satire, and here, as there, whatever his
sympathy for Umbricius, he remains
involved.

The tenth satire is hardly to be under-
stood without an awareness of Epicurean
philosophy. Histories of Epicureanism
are sometimes written as if it ceased with
Lucretius. In fact it can be traced through-
out the early Empire, and the second
century AD saw its zenith, though it
remained prominent in the third and even
the fourth centuries: see J. Ferguson
'Epicureanism under the Roman Empire'
Festschrift für Josef Vogt. J's aim is a
peaceful life (*tranquillae . . . uitae* 10, 364),
and this, and the statement that you cannot
achieve it except through virtue, came
straight from Epicurus. The whole analysis
is Epicurean, the attack on desires which
outrun their natural bounds; on political

ambition, literary ambition, military glory,
all of which the Epicureans disowned: The
attacks on sacrificial superstitions (354-5)
and on the cult of Fortune (365-6) are
characteristic of the Epicureans. The
calculus of pleasure is implicit in the
sections on Old Age and Good Looks: it's
the final equation which must be right.
And 'sound mind in a sound body' is a
good Epicureanism. But J is not a dogmatic
Epicurean, as he tells us himself (13,
120-3), and the ambivalence of his position
is seen in his espousal of Democritean
involvement rather than Heraclitean
withdrawal.

The satire owes some debt to two earlier
works, both by Stoics. These are Seneca *On
Tranquillity of Mind* and Persius *Satire* 2. At
the outset of the former Serenus suggests that
although he is not enslaved by mental
disturbance he is not free from it; he is not
sick, but he is not well (*nec aegroto nec
ualeo*). He is not corrupted by riches,
political power, or ambition for literary
renown, but he is not free from them. He is
in short a typical liberal idealist. Seneca's
answer contains a great deal of good sense.
He identifies a general disease of restless-
ness leading to a state of dissatisfaction,
an absence of *autarkeia.* People in this
state are unstable, and will go to any lengths
to attain their prayers. They must always
be busy and cannot tolerate leisure.
Hence the passion for travel, when (as the
Epicurean Lucretius puts it) they are
trying to escape from themselves. Seneca's
cure is a Stoic answer — public service —
and he does not accept withdrawal as an
answer. But his exaltation of *amicitia
fidelis et dulcis* seems to come from
Epicurus.

Seneca has sensible things to say about
the anxieties arising from property — he
should know! — and even the spiritual
dangers of collecting a private library. His
omnes cum Fortuna copulati sumus (10,
3) is interesting to set against the conclusion
of J's satire. Heights imply precipices, and
men are forced to cling to the eminence
from which they cannot descend without

falling (10, 5-6). His examples of the instability of Fortune include Sejanus and Cicero as do J's and like J he cites Democritus (13, 1), and in fact says *Democritum potius imitemur quam Heraclitum* (15, 2).

Persius's second satire is explicitly on the theme of how to pray, and how not to. By comparison with J he is unmemorable, though it has a clear structure and occasional felicities. How often the prayer uttered audibly for *mens bona, fama, fides* conceals a covert desire for the death of an inconvenient relative, or the finding of treasure trove. Persius starts from wickedness; J from folly. Jupiter is treated like a venal human judge, to be bribed with a greasy sacrifice. So Persius satirises the prayer that a child will grow to be a catch for the girls (37; J 289); for a *corpus . . . fidele senectae* (41; the point is changed by J 188ff); for wealth (44; J 12). Persius's conclusion rises to some eloquence, more pompous than J, but earnest and not ignoble:

Souls bowed to earth and empty of
   heavenly grace,
what value is there in bringing our own
   ways into religion,
in deriving the gods' purposes from our
   sinful flesh?
The flesh it is that ruins oil by mixing in
   casia,
that destroys purple to dye Calabrian
   wool.
The flesh it is that has driven us to rip
   the pearl from the oyster,
and pull the veins of glowing ore from
   natural slag.
It is sinful. The flesh is sinful, yet gains
   by its sin. But, priests,
tell us, what is the use of gold in a
   sanctuary?
No more than dolls dedicated by a girl to
   Venus!
We give to the gods a gift, which for all his
   rich platter
Messala's bleary son cannot offer:
duty to gods and men as a single
   commitment, righteousness
in every corner of the mind, a heart
   prepared for nobility and virtue.
Let me bring these to the gods, and a little
   corn can be my formal offering.
      2, 61-75

J's work in the end has more lasting power than either of these. J drew on other sources for his *exempla*. The account of Sejanus's fall was no doubt derived from the lost books of Tacitus; a former student of mine, Anne Vannan, once showed how well it would transfer to Tacitus's prose (*GR* 4 (1957) 168); J may also have been influenced by broadsheets or other accounts of Domitian's death. Certainly some of his *exempla* were stock themes of the rhetorical schools, and we can see them in the *declamationes* attributed to Quintilian, or in Valerius Maximus (e.g. 6, 9; 7, 2 ext. 1). But J makes them his own: the total result is consistent and individual.

Byron wrote: 'The Tenth Sat[e] has always been my favourite, as I suppose indeed of everybody's. It is the finest recipe for making one miserable with his life, and content to walk out of it, in any language. I should think it might be read with great effect to a man dying without much pain, in preference to all the stuff that ever was sung or said in the churches.' (Letter to F. Hodgson, 9 September 1811, quoted by Highet)

1-22 *How few anywhere in the world make a rational distinction between good and evil. Politicians and soldiers alike, orators and strong men seem determined on their own destruction. Worst of all is the craving for money, though the rich are cut down, while the poor are left in peace, and rich travellers are scared of bandits, while poor travellers whistle in their faces.*

1 *Gadibus:* Gades, the modern Cadiz, was a Phoenician settlement outside the straits of Gibraltar or Pillars of Hercules, and stood for the ancients as the western boundary of the inhabited world. Sil. It. 1, 141 has *hominum finem Gades.* Notice the repetition of sound *Gadibus usque.* Quint. 9, 4, 41 *uidendum etiam ne syllabae uerbi prioris ultimae et primae sequentis sint eaedem.* J knew his Quintilian, and may have been taught by him. He pillories a similar effect in Cicero (122). The effect is presumably deliberate: partly an audible expression of the theme of extension, partly a harshness indicating satirical purpose.

2 *Aurora:* goddess of dawn.
Gangen: the great river of India, taken as the Eastern limit of the world. So Sen. *QN 1 prol. 13 quantum est, quod ab ultimis litoribus Hispaniae usque ad Indos iacet.*

3 *illis* (i.e. *ueris bonis*) *multum diuersa:* i.e. *mala.*

4 *erroris nebula:* not yet a hackneyed cliché. Homer talks of Athene lifting the

mist from the eyes of Diomedes (*Il.* 5,
127ff.) In the pseudo-Platonic 2
Alcibiades 150 D-E Socrates suggests that
in the same way Alcibiades must lift the
mist from his soul in order to distinguish
the good from the bad. J takes the idea
from here. A famous medieval mystical
treatise bears the title *The Cloud of
Unknowing.* Notice how powerfully the
ablative absolute ends the sentence. Chaucer
adapts this passage in 'Troilus and Creseide'
4, 29: 'O Juvenall lord, trewe is thy
sentence,/That litel witen folk what is to
yerne,/That they ne finde in hir desyr
offence,/For cloud of errour lat hem not
descerne/What best is.'
   ratione: 'if we follow reason', a philoso-
phical thought which a Stoic or an Epicurean
might equally voice.
   4-5 *timemus aut cupimus:* Epicurus and
his followers held that the two things
which most assail our peace of mind are
desires which outrun their natural course,
and fears. Epicurus attempted to demon-
strate the rational elimination of fear and
control of desire. J's formulation here is
very Epicurean. But see also Sen. *Ep.* 123, 13
ne haec timeamus (of death, pain, etc.) *ne
illa cupiamus* (of riches, pleasure, beauty,
ambition); Seneca, though a Stoic, was much
influenced by Epicurus in the *Letters.*
   5 *tam dextro pede:* 'so auspiciously'.
It was lucky to enter with the right
foot, ill-omened with the left. So Vitruvius
(3, 3, 4) recommends building a temple
with an odd number of steps so that the
right foot is set on both the bottom and
the top step, and in Petronius (30)
Trimalchio keeps a slave to call to the
guests '*dextro pede*' as they are about to
enter. See also Verg. *A* 8, 302 *tua dexter
adi pede sacra secundo.* But J is wantonly
mixing his metaphors.
   ut te: the monosyllables throw an
offbeat accent on the final syllable.
   7 Note the build-up: 'They (?) have
overthrown families root-and-branch at
(?) the prayers of the heads — they, the
gods, lending a willing ear to the prayers.' This
last is a warning against any suggestion that
J was a full-blooded Epicurean, though
the thought is not incompatible with
Epicurean irony. Martial twice has *faciles*
of the gods (1, 103, 4; 12, 6, 10).
   8 *toga:* 'by politics', as in Cicero's
cedant arma togae (*In Pis.* 30, 73).
Mart. 1, 55, 2 has *clarum militiae, Fronto,
togaeque decus.*
   9 *torrens:* ambiguous between 'blazing'
and 'flooding', but with a strong sense of

destructive power. J has it again at 128
and 3, 74. See also Quint. 3, 8, 60 *torrens
dicentis oratio.* J knows from the inside
the rhetoric in which he decries ambition.
   10 *uiribus ille:* picked out by the
bucolic diaeresis: *uiribus* performs a
double function, with *confisus* and *periit:
ille* is Milo of Croton, a stock example of
brute strength, Olympic victor in the late
sixth century BC, who found an oak-tree
being split and secured with wedges, and in
vanity of strength pulled it further apart
with his bare hands, causing the wedges
to slip out, the wood to snap together
gripping his hands, so that he was held fast
and could neither defend himself against
nor escape from an attack by wolves.
   11 *periit:* the long final syllable is perhaps
an archaism; we find *redieit* in early inscrip-
tions.
   12-4 scornful alliteration on *p* and *b.*
   12 *pluris:* acc. plur. m. not just 'more'
but 'very many', emphatic. For earlier
attacks on man's obsession with money
recall 1, 112; 5, 136.
   13 *strangulat:* a vivid image, perhaps
with reference to Midas, who prayed that
whatever he touched might turn to gold,
so that his food solidified and choked
him.
   patrimonia census: there does not seem
any essential difference between the
words.
   quanto: balanced writing would have
placed *tanto* with *exuperans.*
   14 *ballaena Britannica:* the whale
proper was rare in the Mediterranean, but
relatively common in the North Sea,
which had become more familiar since the
conquest of Britain.
   15 *temporibus diris:* here of Nero's 'reign
of terror' after Piso's conspiracy in AD 65;
at 4, 80 of Domitian: a sure indication that
J believes that history repeats itself, and
that in pillorying the past he is pillorying
the present.
   16 *Longinum:* C Cassius Longinus,
consul suffectus in AD 30, proconsul of
Asia AD 40-1, *legatus* of Syria AD 45-9, a
notable jurist (Tac *Ann.* 12, 12 *ceteros
praeminebat peritia legum*), author of
Liber iuris ciuilis and leader of one school of
juristic interpretation (Plin. *Ep.* 7, 24, 8
Cassianae scholae princeps et parens), exiled
to Sardinia in AD 65, recalled under
Vespasian.
   Senecae praediuitis: for Seneca see on
5, 109: Tac. *Ann.* 15, 64 calls him
praediues et praepotens. He had a large villa
on Mons Caelius. Tacitus records a shatter-

COMMENTARY

ing attack on the gulf between his wealth and his philosophic pretensions by one P. Suillius (*Ann.* 13, 42). Seneca tried to protect himself by handing his fortune over to the emperor. He does not seem to have been privy to Piso's conspiracy, but his nephew Lucan was, and he may have been the plotters' alternative ruler: *tribunus uenit et uillam globis militum saepsit* (*ib* 15, 60); he was forced to suicide.

17 *Lateranorum:* Plautius Lateranus, cos. designate, actively supported the conspiracy and was executed. His villa, also on Mons Caelius, later provided the site for the great basilica of St John Lateran.

18 *cenacula;* orig. upstairs dining-rooms, so upper storeys generally, so garrets or attics (cf 3, 201 *quem tegula sola tuetur*). The whole sentence is one of J's best epigrams.

19 *puri:* emphatic, like *pauca:* the contrasting word is *asperum* or *caelatum* 'embossed', 'chased'. Even the traveller with only a little unelaborate silver is terrified.

22 An even finer epigram: effectively four words (since a prep. forms a single word-group with its noun), patterned by initial letters c-v-c-v: *uacuus* is emphatic and carries the double meaning 'empty-handed' and so 'free from care' (Hor. *O* 1, 6, 19 *cantamus uacui*). Chaucer 'Wife of Bath's Tale' 337 'The povre man, when he goth by the weye,/Bifore the theves he may singe and pleye.'

23-7 *Almost everyone's first prayer is for riches, but earthenware cups do not receive poison, like jewelled goblets with a fine vintage.*

23-7 The epigram marks the end of the introduction. The passage on wealth is very short, because it has already been used as a bridge-theme.

23 *templis:* not places for congregational worship, but for such private offerings and requests.

25 *foro:* the Forum Romanum, where the bankers (*argentarii*) operated: almost exactly the effect of our 'the City'.

25-7 A third variant on the theme of 15-8, and 19-22.

27 *Setinum:* see on 5, 34: wine from Setia was considered one of the best.

ardebit: a beautifully chosen word: 'glows', especially suitable to red wine, but also of the burning, consuming effect of poison.

28-53 *Democritus laughed at the world,*

Heraclitus wept at it. It's easy to laugh; there aren't enough tears to draw on. They didn't have the spectacle of our pompous processions and debased citizens. Democritus found plenty to laugh at; his practical good sense showed that intelligence can be found in a place with a reputation for dullness. He laughed at the man in the street, and dismissed the power of Fortune.

28 *iam:* i.e. 'after all this'.

quod: 'the fact that'.

alter: Democritus of Abdera (c. 459-360 BC) proponent of the atomic theory, and of an ethic in which the aim is contentment founded on moral wellbeing. Horace (*Ep.* 2, 1, 194) has *si foret in terris, rideret Democritus.*

29-30 *quotiens . . . pedem.* The sentence is shaped with asyndeton and chiasmus (*alter ridebat . . . flebat contrarius auctor*). This clause looks both ways, and the separation of *unum* from *pedem* suggests the tentative step out.

30 *contrarius auctor:* 'the exponent of the opposite philosophy', Heraclitus of Ephesus (c. 542-480 BC), exponent of a philosophy of tension between opposites and (according to Plato and Aristotle) of flux controlled by a principle of balance, gnomic and obscure, a soured aristocrat. The contrast between the two is commonplace. Sen. *Tranq. An.* 15, 2 *Democritum potius imitemur quam Heraclitum. hic enim, quotiens in publicum processerat, flebat, ille ridebat.* Lucian contrasts them in *Philosophies for Sale.* Duff quotes Horace Walpole 'Life is a comedy to those who think, a tragedy to those who feel.' See introduction to this satire.

31 'But the censure of stern derision is easy for anyone.' Note that this is a characterisation alike of Democritus and satire.

34 *urbibus illis:* the Greek city states.

35 A good example of J's effective asyndeton. *praetextae:* the purple-fringed toga worn by priests and senior state officials. *trabeae:* the state-dress of *equites. fasces:* the rods and axes carried by lictors before the officers of state. *lectica:* a litter, reserved strictly for senators' wives. *tribunal:* the platform from which the praetor gave judgement.

36 These lines describe the procession (*pompa*) at the *Ludi Romani.* The mockery of Roman tradition is something new in J. *praetorem:* the *praetor urbanus*, chairman for the occasion.

37 *circi:* the Circus Maximus.

38 *tunica Iouis: tunica palmata*
embroidered with a pattern of palm trees,
and kept in the temple of Jupiter on the
Capitol. J writes as if the magistrate
borrows Jupiter's 'frock-coat' for the
occasion.

Sarrana: Tyrian. The Aramaic *Sar*
becomes *Tyrus.* This other robe was purple
with gold embroidery.

39 *aulaea:* 'curtains', a typical
exaggeration.

coronae: a wreath of gold oak-leaves
studded with gems, too heavy to wear, so
held by a slave. See Dio Cass. 6 in
Zonaras 7, 21 for a full account.

41 *publicus:* sc. *seruus.*

sibi consul ne placeat: 'to keep his
lordship from a swollen head'. The praetor
has become a consul; J prefers to alternate
c and p to overdoing alliteration on p.
But he is blurring the games procession
and the military triumph (Suet. *Jul.*
49, 4)

43-7 The grand style used for incon-
gruous effect.

43 *da nunc* 'Next suppose.'

uolucrem: an eagle.

44 *cornicines:* not just trumpeters, but
a whole band of instrumentalists.

45 *officia:* the dutiful attention of
cliens on *patronus.* J likes to put impersonal
for personal in this way: *praecedentium
longum agmen officiosorum* might be a
prosaic version.

niueos: in their snow-white togas, washed
for the occasion, without the purple
fringe.

ad frena: 'to the tune of his bridle-rein'.
Who are more truly bridled — the horses
or the citizens?

46 *defossa:* 'tucked away.' J is suggesting
that the aristocrat supports them simply
to have his *claqueurs,* and they support him
simply for the food or money. For *sportula*
see 1, 95, *amicos* 1, 33.

47 *tum quoque:* 'even in Greek times'
before there were these posturing
aristocrats.

48 *cuius:* referring to Democritus.

50 *ueruecum in patria:* 'in a country of
muttonheads'. Abdera was proverbial for
the dullness of its inhabitants. Democritus
provided an instance to the contrary. There
are some good yarns about the men of
Abdera. One was committing suicide by
hanging. The rope broke; he fell and
cut himself; went to the doctor to have
himself patched up; and then hanged himself
again.

crassoque sub aere: the ancient theorists
were interested in the effect of climate
on intelligence. *Crassus,* like our 'thick',
can be applied to the atmosphere or to the
intelligence; the joke is similar to 'The
population of London is very dense.'

51 *ridebat* + acc: 'laughed at'.

nec non et: piling it on as in 3, 204;
9, 88.

uolgi: they do not escape.

52 *Fortunae:* in Italy originally an
oracular and fertility goddess, here
corresponding to the Greek Tyche, very
much our Fortune. Fortune is important
in Seneca's treatise *On Tranquillity of
Mind.*

ipse: they wept; he behaved differently.

53 *mandaret laqueum:* as we say 'let
her go hang'.

mediumque ostenderet unguem: an
obscene gesture, still in use, designed
originally to avert the evil eye; cf Pers.
2, 33 *digito infami.*

54-113 *What prayers are justified? Power
leads to envy and disaster. Statues of the
once powerful are broken up and
recycled, as with Sejanus, whose fall led to
general rejoicing. Not that the people really
cared; they are interested these days only
in rations and entertainment. Do you really
want to be like Sejanus? Of course you
want power, but do you want its accom-
panying adversities? Better to be a humble
country magistrate. Those who seek
political power are building gimcrack
skyscrapers which topple catastrophically.
There are two things wrong with that
prayer — the request for power and the
fact that the gods grant it. Few autocrats
die in their beds.*

54-5 Knoche omits these intrusive lines,
but Bickel defended them persuasively.

54 *si:* some word has dropped out
between *aut* and *perniciosa:* this makes as
good sense as any: 'Then if the objects of
our prayer are superfluous or dangerous,
for what . . .'. Bücheler proposed *quae,*
Doederlein *uel.*

55 *incerare:* 'to smear wax over'. This
refers to writing petitions on wax tablets
and placing them on the knees of a seated
statue, but we must not lose the vivid
directions of J's phrase.

56 *quosdam:* a muted beginning to a
great build-up.

praecipitat: vivid: 'pushes over the
edge'.

subiecta potentia: almost an oxymoron.

57 *inuidiae:* dat. with *subiecta.*

mergit: a change of metaphor.

honorum: not 'honours' but 'offices held'.

58 *pagina:* a bronze tablet affixed to the statue-base, also called *tabula patronatus.*

descendunt statuae: there are many examples·from first-century history, e.g. Tac. *Ann.* 3, 14 *effigiesque Pisonis traxerant in Gemonias ac diuellebant;* DC 63, 25, 1 of Nero; and especially Domitian (Suet. *Dom.* 23; Plin. *Paneg.* 52, 4-5; Macrob. 1, 12, 37), who may be in J's mind.

secuntur = sequuntur, i.e. 'are pulled away by'.

59 *inpacta securis:* note the difference between Latin and English idiom: we would say 'the stroke of the axe.'

60 *caballis:* dat. of disadvantage. The mood is satirical; the word (from which is derived the French *cheval*) is slangy, 'nags'; the bronze or marble horses suffer for the ambitions of a now dead human, their punishment that of slaves.

62 *ardet:* doubly ironic, for the people had blazed with admiration for Sejanus and he had been voted a statue for energetic action in checking a dangerous fire (Tac. *Ann.* 3, 22).

adoratum: he did receive worship (Tac. *Ann.* 4, 2; DC 58, 4, 3; 58, 11, 2 cited below on 99).

caput et crepat: onomatopoeic of the crackling flames, helped by the offbeat accent in *crepat.*

63 *Seianus:* L. Aelius Seianus of Vulsinii, an *eques,* who became prefect of the praetorians in AD 20, and after the emperor's retirement to Capri was virtually regent. He seems to have been a man of ability, who risked his life for the emperor. But he aspired to the supreme power, murdering those who stood in his way. In AD 31 he was unmasked and on October 18 deposed and executed. Reprisals followed against his associates; the threat of denunciation was enough to intimidate one of them, Pontius Pilatus, into acting against his better judgement. Seneca (*Tranq. An.* 11, 11) takes Seianus as an instance of the fragility of power. Tacitus sketches his character in *Ann.* 4, 1-3; 6, 8; unfortunately his account of the fall, on which this is no doubt based, is missing. Ben Jonson wrote a play on Sejanus and follows J for the fall (5, 10. 'First they tear them down/Then fastening ropes drag them along the streets/ Crying in scorn, "This, this was that rich head/Was covered with garlands, and with odours thus/That was in some so reverenced!

Now/The furnace and the bellows shall to work,/The great Sejanus crack, and piece by piece/Drop in the founder's pit." ') Sam Johnson found his analogue in Wolsey. J builds up to the name, with its three long syllables, as his climax: until the name we do not know who the passage is about.

secunda: second, i.e. to the emperor, but also blessed by fortune.

64 Another characteristic asyndeton, cf 35. *urceoli:* one-handled jugs; *pelues = pedelues:* foot-baths; *sartago:* a frying pan, very modern in appearance; *matellae:* piss-pots, the final degradation. Much the same happened to Domitian's statues (Plin. *Paneg.* 52, 4, 5).

65 Comments by ordinary people.

66 *cretatum:* a white beast was sacrificed to Jupiter; if not pure white, it was smeared with chalk. Lucil. fr. 697 *cretatumque bouem duci ad Capitolia magna.* Also a chalk mark indicated good luck, a charcoal mark bad luck.

unco: used for dragging executed criminals to the Scalae Gemoniae.

67 *quae labra:* a dialogue between two spectators, a dramatic device. The phrase seems to mean 'How scornfully he curled his lip!'

68 *si quid mihi credis:* conversational idiom.

69 *cecidit:* technical term for losing a case. Note the strong alliteration.

70 *delator:* cf 3, 116; ironical, as Sejanus has fostered the practice. The *delator* denounces, sometimes anonymously, and without evidence. The *index* is a minor member of a conspiracy who informs against the others.

71 *uerbosa et grandis epistula:* typical of the emperor's devious approach. The letter was addressed to Macro, who succeeded Sejanus as prefect of the praetorians. He handed it to the consuls, who read it out. Sejanus was expecting high honours and the gradually-unveiled denunciation was thereby an even greater shock (DC 58, 9).

72 *Capreis:* the island in the bay of Naples. Tiberius retired there in AD 27, and Rome seethed with speculation about his private goings-on. His palace is still to be seen, as well as the site of a smaller seaside villa.

bene habet: 'OK'.

sed quid: J slips back into his own persona.

73 *turba Remi:* Remus was strictly Romulus's brother, not the founding father, and in some versions hampered the

foundation and was killed for doing so.
But the interchange of the names means
little, though the phrase in any form is
often ironical, and in this instance an
allusion to the fratricide would be
meaningful. Note the ellipsis of the verb,
easily supplied. Note also the abrupt
breaking of this line into four phrases of
two words each.

74 *Nortia:* Etruscan goddess of Fortune
(Liv. 7, 3, 7), honoured at Vulsinii, and
especially appropriate in relation to the
Tuscus Sejanus.

75 *secura senectus:* another example
of J's liking for the abstract; cf 4, 81
Crispi iucunda senectus; 10, 45 *officia.
secura:* not 'secure' but 'off-guard'.

77 *Augustum:* an honorary title of all
emperors: exactly what Sejanus was
playing for. Highet points out that it
stands in the same position in the verse as
Seianus (63): the fate did overtake
emperors too, especially Domitian.
suffragia nulli: Tiberius in AD 14 took
away the electoral power of the people
and gave it to the senate (Tac. *Ann.* 1, 15).

78 *uendimus:* paraprosdokian. But the
electoral corruption was notorious. Even
Cato stooped to it (Suet. *Caes.* 19), and the
list of Cicero's defence-speeches in trials
for *ambitus* is not short.
effudit: sc. *populus.* They don't bother
any more. Metaphor from a horse throwing
a rider; cf. Verg. *A* 10, 893.
qui dabat olim: note the offbeat rhythm.

79 asyndeton. *imperium:* strictly the
command of armies (not 'empire', though
imperator gives us our 'emperor', and
the *imperium* was, with the *tribunicia
potestas,* one of the pillars of the imperial
power) but here perhaps more broadly
'authority'; *fasces,* the power of corporal,
and with the axe inserted, capital punish-
ment vested in the consul.
se continet: 'they've pulled in their
horns' (Green)

81 *panem et circenses:* J has carefully
prepared this famous climax. Augustus boasts
twelve distributions of corn to the public
in 23 BC, and elaborates on the spectacles
he provided (*RG* 15; 22). C. Gracchus had
begun the practice of subsidising the price
of grain in the capital, and by the time of
Julius Caesar 350 000 were receiving a
monthly dole; he cut the number to
150 000. In addition there were occasional
extra subsidies (e.g. Tac. *Ann.* 2, 87).
Circenses sc. *ludos* are strictly the chariot-
races in the Circus Maximus, but these are
taken as typical of all such public

entertainment. The chariot-races
remained immensely popular in Constan-
tinople, and the factions were a danger to·
public order. At Trèves, with the Empire
falling about their ears, after looting and
in the midst of deprivation, the people were
still crying out for the races (Salvian *Gub. Dei*
6, 15). Fronto, M. Aurelius's friend and
tutor, has some wise words: *populum
Romanum duobus praecipue rebus,
annona et spectaculis, teneri; imperium non
minus ludicris quam seriis probari:
maiore damno seria, grauiore inuidia
ludicra neglegi: minus acribus stimulis
congiaria quam spectacula expeti:
congiariis frumentariam modo plebem
singillatim placari ac nominatim,
spectaculis universum. (Princ. Hist.*
p. 210 Naber). Fronto uses more formal
language to describe the two keys to keep
the people quiet.
perituros: a new conversation. ∘

82 *magna est fornacula:* a kind of
oxymoron, since *fornacula* is a diminutive.
'The furnace is large enough' has a grim
meaning for a century which has known
Auschwitz − or Hiroshima.
pallidulus mi: note the strong break
before the fifth foot, the harsh offbeat
rhythm, the conjunction of the two
diminutives, all placing a strong emphasis
on *pallidulus.*

83 *Bruttidius:* Bruttidius Niger, orator
and historian, aedile in AD 22, prosecutor
of C. Silanus for extortion (Tac. *Ann.*
3, 66). He might be suspected of helping
Sejanus eliminate his opponents. There is a
joke in the application of *pallidulus* to a man
named Niger. ('Mr Black was looking rather
white').
Martis . . . aram: in the Campus Martius.

84 *Aiax:* a complex image. Ajax
contested with Odysseus (Ulysses) for
Achilles's arms and lost. Mad with the
desire for revenge, he tried to murder the
army leaders, but slaughtered a flock of
sheep instead. The theme was a common-
place in the rhetorical schools where
Bruttidius practised. J imagines him making
a demonstration speech in support of
Ajax − unsuccessfully. But Ajax is also
clearly Tiberius, whose interests had not
been properly protected by the senate;
there is some suggestion that his vengeance
might hit the wrong victims.

85 *praecipites et:* again offbeat
rhythm, for J's bitter scorn at the scene.

86 *ripa:* of the Tiber.

87 *uideant serui:* if their masters were
suspected of high treason they were liable to

be compelled to give evidence under torture.

88 *hi sermones:* J has thirty-three spondaic fifth feet, nearly always with a dactyl preceding and a three-syllable word ending. Here there is also a bucolic diaeresis. The effect is to throw great weight on the words.

89 So in this line all the feet are spondaic except the fifth. The movement has suddenly slowed up.

90-1 *habere tantundem:* 'to have his bank-balance'.

91-2 *illi . . . illum:* A and B.

curules: sc. *sellas,* stools of ivory or metal, used formally by the senior magistrates, consuls, praetors, aediles, censors, *praefectus urbi, magister equitum* and a few others.

92 *tutor:* 'Protector'.

93 *Caprearum:* see on 72. The name means 'She-goats' and gives point to *grege.*

94 *cum grege Chaldaeo:* astrology originated in Babylonia, and astrologers were called *Chaldaei* or *mathematici.* Astrology was somewhat suspect among the emperors, who suspected that a favourable horoscope for one of their subjects might foster conspiracy, and that a forecast of their own death might encourage someone to bring it about. But Tiberius had studied the subject at Rhodes, and was *addictus mathematicae* (Suet. *Tib.* 69). So was Otho (Plut. *Galb.* 23, 4). J's picture of the soured old man sitting in a rocky prison of his choice surrounded by a gang of pseudo-scientists is one of his finest strokes.

certe: 'undoubtedly'. Military power is taken to be real power, civil power a mere façade.

95 *egregios:* note the link with *grex.* The *equites* covered a wide range. Those of senatorial riches but not birth were called *illustres* or *splendidi;* this is the group referred to here. They were entitled to wear the broad purple fringe on their toga.

castra domestica: the camp of the praetorian guard; Sejanus brought them into a single barracks.

97 *tanti:* gen. of value, 'worth so much'. The thought is Epicurean: 'sometimes we pass over many pleasures when the discomfort which attends us as a result of them is greater than the pleasure' (DL 10, 129).

99 *trahitur:* picking up 66 *ducitur unco.*

praetextam: see on 35. Sejanus was an *eques* and not entitled to the *toga praetexta;* the right to wear it was con-

ferred on him by special legislation in AD 20; he was in fact consul in AD 31. Dio's account of his fall picks out this privilege in a notable piece of rhetoric: 'At daybreak they had all escorted him to the senate-house as their superior; now they dragged him off to prison as nobody's better. In time past they had honoured him with many crowns; now they set him in chains. Once they had formed a bodyguard for him as their dictator, now they guarded him like a runaway slave, pulling off the cowl with which he tried to hide himself. *They had equipped him with the purple-fringed toga; now they buffeted him.* They had prostrated themselves before him and sacrificed to him as a god; now they were leading him to execution' (58, 11). Macro was wiser and refused the honour (58, 12).

100 *Fidenarum Gabiorumque:* two run-down towns in Latium, a literary allusion to Hor. *Ep.* 1, 11, 7 *Gabiis desertior atque/Fidenis uicus.*

potestas: i.e. magistrate, abstract for concrete.

101 *mensura:* weights and measures, punning with the use in 98.

minora: 'too small', below the statutory size.

102 *pannosus:* contrasting with *praetextam;* cf 3, 179.

aedilis: a general term for a provincial magistrate.

Vlubris: another depopulated town of Latium, also from Hor. *Ep.* 1, 11, 30.

105-7 A vivid and elaborate metaphor, to be read with the Rome of the third Satire in mind.

107 'and the headlong descent of the tottering building once set going becomes disastrous'.

praeceps is substantive, but with a different meaning from 1, 149; *inmane* is predicate; the subj. at *esset* indicates consequence. The *ae* sounds are noteworthy.

108 *Crassos . . . Pompeios:* 'people like Crassus and Pompey. M. Licinius Crassus (c. 112-53 BC) was a man of great wealth, and a dominating figure in Roman politics in the 60s and early 50s. He was consul with Pompey in 70 and 55, having in 60 joined with Pompey and Caesar in the 'first triumvirate'. In 55 he was given an extraordinary command in Syria but was disastrously defeated and killed at Carrhae. Cn. Pompeius Magnus (106-48 BC) exercised greater political power during the same period, often unconstitutionally

and illegally. What Crassus owed to
money, Pompey owed to military skill,
outstandingly exercised in clearing the
eastern Mediterranean of pirates in a
three-month campaign. The high point
of his career was his 'settlement of the
East' in 63. As a statesman he lacked
decisive vision, was outmanoeuvred and
defeated by Caesar, and assassinated as he
tried to take refuge in Egypt.

illum: C. Julius Caesar (102-44 BC), the
great soldier and statesman, left in a
virtually monarchical position on Pompey's
death, and assassinated on the grounds
that he was aspiring to *regnum*. Caesar was
part of the imperial title which is why J
does not use the name.

109 *domitos:* in English we use two
main verbs: 'cowed them and brought
them under the lash' (from Green). The
implication is that he treated them as his
slaves.

Quirites: held up to the end for emphasis,
'citizens though they were'.

110-1 The answer to the question: 'The
fact that they canvassed supreme power . . .
and that the gods granted their prayers.' Note
how the Romans use noun + part. where
we need either 'the fact that' or 'their
canvassing . . . the granting'.

111 *magna . . . uota:* 'prayers for
greatness' with a double meaning,
'colossal requests'.

numinibus: dat. of agent.

malignis: held up in a magnificently
barbed climax.

112 *generum Cereris:* antonomasia for
Pluto, who raped Ceres's daughter Proserpina
(Persephone); cf also 7, 25.

113 *reges: rex* meant to the Romans
the hated kings expelled in 509 BC, or
Oriental potentates like Cleopatra or
Mithradates. The emperors fastidiously
avoided the title.

sicca: 'bloodless'.

tyranni: 'dictator' in our sense, not the
Roman. The Greek states went through a
period when they were ruled by usurping
autocrats, sometimes progressively at
first but with a tendency to degenerate
into what we call tyranny. The parallel
with dictatorial régimes of the 1920s and
1930s is not unjust.

114-32 *Some begin to aspire very young
to the oratorical fame of Demosthenes
or Cicero, but both were destroyed by
their own eloquence. If all Cicero's
writings had been the standard of his
worst verse he would have survived*

*Antony. Better write bad poetry than the
second Philippic. Demosthenes too had a
cruel end. His father did him a disservice
in sending him from the smithy to the
orator for training.*

114 *eloquium ac famam:* virtually
'reputation for eloquence'.

Demosthenis: the greatest of
Athenian orators (384-322 BC). He is said
to have had a weak delivery in his younger
days, and to have disciplined himself by
standing on the shore with pebbles in his
mouth declaiming against the sea. He made
his name as a civil advocate and prosecutor.
His major political speeches are associated
with the rise of Philip of Macedon in the
north (hence *Philippics*). His magnificent
speech *On the Crown* is an eloquent defence
of his policies, which were perhaps not quite
as far-seeing and altruistic as he made out.
In 324 he was condemned for corruption
and went into exile. After Alexander's
death he tried to stage a comeback, was
condemned to death, and committed
suicide. A.W. Pickard-Cambridge's study
of him, though old, is still perhaps the best.
See also W. Jaeger (1938).

aut Ciceronis: a slightly irregular
rhythm, not uncommon with proper names,
but introducing a jarring note into the
stream of eloquence. M. Tullius Cicero
(106-43 BC), the greatest of Roman
orators, a *nouus homo* from Arpinum, who
made his reputation by eschewing
eloquence for evidence in his prosecution
of the corrupt Verres in 70, became
consul in 63, suppressed the conspiracy of
Catiline, was exiled for a period, served
as proconsul in Cilicia, spent a few years
·in retirement compiling an encyclopedia of
philosophy for Rome, re-emerged after
Caesar's death, flayed Antony with his
tongue, and was consequently proscribed
and executed. There is a valuable recent
study by D. Stockton (1971); another by
Elizabeth Rawson (1975).

quinquatribus: the festival of Minerva,
goddess of wisdom, so called because it
began five days (counting inclusively)
after the Ides of March, 19-23 Mar. Orators
naturally took Minerva as their patron.
It was also a school holiday.

116 The succession of two-syllable
words, each accenting on the first syllable,
expresses the young boy's rhetorical
limitations.

uno . . . asse: probably not the school-fee,
which was higher (Hor. *S* 1, 6, 75 quotes
eight asses a month), but his contribution
to the 'collection'.

parcam: not quite clear. Perhaps 'worships Minerva on the cheap'; the epithet is then neatly transferred from *asse.*

117   *capsae:* a cylindrical beechen book box (the books being of course cylindrical rolls). The attendant slave was called *capsarius.* School began before dawn, and in the city the boy needed an escort.

118   *perit:* pf., contracted from *periit,* the *i* therefore long cf 3, 174 *redit.*

119   *ingenii fons:* the offbeat rhythm and emphasis on the final syllable expresses the abrupt ceasing of the stream, like the thud of the falling ox in Verg. *A* 5, 481 *procumbit humi bos.*

120   Antony had Cicero's head and hands cut off and affixed to the rostra, the stage for orators in the forum. *ingenio* is dat. of disadvantage.

122   Cicero had a good reputation as a poet in his day (Plut. *Cic.* 2, 2), and some surviving passages are not without power. This is one of his unhappiest lines, partly for its boastfulness (Quint. 11, 1, 24), partly for the repetition of *natam (ib.* 9, 4, 41), but the effect is deliberate, as he could easily have written *O fortunatam Romam me consule natam.* Dryden imitated the effect as 'Fortune fortun'd the dying notes of Rome,/Till I, thy consul sole consol'd thy doom'. The lines come from his poem on his consulate. Tacitus (*Dial.* 21) remarks that Caesar and Brutus wrote poetry no better than Cicero, but with better fortune, since fewer people know that they did so.

123   *Antoni:* M. Antonius (c. 82-30 BC), consul at the time of Caesar's assassination; as triumvir with Octavian (the future Augustus) and Lepidus, he was responsible for Cicero's death. A gifted soldier, his entanglement with Cleopatra led to his downfall. J is alluding to Cicero's words to Antony: *contempsi Catilinae gladios, non pertimescam tuos* (2 *Phil.* 46, 118).

potuit: technically a mixed conditional, but *posse* already has the idea of potentiality and regularly falls into the indicative (Woodcock § 200).

si sic: echoing the Ciceronian effect (continued in *dixisset*).

125   *Philippica:* Cicero's fourteen speeches against Antony were so called because they rivalled Demosthenes's attacks on Philip. Curiously, the most famous, the second, referred to here, circulated as a pamphlet and was never actually delivered.

126   *uolueris:* being in scroll form, Roman books were unrolled, the pages being glued together at the margins; *quae* is subject.

a prima . . . proxima: a riddling way of saying 'second'.

illum: Demosthenes. Note how the bucolic diaeresis emphasises the end of the line.

128   *torrentem:* cf 3, 73; 10, 9.

moderantem frena: a quick change of metaphor.

theatri: theatres were frequently used for political assembly.

130   *pater:* the game of playing down the profession and status of your opponent's parents was a standard rhetorical trick which Demosthenes himself used. His father was not a blacksmith, but the owner of a sword-factory.

132   *luteo Volcano:* the god of the furnace: he is paraprosdokian *lŭteo,* 'grimy', where we expect *lūteo,* 'flame-coloured'.

rhetora: Isaeus (see on 3, 73), with whom Demosthenes studied. But his father did not send him as he was only 7 at his father's death.

133-87   *Many people think military glory something superhuman. Would they pursue the military virtues if it were not for the rewards? Those who seek glory bring their country to disaster to leave an inscription on a perishable tombstone. Witness Hannibal, the one-eyed commander on an outlandish monster. The rings from the Roman dead at Cannae were avenged by his own poison-ring. Alexander was frustrated within a single world, but died at Babylon. Xerxes whipped the winds and fettered the waves, to limp home after the destruction of his fleet at Salamis.*

133   *bellorum:* J makes clear at the outset the subject of each section.

truncis . . . tropaeis: the simplest form of trophy was formed from a couple of broken boughs fixed together to act as a kind of scarecrow for hanging up enemy armour.

134   *buccula:* 'cheek-piece' from *bucca,* though it gives us our 'buckle'.

135   *curtum temone iugum:* the meaning is clear, the construction less so. The chariot-yoke is either shortened from its pole (separation) or by a pole (measure of difference).

triremis: a war-galley, not with three bank of oars, which would be impossible to control, but with slanted benches, and three rowers to a bench, each with his own oar.

136 *aplustre:* Gk, ἄφλαστον, the curved poop with ornamental decorations attached.

arcu: i.e. a triumphal arch, as on the arches of Septimius Severus or of Constantine in Rome. But they appear near the base, not in an elevated position.

137 *ad hoc se:* harshly breaking the rhythm.

138 *barbarus:* 'foreign'; his example will be Hannibal.

induperator: cf 4, 29. There is some irony: a build-up of dignity to be deflated.

140 *inde:* from the desire for military glory.

uirtutis: originally the quality of a *uir*, courage, toughness, later more widely 'virtue'. Note that the Roman did not have to choose between two meanings: they formed a single whole for him. The Epicureans, like the Cynics, were particularly sceptical about the military virtues.

sitis est quam: offbeat rhythm.

141 *amplectitur:* an excellent example of a mixed conditional made more vivid and pungent by the indicative.

ipsam: 'for its own sake'. The whole sentence makes a memorable epigram. (Note the 'rhyme' with the previous line.)

142 *tollas:* the second person gives a conversational touch, as in Hor. *S* 1, 4, 55.

patriam: J begins from the damage to others.

olim: 'time and again', a frequent poetical use. Note the alliteration reinforcing the point.

143 *tituli:* the funerary inscription on the tombstone; cf 1, 130.

144 *haesuri:* 'intended to stick to', a common use of the fut.

quae: the antecedent is *saxis*.

145 *sterilis:* ironical. J's addition to a commonplace cf Mart. 10, 2, 9 *marmora Messallae findit caprificus.* Fig trees do indeed break slabs of stone in this way.

146 A clinching, brilliant conclusion.

147 *expende:* 'weigh': an unexpected metaphor. This sentence was a favourite with Byron.

Hannibalem: the great Carthaginian commander (c. 247-182 BC) who occupied Italy for sixteen years during the Second Punic War. He was defeated by Scipio at Zama in North Africa in 202, showed himself something of a domestic statesman in the years which followed but was eventually driven to take refuge in the East, and finally harried to suicide by Roman hostility.

148 *non capit:* 'cannot contain'.

Africa: what we call North Africa from the Atlantic to Egypt and south to the Negro peoples of the Sahel.

149 *Niloque . . . tepenti:* a commonplace phrase (Prop. 2, 33, 3). Lucan (10, 210ff) explains that the unknown sources of the Nile lie under that part of the sky where Sirius blazes.

150 *Aethiopum:* lit. 'the burnt-faced people', a general term for the black and brown races.

aliosque elephantos: i.e. different from the Indian variety.

151 *Hispania:* his father Hamilcar had secured a base for Carthaginian operations in her Spanish empire: Hannibal consolidated this. Hostilities with Rome began when he captured her ally Saguntum in 219.

Pyrenaeum: a spondaic fifth foot, not uncommon with foreign names.

152 *transilit:* in swiftness of movement he rivalled Alexander or Caesar: the first stage of the march on Rome. Note how the asyndeton expresses this.

Alpemque niuemque: 'the Alpine snows'. The crossing of the Alps was his most sensational achievement. Sir Gavin de Beer traces his route across the Rhône north of Arles, then northwards till the junction with the Drôme, up the Drôme past Die, and over the Col de Grimone through Bassin de Gap to the Durance and over the Col de la Traversette down to Turin: see *Hannibal's March* (1967), *Hannibal* (1969). For a criticism see F. W. Walbank in *JRS* 46 (1956) 37-45, and for a more recent treatment, bringing him over either the Col du Clapier or the Col de la Traversette see D. Proctor *Hannibal's March in History* (1971).

153 *aceto:* Livy (21, 37) mentions this: not Polybius. But the method is well attested in antiquity (Plin. *NH* 33, 21, 71; 23, 27, 57; Vitr. 8, 3, 19; DC 36, 18, 2), and de Beer experimented successfully with it. The rock is first heated by a bonfire and then douched with vinegar. The troops would have plenty: vinegar and water was the regular drink of the private soldier.

155 *acti:* partitive gen.: 'there is nothing within the field of the accomplished'. Lucan (2, 657) says of Caesar *nil actum credens, cum quid superesset agendum,* which would account for the alternative reading *actum.* The sudden change to direct speech is dramatic and vivid; cf 291.

Poeno milite: the soldiers are treated as an instrument.

156 *Subura:* see on 3, 5. Satirical: it was the 'red-light' area.

157 *tabella:* the diminutive suggests scorn: perhaps 'cartoon'.

158 *Gaetula:* the Gaetuli were a Saharan tribe. By 217 Hannibal had one elephant left which he rode himself.

luscum: he lost the sight of one eye. The whole portrait (derived from Liv. 22, 2) is satirical.

159 *uincitur:* at Zama in 202.

160 *praeceps:* not immediately; J has condensed the events for rhetorical effect. He did not reach the court of Antiochus of Syria till 195.

161 *cliens:* J imposes the picture he has already drawn in several satires, of the *cliens* dependent on a *patronus.*

praetoria: 'palace'.

regis: Prusias of Bithynia (in north-west Asia Minor).

162 *uigilare:* again from his picture of the *cliens* at Rome (5, 19).

163 *animae:* dat. with *dabunt.*

res humanas miscuit: 'turned the world topsy-turvy'.

olim: here 'in the past' (contrast 142).

164 *saxa:* Pyrrhus of Epirus was so killed in 272 BC.

165 *Cannarum:* Hannibal's greatest victory₁ In 216 BC he faced the consuls L. Aemilius Paullus and C. Terentius Varro. Much outnumbered, he weakened and advanced his centre with instructions for an orderly withdrawal; his cavalry routed the Roman wings leaving their centre encircled.

uindex: he had collected the gold rings from the Roman dead and sent them to Carthage.

166 *anulus:* an unexpected and brilliant climax held up till the end. He kept the poison which he used for his suicide in a ring.

i: addressed not to Hannibal but to the hearer ambitious for military glory.

167 *pueris placeas:* presumably as an eventual triumph over disaster for Rome.

declamatio fias: Hannibal was indeed a theme for the *suasoriae* of the rhetorical schools: see on 1, 16; 7, 161. The line forms a brilliant epigrammatic climax, with its suggestion that this was the purpose of all his endeavours. Johnson in his imitation, with Charles XII of Sweden as his subject, has the excellent couplet: 'He left a name, at which the world grew pale,/To point a moral, and adorn a tale.' J's section, like Johnson's, might have been better ended here.

168 *Pellaeo iuueni:* antonomasia: Alexander the Great (356-323 BC), who in a brief life of conquest had swept halfway across Asia and far into India. He was born in Pella in Macedonia. The picture of Alexander sighing for fresh worlds to conquer is unauthentic but *ben trovato.* It comes from Valerius Maximus 8, 14, who tells how Alexander, hearing the philosophical view that there were many worlds, cried *heu me miserum, quod ne uno quidem adhuc sum potitus.* But he did have a kind of inner drive, a sudden almost mystical desire to reach out beyond the horizon: see V. Ehrenberg *Alexander and the Greeks* 1938 (c.2) 'Pothos'. The idea is well illustrated by Arrian *Alex.* 7, 1. There is an excellent Latin epigram on Alexander: *sufficit huic tumulus cui non suffecerat orbis;/res breuis huic ampla est, cui fuit ampla breuis (Anth. Vet. Lat. Epig.* 2, 15; cf 2, 17, 33 *non satis mundus fuit unus illi).* The comparison between Hannibal and Alexander is a commonplace (e.g. Liv. 35, 14, 6-11). *non sufficit orbis* comes from Lucan 5, 356. For Roman criticism of Alexander, cf Quint. 1, 1, 9.

169 An excellent image of the sea seething through a narrow strait: *limite:* abl. of cause. It is a parody of Luc. 6, 63 *aestuat angusta rabies ciuilis harena.*

170 *Gyarae . . . Seripho:* two minor Aegean islands: see on 1, 73; 6, 564. Note that Seriphus, an island, is fem.

171 *a figulis . . . urbem:* typical J antonomasia: Babylon, famed for its brick construction (Hdt. 1, 178ff). Alexander died there, after defying warnings by seers not to enter. As he sickened, they asked a god if they should move him: the answer was 'Leave him; that is best.' 'Whom the gods love, dies young.'

173 *quantula . . . corpuscula:* the double diminutive is pointed.

creditur olim: 'It has long been believed that'. *Athos* is the grammatical subject. The words, and so J's scepticism, are picked out by the bucolic diaeresis.

174 *uelificatus Athos:* Athos, the Sacred Mountain, 2100 metres high, stands at the tip of the most easterly of the three promontories of Chalcidice in the north Aegean. In 492 BC a Persian fleet was wrecked there. When Xerxes was planning his expedition against Greece in the late 480s he determined to avoid the danger by digging a canal through the neck of the peninsula, to a

length of nearly 2½ km (Hdt. 7, 22ff).
Despite the scepticism of J and others
the canal was completed. *uelifico* and
uelificor are both found. 'Athos took
sail', an amiable hyperbole, is perhaps
better than the awkwardness of 'Athos
was sailed'.
  Graecia mendax: back to the prejudices
of the third Satire. This was a Roman
prejudice: see Vergil's picture of Sinon
(*A* 2, 152; 2, 195). The Romans were not
always innocent (cf Liv. 42, 47).
  175 *historia:* a jibe at Herodotus, the
fifth-century historian, whose accuracy is
sometimes excessively impugned and
sometimes indiscreetly exaggerated. The
Latin word means very much our 'history'
but to Herodotus it meant 'researches'.
  175-6 This is a reference to the bridge
of boats which Xerxes used to enable
his army to cross the Hellespont (Hdt. 7,
33-6). J makes a neat antithesis:
Herodotus turns the land into sea and the
sea into land.
  177 *amnes:* Herodotus (7, 21) says
that only the larger rivers were not drained
dry.
  178 *prandente:* this touch is J's
hyperbole.
  madidis . . . alis: a complex image. The
poet taking wings is a commonplace. Why
are the wings wet? The scholiast says
because poets who take a lot of pains over
their recitals sweat under the armpits.
Others have supposed that Sostratus was
seeking his inspiration in wine, not
finding it elsewhere. But surely the
reference is to Icarus. Sostratus, who is
not otherwise known, was too high-flying
and came a flop.
  179 *ille:* Xerxes, who is characteristically
not named.
  Salamine: island not far from Athens,
in whose bay was fought the famous
sea-battle of 480 BC in which the Greeks,
through the genius of Themistocles,
defeated the Persian armada.
  180 *Corum atque Eurum:* the NW
(often Caurus) and SE winds. Herodotus
tells how Xerxes gave the Hellespont a
whipping, but the whipping of the winds
is not otherwise recorded.
  181 *barbarus:* non-Greek in birth and
behaviour.
  Aeolio: the Romans use an adj., where
we use a gen., 'of Aeolus', god of the
winds.
  carcere: he kept the winds in a cave
(Verg. *A* 1, 52ff).
  182 *Ennosigaeum:* a five-syllable

foreign name to end the line: it does not
affect the basic rhythm. 'Earth-shaker'
is a Homeric description of Poseidon-
Neptune, god of the sea: earthquakes and
tidal waves go together. The first bridge
of boats was destroyed by a storm; in addi-
tion to the flogging mentioned above (on
180) Xerxes had manacles thrown in
(Hdt. 7, 35).
  183 *mitius id sane:* 'I suppose it was
an act of some clemency'.
  et stigmate: 'branding as well': a
satirical touch, since the water would
quench the branding iron: but there were
rumours of this (Hdt. 7, 35; Plut. *Mor.*
455d). The text is due to E. W. Weber.
  184 *huic . . . deorum?:* all three
punishments were appropriate to slaves,
flogging, fettering and branding. There
are myths of gods and demi-gods acting as
slaves to mortals, Poseidon-Neptune
himself and Apollo to Laomedon, Apollo
to Admetus, Heracles-Hercules to
Omphale. But Xerxes would be an impos-
sible master.
  185 *una naue:* a later exaggeration.
  186 Characteristic hyperbole, matched
by striking sound-effect.
  187 *totiens* with *optata* and *exegit.*

188-288 *'Grant long life.' But old age
is full of misfortunes. Young men differ
from one another, old men are all the
same, helpless, hostile, pleasureless,
impotent, deaf, subject to every disease,
including the loss of mental faculties.
And if they remain fit, it is only to watch
their family dying round them. Nestor
mourned Antilochus, Peleus Achilles,
Laertes Ulysses. Priam would better have
died young. To pass over Mithradates and
Croesus, Marius would better have died in
triumph than become a refugee, Pompey
would better have died of fever than lose
his head, a fate which even the
Catilinarians escaped.*
  188 Again a clear beginning to the new
section. There is a parody of Verg. *A* 3,
85 *da propriam, Thymbraee, domum, da
moenia fessis.*
  189 *recto uoltu:* cf 6, 401 *recta facie.*
The general effect is that when young and
fit this is your prayer, when older or ill
(*pallidus* covers both) it is your sole
prayer. The scholiast explains it *laetus
et tristis uitam longam optas.*
  192 *deformem:* a slightly odd rhetorical
repetition.
  194 *Thabraca:* a town on the coast of
Numidia, later the site of a Christian

bishopric, and in AD 398 the deathplace of Gildo.

195 An excellent and amusing picture. The MS *iam mater* makes no sense. I have ventured *Garamantis* in parody of Verg. *A* 4, 198, from the African tribe.

197 The MS *ille alio* can hardly be right, as it breaks the *ille hoc . . . hic illo* contrast. Giangrande ingeniously proposes *ardalio* (Mart. 2, 7, 8; 4, 78, 10), a person who is always on the go.

198 *facies:* sc. *est: membra,* etc. are best taken in apposition.

cum uoce: effective: the limbs shake in rhythm with the voice.

199 *lēue:* 'smooth'.

infantia: 'an incapacity to talk properly coming from a running nose'.

200 *misero:* dat. of the agent: 'the poor fellow has to break'.

gingiua . . . inermi: precisely 'with nonviolent gum(s)'.

202 *captatori:* dat. of the person or thing indirectly concerned: we can say 'turns the stomach *of*'. We have met the legacy-hunters several times (e.g. 1, 146; 3, 129; 3, 221; 4, 19; cf Petronius *Sat.* 124ff). Cossus has appeared at 3, 184, as a man worth having as a *patronus:* conceivably the same, though the admirable exemplar of 8, 21 is clearly different.

203 *torpente palato:* abl. abs.

205-6 *iacet . . . et . . . iacebit:* cf Verg. *A* 6, 617 *sedet aeternumque sedebit.*

205 *ramice:* a varicose deformation of the testicles.

neruus: the penis, as the scholiast tells us.

206 *palpetur:* stroked, coaxed, worked on.

208 *canities:* the application of greyness to the pubic hair is an amusing displacement.

quid quod: 'what of the fact that'.

209 *quae . . . uiribus:* Green 'when desire outruns performance'.

partis . . . alterius: the ear, as we soon find.

210-2 The writing is elliptical. 'For what pleasure is there, when *someone* is singing, even though he be outstanding, or when the harpist *is* Seleucus, or *when the harpists are* those who are usually resplendent in gold costume?' Seleucus is otherwise unknown. The *cithara* was an elaborate lyre, seemingly with twelve strings, though some writers speak of fifteen or even eighteen, plucked either with the fingers of the left hand, or with a plectrum held in the right. The elaborate costumes are well-attested, Lucian (*Adv. Indoct.* 8-9) has an account of one

Euangelos who appeared at Delphi with a purple robe embroidered with gold, a gold laurel-wreath with emeralds for berries, and a golden lyre encrusted with beryls and sapphires and decorated with reliefs of the Muses, Apollo and Orpheus. His performance was not up to his appearance.

213 *magni . . . theatri:* a slight pun: the reference is to the theatre of Pompey of 55 BC (Pompeius Magnus), the largest of the three in Rome at this period. It had 40 000 *loca,* but these seem to have been estimated in units of one foot, and even in a crowd a spectator needs more than that, and we should think of a maximum of 27 000. Only foundations remain, though the modern street-system shows the site plainly enough. It was part of an arts complex; it was in its meeting hall that Julius Caesar was assassinated. The other theatres were the theatre of Balbus of 13 BC with 11 510 *loca* or 7-8 000 seats, and the theatre of Marcellus of 11 BC with 20 500 *loca* or 14 000 seats. The figures are small compared with the Circus Maximus with its quarter of a million capacity, but colossal compared with even the largest modern theatre (La Scala at Milan seats 3 600).

215 *auris:* subject.

216 *puer:* the 'boy', a slave called *cubicularius* who announced visitors. We have moved from the theatre to the home. Cicero has a good story (*De Or.* 2, 68, 276). Nasica called on Ennius. The maid said 'He's not at home' — but he was. A few days later Ennius called on Nasica. Nasica shouted that he wasn't at home. 'But surely I recognise your voice?' 'Impudent fellow! I believed your servant's word; you won't believe mine.'

quot nuntiet horas: the Romans had no mechanical clocks. For the most part they would go by the position of the sun. The passage of time could be calculated by a water-clock (*clepsydra*) or the burning of a marked candle. In the daytime the exact hour would be taken from a sundial (*solarium*); a *puer* had the duty of keeping an eye on this to ensure his master was not late for his engagements (Mart. 8, 67, 1).

218 *febre calet sola:* a good joke, though a stock one (cf. Mar. 3, 93).

agmine facto: cf Hor. *Od.* 1, 3, 30 *noua febrium/terris incubuit cohors:* military metaphor, none the worse for being obvious.

220 *expediam:* fut. ind.: the 'mixed'

conditional with the if-clause more remote
and the main clause more vivid is neither
rare nor difficult.

220-6 Parody of elegiac writing as Ov.
Tr. 4, 1, 55-60; *Pont.* 2, 7, 25-30. It is
brilliantly carried out. Imitated by Boileau,
and in turn by Sir Samuel Garth (1714):
'Can you count the silver lights/That deck
the skies and cheer the nights;/Or the
leaves that show the vales,/Where graves
are stripped by winter gales;/Or the drops
that in the morn/Hang with transparent
pearl the thorn;/Or bridegroom's joys, or
miser's cares./Or gamester's oaths, or
hermit's prayers:/Or envy's pangs, or
love's alarms./Or Marlb'rough's acts, or
Wharton's charms?' See also John Donne,
Sat. 1, 53ff.

Oppia: also at 322. The name may be
taken from the Vestal condemned for
unchastity in 483 BC (Liv. 2, 42).

221 *Themison:* a famous medical
name, a doctor from Laodicea in the first
century BC, who founded the 'Methodist'
school of medical practice under
Epicurean influence. He is said to have
developed bloodletting through leeches,
and to have encouraged the systematic
study of chronic diseases. It is part of J's
wit to have applied this name to the sort
of doctor who buries his mistakes.

autumno: the worst season for disease.

222 *Basilus:* a businessman not other-
wise known: the lawyer of 7, 145 seems
different.

socios: 'partners'.

circumscripserit: almost as we say 'run
rings round'; cf Cic. *Ac.* 2, 15, 46.
circumscripti atque decepti.

Hirrus: not known.

223 *exorbeat:* from *ex-sorbere*
'drain dry'.

224 *Maura:* perhaps a black girl: at
6, 308 she has no place for the Altar of
Chastity.

inclinet: 'lays', like *resupinat* (3,
112). The homosexually amorous
schoolmaster is otherwise unknown (but
cf Mart. 7, 62). For such corruption,
cf Hor. *S* 1, 6, 81ff.

226 Repeated from 1, 25 q.v.

227 *ille umero, hic:* the elisions help
the sense of something wrong at the
joints.

debilis: from *de-habilis*, 'disabled'
and so 'weak'. Maecenas (cf 1, 66) had
some verses *debilem facito manu,
debilem pede coxo/ . . . /uita dum superest,
benest,* of which Seneca (*Ep.* 101, 11) is
very critical. Note how two successive

lines have a break after the fifth foot. It has
the effect of holding up the end of the
line, followed by a rapid acceleration
into the next.

228 *ille oculos:* another effective
symbolic elision.

luscis inuidet: so the proverb, out of
which H. G. Wells spun a powerful short
story, 'In the country of the blind the
one-eyed man is king'.

229 *cibum accipiunt:* the elision when
we are expecting the third-foot caesura
express the gulp which sucks down the
food.

digitis alienis: the four-syllable ending
creates a harsh, alien, offbeat rhythm.

231 *pullus hirundinis:* a good simile,
parodying Hom. *Il.* 9, 323-4.

232 *ieiuna:* 'depriving herself'.

omni: we say 'than any'.

233 *dementia:* not 'madness' but
'loss of mental faculties'.

234 *nomina seruorum:* Plin. *NH*
7, 90 has an interesting passage on
examples of loss of memory, including
one man who did not remember his
mother and relatives, another who forgot
his slaves' names, and a third (Messala
Corvinus) who could not remember his
own.

235 *praeterita cenauit nocte:*
compare the Cambridge story of a well-
known Congregational minister meeting a
Girtonian in the street. 'You must come
and have a meal with us some time.'
'I've just been having lunch with you.'

237 *heredes uetat esse suos:* 'legally
prevents his own family from being his
heirs'. This seems the structure, though
sui heredes is a legal term for a wife and
dependent children. By Roman law a
testator who wished to disinherit his
natural heirs must do so expressly. J's
point is not quite clear: he seems to have
moved from forgetfulness to eccentricity,
and returned to 201 unless the point is
that he forgets he has flesh-and-blood
relations.

238 *Phiale:* his mistress.

artificis: she's a professional. The
wording suggests *fellatio.*

239 *quod:* 'because', 'in view of the
fact that'.

steterat: for *prostiterat* 'had been a
prostitute'.

fornicis: see on 3, 156.

240 *ut:* 'although', picked up by
tamen. Even full possession of the senses
means only that you are in full receipt of
sorrow.

243 *renouata:* with *clade.* There is a slight irregularity of rhythm, with a secondary accent on the first syllable of *renouata,* which intensifies the distress.

244 *inque:* for *in* at the end of a line, cf 6, 58.

245 *nigra ueste:* with the Romans, as with us, for mourning: it is not so in all cultures.

246 *rex Pylius:* Nestor, king of Pylos, whose palace has been unearthed by Carl Blegen on the coast of the Peloponnese in our own day.

Homero: Il. 1, 250. Homer was regarded as the major authority on anything under the sun: the theme is excellently treated in E. A. Havelock's controversial *Preface to Plato* Oxford 1963 c. 4 'The Homeric Encyclopedia'. The slightly apologetic *si credis* is standard cliché with reference to Homer: Thuc. 1, 9, 4; Sen. *QN* 6, 26, 1; *Priap.* 80, 5.

247 *a cornice:* we say 'second only to', the Romans 'second counting from'. The crow proverbially lived nine human generations, Nestor three (Hesiod in Plut. *Mor.* 415 D).

249 *dextra:* ones and tens were counted on the left hand, hundreds on the right. J is reckoning three generations to a century.

250 *quique . . . bibit:* satirical climax. Every word in this line, if we allow the *n-m* equivalence in *nouum,* has a kind of internal alliteration. Note how the diaeresis after *bibit* injects great earnestness into the words which follow.

251 Not a Homeric scene, though cf *Od.* 3, 111ff. The story was told in Arctinus's lost *Aethiopis;* cf Pind. *Pyth.* 6, 28. But proximately J is parodying Prop. 2, 13, 47-50 *cum si longaeuo minuisset fata senectae/Gallicus Iliacis miles in aggeribus,/non aut Antilochi uidisset corpus humari,/diceret aut 'o mors, cur mihi sera uenis?'.* For similar thoughts see Cic. *De Or.* 3, 3, 12 on Crassus; Plut. *Mor.* 113F on Priam.

252 *stamine:* mythology told of the three Fates, Lachesis, who allots to each his destiny, Clotho, who spins the thread of his life, Atropos, who cannot be turned aside from severing the thread at the appointed time.

acris Antilochi: Nestor's son, killed by Memnon when seeking to save his father. *acris* gives the impression of being padding; but (a) it is alliterative, (b) it sums up in one word Homer's description (*Od.* 3, 111-2), (c) it represents his

eagerness to save his father, (d) it contrasts the dynamic of youth with the despondency of age, (e) it is ethically ambiguous (eager and impetuous), (f) it is synonymous with the metaphorical use of *ardens.*

253 *barbam:* an incongruous detail, but it emphasises his youth, since at this period the Romans were cleanshaven in middle life, cf 6, 105; 8, 166.

ardentem: on the funeral pyre, a sick joke, since *acer* = (in another sense) *ardens.*

ab omni: with *socio.*

255 *admiserit:* 'committed'. Servius, the Vergilian commentator, says that J borrowed the rhetorical *color* of this line from *A* 9, 497 *quando aliter nequeo crudelem abrumpere uitam.*

256 *Peleus:* husband of the sea-nymph Thetis, father of Achilles, who chose a short glorious life rather than a long inglorious one. At Hom. *Il,* 24, 534-49 he laments the sorrow his death will bring his father; cf also Quint. Smyrn. 3, 450-8. We must supply *queritur.*

raptum: often of death in poetry. In one funerary inscription (Orelli 4475) *rapta est* appears.

Achillem: greatest of the Greek soldiers at Troy. The poem we call *The Iliad* is about his Wrath. He was killed by an arrow shot by Paris: according to one story his mother had dipped him in the river Styx to make him invulnerable, but the arrow hit the heel at the point where the grip of her fingers prevented the invulnerability reaching: hence our proverbial 'Achilles's heel'.

257 *alius:* Laertes, father of Odysseus-Ulysses. For the riddling use of *alius,* cf 1, 10.

fas: it was normally *nefas* to mourn the living, but Ulysses was 'missing, presumed dead'.

Ithacum: Ulysses, whose home was on the island of Ithaca. Archaeologists and antiquaries still differ about its identification: the majority opt for either Thiaki or Leucas, one of the Ionian islands off the west coast of Greece.

natantem: 'at sea': at one point he did in fact 'swim for it'.

258 *Troia:* the city commanding the north-west point of Asia Minor, excavated by Schliemann and later by Blegen, who revealed a complex of cities of different dates, Priam's city being seemingly VII A. The construction is abl. abs.

Priamus: King of Troy in Homer's *Iliad.* He became a stock example of the reverse

of fortune: Πριαμικαὶ τύχαι. The whole
passage is based on Cic. *TD* 1, 35, 85.

uenisset: the if-clause is held up till 263.

259 *Assaraci:* Priam's great-uncle,
Tros, the eponymous city-founder had
three sons, Assaracus, Ilus, Gánymedes.
Priam was Ilus's grandson.

sollemnibus: noun. The root seems to
be *sollus-annus* 'whole year'; annual
ceremonies. We derive 'solemn' from it.

Hectore: one of Priam's fifty sons, the
heroic defender of Troy, whose death at
Achilles's hands is the climax of *The Iliad,*
so that in fact Priam mourned Hector.

funus: the body, as in Verg. *A* 9, 491;
Prop. 1, 17, 8 (*haecine parua meum funus
harena teget*).

261 *Iliadum:* the women of Troy or
Ilion. In *The Iliad* the men begin the
mourning, and the women follow with
Hector's wife Andromache first (24,
722-3). In Roman ceremonies a woman
known as *praefica* was hired to lead the
keening.

ut: used loosely. Note that in translation
we have to choose between saying that *ut*
introduces a clause defining *Iliadum lacrimas*
and that *ut* means 'when' (the subjunctive
being explained by the conditional), but
to the Roman listener *ut* was *ut*, blending
the senses we analyse as 'when', 'as', 'in
order to', 'with the result that', etc. We
can get round it by 'with Cassandra leading'
or 'and Cassandra would have led'.

262 *Cassandra . . . Polyxena:* two of
Priam's daughters. They in fact survived
Priam, but as prisoners of war were in no
position to lead the mourning. Cassandra
became Agamemnon's concubine, to be
killed with him on his return home;
Polyxena was sacrificed to the dead
Achilles.

palla: a large rectangular shawl, sometimes
but not always drawn over the head, falling
to the knees, and fastened with brooches.
The tearing of the clothes in sorrow is a
widespread custom, e.g. among the
Hebrews (2 Sam. 1:11; 3:31), among the
Greeks (Aesch. *Choeph.* 27-8; Lucian *De
Luctu* 12). Nero tore his clothes when he
heard of Galba's revolt (Suet. *Ner.* 42).
See also Stat. *Theb.* 3, 125; 9, 154.

263 *diuerso:* 'different'.

264 *audaces:* often in Latin of criminal
enterprises: note the personification of the
ships as members of the gang.

Paris: Priam's son whose elopement
with Helen, queen of Sparta, was the *casus
belli.* Note the swift movement of the
second half of the line.

265 *omnia uidit:* the bucolic diaeresis
creates a dramatic pause.

266 J is alluding (without parody) to
Verg. *A* 3, 1-2 *postquam res Asiae
Priamique euertere gentem/inmeritam
uisum superis;* cf 2, 554-7. Asia, originally
a town in Lydia, is often used of the
dominion of Troy. The Roman reader
thought naturally of the province which
covered western Asia Minor.

267 *miles:* 'as a soldier'.

tiara: a foreign word to give colour.
J wants to convey an Eastern royal
headdress without precisely envisaging it.
Note the powerful alliteration and
assonance.

268 *summi Iouis:* Verg. *A* 2, 550 has
altaria ad ipsa; that it was the altar of Zeus
Herkeios comes from Arctinus, who was
followed by Euripides (*Tro.* 483) and
Quintus of Smyrna (13, 222).

ut uetulus bos: the offbeat rhythm with
the monosyllabic thud of the falling body
is imitated from Verg. *A* 5, 481
procumbit humi bos. Note how J elaborates
the simile. The comparison of Priam to an
ox is intentionally ludicrous.

270 *ab ingrato:* both words personify
the plough.

271-2 Hecabe-Hecuba, Priam's queen,
was turned into a kind of hellhound (Eur.
Hec. 1265; Ov. *M* 13, 565ff; Sen. *Agam.*
705ff).

273 *nostros:* Romans.

regem . . . Ponti: Mithradates VI
Eupator (130-63 BC), King of Pontus on
the south coast of the Black Sea. It would
be hard to better J. E. B. Mayor's word-
picture: 'Gigantic of stature, hardy and
fleet of foot, restless in enterprise, he
fought in the thickest of the fight in his
old age, could speak all the 21 tongues
spoken by his subjects, and was the one
formidable obstacle to Roman power in
the East before the Parthian Wars.'
Checked by Sulla, he defied his successors
among the Roman commanders, but was
weakened by Lucullus and finally
defeated by Pompey.

274 *Croesum:* King of Lydia (c. 560-
546 BC), proverbial for his wealth and
the overthrow of his power by the Persians.
He is one of Seneca's examples of the
instability of Fortune (*Tranq. An.* 11, 10).

Solonis: Athenian statesman (c. 640-
560 BC), one of the proverbial Seven
Sages. Herodotus (1, 29ff.) tells the
story of their encounter incomparably.
Croesus fêted Solon, and asked him
whether he had ever seen anyone more

blessed. Solon promptly adduced Tellus, an Athenian patriot who died in battle, and Cleobis and Biton, men of Argos, who did religious duty to their mother and were granted an immediate peaceful death. To Croesus he said 'Man is wholly chance . . . I cannot answer your question until I hear that you have ended your life with glory . . . . Until a man is dead, we must suspend judgement and call him fortunate not blessed.' The historicity of the story is chronologically unlikely.

276ff: this is C. Marius (157-86 BC), Roman general and populist leader. After saving Rome from the northern invaders, and being consul six times, he was ousted by Sulla and the right wing, hid in the rushes in the marshes of Minturnae by the *Via Appia,* and was captured and imprisoned for execution, but the executioner refused to kill him and helped him to escape to Carthage where he lived as a beggar. The story is taken from Velleius Paterculus 2, 19. It is not to J's point to recall that Marius in fact returned to a seventh consulate and died in office.

277   *uicta Carthagine:* Carthage had been destroyed in 146 BC. C. Gracchus's attempt to redevelop the site failed, and it was not till the early Empire that there was much more than shacks and squatters there. Plut. *Mar.* 40 tells of Marius's retort to the Roman administrator 'Report that you have seen Gaius Marius sitting as a refugee in the ruins of Carthage.' Some of Marius's own victories were won in North Africa against Jugurtha.

278   *hinc:* from living too long.

illo ciue: abl. of comparison with *beatius: ciue* is emphatic, contrasting with the 'enemy of the state' which he was declared.

279   *quid:* emphatic anaphora.

Roma: even more of a climax than *natura in terris.*

280   *circumducto:* the triumphal procession winding through the capital.

281   *pompa animam:* hiatus, giving the effect of the last gasp.

opimam: a joke since the *opima spolia* were the spoils of honour in war.

282   *Teutonico:* Marius defeated the Teutones at Aquae Sextiae in 102 BC and the Cimbri near Vercellae in 101 BC; he refused to accept more than one triumph for both victories.

283   *Pompeio:* see on 108.

Campania: the region round Naples. Pompey fell ill there in 50 BC. The passage is derived from similar reflections in

Cic. *TD* 1, 35, 86; cf on 258.

284   *urbes et . . . uota:* hendiadys.

285   *Fortuna:* often of a man's personal 'lucky star'; contrasted in this way in Lucan's Stoic epic with *fatum,* Destiny.

urbis: the Greek Tyche becomes a city-goddess; there is a famous statue of the Tyche of Antioch by Eutychides: a good copy is in the Vatican Museum. *FORTVNA VRBIS* appears on Roman coins. There is an implication that Pompey's good luck and Rome's ran out simultaneously: J is not afraid to express opposition to the imperial régime.

286   *uicto:* dat. of disadvantage.

hoc cruciatu: bucolic diaeresis followed by offbeat rhythm: emphatic and contorted.

287   *Lentulus:* P. Cornelius Lentulus Sura, consul 71 BC, expelled from the senate for immorality in the following year, praetor in 63, Catiline's chief lieutenant, arrested for conspiracy and executed by strangulation.

Cethegus: C. Cornelius Cethegus, senator and another conspirator who suffered the same fate. Note the alliteration (including Q and G) which is very sharp, and extends over three lines.

288   *Catilina:* L. Sergius Catilina, defeated for election as consul for 63 and again for 62, planned a conspiracy which was foiled by Cicero, and died fighting *pulcherrima morte, si pro patria sic concidisset* (Flor. 2, 12).

toto: i.e. unmutilated, though Dio Cassius 37, 40 says that the head was cut off. The fear of mutilation is striking; to our way of thought it is an odd ending to the section.

289-345   *Many mothers pray for good looks for their children. Good looks brought disaster to Lucretia and Verginia; they bring parents nothing but anxiety; they kindle illicit passions in those who see them, and lead their possessors to adultery and its consequences. They did nothing but harm to Hippolytus and Bellerophon, and brought C. Silius to the point where he had to choose between an immediate death for offending Messalina or death a few days later for offending the emperor.*

289   *formam:* the first word of the section, making clear the theme.

modico . . . murmure: the patterned alliteration is very skilful, the *m* onomatopoeic of the murmured prayer, the *p* letting the satirist's scorn break through.

290   *Veneris:* the goddess of love will naturally grant beauty; cf *uenustas.*

anxia mater: from Prop. 2, 22, 42, a poem which contains the assertion that it is never hard work to serve Venus.

291   *usque . . . uotorum:* 'to the point of the most extravagant requests'.

292   *corripias?:* 'Why should you criticise that?' The sudden change to direct speech is dramatic and vivid; cf 155.

Latona Diana: Hom. *Od.* 6, 102-8 and Verg. *A* 1, 498-502 speak of Leto-Latona's joy in the beauty of her daughter Artemis-Diana.

293   *Lucretia:* a famous Roman legendary figure, wife of Collatinus; her beauty inflamed Sextus, son of Tarquinius Superbus, last of the seven kings of Rome, who raped her. She told her story and committed suicide: a popular uprising expelled the Tarquins and established the Republic in 509 BC. The tale is excellently told by Livy (1, 57-8) and Ovid (*F* 2, 721-852). It has attracted post-Renaissance western painters, e.g. for the rape Titian in the Fitzwilliam Museum, Cambridge; for the suicide the elder Cranach in the Munich Pinakothek, Rembrandt in the Minneapolis Art Institute.

294   *cuperet:* 'would be passionately anxious to' (if she could): a strong word. Note the asyndeton and change of form between the two parts of the sentence.

Rutilae: not otherwise recorded, but presumably a well-known hunchback.

Verginia: another familiar tradition of sixty years later: she was *forma excellentem,* daughter of L. Verginius, engaged to L. Icilius. Appius Claudius, the decemvir, tried to do violence to her. Her father stabbed her to save her from further degradation, and a rising ousted the decemvirs (Liv. 3, 44-51 who speaks of *puellae infelicem formam;* DH 11, 28-40).

295   *suum:* the best reading, referring to *gibbum,* used with grim irony of Verginia's bosom. The inferior reading *suam* would refer to *faciem.*

filius autem: emphasised by the bucolic diaeresis. *autem* expresses either a strong additional assertion, as here ('Yes, and'), or a strong counter-assertion ('Yes, but').

296   *corporis egregii:* gen. of description with *filius.*

miseros trepidosque: predicate: he keeps them in a state of tortured fearfulness.

298   *licet:* 'although'; the main verb in 304 is also *licet.*

horrida: 'unsophisticated'.

299   *Sabinos:* the type of honourable simplicity; cf 3, 85; 3, 168; 6, 164.

300   *praeterea:* continuing the 'although' clause.

301   *sanguine:* Diogenes the 'dog', seeing a boy blushing, said 'Cheers! that's the colour of virtue' (DL 6, 54).

302   *conferre potest plus:* the offbeat rhythm and alliteration on p run counter to the seeming optimism of the words.

304   *uiro:* i.e. he is the object of homosexual attention.

corruptoris: fifth foot spondee laying great weight upon the word.

306   The bucolic diaeresis isolates the epigram in the first part as well as picking out what follows.

ephebum: Greek term, technically at Athens of the 18-20 age-group, but more loosely of adolescents. J perhaps uses it to allude adversely to Greek homosexuality, though his purview is wider.

307   *deformem:* a brilliant touch. No one who is already *deformis* is castrated so as to become *deformis.*

castrauit: note the word order: the castration takes place in the inside of the fortress: also the pun on *castra (= arx).*

308   In its own way a model line. The non-bandy-legged adolescent embraces Nero and the rape: the two four-syllable words set off the two sharply definite words between: the offbeat rhythm at the end marks the satirical contempt. For *praetextatus* see 1, 78, but note a double meaning, since *praetextata uerba* are obscenities. *loripedem* seems to mean 'with feet or legs like thongs', i.e. not rigid. Nero's amorous adventures with the attractive of both sexes were notorious. The young eunuch Sporus was with him at his death; a current joke ran that it was a pity that Nero's father hadn't been satisfied with a similar wife (Suet. *Ner.* 28). Domitian (who is always to be considered when J mentions Nero) was alleged to have been the object of others' homosexual attentions in his youth, but heterosexual in his own lusts (Suet. *Dom.* 1; 22).

309   *strumosum:* scrofulous.

utero: of the male paunch; cf Verg. *A* 7, 499.

310   *i nunc:* a favourite phrase of J, as generally in first-century rhetoric; cf 6, 306; 12, 57.

iuuenis: common in verse for the unmetrical *filii* (cf 3, 158; 8, 262), though the word has additional bite.

laetare tui, quem: the irregular rhythm emphasises the sarcasm.

311 *discrimina:* double meaning: he already has *distinction* of appearance: it will lead him into *danger.* The bucolic diaeresis picks out the next two words.

312 *publicus:* with many shades of meaning, 'notorious' 'promiscuous', 'common-or-garden'.

313 *ex ira:* Clausen's suggestion (*CR* 1 (1951) 73-4); the MSS have *irati, exire irati* or *exigere irati.* Housman's *lex irae* is also attractive.

debet: Valerius Maximus (6, 1, 13) cites examples where the adulterer was whipped, castrated or *familiae stuprandus* (i.e. subjected to sexual degradation by the slaves of the injured husband). At Athens there was a revenge known as *raphanidosis,* which consisted in thrusting a radish up the offender's rear (Ar. *Clouds* 1083). Catullus (15, 19) links this with the similar use of a mullet mentioned below (317). Augustus tried to legislate against adultery, to check both immorality and excessive vengeance.

nec erit . . . Martis: sense-construction: strictly 'his star will be no luckier than Mars's'.

astro: in astrological thought the position of the heavenly bodies at a person's birth affects his destiny: the joke here is that Mars is one of the heavenly bodies.

314 *Martis:* caught in adultery with Aphrodite-Venus by the injured husband Hephaestus-Vulcan through a mechanical net (*laqueos*), and exposed in the act to the other gods. But Hermes's comment was that it would have been worth it (Hom. *Od.* 8, 266-369).

exigit autem: again picked out by bucolic diaeresis.

315 *ille dolor . . . ulla dolori:* an extraordinary assonance.

316 *necat:* justified in Athenian law, and in earlier Roman times provided both wife and adulterer were killed: later the wife was spared and the adulterer subject to death from the husband only if he were a slave or ex-slave or condemned criminal. See Mayor ad loc. Note *necat - secat.*

cruentis uerberibus: based on Hor. *S* 1, 2, 37-46 who is referring to Milo's flogging of Sallust for adultery with his wife Fausta.

317 *mugilis:* peculiarly painful because of its large spined head: the scholiast says *mugilis piscis grandi capite postremus exilis qui in podicem moechorum*

deprehensorum solebat immitti. The French call it *diable de mer,* the Americans bullhead. See on 313.

318 *Endymion:* handsome young man, a prince or shepherd in different versions, who attracted the love of Selene, the Moon, and was put to sleep so that she could come down each night and embrace him. Their love forms an attractive episode in Cavalli's opera *La Calisto.* Endymion is the subject of poems by Keats and Longfellow and a novel by Lord Beaconsfield.

fiet adulter: picking up 311.

319 *Seruilia:* general rather than referring to one particular person. The *gens Seruilia* was ancient and respected.

320 *fiet:* sc. *adulter matronae,* i.e. of Servilia.

illius: referring to Servilia.

322 *Oppia:* cf 220.

Catulla: the name appears at 2, 49; perhaps from Mart. 8, 53 where she is very beautiful with the morals of an alley-cat.

323 Self-contained epigram. *Illic:* in their sex-organs.

324 *immo:* 'on the contrary'.

325 *Hippolyto:* son of Theseus, King of Athens; his stepmother Phaedra fell in love with him with disastrous results for both of them, though he refused her. In Euripides's play he is *castitas* personified; cf Mart. 8, 46, 2 *caste puer, puero castior Hippolyto.*

graue propositum: 'virtuous resolution'.

Bellerophonti: a similar story: Sthenoboea, wife of Proetus, King of Argos, fell for him and accused him falsely to her husband when he rejected her. Unlike Hippolytus, he escaped the death planned for him, though he ended his life lonely and god-forsaken.

326 *haec:* Phaedra. Most often *hic . . . ille* means 'the latter . . . the former', but the usage, especially in Silver Latin, is fairly free.

327 *Cressa:* Phaedra was a Cretan princess.

excanduit: 'glowed white' with passion: there is a joke, since *creta* ('Cretan earth') is chalk.

se concussere: 'got worked up'.

328 *mulier:* J cannot resist this digression: we must not expect satire to be tidy: the observation is a shrewd one. Compare Congreve *Mourning Bride* 3, 8 'Heav'n has no rage like love to hatred turn'd,/Nor Hell a fury like a woman scorn'd.'

329 *elige quidnam:* given weight by the bucolic diaeresis.

330   *cui:* i.e. *ei cui.*
nubere: ambiguous; she is of course
already married but cf 338.
Caesaris uxor: at this point we don't know
which Caesar, and perhaps think immed-
iately of Julius ('Caesar's wife must be
above suspicion'; cf Plut. *Caes.* 10).
Only at 333 *Messalinae* is the reference
clear: the lines before are almost a riddle
to which this gives the answer. Messalina,
the profligate wife of the emperor
Claudius, fell in love with the consul
designate, C. Silius, and went through some
kind of marriage ceremony with him in
AD 48 while Claudius was away at Ostia.
This was now clearly treasonable, and it
was exposed through one of the senior
imperial administrators, the freedman
Narcissus. The whole story is brilliantly
narrated by Tacitus (*Ann.* 11, 12, 26-38);
also (though the portrait of Claudius is
something of a caricature) in Robert
Graves's novel *Claudius the God and his
wife Messalina.*
331   *destinat:* the strong break after the
first foot is noteworthy.
optimus: the only instance in J of a self-
contained dactyl in the second foot: one
effect is to produce a line without the
normal clash between metrical ictus and
natural word-accent in the middle.
formonsissimus: Tac. *Ann.* 11, 12
iuuentutis Romanae pulcherrimum.
332   *gentis patriciae:* a mistake: Silius
was of plebeian family.
rapitur: more often of the woman:
strongly ironical here: she 'wears the
trousers'. A fifth-foot spondee follows.
334   *flammeolo:* the bride's orange-
coloured veil; cf Cat. 61, 115 *flammeum
uideo uenire:* the diminutive is found here
only, and Prud. *Psych.* 449. But again the
rôles are reversed: in Roman marriage the
bride went to the groom.
Tyrius: i.e. with a coverlet dyed purple:
the shellfish from which the dye was
made was found off the coast of Palestine.
Purple is the imperial colour, appropriate
to Messalina, treasonable in Silius.
genialis: sc. *lectus,* the marriage-bed.
hortis: the gardens of Lucullus on Mons
Pincius, which Messalina had secured
through the murder of their previous owner
(Tac. *Ann.* 11, 1). Tacitus does not say
that the 'marriage' was celebrated there,
but that Messalina took refuge there after
the denunciation (*ib.* 11, 37).
335   *ritu ... antiquo:* dowry, in this
instance 1 000 000 sesterces, was part
of the traditional ritual. The figure is

paralleled in marriage into a wealthy
family (Tac. *Ann.* 2, 86).
336   *signatoribus:* the witnesses.
auspex: strictly one who takes omens
from watching birds, but extended to
include the *haruspex* who used the
entrails of sacrificial victims. Cicero (*Div.*
1, 16, 28) notes the survival of 'nuptial
auspices'.
337   *tu:* the sudden apostrophe to
Silius is startling.
quid placeat dic: very harsh, with the
bucolic diaeresis and the offbeat rhythm.
339   *pereundum est:* if he says no,
Messalina will have him disposed of before
dark; if yes, he won't last much longer.
340   *admittas:* 'commit'.
paruula: contemptuous diminutive.
dum: 'until'.
342   *ille:* Claudius's blindness to his
wife's offences was notorious.
interea tu: yet again bucolic diaeresis and
offbeat rhythm.
343   *imperio:* i.e. Messalina's, but the
irony is strong, since *imperium* belonged
to the emperor.
tanti: sc. *est:* gen. of value, 'is worth so
much'.
344   *quidquid:* 'whichever line'.
leuius: from *lĕuis,* 'light, easy'.
melius: ironical, as often.
345   *praebenda est:* used particularly of
those who weakly accept their fate.

346-66   *Are men then to offer no prayers?
If you have any sense you will leave it
to the gods to decide what is best for us:
they know better than we do. Best to
pray for a healthy mind in a healthy
body, for a mind free from fear of death,
tough, free from anger and desire, with
no urge to luxury. You can answer that
prayer yourself. There is only one path
to peace of mind — through virtue. It is
we who have the folly to make Fortune a
goddess.*
346   Picking up 54-5. Note again bucolic
diaeresis and offbeat rhythm, emphasising
the importance of the end of the line, but
with a touch of scornful pessimism.
347   *numinibus:* 'to the powers that be',
vaguer than 'gods'. The word means literally
'nodding': the power of fertility was believed
to reside in the head, and to nod was to set
it in motion. In the ancient Roman religion
there were many 'powers', scarcely
anthropomorphic (the word is neuter).
Horace, an ex-Epicurean, has *permitte
diuis cetera (O* 1, 9, 9); cf Jesus 'Your

Father knows what your needs are before you ask him' (Matthew 6:8).

348 *utile:* an Epicurean concept (not, however, exclusively), though the Epicurean gods did not intervene directly in human affairs.

349 *pro iucundis aptissima quaeque:* Epicureanism nominally made 'pleasure' the end or aim of life. But Epicurus was something of a pessimist, and found the most pleasurable action often consisted in the one with the smallest excess of pain over pleasure, and he would not have disowned these words.

aptissima quaeque: 'the most appropriate things in each case'.

dabunt di: alliteration and offbeat rhythm.

350 *carior ... sibi:* a flashing epigram.

nos animorum: bucolic diaeresis for emphasis: the four-syllable final word, though Vergil generally avoids it, creates only a slight offbeat effect.

352 *illis:* the gods.

353 *qui:* i.e. *quales.*

354 *et ... que:* fairly common in combination in Silver Latin.

354-5 *sacellis ... candiduli ... tomacula:* scornful diminutives.

355 *diuina:* double meaning, 'offered to the gods', 'for purposes of divination'.

tomacula: 'hot dogs': satirical. He has in mind the similar passage in Persius (2, 30).

356-64 In these lines Juvenal gives, in reverse order, the true prayers to balance the false ones, though the parallelism is not to be pressed too far.

TRUE	FALSE
Health and good sense (356)	Beauty (289-345)
Freedom from fear of death (357-8)	Long life (188-288)
Strength to endure (359)	Military fame (133-187)
Freedom from anger (360)	Eloquence (114-32)
Freedom from desire (360)	Political power (56-113)
Freedom from luxury (360-2)	Riches (12-27)

Freedom from anger is not parallel to eloquence, and freedom from desire is wider than political power. The whole collection of true prayers is derived from the commonplaces of Hellenistic philosophy: we may see something similar in Cic. *Tusc. Disp.* 5. See also Martial 10, 47.

356 J's most familiar epigram, usually quoted as something to be cultivated

rather than prayed for. It is in fact a variant of a stock prayer, cf Petr. 61 *omnes bonam mentem bonamque ualetudinem sibi optarunt;* Sen. *Ep.* 10, 4 *roga bonam mentem, bonam ualetudinem animi, deinde tunc corporis.*

357: so Hor. *S* 2, 7, 82-6 *quisnam igitur liber? sapiens, sibi qui imperiosus,/ quem neque pauperies neque mors neque uincula terrent,/responsare cupidinibus, contemnere honores/fortis.* That is very Epicurean. The third book of Lucretius is directed against the fear of death.

358 *extremum:* 'lowest', predicative. But some people (less probably) take *spatium uitae extremum* together, meaning 'death', considered as a blessing when granted by nature. So Johnson: 'For faith, that panting for a happier seat,/Counts death kind Nature's signal of retreat.'

359 *quoscumque:* indefinite.

labores: uirtus, the quality of being a *uir* is in origin something like our 'toughness', the quality of a soldier-farmer. See J. Ferguson *Moral Values in the Ancient World* London 1958 c. ix.

360 *nesciat irasci:* part of Stoic apatheia. Sen. *Ira* 2, 6, 3 *atqui si nec magnam iram nec frequentem in animo sapientis locum habere credimus, quid est quare non ex toto illum hoc adfectu liberemus?*

cupiat nihil: to Epicurus fear and desire were the main factors disturbing peace of mind.

361 *Herculis aerumnas:* in myth the ten Labours of Hercules were laid on him by the tyrannical Eurystheus, but later philosophers saw them as works for the service of mankind, and Hercules became the type of the Stoic or Cynic ideal sage.

labores: three successive lines end *labores, potiores, labores.*

362 *Sardanapalli:* the last king of Assyria, known also as Assurbanipal; his name was a byword for luxury. His end was legendary: he collected together his treasures, including his concubines, and had them all killed with him: the scene was exotically depicted in Delacroix's painting (now in the Louvre). Byron wrote a poetic drama *Sardanapalus.* A five-syllable foreign name is not infrequent at the end of a hexameter.

363 *ipse tibi:* the aim of the Hellenistic philosophies was *autarkeia,* self-sufficiency. This is the point: action not prayer is called for.

semita certe: picked out by the bucolic diaeresis. The Pythagoreans used the

figure Y to denote man's choice of paths,
one to bliss and one not. So in the Sermon
on the Mount, Jesus presents his followers
with the choice of the broad road of
destruction or the narrow road of life
(Matthew 7:13-4).

364 *tranquillae:* the Epicurean ideal:
ataraxia, not being shaken or disturbed.
Seneca, a Stoic but open to Epicurean
influence, wrote *De tranquillitate animi.*

uirtutem: Epicurus KΔ5 'It is not possible
to live in pleasure, without living in wisdom,
honour and justice.'

365 *habes, si sit:* technically a mixed
conditional: the effect is to make the
apodosis more vivid, the protasis more
remote. The subject of *habes* is held up in a
riddling way: it is Fortune.

nos te: very emphatic: the last foot is
isolated by punctuation: it has two word-
accents: it is the culmination of three lines
ending -*te,* -*tae,* -*te,* paralleling 359-61:
and *nos* is repeated.

366 An eloquent line with alliteration
on *f* and assonance on *n-m,* picking up
the sound in *nullum numen.*

Fortuna: see on 52, 285. The attack
on Fortune comes as an unexpected climax
to a satire on How Not to Pray. For
Epicurus's attack on the idea of Chance
(Tyche) as a god or controlling element
see DL 10, 134. The elder Pliny (*NH*
2, 5, 22) has a scathing passage from some
Hellenistic source on the same subject
(. . . *ut sors ipsa pro deo sit, qua deus
probatur incertus*). Lactantius, writing as a
Christian attacking the pagans, quotes, or
rather misquotes, these last two lines
(*Inst. Div.* 3, 29).

General comments

This masterly satire calls for little general
comment.

Its strength is fourfold.

First, the structure is, in Highet's terms,
'bold and simple'. It is not too slick; we
might expect a fuller and later treatment of
wealth; and 54-5, if they are genuine, are
curiously abrupt. But in general the
sequence of thought is clear and logical.
Each section begins with a clear direction.
It is in fact a magnificent piece of well-
ordered rhetoric, with *exordium* (introduc-
tion), merging into *narration* of the case,
represented by the attack on wealth,
followed by a *digression* on Democritus
and Heraclitus, the *confirmation* of the case
and the *refutation* of the counter-position
being carried out through a succession of
topics and *examples,* the whole culminating

in a *peroration.* It is remorseless in its
forensic outset.

Secondly, J's capacity for acting as a kind
of verbal cine-camera is nowhere better
displayed, supremely in the shots of
Sejanus's toppling statues (56-64) but
also in the distant shot of a precipitous
cliff standing out from the sea, and, as we
pan in, the emperor surrounded by men in
foreign dress drawing triangles and circles
in the dust of the garden (93-4), or in the
ornate tomb with its elaborate inscriptions
shattered by a fig-tree (the camera 'mixes'
from marble glory to broken neglect)
(143-5), or in the one-eyed African riding
the elephant (158), or in the portrayal of
quavering, quivering old age (198-200),
or in C. Silius unresistingly bending his
smooth white neck as the sword flashes
down, an effect which has been powerfully
used by film-makers (345).

Thirdly, there is, as always, the brilliance
of the epigrams: *cantabit uacuus coram
latrone uiator* (22); *Antoni gladios potuit
contemnere si sic/omnia dixisset* (123-4);
*expende Hannibalem. quot libras in duce
summo/inuenies?,* which Byron greatly
admired (147-8); *deterior totos habet
illic femina mores* (323); *carior est illis
homo quam sibi* (350); and of course
*orandum est ut sit mens sana in corpore
sano* (356); and many more beside. These
must have brought a buzz of appreciation
at the *recitatio,* and been retained in many
memories.

But, fourthly, brilliances of structure,
word-painting and epigram are ephemeral
unless the writer has something to say.
What is particularly compelling about the
mood of this poem is its brooding pessimism.
Some critics have spoken of it as bitter
and cynical. This is surely wrong. It is a
reflective poem, not a strident one. But it is
certainly a pessimistic one. The appeal of its
theme is the appeal of the *Rubaiyat* or of
Housman to different generations. 'O
eloquent, just and mighty Death!' wrote
Raleigh in his *History of the World;*
'whom none could advise thou hast per-
suaded; what none has dared, thou hast
done, and whom all the world hath
flattered, thou only has cast out of the
world and despised. Thou hast drawne
together all the farre stretched greatnesse,
all the pride, crueltie and ambition of men,
and covered it all over with these two
narrow words: Hic Jacet!' For though J
speaks of the uncertainties of life, which
turn Marius from a conquering hero into a
beggared exile, he will not have men blame

some goddess of uncertainty, and behind all the uncertainties is the certainty of death, which takes Sejanus, Crassus, Pompey, Cicero, Hannibal, Alexander, Antilochus and Achilles, Mithradates and Croesus, Lentulus and Cethegus and Catiline, Lucretia and Servilia and Silius, some earlier but sooner or later, all. And beyond, our glory becomes a tombstone cracked by a barren fig-tree. This is, without misusing the word, the tragedy of human ambition.

But in this poem J's pessimism is almost urbane. He has his positive word to say. There are two things in life worth having. Neither is wholly within our power; both are appropriately the object of prayer. The greatest of external goods is physical health; the greatest of internal blessings is good sense and sound judgement. *Orandum est ut sit mens sana in corpore sano.* It is no bad prescription.

For, as has been amply shown, the key to the mood of the satire lies in the figure of Democritus. Heraclitus too, but to a lesser extent. The indignation, the fulmination of the earlier satires is here gone. We are given a choice between weeping and laughing, and J comes down on the side of Democritus. There *is* pathos, in the portrayal of Nestor, Peleus and Priam, or, in marked contrast with Tacitus, in that of C. Silius. But mockery, as with Sejanus, or Cicero, or the great generals, or old age, is uppermost. In the first satire *facit indignatio uersum* (1, 79). And his theme? *quidquid agunt homines, uotum, timor, ira, uoluptas,/ gaudia, discursus, nostri farrago libelli est* (1, 85-6). But what is Democritus's mood? *ridebat curas nec non et gaudia uolgi,/interdum et lacrimas* (10, 51-2). And *uotum* is the theme of the tenth satire, and, as Anderson puts it, 'Describing the folly of *vota* (cf 10, 23), the vain *voluptas* imagined in prolonged life or physical beauty, the satirist demonstrates how briefly endure the *gaudia* for those who gain their wishes, how rapidly follow

timor and destruction, often caused by the *ira* of a jealous or anxious ruler.' So the theme is unchanged, but J offers a fresh response. That response still means involvement; J does not follow Umbricius into withdrawal. But whereas earlier J has been the detached observer, now we feel a deeper sense of identity with others; compassion has replaced indignation. And the laughter which was bitter has a gentler, autumnal tone. It is almost as though laughter has become his protection. For in the end the poem is a satire upon those who take themselves too seriously, and when things go wrong, blame Fortune. J laughs at them, and laughs at himself, and contents himself with a more modest aim.

Bibliography
Anderson, W. S. 'The Programs of Juvenal's Later Books' *CP* 57 (1962) 145-60
Bickel, E. 'Juvenaliana' *RhM* 67 (1912) 142-6
Dick, B. F. 'Seneca and Juvenal 10' *HSCP* 73 (1969) 237-46
Eichholz, D. E. 'The Art of Juvenal and his Tenth Satire' *GR* 3 (1956) 61-9
Elmore, J. '*Recto vultu* and *recta facie* in Juvenal' *AJP* 46 (1925) 268-70
Fox, W. S. 'Note on Juvenal x 188-89' *CP* 9 (1914) 193-6
Gifford, W. 'The Vanity of Human Wishes' *Review of Eng. Studies* 6 (1955) 159-65
Lawall, G. '*Exempla* and Theme in Juvenal's Tenth Satire' *TAPA* 89 (1958) 25-31
Lelièvre, F. J. 'Juvenal: Two Possible Examples of Word-Play' *CP* 53 (1958) 241-2
Lutz, C. 'Democritus and Heraclitus' *CJ* 49 (1953-4) 309-14
Nutting, H. C. 'Three Notes on Juvenal' *AJP* 49 (1928) 258-66
O'Neil, E. N. 'Juvenal 10, 358' *CP* 47 (1952) 233-6
Rudd, N. and Courtney, E. *Juvenal: Satires I, III, X* Bristol 1977
Wiesen, D. 'Juvenal 10, 358' *CP* 64 (1969) 73-80

SATIRE 11

Not merely was the dinner party a natural theme for satire (and after all, Plato's *Symposium,* Xenophon's *Symposium,* and Athenaeus's *Deipnosophists* are all in their

different ways *saturae*), but the contrast between the simple meal and all the elaboration of the *cena* had already been used, possibly by Lucilius (frr. 1173,

1188, 1198 look as if they might come from such a topic), exquisitely by Horace (*S* 2, 2; cf. 1, 6, 114-8; 2, 6, 63-76), and epigrammatically by Martial, who reflects as well as supplying satiric themes (5, 78; 10, 48; 11, 52). It was easy and natural for J to turn his invective against aristocratic *luxuria* into such a form. He was now mellower: somewhere he had come under Epicurean influence (see on 148, 208). The tenth satire had offered a constructive message. This too is positive: the invective is there, but it is primarily by contrast: there is more of the delights of simplicity (notice the very personal 203-4), and a deal of praise of the past: it is more effective criticism for being less aggressive: the conclusion is the philosophical *uoluptates commendat rarior usus* (208). In one sense this is a companion-piece to the Horrible Dinner-party in the fifth satire: this is constructive where that is destructive.

The basic structure is simple and direct: a long discursive introduction, a dinner invitation, four themes, and an epilogue. But it is worth seeing in some detail how J controls the apparently loose structure of the introduction.

1 (a) The theme: living beyond your
     means 1-2
    (b) The theme elaborated 2-20
    (c) The theme: living beyond your
     means   21-3
2 (a) Restatement of theme: be aware
     of the state of your finances 23-7
    (b) 'Know yourself' as a major
     proposition of life 27-34
    (c) Be aware of your limitations even
     in buying fish 35-8
3 The results of extravagance:
    (a) beggary 38-45   (b) exile 46-51
    (c) shamelessness 52-5

The whole forms a pattern of strophe, antistrophe and epode.

The general pattern of the poem then is:

1 Introduction: Living beyond your
    means 1-55
2 Invitation to a simple dinner 56-182
    (a) The invitation 56-63
    (b) The dinner
        (i) food 64-89
        (ii) furniture 90-135
        (iii) servants 136-61
        (iv) entertainment 162-82
3 Epilogue 183-208

J takes care to link different parts of the satire by cross-reference. It will be noticed that the two sections on food and furniture together form roughly the central third

of the poem: each of these contains reflections on the life of the great Romans of old, *mos maiorum*. Notice too how the reference to the exiled bankrupt who misses only the races (53) prepares us by contrast for J's own indifference to them as a source of pleasure (204). Again we have a picture of the town-slave forced to work in the country and yearning for even the lowest delights of city-life (80) balanced by the country-slave forced to work in the town and yearning for the healthy and basic existence in the country (153). By such devices J holds his work together. It is a well-structured poem, mature and reflective, not without bite, but not without charm either.

1-55 *If you're a millionaire, you can dine well, but a poor man trying to be an epicure is making a spectacle of himself. Disaster is near; property is sold; soon he's fighting as a gladiator. The most important knowledge is self-knowledge. Live according to your means. Old age is worse than death to the extravagant. They borrow money, waste it before the owners' eyes, and then flit, regretting only that they are missing the races: they have lost all sense of shame.*

1 *Atticus:* Ti. Claudius Atticus Herodes, whose accidental discovery of a treasure in the last years of the first century AD was the foundation of the fortune of his millionaire son, the benefactor Herodes Atticus. The father was twice consul and served as governor of Syria under Trajan. This is one almost certain mention of someone who was still alive.

lautus: 'a gentleman'.

2 *Rutilus:* cf 14, 18, unknown but clearly an impoverished nobleman.

demens: just 'he's crazy', but the thought would be differently meaningful in Stoic terms: he is not a sage, since he is not living in acceptance of his destiny, and anyone who is not a sage is a madman. *maiore cachinno:* cf 3, 100.

3 *pauper Apicius:* a controlled oxymoron, for an epicure must be rich. tr. 'a poor man playing Apicius'. For M. Gavius Apicius see 4, 23 n.

4 All places where people meet and talk. For *stationes* see Plin. *Ep.* 1, 13, 2 *plerique in stationibus sedent, tempusque audiendi fabulis conterunt.*

5 *de Rutilo:* sc. *colloquuntur.* *iuuenalia:* i.e. of military age: did J have a wry smile as he used the word?

6 *galeae:* i.e. military service.

fertur: 'gossip says that he is going to . . .'.

7 *sed nec:* 'but not . . . either'.

8 *tribuno:* sc. *plebis* who had to authorise the contract of service to a *lanista* on the part of a citizen.

regia: we would say 'dictatorial'; cf Petron. *Sat.* 117 *tanquam legitimi gladiatores domino corpora animasque religiosissime addicimus.*

10 *creditor:* 'moneylender'.

macelli: almost a supermarket, since meat, fish and vegetables were all available. There were in fact two main ones at this period, the Macellum Liviae on the Esquiline built by Augustus, and the Macellum Magnum on the Caelian built by Nero. The market was an obvious place to catch someone.

11 *uiuendi causa:* ironical in view of 8, 84.

12 *egregius:* there is a double-take here. When we hear the word *egregius* we naturally take it as nom. sing.: only when we reach *meliusque* do we realise that it is 'really' the comparative adv. from *egregie.* But the other sense, once in our minds, is not wholly eliminated: the man, not merely the meal, stands out.

miserrimus: J means that the more wretched he is the better he dines.

13 *perlucente ruina:* a vivid phrase within an excellent metaphor: the house's imminent fall is shining like a shaft of light through the cracks.

14 *gustus:* 'delicacies' (lit. 'flavours').

elementa: earth for truffles, meat, etc., air for birds, water for fish, and fire to cook them.

15 Abl. abs. at the end of the sentence and bucolic diaeresis pick out the words.

16 *pluris:* gen. of price.

ementur: note the fut.: 'the greater their prospective cost, the greater the pleasure.'

18 *oppositis:* sc. *pignori* i.e. 'pawned'. Catullus (26) makes a joke of it: his villa is not *opposita* to the winds but to a mortgage — an overdraft.

fracta: breaking it up and melting it down, presumably a silver bust done by a not very good artist.

20 *fictile:* the silverware is pawned.

miscellanea: 'stew'; he will get coarse fare but adequate.

ludi: the gladiators' training-school.

21 *paret:* 'who's doing the buying': epigram picked out by bucolic diaeresis.

in Rutilo nam: offbeat rhythm, as usual emphasising distaste.

22 *luxuria:* more than our 'luxury',

excess and extravagance in all forms, the main object of satiric attack in Petronius and an important one in J.

Ventidio: we have met P. Ventidius Bassus at 7, 199. Ventidius is not a name from the ancient aristocracy, nor do we particularly know of any appropriate millionaire. The point is sure that Rutilus has been rich, is poor, but is trying to keep up pretences. Ventidius has been poor, and is now rich: his expenditure would now be within his means.

23 *sumptus:* Heinrich for the weakly repetitive *sumit.*

a censu famam trahit: bucolic diaeresis isolates the epigram.

illum ego iure: the three word-accents stress the point.

24 *quanto:* a trivial piece of information. J is contrasting the accumulation of useless book-knowledge with a genuine understanding of life.

Atlas: really a range of mountains from Carthage to the Atlantic: the high point is the Jebel Toubkal (4165 m: 13 665 ft) towards the Atlantic. The Romans were more familiar with the northern section whose highpoint is Jebel Tidirhine (2456 m 8058 ft). It would be interesting to have J's comment on this note.

25 *Libya:* Africa.

27 *e caelo:* the saying was inscribed on the Temple of Apollo at Delphi (Xen. *Mem.* 4, 2, 24) together with the other piece of proverbial wisdom μηδὲν ἄγαν ('Avoid excess'), and attributed by one tradition to Apollo himself: in other versions it originates from one of the Seven Sages. Cic. *Fin.* 5, 16, 44 says *quod maius erat quam ut ab homine uideretur, idcirco assignatum est deo;* Aristotle discussed it in his early *On Philosophy,* and thought that it came from the Pythia.

γνῶθι σεαυτόν 'Know yourself': *nosce te (ipsum).* There are references to the injunction all through Greek and Roman literature. See for one example only Plat. *Phileb.* 48 c where he discusses self-ignorance relating to possessions, physical qualities and inner personality. Sophocles's King Oedipus is a man who knows everything except himself. Seneca refers to a man *qui notus nimis omnibus,/ignotus moritur sibi (Thy.* 403); cf in English Thomas Fuller, in an age of exploration, 'Who hath sailed about the world of his own heart, sounded each creek, surveyed each corner, but that there still remains much *terra incognita* to himself?' Sir John Davies in a poem

'Nosce te ipsum', 'We seek to know the
moving of each sphere,/And the strange
cause of th'ebb and flow of Nile;/But of
that clock within our breasts we bear,/The
subtle motions we forget the while.//We
that acquaint ourselves with every zone,/
And pass both tropics and behold the
poles,/When we come home, are to our-
selves unknown,/And unacquainted still
with our own souls.' The extension of
acquaintance to the Moon and Mars
merely intensifies the point. J's application
of the words to one's bank-balance is
excellent satire.

29 *coniugium . . . senatus:* the state of
those addressed in Satires 6 and 8.

sacri: apparently a Greek idea: ἡ ἱερὰ
σύγκλητος is common.

30 *loricam . . . Achillis:* after Achilles's
death there was a contest to possess his
armour: it was awarded to the cunning
Ulysses rather than the gallant Ajax.

31 *Thersites:* see on 8, 269. But
according to the usual story, Achilles had
in fact himself killed Thersites.

se traducebat: 'made an exhibition of
himself'. J may have in mind Ov. *M*
13, 1-383 where Ulysses as the skilful
orator defeats Ajax as the man of action.
But he seems also to be thinking of some
discreditable episode while he was wearing
the armour, similar to his being chased off
the field of battle by Telephus, an episode
recorded by Dictys of Crete (2, 3). There
is a magisterial work on the rise and fall of
Ulysses in the opinions of men: W. B.
Stanford *The Ulysses Theme.*

33 *protegere:* 'act as advocate for'.

te consule: 'look to yourself': the same
words occur at 8, 23 with *consule* a noun.

dic tibi qui sis: four word-accents in the
last two feet place great weight on the
words: *qui* for *quis* appears here only in J:
to avoid hissing.

34 *Curtius et Matho:* schol. *iactanticuli,
qui tantum buccas inflant, et nihil dicunt.*
Curtius is unknown: for Matho cf 1, 32;
7, 129.

37 *mullum:* for this luxury fish see
on 4, 15; 5, 92; 6, 40.

gobio: i.e. enough to buy one: a small
fish: strictly the *gudgeon,* one of the gobies,
of which there are some thirty Mediterra-
nean species, now as then eaten by the
poor only: we might say 'sardine'.

38-9 *deficiente crumina et crescente
gula:* J has taken a phrase from Hor.
Ep. 1, 4, 11 and by adding a contrasting
phrase, pointed it sharply.

41 *argenti grauis:* 'solid silver'.

capacem: a good instance of J's satiric
method: we get a vivid cartoon of a giant
maw engulfing herds and fields, and then
realise that the truth is not so hyperbolic,
that the food consumed is the cost of all
those.

42 *exit:* 'passes from their possession',
a legal term. But the phrase *nouissimus exit*
comes in Ovid (*H* 13, 99; *M* 2, 115; 11, 296),
who also uses *exire* of a ring being drawn
off (*A* 2, 15, 19).

43 *anulus:* marking the *eques.*

Pollio: for a bankrupt Pollio see 9, 6. The
Pollios had Jewish connections which will
not have endeared them to J: we even find
a Pharisee of the name (Jos. *Ant.* 15, 3-4).

45 *luxuriae:* the abstract quality
standing for the people who show it.
Apicius committed suicide when his
resources diminished (cf 4, 23 n).

46 *gradus:* exactly our 'steps'.

47 *dominis:* the real owners of the
borrowed money.

49 *uertere solum:* they change their
territory, i.e. 'do a bunk'. (The phrase
comes at Cic. *Caec.* 34, 100; Petron. 81:
schol. *exsilium pati.*)

Baias: a fashionable resort on the bay of
Naples. Seneca *Ep.* 57 gives a grim
account of what it was like.

ostrea: the oysters from the nearby
Lucrine lake; cf 4, 141; 9, 57. A well-
known story tells how Milo, in exile,
on receiving a copy of the speech Cicero
had intended to deliver in his defence, said
he was glad it had not been given, or he
would never have enjoyed the mullets of
Marseilles (Dio Cass. 40, 54, 3).

50 *cedere foro:* 'to evade one's creditors',
since the forum was the business-centre
of the city: the phrase is idiomatic.

51 *Esquilias:* cf 3, 51; 5, 77.

feruenti: 'seething with people'.

Subura: cf 3, 5; 5, 106; 10, 156.

54 i.e. they are no longer capable of
blushing.

55 *pauci:* i.e. no one cares.

Pudorem: compare the disappearance
of Pudicitia from earth (6, 20), and of
course the departure of Umbricius from
Rome in the third Satire.

56-63 *Persicus, see whether I practise
what I preach. You've accepted my
invitation to dinner: expect the
hospitality of an Evander: you can be a
Hercules or Aeneas, both due to be deified.*

57 *Persice:* not, one would think, the
wealthy, childless, fraudulent arsonist of
3, 221. Paulus Fabius Persicus was consul

in AD 34, not a desirable character either, but we may be dealing with a direct or collateral descendant. One has the feeling, not of a close friend, but of an ambitious man (62-3), whom J wants to show the possibilities of simpler living. The name itself is suggestive of extravagance, and is possibly fictitious, from Hor. *O* 1, 38, 1 *Persicos, odi, puer, apparatus* also in the context of a simple celebration. Note harsh hiatus (*uita et*).

praestem: 'practise (what I preach)': it is the Greek *logos-ergon* contrast.

58 *siliquas:* 'pulse' made from the green pods of leguminous vegetables.

occultus ganeo: 'a gourmand on the sly'.

pultes: a porridge made of spelt, the basic traditional common Roman meal, not unlike the modern Italian *polenta.*

59 *placentas:* 'scones', made of wheat-flour, cheese and honey.

60 *cum:* 'since'.

promissus: i.e. you've accepted my invitation.

61 *Euandrum:* schol; *excipieris . . . a me hospitio paupere ut scilicet Hercules ab Euandro aut Aeneas.* King Evander came from Arcadia and settled on the Palatine where he offered simple hospitality first to Hercules, then to Aeneas; cf Verg. *A* 8, 100 *tum res inopes Euandrus habebat;* cf 364-5.

Tiryntheus: Hercules was born at Tiryns near Argos where there are the mighty remains of a Mycenaean fortress-palace.

minor illo: Aeneas: the audience would identify the *Aeneid* reference: *minor* is neat: Aeneas was smaller than Hercules, hardly less important in Roman eyes, though Hercules was a more important god.

62 *et ipse:* Aeneas was son of Venus and Anchises, Hercules of Jupiter and Alcmena.

63 Aeneas died by drowning in the river Numicius, Hercules on a pyre on Mount Oeta: both deaths can be regarded as purifying them for deification.

64-89 *The main courses will be home-grown: a young kid, mountain asparagus, eggs, chicken, grapes, pears, ripe apples. It's the sort of meal our senators enjoyed when they cooked their own vegetables instead of having them farmed by a slave-gang, in the days when ham came out for a festival, bacon for a birthday, and fresh meat at sacrifices only, when those who'd held high office knocked off work early on the farms for a special occasion.*

64 *fercula:* 'main course'; cf 1, 94. It is a little more complex than this, as the outcome shows, but the Romans marked off the main part of the meal from *hors d'oeuvres (gustus, promulsis,* the modern Greek *mezes)* and dessert (*mensae secundae*).

nullis ornata macellis: 'elaborated by no markets' a slightly odd phrase. If this is J, and not just a *persona* he is adopting, it means that he has a little farm outside the city in Tivoli.

65 *Tiburtino:* Tibur is in the hills a few miles from Rome. Hadrian built a magnificent villa nearby; cf 3, 192; 14, 87.

66 *inscius herbae:* i.e. not yet weaned.

69 *asparagi:* nom. pl.: Mart. (13, 21) writes in its praise. Pliny the Elder (*NH* 16, 67, 173; 19, 42, 145) identifies it as a delicacy: the wild variety from the mountains being somewhat coarser.

uilica: J can afford a farm-manager.

70 *feno:* to prevent them from breaking in transit; cf Mart. 3, 47 *tuta faeno cursor oua portabat.*

71 *matribus:* a whimsical way of referring to the hens. Spondaic fifth foot; cf 68.

72 *parte anni:* 'half the year', a regular idiom: one part = one half, two parts = two-thirds, etc. The dinner is on April 10 (cf 193), so that this would be roughly the period since the vintage.

73 *Signinum:* Signia (today Segni) is in Latium: Columella (5, 10, 18) says that the best pears come from Signia and Tarentum; cf Plin. *NH* 15, 16, 55 *Signina quae alii a colore testacea appellant.*

Syrium: this was a transplant from Syria to Tarentum in southern Italy: it is slightly unexpected to find it successfully cultivated as far north as Tibur.

74 *Picenum:* in eastern Italy, famous for apples, pears and olives (cf Hor. *S* 2, 3, 272; 2, 4, 70).

76 *autumnum:* i.e. their unripeness, an enterprising use. Many apples need to mature after picking.

77 *iam:* 'quite', an idiomatic use.

78 *Curius:* see on 2, 3. There was a famous story of a Samnite delegation finding him cooking a turnip at his own fireside (Sen. *Cons. Helv.* 10, 8; Plin. *NH* 19, 27, 87).

80 *conpede:* chain-gang labour on the estates was a punishment for town-slaves; cf 8, 180.

81 *uolua:* i.e. 'tripe'.

82 J wants us to recognise the dinner the poor cottagers Philemon and Baucis offer the disguised gods Ov. *M* 8, 648 *sordida terga suis nigro pendentia tigno:*

this too is 'a feast for the gods'. Ham was
hung for curing from a hook or on an
open frame suspended from the ceiling.

83 *moris:* 'it was a sign of accepted
behaviour'.

84 *natalicium:* we would say 'on a
birthday'.

85 *hostia:* we should remember that
in ancient Greece and Rome, as in Africa
until recent times, meat was not part of the
staple diet, and was the more enjoyed at
the feast which accompanied a sacrifice.

86 *titulo ter consulis:* not many could
claim this. From 342 or a little later there
was a constitutional gap of ten years
between two consulships, and in the
middle of the second century it was
forbidden to hold the office more than
once. This did not prevent C. Marius
from being consul seven times, or his
follower Cn. Papirius Carbo three times.
Crispus (4, 81) was consul three times,
according to Statius.

87 *castrorum imperiis:* perhaps with a
sideblow at Domitian and his like, who
took the title *imperator* without exercising
it in the *castra.*

dictatoris: cf 8, 8 n.

89 *domito:* the military metaphor,
though commonplace, is here deliberate;
they showed military toughness in the
field of the farm as well as the field of
battle.

90-135 *In the days of the great censors of
old, no one was worried about tortoiseshell
veneers: a bronze donkey's head was
enough decoration for a dining-couch.
They had not learned to admire Greek
craftsmanship and used works of art to
make their armour more hostile. Silver
was used for armour only. Those were the
days when the gods protected Rome —
and their statues were of terracotta. The
furniture was home-made. Now luxury
dishes must be eaten off imported
citrus-tables with ivory supports. You won't
find any ivory in my house — and the
food tastes no worse.*

90 *Fabios:* cf 2, 146. One of this great
family, Q. Fabius Maximus Rullianus, was
a noteworthy censor in 304 BC; Seneca
also couples him with Cato (*Ep.* 86, 10).

durumque Catonem: cf Mart. 11, 2, 1
durique seuera Catonis/frons. For Cato, cf
2, 40. M. Porcius Cato Censorinus
(234-149 BC) was a traditionalist,
chauvinist and puritan. As censor in 184
he imposed a tax on luxury. His great
constructive contribution was to develop

Rome's sewage-system. He gave the impulse
to the destruction of Carthage three years
after his death.

91 *Scauros:* cf 2, 35; 6, 604. M. Aemilius
Scaurus was consul in 115 BC passing a
sumptuary law to check extravagances,
and censor in 109. The pl. may be
generic ('men like) or simply a metrical
convenience.

Fabricium: the incorruptible censor of
275 BC; cf 2, 154; 9, 142.

92 *censoris:* a civil magistracy initiated
about 443 BC to relieve the consuls of
responsibility for the *census,* or citizen-
roll. Appointments were for eighteen months:
they were made once every five (originally
four) years. The association of the censor-
ship with morality arose from their right
to remove names for improper behaviour.

collega: in 204 BC the censors, M. Livius
Salinator and C. Claudius Nero, were
mutually hostile: each compelled the
other to sell his horse (Liv. 29, 37; Val.
Max. 2, 9, 6).

94 *Oceani fluctu:* to the ancients, the
Mediterranean was a kind of salt lake: all
round the land-mass of the world flowed
the river Oceanus.

testudo: for a veneer for the head of the
dining-couch cf Mart. 12, 66, 5 *gemmantes
prima fulgent testudine lecti.*

95 *Troiugenis:* 'the blue-blooded
aristocracy'; cf 1, 100; 8, 181.

nobile: sarcastic.

fulcrum: see W. C. F. Anderson 'The
meaning of "fulcrum" and "fulcri
genius" ' *CR* 3 (1889) 322-4, a still useful
article: see on 6, 22.

96 *nudo latere:* it is hard to know whether
to take this as abl. abs. parallel to
paruis . . . lectis, as an adjectival phrase
parallel to *paruis* qualifying *lectis,* or as an
abl. of quality in the thought *lectus paruus
nudo latere et fronte aerea,* which has been
loosely and emphatically expressed. J,
who thought in meaning not grammar, might
not have understood the question!

97 *coronati . .. aselli:* a bronze head;
examples have survived. The donkey had
his part in the Bacchic processions, and
was crowned with vine-leaves.

98 *lasciui:* 'playful'.

ruris alumni: schol. *rustici infantes.*

99 The line is not merely weak, but
coming in the middle of an account of
furniture it is totally inept.

100 *Graias . .. artes:* J may have in mind
Livy's comment on Roman contact with
Syracuse in 212 BC *inde primum initium
mirandi Graecarum artium opera* (25,

40, 1). He cannot resist a dig at the Greeks. A high proportion of Roman craftsmen were Greek.

101   *praedarum:* Polybius, the historian, was actually present at the sack of Corinth in 146 BC and saw the damage to priceless treasures (Strab. 8, 6, 381). Velleius has a good story of Rome's Philistine commander Mummius telling the soldiers that if they broke anything they would have to replace it (1, 11, 4-5).

102   For such work see Plin. *NH* 33, 153.

103   The scenes are used for two purposes: (a) horse-trappings, (b) helmet-fittings, and three examples of the latter are given (i) the wolf (ii) the twins (iii) Mars. The verb with *cassis* is *ostenderet*.

104   *Romuleae . . . ferae:* the she-wolf which in the legend suckled Romulus and Remus: she was portrayed, as were the twins, on Aeneas's shield (Verg. *A* 8, 630-4). There is a magnificent bronze she-wolf in the Capitoline museum in Rome: the accompanying figures of the twins are not original. Note how *-ae* shapes the line.

105   *Quirinos:* Quirinus was an ancient god (2, 133; 3, 67; 8, 259), later identified with Romulus as founding father. Here the pl. is used for the twins.

106   *uenientis:* 'advancing to the attack',

107   *dei:* Mars, in myth the twins' father, god of agriculture and war, here not on a love-journey to Rhea Silvia, but ready for battle.

108   *Tusco:* cheap crockery: it is ironical that Etruria in the English Potteries should make some of the finest Wedgwood ware.

farrata: i.e. *pultes* (58), made of *far*.

109   *argenti:* partitive gen. J seems to have in mind Livy's account of the spoil captured by Hannibal at Cannae in 216 BC (22, 52, 4).

110   *si liuidulus sis:* the offbeat rhythm gives a harsh effect. The diminutive: 'If you're inclined to be envious'. The line is ironical.

111   *uox:* cf Liv. 5, 32, 6. The voice warned that the Gauls were coming, and as little notice was taken as the Americans took of human warnings about Japanese intentions in the early 1940s.

112   *media mediamque:* for a similar repetition — almost a wordplay — see Ov. *A* 1, 5, 1-2 (ref. due to Prof. G. B. A. Fletcher).

audita: sc. *est*.

113   *litore ab Oceani:* from Liv. 5, 37, 2: J's use of historical sources is not without interest.

uenientibus: 'advancing', a military term.

114   *his monuit nos:* bucolic diaeresis and offbeat rhythm stress the disregarded warnings: *his* = 'by these means'.

115   *Latiis:* i.e. *Romanis*.

116   *fictilis:* i.e. terracotta, the material of early statues.

Iuppiter: not the earliest of Roman divinities, but from a very early period the high-god of Rome, with his temple on the Capitol. He, like the Greek Zeus, is derived from the Indo-European sky-god Dyaus: *-piter* means 'Father'. A. B. Cook's huge *Zeus* is a treasury of information, though care must be taken over his interpretations.

117   *domi natas:* literally 'home-grown'. J is girding at expensive tables of imported citrus-wood.

119   *nucem:* 'walnut'.

121   *rhombus:* for this luxury fish see 4, 39.

damma: 'venison': Martial (1, 49, 23) mentions it with hare and boar.

122   *unguenta atque rosae:* features of parties; cf Mart. 10, 19, 20 *cum regnat rosa, cum madent capilli*. Athenaeus (15, 685c) says that they were brought in with the dessert.

orbes: round cross-sections of citrus-wood used as table-tops. Plin. *NH* 13, 29, 91-9 has an elaborate account of their manufacture, size and price. They might be as much as 1¼ metres in diameter; larger tables were known formed of two semi-circular pieces.

123   *ebur et . . . pardus:* a complex hendiadys: 'an ivory panther': the adj. with each noun complicates the structure.

124   *porta Syenes:* Aswan, where the dam now stands, a frontier-post to which J may perhaps have been sent. *Porta* is uncertain: it may refer to the frontier-post, through which imports passed from the south, or to the town-gate, or to the narrows of the Nile just to the north. In 10, 150 J mentions 'Ethiopia' (the Land of the Blacks) as a source of elephants.

125   *Mauri:* here strictly the inhabitants of Mauretania.

obscurior Indus: the Indian is not darker than the African Negro, but is darker than the North African peoples with whom the Romans had more contact. Lucan 4, 679 has *concolor Indo/Maurus*. J's three sources of ivory correspond to those given in Plin. *NH* 8, 11, 32.

126   *deposuit:* an old wives' tale, typical of many which circulate in natural history.

Nabataeo: the Nabataei inhabited

Arabia Petraea. Elephants were never found there, but ancient geography is vague, and they become a symbol of the mysterious East (Ov. *M* 1, 61, *ad Auroram Nabataeaque regna;* Luc. 4, 63). In any case the Nabataeans were efficient middlemen, and did not reveal their sources.

127   *hinc surgit orexis:* 'The table gives an edge to the appetite.' It is typical of J to use a Greek word here.

129   *anulus . . . ferreus:* an iron ring, once generally worn, was now the sign of a nobody (Plin. *NH* 33, 4, 9-12; 33, 6, 17-23). Statius calls it *laeuaeque ignobile ferrum (Silv.* 3, 3, 144). J is saying that the snobs of his day take the same attitude to silver table-supports.

ergo superbum: the bucolic diaeresis isolates and stresses these words.

132   *tessellae:* 'dice'.

calculus: 'draughtsman'.

135   *rancidula:* 'off in the slightest degree'.

136-61   *I don't have a professional carver either, trained on wooden models of exotic animals. My boy's a novice from the country, Latin-speaking, with short straight hair, combed only for the occasion, longing to be back in the country, of natural decency, not like those others who show off their sexual attractions in the baths. And the wine, like the server, is mountain-bred.*

136   *nec:* 'not . . . either'.

137   *pergula:* 'the domestic science lab', in the form of a verandah or studio attached to another building. Here it stands for its student-occupants, a common device in J. But the word also means 'brothel', and as the Subura was Rome's red-light area there is an underlying innuendo throughout.

Trypheri: a Greek word, dainty of food, effeminate of character. The Professor of Carving is diabolically well-named, as Green puts it.

138   J starts from the familiar and goes through to the more and more exotic.

sumine: 'hog's paunch', a luxury dish. Pliny (*NH* 8, 77, 209) says that the mime-writer Publius ate it as a mark of his freedom. It was the subject of sumptuary laws. cf also Mart. 7, 78, 3 *sumen, aprum, leporem, boletos, ostrea, mullos.* The emperor Julian, looking for hard military fare, banned it as a luxury (Amm. Marc. 16, 5, 3).

et pygargus: schol. *fera est in specie cerui, quae retriores partes albas habet.* Note the spondee in the fifth foot, suggesting the unusual. The very word is harsh, and *y* is un-Latin.

139   *Scythicae uolucres:* i.e. pheasants: the English word comes from the more usual Latin *phasianae aues,* from the river Phasis in Colchis. This was a rare luxury. The emperor Pertinax refused to serve it (SHA *Pert.* 12); Alexander Severus confined it to special festivals (SHA *Alex. Sev.* 37); Julian banned it (Amm. Marc. 16,5,3).

phoenicopterus: flamingo: the tongue and brain were special delicacies.

140   *Gaetulus:* the Gaetuli were an African people (not, it seems, Negroid) who lived south of the coastal plain and controlled the Sahara trade; cf 5,53; 10,158; 14,278.

oryx: an antelope, fierce, and allegedly with one horn. For Pliny's account see *NH* 10, 94, 201. The word is alien; *y* is un-Latin.

hebeti: a totally unexpected twist.

141   *ulmea:* only here is the riddle solved: this luxuriously appetising meal *(lautissima)* consists of wooden practice-dummies.

Subura: see on 3,5. The idea of the sounds of the domestic science class ringing through the whole of this noisy region is typical and effective hyperbole.

142   *subducere:* jokes about servants as snappers-up of unconsidered trifles are common in all cultures which have domestic service, cf the butler who drinks the port.

142-3   *Afrae . . . auis:* 'guinea-fowl' (similarly named from Guinea).

143   *nouit:* + inf. = 'has learnt how to'.

noster: 'my own ("boy")'.

tirunculus: a delightful affectionate diminutive.

144   *ofellae:* diminutive of *offa* (as *mamilla* from *mamma),* which like our hamburger, did not require carving, cf Mart. 10, 48, 15 *quae non egeant ferro structoris ofellae.*

146   *incultus:* a neat piece of writing: the boy is untrained: he is not dolled up in finery; he is not idolised (as Hadrian's Antinous was to be).

a frigore tutus: 'warmly wrapped', not in silks, or naked to show off his sexual attractiveness. C. Gracchus, speaking of his period as governor of Sardinia, boasted *si cuiusquam seruulus propter me sollicitatus est, omnium nationum postremissimum nequissimumque existimatote* (Aul. Gell. 15, 12, 2).

147   *non Phryx aut Lycius:* fashionable cupbearers came from Asia Minor.

148   *magno:* sc. *pretio.* There is an

Epicurean joke here. The Epicureans believed that language is natural, so that a relationship between words must reflect a relationship between the objects they denote. Thus the common element between *lignum* and *ignis* reflects the fact that wood can be transformed into fire (Lucr. 1, 914). J is joking on this: the common element between *mango and magno* means slave-dealers sell at high prices. (Guyet proposed deleting *non a . . . magno*.)

Latine: not Greek; cf his bitter *omnia Graece* (6, 187).

149   *tonsi rectique:* by contrast with the long curled hair of the fashionable *capillati*.

151   *bubulci:* the common word suits the simplicity: contrast 7, 116.

153   *casulam:* this satire has an unusual number of diminutives, mainly affectionate. Note the contrast with the town-slave in the country longing for his low dive in the city (80).

154   One of J's more famous lines: the coupling of outward and inward qualities is beautifully done: *ingenui* too is neat: it means literally something like 'natural' or 'inborn'; it means 'decent', 'frank', 'open'; and it means 'freeborn'. The second is the primary meaning here, but there are strong elements of the first, and the third forms a transition to the next line. For the shape of the phrase, cf Phaedr. 1, 5, 5 *ceruus uasti corporis*.

155   Steel comes into the voice as he speaks of the degenerate aristocrats.

purpura: the *toga praetexta* with a purple stripe worn by curule magistrates and freeborn boys who had not yet put on the white *toga uirilis*.

156   *draucus:* 'a sodomite', the reading of some minor MSS, not cited by Clausen, But see R. Verdière in *Latomus* 11 (1952) 25-6.

157   *alas:* 'armpits'.

158   A parody of the statues of *Venus pudica*, naked, with one hand vaguely masking the breasts and the other the genitals. The country boy is not like those who hold the oil-flask (oil was used in the baths where we use soap) in front of his swelling member. J has in mind Giton in Petron. 92: note his punning contrast *ingenui — inguina.*

159   *uina:* grown and bottled on his little farm, not vintages to be conjured with from Campania.

161   The wine, like the boy, is rough but honest: a line remarkable for five elisions, including one over the end of the

fourth foot, and possibly a versified gloss.

162-82   *No use expecting salacious Spanish song and dance, such as young couples like to watch and are ashamed to be told about, arousing sexual reactions especially among the women. Not in my humble establishment. Leave such obscenities to the idle rich. We forgive anything to money. Gambling or adultery is a disgrace to the poor. My entertainment is Homer or Vergil, worthwhile however badly read.*

162   *Gaditana:* sc. *cantica.* For Gades (the modern Cadiz) see on 10, 1. Martial often refers to their sexy dances: see especially 5, 78, 26, an invitation to a simple meal which J is here drawing on: *nec de Gadibus improbis puellae/uibrabunt sine fine prurientes/lasciuos docili tremore lumbos.* They were an expensive luxury (Plin. *Ep.* 1, 15, 2).

163   Scornful alliteration on *p*.

165-6   Omitted in some MSS, found in different MSS after 159, after 160, after 161 in reverse order, after 164, 171, 172, 175 or 205, placed after 170 by one editor (who reads *spectent*) and generally suspect. Yet the thought and expression are not unworthy of J.

168   *urticae:* an aphrodisiac, so the passions it arouses, cf 2, 128. Jachmann would delete *maior . . . sexus.*

169   *ille:* sc. *sexus,* i.e. women.

170   *urina:* J is depicting *patratio* or orgasm.

171   *non capit . . . domus:* isolated and emphasised by the bucolic caesura.

ille: antecedent to 175.

172   *testarum:* 'castanets'.

172-3   *nudum olido stans fornice:* from Hor. *S* 1, 2, 30 *olente in fornice stantem.* Note the harsh elision and offbeat rhythm at the end of 172.

173   *mancipium:* lit. 'right of ownership', so 'slave': the neut. for personal which J likes is here commonplace: we may legitimately tr. 'tart'.

175   *Lacedaemonium . . . orbem:* a circular floor of marble from Mount Taenarus near Sparta: J repudiates the use of Greek marble.

pytismate: the Greek word expresses still more strongly the rejection of the Greek practice of tasting wine and spitting it out on the floor.

176   *fortunae:* i.e. 'the rich'.

176-7   *alea . . . mediocribus:* the epigram is carefully picked out by the double bucolic caesura: *mediocribus* are the poor, not the middle class.

177   *illi:* the rich.
178   *hilares nitidique:* 'gay dogs'.
180   A *lector* was employed for this purpose (Plin. *Ep.* 1, 15, 2). Seneca has an account of a rich man of no education, Calvisius Sabinus, who kept eleven slaves each of whom had all the works of a different poet by heart (Sen. *Ep.* 27, 5). The 'entertainment' might become a detraction, especially if the host produced his own poetry (cf Mart. 11, 52, 16 *nil recitabo tibi*). Homer and Vergil were safer. As to their relative merits, 'caparisons are odorous': they were debated in antiquity: Domitius Afer said *secundus est Vergilius, propior tamen primo quam tertio* (Quint. 10, 1, 85-6). See also 6, 436-7.
182   Sound advice: an amateur operatic society does not act stupidly in essaying Mozart, for something survives even the worst performance, whereas trivialities have to be superbly performed to come off.
183-208   *So cast care aside. No mention of money. No jealousy of your wife. Drop it all at my door. It's the festival of the Great Mother; all Rome's at the races; and the shouting shows that the Green has won. That's a young man's game: I prefer to be out of my toga, sunning myself. All right to go to the baths early today. But such a life would soon pall. Pleasures are keener when infrequent.*
183   Horace has a similar sentiment in a similar situation (*Ep.* 1, 5, 8). The theme is also highly Plautine; cf. *Cas.* Prol. 23 *eicite ex animo curam atque alienum aes.*
185   *non:* sc. *sit:* we might expect *ne* but *non . . . ulla* is more emphatic.
fenoris: another Plautine theme: see esp. *Most.* 603-6 where the word comes eight times.
186   *nec:* again strictly *neue* or *neu* (which J uses only at 14, 203), but J prefers the more conversational *nec,* which corresponds to *non.*
187   i.e. 'don't let suppressed jealousy get the better of you'.
188-9   A nicely observed description.
191   *pone domum:* 'leave domestic worries behind'.
illis: dat. of the agent: 'is broken so far as they are concerned', i.e. 'by them'.
192   *ingratos . . . sodales:* we say 'the ingratitude of friends'. If Persicus really existed there may be some point here which we have lost.
193   *Megalesiacae:* the cult of Cybele

was introduced to Rome in the last days of the Second Punic War in 204 BC. The Roman intelligence service had not done their work properly, and the Romans were shocked by the eunuch priests. It was not until the reign of Claudius that the cult became officially respectable, and the priesthood opened to citizens. However, she had her temple on the Palatine, and the festival of the Megalesia, 4-10 April, was popular: the name is derived from *Megale Meter,* the Great Mother. The races were on the last day.
spectacula: i.e. 'spectators': J likes the neut. for people.
mappae: where we use a starting-pistol, or in motor-racing a chequered flag, the Romans used a white cloth; cf Mart. 12, 29, 9 *cretatam praetor cum uellet mittere mappam.*
194   *Idaeum:* cf 3, 138: Cybele was also called *mater Idaea* from Mount Ida in Asia Minor: she was in origin a mountain mother, a power of nature in the wild, attended by lions.
triumpho: strictly we would expect *triumphanti,* but it is an easy sense-construction.
195   *praeda caballorum:* a very bold phrase: he is the prey or booty of the horses, i.e. the games have emptied his purse.
195-6   *pace . . . plebis:* 'with the permission of the people'. *Pax deorum* $=$ the gods' favour.
197   *totam . . . Romam:* the Circus Maximus had recently been extended to accommodate somewhat over 300 000: the population of Rome must have been between one and two millions: but it is a legitimate exaggeration.
198   *uiridus . . . panni:* the four stables or *factiones* wore tunics of the appropriate colour; cf on 7, 114. At this period the green (more often *prasinus*) was as popular as the red was unfashionable; the aristocrats supported the blue (see R. Goossens in *Byzantion* 14 (1939) 205-9).
200   *Cannarum in puluere:* the great disaster the Romans suffered at Hannibal's hands in 216 BC. Even three-hundred-odd years later the ignominy is vivid; cf 2, 155; 7, 163; 10, 165. Livy mentions the dust (22, 46, 9).
201   *consulibus:* both were in the field: L. Aemilius Paullus was killed, C. Terentius Varro escaped.
202   *sponsio:* 'betting'.
cultae: 'well-dressed' as at 3, 189; Ov. *Am.* 2, 4, 37-8.

puellae: one of Ovid's wittiest love-poems shows him seated by a girl at the races (*Am.* 3, 2 wittily rendered by L. P. Wilkinson *Ovid Recalled* p. 57). Compare his advice in *AA* 1, 136 *quisquis erit, cui fauet illa, faue.* In the theatre and amphitheatre there was segregation.

203 *contracta:* 'wrinkled', implying advancing years.

204 *togam:* the *toga* was obligatory wear for citizens at the Circus: it might be too hot on a bright spring day, so J, or his *persona*, avoids going out. J has prepared us for his refusal to go to the races by the account of the exiled bankrupt who misses only the races (53). His rejection of the toga is ironical in view of the traditionalism in this satire. Mart. 12, 18 (addressed to J) equates throwing off the toga with freedom from care; cf Sen. *Ep.* 18, 2 on the Saturnalia *hilarius cenandum et exuendam togam.* E. Segal in his lively *Roman Laughter* identifies the purpose of Plautine comedy with escaping the toga — ironically into a Greek masquerade.

204-5 *salua fronte:* 'without blushing', with reference to the hour.

205 *solida hora:* we can say 'a solid hour'.

206 *sextam:* 'noon'. The period of daylight was divided into twelve equal parts, each lasting about an hour around the equinoxes, longer in summer, shorter in winter. Dinner was usually at the ninth hour. Hadrian forbade the use of the baths before the eighth hour (SHA *Hadr.* 22), except for the ill: this shows that some people were bathing earlier. But the restrictions may not have applied to festivals and public holidays, and in any case there were private baths available; cf on 7, 233.

quinque diebus: our 'a few days running'.

208 *commendat:* 'enhances', 'sharpens'. Only 2 and perhaps 10 end with as pointed an epigram, and they have a mordancy which is lacking here. The thought is Epicurean: Epicurus enjoyed his diet of bread and water, because he received more pleasure from an occasional cheese than anyone could get from his food who banqueted every day (C. Bailey *Epicurus* V B 37; 39). See too Milton 'He who of such delights can judge, and spare/ To interpose them oft, is not unwise.' (*Sonn.* 20, 13-4).

General comments

This poem raises two major questions.

First, is it an actual dinner invitation?

Although nearly all interpreters so write about it, it obviously is not. Common sense shows this. J was a meticulously careful artist: he did not write a poem of 200 lines on the spur of the moment. He did not wait until the shout went up from the Circus Maximus before sending his dinner-invitation for that evening. It is possible that he constructed his invitation some weeks in advance. It is more likely, though still not probable, that he reflected after the event on his simple dinner-party, and wrote a poem about it. It is most likely that the dinner party did not take place at all. Persicus is not a very plausible friend for J. Some critics talk about 'the two old gentlemen sitting together in the sun'. Persicus seems rather to be an aristocrat, perhaps of quite inordinate ambition (cf 62-3), and presumably still quite young. We know some aristocrats of the name (see on 57), but the allusion seems rather to be Horace's rejection of *Persicos . . . apparatus* for his own simple celebration (*O* 1, 38, 1). If there was a Persicus it is a pseudonym: he is more likely a generalised young aristocrat who needs a lesson.

This leads to the second question. The dinner-invitation starts at 56. What is the function of 1-55 in the poem?

Once we have seen that the poem is not a dinner-invitation, but a lesson in simple living, this question is much easier to answer. For the first 55 lines are an injunction against living beyond one's means. So that the poem is in fact about *luxuria*, extravagance. The first section is an attack on aristocratic extravagance. The rest is a demonstration of the way in which it is possible to serve a delightful meal without extravagance. (Incidentally, J's meal is not to our minds so very simple, and we are reminded that he (or his *persona*) had a small estate at Tivoli. This both reminds us that the aristocratic *luxuria* was indeed excessive, but that none the less J was fairly middle-class: he was not living near the borderline of poverty either through deprivation or sanctity.) The linking of this theme with the *mos maiorum* shows that it is an attack on the habits of the aristocracy, of whom Persicus is presumably one, as much as any of the earlier poems.

With one difference. There the critique is largely negative. Now it has become far more positive, still scathing, but also gentler. We have to see the fourth book as a whole. We have to see 11 (and 12) as almost an appendage to the long and brilliant 10. One of the false prayers is for wealth, for power: this is an exemplification of the theme in one single field: and it is not unworthy.

Bibliography

Adamietz, J. *Untersuchungen zu Juvenal (Hermes* Einzelschriften Haft 26) Wiesbaden 1972

Felton, K. and Lee, K. H. 'The Theme of Juvenal's Eleventh Satire' *Latomus* 31 (1972) 1041-6

McDevitt, A. S. 'The Structure of Juvenal's Eleventh *Satire' GR* 15 (1968) 173-9

Smutny, R. J. 'Juvenal 11, 162-75' *CP* 52 (1957) 248-51

Weisinger, K. 'Irony and Moderation in Juvenal XI' *UCS* 5 (1972) 227-40

SATIRE 12

This is the shortest of the satires. It purports to be a thanksgiving for a rescue from shipwreck; as such it gives scope for epic parody. It is in fact a warning against greed, hung loosely on to that theme. It falls sharply into two parts, each introduced by the ceremony of thanksgiving:

1-16 The ceremony of thanksgiving
17-82 The greed of the merchant endangering his life at sea
83-92 The ceremony of thanksgiving
93-130 The greed of the legacy-hunter leaving him unloved.

1-16 *Corvinus, this is a more brilliant day than my birthday, a day for sacrifice to the Capitoline gods: if I could afford one, it would be a bull fatter than Hispulla. It is for the miraculous escape of a friend.*

1 The Romans kept their birthdays as special occasions. Sacrifice was offered to the *Genius*, or Juno, and friends and relations came to a party (*nataliciae dapes*) wearing white and bringing presents. Seneca has good advice on the choice of a present: don't send books to the illiterate, sporting equipment to the recluse; don't send wine to an alcoholic; choose something unusual, personal, permanent (Sen. *Ben.* 1, 11ff.). Martial has a number of epigrams on the subject (8, 64; 9, 53; 10, 24; 10, 29; 10, 87; 11, 65).

natali . . . die: Servius on Verg. *Ecl.* 3, 76 comments on J's use of the full phrase though *natalis* was used earlier.

Coruine: not otherwise known: it was a cognomen of the gens Valeria, so the recipient is an aristocrat.

dulcior: cf Hor. *O* 4, 11, 17-8 *sanctiorque/ paene natali proprio (dies).*

lux: 'day' but warmer and more joyful.

2 *caespes:* a turf altar. A temple was the god's home, not a place for congregational worship like a church or mosque. Offering

was generally made at an altar standing in front of the temple.

3 *niueam:* white victims were sacrificed to the Olympian gods, black victims to the powers of the underworld.

Reginae: cult-title of Juno: she was so worshipped at Ardea, Lanuvium, Pisaurum, and elsewhere among the Etruscans, on the Capitol, in her special temple on the Aventine dedicated in 392 BC, and in another temple near the Circus Flaminius (187 BC).

4 *uellus:* i.e. lamb, 'part for whole', cf *ebur* (112).

5 *pugnanti Gorgone Maura:* Minerva who carried a shield bearing a head of the snake-headed Gorgon Medusa at its centre to strike her enemies to stone with fear. J likes such circuitous descriptions; cf 5, 45 *zelotypo iuuenis praelatus Iarbae* (= Aeneas); 10, 171 *a figulis munitam . . . urbem* (= Babylon). The Gorgons' home was in Libya: hence *Maura*, 'black'.

6 *Tarpeio:* i.e. Capitoline. The Tarpeian rock was a crag on the Capitol (cf 6, 47). Jupiter, Juno and Minerva shared the Capitoline temple: they were the presiding deities of the Roman people: similar temples were found all over the empire: there was, for example, a spectacular one at Timgad in Algeria. On this great occasion J offers sacrifice to all three.

7 *uitulus:* the description deliberately recalls Horace's thank-offering for Augustus's safe return (*O* 4, 2, 54-6).

8 *spargendusque mero:* the victim was consecrated by pouring wine between the horns; cf Verg. *A* 4, 61 *candentis uaccae media inter cornua fundit.*

10 *res ampla domi:* cf 3, 165; 6, 357 *res angusta domi.*

similisque adfectibus: 'to match my emotions'.

11 *Hispulla:* the first touch of humour. She was obviously a phenomenally fat

woman, *ipsa mole pigra*: we have met her as debauched (6, 74); the name is found of the wife and daughter of Corellius Rufus, and of the younger Pliny's aunt-in-law: see on 6, 74; cf 2, 50.

13 *Clitumni*: a river of Umbria, a tributary of the Tinia, which is a tributary of the Tiber, extolled by Vergil for its flocks and herds (*G* 2, 146-8), by Propertius (2, 19, 25-6), and by Pliny for its charm and translucency (*Ep.* 8, 8); it is the subject of an attractive chapter in Gilbert Highet *Poets in a Landscape*.

13-4 *sanguis . . . ceruix*: again part for whole (cf 4); we might say 'with his rich blood showing . . and firm neck requiring . . . he would move forward.'

14 *a grandi . . . ministro*: gerundive with *a* + abl. is found in place of the commoner dative occasionally, e.g. Cic. *Leg. Agr.* 2, 35, 95 *uenerandos a nobis*; cf *Imp. Pomp.* 2, 6; *Caec.* 12, 33 Servius (on Verg. *A* 8, 106) cites the line in this form, and there is no need to alter it. (See J.G. Griffith in *CR* 10(1960) 189-92). The language is derived from juridical and religious texts and strikes a note of formalism.

16 *amici*: for the difficulties see General comments: can it mean '*your* friend'?

17-82 *He escaped a thunderstorm at sea, the sky a single cloud, lightning striking. It was a real poet's storm, but no different from hundreds of others, which hit Catullus. The captain was helpless. 'Throw out all my goods,' cried Catullus: purple cloth, silver, huge pots, baskets, chased work. Not worth sacrificing one's life for a fortune. The captain even cut down the mast. (Don't forget your axe next time). The Fates were kind: the winds dropped; they limped into Ostia and gave thanks.*

17 *et*: 'as well'.

19 *nube una*: Duff excellently quotes Charlotte Brontë *Shirley*, 'there is only one cloud in the sky; but it curtains it from pole to pole.'
inpulit igni: note the alliteration.

21 *attonitus*: 'thunderstruck', an almost grotesque mixture of the literal and metaphorical.
posse putaret: alliteration again.

22 *omnia fiunt*: the bucolic diaeresis is a sign of satiric intent adding weight to what is said on either side.

23-4 *poetica . . . tempestas*: this is very sarcastic: 'it was just like a storm in a poem', or rather ' a storm in a poem is just like that.' There are fine storms in Hom. *Od.* 5, 291ff; 9, 67ff; 12, 403ff; Verg. *A* 1, 81ff; Ov. *M* 11, 478-565; *Tr.* 1, 2;

Sen. *Agam.* 483-599; Luc. 5, 577ff; Stat. *Theb.* 5, 361ff; Val. Fl. 1, 574ff.

25 *quamquam sint*: taking the sting out of *miserere*: 'show pity — although it's all the same story.' Note the change in Latin: Cicero uses the indic. with *quamquam*; cf 7, 14. I take the structure to be loose and conversational, allowing the *quamquam* clause to look both forward and back so that we also have 'although it's all much the same, some is grim.'

26 *sed* again taking the sting out of *dira*. Note the harsh repeated *-dem*.

27 *uotiua . . . tabella*: those saved from shipwreck hung up the clothes in which they were saved, and a picture of the danger escaped in the temple of Neptune (Poseidon). There is a story told of the atheist Diagoras (or the debunking Cynic Diogenes) that he was shown the offerings of those saved from shipwreck as evidence of the existence of the gods, and replied 'Where are the offerings of those who were not saved?' (Cic. *ND* 3, 37, 89; Diog. Laert. 6, 59). Horace has a delightful twist about his escape from the attentions of Pyrrha *me tabula sacer/uotiua paries indicat uuida/suspendisse potenti/uestimenta maris deo (O* 1, 5, 13-6).

28 *Iside*: cf 6, 529. The worship of Isis was patronised by Domitian and was spreading rapidly at this period. She made universal claims: she was the sole reality of all the gods and goddesses (Apul. *Met.* 11,5; P. Oxyrh. XI, 1380; the last written at much the time of this poem). She was indeed mistress of the sea, Isis Pelagia and offerings were so made to her (Tib. 1, 3, 23-8; Stat. *S* 3, 2, 103; *Anth. Pal.* 6, 231; Orelli 1871-2; 2494. See Roscher *Lexicon* 474-80; R.E. Witt *Isis in the Graeco-Roman World* c. VIII n 2). One of her loveliest titles, *Stella Maris*, was taken over by Mary. But J will not have been sympathetic to a goddess from the East ousting Neptune, especially one patronised by Domitian, and there is strong sarcasm.

29 *Catullo*: not the lyric poet, nor the mime-writer (8, 186; 13, 111); possibly the informer (4, 113); it is an illusion to think that this is a friend: see General comments on this satire.

31 *alternum*: 'first one, then the other'.
puppis: Highet (*CR* 2 (1952) 70-1), following Ruperti, suggested that this was a gloss on *arboris* and the right reading *saeuis* or some similar adjective.

32 *arboris*: 'mast': dependent on *alueus*: the boat was 'of unstable mast' (R.S. Kilpatrick *CP* 66 (1971) 114-5 proposes

arbore et incerta, which is undoubtedly easier).

cani: 'grey-haired' and therefore rich in experience.

33 *rectoris*: 'helmsman': schol. *gubernatoris*.

decidere: a splendid piece of satire. Catullus begins a business negotiation with the winds: it is the technical term for a bankrupt compounding with his creditors for a partial payment.

iactu: *iactura* is commoner, but cf. *Dig.* 14, 2 *de lege Rhodia de iactu;* Sen Eld. *Contr.* exc. 4, 4 *nauigia iactu exonerat*; Sen. *Tro.* 1037 *medioque iactum/fecit in ponto.*

33 *castora*: the beaver was hunted not for its fur but for *castoreum*, a glandular secretion, not actually from the testicles, but near them. It was once used by physicians in the treatment of nervous disorders. (NB Our castor-oil is a vegetable oil.) The story of the beaver biting off its testicles in order to escape is of course an old wives' tale, though Pliny believed it (*NH* 8, 47, 109); cf Sir Thomas Browne *Vulgar Errors* III c. 4. But the beaver normally has its testicles retracted into its abdomen, and this may explain the story. There is an implicit pun with *castrare* which Tertullian makes explicit *(Marc.* 1, 1 *castrator carnis castor).* The whole mood of the metaphor should warn us of satirical purpose.

36 *testiculi: adeo:* the only example of hiatus at this point of the line in J: it occurs seven times in the third foot and three in the fourth.

medicatum: sc. *esse*: we would tr. 'it knows that a drug is secreted in its groin.'

37 *cuncta*: emphasised by the place of *dicebat.* Catullus's reaction is extravagant: he does not proceed piecemeal.

39 *teneris*: 'effeminate': J does not approve of the cargo.

Maecenatibus: 'people like Maecenas'; see on 1, 66.

40 *alias*: sc. *uestes.*

quarum: with *pecus*: the construction is clumsy, 'whose flocks are dyed', 'supplied by flocks which are dyed'. The sheep walking around with their fleeces ready-dyed recalls the Messianic vision of Verg. *Ecl.* 4, 42-5.

41 *egregius fons*: the Baetis, or Guadalquivir. J's friend Martial insists on this; cf. 12, 98, 1-2 *Baetis . . . aurea qui nitidis uellera tinguis aquis.* The offbeat rhythm may lead us to suspect that J does not take the claim too seriously.

42 *uiribus occultis*: some people think that iron oxide in the water may have had some such effect. J offers three explanations — the grass, the water or the climate.

Baeticus: Baetica is the modern Andalusia.

44 *Parthenio*: schol. *caelatoris nomen,* probably rightly, a silversmith, obviously of distinction and Greek, otherwise unknown: dat. 'of the agent'.

urnae: half an amphora, twenty-four *sextarii,* about fifteen litres (three gallons).

cratera: a large two-handled bowl into which the wine was decanted for mixing and from which it was drawn for drinking.

45 *Pholo*: a Centaur, who offered Hercules a formidably large *crater* of wine (Stesich. fr. 7) and is portrayed in the battle with the Lapiths as using a crater as a club.

coniuge Fusci: we do not know this allegedly bibulous lady: for one possible Fuscus see 4, 112; also 16, 46. The style is mock-epic with bathos at the end.

46 *bascaudas*: schol. *uasa ubi calices lauabantur uel cacabus.* This does not seem likely. The word is Celtic, Welsh *basgawd,* English 'basket', and some were imported from Britain, cf. Mart. 14, 99, 1 *barbara de pictis ueni bascauda Britannis.* The word is otherwise found only in the glossaries. The passage is sarcastic. Catullus throws even his fancy basketwork overboard, though that must have been far too light to affect the ship's stability.

escaria: sc. *uasa* 'meat-dishes'.

47 *caelati*: sc. *argenti*: partitive gen.

callidus emptor Olynthi: Philip II of Macedon, who in 347 BC used bribery to secure Olynthus, a key town in the north of Greece, excavated in an exemplary manner by the American School at Athens: *callidus* is not complimentary: Philip 'tricked boys with dice, men with oaths' (Ael. *VH* 7, 12) and said that no city was safe into which a donkey carrying gold could go (Plut. *Mor.* 178B). Philip was a hard drinker: one sentenced by him appealed 'from Philip drunk to Philip sober' (Val. Max. 6, 2 ext. 1). The Romans set some store by previous owners of silver plate, ornaments, etc. (as we do with books); cf Hor. *S* 1, 2, 91; Sen. *Dial.* 9, 1, 7.

48 *qua . . . quis*: as at 10, 69 two interrogatives in one sentence: we should add 'and'.

50-1 The great Richard Bentley was scathing about these lines *quale autem illud 'faciunt patrimonia'? quae scabies locutionis? quam alienum et pannosum illud 'uitio caeci'?* That Bentley might have improved on them does not mean that J did not write them. Indeed they seem needful to J's theme, for this is what Catullus was doing.

50 *patrimonia*: 'a fortune', not (despite the derivation) necessarily inherited.

52 *rerum utilium*: in sharp contrast with what has gone before. They have dumped the necessities as well as the luxuries. There is a kind of Epicurean paradox here: it may be *utile* to abandon *res utiles.*

nec damna leuant: 'not even those losses free (the ship)'.

54 *malum ferro summitteret*: the regular phrase for lowering the mast, made unexpected by the use of the axe. Double letters indicate repeated blows.

55 *angustum*: i.e. *in angusto conclusum.*

discriminis ultima: neut. plur. with partitive gen. is less common than sing. but cf. Luc. 8, 665 *ultima mortis.*

57 *i nunc et*: often sarcastic; cf. 6, 306; 10, 310.

58 *digitis*: 'finger's breadths', the lowest unit of length, roughly two centimetres.

59 *taedae*: 'pitch-pine', gen. with *digitis.*

60 *mox*: 'next time': J does not doubt that there will be one. Others take 'at the next stage'.

reticulis: string-bags for provisions.

61 *secures*: cf *ferro* (54): the passage is charged with irony.

63 *uectoris*: 'our traveller'. Some interpreters take *uectoris fatum* as a single phrase. There are two objections to this (postponed *-que* is not one). One is the rhythm of the line, which has only one strong caesura, after *uectoris.* The other (less weighty in view of what follows) is that *fatum*, a strongly Stoic concept, is not usually personal: in Lucan's epic there is interplay between *fatum*, Destiny, and *fortuna*, Caesar's personal 'lucky star'. But if *uectoris* is the right reading (the MSS evidence is clear, but *uectori* is tempting), there is some irony: whether or not he has his own destiny he has his own fine weather.

euro: 'the wind' without reference to direction; cf 69.

64 *Parcae*: the Fates, Greek *Moirae*, who spin the thread of our lives.

65 *staminis*: objective gen. with *lanificae.*

albi: white wool was favourable, black sinister; cf Cat. 63, 318 *ante pedes autem candentis mollia lanae/uellera*; Mart. 6, 58, 7 *si mihi lanificae ducunt non pulla sorores/ stamina.*

69 *uelo prora suo*: the only sail left is the jib.

austris: see in 63 *euro.*

70-4 Iulus (=Ascanius), Aeneas's son, migrated from Lavinium, named after his stepmother (cf *nouercali*) Lavinia, and founded Alba Longa on Mount Alba, at a place identified by the portent of a white sow with a litter of thirty (Verg. *A* 3, 389ff; 8, 43ff; Liv. 1, 3, 3).

71 *Lauino*: normally Lavinium, but the adj. *Lauinus* is found (Verg. *A* 1, 2 *Lauinaque litora*).

72 *sublimis apex*: Mount Alba, just under 1000 metres high, visible from the sea.

73 *Phrygibus*: Iulus had of course come from Troy.

mirabile sumen: Verg. (*A* 8, 81) has *mirabile monstrum*: J deflates.

74 *numquam uisis*: J is still deflating: they didn't actually see the udders because the piglets were at them. This seems better than taking it to mean 'never seen before'. 'unprecedented'. cf 4, 114.

75-9 A vivid account of the harbour at Ostia, at the mouth of the Tiber, the port of Rome. This was much developed by Claudius who formed the *portus Augusti* or *portus Romanus* (Suet. *Claud.* 20; Dio Cass. 60, 11, 3); this may be seen on coins of Nero (M. Grant *Roman History from Coins* p. 19 no 2.); Trajan added an inner hexagonal basin with elaborate quays and facilities. R. Meiggs *Roman Ostia* is the standard work; there is an attractive brief description in Paul MacKendrick *The Mute Stones Speak.* Anyone visiting Rome should take the train to Ostia Scavi and get the feel of an ancient port-town. Sometimes if one flies in to Rome it is possible to get a clear view of the harbour lay-out.

75 *moles*: the docks, etc.

76 *Tyrrhenamque pharon*: the *Pharos* was the island off Alexandria carrying a world-famous lighthouse (cf 6, 83); so the name was applied to lighthouses elsewhere. This one stood on an artificial island just outside the harbour; it is Etruscan because the sea was known as *mare Tuscum* or *mare Tyrrhenum.*

bracchia: the two massive moles built by Claudius.

77 Typical hyperbole.

78 *similis*: Housman for *igitur*, which makes no sense: see his note.

79 *sed*: 'anyway', coming back to the narrative.

80-1 *interiora ... stagna*: Trajan's hexagonal inner basin, as smooth as a mill-pond, where even pleasure-boats could sail in safety.

Baianae: such as you might find at Baiae, the fashionable resort on the bay of Naples.

81 *uertice raso*: those saved from disaster

at sea shaved their heads: the hair, a symbol of life, was offered to the god (Petron. 103). Artemidorus in his dream-book (1, 22) tells us that for sailors to dream of a shaved head was a forewarning of shipwreck.

83-92 *Come on then, lads, a proper thank-offering on the altars, and to Jupiter and the Lares at home, incense, flowers, branches at the door, and lamps lit in the day time.*

linguis . . . fauentibus: the Greek εὐφημεῖτε and Latin *fauete linguis* were a call to silence preceding a sacrifice (Sen. *Dial. 7, 26, 7 hoc uerbum non, ut plerique existumant, a fauore trahitur: sed imperatur silentium, ut rite peragi possit sacrum nulla uoce mala obstrepente.*) The phrase *linguis animisque fauete* comes e.g. at Ov. *M* 15, 677.

84   *delubris*: we are back to the scene of 3-6.

farra: Servius on Verg. *A* 2, 133 *sal et far quod dicitur mola salsa, qua et frons uictimae et foci aspergebantur et cultri.*

85   *mollis*: because they are of turf.

86   *quod praestat*: 'which is of primary importance': the absolute usage is unusual but cf Asinius Pollio in Cic. *Fam.* 10, 32, 4 *nunc, quod praestat, quid me uelitis facere, constituite.*

88   *fragili . . . cera*: wax was used for varnishing the statues; it was crumbled for melting for use as polish.

89   *nostrum . . . Iouem*: he has his own statue of Jupiter in his *lararium.*

Laribusque paternis: the Lares presided over the fortunes of the family from one generation to another: they were perhaps in one aspect the ancestors guarding the estate: see 8, 110; 9, 137.

90   *omnis uiolae colores*: Plin (*NH* 21, 14, 27) identifies crimson, yellow and white: it is not our violet, but seems to cover the pansy and the wallflower, among other flowers.

91   *ianua*: the door, the protector of the house, is personified.

92   *operatur*: schol. *sacrificat.*

lucernis: the lighting of lamps in the daytime meant religious ceremonial.

93-130 *Don't suspect that I'm legacy-hunting. Catullus has three children. No one offers sacrifice of a half-dead blind hen with so little hope of return. But if a childless millionaire is ailing, the promises are extravagant, hecatombs — of elephants, if they were available, Novius or Pacuvius Hister would offer an elephant gladly. Pacuvius would offer his own daughter — like Iphigenia. I congratulate him: an inheritance*

is more important than a thousand ships. If the sick person recovers, everything is going to be willed to Pacuvius. The only thing he will lack is affection.

93-5   i.e. You must not charge me with legacy-hunting.

95   *tres heredes*: see on 5, 141; 9, 90.

libet expectare: 'I should like to see'.

97   *tam sterili*: beautifully ironical: the more fertile he is physically the more barren he becomes to the *captatores.*

98   *sentire calorem*: the beginning of an enormous, sprawling sentence which goes down to 110: *calorem*: 'fever .

99   *Gallitta*: cf 2, 68 *Pollittas*: it is an affectionate form of Galla, found in Plin. *Ep.* 6, 31, 4 of the daughter of Aurelius Gallus, condemned by Trajan for adultery with a centurion. The use here is pointed; the *captator* addresses the woman (not the man) in terms of endearment.

Pacius: a name found in Praeneste, Capua and elsewhere: not to be identified.

orbi: emphatic.

100   *legitime*: 'officially'.

libellis: i.e. *tabellis uotiuis* making sometimes extravagant promises in the event of recovery. Caligula unsportingly insisted on such promises being kept (Suet. *Cal.* 27, cf 14).

101   *porticus*: of the temple of Aesculapius on the Isola Tiberina.

hecatomben: the Greek ending is a sure index of J's satirical sneer. Such offerings of 100 oxen were known, by the Athenian general Conon (Ath. 1, 3C), by C. Marius for his victory over the Cimbri (Plut. *Mar.* 26, 3), by Ti. Claudius Atticus Herodes (cf 11, 1) to Athene (Philostr. *V. Soph.* 2, 1, 5), later by the emperor Balbinus on receiving the head of Maximin (SHA *Max. et Balb.* 11), by the senate when they recovered some say in selecting the emperor (SHA *Tac.* 12). Livy cites from the Second Punic War a vow of 300 oxen (22, 10, 7).

102   *quatenus*: 'insofar as', i.e. they would offer elephants if they could.

nec uenales: as in Oscar Wilde's *The Importance of Being Earnest* 'not even for ready money'.

105   *Rutulis*: the imperial elephants were stabled at Ardea in Rutulian territory. For the Rutuli and their hero Turnus see 1, 102; 6, 637; 7, 68; 15, 65. The reference helps the mock-epic effect.

107   *Tyrio*: i.e. Carthaginian, Carthage having been founded from Tyre.

108   *Hannibali*: cf 10, 158: he incredibly brought elephants across the Alps: the survivors fought in the battle of Trebia

(Liv. 21, 55); in his homeland he had fifty at the battle of Zama in 202 BC (Liv. 30, 33, 4).

nostris ducibus: the Romans used them first against Philip V of Macedon in 200 BC (Liv. 31, 36, 4); L. Cornelius Scipio had sixteen at the battle of Magnesia in 190 (Liv. 37, 39, 13); Cn. Domitius Ahenobarbus used them in his victory over the Allobroges in 121 (Oros. 5, 13).

regique Molosso: Pyrrhus, king of Epirus, of which the Molossi were one tribe: the Romans' first encounter with elephants was in Lucania in 281 BC during his invasion: hence their Latin name *boues Lucae.* This parade of learning on elephantine history is typical of Silver Latin Poetry: Lucan has an inordinate account of the snakes of North Africa (9, 607-937).

109 *maiores:* the suggestion is that the present day imperial herd is descended from these.

110 *partem:* in apposition to *cohortis.*

belli, et: hiatus at this point occurs seven times in J: it is eased by the marked break; cf 3, 70; 6, 274; 6, 468; 10, 281; 14, 49; 15, 126.

turrem: a second object to *ferre.*

111-2 Novius and Pacuvius Hister are obviously *captatores,* not otherwise known, except that Hister appears at 2, 58. The last name suggests an origin for him or some ancestor on the Danube.

112 *ebur:* i.e. 'elephant', part for whole.

114 *deis:* i.e. Laribus Gallittae.

captatoribus horum: strongly ironical.

115 *alter:* Pacuvius Hister.

116 *magna et pulcherrima quaeque:* the combination of positive and superlative in this order is curiously rare, seeing that it offers a neat built-up.

117 *ancillarum:* there are thirty-three spondaic fifth feet in J, cf 121.

119 *Iphigenia:* d. of Agamemnon and Clytemnestra, brought to Aulis under the pretext of marriage to Achilles, and offered as human sacrifice to the offended Artemis (Agamemnon impiously boasted that he was a finer hunter than the goddess) to secure favourable winds for the Trojan expedition. Lucretius (1, 84-100) tells the story with power and pathos as one of the crimes of traditional religion; the scene of sacrifice is portrayed in a wall-painting from the House of the Tragic Poet in Pompeii. Hister would slit his own daughter's throat for a legacy.

120 In what is obviously a more refined, and later, version of the story Artemis miraculously saves Iphigeneia, substituting a deer: this version appears first in

Euripides's play *Iphigeneia in Tauris* (cf *tragicae*).

121 *ciuem* doubly sarcastic if Pacuvius came from the Balkans.

122 *mille rates:* the traditional size of the Greek fleet (Varro *RR* 2, 1, 26 *mille naues isse ad Troiam*), though the Homeric number is 1186 (*Il.* 2). Note the way this phrase links together the poem's two main sections.

Libitinam: the *numen* of funeral rites; the undertakers' equipment was kept in her sacred grove. She was sometimes identified with Proserpina, less obviously with Venus, through confusion with Lubentina (Plut. *Num.* 12,1); cf Horace's claim to immortality through his poetry *O* 3, 30, 6 *multaque pars mei/uitabit Libitinam.*

123 *tabulas:* i.e. his previous will.

nassae: a fish-trap of wickerwork, allowing the fish in but not out.

125 *ille superbus:* the bucolic diaeresis isolates these words, and gives us a blow-up of the man in his pride.

127 *iugulata Mycenis:* 'we say 'the murder of the girl from Mycenae'', sc. Iphigeneia, Agamemnon being king of Mycenae, the great citadel excavated by Schliemann and again Wace, in the foothills above Argos: the image is continued from 119.

128 *uiuat... Nestora totum:* an extension of the cognate acc.: 'may he live a life as long as Nestor's', lit. 'may he live out a complete Nestor'. Nestor was the classical Methuselah, proverbial for longevity (Hom. *Il.* 1, 250ff), and the wisdom that goes with it. The palace at Pylos associated with him has been excavated by Carl Blegen.

129 *rapuit Nero:* he pillaged Greece for works of art (Tac. *Ann.* 15, 45): one writer says that his taste for the arts did more damage to Greece than the conflagrations of Xerxes (Philostr. *V. Ap.* 5, 7, 3).

130 The sting in the tail: *nec,* as often in J for the more regular *neu.* The words are a brilliantly concise summary of a passage in Cic. *Am.* 15, 52 *nam quis est... qui uelit, ut neque diligat quemquam nec ipse ab ullo diligatur, circumfluere omnibus copiis atque in omnium rerum abundantia uiuere?* See J.E.B. Mayor *JP* 12 (1883) 269. We should however not forget that J seems to have been influenced by Epicureanism at this time, and that Epicurus laid great stress on friendship: 'Friendship dances round the world, calling us to awaken to the praises of the life of happiness' (fr. 52 Bailey). It is this which Pacuvius has thrown away.

General comments

It is hard to see how anyone has ever
taken this poem as a serious expression of
friendship. Yet Duff has the heading
'Welcome to a friend on his escape from
shipwreck'; Humphries has 'On the near-
shipwreck of a friend'; and this is the general
mood of the commentaries. This is to miss
the satirical note altogether.

This is in effect a scenario with four
characters. Corvinus is in the background. We
know nothing about him but his name, which
is that of a blue-blooded aristocrat of the gens
Valeria. He is unlikely to be one of J's
friends. He might be a patron, but the more
we look at the poem the more unwelcome it
would seem to an aristocratic patron, for it is
an attack on the values which to J's
disgust permeated Roman society. The note
sounded seems to be a warning-bell. Still, we
should not rule out the possibility that
Corvinus was or (if he be fictitious) stands
for an aristocrat of the old school who
upholds the *mores maiorum* and deplores the
monetary values and the *nouveaux riches.*

The second half of the poem is dominated
by Pacuvius Hister. This is clearly a hostile
portrait of a notorious *captator,* who is
interested only in money, will swear
his soul away, and sacrifice his daughter, and
throw away the supreme happiness of all that
is included in friendship and family love.

If the dominant figure of the second
half is portrayed with hostility because of
valuing money above everything, what of the
dominant figure of the first half, Catullus?
The only Catullus elsewhere in the poems
who this could be is the informer (4, 113).
This is not conclusive, as it is not an un-
common name. Still, if it were not for the
two passages about the sacrifice no one would
have thought of him as a friend of J. *Nostro . . .
Catullo* (30) is no more than 'our central
character Catullus'; if anything it is rather
less, seeing that J calls Pacuvius *meum ciuem*
(121). Catullus is not sympathetically
portrayed. He is a typical exponent of *luxuria,*
with his purple clothes and his silver plates.

He is grievously subject to the perturbation
of panic: 'Throw the lot out' (37). There
seems some sense that his description of his
perils was somewhat overplayed; cf the almost
grotesque *attonitus* (21). It was a storm
worthy of imaginative writing (*poetica* 23) —
but no different from hundreds of others
(26). More, he is a fool, if he thinks that
baskets will make any difference to the
boat's stability (46). And J obviously does
not think that he has learned any lesson
at all (*mox* 60). So that his description of
him as a friend (16) is charged with diffi-
culties.

What then of J himself, our fourth
character? This is the point. The account of
the sacrifice is overstated from the first. We
suspect it at the very beginning. When we
read of 'a bull fatter than Hispulla' (11) we
cannot take it wholly seriously. And yet there
is a point and it is connected with the
influence of Epicurus on J at this period.
Epicurus did not believe that the gods
consciously intervened to affect human
destiny. But he did believe that the sort of
person who gave thanks to the gods was,
or might be, an admirable person for that
reason. J is teasingly saying that he gives
thanks for Catullus's deliverance no matter
how undesirable Catallus is. For J in the poems
of this book is showing the simple life in
contrast to the life of *luxuria.*

This is important. 11 and 12 are appendages
to 10. 10 is an attack on ambition. So in
different ways are both of these. *Nos te, nos
facimus, Fortuna, deam caeloque locamus*
(10, 365-6). So J ended the tenth satire, and
Catullus and Pacuvius both in different
ways have put themselves at the mercy of
Fortune. J not merely indicts them: he shows
them a better way.

Bibliography

Colton, R.E. 'Echoes of Martial in Juvenal's
        Twelfth Satire' *Latomus* 31 (1972) 164-73
Helmbold, W.C. 'Juvenal's Twelfth Satire'
        CP 51 (1956) 14-23

SATIRE 13

The last book shows little diminution of J's
vigour. The first satire is in the form of a con-
solation, a technical rhetorical and philo-
sophical literary genre, written to a nobleman
who has been cheated out of a relatively
small sum of money. The point of the poem

is that it is not a consolation, but a satire
on consolatory writings cast into the form
of a consolation: unless we see the satirical
intent we shall not understand it. Calvinus,
to whom it is addressed, belongs to a noble
house: he is elderly (17) and well-off, and

there is no reason to suppose him a particular friend to J, even if he is an actual person, and the whole situation is not invented for satirical purposes.

I accept then Highet's analysis of the structure, which I reproduce here:
(a) 1-12 Introduction
(b) 13-173 *de crimine*
    (i) *usitatum* 13-70
    (ii) *necessarium* 71-119
    (iii) *leue* 120-73
(c) 174-249 *de ultione*
    (i) *neglegenda* 174-92
    (ii) *certa ex conscientia* 192-239
    (iii)*certa ex natura* 239-49.
That is right, but Highet takes it as a serious *consolatio*. That it is not. It is a mock-*consolatio*.

It is in fact an excuse for castigating the criminality of the age, and if we look at any of the sections in detail we shall find that this is J's point. Crime is now rampant. There is no divine providence. There can be no *consolatio*. Crime is victorious. There is no hope in human judges: the world will not give him justice. There is no hope in the gods. Calvinus can avenge himself only by letting nature take its course. The successful criminal is always uneasy, yet always thinks that he will get away with it again, and sooner or later overreaches himself. This is set as a final consolation to Calvinus. It is not really so. It is the nearest J comes to asserting a moral order in this poem, pessimistically but positively.

1-12 *Bad actions damage the doer. A person who evades legal judgement stands condemned at the bar of conscience. Calvinus, you can stand your loss, and it's not unique: don't be indignant to excess.*

1 'Everything that is done in the way of setting a bad example' – abl. of manner.

2 *displicet*: 'is to the disadvantage of'.
ultio: 'punishment'.

2-3 *se iudice*: 'at the bar of conscience' (Green).

4 *fallaci praetoris . . . urna*: we may tr. 'a rigged verdict'. Servius on Verg. *A* 6, 431 quotes this line and refers it to the ballot to determine the order of the cases to be tried, which is presumably right: in the long run this might lead to the case being adjourned *sine die*.
uicerit: 'has gained a favourable verdict'.

5 *Caluine*: not otherwise known; the name is found in a number of *gentes*. He is aged 60 (17).
recenti: dramatically important.

6 *fidei*: the cement of human society

(Arist. *Rhet.* 1, 15, 22; Cic. *Rosc. Am.* 38, 111).

6-11 J's source is Sen. *Ep.* 93, 12 *minimum est de quo sollicitissime agitur.*

8 *iacturae. . . mergat onus*: a very odd mixed metaphor: both parts are from sea-trading, but *iacturae* refers to the loss of what you throw overboard to avoid shipwreck (cf 12, 37), *mergat onus* to the ship sinking through the weight of what is left on board.

9 *multis hic cognitus*: cf 12, 26 *cognita multis*: where the point, also to a rich man, is the same.

11 *Fortunae*: it is hard to know whether to capitalise or not. J does not believe in Fortune as a goddess (10, 366), but here she is personalised.

12 *uiri*: 'a real man': *uirtus* is what it means to be a *uir*. Kipling's 'If' ('And – which is more – you'll be a Man, my son!') sums up *Romana uirtus* well enough. It prepares us for the mordant *femina* at 192.

13-70 *Your trust's been broken over money. You're 60, and should hardly be surprised. Every festival brings crimes. Good men are rare. Yet we noisily protest. You're behaving like a child if you believe in religious sanctions. That's all pre-Jupiter, long before the present overcrowding of Olympus. No punishments in Hades then. The young deferred to their elders. Today honesty's the portent.*

13 *quamuis*: closely with *leuium*.

14-5 *spumantibus ardens uisceribus*: over-written language for Calvinus's overreaction.

15 *sacrum*: i.e. entrusted under oath: it is an ironic keyword.

17 *Fonteio consule*: this gives us an approximate date for the satire.
Fonteius Capito was consul in AD 67: the satire was written not later than AD 127.

18 *tot rerum. . . usu*: 'a lifetime's experience' (Green): this is right but it omits two elements in the words: one is *rerum* as 'property', so that it is 'experience in the handling of property': the other is the Epicurean element in *usus*, which means the possessions should be usefully employed, not left to accumulate.

20 *sapientia*: 'philosophy'. This is the view of all Hellenistic schools: the chief work of philosophy is to protect us against 'the slings and arrows of outrageous Fortune', to lead us to *autarkeia*, self-sufficiency, non-attachment: cf Sen. *Ep.* 71, 30 *sapiens quidem uincit uirtute fortunam.*

22 *iactare*: 'to try to throw off'.
uita . . . magistra: 'in the school of life'.

23 *cesset prodere*: 'it fails to bring to

light'. The inf. is conversational. For the thought, cf Suet. *Tib.* 61 *nullus a poena hominum cessauit dies, ne religiosus quidem ac sacer.*

furtum: Nisbet for *furem*: all the others are crimes, and *prodere furem* is a stock phrase, which would explain the error.

25   *puxide*: 'the poison-cabinet'.

27   *Thebarum portae*: the town in Greece in Boeotia, with seven gates: in Aeschylus's *Seven Against Thebes* one champion assails each gate. J has in mind the Seven Sages, traditional in antiquity, though the lists vary.

diuitis ostia Nili: the seven mouths of the delta of the Nile, which Catullus calls *septemgeminus* (11, 7): *diuitis* because of its power to fertilise the land as it floods.

28   *nona aetas*: a problem. Hesiod in *Works and Days* 109-210 has five, and this seems to be not paralleled earlier in the Near East: the metal (30) links it with this, for Hesiod has Gold, Silver, Bronze, Heroic (out of pattern to emphasise later degeneracy) and Iron (cf *ferri*). Many explanations have been given. The right explanation is contained in the Judaeo-Christian *Oracula Sibyllina* where human history unfolds itself in ten ages. The tenth is the peaceable kingdom, but it is inaugurated by apocalyptic disasters. To live in the ninth age is to face this last prospect. It is to experience it indeed, for the ninth age contains darkness at noon, wars and rumours of war, eruption and earthquake. That the oracles were known in Rome is clear from their propaganda-use in the confrontation between Octavian and Antony, and in the first century AD from Dio Cass. 57, 18, 3ff; 62, 18, 3ff.

31   *hominum diuumque*: epic parody.

32   *Faesidium*: an unknown advocate *(agentem)*.

33   *sportula*: i.e. his *clientela*: J continually uses the impersonal for the personal cf 10, 45 *officia*; for *sportula* see on 1, 95: Pliny *(Ep.* 2, 14, 4) says that the *sportula* was actually distributed to the *claqueurs* in the courtroom.

bulla: a phallic amulet worn by freeborn children for good luck.

34   *ueneres*: 'attractions': note the linking of sex and money.

nescis: rhetorical *repetitio* at the same point in the line.

35   *simplicitas*: cf 1, 153; 2, 18; 6, 206.

moueat, cum: offbeat rhythm, as usual, for scorn.

37   *esse aliquod numen*: a bitter attack on conventional religion, reminiscent of Lucr. 1, 62-101. For the shape of the phrase,

cf 2, 149 *esse aliquos manes.*

rubenti: with fire and blood.

38   *indigenae*: primitive man, the *autochthones*; again we may think of Lucretius's account of the emergence of civilisation (5, 783ff, esp. 925ff).

40   *Saturnus*: Greek Cronus or Kronos, ruler of the Golden Age, ousted by Jupiter; cf *redeunt Saturnia regna* Verg. *Ecl.* 4, 6). According to Roman myth — one of the relatively few indigenous Roman myths about the gods; mostly they borrowed from the Greeks — he settled in Latium and taught the people agriculture (Verg. *A* 8, 319-20).

Iuno: sc. *erat*: originally the numen of fertility in women, corresponding to the male *Genius*: later consort of Jupiter, identified with Hera.

41   *priuatus adhuc*: i.e. not yet king of gods and men: the language is satirical throughout; cf *uirguncula*. It is especially ironical as Jupiter was guardian of oaths.

42   *super nubes*: the lower atmosphere was the domain of *aer*, the foggy air we breathe; the higher consisted of fiery *aether*, divinely nourishing. The ancients had a picture of the universe as a sphere: all round it is the 'boundless mind-stuff' which seeps in at the top. So sun, moon and stars are divine. In Aristophanes's *The Clouds* 225 Socrates walks on air and contemplates the sun: this nourishes the intellect. Mount Olympus reached out of the *aer* into the *aether*: in fact from the sea you can sometimes see a belt of clouds and the peak reaching clear above them.

caelicolarum: an archaic, Lucretian word, giving a five-syllable ending to the line. The idea is that simple honesty belongs to a bygone world.

43   *puer Iliacus*: Ganymede, swept up to Olympus by the eagle, to be Jupiter's cupbearer and lover.

formonsa . . . Herculis uxor: Hebe, goddess of youth, married to Hercules in a kind of beauty-and-the-beast folk-tale. Again note the archaism.

44   *ad cyathos*: sc. *stabat.*

saccato: so the schol.: 'strained', which gives better sense than *siccato* 'drained'. Vulcan, also one of the cupbearers (Hom *Il.* 1, 597), was still washing himself while the others got on with the work. Again strongly satirical (Green suggests that with either reading, the ablative is instrumental: he scrubs himself with distilled nectar: this may be right).

nectare: the drink of the gods, ambrosia being their food. They smelt sweet, and conferred immortality: nectar is conceived as a honey-mead.

45 *Liparaea ... taberna*: Vergil (*A.* 8, 422) calls Hiera, the southernmost of the Lipari Islands off southern Italy, *Vulcani domus*: it is still called Vulcano: *taberna* is his smithy.

46 *prandebat sibi quisque*: from Lucr. 5, 961 *sibi quisque ualere* of primitive man: there is thus a double satirical twist.

turba: 'rabble': the number of the gods has been increased by imports from the East (Mithras, Isis, Osiris, Sarapis, YHWH, not to mention Jesus), and by the deification of emperors.

48 *Atlanta*: the giant who sustains the sky on his shoulders: the fewer gods, the less weight!

49 *sortitus*: the three brothers, Jupiter, Neptune and Pluto cast lots for their spheres of dominion: Jupiter received the sky, Neptune the sea, Pluto the underworld; *imi* Housman for MS *aliquis*.

50 *Sicula ... coniuge*: Proserpina, whom he kidnapped as she picked flowers at Etna in Sicily ('herself a fairer flower' — Milton *PL* 4, 270) to be his queen.

toruos: n. sing. masc.: archaic ending; see on 42.

51 These are allusions to the myths of everlasting punishment in Hades. The wheel is Ixion's: he killed his father-in-law-to-be, failed to achieve purification from blood-guilt, took refuge with Zeus, tried to seduce Hera, was fobbed off with a cloud in her likeness, on whom he fathered the first Centaur, and was punished by being bound to an ever-turning wheel. The Furies, in Greek Erinyes or Eumenides, are the snake-haired ministers of vengeance. The rock is that of Sisyphus who was doomed to push a stone up hill; when it had almost reached the top it would roll down again. Homer gives no reason for the punishment: other sources cite treachery to the gods, violence to men, or the tricksterly outwitting of Death. Another rock was in one version hanging over the head of Tantalus, who stole the food of the gods. The vulture is that of Tityos (not Prometheus, as Green oddly suggests), who attempted to rape Artemis, and was punished by the eternal pecking at the liver, the seat of desire. The whole passage is taken from Epicurean critiques (cf Lucr, 3, 978-1023) but differently applied. The Epicureans rationalised: these are mythical expressions of our fears and guilt. J is merely saying that in the good old days there was no crime and therefore no punishment.

53 *admirabilis*: 'profoundly shocking'.

57 High irony, for after all the food was of practical use: a searching assault on monetary values.

59 *adeo*: with *par*.

61 *aerugine*: more satire: the coins are not used: they are green with mildew.

follem: a leather money-bag.

62 *prodigiosa*: 'portentous', i.e. requiring religious expiation.

Tuscis ... libellis: the Etruscans were the diviners of the Roman world: these volumes of their lore are referred to by Cicero (*Har. Resp.* 12, 25 *Etruscorum scriptis; Div.* 1, 12, 20 *chartis ... Etruscis*; 1, 33, 72 *Etruscorum ... libri haruspicini et fulgurates*); they were attributed to one Tages.

63 *coronata*: for sacrifice.

64 *bimembri*: 'with a double member'. Livy (41, 21, 12) has *biceps puer*.

65 *miranti ... aratro*: an easy and vivid personification: compare Vergil's grafted tree *miraturque nouas frondes et non sua poma* (*G* 2, 82). Note hiatus and offbeat rhythm.

66 *piscibus*: Livy (42, 2, 5) records this from Gaul.

fetae ... mulae: Liv. 37, 3, 3: the portents are taken from Livy with several pinches of salt.

67 *lapides*: pebble-rain is not uncommon in volcanic countries: there are many examples in Livy (26, 23, 5; 34, 45, 8 etc.).

68 *uua*: 'cluster': Vergil (*G* 4 558) uses the same image of bees. For the portent Liv. 21, 46, 2.

70 Liv. 34, 45, 7.

71-85 *Others have been robbed of larger sums than you, and the thieves swear by everything that is holy; they even swear to eat their own children if they're lying.*

72 *sacrilega*: referring with pointed irony back to *sacrum* (15).

73 *arcana*: deposited without witnesses.

76 The bucolic diaeresis picks up the preceding epigram. Critias, the Athenian politician who became leader of the Thirty Dictators in 404 BC, wrote a play in which a character (Sisyphus) reflects cynically on the role of religion. In the state of nature force ruled. Laws were invented to protect the weak against open violence. Covert crime continued. Then some ingenious person invented the gods as a threat against secret crime. J is saying that this sanction has worn thin.

76-7 *quanta uoce*: in the margin of a minister's sermon were pencilled the words 'Argument weak. Shout like hell.'

77 *ficti constantia*: almost an oxymoron.

78 He goes through the gamut of adjurations, familiar and unfamiliar, in parody of Lucan 7, 145-50.

solis radios: the all-seeing Sun is naturally a guardian of justice.

Tarpeiaque fulmina: the thunderbolts of Jupiter Capitolinus; cf 6, 47; 12, 6.

79 *Martis frameam*: a German word for 'spear' (Tac. *Germ.* 6): the oath is more recondite, but Mars's spear was sacred enough, and Mars was identified with various Celtic and Germanic gods.

Cirrhaei . . uatis: Apollo, a notable archer, as Niobe's sons found to their cost. Cirrha was the port for Delphi, cf 7, 64.

80 *uenatricis . . . puellae*: Diana.

81 *pater Aegaei*: the Roman gods take over the attributes of their Greek counterparts lock, stock and barrel. cf Verg. *A* 3, 74 *Neptuno Aegaeo*.

82 *Herculeos arcus*: Hercules is familiarly portrayed in sculpture with a club, but in myth he is a great bowman. This is the bow which Philoctetes took over, without which Troy could not be taken.

hastamque Mineruae: a moving relief in the Acropolis Museum at Athens shows her leaning on her spear in sorrow at the Athenian fallen.

83 *armamentaria*: a grandiose word, and an excellent satirical climax to this epic parody.

84-5 Or so we think till we come to this second deflating climax.

85 *Phario*: i.e. Egyptian. Pharos is the island off Alexandria where the famous lighthouse was built. For the vinegar cf Mart. 13, 122, 1 *amphora Niliaci non sit tibi uilis aceti*.

86-119 *Some people think fortune rules; others believe in the gods and disregard them; they'll face divine punishment for money — always hoping to escape. So they forswear themselves enthusiastically. You shout your complaints to Jupiter. He doesn't answer.*

86 *fortunae*: the concept of Fortuna or Tyche is not an easy one. The root meaning of *tyche* is 'chance happening'. In Hesiod Bounty and Tyche are primal beings, daughters of Ocean (*Theog.* 360). In Archilochus Tyche and Moira give everything to men (Stob. 1, 6, 3). In Pindar Tyche is the saviour, daughter of Zeus the deliverer, good fortune divinely bestowed and success won by innate gifts (*Ol* 12, 1-5). But Tyche works unpredictably (Soph. *Ant.* 1158). In some strands of thought *tyche* is personal; we each have our own (Dem. 18, 208). In the fourth-century philosophers *tyche* is the sphere neither of will (divine or human) nor of pure chance (*automaton*), but almost of what we would call natural law. In the

uncertainties, the failure of nerve, of the Hellenistic Age the old gods weakened, and people turned increasingly to Tyche. But ambiguity remained: in Menander she varies from a blind, wretched thing (Stob. 1, 7, 3) to a divine breath (Stob. 1, 6. 1). The thought of personal Tyche is taken up almost as a guardian angel; cities also have their own Tyche, like the famous statue of the Tyche of Antioch. Stoic determinism had little place for Tyche except as something to be defied. The Epicureans did not believe in a purposive creation but in a chance aggregation of atoms, *tyche* with a small *t*. Fortuna, an Italian fertility and oracular goddess, was by now totally identified with Tyche. The lines here are a garbled Epicureanism, linked to the popular idea of Tyche. They are a clear indication that J. although influenced by some Epicurean thought, was not a committed Epicurean. Nothing would be further from Epicurean practice than false oaths: in many ways they appear as the Quakers of antiquity. See further 3, 40; 6, 605; 7, 197; 9, 148; 10, 42; 10, 284; 10, 366.

87 *mundum*: 'the sky', the framework of the universe.

90 This in fact looks like an Epicurean gloss, for the Epicureans, whose theory was far more self-centred than their practice, argued against crime because of the danger of exposure. So whether the line is authentic or not it means 'some people hold this view of nature combined with a fear of punishment'.

91 *hic*: a fresh person.

et: 'and still'. cf 1, 74; 1, 93; 7, 124.

secum: sc. *loquitur*.

93 *Isis*: the Egyptian goddess who at this period was making universal claims. Blindness in Egypt, one form of which is due to a water-organism ('river-blindness'), was attributed to Isis's anger. J will not be surprised at perjury associated with an oriental goddess.

sistro: the rattle with which the goddess is portrayed, and which was used in her worship. It can be held easily in the hand, and consists of bent metal strips across a metal frame, which do indeed rattle when shaken. Note the transferred epithet *irato*.

95 *pthisis*: 'TB'.

uomicae putres: 'festering ulcers'.

dimidium crus: offbeat rhythm in J's scorn.

96 *sunt tanti*: 'are worth it': gen. of value: sc. *ut teneam nummos*, the desired prize. The construction would be more obviously reversed as at 3, 54.

locupletem . . . podagram: the disease is

personified: there is an illusion that gout is a rich man's complaint: it is certainly aggravated by excessive port-drinking.

97 *Ladas*: a champion runner: we know two of the name, one of whom died in the moment of victory and was portrayed by the sculptor Myron: this last statue may have been 'liberated' from Olympia to Rome, as Pausanias does not mention it, and Roman writers seem curiously aware of the name.

Anticyra nec: again offbeat rhythm. There were two towns of the name, one on the Gulf of Corinth, the other in Thessaly: both famous for hellebore, which was used in the treatment of mental disorder. The Romans said of a person acting crazily *nauiget Anticyram* (Hor. *S* 2, 3, 166).

98 *Archigene*: a doctor; cf on 6, 236.

99 *esuriens*: around here J has a number of transferred epithets; cf 93, 96.

Pisaeae . . .oliuae: the victor's prize; at Olympia: Pisa is a town near the sanctuary of Zeus.

100 *ut*: 'although'.

A brilliant inversion of the normal cliché; cf. Sen. Eld. *Contr*. 10, 6 *sunt di immortales lenti quidem sed certi uindices generis humani*: H.W. Longfellow 'Retribution': 'Though the mills of God grind slowly, yet they grind exceeding small;/Though with patience he stands waiting, with exactness grinds he all.' The first line is translated from a Greek proverb.

102 *exorabile numen*: to Plato this was one of the great blasphemies (*Laws* 10, 901-7).

103 *his*: 'acts like these'.

105 So did the brigand say to Alexander the Great that the king operated the same profession on a larger scale (Aug. *CD* 4, 4).

tulit: this is the Greek aorist, a timeless tense for generalised statements.

108 *immo ultro*: 'furthermore'.

uectare: Nisbet for *uexare*: he will precede you, drag you along, have you carried there.

109 *audacia*: 'brazenness'.

110 *mimum agit ille*: 'it's play-acting': the bucolic diaeresis and the additional word-accent emphasise the point: traditional religion has become a theatrical show.

111 *Catulli*: see on 8, 186. According to the scholiast there was a rôle-reversal, and the runaway slave arrested the master and demanded that he prove his free birth.

112 *exclamas*: what follows recalls earlier apostrophes, e.g. 2, 126; 6, 393. J is satirising his earlier self.

Stentora: Gk acc.: the 'brazen-voiced' herald whose decibels equalled those of fifty normal men (Hom. *Il.* 5, 785-6).

113 *Gradiuus*: 'Infantryman' (from *gradior*), a title of Mars, the Roman god of war and agriculture, who was equated with Ares, the Greek god of war, who in Homer, when wounded by Diomedes, bellowed like nine or ten thousand (*Il.* 5,850). The prayer is a parody of Verg. *A* 4, 206ff.

116 *carbone*: 'censer'.

charta: the incense was carried in a screw of paper.

pia tura: another transferred epithet.

117 *albaque porci*: cf 10, 355.

119 *Vagelli*: cf 16, 23 *declamatoris mulino corde Vagelli*. A L. Vagellius was consul suffect under Claudius: another, a poet, is mentioned in Sen. *QN* 6, 2, 9. There must be some point in the reference which we cannot see: either Vagellius had the *ius imaginum*, or some grateful client had his statue erected. Possibly he was a nonstop talker; it was a miracle that his statue didn't talk.

120-73 *I'm no philosopher. But there's a simple solution. Realise that there's plenty worse going on. Why should you expect special treatment? Think of the arsonists, the temple-robbers, the petty thieves who scrape the gilt off statues, the poisoners. If you want to understand human nature, spend a day or two in the courts. We shouldn't be surprised at the consistency of human nature.*

121-3 This is a clear statement that J does not align himself with either Stoics or Epicureans. But he is aware of both schools. Stoicism permeated Roman thought generally, Epicureanism was aloof from the other schools, and J must have had some close association with Epicureans to have had such a fair and sympathetic knowledge of them. Note the omission of Platonists and Aristotelians. The Platonists were about to stage a comeback.

121 *Cynicos*: a movement of protest, to be traced back to Diogenes the 'dog' (c. 400-325 BC), a lovable, infuriating figure, who went round shocking convention, 'putting false currency out of circulation' (as he put it), stripping himself of ties of country, home, family and possessions and inuring himself to hardship till he could face all that life might do to him. (His association with Antisthenes is an illusory attempt to trace the movement back to Socrates.) The movement tended to produce exhibitionists, but its protests were also usually soundly based. It was strong under the early Empire: Dio Chrysostom, who became one of Trajan's leading advisers, when in exile, became caught up in the

movement. The word Cynic has changed
its meaning entirely: in origin it means
'doglike' or 'dogged'. See the useful study
D.R. Dudley *A History of Cynicism*.

Stoica dogmata: the phrase is pointed: the
Stoics were dogmatists. The movement goes
back to Zeno of Citium (335-263 BC) in the
late fourth century. It takes its name from
the Stoa Poikile on the north side of the
agora at Athens where he taught in public.
The Stoics, especially from the time of
Chrysippus (c. 280-207 BC), the third
head of the school, were great systematisers,
and built up a complete system of logic,
physics and ethics integrated by a panthe-
istic and deterministic theology. For a good
general account showing great learning
carried lightly see F.H. Sandbach *The Stoics*.
An old book E.V. Arnold *Roman Stoicism*
remains the most comprehensive study in
English.

122 *tunica distantia*: the Cynics discarded
conventional clothing, the Stoics did not.
In fact the links are closer than might
appear likely. Zeno was directly associated
with Crates the Cynic. More, two of the
leading Stoics of the imperial period,
Musonius Rufus under Nero, and Epictetus,
an older contemporary of J, hold views
scarcely distinguishable from those of the
Cynics. The truth is that Stoic determinism
led to resignation to circumstances, so that
a Stoic in misfortune might appear very like
a Cynic (though Seneca, it is to be feared,
whined and grovelled in exile), but no Cynic
would on principle accept the political
power and wealth which Seneca accepted
'because they came his way'.

Epicurum: (341-270 BC) except for his
arrogant claims of independence from
other thinkers, one of the most attractive of
ancient philosophers, not least in his exalta-
tion of friendship, charmingly revealed in his
letters (cf 12, 130 n). Epicurus was maligned
in antiquity. He held the end of life was
pleasure, but, being a pessimist, held that we
should normally seek the action which led
to the least excess of pain over pleasure (not
achieved by grabbing at 'pleasures') and
that pleasure was not attainable without
righteousness. We must therefore free our-
selves from desires which outrun their
natural stations — unnatural desires for
fame, military glory, power, riches (such as
the tenth satire attacks). Live therefore in
retirement: Epicurus bought a 'garden' just
outside Athens. We must free ourselves from
fears, through a scientific understanding of
the atomic structure of the universe, through
the realisation that the gods do not reward or

punish, and that the soul does not survive
death. J's understanding of the philosophy
of pleasure (*laetum*), the simplicity (*exigui*),
the vegetarianism *(plantaribus)* confirms
inside knowledge. Lucretius is the great
Roman exponent of Epicurean thought:
Cicero presents it fairly while rejecting it:
Vergil and Horace were both involved with it
in their youth, but moved away from it. It
was in bad odour with the establishment at
Rome, partly because of its indifference to
public office and public service and scepticism
about established religion, but the second
century AD was its greatest period. See
N.W. de Witt *Epicurus and his Philosophy*,
and for a delectable short account A. -J.
Festugière *Epicurus and his Gods*. His
surviving work was collected in C. Bailey
Epicurus.

124 This medical metaphor is vital: it is
the pivot on which the poem turns; it was a
commonplace of the *consolatio*: its origin goes
back to the Greek Antiphon. Cicero uses it
frequently e.g. *TD* 3, 76-83.

125 *Philippi*: an unknown Greek doctor,
possibly but not necessarily a quack: the
emphasis is on *discipulo* (Green's 'first-year
medical student').

126-34 This whole passage should be read
aloud to follow the soundplay on *t*, *p*, and
m-n.

127-8 Signs of mourning.

129 *claudenda est ianua*: as when a death
has occurred (e.g. Tac. *Ann*. 2, 82 at the time
of Germanicus's death).

131 The climactic epigram, picked out
by the bucolic caesura.

132 *uestem ... summam*: a token act of
mourning.

134 *ueris*: the ironical point is held to the
last. J does not often repeat himself, but he
conducts ingenious variations on a theme; cf
1, 145.

135 See plan of Rome. The emperors
developed areas adjacent to the original
forum Romanum. Other forums were due to
Caesar, Augustus, and (after a century)
Nerva, and in AD 113 most recent and most
palatial, Trajan. These were the nerve-centres
of business, law, politics.

136 *diuersa parte*: i.e. on your opponent's
side.

137 An excellent line, 'golden' in form,
with both adjs. effectively predicative: 'they
affirm that the bonds' — note the Greek word
— 'are forged, and the tablet on which they are
written' — a wooden board smeared with
wax — 'worthless'. At 16, 41 J virtually
repeats this line.

138 *littera*: 'handwriting'.

139 *sardonychum*: see on 6, 381: this is a 'prince of sardonyxes' too precious to wear as a ring, and kept in a box: a seal was less easy to forge than a signature.

140 *o delicias*: best taken as personal, attracted from the vocative into the case of *ten*: 'you precious ass'.

141 *gallinae . . . albae*: a puzzle: schol. *prouerbium uulgare: id est, nobilis*. It is not so vulgar as to have survived elsewhere, and white hens are not specially rare, though they were perhaps less common in the past. Mayor cites, I cannot tell with what cogency, the French *le fils de la poule blanche*. French linguists do not know the phrase. White is on the whole regarded as a lucky colour. Burton cites the Latin in *The Anatomy of Melancholy* 1, 2, 3, 10 as 'a happy and fortunate man'.

142 *pulli*: a pun here, and J may have coined the previous phrase to make it: for *pullus* = 'pullet', but also 'black'.

143 *modicam . . . mediocri*: a neat effect, as if we were expected to control our indignation according to a nicely proportioned scale of causes.

144 *flectas*: a 'mixed conditional': the effect is 'you are suffering . . . (and you would realise it) if you would only . . .'

145-6 *sulpure . . . atque dolo*: zeugma (like Housman's parodic 'I go into the house with heels and speed'). For the use of sulphur as tinder see Plin. *NH* 36, 30, 138. In fires *dolus* = arson, cf *Dig.* 1, 15, 4 *qui dolo fecisse incendium conuincentur*.

148 *adorandae robiginis*: there is a complex irony here, though to spell it out tends to dispel it: for (a) antiquity *is* or may be venerable, (b) it is bathetic to suggest that the staining on the chalices is venerable, (c) there is some irony in suggesting that adoration is due to the chalice or any part of it rather than to the deity, (d) none the less the Romans did in fact recognise and propitiate Robigus, the *numen* or power of 'rust', particularly as a disease of wheat.

150 *haec ibi si non sunt*: deliberately bathetic words in preparation for what follows.

152 *bratteolam*: gilding was laid on in thin leaves which might be prised off.

Castore: the Heavenly Twins, Castor and Pollux, were honoured by the Romans whom they were believed to have supported at the battle of Lake Regillus.

153 This line can hardly be authentic, for this is hardly petty crime. The Thunderer is a cult-title of Jupiter. No emendation seems satisfactory: one recent suggestion is D.R. Shackleton Bailey's *solidum* for *solitus*, which removes one difficulty (*CR* 9 (1959) 201-2).

155-6 See on 8, 214.

155 *deducendum*: metaphor from launching a ship.

cum quo: for *quocum*, as at 4, 9; 4, 87.

157 *haec*: we do not have to decide whether this is neut. pl. or fem sing.: it covers both.

Gallicus: Rutilius Gallicus was *praefectus urbi* and therefore responsible for order under Domitian. He appears in Statius (*Silv.* 1, 4). He died in the early 90s, one of those *quorum Flaminia tegitur cinis atque Latina* (1, 171).

158 *donec lux occidat*: the sessions usually ended at the tenth hour, but there is too much business. The language is sharp, for it is almost as if the day is murdered: the collocation of the two verbs is harsh, and the line has a kind of infernal repetition — *luc-* . . . *lux, occidat audit*. The phrase *occidit breuis lux* can however be poignant (Cat. 5, 5).

160 *domus*: 'office' (not 'private house'): the sense is 'police court'.

consume dies et: clever writing: the offbeat rhythm, the additional word-stress in the last two feet, and the succession of words of three syllables, two syllables, one syllable all effect a sense of tedium.

162-5 The source of this passage is Sen. *Dial.* 5, 26, 3: but the observation of African women seems to be original with J, which makes it more likely that he had in fact been there.

162 *tumidum guttur*: 'the goitre', which was was at least until this century common in Switzerland. It used to be common in hill districts of Britain, being sometimes known as 'Derbyshire neck'.

163 *Meroe*: see on 6, 528.

164 *caerula . . . lumina*: cf Tac. *Germ.* 4 *truces et caerulei oculi, rutilae comae*.

165 *madido*: with *spuma Bataua*, a soap-mixture used to make the hair greasy.

torquentem: parallel to *flauam*, agreeing with *caesariem*: for the practice, cf Tac. *Germ.* 38 *obliquare crinem nodoque substringere*; Mart. *Spect.* 3, 9 *crinibus in nodum torti uenere Sicambri*.

cornua: at the sides therefore, rather than the back or top of the head.

166 This looks like a marginal gloss, answering the question.

167 The legend of the battle of cranes and Pygmies goes back to Homer (*Il.* 3, 3-6). Even as reputable a scientist as Aristotle accepted it (*Hist. An.* 8, 597a4). The geographer Strabo however treated it as fabulous (15, 1, 711; cf 17, 2, 821). Cranes do indeed migrate south in winter. For the Pygmies, cf on 6, 506.

170 *si uideas hoc*: J marks his point by

bucolic diaeresis and offbeat rhythm.

174-249 *'Is wrong to go unpunished?'*
To punish the crook doesn't restore your
money. 'Vengeance is lovely.' Not to the
philosophical, only to the small-minded,
to women. But does he escape? What about
conscience? Remember the Spartan who
tempted Delphi: his whole house vanished.
Conscience affects eating and drinking,
sleeping and dreaming. Any illness seems
a punishment. Bad men have shifty natures.
The man who did you down will trip up
sooner or later, and you'll agree then that
the gods see and care.

174 The discussion of punishment which
begins here has not lost its relevance.

175 *grauiore*: pointed: 'heavier than
usual'.

178 *corpore trunco*: J has in mind Paris
in Vergil's epic (*A* 2, 557-8), and still more
vividly the fate of Pompey the Great (Plut.
Pomp. 80; Lucan 8, 667 *lacerum . . . caput*).

179 *nimius . . sanguis*: 'a shower of
blood': for this reading see J.R.C. Martyn
in *Hermes* 102 (1974) 341-3; the MS
minimus makes no sense.

180 *indocti*: sc. *dicunt*: not so much the
uneducated as the unphilosophical. It must
be realised that philosophy was not an
academic discipline but a way of life, and
the philosopher was more of a *guru* than a
university professor: the philosopher attached
to the upper-class house was more of a
chaplain than a tutor.

183 *adeo*: modifying what's gone
before: almost 'you see'.

184 *Chrysippus*: the great systematising
head of the Stoa: see on 121; also 2, 5. At
15, 106-7 J cites Zeno *melius nos/Zenonis*
praecepta monent.

184-5 *mite Thaletis ingenium*: for the
circumlocution, cf 4, 81 *Crispi iucunda*
senectus. Thales was the effective founder
of Ionian natural philosophy, seeking
material rather than purely mythological
answers to questions about the nature of the
world. But he was a man of diverse talents
and concerns, one of the legendary Seven
Sages, and on all the various lists, and
putative author of gnomic wisom. Curiously,
one saying attributed to him suggests that
the best way to bear misfortune is by seeing
your enemies doing worse (Diog. Laert. 1,
36). More apposite is that the best life
consists in not doing what you criticise in
others (*ib.* 1, 37).

185 *dulci . . . Hymetto*: the bare rocky
ridge which dominates Athens lying like a
stranded whale to the east; it produced
superb honey, and still does.

senex: Socrates, 70 years old at his
execution in 399 BC. Calvinus too is *senex*.
J's source, as for much in this poem, is
Seneca (*Ep.* 24, 4).

186 *cicutae*: the Athenian method of
execution was by drinking hemlock, a
paralysing poison. Plato's *Phaedo* contains
the record of the death-scene marvellously
written. See also the painting by J.L David,
now in the Metropolitan Museum, New
York.

187 *accusatori*: there were three, named
Meletus, Anytus and Lycon. The charges
were corrupting the youth and religious
innovation, but they masked accusations of
antidemocratic influence which could not
be put overtly owing to a political amnesty.

nollet: vivid for *noluisset*: it makes the
scene present to us.

187-9 The characteristic functions of
Hellenistic philosophy are here. All Hellen-
istic philosophies are primarily concerned
with how people live, what is their 'end'
(*telos*), and what are the effective means to
that end.

189 *minuti*: exactly our 'small mind'.

191 *collige* 'draw your conclusion from
the fact that'.

quod uindicta: emphatic fifth-foot spondee.

192 *femina*: J's male chauvinism asserts
itself. For the *topos* see Sen. *Clem.* 1, 5, 5
muliebre est furere in ira.

cur tamen hos tu: note the bucolic
diaeresis and the four short words in the
last two feet.

193 *facti*: objective gen.: but J is
calling to our minds the Epicurean Lucretius
3, 1018 *at mens sibi conscia factis/praeme-*
tuens adhibet stimulas terretque flagellis.

194 *attonitos*: a strong word, 'benumbed
with horror'.

surdo uerbere: a brilliant touch of J's own.

197 *Caedicius*: schol. *aulicum Neronis*
crudelissimum fuisse uult intelligi: this is
possible. A lawyer of the name is mentioned
at 16, 46. The name is that of a plebeian gens.

Rhadamanthus: one of the three inexorable
judges of the dead. He was said to have
been an incorruptible judge in Crete in his
life.

199 *Spartano cuidam*: Glaucus (Hdt. 6, 86)
who consulted the Delphic oracle about his
attempt to withhold money deposited with
him for the depositor's children. He was
told that the family of such a perjurer
would be annihilated. He thereon restored
the money, but he had tempted the oracle,
and his family became extinct. J is emphasis-
ing his conclusion that even the secret will
to crime brings with it its own penalty in

the nature of the universe, and it's none of our business to inflict it. E. Courtney in *Hermathena* 118 (1974) 15-21 draws attention to a typical device of J here as he moves away from the theme of conscience, and then returns to it.

200 *dubitaret*: 'was wondering about' with a positive aim.

203 *illi*: we might expect *sibi.*

204 *metu, non moribus*: admirably phrased.

tamen: despite his action.

205 From Lucan 9, 565 *effudit dignas adytis e pectore uoces*, giving an epic tinge.

208 A memorable conclusion, marked by alliteration.

210 *crimen*: 'guilt'. This is very close to the Sermon on the Mount, cf Matthew 5:28 'But I say to you that every one who looks at a woman lustfully has already committed adultery with her in his heart.'

cedo: see on 6, 504.

211 *perpetua*: sc. *est.*

213 *crescente cibo*: for this sensation that the food in the mouth is bigger than actuality, cf Ov. *Her.* 15, 122 *crescit et inuito lentus in ore cibus*; Sen. *Ep.* 82, 21 *non in ore creuit cibus.*

Setina: an excellent emendation by Herel and Withof of MS *sed uina*. See on 5, 33.

214 *Albani . . . senectus*: a periphrasis of the type of 4, 81 *Crispi iucunda senectus*, the neater for its personal use there: cf 184-5. For the wine see 6, 015.

216 *acri . . . Falerno*: unexpected, since Falernian was reckoned better than Alban: see on 4, 138; 6, 150, etc. The point seems to be that Falernian grew rich and mellow after about fifteen years (Cic. *Brut.* 83, 287; Plin. *NH* 23, 20, 34); even then it was blended with honey or a sweet wine from Chios. In general the ancient world liked its wines sweeter than we do, but as they were for drinking after rather than with the meal, this makes gastronomic sense too.

221 *sacra*: 'awesome', 'supernatural': remember it is a keyword in this satire. The dream-appearance is ironical, for the sight of the dead in dreams is a standard feature of the *consolatio.*

221-2 *maior . . . humana*: like Pliny's ghost *Ep.* 7, 27, 2 *mulieris figura humana grandior pulchriorque.*

223 *fulgura*: Jupiter's wrath against oathbreakers, cf the Christian Tertullian's sarcasm *nos unum Deum colimus, quem omnes naturaliter nostis, ad cuius fulgura et tonitrua contremiscitis.* (Scap. 2)

225 *fortuitus*: the Epicurean view: the word is seemingly treated as a trisyllable

(cf Manil. 1, 182; Stat. *Th.* 7, 449), though possibly the *i* is shortened in the unemphatic position.

nec uentorum rabie sed: i.e. by personalised but wild and random action, well expressed by throwing the end of the line off beat.

226 *iratus . . . uindicet*: note that the fire itself is personalised: *uindicet*, found in some lesser MSS, is approved by Nisbet for *iudicet.*

227 *illa*: explained by *tempestas* in 228.

228 *sereno*: 'calm weather'; cf 7, 179.

229 *uigili cum febre*: transferred epithet, such as J uses freely.

230 *morbum*: like the plague which Apollo spreads in Hom. *Il.* 1, 43ff. Disease is so interpreted in many cultures.

231-2 *saxa . . . et tela*: the weapons with which they repelled the Giants.

233 *Laribus*: see 8, 110; 9, 137; 12, 89.

cristam . . . galli: i.e. a crested cock, a common offering to Aesculapius, as in Herodas *Mime* 4, or Plato *Phaedo* 118 A (Socrates's dying words, 'Crito, we owe a cock to Asclepius': after life's fitful fever he would sleep well).

236 Taken mischievously from Verg. *A* 4, 569-70 *uarium et mutabile/femina: malorum* is masc.

237 *admittunt*: 'are committing'.

constantia: 'determination'.

238-9 *peractis criminibus*: abl. abs. at the end is always emphatic in J.

239 *natura recurrit*: recalling Hor. *Ep.* 1, 10, 24 *naturam expelles furca, tamen usque recurret.* Conscience is not a restraint.

241 The bucolic diaeresis marks off the epigram on either side,

242 *attrita*: 'hardened'.

244 *dabit in laqueum uestigia*: 'will put his foot into a snare': see also on 245.

245 *uncum* see on 10, 66. The *uncus* and the *laqueus* both have to do with political criminals. cf Suet. *Tib.* 54 *laqueos et uncos.* J ironically suggests that the criminal will fall foul of his equally corrupt political masters — poetic justice.

246 cf 10, 170.

249 *Drusum*: for the MS *surdum*: E. Courtney in *U. of London Bull. of Class. Stud.* 13 (1966) 42: for the emperor Claudius's propensity to sleep on the bench see 3, 238.

Teresian: note the Greek ending. Teiresias was the blind prophet of Thebes. The conclusion is ironical, for in Hor. *S* 2, 5 Ulysses asks Teiresias how to restore his lost fortunes — *quid rides?* We too are meant to see that smile.

General comments

J begins his last book with a programmatic
satire, as certainly programmatic as the
first satire of the first book, and as dramati-
cally contrasting. There his opening line
expressed the desire for revenge: *num-
quamne reponam . . .?* (1, 1). *Indignatio*
dipped his pen in gall (1, 79). Now he
asserts that the desire for revenge belongs
to the *indocti* (181), to children (33; 181-90)
and women (192). J is of course still capable
of *indignatio*: but his general message is
aloofness not involvement. He is satirising
his earlier self: compare the apostrophe at
112 with his own at 2, 126 or 6, 393.

The satirical point of the poem is direct-
ed first against Calvinus. He has suffered
loss, it is true, but he overreacts. His moral
posturing comes down to *auaritia*: when it is
not that (and J shows that punishing the
criminal does not bring back the money),
it is the merest petulance. Calvinus has not
learned the lesson of *tranquillitas*; at the very
last, in the ironical conclusion, he still has
not learned it, and J dissociates himself from
Calvinus at the end as at the beginning.

This is why the poem is a mock-consola-
tion, a satire on consolations, as Pryor and
Edmunds have pointed out with particular
skill and sensitivity. The form is that of the
consolatio. But the cause of the sorrow is
loss of money not bereavement. Further,
the corruption of society is such that there
is no legal remedy for Calvinus. There is no
religious remedy either: men are indifferent
to the gods, and the gods are indifferent to
men. In some earlier satires J has used
mythology as offering a positive alternative
to his satirical view of society. Here the
mythology is twisted and jaundiced.

A *consolatio* was not usually given while
the wound was recent (Sen. *Helv. Matr.*
1, 2; Stat. *S* 5, 1, 18); J uses the word
recenti (5), for his purpose is satirical. Cicero
spells out the lines of a *consolatio*: *est autem
consolatio peruulgata quidem illa maxima,
quam semper in ore atque animo habere
debemus, homines nos ut esse meminerinus
ea lege natos, ut omnibus letis fortunae
proposita sit uita nostra, neque esse
recusandum, quominus ea, qua nati sumus,
condicione uiuamus, neue tam grauiter eos
casus feramus, quos nullo consilio uitare
possumus, euentisque aliorum memoria
repetendis, nihil accidisse nobis noui
cogitemus (Fam.* 5, 16, 2). This is exactly
what J offers. But it is for the loss of money,
not the loss of a son. Later (129-31) he
makes the point explicitly: here it is more
strongly ironical. So the words *dolor, uiri,*

uolnere (12) are effective because misapplied.
The technical terms of the *consolatio,* and
the technical structure of the *consolatio,*
reinforce the emptiness of Calvinus's
'bereavement'.

Through Calvinus the satire reaches
out to society, which is relentlessly exposed.
Fides is the cement of society (6). It is
broken; it is broken on all sides. Calvinus
does not care about the breaking of *fides*; he
is concerned only about his own loss. Social
values are his concern only when they
touch him directly. But Calvinus's *auaritia,*
his monetary values, are destructive of
fides. What would Calvinus say about *fides*
if its absence would gain him a fortune with-
out danger to himself? So each has an eye
on the main chance; religious and moral
values go for nothing. This is J's exposure of
Roman society. The ironical conclusion is
that the successful criminal does not know
where to stop, and comes up against a
political establishment as corrupt as he,
but far more powerful. This is no *consolatio.*

What of conscience? J's appeal to
conscience is ironic. This can be seen by the
dream-appearance of Calvinus to his defrauder.
Such apparitions were part of the stock-in-
trade of the *consolatio.* If J had wanted one
twist he could have had a differently ironic
passage in which Calvinus's money appeared
to him in a dream to assure him it was
happy in another existence. That he does not
do that shows that this poem is not about
Calvinus at all. He gives the dream-sequence
a still more savage twist: it is Calvinus who
is the theme, not the recipient of the dream,
and it is in consequence a nightmare.
Calvinus is an avenging Fury. But J's irony
has its serious side. He has learned enough
from Epicurus to believe that consciences
are uneasy, that the life of fools is a hell
on earth. This is not a consolation: it is rather
a lesson. It is not needful or desirable to
busy ourselves with thoughts of vengeance.
J does not speak with any seriousness of a
divine order. But he does believe that crime
overreaches itself and that criminals are
uneasy within. He is telling Calvinus not to
add to the sum of uneasiness and violent
over-reaction. For these things escalate.
Chesterton once said that the confidence-
trick was the work of man, but the want-of-
confidence trick was the work of the devil.
Calvinus is adding the want-of-confidence
trick to the confidence-trick. Violence
escalates: this is Archbishop Helder
Camara's 'spiral of violence'. J is telling
Calvinus not to add to the escalation. This
is a single-minded satire.

J's satire has not lost its power. It has fewer brilliances. The epigrams are there, glowing rather than flashing. There is hardly a single visual picture which stays in the mind. But the handling of satiric structure is firmer and surer than it has ever been: in this the power of this remarkable poem consists.

Bibliography

Anderson, W.S. 'The Programs of Juvenal's Later Books' (*CP* 57 (1962) 145-60 esp. 149-52.

Edmunds, L. 'Juvenal's Thirteenth Satire' *Rh. M.* 115 (1972) 59-73

Fredericks, S.C. 'Calvinus in Juvenal's Thirteenth Satire' *Arethusa* 4 (1971) 219-31

McGann, M.J. 'Juvenal's Ninth Age (13, 28ff)' *Hermes* 96 (1968) 509-14

Morford, M. 'Juvenal's Thirteenth Satire' *AJP* 94 (1973) 26-36

Pryor, A.D. 'Juvenal's False Consolation' *AUMLA* 18 (1962) 167-80

SATIRE 14

There is a small question-mark against the date of this satire. The third book is reasonably placed between Hadrian's arrival in Rome in 118 and his departure in 121. The fourth book, except that it is a work of old age, bears no indication of date. The fifth book contains two precise references to the year 127 (13, 17; 15, 27). But this poem suggests that the places to campaign are Mauretania and Britain (196), places with which Hadrian was involved in the first five years of his reign. Either then this satire was written earlier, put on one side, and added to the last book, or there is a satirical anachronism.

The structure has been analysed in detail by O'Neil, and I broadly follow his account.

I The Bad Influence of Parental Education 1-106
  A The parent teaches 1-3
    1 Gambling 4-7
    2 Gluttony 7-14
    3 Cruelty 15-24
    4 Adultery 25-30
    The parent teaches 31-7
  B Parents, refrain from bad conduct 38-43
    1 Wantonness 44-58
    2 Moral uncleanliness 59-72
  C All animals follow parental example 73-85
    1 Children learn extravagance 86-95
    2 Children learn superstition 96-106
II *Auaritia*: the worst vice learned 107-316
  A Its double nature
    1 Miserliness 107-14
    2 Greed 114-8
  B The parent teaches *auaritia* 119-25
    1 Miserliness 126-37
    2 Greed 138-60
    This contrasts with Roman tradition 161-72

  C *Auaritia* leads to other crimes 173-8
    This contrasts with Roman tradition 179-88
    1 Greed leads to
    (a) ambition 189-98
    (b) dishonesty 198-209
    The son will outstrip the father 210-34
    2 Miserliness leads to
    (a) chicanery 235-43
    (b) to patricide 244-55
    (whereby the son outstrips the father)
  D Disadvantages of *auaritia*: dangers 256-302
    difficulties 303-15
III Epilogue
  A How much is enough? 316-7
  B Enough to satisfy nature 318-31
There remains a question whether J has successfully integrated what seem to be two themes, parental miseducation, and *auaritia*, but O'Neil has successfully shown that the poem as a whole is planned and executed with meticulous care.

1-37 *Fuscinus, much that is shameful comes to children from their parents. Gambling for example, or gluttony. Rutilus teaches no lesson of mildness; his treatment of his slaves is sadistic, and he passes it on. If the mother sleeps round, so will the daughter. She was privy to her mother's secrets, and soon sends her own letters by the same go-between. That is nature: we follow our fathers' footsteps into vice.*

1 *Fuscine*: the name appears only in the first line: the person addressed is as dark as his name, and J promptly forgets him for the general reader.

1A Almost universally omitted: not in the best MSS.

3 *monstrant . . . traduntque*: example

and precept.

parentes: the unexpected word: the guardians of tradition are the sources of corruption.

5 *bullatus*: i.e. *praetextatus* (1, 78): the *bulla* (5, 164; 13, 33) was an amulet laid aside on donning the *toga uirilis*.

eadem . . . arma: i.e. *tesserae* or *tali*: the metaphor is a common one.

7 *iuuenis*: 'as a young man' in contrast to *bullatus*. The punctuation and interpretation are due to Nisbet.

7-9 *luxuries*: *ficedulas* are beccaficoes (Petron. 33).

10 *cana*: transferred epithet, cf Mart. 2, 34, 3; 9, 37, 7.

12 *barbatos*: i.e. philosophers, marked out among the other clean shaven elders. But see the remark of Herodes Atticus to a self-professed *guru*: *uideo barbam et pallium, philosophum nondum uideo* (Aul. Gell. 9, 2, 4).

15 Alliteration on *m*.

17 *paribusque elementis*: the Stoic and general philosophic view, cf Macrob. 1, 11, 6 *ex isdem tibi et constent et alantur elementis eundemque spiritum ab eodem principe carpant*. Note the fifth-foot elision and the four-syllable ending.

18 *Rutilus*: possibly the spendthrift of 11, 1-8.

19 *Sirena*: one of the monstrous bird-women who lured sailors to their doom by the magnetic power of their voices, cf on 9, 149.

20 *Antiphates*: a typical ogre, king of the cannibal Laestrygones (Hom. *Od.* 10, 80-132).

trepidi laris: 'to his trembling household'.

Polyphemus: the one-eyed monster of *The Odyssey*, who eats Ulysses's companions (Hom. *Od.* 9, 176-555). The four-syllable ending is not uncommon with a foreign word; the use of a preceding monosyllable prevents it from being thrown off beat.

22 *uritur*: 'is branded'.

duo propter lintea: napkins or towels, lost or stolen. Catullus 12 is a picture of a napkin-stealer of good family.

23 *quid suadet*: 'what is the effect of?' *stridore catenae*: from Verg. *A* 6, 558; epic flavour.

24 *inscripta*: 'brandings'.

ergastula: see on 8, 180.

25 *rusticus expectas*: 'are you such a country-bumpkin as to imagine?' The phrase is borrowed and turned from Hor. *Ep.* 1, 2, 42 *rusticus expectat dum defluat amnis*.

Largae: not otherwise mentioned: she is 'generous' in her favours. Renier (See*PW*) identified her with either Caecinia A. F. Larga

or Larcia Priscilla, wife and daughter of A. Larcius Lepidus (*CIL* 10, 6659) of Antium.

27 Note the play on *t* and *c*.

28 The bucolic diaeresis picks out the phrases.

29 *ceras*: tablets, of wax on a wood base, on which love-letters were written. See also 191.

hac: her mother.

30 *dat . . . ferre*: the inf. is a verb-noun and may be in the dat., so 'gives them for carrying' is not unnatural Latin; cf Hor. *O* 1, 26, 23 *tradam . . . portare*.

cinaedis: 'go-betweens'.

31 *et citius nos*: J points his dislike of the situation by offbeat rhythm.

33 *unus et alter*: again bucolic diaeresis to pick out the point.

35 *Titan*: Prometheus, one of the Titans or old gods (Hes. *Theog.* 424), ousted by Jupiter and the Olympians; they included Cronos, and Iapetus. Prometheus was s. of Iapetus and of a d. of Oceanus. He is a fire-spirit, who steals fire from heaven for men. In one myth he creates mankind of clay; cf 6, 13. See the sarcophagus in the Naples Museum.

36 *reliquos*: J scans this as an anapaest; cf 5, 149; 10, 260; Vergil, Horace and Ovid did not use it.

38-58 So refrain from bad conduct: or our children will follow our crimes, Catilines not Catos. Show respect for children when you're about to do something nasty. It's no good later blaming him for the crimes you've taught him.

38 The first four feet are a self-contained epigram.

huius enim uel: extra word-accent for emphasis.

41 *Catilinam*: taken as a notorious criminal, cf 2, 27; 8, 231; 10, 288.

43 *Brutus*: M. Brutus, the 'honourable man' who killed Julius Caesar, rather than the founder of the Republic, as the context shows: he had a high reputation for philosophic integrity, but this did not prevent him charging 48% interest on a loan to a town in Cyprus, and sending a private army to collect.

Bruti . . . auunculus: M. Porcius Cato Uticensis, whose sister Servilia was Brutus's mother: see on 2, 40.

44 *dictu . . . uisuque*: supines.

45 *procul, a procul*: formula from the Mysteries; cf Verg. *A* 6, 258 *procul o procul este, profani*. The implication is the sacredness of the child.

46 *pernoctantis parasiti*: alliteration and offbeat rhythm point the line. J uses the

dissolute characters of the comic stage to depict the corruptions of real life. For *leno* and *parasitus* see G.E. Duckworth *The Nature of Roman Comedy* pp. 262-7.

47 A notable epigram, usually however cited without the sting in the tail, *si quid/turpe paras*, the unexpected twist.

49 *peccaturo obstet*: hiatus: seven times in J in this position; cf 3, 70; the caesura provides a break.

infans: younger than *puer*: an additional point.

50 *censoris*: an old Republican office, concerned with the list of citizens, which involved striking off the unworthy. Under the Empire there were no censors, except occasionally the emperor. As Domitian was a censor of notorious rigidity, the irony is increased.

53 *omnia*: obj. of *peccet*.

peccet: consec. 'of such a character that'.

55 *tabulas mutare*: 'cut him out of your will'.

58 *uentosa cucurbita*: lit. 'gourd', so 'cupping-glass' from the shape: the release of blood was believed to relieve madness. J was evidently not quite sure how it worked: in fact the burning of linen inside created a vacuum, which helped to draw the blood through different air-pressure. Hence *uentosa*, which was the medieval Latin and early Italian word. *uacuum* thus becomes a double joke: the vacuum is in the head, where it should be in the glass. *cucurbita* too, since it is the Latin for a blockhead (Petr. 39); we are applying a *cucurbita* to a *cucurbita*! More than a dozen cupping-bronzes were found in Pompeii and Herculaneum. In general see F.A. Todd in *CQ* 37 (1943) 101-11.

59-72 *When you expect company, you keep the house clean and neat. But you present your son with a blemished home. It's a fine thing to present your country with a citizen, provided that he'll be a useful citizen.*

59 The theme is brilliantly treated in a seventeenth-century anon. English poem, which describes the spit and polish to entertain an earthly king: 'but at the coming of the King of Heaven,/All's set at six and seven.' (Oxford Christ Church MS 736-8: *Oxford Book of Seventeenth Century Verse* 308).

60-2 Note the specialised work of the *serui ad argentum*. Charcoal was used to remove tarnish, and chalk for polishing: sometimes vinegar or sodium carbonate was used (Plin. *NH* 33, 131; 35, 199; Theophilus 80). The palace had a steward *praepositus argenti escari*.

62 *leue*: 'smooth', i.e. not embossed, by contrast with *uasa aspera*.

67 *scobis*: 'sawdust', costing nothing. It was spread on the floor before a feast and swept up afterwards. Elagabalus used gold dust for the purpose (SHA *Elag.* 31); the mind boggles to think what J's comments might have been.

70 *gratum est quod*: 'thank you for'.

71 *ciuis*: Housman, for MS *patria* or *patriae*, both weak after *patriae*... *populoque*: the word would easily have dropped out after *-cis ut*.

73-85 *Your moral training is vital. All birds learn from the example of their parents.*

73 *plurimum enim intererit*: a rare elision in J; cf 6, 151 *quantulum in hoc*: the whole phrase is prosaic.

77 *crucibusque*: a typical twist on J's part.

80 *arbore*: J is wrong: vultures nest in rocks.

81 *famulae Iouis*: i.e. eagles; cf Hor. *O* 4, 4, 1 *ministrum fulminis alitem*.

86-95 *Caetronius was mad on building, putting up villas all over the place. He made a hole in his fortune, for his son to squander the rest on even more extravagant building.*

86 *Caetronius*: not a very common name: we know of two commanders of the name in the first century AD (Tac. *Ann.* 1, 44; *Hist.* 4, 50).

87 *Caietae*: a seaside town between Terracina and Minturnae, the modern Gaeta, according to myth named after Aeneas's nurse.

Tiburis: see on 3, 192; 11, 85.

88 *Praenestinis*: see on 3, 190. The musician Palestrina took his name from the town.

89 *Graecis*: even in old age J carries on the battle against Greek ways. A green marble from Laconia was especially in demand.

90 *Fortunae atque Herculis aedem*: Fortuna had a temple at Praeneste, Hercules one at Tibur: J's point is that Caetronius's private houses outvie these in splendour.

91 *Posides*: a eunuch-freedman of Claudius (Suet. *Claud.* 28): he built baths in Baiae (Plin. *NH* 31, 2, 5) and evidently built an extravagant house in Rome, though the suggestion that it outstripped the Capitoline temple is hyperbolic.

92 *inminuit rem*: the offbeat rhythm for rejection.

94 *turbauit*: i.e. *conturbauit*: see on 7, 129.

96-106 *Some follow Sabbath-fearing*
fathers into abstinence from pork, circum-
cision and the law of Moses. It's their father's
fault.

96 *quidam*: for the Jews under the
Romans see E.M. Smallwood *The Jews*
under Roman Rule; H.J. Leon *The Jews of*
Ancient Rome. This was a period of some
tension: the rising of Bar Kochba took place
in AD 132. As an account of external
observances, sabbath-keeping, refusal to
worship images, refusal to eat pig's flesh,
circumcision, observance of the Torah, it is
fair. For a more elaborate account see
Tac. *Hist.* 5, 1-9.

metuentem: Jewish proselytes were
called 'God-fearers'.

sabbata: the seventh day, our Saturday,
observed as a day of rest.

97 A somewhat garbled idea. The
absence of images led to all kinds of fantastic
fables, e.g. that the Jews worshipped a
donkey's head (Jos. *C. Ap.* 2, 7; the
graffito on the Palatine of a man with a
donkey's head on a cross, 'Alexamenos
worships his god', is a hostile muddle of
Judaism and Christianity). The reluctance to
use the name God and the preference for
'heaven' led to the idea that the Jews were
sky-worshippers; some of the Psalms could
be interpreted to support this; one sect
was in fact called the Caelicolae (*Cod. Just.*
1, 9, 12).

98 Cannibalism was a slander on Jews
and Christians alike; abstention from pig's
flesh (a reasonable health precaution in a hot
climate) is common to Judaism and Islam.
Hence Augustus's joke (a pun in Greek)
mallem Herodis porcus esse quam filius
(Macrob. 2, 4, 11).

99 *praeputia ponunt*: circumcision is also
common to Judaism and Islam; it was
found in ancient Egypt and is general in
African traditional religion. Hadrian banned
it (SHA *Hadr.* 14, 2) but Antoninus re-
pealed the ban. Elagabalus was circumcised
(D. Cass. 79, 11, 1-2). The origin is
obscure: it is an initiatory rite: possible
explanations include an endurance test, a
sacrificial offering, a sanctification of the
sex-organ, a hygienic act, a mark of tribal
distinction.

101 *ac metuunt ius*: offbeat rhythm for
scornful pointing. But J is right in stressing
the Torah. The line seems to parody
Biblical language.

102 *arcano . . . uolumine*: the Pentateuch,
the first five books of the Bible, which were
attributed to Moses.

Moyses: the great Jewish leader who led

his people out of slavery in Egypt towards
their new home in Palestine, and at Mount
Sinai received the Ten Commandments as a
basis for the moral life of the people and
part of their covenant with YHWH. 'The
legislator of the Jews' is mentioned by the
author of the treatise *On the Sublime*,
as author of the words 'Let there be light'
(9, 9). The second-century philosopher
Numenius actually calls Plato 'Moses
speaking Greek' (Clem. Al. *Strom.* 1, 22,
148).

103 *non monstrare*: explanatory of *ius*:
J is attacking Jewish exclusiveness, cf Tac.
Hist. 5, 5 *aduersus omnes alios hostile odium.*
Christians too were charged with *odium*
humani generis (Tac. *Ann.* 15, 44). There
seems to be ambiguity between 'the way' in
an everyday sense and the way of life: the
metaphor was common in Graeco-Roman
and Judaeo-Christian religion.

104 *quaesitum ad fontem*: again a
double-take between an ordinary request for
water, and baptism: this was not purely
Christian, since a sect associated with John
the Baptist lingered on, but in any case
Roman writers of this period had not
necessarily a clear distinction between Jews
and Christians in their mind.

106 *ignaua*: the Romans had no regular
weekend, free from work, and attributed
this to laziness. So Tac. *Hist.* 5, 4 uses
otium, inertia, ignauia.

107-37 *The worst vice for children to*
imitate is avarice. It leads to miserliness and
a passion for money-making. The avaricious
father drums the lesson into his son. He
is miserly to his slaves, miserly to himself,
living in poverty so as to die in wealth.

109 *specie uirtutis*: even today, when it
goes by the name of the Protestant Ethic.

110 *cum*: 'since'.

112 *tutela*: as often, J applies the im-
personal to the personal.

114 *Hesperidum serpens aut Ponticus*:
two dragons or snakes guarding legendary
treasures, one the golden apples of the
Daughters of the West, which it was a labour
of Hercules to secure, the other the Golden
Fleece of Colchis, which Jason secured with
the magical help of the princess Medea.

adde quod hunc de: bucolic diaeresis and a
broken prosaic ending in contrast with the
preceding mock-epic. For final *de*, cf 5, 33.

115 *adquirendi*: in seventeen of the
thirty-three lines with spondaic fifth feet the
last two feet form a single four-syllable word.
The word here emphasised is a keyword for
the satire (cf 125; 223; 238; 269): it does

not occur elsewhere in J.

116 *artificem*: as if a money-maker coined his own money as a craftsman: the metaphor is carried on in *fabris, incude, camino*.

118 The money-lender is always on the go and ready for more.

119 It is surely right to delete this line: if it stands *et* means 'as well as the man in the street', and *animi* is locative with *felices*.

120 The language is indebted to Hor. *O* 3, 29, 11-2, an injunction not to admire the riches of Rome.

120-1 *beati pauperis*: the Latin of Luke 6:20 is *beati pauperes*: this is presumably coincidental: the Latin NT was not yet shaped: but in view of the awareness of Judaism it is just possible that J had come across some Christian teaching. But the schol. recalls Aglaus, a poor man of Arcadia, held by Delphi to be happier than King Gyges of Lydia; cf also Hdt. 1, 30.

122 *sectae*: 'way of life', 'school of thought'.

123 *elementa*: 'first principles'.

125 A mock-heroic line.

126 *modio . . . iniquo* 'short measure'. Seneca gave his slaves five *modii* and five *denarii* a month. A *modius* is about 8½ litres.

127 *neque . . . sustinet*: 'he can't stand'.

128 *caerulei*: i.e. blue with mould.

129 *seruare*: cf Mart. 3, 58, 42 *nec auara seruat crastinas dapes mensa*.

minutal: 'mince', cf Mart. 11, 31, 11.

130 *Septembri*: the hottest, most unpleasant, most unhygienic month in Rome.

131 *conchem*: cheap food, coupled with *lacertus* at Mart. 7, 78, 1-2.

aestiuam: so likely to 'go off'.

lacerti: an unknown sea-fish.

132 *signatam*: under seal, as we would say 'under lock and key'.

siluro: see on 4, 33.

133 *sectiui . . . porri*: early-picked leeks: see 3, 293.

numerata: he counts them before putting them away.

134 *de ponte*: i.e. 'a beggar': see on 4, 116.

136 *phrenesis*: Cels. 3, 18 *phrenesis tum demum est cum continua dementia esse incipit*: the Greek word adds to J's scorn.

137 A splendid epigram.

138-72 *Greed for wealth increases as wealth expands. You begin to covet your neighbour's land, and if he refuses to sell, send your cattle in to devour his crops. You are not interested in the good opinion of others, provided you are protected from real work. The panacea is to have as much yourself as once constituted the whole territory of Rome. Once heroes were content with a hectare: that's not enough for a vegetable-plot for us.*

139 A Parkinsonian law of money-making.

140 The bucolic diaeresis picks out the points on either side.

141 *rus*: 'country estate'.

144 *arbusta*: 'vineyards', the vines being trained on other trees.

canet: the olive leaves are a grey-green on the upper side and hoary on the other: they are of great beauty from a distance, e.g. looking down on the olives round the river Pleistos from Delphi.

146 A crooked act for which the Twelve Tables prescribe penalties *de pastu pecoris*. The cattle are lean, half-starving and hard-worked, so will do the maximum damage (148 *saeuos*).

152 *foede*: sc. *sonat*.

famae: 'gossip'.

153 *tunicam . . . lupini*: a bean-pod, something worthless, like the brass farthing, tinker's cuss, and all such.

155 *exigui ruris*: J is thinking of Verg. *G* 2, 412-3 *laudato ingentia rura,/exiguum colito*, advice which is here rejected.

159 The vast estates were called *latifundia*; cf Plin. *NH* 18, 7, 35 *uerumque confitentibus latifundia perdidere Italiam, iam uero et prouincias*. See also Sen. *Ep.* 89, 20.

160 *Tatio*: Titus Tatius, the Sabine king who ruled jointly with Romulus, subject of a famous alliterative line by Ennius *O Tite, tute, Tati, tibi tanta, tyranne, tulisti (Ann.* 109).

161 *Punica*: the Romans identified three Punic Wars (i.e. against Carthage). The first (264-241 BC) was much concerned with Sicily, and ended in a Roman naval victory. The second (218-201 BC) was the war with Hannibal. The third (149-146 BC) led to the final annihilation of Carthage.

162 *Pyrrhum*: Pyrrhus (319-272 BC), king of Epirus, where the Molossi lived (cf 12, 108), was campaigning in Italy from 280-275 BC; his victories were so costly that a Pyrrhic victory has become proverbial ('Another such victory and I shall have lost the war'); when he withdrew he said 'What a battleground I am leaving to Rome and Carthage!' Note the alliteration

166 *curta fides*: 'a breach of faith'.

171 *pultibus*: 'porridge': the basic farm-workers' diet was a bowl of porridge with eggs and honey stirred in.

172 *horto*: 'allotment', 'vegetable patch'.

173-88 *Avarice leads to other crimes, like murder. In the old days people taught contentment.*

173 *inde*: i.e. from the desire to pile up property.

177 *et*: 'also': an excellent epigram: our phrase is 'get-rich-quick'.

180-1 The Marsi (one of the Italic tribes dedicated to Mars) lived on the Lacus Fucinus; the Vestini lay to the north-east over towards the Adriatic; the Hernici were in Latium with their capital at Anagnia; all were small, hardy, farming peoples.

182 *numina ruris: numen* (lit. a nodding, because the power of fertility was believed to reside in the head, and to nod or shake the head was to stir the life-force) is a general term for divine power; it can be used of gods and goddesses, but also of divine powers not conceived in human form. J has in mind Verg. *G* 1, 7-8 *Liber et alma Ceres, uestro si munere tellus/Chaoniam pingui glandem mutauit arista.* Liber Pater was an Italic power of fertility and wine, Ceres (cf *creare*) the power of growth in crops.

183 *ope et auxilio*: there is not much difference: J, like other Latin authors, likes the rhetorical effect of duplication.

184 *fastidia quercus*: a variant on Lucr. 5, 1416 *sic odium coepit glandis.*

186 *perone*: a farm-worker's boot; cf Pers. 5, 102 *peronatus arator.*

summouet: 'withstands'.

187 *pellibus inuersis*: i.e. lined with fleece.

188 *purpura*: 'luxurious clothes'.

189-255 *Nowadays the father drives his son to economic ambition, making a career in the army, or if he's lazy or cowardly, then through trade. The maxim is 'Get money — no questions asked about the source.' There's no need to din this into children's heads; they learn it for themselves and outstrip their parents. If your daughter-in-law has a dowry she's as good as dead. It's your doing. If you are acquisitive your son's only values will be monetary. He's off, you can't call him back. To tell him that charity's childish is to teach him crime. And you're not immune: your own life's in danger.*

189 *minoribus*: ambiguous between 'children' and 'future generations'.

190 *post finem autumni*: with the long nights, energetic Romans would rise early and work by lamplight (Plin. *Ep.* 3, 5, 8).

191 *ceras*: tablets of wax on a wood base, used for notebooks. For another use see on 29.

192 The peremptory, staccato instructions are excellently conveyed.

causas age: i.e. practise preparing speeches.

rubras: the titles and first words of a law were written in vermilion (*minium*): so our 'rubric'.

193 *uitem*: see on 8, 247: the baton of vinewood was the centurion's badge of authority. A senator would begin public life by military service as *tribunus legionis*; an *eques* went through four grades, as *centurio, praefectus cohortis sociorum, tribunus legionis,* and *praefectus alae*; a plebeian might make the army his career, aiming at the post of *primipilaris* or senior centurion. It seems that the last is the present point.

libello: 'petition': the regular word: there was a permanent imperial secretary *a libellis*.

194 *buxo*: 'the comb', made of boxwood.

195 *Laelius*: the commanding officer: no one appropriate is known at this period; there is probably a reference to Scipio Aemilianus's friend Laelius, who took an immediate admiration for the bulk and rough vigour of C. Marius (a story more commonly told of Scipio himself).

alas: 'shoulders'.

196 *Maurorum*: Hadrian was campaigning in Mauretania in the first years of his reign.

attegias: a very rare word, found once in an inscription (Orelli 1396): the usual word for African huts is *mapalia.*

Brigantum: the dominant tribe of northern England. Hadrian was in Britain in 121, and put in hand his celebrated wall. These references to the Mauri and Brigantes are strange, as other indications place this book to 127 or later (see Introduction): there may be a satirical point: the father who is so busy with his son's career is out of touch with the real world.

197 *locupletem aquilam*: the legionary standard or eagle was in the charge of the senior centurion, *centurio primi pili*: such a one might expect rewards; cf Mart. 1, 31, 2 *grata Pudens meriti tulerit cum praemia pili*; 6, 58, 10. Note the transferred epithet.

sexagesimus annus: retirement was permitted after twenty years' service, but not obligatory. Sixty was reckoned a good age for retirement. Aug. *QE* 19 *solet enim otium concedi sexagenariis post militiam.*

199 *cornua*: large curved trumpets.

200 *litua*: the cavalry bugles, straight with a slight curve near the mouthpiece.

pares: from *parare.*

201 *pluris dimidio*: 'at a 50% profit', gen,

of price + abl. of the measure of difference.
This too makes it likely that J is satirising
a plebeian household: senators, at least,
might not engage in trade.

202 *Tiberim ultra*: the more odoriferous
professions (e.g. tanning) were confined to
the Transtiberine area towards Janiculum.

204 *est odor ex re*: additional word-
accents in the last two feet for emphasis.
There is an excellent story of Vespasian, who
put a tax on urine (used in fulling). His
son Titus thought that this was a bit off,
but Vespasian asked him whether he found
that the money smelt any worse (Suet. *Vesp.*
23).

206 *dis atque ipso Ioue*: the combination
of general plural and particular sing. is a
poetical figure; cf Verg. *A* 1, 30 *Danaum
atque immitis Achilli*; Cic. *Cat.* 1, 5, 11 *dis
immortalibus . . . atque huic ipsi Ioui Statori.*
The idea of Jupiter as a poet is a pleasant
conceit.

207 A rhetorical *sententia*; cf Sen. *Ep.*
115, 14 *non quare et unde, quid habeas
tantum rogant.* Long *ō* in *nemo* shows that
it is not of J's coining, since elsewhere in J
it is short.

208-9 Jahn bracketed these lines. It is
true that we are concentrating on parental
influence, but even in mature old age J is
not afraid of diversion, and in any case the
influence of nurses is not to be totally dis-
sociated from that of parents. These are
strong lines, not those of a hack gloss-writer.

208 *repentibus*: 'still crawling'.
assae: 'dry-nurses' schol. *'assa nutrix'
dicitur quae lac non praestat infantibus
sed solum diligentiam et munditiam
adhibet: nutricula sicca uetusta infantibus
monstrat.*

209 *alpha et beta*: our 'alphabet', from
the first two letters in Greek: the Romans
learned Greek and Latin together from the
first.

212-3 *meliorem . . . discipulum*: a
satirical twist to his advice.

213-4 *Aiax. . . Telamonem*: Telamon
was in myth brother of Peleus, one of the
Argonauts. He settled on the island of Salamis,
where he became king, and fathered Ajax,
who was second only to Achilles among
the Greek fighters at Troy.

214 *Pelea . . . Achilles*: from Ov. *M*
15, 856 *sic Pelea uicit Achilles*, a general
passage about sons outstripping fathers.
The son of Thetis was fated to surpass his
father; this knowledge was Prometheus's
secret since Zeus was pursuing Thetis;
the fate and fortune were passed on to
Peleus. Note the Greek acc.: the final

syllable is shortened, as often in Latin
verse; cf 3, 266 *porthmea*; 7, 12 *Terea*;
8, 133 *Promethea.*

215 *parcendum est teneris*: a witty
adaption of Vergil's instructions about
young vines (*G* 2, 363).

215-6 An impressively-sounding combina-
tion of *m* and *n.*

218-9 *summa exigua*: 'for a trifling sum'.

219 *et Cereris*: 'even Ceres': here Demeter
of the Mysteries of Eleusis, guardian with her
daughter Kore (Persephone, Proserpina),
Queen of the Underworld, of the most
sacred of all oaths. See also 3, 320.

aramque pedemque: to touch the sacred
altar and statue was stringent ratification:
to be perjured so doing was utterly shame-
less: cf Plaut. *Rud.* 1333 *tange aram hanc
Veneris.*

220 *elatam*: 'has already been carried
out to burial'.

221 *mortifera*: an unexpected and
brilliantly pregnant word.

224 *haec ego numquam:* the bucolic
caesura isolates and points the previous
epigram: the additional word-accent lays
extra weight to these words.

228 *laeuo*: 'sinister', 'perverted'.
auaros: proleptic.

229 The reading is due to D.A. Amyx in
CP 36 (1941) 278-9. The line is splendidly
sonorous.

230 *totas effundit habenas*: from Verg.
A 5, 818 *omnis effundit habenas.*

231 *quem*: the Roman grammarians give
a masc. form *curriculus*: the implication is
that *curriculo* may be the antecedent: this
is not impossible as J likes to use the thing
for the person.

reuoces: the technical term for calling
the competitors back after a false start.

232 *metis*: 'the turning-posts': the
metaphor from racing is skilfully sustained.

233 *credit . . . delinquere*: 'believes in
doing wrong'.

235 *stultum*: sc. *esse.*

236 *propinqui*: 'of a relation'.

237 *doces*: the main verb.
circumscribere: 'to practise chicanery', cf
10, 222; 15, 136.

238 *quarum amor in te*: the elision and
additional word-accent mark the point.

239 *Deciorum*: see on 8, 254.

240 *si Graecia uera*: J is sceptical of all
things Greek, even their patriotism; cf 10,
174-5 *quidquid Graecia mendax/audet in
historia.*

Menoeceus: there were two heroes of the
name, and two variants of the myth, oddly
paralleling the Decii. The elder was f. to Creon

and Jocasta (queen to Laius and then
Oedipus), himself Oedipus's grandfather and
father-in-law. When plague hit Thebes the
prophet Teiresias declared that one of the
descendants of the Sparti (see on 241) must
sacrifice himself for the city: Menoeceus
threw himself from the walls. When the
Seven marched against Thebes, Teiresias again
declared the need for a similar sacrifice, and
Creon's son Menoeceus, grandson of the
other, stabbed himself.

241 *quorum*: i.e *Thebani.*

The myth here is that Cadmus killed
the dragon of Ares which was guarding a
spring; on Athene's advice he sowed
the teeth, from which sprang armed men, the
Sparti, or Sown Men. By throwing stones
among them he started a quarrel in which
there was a general massacre with only
five survivors. These five helped Cadmus
found the city. The treatment is of course
satirical: J is suggesting that such things
are everyday occurrences — in Greek accounts
of their own history.

244-5 A change of metaphor but an
effective one.

246 *nec tibi* 'not you either'.

247 *leo alumnus*: a third rich metaphor,
derived from a theatre in Aesch. *Agam.*
717-36; cf Ar. *Frogs* 1431-2, but overlaid
with the associations of the rich eccentric
Romans and the arena; cf Mart. *Spect.*
10, 1 *laeserat ingrato leo perfidus ore
magistrum.*

248 *mathematicis*: 'astrologers' cf 3, 43;
6, 553; 10, 94: it is historically true that in
Babylonia mathematics developed in the
service of astrology.

genesis: 'horoscope', cf 6, 579.

graue: 'it's grim'.

249 *colus . . . stamine*: the three Fates
mythologically spin the threads of a man's life.

251 *ceruina*: Plin. *NH* 7, 48, 153 quotes
Hesiod to the effect that the stag lives four
times as long as the crow and the crow nine
times as long as man: the scholiast's 900
years seems short by comparison. Aristotle
HA 6, 29, 578b23 rightly identifies the
longevity as a vulgar error.

252 *Archigenen*: a distinguished doctor:
see on 6, 236.

Mithridates: see on 6, 661.

253 *aliam decerpere ficum*: i.e. live
another year.

255 *et pater et rex*: i.e. the Roman pater-
familias today is in as much danger as the
eastern potentate of old.

256-302 *It's as good as a play to watch
the dangers the avaricious face in pursuit of
wealth, better entertainment than the tight-*

*rope-walker. He does it for a living, you for
a luxury. Look at the merchant fleets which
face strange seas and sea-monsters. There
are many forms of madness: one is sea-
trading — all those hardships for pieces of
metal. The stormclouds rise. 'Cast off,'
says the trader. His ship is a wreck, and
he becomes a beggar.*

257 For the praetor at the Games see
11, 195.

258 *spectes*: taking its point from
spectaculum: J is playing on the common-
place of life as drama: he is somewhere
in the line of ascent from Shakespeare's
'All the world's a stage' (*As You Like It*
2, 7, 139). Compare also Raleigh's lines,
set by Orlando Gibbons, 'What is our life?
A play of passion', ending, 'Only we die in
earnest, that's no jest.'

capitis discrimine: 'peril to life'.

260 *Castora*: the temple of Castor in
the forum, whose three surviving
Corinthian columns remain a landmark.
It was really a temple of Castor and Pollux,
but Pollux was squeezed out in popular
parlance. Bibulus complained that the
same thing happened to him as consul
with Caesar (Suet. *Caes.* 10). To deposit
treasures in a temple was a normal precaution.
It seems that this temple had a military guard:
hence *uigilem.*

261 *Mars Vltor*: in the forum Augusti:
it had apparently suffered a burglary.

262 *Florae*: the goddess of flowers:
for the Floralia see on 6, 250.

263 *Cereris*: the ludi Ceriales were held
12-9 April in honour of Ceres.

Cybeles: the Megalesia 4-10 April: see on
11, 193. The three great spring festivals
are named in reverse order.

aulaea: all three included theatre.

264 sc. *sunt: humana negotia* is subj. A
good epigram.

265 *petauro*: seemingly a springboard,
certainly a part of the acrobat's equipment:
sometimes it is a trapeze, and sometimes a
wheel. Mart. 2, 86, 7 *graciles uias petauri*;
cf 11, 21, 3.

266 *rectum descendere funem*: evidently
a tightrope slanting down to the ground
from a height.

267 *Corycia*: Corycus was a town in
Cilicia, celebrated for saffron (269 *sacci
olentis*), which was used in the form of a
spray to perfume the theatre (Mart. 5, 25, 7).

268 *coro*: the west-north-west wind.

tollendus: blending 'fit to be' and 'about
to be'.

269 The reading of this line is quite
uncertain. The MS *acullis* or *ac uilis* or

a siculis is impossible, as Housman showed: suggestions include *ac similis* (Housman), *ac facilis* (Green), *ac fatuus* (Griffith). I have accepted, but without any certainty, *adquirens:* see F. Schreiber in *Hermes* 99 (1971) 383-4, who argued that *adquirere* is the satire's keynote; cf 115; 125; 223; 238. *Perditus* means 'desperate', 'reckless'. The *mercator* has a bad press from Roman poets, e.g. Hor. *O* 1, 1, 16; 1, 31, 11ff; 3, 24, 35ff; *S* 1, 4, 29ff; *Ep.* 1, 1, 45ff; Tib. 1, 3, 39-40; Verg. *Ecl.* 4, 31-2. It is a relic of Greek philosophy: trade was for foreigners. Cic. *Off.* 1, 151 is interesting: if profit is small, trade is despicable; if it is large without extravagance it may be praised.

271 *passum* 'raisin wine', so called because the grapes were spread out (*pandere*) to dry. Mart. has an epigram on *passum* (13, 106): *Gnosia Minoae genuit uindemia Cretae/hoc tibi, quod mulsum pauperis esse solet.*

municipes Iouis ... lagonas: J mingles the personal and impersonal, and interchanges nouns and adjs with some freedom; cf 4, 33 *municipes ... siluros*; Mart. 10, 87, 10 *Cadmi municipes ferat lacernas.* Jupiter according to one myth was born in Crete.

272 *hic:* the tightrope-walker: the line excellently describes the profession.

273 *uictum ... parat:* 'makes his living'.

276 *plenum:* with both nouns: this is the idiomatic position; cf 8, 129; Verg. *A* 4, 588 *litoraque et uacuos sensit sine remige portus.* The moralists are frequently on about the sinfulness of seafaring. So in Horace the *mercator* is the type of sinful ambition (*O* 1, 31, 10; 3, 24, 40; *Ep.* 1, 1, 45). In Vergil's golden age *cedet et ipse mari uector, nec nautica pinus/mutabit merces* (*Ecl.* 4, 38-9). J echoes *A* 4, 566.

plus hominum est iam: J points his hyperbole by bucolic diaeresis and extra word-accents in the last two feet.

278 *Carpathium:* around the island of Carpathus, between Crete and Rhodes.

Gaetula: waters off the North African coast.

279 *Calpe:* abl.: Gibraltar, the northern pillar of Hercules, the other being Abyla.

280 *Herculeo ... gurgite:* the Atlantic: Hercules reached there in seeking the golden apples of the Hesperides.

stridentem: the red-hot sun hisses as it dips into the waters.

281 *tenso folle:* 'with money-bags bursting'.

282 *aluta:* a leather purse.

283 *iuuenes ... marinos:* Tritons and other mermen: note that these are regarded as perils, not curiosities.

uidisse: strictly the subj. of the whole sentence.

284 *non unu. ... furor:* 'more than one form of': epigram self-contained in first four feet.

ille: Orestes, seeing the Furies pursuing him with flaming torches for his murder of his mother and being cared for by his sister Electra: the closest parallel in surviving literature is Eur. *Or.* 260-4.

286 *hic:* Ajax, who went mad when Ulysses, not he, received the arms of Achilles, and slaughtered cattle under the impression they were the Greek commanders: see Soph. *Ajax.*

287 *Ithacum:* Ulysses, who came from Ithaca.

parcat ... licet: 'even though he does not tear'.

288 *curatoris eget:* exactly our 'needs a keeper'.

289 *tabula distinguitur unda:* 'is separated from the waves by a single plank'.

291 *titulos faciesque:* the 'image and superscription' of Mark 12:16. The satirical description of the coinage is excellent.

292 *'soluite funem':* 'cast off', i.e. 'put out to sea'.

293 *frumenti:* Africa was now the granary of Rome, and corn-shipping must have been profitable.

piperis: imported from India overland to Alexandria and shipped to Rome from there.

294 *color* 'darkness'.

fascia: 'cloud-bank': schol. *nubes ducta per caelum.*

295 *aestiuom tonat:* we speak more readily of summer lightning.

297 *zonam:* 'money-belt', the regular way of carrying money while travelling.

laeua morsuque: it is weighing him down, but he won't let go and is holding it above the water: with his right hand he is clinging to a spar.

299 *Tagus:* river of Spain, reputed to carry gold-dust; cf 3, 55; it is one of those listed in Plin. *NH* 33, 21, 66; cf Cat. 29, 19 *amnis aurifer Tagus.*

Pactolus: river of Lydia, with the same properties, the source of the wealth of Sardis; cf Plin. *NH* 33, 21, 66; Hor. *Ep.* 15, 20 *tibi Pactolus fluat.*

300 *inguina:* all that makes for life is chilled: strong and skilled satire.

302 *picta:* those shipwrecked begged for money displaying a picture of the wreck painted on a fragment from the wreck (Pers. 1, 88-90).

303-15 *Riches are as hard to keep as to get.*

*All those fire-precautions! The Cynics' jar
doesn't catch fire. Alexander knew that
Diogenes was happier in freedom from
desire than he himself was in ambition.
No divinity there!*

304 *misera est magni custodia census*:
a good epigram pointed by alliteration:
m here and in the previous line expresses
fearfulness. For the thought, cf Hor. *O*
3, 16, 17 *crescentem sequitur cura pecuniam*;
Sen. *Ep.* 115, 16 *maiore tormento pecunia
possidetur quam quaeritur.*

305 *praediues*: a neat ironical touch:
J's theme is from Seneca, but it applies to
Seneca himself (cf 10, 16 *praediuitis*).

amis: 'fire-buckets'. For urban fire-hazards
see 3, 197ff. The Great Fire of AD 64
was still within living memory.

306 *Licinus*: see on 1, 109. According
to the schol. and other sources, a Gaul by
birth, a freedman whom Augustus made
procurator in Gaul, and who died in Tiberius's
reign. His name was C. Julius Licinius, here
shortened *metri causa.*

attonitus pro: 'frozen with fear for': the
offbeat rhythm adds to the effect. For a
final monosyllabic prep. see on 5, 33; 6, 58.

307 *electro*: probably 'amber' (cf 5, 38),
though the word is also used of an alloy
of gold and silver.

Phrygiaque columna: marble from Synnada
was valued highly (Hor. *O* 3, 1, 41; Strab. 12,
577; Plin. *NH* 35, 1, 3; 36, 24, 102).

308 *testudine*: see on 11, 94.

dolia nudi: the bucolic diaeresis empha-
sises these words. For Diogenes the 'dog'
and the Cynics see on 13, 121. Diogenes
stripped himself of all possessions (*nudi*)
except a large earthenware jar (*dolium*)
for protection against the weather, a scrip,
and in old age a staff. He is shown in his
jar in a relief in the Villa Albani, and on
gems in Thorwaldsen Museum, Copenhagen,
in Leningrad and Berlin. (See G.M.A. Richter
Portraits of the Greeks figs 1067-8.)

309 *non ardent*: 'do not catch fire'.

310 *atque*: virtually 'or'.

plumbo commissa: 'stapled together with
lead'.

311 *Alexander*: stories of the confronta-
tion between the soldier-statesman and the
ascetic were popular and no doubt
apocryphal. 'I am Alexander the Great King.'
'I am Diogenes the dog.' 'Ask me any favour
and it shall be granted.' 'Would you mind not
keeping the sun off me?': see e.g. Diog. Laert.
6, 38; Plut. *Alex.* 14; Val. Max. 4, 3E4.

testa: the jar.

313 cf Sen. *Ben.* 5, 4, 4 on Diogenes
multo potentior, multo locupletior fuit

*omnia tunc possidente Alexandro; plus
enim erat quod hic nollet accipere quam
quod ille posset dare.*

cuperet . . . posceret: subj. because these
are Alexander's thoughts.

totum . . . orbem: cf 10, 168.

315-6 Something is plainly wrong with
the text: *nullum . . . deam* is taken directly
from 10, 365-6: J seldom repeats himself
exactly, and here the repetition is inap-
propriate. It is possible that *nullum numen
habes* can stand, since Alexander was
worshipped, and another story was told of
Diogenes's rejection of that worship (Diog.
Laert. 6, 63 'Make me Sarapis while you're
about it' — again apocryphal but *ben
trovato*). The words were then glossed by the
familiar quotation. But more has probably
dropped out. J usually begins a new para-
graph for his conclusion, and I suspect that
something led into *mensura tamen quae.*

316-31 *So where are we to draw the line?
Enough to keep off cold, thirst and hunger.
The example of Epicurus and Socrates.
Philosophy and nature tell the same story.
Do you find this harsh? Go for the qualifica-
tion of a knight — two knights — three
knights. If you're not satisfied then, nothing
will satisfy you, not even the power to
execute an empress.*

319 *Epicure*: see on 13, 122: J has a
proper appreciation of Epicurus's cult of the
simple life. There is irony in J taking two
Greek models: they are the more telling
just because they are Greek.

320 *Socratici . . . penates*: the *penates*
were the spiritual powers guarding the larder,
pantry (and today refrigerator and deep
freeze). Socrates had a reputation for
simple living: see Xen. *Mem.* 1, 2, 1; 1, 3, 5;
1, 6, 2; 2, 1, etc.

321 *sapientia*: 'philosophy': a good
epigram and a searching one: the Stoics were
always insisting *secundum naturam uiuere.*

322 *acribus*: 'harsh'.

323 *nostris*: 'our present-day', not those J
is advocating.

summam: 400000 sesterces, the amount
required for registration as an *eques.*

324 In the theatre the fourteen front
rows were reserved for the *equites* by the
lex Roscia theatralis of 67 BC, due to the
tribune L. Roscius Otho: the law was re-
affirmed by Domitian; cf 3, 154. (Humphries'
reference to the emperor Otho is wrong.)

325 *haec*: sc. *summa.*

rugam trahit extenditque labellum:
'brings a frown to your brow and a pout
to your lips'.

326 *duos equites*: a very daring phrase:

'take a couple of knights', i.e. a fortune enough for two: but the direct thought has satirical power: why should anyone want two men's fortunes?

tertia: this would bring him up to qualify as a senator.

328 *Croesi*: cf 10, 274: king of Lydia, proverbial for his wealth.

Persica regna: cf Hor. *O* 2, 12, 21 *diues Achaemenes*; 3, 9, 4 *Persarum rege beatior.*

329 *Narcissi*: a freedman, who became Claudius's secretary, handling the imperial correspondence (*ab epistulis*). He was one of three immensely rich and powerful freedmen, the others being Pallas and Callistratus. His fortune was reputed to exceed 400 000 000 sesterces, i.e. 100 times that of the *census equester.* See Suet. *CL* 28; Plin. *NH* 33, 47, 134. Spondaic fifth foot; cf 326.

331 According to Tacitus (*Ann.* 11, 30-8), when Messalina had her mad marriage with C. Silius, it was Narcissus who gave orders for her execution, telling the emperor afterwards. The line forms a bitter despondent climax to this trenchant satire.

General comments

This satire has attracted curiously little attention, for it is a poem of considerable power, and one which speaks strongly to the mood of many of the student generation of the second half of the twentieth century. It has been criticised on the grounds of inconsistency. Such critics claim that it starts from an attack on the miseducation of children by parents, and switches to an offensive against *auaritia.*

J is attacking the values of upper-class and middle-class Roman society, and in this poem he focuses his attention on the values expressed in family life. No American student could misunderstand the point of the satire. The 'generation gap' and the 'Protestant ethic' are part of the same pattern. *Auaritia* is shown in both parental indifference and public corruption. But student protest has been ambiguous. For, as Harold Loukes, the Oxford educationalist, commented with reference to the British scene, the protesters are moulded by the very system against which they are protesting, and use the categories and weapons of that system. And it is frighteningly easy to be caught up in the system. I have seen a student engaged in a wholly justified movement of protest, shaken because his mother threatened that if he ever did so again she might 'lose her cheque-book'. And, less blatantly but no less effectively, once students leave the shelter of university or college, it is easy to get caught up in the old order, willy-nilly. This is not a digression from J: it is exactly what J was talking about — a total environment, based on the family.

Auaritia is for J the spring of Roman life. It is the spirit which puts monetary values first. It is the acquisitive society: only in this poem does he use the word *adquirere,* and it recurs (115; 125; 223; 238; cf 269). J has taken a hint from Horace *Sat.* 1, 1, 92 *denique sit finis quaerendi. Auaritia* has a double meaning, miserliness and greed, and the combination of the two permeates social life at all levels. In earlier poems J has attacked single vices. Here he sees them all as part of the single, comprehensive, vicious system of *auaritia.*

The family is caught up in the system: it is decadent, corrupt, and complacent. J starts from the family which is the basis of society, and extends from there to society at large. The family, more than the school, is the instrument of education. But society as a whole educates. It is not easy to foster cooperation through the home when society is competitive, peace through the home when the media screen violence, sexual integrity through the home when the billboards carry salacious advertisements, service through the home when only monetary success is recognised in society. This dichotomy could be a theme for satire: not for J, since he sees the family as pulling in the same disastrous direction as society. This gives the satire its unity. There are not two themes but one. J passes from the general theme of the bad influence of parents to concentrate on *auaritia.* But the thought of *auaritia* has already been implicit: gambling is an expression of *auaritia,* so is gluttony, so is architectural extravagance. Further, when J passes explicitly to *auaritia* he is continually concerned with education in *auaritia,* with the influence of parents on children. It is only at 256 that he seems to pass to *auaritia* in itself, but here too we must sense the thought of precept and example in the background.

In this poem J uses the traditions of ancient Rome as a check. He treats them both positively and negatively. The (very interesting) passage about Judaism (96-106) is not just a side-swipe at Orientals: the point is that education in superstition is education away from traditional Roman religious values. The same is true of the use of Greek words (136), letters (209), forms (214), myths (240): they are not arbitrary: they are all parts of the un-Roman behaviour of J's Romans. Positively, two extended passages exalt the simple traditions of ancient Rome (159-71; 179-89; cf 71-2).

This is J's answer: this satire is positive: simplicity of life. His models are Epicurus and Socrates. It is ironical that they should be Greek: it is as if he is saying, 'If you will be Greek, at least go to the best Greeks.' The Romans he is attacking have fallen far below the standards not merely of Rome but even of Greece. He insists, brilliantly, that philosophy does not require unnatural behaviour (321). But J is pessimistic. The positive pleas of the first section (38; 44-9; 68-9) fade away. The conclusion is masterly and depressing. He does not expect his advice to be followed. The point of the last ten lines is that there is no logical stopping-place between living a life of basic simplicity, and total dominance by *auaritia.* If you seek the *census equester*, why stop there? Why not enough for two? Or three? Why not become a senator? Why not become a millionaire? A multi-millionaire? Why not dominate the emperor? Why not cut off the empress's head? So the fantasies grow to the pungent conclusion.

This is the third longest satire, exceeded only by the sixth and tenth. Its theme is expressed in the third line by the shocking paraprosdokian on *parentes.* It is marked by

brilliant epigrams (47 *maxima debetur puero reverentia, si quid/turpe paras*; 137 *ut locuples moriaris, egentis uiuere fato;* 207 'unde · habeas quaerit nemo, sed oportet habere'; 276-7 *plus hominum est iam/in pelago;* 285 *non unus mentes agitat furor;* 308-9 *dolia nudi/non ardent Cynici*; 321 *numquam aliud natura, aliud sapientia dicit* — to name but a few). There is admirable use, including parody, of previous authors, Vergil in particular (e.g. 155; 215). The handling of language shows great skill: see for one thing the extraordinary concatenation of double meanings at 57-8. The verse too is treated with considerable art: notice the sound-effects at 27 or 303-4, or the contrasting effect of the two parts of 114. But the power of this unjustly neglected poem does not lie in details, but in the total effect, the unremitting assault on the corruption of the family, of education, of society by *auaritia.*

Bibliography
D'Agostino, V. 'La Satira XIV di Giovenale' *Convivium* 4 (1932) 227-44
O'Neil, E.N. 'The Structure of Juvenal's Fourteenth Satire' *CP* 55 (1960) 251-3
Stein, J.P. 'The Unity and Scope of Juvenal's Fourteenth Satire' *CP* 65 (1970) 34-6

SATIRE 15

This poem is one of the few to which a relatively firm date may be assigned. J explicitly declares that the events took place *consule Iunco* (27), i.e. AD 127. This does not precisely date the poem, as they are described as *nuper*, which can allow much water to flow under the bridges or down the Nile, but we shall not be far out if we date the poem to AD 127-30.

Otherwise there is little that needs saying by way of preliminaries. The structure is clear:

1-32   Introduction
33-92 Narrative of mob murder and cannibalism in Egypt
93-131 Other examples of cannibalism and murder: none comparable
131-74 Moral: man is more brutal than the brute beasts.

One interesting feature is that though J usually marks his paragraphs firmly and clearly, the last two sections flow into one

another in the middle of a line. (But cf 14,316.)

J is not the only satirist to use cannibalism as a symbol of violating violence. Petronius had done so before him, and Swift, in *A Modest Proposal,* Byron in 'Don Juan', and Evelyn Waugh in *Black Mischief* were to do so later.

1-32 *Volusius, everyone knows the extravagances of Egyptian religion, the worship of crocodiles, cats, fish, dogs. Yet people who will not eat animals eat their fellow-humans. Cannibalism was the worst horror of Ulysses's saga. That was an unsupported yarn. I have a piece of recent history, worse than any tragedy because committed by a whole people.*

1 *Quis*: in Satires 8, 15 and 16 the theme is put in the form of a question.

Volusi Bithynice: unknown: sometimes one wonders whether the recipient is fictitious, but this looks genuine. Bithynicus was a cognomen of the gens Pompeia: a

Bithynicus appears at Mart. 6, 50, 5. There was a jurist named L. Volusius Maecianus who was an *amicus principis* of Antoninus Pius.

2 *Aegyptos*: the Greek ending creates an initial alienation: note also the personification implied in *demens*.

portenta: Cic. *ND* 3, 15, 39 *omne fere genus beluarum Aegyptii consecrauerunt*; cf *TD* 5, 27, 78. Verg. *A* 8, 698 has *monstra* of the Egyptians; Cyprian (*Quod idola di non sint* 4) has *Aegyptia portenta non numina*: Plutarch *Is. et Os.* has a fairly full account.

crocodilon: Hdt. 2, 68-70; Strabo has an account of feeding a sacred crocodile (17, 811-2); Plut. *Is. et Os.* 381 B has an unsatisfactory account of the religious significance. Again note the Greek ending.

3 *pars haec*: 'one region'.

ibin: Hdt. 2, 75-6: the ibis is a long–beaked water-bird: it apparently kept the snakes under control; cf Cic. *ND* 1, 36, 101 *ibes maximam uim serpentium conficiunt*. It was sacred to Thoth.

4 *cercopitheci*: a long-tailed ape; cf Mart. 14, 202, 2 on the *simius: si mihi cauda foret cercopithecus eram*. Their mummified remains have been found.

5 *Memnone*: Memnon was in legend an Ethiopian, son of Dawn. The statue to which J refers was in fact of king Amenophis III. Something in the stone caused a twanging sound to emerge with the change of temperature at sunrise: Tac. *Ann.* 2, 61 *Memnonis saxea effigies, ubi radiis solis icta est, uocalem sonum reddens*: Strabo heard the effect (17, 816). The statue survives: various visitors of the period (including the emperor Hadrian) regrettably carved their names on it. It was at this time in a broken condition (*dimidio*): Septimius Severus restored it (SHA *Sept.* 17), and the phenomenon ceased. *dimidio . . . Memnone* is perhaps abl. abs.

6 *Thebe*: the hundred gates of Thebes, one of the great cities of early antiquity, are mentioned by Homer (*Il.* 9, 383).

7 *aeluros*: a certain emendation by Brodaeus of *illicaeruleos*. The cat was domesticated in Egypt: curiously not in Greece or Rome, where weasels and martens were used to keep down rats and mice. The goddess Bast was depicted with a cat's head (Hdt. 2, 66-7).

piscem fluminis: Hdt. 2, 72: we know of several sacred fish, particularly the eel and the *lepidotos* (perhaps the Nile perch): the priests were forbidden to eat fish. The river is of course the Nile.

8 *canem*: Hdt. 2, 66; Cic. *Leg.* 1, 11, 32

qui canem et faelem ut deos colunt. Anubis (cf 6, 532) was depicted with the head of a dog or jackal.

Dianam: as huntress she was mistress of the hounds. Some commentators say that dogs were sacrificed to her. I do not know of evidence for this, though they were sacrificed to Hecate, one of her triple identities (Ov. *F* 1, 389). Dogs were garlanded at Diana's festival (Stat. *S* 3, 1, 57). In actual fact Artemis-Diana was regarded as one with the Egyptian goddess Bast (Hdt. 2, 59).

9 *porrum et caepe*: cf Hor. *Ep.* 1, 12, 21 *seu pisces seu porrum et caepe trucidas*; Plin. *NH* 19, 32, 101 *alium caepasque inter deos in iureiurando habet Aegyptus.* Diod. Sic. 1, 89 speaks of Egyptians who do not eat lentils, beans, cheese or onions.

10 Sarcasm.

11-2 Hdt. 2, 42: in the Theban nome sacrifice is of goats not sheep, in the Mendesian sheep not goats.

13 *carnibus . . . licet*: the grim assertion (denied by Hdt. 2, 45) is picked out by the bucolic diaeresis.

attonito cum: the offbeat rhythm continues the sense of shock.

14 *Vlixes*: Hom. *Od.* 9-12 is the lengthy narrative by Ulysses (Odysseus) of his adventures to Alcinous and the Phaeacian court: these included encounters with cannibals — hardly the most fantastic part of the tale: *attonito* alludes to Homer's account of the spellbound audience (Hom. *Od.* 13, 2).

16 *mouerat*: the plpf. has the force of the Greek aorist or French *passé défini.*

aretalogus: the sarcastic Greek word is emphasised by the bucolic diaeresis following: it means 'one who tells of glorious exploits': it is particularly appropriate here in that we have a number of aretalogies of the Egyptian goddess Isis. The use of such a strong word with a neutral meaning was technically called *amplificatio*, a rhetorical device (Quint. 8, 4, 1). Augustus used *aretalogi* as dinner-party entertainers (Suet. *Aug.* 74); they were notorious for drawing the long bow at great length; cf Porphyrio on Hor. *S* 1, 1, 120 *Crispinus carmina scripsit sed tam garrule ut aretalogus diceretur.*

17 *abicit*: we would say 'Will no one throw . . .?'

dignum uera: cf 8, 188 *dignus uera cruce.*

Charybdi: a whirlpool, supposedly by the Straits of Messina between Sicily and the mainland. The real one is contrasted with Ulysses's fictitious account (Hom. *Od.* 12, 234ff).

18 *Laestrygonas et Cyclopas*: the cannibals of *The Odyssey*: see on 14,20. Note the Greek endings, and the spondaic fifth foot.

19 *Scyllam*: a sea-monster opposite Charybdis (Hom. *Od.* 12, 80ff).

concurrentia saxa: J identifies the Wandering Rocks of Hom. *Od.* 12, 59-72 with the Clashing Rocks or Symplegades of the voyage of the Argonauts.

20 *Cyaneas*: the MS *Cyaneis* really makes no sense: *Cyaneas* is in apposition, like Hor. *O* 1, 3, 20 *infames scopulos Acroceraunia*: the Dark Rocks was another name for the Symplegades (Eur. *Med.* 2).

utres: Aeolus's bag of wind (Hom. *Od.* 10, 1ff).

21 *Circes:* the sorceress who turned Ulysses's companions into pigs (Hom. *Od.* 10, 210ff). The form is a Greek genitive.

22 *Elpenora*: oddly he is not mentioned as one of those transformed: later while drunk he fell from the roof and broke his neck (Hom. *Od.* 10, 552-60). Greek acc.

24 *et minimum qui*: offbeat rhythm.

25 A line with only twenty-nine letters is unusual: see on 9, 149. It is spondaic.

Corcyraea . . . urna: Phaeacia is identified with Corcyra (the modern Corfu); cf Mart. 8, 68, 1 *Corcyraei pomaria regis*.

temetum: an anteclassical and poetic word for intoxicating liquor: J probably took it from Hor. *Ep.* 2, 2, 163.

duxerat: 'decanted'.

26 *solus*: all his companions being dead.

Ithacus: Ulysses came from Ithaca: most people however identify the ancient Ithaca with the modern Leucas rather than Ithaki.

27 *consule Iunco*: a clear date: L. Aemilius Iuncus was cos. in AD 127 with Sex. Julius Severus (*Dig.* 40, 5, 28, 4); he came from Tripoli in Phoenicia, and was perhaps later proconsul of Asia.

28 *Copti*: a city of Upper Egypt, 16 km north of Thebes.

29 *coturnis*: i.e. 'tragedies', cf 6, 634.

30 *a Pyrrha*: i.e. 'from the Flood'; cf 1, 84 (perhaps a deliberate reference back).

syrmata: again 'tragedies', cf 8, 229.

uoluas: i.e. 'read': the scroll (*uolumen*) was unrolled from one stick and rolled on to another.

31 *populus*. emphatic: this is a collective action.

accipe nostro: bucolic diaeresis emphasising the words on either side.

33-92 *There was an ancient religious rivalry between Ombi and Tentyra. They waited for a religious festival to attack. There were fisticuffs, bruises, broken noses, blood.*

But it did not stop there. Next stones (though not of heroic dimensions). Then the men of Ombi rallied with swords. One of the others slipped. They fell on him, rent him limb from limb and ate his flesh raw. At least they didn't dishonour fire!

33 *uetus atque antiqua*: 'of long standing and of remote origin'.

34 *numquam sanabile uulnus*: the language is mock-epic: Vergil likes this form of adj. at this point of the line (e.g. *A* 5, 591 *irremeabilis error*).

35 *Ombos et Tentura*: in apposition to *finitimos*. Tentura or Tentyra is the modern Dendereh: the inhabitants worshipped the gentle Hathor, the cow-headed goddess, and abhorred the crocodile (Ael. *Nat. An.* 10, 21). Ombi, discovered by Flinders Petrie in 1895, was some 16 km away, and honoured the harsh Set, the crocodile-god (Ael. *Nat. An.* 10, 24). There was a defensive wall separating the territories.

summus utrimque: emphasised by the bucolic diaeresis.

36 *uicinorum*: the spondaic fifth foot adds weight: there are thirty-three in all: in 17 the fifth and sixth feet contain a single word.

39 *alterius*: he does not specify who started it, though it becomes clear or at least probable that Tentyra attacks Ombi.

40 *ac ducibus, ne*: offbeat, harsh rhythm.

42 *compita*: for the practice of open-air dining see Hdt. 2, 35; Mela 1, 57 *cibos palas et extra tecta sua capiunt*.

43 *toro*: they reclined on couches while feasting.

44 *horrida sane*: 'uncivilised, of course': the phrase is emphasised by the bucolic diaeresis.

45 *ipse notaui*: for J's knowledge of Egypt see Introduction, 'Life of Juvenal'.

46 *Canopo*: a fashionable Greek city near Alexandria: the *barbara turba* are the fellaheen of Upper Egypt. Sen. *Ep.* 51,3 couples Canopus with Baiae as a *diuersorium uitiorum*.

48 *mero titubantibus*: from Ovid's description of Silenus (*M* 11, 90; cf *F* 6, 677).

inde uirorum: the words are pointed by the bucolic diaeresis: *inde* 'on the one side' contrasting with *hinc* (51): *uirorum* satirical since dancing was regarded as effeminate.

49 *nigro tibicine*: abl. abs.: Upper Egypt had commerce with the black kingdom of Meroe.

qualiacumque: 'such as they were'.

51 *ieiunum*: 'ravenous', an effective

contrast with the sated condition of Ombi.

52 *tuba*: an appropriate metaphor.

53 *concurritur*: impers. pass.

55 *nasus*: a satirical detail.

57 *dimidios*: 'broken'.

alias: 'unrecognisable'.

58 *sanguine*: J uses abl. not gen. with
plenus; cf 1, 33 *plena ipso*.

59 *ipsi tamen*: i.e. 'you listeners might
think that they'd gone far enough, but . . '.

60 *calcent*: subj., because it is the
thought in their minds.

63 *inclinatis . . . lacertis*: a pictorial detail.

65 *qualis*: acc. pl.; sc. *torquebant*.

65-6 *Turnus . . . Aiax . . . Tydides*: epic
heroes hurling colossal rocks, Turnus
against Aeneas (Verg. *A* 12, 896-902), Ajax
against Hector (Hom. *IL* 7, 268-70),
Diomedes (s. of Tydeus) against Aeneas
(Hom. *IL* 5, 307-8). Pope in *Essay on
Criticism* 370-1 used the Ajax episode to
illustrate the matching of sound to sense
('When Ajax strives some rock's vast weight
to throw,/The line too labours, and the
words move slow.') J does the same in 66
with its heavy spondees: note also the
heavy *Aeneae* to start 67.

68 An ironical hit at contemporary
degeneracy. There were conflicting views
in antiquity. One, the Hesiodic, told of
degeneration from a state of primal
bliss; the other, the Epicurean, told of a
rise from a state of primitive savagery.
Sometimes they were combined, e.g. a
cataclysmic fall followed by a steady rise;
sometimes we encounter a cyclic view, cf
A.O. Lovejoy and G. Boas *Primitivism and
Related Ideas in Antiquity*.

69 *Homero*: Velleius Paterculus, writing
under Tiberius, placed his floruit 950 years
before, i.e. 925 BC; today we might date
The Iliad to 800 BC or shortly after.

70-1 Note the chiasmus: *malos . . .
pusillos . . . ridet . . . odit*.

73 *pars altera*: the Ombitani.

75 *Ombis*: the place for the inhabitants.

76 *umbrosae . . . palmae*: gen. of quality;
cf 3, 5.

81 *nec . . . decoxit*: the French anthro-
pologist Claude Lévi-Strauss has made the
antithesis between 'the Raw and the Cooked'
a cardinal point in his structural anthropology.

82 *ueribus*: strictly we must supply a
word for 'roasted' to parallel *decoxit*.

83 Note the cutting alliteration.

84 Satirical.

85 *Prometheu*: cf 4, 133; 8, 133; the
Titan who stole fire from heaven for men,
thus founding technology, and being
granted the great title *philanthropos*

'lover of man' (Aesch. *PV* 11). The reading
(for the MS *Prometheus donauit*) is due to
J.G. Griffith in *CQ* 19 (1969) 387: it
makes sense of *te* (86).

88 *sustinuit*: for the use + inf. see 6, 105;
14, 127.

89 *et dubites an*: harsh, offbeat rhythm.

90 *ante*: Housman's emendation of the
impossible *autem*, subsequently confirmed
by a MS in the British Museum. The pleasure
was felt not only by those who started the
cannibal feast: the man who previously
had been on the edge of the crowd now
rushed forward to pick up some blood
with his fingers and lick it up.

93-131 *There are other historical horror-
stories — Spaniards who, besieged, turned
to cannibalism. But that was under extreme
privation, and before Graeco-Roman
civilisation had reached them. The
Egyptian business is worse than human
sacrifice in the Crimea; that ended with
the execution. The Egyptian crime is not
paralleled even among the most savage tribes.
It equated hunger and rage.*

93 *Vascones*: a Spanish tribe, whose main
town Calagurris, on the Ebro, was the birth-
place of Quintilian. In 75 BC Sertorius with-
stood a siege by Metellus and Pompeius:
after his death the town faced a further siege
by Afranius, and were reduced to killing
and eating the weaker among them (Val. Max.
7, 6E3).

94 *sed res diuersa*: 'but the situation was
different'.

97-8 These lines are so awkward and
contradictory in meaning that it is hard to
believe that they are genuine.

102 *fame*: for the long *e* cf 6, 424; 14, 84.

106 *uescebantur? melius nos*: strikingly
offbeat.

107 *Zenonis*: for the Stoics see on 13,
121. Their general view was that virtue was
the only good, and that a wise man should
die, even committing suicide, rather than
do wrong. Oddly, however, there is
evidence that the Stoics placed cannibalism
among 'things indifferent', i.e. which were
acceptable if forced upon us: this no doubt
applied to eating dead bodies, not to killing
for food (Diog. Laert. 7, 121; 7, 188; Sext.
Emp. *Pyrrh.* 3, 207; 3, 247-8). J obviously
did not know this.

108 *Cantaber*: strictly a different Spanish
tribe, but J is not beyond a little geographical
confusion.

109 *Metelli*: Q. Caecilius Metellus Pius: J is
slightly confused: Metellus was the besieger in
75 not in 72.

110 *Athenas*: i.e. 'education', cf Val.
Max. 2, 1, 10 *quas Athenas, quam scholam
huic domesticae disciplinae praetulerim?*
Pericles had called Athens 'an education to
Greece' (Thuc. 2, 41). Diod. Sic. 13, 27, 1
echoes this: Athens is a common school
to all mankind. The passage is notable because
J acknowledges a common Graeco-Roman
culture and because he uses Athens as a
symbol of higher education. Not so did he
treat the Greeks in 3, 58ff or 6, 184-99. There
is possibly a reference to Hadrian's Athenaeum,
an institute for the encouragement and
control of literature.

111 *Gallia*: human sacrifice by the
Druids had been abolished by Augustus (Suet.
Claud. 25). Massilia had become a centre of
Graeco-Roman education before the end of
the Republic; Agricola was educated there
(Tac. *Agr.* 4). Augustodunum (Autun) and
Lugdunum (Lyons) were other early
cultural centres: see also Suet. *Cal.* 45. Later
Gaul became the major centre of Latin
culture: in AD 376 the emperors established
professors of rhetoric and grammar in all
the main cities.

Britannos: Tac. *Agr.* 21 has an amusing
picture of Agricola encouraging the
emergence of literary and rhetorical education
in Britain by comparing the British favourably
with the Gauls in brightness and receptivity.

112 *Thyle*: cf Verg. *G* 1, 30 *ultima
Thule*, the extreme north, compounded of ex-
periences and stories of Shetlands, Orkneys,
Iceland and Jutland: a pleasant climactic
hyperbole.

113 *ille*: the Vascones.

114 *Zacynthos*: Saguntum in Spain,
supposedly founded by Zacynthus (Zante)
in Greece. The reference is to the siege by
Hannibal in 219-8 BC (Liv. 21, 14-5). The
inhabitants suffered terrible privation, but
there is no reliable mention of cannibalism in
the historians, cf Petron. 141 *Saguntini
oppressi ab Hannibale humanas edere carnes.*

115 *Maeotide . . . ara*: the Taurians of
the Crimea offered human sacrifice of
foreigners who came among them, to a
goddess Opis whom the Greeks identified
with Artemis; cf Eur *IT* 28ff. Strictly the
palus Maeotica (cf 4, 42) is the Sea of
Azov, further to the north.

116 *illa . . . Taurica*: Opis-Artemis.

117 *carmina*: like Euripides's play.

118 *tantum*: 'only': they didn't eat the
bodies.

ulterius nil: the sentence beginning here
is isolated by bucolic diaeresis at either end,
and emphasised by this offbeat rhythm.

122 *Memphitide*: i.e. Egyptian, Memphis

being the traditional centre of Lower Egypt,
later second to Alexandria, then under the
Romans in decline.

123 *inuidiam facerent . . . Nilo*: 'make the
Nile feel ashamed'. The land of Egypt was
and is totally dependent on the Nile for
water. The Nile is here conceived as a god –
there is in the Vatican a famous statue of
the Nile as a river-god. In the event of a god
not performing his expected function
worshippers would sometimes abuse him in
word and action in the hope of provoking
him.

124 *Cimbri*: a military Germanic tribe,
cf 8, 249.

Brittones: the Britons; cf Hor. *O* 3, 4, 33
Britannos hospitibus feros; Ov. *Am.* 2, 16,
39-40.

125 *Sauromatae*: from Poland and Russia.
Ovid (*Tr.* 3, 10, 5) called them *fera gens.*

immanes Agathyrsi: the four-syllable
ending with a foreign name is not
uncommon, but J has effectively used the
fact that it throws the rhythm offbeat. They
seem to come from Transylvania: Vergil (*A*
4, 146) calls them *picti.*

126 *rabie imbelle*: the hiatus is made
easier by the strong caesura: J has it seven
times at this point; cf 3, 70: there is a
gulping effect.

127 *paruula*: J's use of the diminutive
is often hostile; cf 10, 340.

fictilibus: the detail is confirmed by
Strab. 17, 788.

phaselis: a boat shaped like a bean: J has
in mind the same word in Verg. *G* 4, 289
who calls them *pictis.*

128 *testae*: sarcastic: we should not
interpret but tr. 'tile': it is gen. with *remis.*

131-74 *Man is distinguished from the
animals by a capacity for tears and tender-
ness. A good man cares for all human
concerns. Mankind had reason, common
partnership, collective security. Today
snakes cooperate better than men. Lions,
boars, tigers, bears spare their own kind.
Men have passed from agricultural
implements to weapons of destruction,
and treat their fellows as food. What would
Pythagoras say?*

133 *haec*: emotionalism, tenderness.

134 *iubet*: sc. *natura.*

135 *squaloremque rei*: the accused
affected an unkempt appearance to arouse
pity.

136 A sonorous spondaic line.

136-7 'whose adolescent curls make
that tear-stained complexion ambiguously
a girl's or boy's'.

138-40 This tenderness has hardly been

allowed to appear before in J.

140 *minor*: 'too young for'; cf Plin. *NH* 7, 16, 72 *hominem prius quam genito dente cremari mos gentium non est.*

140-1 *face dignus arcana*: 'worthy of the mystic torch', carried by the initiate in the great procession at the Eleusinian Mysteries. The hierophant proclaimed the need for religious and moral purity: Celsus, who in c. AD 175 wrote an attack on Christianity entitled *The True Word,* explicitly contrasted this with the Christian invitation to sinners of all sorts (Orig. *Cels.* 3, 59).

141 *Cereris . . . sacerdos*: the hierophant: the goddesses of the Mysteries were Demeter (Ceres) and her daughter Kore ('the Maid'). For a full account, see G.E. Mylonas *Eleusis and the Eleusinian Mysteries* also C. Kerenyi *Eleusis.* See also 3, 320.

142 *aliena sibi*: cf the famous words of the neighbour in Ter. *Haut.* 77 *homo sum: humani nil a me alienum puto.*

separat hoc nos: the bucolic diaeresis places great weight on the telling epigrams on either side.

143 *mutorum*: the contrast is common in Seneca (e.g. *Ep.* 124, 16). An extended passage in Ps-Quint. *Decl.* 12, 26-7 draws the contrast well, and shows that it was a rhetorical commonplace.

adeo: Nisbet for *ideo*: not 'for that reason' but 'what is more it is from heaven that'.

144 *diuinorumque capaces*: 'capable of receiving inspiration from the gods'.

146 *sensum*: not the power of sensation, which animals possess, but a higher sensibility. So Ps-Quint. *Decl.* 12, 27 *quamuis sensu careant muta animalia.* The thought is Stoic: there is implanted in man a spark of the divine fire.

147 *cuius*: with *egent,* a Greek ablatival gen.

terram spectantia: man's upright stature and capacity to look upwards is taken as a sign of his peculiar divine endowment; cf Xen. *Mem.* 1, 4, 11; Arist. *Part. An.* 4, 686 a 27; Ov. *M* 1, 84-6 *pronaque cum spectent animalia cetera terram,/os homini sublime dedit caelumque uidere/iussit et erectos ad sidera tollere uultus.*

mundi : note how this break at the end of the fifth foot is parodied at 159.

148 *communis*: i.e. of men and animals.

149 *animas . . . animum*: i.e. life and intelligence; cf Non. 426 *animus est quo sapimus, anima qua uiuimus.*

ut: 'with the intention that'.

150-1 J very boldly contructs these lines in a closely similar verbal pattern as if insisting on his point.

151ff The thought is from the account of the emergence of civilisation in the fifth book of Lucretius, but J has a creator-god and a teleology which the Epicurean account denies. Nothing more clearly shows his eclectic position, but one with a more intimate and sympathetic knowledge of Epicureanism than most.

153 *laribus*: perhaps a little more than a periphrasis for 'home'; 'adding a next-door neighbour for our household gods'.

155 *conlata . . . fiducia*: 'collective security'.

157 *defendier*: archaic for *defendi.* Such archaisms are rare in J; cf 1, 169 *duelli*; 10, 138 *induperator.* Probably he is simply acknowledging his debt to Lucretius (C. Bailey *Lucretius* I p. 84, e.g. Lucr. 1, 710 *uertier*), but he may also mean that he is writing in a more serious vein like Persius, who has *dicier* (1, 28), *fallier* (3, 50).

159 A biting epigram.

159-60 i.e. 'Leopard does not prey on leopard'. But there is a double meaning since *macula* = 'moral blemish': J implies that humans, themselves 'spotted', do not spare the 'spottedness' of other humans. He points the epigram by the bucolic diaeresis.

166 *produxisse parum est*: the biting alliteration makes the point: killing is not enough for men today: they eat the dead bodies.

167 *coquere*: a brilliant touch: he means 'to forge', but the connection with cooking and eating must not be lost. J derives a fourfold fall: the 'cooking' of agricultural implements, the 'cooking' of weapons, the 'cooking' of human flesh, the eating of human flesh raw.

168 *gladios extendere*: i.e. to lengthen knives (a useful tool) into swords. Epicurean pacifism breaks through here, though Lucretius was more historically pessimistic (5, 1283-96), and J himself has shown some enthusiasm for common military action (155-8).

171 *crediderint*: supply *qui*: the change of mood is odd: it may be primarily metrical convenience, but there is an implied change from 'this happens' to 'they are the sort of people who'.

172 *monstra*: abnormal portents.

173 *Pythagoras*: a rather shadowy Greek thinker of the sixth century BC, born in Samos, who travelled widely, must somehow have come in touch with Indian thought, and held a kind of mathematical mysticism, which included belief in the transmigration of souls; he settled in southern Italy, which

became the centre of the school's activities.

abstinuit qui: offbeat rhythm: it probably indicates that J is not a vegetarian, but is using Pythagoras as an extreme example in the opposite direction.

174 *tamquam homine*: since he believed in transmigration into animals.

non omne legumen: the Pythagoreans abstained from beans: one view is that it is because they cause flatulence and endanger the soul (which is breath) (Diog. Laert. 8, 24): other explanations include their phallic shape, resemblance to the universe, origin in primal matter, association with souls of the dead (ib. 8, 34; Plin. *NH* 18, 30, 118; Plut. *Q. Conv.* 727-8). Recently Richard and Eva Blum in *Health and Healing in Rural Greece* 1965 p. 78 have put forward an explanation in terms of the tendency of the fava bean to cause in some people a disease called favism. No doubt some tabus do have such rational explanations. There is an ancient view (cited by Pliny) that beans cause dullness or sleeplessness, and this is a more likely explanation.

General comments

This is unique in J's satires in that its target is not the Roman power-élite. The attack is totally on a scene far from Rome. The weakness of the satire is J's self-righteousness. In other satires he is not too far from the receiving-end of his own shafts.

He hated the Egyptians. He hated all Easterners, and most foreigners. The remarkable feature of this satire is that whereas in other satires he attacks the Greeks with particular ferocity, here the Greeks are part of a Graeco-Roman civilisation which he characterises as *Athenas* (110), Athens, the school of the world. His hostility to the Egyptians seems to be due to three factors. First, Egypt, if we accept the tradition as authentic, was the scene of his exile, and he loathed it as such. Secondly, there was in the reign of Hadrian an outbreak of Egyptomania sweeping across Italy: it was this no doubt that brought back his memories of loathing. Thirdly, there was the incident itself, the religious feud between two village-communities, mob violence, and the killing and eating of a man who failed to make good his escape. There is no reason to doubt the historicity of the incident, which J is careful to date. Attempts to interpret it in a pattern of religious ritual run counter to the narrative; if it had been so, J would have made still more of it. Rather are we to see the events as not

atypical. Thus we hear of an Egyptian who would eat raw flesh in the reign of Nero, who toyed with the idea of giving him a live man to eat (Suet. *Nero* 37, 2); and we know of very similar religious feuds (Plut. *Is. et Os.* 72, 380 B-C), and, a little later, of a similar instance of cannibalism (Dio Cass. 71, 4). We may think that J was unsympathetic to the positive side of Egyptian culture, but there was plenty to which he might reasonably and understandably and without racial prejudice be unsympathetic.

It is remarkable, however, in view of his past record, that he should have been so single-minded in his attack. We would have expected him to take this as his text and turn to lambast the sadism of the gladiatorial displays, which in other satires he abominates, or the treatment of the Christians by Nero (and indeed Domitian), to be renewed and intensified at Lyons under Marcus Aurelius, who was not always as humane and philosophical as his faith should have made him, and some of the other cruelties of Roman life. We can reconstruct the satire which he might have written in different ways. He could have made the Roman appear worse than the Egyptian. (There is an apocryphal story of a cannibal hearing about the dead in the 1914-18 war and asking, 'How did you eat them all?' His informant said icily that Europeans do not eat their dead. 'Barbarians! We only kill for food. You kill for no purpose at all.') Or he could have treated both as aspects of a degenerate age: he comes near to this (31-2 *nostro . . . aeuo*; 159 *iam*) but he makes nothing of it.

There is however one possible explanation. J may have planned satires 15 and 16 together, and felt that the attack on the Roman soldiery, as representative of Roman brutality, would be more effective if placed in stark contrast with the story of Egyptian brutality — *reculer pour mieux sauter*. If so the conclusion of that will have been that despite their privileges they behave no better than animals.

This single-mindedness also explains why he makes little use of the mythological examples of cannibalism. In one celebrated story, which Pindar rejects, the gods are tricked into a cannibal feast — which is why Pelops ended up with an ivory shoulder. Cannibalism in the heroic age is found in the stories of Tereus and Thyestes, to which J alludes elsewhere. But these would here have distracted from his purpose. He wants to present the crime as a unique barbarity: it does not help to say that gods or heroes have also perpetrated it.

The fifteenth is an ugly, humourless satire, totally unredeemed by laughter. What is unusual in it is that J stresses what one might almost call a positive faith to a greater extent than anywhere else. The last part of the poem is sustained by a high seriousness, comparable to the high seriousness which more briefly (at least in proportion) ends the tenth. J's philosophy of life is eclectic. He values Stoic universalism, and Epicurean friendship and belief in the emergence of civilisation. He alludes with approbation to the great line from Terence 'I am a man, and count nothing that affects any man as foreign to me.' (142). He compares the contemporary behaviour shown by the Egyptians unfavourably with that of animals (Green comments neatly that 'a collector of natural history fallacies would do quite well out of J'). But his positive assertion is that what marks man's essential nature off from that of dumb animals is tenderness, sympathy, fellow-feeling, the capacity for tears. For that alone the poem deserves to survive.

Bibliography

Boussac, P.H. 'L'exil de Juvénal et l'Ombos de la XVe satire' *R. Phil.* 41 (1917) 169-84

Fredericks, S.C. 'Juvenal's Fifteenth Satire' *Ill. Class. Studies* 1 (1976) 174-89

Highet, G. 'A fight in the desert: Juvenal XV and a modern parallel' *CJ* 45 (1949) 94-6

Lindsay, J. *Daily Life in Roman Egypt* London 1963 pp. 109-21.

Moreau, J. 'Une scène d'anthropophagie en Egypte en l'an 127 de notre ère' *Chroniques d'Egypte* 15 (1940) 279-85

Palm, G. *De Juvenalis satira quinta decima* Halle 1882

Pryor, A.D. 'The best satirists either for satirical, tragical, satirical-tragical, satirical-tragical-comical, together with some observations on Juvenal's anthropophagous comedy' *AUMLA* 14 (1958) 44-55

SATIRE 16

The last poem is patently unfinished: it breaks off in mid-sentence, and it does not by any means fulfil the programme implicitly offered in *primum* (7). No fragments are quoted elsewhere: the ancient commentators had the defective version. Three explanations have been given. One is that the attack on the army was censored by Hadrian. There is no inherent improbability in this, but surely the whole poem would have gone: what is left is not exactly complimentary. The second view is that of Gilbert Highet, that the poem was completed but that at an early point in the MS tradition a MS which happened alone to survive was mutilated, and one or two parchment quires were lost. There are two major problems about this. One is that it is very odd that no trace of even a single line has been preserved in either quotation or allusion. The other is the length of this book. It already contains 814 lines: Highet's shorter version would extend it to 1054; his longer one to nearly 1300. No book of J exceeds 1000 lines, and Lucretius apart, books of that length are almost unknown in Latin poetry. On the whole then it seems better to believe that J died without completing his poem. Highet's case against this, that J's editor would have tidied it up is reasonable enough but not completely

cogent; it seems the most likely of the explanations.

The ancient commentators say that some doubt was cast on the authenticity of the satire in antiquity. Such doubt (which Gibbon shared) was not well founded. It is, to say the least, unlikely that anyone would compose a fragment. Mood, technique and vocabulary are authentically those of J: indeed one might argue that the return to an attack on the power-structure of Rome is a return to his old self.

It is temerarious to reconstruct what has been lost. Highet does so, but the reconstruction must surely be too expansive. What we have does, however, give some indication of what J must have intended, and in his general outline Highet is certainly right.

Introduction 1-6
General advantages common to all soldiers
    legal 7-60 . . .
    other
Special stories of particular advantages
Conclusion

My own estimate would be of a satire 200-250 lines long. It is interesting to speculate, as Highet does, that among J's special stories may have been the achievement of imperial power.

1-6 *Who can enumerate the fringe-
benefits of military service, Gallius —
provided that you're lucky? A lucky star
counts more than direct commendation to
Mars from Venus or Juno.*

1 *Quis*: see on 15, 1.

felicis: J lays it on thick; cf *prospera* (2),
secundo (3), *benigni* (4). It was the nick-
name of Legio IV Flavia Felix.

praemia: in material terms a member of
the praetorian guard received two denarii a
day (Tac. *Ann.* 1, 17), increased to 1000 a
year under Domitian, a lump sum of 5000
denarii on discharge and extra gratuities on
special occasions. A legionary's pay was one
denarius a day. Durry has shown that J is
referring to the praetorians.

Galli: a better reading than *Galle*: the name
Gallius is less common, but the name is
found in the time of Cicero (e.g. *Fam* 13,
44). J's Gallius is unknown, but not
necessarily non-existent: indeed there would
be no point in inventing a character and
not using him.

2-3 Jahn proposed a missing line
here: Green supplies 'The sky's the limit,
there's nothing you can't hope for.'

3 *porta*: sc. *castrorum*.

5 *Veneris*: the love-affair between
Venus and Mars (Aphrodite and Ares)
goes back to Homer (*Od.* 8, 266ff):
perhaps originally a projection of the inter-
play on a human scale between feminine
beauty and masculine toughness: it
becomes a parable of the subduing of violence
by the power of life (Lucr. 1, 31-40).

commendet epistula: Cic. *Fam.* 13 consists
of such commendatory letters. We should
not forget that the emperor was the Roman
commander-in-chief. How many commenda-
tory epistles came from the women of the
court?

6 *Samia . . . harena*: Juno (Hera), mother
of Mars, was patron goddess of the island
of Samos. A stele containing a treaty
between Athens and Samos, now in the
National Museum, Athens, portrays Hera
and Athene greeting one another.

7-34 *First look at all that the military
enjoy in common. No civilian would dare
assault a soldier, and if assaulted by a soldier
either dares not seek redress or faces a
military court. If he expects justice he'll be
disappointed. No witness would dare to
support his story.*

7 *primum communia*: no others are
treated: this alone shows that the poem is
incomplete. Notice the alliteration on
c (q), the assonance on *m (n)* and the pre-
dominance of *u* in the vowels.

8 *ne*: we might expect *ut non*, but
there is an element of purpose.

togatus 'civilian'.

9 *dissimulet nec*: the offbeat rhythm
suggests that J is being bitterly satirical.

10 *audeat*: rhetorical repetition.

excussos . . . dentes: the soldier behaves
in the same way as the tough in 3, 288-301
(*paucis cum dentibus*).

praetori: sc. *urbano*.

11 *offam*: 'bruise', 'raw lump'.

13-4 *Bardaicus . . . calceus*: the Bardaei
or Vardaei were a people of Illyria who had
been Marius's bodyguard (Plut. *Mar.* 43,4)
and who gave their name to a military boot.
Bardaicus calceus here stands for the
centurion who wears it. But the effect of
the word-order is more satirical than that,
for we cannot avoid understanding 'a judge
from the Bardaei is awarded — a boot'.
Hadrian among his measures to keep the
support of the army ruled that soldiers
should not leave their units to engage in
the law courts, and any charges against them
should be referred to a military tribunal
(*Dig.* 22, 5, 3, 6).

15 *Camilli*: M. Furius Camillus, who
saved Rome from the Gauls in 387-6 BC,
introduced a standing army (Liv. 5, 2),
which made it less easy for soldiers to engage
in the law courts.

17-9 The optimistic and unfulfilled
assumption of the injured person (*mihi*).

18 *exigitur*: Bücheler for *est igitur*.
R.S. Kilpatrick in *CP* 66 (1971) 114-5 argues
for *est; agitur*.

20 *cohors*: there were ten of 1000 men
constituting the praetorian guard, each
divided into three maniples (M. Durry,
however, argues that at this period they
were at half-strength).

21 *curabilis*: 'easily remedied' and so
ineffectual: this view seems better than
'requiring medical treatment'.

22 *dignum erit ergo*: bucolic diaeresis and
three word-accents giving emphasis.

23 A slow, spondaic, mulish, four-word
line. For Vagellius see 13, 119.

24 *duo*: 'only two' in contrast with *tot.*
tot caligas, tot. offbeat, harsh rhythm:
the soldiers' hobnailed boots stand for the
soldiers, but also add a frightening detail.

26 *Pylades*: i.e. a true friend: for this
device, cf 1, 61 *Automedon*; 4, 133
Prometheus; 5, 139 *paruulus Aeneas*.
Pylades was friend to Orestes, and becomes
a type of friendship; cf Ov. *RA* 589 *semper
habe Pyladen aliquem, qui curet Orestem.*

molem aggeris ultra: see on 8, 43: the
camp was between the Colline and
Viminal Gates outside the *agger*.

28 A rotund, sonorous, sarcastic line for the friends 'who are sure to make excuses'.

29-31 *audeat . . . et credam*: i.e. *si audeat . . . credam.*

31 *barba . . . capillis.* for the shagginess of the ancient Romans, cf 4, 103 *barbato . . regi;* 5, 30 *capillato . . . consule.*

34 *paganum*: a countryman (from *pagus*), so a civilian in contrast to *armati*, cf Plin. *Ep.* 10, 86, 2 *et milites et pagani.* Our word 'pagan' probably comes from the religious conservatism of the countryside, possibly from the fact that they were not enrolled in the army of Christ.

fortunam: 'purse'.

pudorem: 'honour': satirical view of the behaviour.

35-50 *More military emoluments. A civilian who goes to law faces impossible delays. Soldiers don't have the brakes put on their actions.*

35-6 A rattling dactylic line followed by heavy spondees.

36 *sacramentorum*: i.e. the soldiers, from their oaths of allegiance.

38 *sacrum . . . saxum*: the boundary-stone, sacred to the god Terminus, its personification; cf Ov. *F* 2, 641 *Termine, siue lapis siue es defossus in agro/stipes.*

39 *puls annua*: on the Terminalia on 23 Feb.: sacrifices to Terminus were bloodless (Plut. *QR* 15).

40 *pergit non reddere*: 'persists in refusing to return'.

41 A rare example of repetition in J, see on 13, 137.

42 *annus*: Serv. on Verg. *A* 2, 102 cites this passage and refers it to the *annus litium*, i.e. the period of the year in which the courts are sitting (as we might speak of 'the school year'), and when of course everyone else was waiting for their cases to be heard. There is no reason to suppose Servius wrong.

45 A solemn spondaic line.

sternuntur: attendants placed cushions on the benches.

ponente lacernas: in order to put on the toga, formal wear being necessary for pleading, cf 9, 28-9.

46 *Caedicio*: cf 13, 197.

Fusco: cf 4, 112; 12, 45, but this lawyer is not necessarily connected with those.

47 *digredimur*: i.e. the case is adjourned. *lentaque*: the emphatic word.

48 *balteus*: a leather sword-belt worn over the shoulder; cf 6, 256; Verg. *A* 12, 941-2 *umero cum apparuit alto/*

balteus.

50 *res*: 'substance'.

sufflamine: 'brake': Augustus said of an orator who spoke too quickly *Haterius noster sufflaminandus est* (Sen. Eld. *Contr.* 4 pref. 7). The idea is that when braked the wheel drags and so wears down.

51-60 *Again a soldier does not have to surrender his earnings to his father and can dispose of his own property. So that fathers try to be named in their sons' wills. Military commanders find it useful to see that good soldiers are well-off.*

51 *testandi militibus ius*: the extraordinary assonance and offbeat rhythm show just what J thought of this. Officially a son had no property of his own, but a soldier was given his *castrense peculium* as an inalienable right: see *Dig.*49, 17; *Inst.* 2, 12 pref.

53 *in corpore census*: 'in the main body of the family property'.

54 *ergo Coranum*: picked out by bucolic diaeresis. J is alluding to Hor. *S* 2, 5, 55-69 where a son-in-law Coranus evades the attentions of his father-in-law Nasica *captatorque dabit risus Nasica Corano.*

56 *iam tremulus*: i.e. getting on in years. *captat*: a *captator* is a legacy-hunter: see on 3, 129; 4, 19; 5, 98; 12, 93.

hunc fauor aequus: bucolic diaeresis and three word-accents for emphasis: *fauor* is Ruperti's emendation for *labor: fauor aequus* is an oxymoron.

57 *pulchro*: satirical, as the alliteration on *p* suggests.

60 *phaleris et torquibus*: we would say 'medals and decorations': they were bronze or silver medals and necklaces.

omnes: the poem breaks off in mid-sentence: see introduction.

General comments

There is little that calls for extended comment in the final fragment of J's writing. It is an attack on the standing army. It is clearly an attack on the privileges and behaviour of the standing army of J's own day; no longer is he trying *quid concedatur in illos/quorum Flaminia tegitur cinis atque Latina* (1, 170-1). The army had already shown themselves as king-makers. J concentrates his satirical attention on the praetorian guard, the élite whom the people of Rome knew and perhaps feared. They had unmade Caligula, and made Claudius and Trajan: in the year of the four emperors it was the legions in the provinces who jostled to put their nominees on the throne. Before another century had passed Septimius Severus was to tell his sons to stick together and keep the troops contented: no one else mattered (Dio Cass. 76, 17, 4). It was courageous to attack the real seat of power.

The satire marks a return to the old J. The picture of the civilians waiting in the law courts where the military get prompt service is exactly parallel to the fate of the humble *cliens* in the first and third satires. J is not unlike an American satirist who has discovered that the real power has passed from the businessmen to the Pentagon, and has found his satirical strength renewed accordingly.

His opening lines are gentle enough. He is going to write about privileges. But there is a stress on fortune (1 *felicis*; 2 *prospera*; 3 *secundo*; 4 *benigni*) which makes us suspicious. J does not believe in fortune (10, 365-6). And there is a glorious picture of Mars as commander-in-chief receiving commendatory letters from his mother Juno and his lover Venus. J begins with general advantages, and repetitive alliteration (*commoda . . . communia*) and a humming assonance (7) make us suspicious, and two lines later (9 *dissimulet nec*) offbeat rhythm makes certain that his purpose is a savage rejection of army privilege. The civilians are beaten up without redress. The account of the legal privileges of the military

is a masked attack on their brutality. We may suspect that the account of the *castrense peculium* was going on to a denunciation of confiscations and depredations such as have taken place under military régimes our own day.

We do not know how the satire ended. Clearly the poem went on from communal advantages to at least one pen-portrait of an individual who rose to the top through a military career — from the opening words we may assume by luck rather than merit. As some of the emperors had risen as soldiers this was a dangerous theme. If I am right in thinking that the single-minded attack on the Egyptians and their cruelty in 15 was matched by a single-minded attack on the Roman soldier and his cruelty in 16, we may reasonably think that the personal section was about someone with a gory record and that the final section set the cruelties against the privileges. We cannot be certain. But we can regret the loss of the rest of what promised to be a satire of considerable power.

Bibliography

Durry, M. 'Juvénal et les Prétoriens' *REL* 13 (1935) 95-106

Ercole, P. 'La Satira XVI de Giovenali' *Ath.* 8 (1930) 346-60